Benefits for Migrants Handbook

12th edition

Rebecca Walker, Kamla Adiseshiah, Ravi Low-Beer,
Ruth Mercer and Henri Krishna

Child Poverty Action Group

Child Poverty Action Group works on behalf of the more than one in four children in the UK growing up in poverty. It does not have to be like this. We use our understanding of what causes poverty and the impact it has on children's lives to campaign for policies that will prevent and solve poverty – for good. We provide training, advice and information to make sure hard-up families get the financial support they need. We also carry out high-profile legal work to establish and protect families' rights. If you are not already supporting us, please consider making a donation, or ask for details of our membership schemes, training courses and publications.

Published by Child Poverty Action Group
30 Micawber Street
London N1 7TB
Tel: 020 7837 7979
staff@cpag.org.uk
cpag.org.uk

A CIP record for this book is available from the British Library.

ISBN: 978 1 910715 62 8

Child Poverty Action Group is a charity registered in England and Wales (registration number 294841) and in Scotland (registration number SC039339), and is a company limited by guarantee, registered in England (registration number 1993854). VAT number: 690 808117

Cover design by Colorido Studios
Internal design by Devious Designs
Content management system by Konnect Soft
Typeset by DLxml, a division of RefineCatch Limited, Bungay, Suffolk
Printed by CPI Group (UK) Ltd, Croydon CR0 4YY

The authors

Rebecca Walker is an advice worker at Sheffield Citizens Advice and Law Centre, and a freelance trainer and writer on welfare rights.

Kamla Adiseshiah is a senior solicitor at Southwark Law Centre.

Ruth Mercer is an immigration and housing solicitor at Southwark Law Centre.

Ravi Low-Beer is a legal advisor at the Asylum Support Appeals Project.

Henri Krishna is a welfare rights worker at CPAG in Scotland.

Acknowledgements

The authors would like to thank everyone who has contributed to this book and all the authors of previous editions.

Thanks are particularly due this year to Alice Tichborne, Dave Kelly, Nick Turnill and Mark Rogers.

We would also like to thank Bridget Giles for editing and managing the production of the book, Katherine Dawson for compiling the index and Kathleen Armstrong for proofreading the text.

The law covered in this book was correct on 1 March 2021. It includes regulations laid and judgments delivered up to this date.

Contents

Abbreviations

AA	attendance allowance
ARC	application registration card
ASAP	Asylum Support Appeals Project
ASU	Asylum Screening Unit
BIA	Border and Immigration Agency
BRP	biometric residence permit
CA	carer's allowance
CJEU	Court of Justice of the European Union
CTC	child tax credit
DLA	disability living allowance
DWP	Department for Work and Pensions
EC	European Community
ECAA	Turkish EC Association Agreement
ECHR	European Convention on Human Rights
ECtHR	European Court of Human Rights
EEA	European Economic Area
EFTA	European Free Trade Association
EHIC	European health insurance card
ESA	employment and support allowance
EU	European Union
EUSS	European Union Settlement Scheme
FNO	foreign national offender
FSU	Further Submissions Unit
HB	housing benefit
HMCTS	HM Courts and Tribunals Service
HMRC	HM Revenue and Customs
IB	incapacity benefit
ICE	Independent Case Examiner
IS	income support
ISA	individual savings account
JSA	jobseeker's allowance
MA	maternity allowance
MP	Member of Parliament
MSP	Member of the Scottish Parliament
NASS	National Asylum Support Service
NI	national insurance
OISC	Office of the Immigration Services Commissioner
PC	pension credit
PIP	personal independence payment
REA	reduced earnings allowance
SAL	standard acknowledgement letter
SAP	statutory adoption pay
SDA	severe disablement allowance
SIAC	Special Immigration Appeals Commission
SMP	statutory maternity pay
SPBP	statutory parental bereavement pay
SPP	statutory paternity pay
SSP	statutory sick pay
SSPP	statutory shared parental pay
SSS	Social Security Scotland
TFEU	Treaty on the Functioning of the European Union
UC	universal credit
UK	United Kingdom
UKBA	UK Border Agency
UKVI	UK Visas and Immigration
UN	United Nations
WTC	working tax credit

Part 1

Introduction

Chapter 1

How to use this book

This chapter covers:

1. About this *Handbook* (below)
2. Checking the rules that affect you (p4)
3. Finding the relevant law (p6)
4. Immigration advice (p7)

1. About this *Handbook*

This *Handbook* is for migrants and their advisers wanting information on how entitlements to social security benefits are affected by the country in which someone lives, absences abroad, nationality and immigration status. It also provides an overview of the main types of immigration status and covers the support available for people who have applied for asylum in the UK. By 'migrants' we mean people, including British citizens, who have come or returned to Great Britain from abroad and people who have left Great Britain either temporarily or to live abroad.

The law on benefit entitlement for migrants is complex and frequently changing. As a result, migrants are often refused benefits to which they are entitled, or are not paid for family members when they should be.

This *Handbook* explains the different requirements that must be satisfied in order to be entitled to benefits, so that you can understand whether or not you satisfy them and effectively challenge incorrect decisions.

This *Handbook* covers the rules that are most likely to affect migrant claimants and their families, and the practical problems that can arise. It is not a complete guide to the benefit rules and should be used together with general guides on social security benefits, such as CPAG's *Welfare Benefits and Tax Credits Handbook*.

How this book is organised

The book is split into parts, and related chapters are grouped under these parts. For a description of the information covered in each part, see below. For the chapters included in each part, see the table of contents on pv.

Part 1 is an introduction to this *Handbook*.

Part 2 gives an overview of immigration law to help you identify your immigration status and understand the immigration terms that appear in the rest of this *Handbook*.

Part 3 covers the way your, and your family members', immigration status affects your entitlement to benefits. If you and all the people included in your claim are British or Irish citizens, the rules in this part do not apply to you.

Part 4 covers the residence and presence requirements for all benefits and how you satisfy them, including details on how you satisfy the 'right to reside' requirement.

Part 5 explains the way your entitlement to benefits is affected if you, or a family member who is included in your claim, go abroad.

Part 6 describes the way in which the European Union social security co-ordination rules and international agreements on social security can assist you to satisfy entitlement conditions in the UK, or to be paid UK benefits abroad, or, in limited circumstances, can prevent you being entitled to UK benefits.

Part 7 covers some issues that can be particularly problematic for migrants – delays, satisfying the national insurance number requirement and providing evidence to show you meet the immigration status, residence and presence rules.

Part 8 covers the rules on asylum support for people who have made an application for asylum in the UK.

Part 9 gives an overview of other possible sources of help that may be available to migrants.

Finding information

The two most efficient ways of finding information in this *Handbook* are to use the contents page and the index.

The contents shows the structure of the book and lists the parts, the chapters and the sections within each chapter.

The index contains entries in bold type, directing you to the general information on the subject or to the page(s) where the subject is covered more fully. Sub-entries under the bold headings are listed alphabetically and direct you to specific aspects of the subject.

Throughout this *Handbook* the text is referenced with the source of information, given in endnotes which are at the end of each chapter. For more information on finding the relevant law, see p6.

2. Checking the rules that affect you

As the rules are complicated, it is helpful to approach them systematically.

If you are not a British or Irish citizen, or if anyone you could include in your claim is not a British or Irish citizen, work through the following steps.

- **Step one:** be clear about your immigration status and that of anyone you could make a joint claim with or include in your claim. See Chapter 6 for how to check the status you have in the UK. If you are unsure about your immigration status, get specialist immigration advice (see p7).
- **Step two:** check whether you are defined as a 'person subject to immigration control' (see Chapter 7). If you are not, your immigration status does not exclude you from benefit entitlement, but you must still satisfy the rules on residence and presence. If you have a partner or child who is subject to immigration control, check the rules on partners and children for how your benefit is affected (see p104).
- **Step three:** if you are defined as a 'person subject to immigration control', check whether the rules on the particular benefit exclude people subject to immigration control (see p81). If not, your immigration status does not exclude you from entitlement to that benefit, but you must still satisfy the rules on residence and presence.
- **Step four:** if the benefit you want to claim is one from which people subject to immigration control are generally excluded, check whether you come into an exempt group. These vary between the different benefits (see p96). If you are exempt, you must still satisfy all the other conditions of entitlement, including the residence and presence requirements.
- **Step five:** if you cannot claim the benefit you want because you are defined as a 'person subject to immigration control', but you have a partner who may be able to claim, check the rules on partners (see p104).
- **Step six:** if you or a member of your family have leave to enter or remain in the UK that is subject to a no recourse to public funds condition, check whether any claim for benefits could breach this condition because this could jeopardise your (or her/his) current or future immigration status (see p87).
- **Step seven:** if you are an asylum seeker or are dependent on an asylum seeker, check whether you are entitled to asylum support (see Chapter 21).

If you are a British or Irish citizen , or your immigration status does not exclude you from benefit entitlement, work through the following steps.

- **Step one**: check the residence and presence requirements for the benefit you want to claim (see Chapter 13).
- **Step two**: if the benefit you are claiming requires you to be 'habitually resident', check whether you are exempt from, or satisfy, this requirement (see Chapter 11).
- **Step three**: if the benefit you are claiming requires you have a right to reside, check whether you have a right to reside (see Chapter 12), and note the some residence rights are excluded for particular benefits (p151).
- **Step four:** if you are claiming universal credit and you have a partner, check whether s/he is exempt from, or satisfies, the habitual residence test, including having a right to reside, and check how this affects your award (see p142).

- **Step five:** if you are claiming a disability or carer's benefit, check Chapter 16 to see whether you are covered by the European Union (EU) social security co-ordination rules. If so, check whether the UK is the 'competent state' to pay these benefits (see p369).
- **Step six:** if you are entitled to benefit and want to know whether you can continue to be paid when you, or someone who is included in your claim, go abroad, see Chapter 14 for an overview of the rules and Chapter 15 for the specific rules for individual benefits.
- **Step seven:** if you do not satisfy the residence and presence rules, check whether the EU co-ordination rules can assist you. The ways these rules can assist you to be entitled is explained for specific benefits in Chapter 13, and to continue to be entitled when you move to a European country is explained for specific benefits in Chapter 15. An overview of the different rules and who each applies to is covered in Chapter 16.

Note: the rules for European Economic Area (EEA) nationals changed significantly at the end of 2020, and, in most cases, entitlements were reduced. However, if you are an EEA national already living in the UK before the end of 2020, or you are a family member of such an EEA national, you may be in a protected group able to claim benefits under the rules that applied previously. Similarly, if you were an EEA national living in the UK, or a British citizen living in an EEA country, before the end of 2020, you may be covered by protections that mean the main EU co-ordination rules apply to you. For an overview of changes due to the UK leaving the EU, which apply after the end of 2020, see p164 and p350.

3. Finding the relevant law

The complexity of the rules that specifically affect migrants means that it can be useful to refer to the relevant law not only when you are challenging a decision, but also when you make your claim. In order to ensure that the decision maker makes the correct decision on your claim, it is advisable to provide a letter setting out the legal requirements that you must satisfy for the particular benefit (eg, the immigration status, residence or presence requirements) and the ways in which you satisfy them. You may need to set out additional law (eg, the legislation and caselaw on when you have a right to reside) and provide evidence to show how this applies to you.

However, this does not guarantee that the correct decision will be made. If you are refused benefit when you believe you are entitled to it, you should challenge the decision. In any challenge, wherever possible, try to set out the relevant legal requirements and explain clearly how you meet them, citing the relevant law as appropriate and providing as much evidence as you can to show you meet the requirements.

This *Handbook* provides references to the law (both legislation and caselaw) and to guidance, so you can locate the source of the information given in the text.

- Find the information in the book relevant to the legal requirement you must satisfy and the text on how you satisfy it that applies to you.
- Find the endnote for that information and check the endnote text at the end of the chapter for the legal reference.
- Check Appendix 7 for an explanation of the abbreviations used in the references.
- See Appendices 2 and 4 for where to find the law and guidance online and for other useful sources of information.
- See Chapter 20 for information about providing evidence to show you satisfy legal requirements.

For a useful introduction to using legal sources, see CPAG's *Welfare Benefits and Tax Credits Handbook.*

Note: the law referred to in this *Handbook* applies in Great Britain. The equivalent law in Northern Ireland is often very similar and, in most cases, has the same effect. Many of the differences are due to the fact that the legislation and the administrative and adjudicating bodies in Northern Ireland are named differently. However, sometimes the law in Northern Ireland on a particular rule is different.

4. **Immigration advice**

If you are unsure about your immigration status, or that of anyone you could include in your claim, or you need to know what the immigration options are for you and your family, get specialist advice from your local law centre, Citizens Advice or other advice agency that gives immigration advice (see Appendix 2).

Anyone who gives immigration advice must be:

- a solicitor, barrister or legal executive, or supervised by such a person; *or*
- registered by the Office of the Immigration Services Commissioner (OISC); *or*
- an adviser with an organisation that is exempt from registration. For example, Citizens Advice offices are exempt, but only to give basic immigration advice.

It is a criminal offence for someone not covered by one of the above groups to give immigration advice.

Every OISC-registered or exempt advice agency should display a certificate issued by the OISC to show it meets the OISC standards.

A list of all OISC-registered and exempt advisers and advice organisations is on the OISC website, which also includes details of how to make a complaint about an immigration adviser.

Part 2

Immigration law

Chapter 2

Immigration and nationality law: overview

This chapter covers:

1. Immigration and nationality law

The right to live, work and settle in the UK is regulated and controlled by a complex system of laws. These are amended frequently. If you are unsure about your immigration status, or about the immigration status of anyone you could include in your benefit claim, get specialist advice from a regulated provider of immigration services. Citizens Advice can signpost or refer you (see p7).

Sources of law

The main UK Acts of Parliament that are concerned with immigration and nationality law are:

- Immigration Act 1971;
- British Nationality Act 1981;
- Immigration Act 1988;
- Asylum and Immigration Appeals Act 1993;
- Asylum and Immigration Act 1996;
- Human Rights Act 1998;
- Immigration and Asylum Act 1999;
- Nationality, Immigration and Asylum Act 2002;
- Asylum and Immigration (Treatment of Claimants, etc.) Act 2004;
- Immigration, Asylum and Nationality Act 2006;
- UK Borders Act 2007;

- Borders, Citizenship and Immigration Act 2009;
- Immigration Act 2014;
- Immigration Act 2016.

These Acts are supplemented by:
- statutory instruments (regulations);
- the Immigration Rules;
- government policies.

You can find the original (as enacted) and revised versions of Acts of Parliament and statutory instruments at legislation.gov.uk, although more recent revisions may not be included.

The Immigration Rules and most government policies concerning immigration can be found at gov.uk/guidance/immigration-rules and gov.uk/topic/immigration-operational-guidance.

The UK has also signed various international treaties and conventions, which guarantee certain rights. These include the:
- European Convention for the Protection of Human Rights and Fundamental Freedoms 1950 (the 'European Convention on Human Rights'), incorporated, in part, into UK law by the Human Rights Act 1998;
- 1951 United Nations (UN) Convention Relating to the Status of Refugees and its 1967 Protocol, commonly referred to as 'the Refugee Convention';
- 1954 UN Convention Relating to the Status of Stateless Persons and the 1961 Convention on the Reduction of Statelessness;
- European Council Directive 2003/9/EC, laying down minimum standards for the reception of asylum seekers ('the Reception Directive');
- European Council Directive 2004/83/EC on minimum standards for the qualification and status of third-country nationals or stateless people as refugees or as persons who otherwise need international protection, and the content of the protection granted ('the Qualification Directive');
- European Council Directive 2004/38/EC on the right of citizens of the European Union (EU) and their family members to move and reside freely within the territory of the member states ('the Citizens' Directive');
- 2005 Council of Europe Convention on Action Against Trafficking in Human Beings.

The UK left the EU at 11pm on 31 January 2020. This was followed by a transition / implementation period, which ended at 11pm on 31 December 2020. At the end of the transition / implementation period, existing EU law was incorporated into domestic law and is known as 'retained law'. As for all UK law, retained law can be amended or revoked. Please see p171 for details of European free movement rights that can apply for 'protected groups' after the end of the transition / implementation period.

Caselaw of the tribunals and higher courts in the UK and Europe is also important in immigration and nationality law. Much of this can be accessed free of charge on the British and Irish Legal Information Institute website at bailii.org. See p174 for the status of decisions of the Court of Justice of the EU after the transition / implementation period.

Relevant institutions

The **Home Secretary** (Secretary of State for the Home Department) is responsible for the **Home Office.** The department within the Home Office that deals with immigration control is called **UK Visas and Immigration (UKVI)**. Home Office is used throughout this *Handbook*.

Immigration officers are generally responsible for granting permission to enter the UK to people who arrive at the various ports of entry, and for arresting, detaining and enforcing the removal of people from the UK. They have powers of search, entry, seizure and arrest of those suspected of having committed a criminal offence under immigration law, and may arrest and detain people who can be lawfully removed to enforce their departure from the UK under immigration law.

Entry clearance officers stationed overseas are responsible for immigration control prior to entry to the UK. They process applications made outside of the UK and decide whether to give **entry clearance** or **visas** to applicants under the Immigration Rules and on human rights or on other grounds (see Chapter 3).

Civil servants in the Home Office are mainly responsible for deciding immigration and nationality applications made in the UK. Some applications made from outside the UK are referred to civil servants in the UK by entry clearance officers stationed overseas.

HM Passport Office is responsible for issuing UK passports. The General Register Office is the part of HM Passport Office that administers the civil registration process in England and Wales – eg, births, deaths, marriages and civil partnerships.

Police officers are responsible for registering people who are required to register with police after their arrival in the UK. They may also arrest people suspected of having committed a criminal offence under immigration law, and arrest and detain people in order to enforce their departure from the UK under immigration law.

Judges of the **Immigration and Asylum Chambers of the First-tier Tribunal and the Upper Tribunal** are responsible for hearing and determining appeals against decisions made by entry clearance officers, immigration officers and the Home Office, applications for bail and most immigration-related judicial review applications.

Judges of the **Social Entitlement Chamber of the First-tier Tribunal** are responsible for determining appeals against decisions refusing asylum support.

Judges of the **Court of Appeal (in England and Wales), the Court of Session (in Scotland) and the UK Supreme Court** hear appeals from the Upper Tribunal, and judges of the **High Court** (in England and Wales) and the Court of Session (in Scotland) continue to decide applications for judicial review of certain types of decisions by the Home Office and the Upper Tribunal.

Cases may also be brought in the **European Court of Human Rights** if the matter concerns the European Convention on Human Rights.

2. The main types of immigration status

There are five main types of immigration status in the UK.

- British citizens and people with the right of abode. These people are not subject to immigration control (see p15).
- People who have limited leave to enter or remain (see Chapter 3).
- People who have indefinite leave to remain (see Chapter 3).
- People who have pre-settled or settled status under the European Union (EU) settlement scheme and some citizens of the European Economic Area (EEA) whose rights to reside are protected from 31 December 2020 to 30 June 2021 (see Chapter 5).
- People who do not have an immigration status:
  - illegal entrants are people who have entered the UK without leave to enter or remain, including those who have made an in-country immigration application or an asylum claim (see Chapter 4);
  - 'overstayers' are people who had leave to remain and who stayed in the UK after the expiry date of their leave and did not make an in-time extension application.

  If you do not have immigration status, you are liable to be detained, but you may be granted immigration bail (previously called temporary admission, temporary release or bail – see below) as an alternative to detention.

Note: the term 'person subject to immigration control' is important for establishing someone's entitlement to benefits. It has a specific meaning that is explained on p81.

Immigration bail

The Home Office has the power to detain you if you require, but do not have, leave (permission) to remain in the UK. As an alternative to detention, the Home Office may grant you immigration bail. **Note**: immigration bail replaced all forms of bail, temporary admission and temporary release from 15 January 2018. Immigration bail is retrospective, so all types of bail granted before 15 January 2018 are known as immigration bail.

If you apply for leave to enter or remain (including an asylum or a human rights claim) at a port of entry or while in the UK when you do not have leave, you may be given immigration bail until your application is decided. If you are in immigration detention, you may be released on immigration bail. Immigration bail may also be given if:

- you remain in the UK after your application for leave to remain has been refused; *or*
- you remain in the UK after your limited leave to enter or remain has expired; *or*
- you are discovered in the UK without leave to remain.

Immigration bail is an alternative to detention and may continue after the refusal of asylum or any other type of application. Immigration bail may also continue during Home Office consideration of further submissions or a new application (see p46).

If you were granted immigration bail (or temporary admission before 15 January 2018) at a port of entry, you are considered to be 'lawfully resident in the UK', if you are later granted leave to enter or remain. This can be significant if you must meet the requirement to have resided lawfully in the UK for a specified period of time to become eligible for citizenship or for leave to remain on the grounds of long residence. It can also be relevant to your eligibility to claim benefits.

Immigration bail includes at least one condition, such as a requirement to live at a specified address, to report to an immigration officer at a specified time and place, and not to engage in paid or unpaid employment. There can be criminal penalties if you do not adhere to these conditions, and failing to do so will be taken into account in any decision on whether to place you into immigration detention.

If you are on immigration bail, you should have been issued with a notice (form BAIL 201) informing you of your status and any conditions that apply.

Note: in certain circumstances, the Home Office must provide accommodation to people with, or applying for, immigration bail (see p507).

3. British nationality

You can acquire British nationality:

- at birth, depending on the date and place of your birth, and on the nationality/citizenship and immigration and/or marital status of your parents; *or*
- on adoption; *or*
- by applying to the Home Office for naturalisation or registration; *or*
- as the result of legislative change.

Note: the examples given in this *Handbook* of how British citizenship may be acquired are basic. British nationality law is complex and there are many other routes that are not covered here.

There are six different forms of British nationality, only one of which (British citizenship) gives the right of abode in the UK (see below). A British national may be a:

- British citizen;
- British overseas territories citizen;
- British subject;
- British protected person;
- British national (overseas);
- British overseas citizen.

Some of the above forms of British nationality are rare and can no longer be acquired. In time, only British citizenship and British overseas territories citizenship will exist.

Multiple nationalities

Although some countries do not allow dual or multiple nationality or citizenship, UK law permits you to be a British national and a national of any number of other countries.

British nationals and the right of abode

The **'right of abode'** gives you the freedom to enter, live in and leave the UK at any time.

All full British citizens have the right of abode, but most people who have some other form of British nationality do not have this right. Some Commonwealth citizens also have the right of abode, including people who are British nationals and not British citizens. However, it has not been possible to gain the right of abode since 1983 without also being a British citizen.

A British national who does not have the right of abode generally requires leave to enter or remain in the UK but may be able to apply to register as a British citizen.

Acquiring British citizenship at birth

Most people, except children of diplomats and 'enemy aliens', born in the UK before 1 January 1983 automatically acquired British citizenship on that date.[1]

If you were born in the UK on or after 1 January 1983, you only acquired British citizenship if, at the time of your birth:

- your mother was a British citizen or was 'settled' in the UK – eg, she had indefinite leave to remain or permanent residence;[2] *or*

- your father was a British citizen or was 'settled' in the UK. If you were born before 1 July 2006, you could only gain citizenship from your father in this way if your parents were married, either at the time or subsequently. Since 1 July 2006, this restriction has no longer applied. If you are affected by the restriction, you may be able to apply to register as a British citizen.

From 1 January 1983, if you were born overseas, you would have acquired British citizenship at birth if either parent was a British citizen, unless that parent was her/himself a British citizen 'by descent' – ie, because s/he was also born overseas.[3] The same provisions as above apply to unmarried British fathers of children born abroad.

---

4. Immigration and nationality applications

Applying from outside the UK

If you do not have the right of abode, you have must obtain entry clearance before travelling to the UK to seek entry for most purposes.

Nationals of countries or territories listed in Appendix V of the Immigration Rules are known as '**visa nationals**'. See gov.uk/guidance/immigration-rules/immigration-rules-appendix-v-visitor. If you are a visa national, you must obtain a visa before travelling to the UK for any purpose (unless you are a refugee – see Chapter 4).

Nationals of all other countries ('**non-visa nationals**') may apply to an immigration officer at the port of arrival for entry for certain purposes, mainly for short-term visits. If you are a non-visa national and you intend to stay for a longer period, you must usually obtain entry clearance before travelling.

Note: from 1 January 2021, the non-European Economic Area (EEA) national family member of an EEA national must obtain an EEA family permit before s/he travels to the UK.

An exempt vignette is issued to people, such as diplomats, who are exempt from the requirements of the Immigration Act 1971.

In most countries, you can apply for entry clearance online. In some countries, you must complete a printed application form. All applicants must attend a visa application centre in person. There is not a visa application centre in every country in the world, so you may have to travel to a different country to apply. Most applicants must have their fingerprints and photograph (known as 'biometric information') taken at the visa application centre.

To apply for British nationality from outside the UK, you must either make an online application or send your application to the Home Office in the UK.

Applying from within the UK

The Home Office is responsible for processing applications made by people in the UK:

- for leave to remain in the UK, including for asylum;
- to extend their leave to remain;
- to vary their leave to remain – ie, to change the type of leave;
- for indefinite leave to remain;
- for settled status or pre-settled status under the European Union (EU) Settlement Scheme;
- for British nationality.

Application procedure

Most applications must be made online. That includes human rights applications in which the applicant is not making a protection claim. Protection claims, which include asylum, humanitarian protection and some human rights claims, must be made in person at the Home Office (see Chapter 4).

Certain types of application must usually be made in person at a specified location. These include applications for asylum (except those made under Article 3 of the European Convention on Human Rights solely for health reasons), which are known as 'protection claims'. Other types of application may also be made in person. A 'premium service' is available, with a shorter processing time (applications are sometimes dealt with on the same day), at an increased cost.

Home Office application fees

A fee is charged for most applications and for biometric enrolment. Some types of application are exempt from the fee, including:[4]

- an application for leave to enter or remain on protection grounds, including asylum, humanitarian protection and human rights claims (note that stand-alone human rights claims, that do not rely on Article 3, are not exempt from the fee);
- an application made under Article 3 of the European Convention on Human Rights on medical grounds;
- an application for leave to enter or remain by a child who is being looked after by a local authority;
- a 'Windrush' application for citizenship, a document confirming the right of abode or settled status, or indefinite leave to remain by a Commonwealth citizen who was either settled in the UK before 1 January 1973 or has the right of abode, or by her/his child, or by someone of any nationality who arrived in the UK before 31 December 1988 and is settled in the UK;
- an application for limited leave to enter or remain by a victim of trafficking (in limited circumstances only);
- an application for limited leave to enter or remain for certain purposes if the Home Office accepts that the applicant is destitute or that other exceptional

circumstances apply. In these circumstances, you must complete an application form for a fee waiver (available at gov.uk/government/publications/applications-for-a-fee-waiver-and-refunds) and provide evidence. See below;

- an application for settled status or pre-settled status by an EEA national or the family member of an EEA national under the EU Settlement Scheme.

Home Office fee waiver policy

A fee waiver is an application to avoid paying the Home Office application fee and immigration health surcharge, on the basis that the person cannot afford to pay. Fee waivers are only possible for certain types of immigration application.

- An application for limited leave to enter or remain for certain purposes if the Home Office accepts that the applicant is destitute or that other exceptional circumstances apply. In these circumstances, you must provide evidence and complete an application form for a fee waiver (available at gov.uk/government/publications/applications-for-a-fee-waiver-and-refunds).
- Applications for leave to remain under the five-year partner route from applicants who are not required to meet the minimum income threshold because their sponsor is in receipt of one or more specified benefits and who instead must demonstrate that their sponsor can provide adequate maintenance.
- Applications for leave to remain under the five-year parent route.
- Applications for leave to remain under the 10-year partner, parent or private life route in which the applicant claims that refusal of that application for leave to remain would breach her/his rights (or the rights of other specified persons) under Article 8 of the European Convention of Human Rights (ECHR) (the right to respect for private and family life).
- Applications for leave to remain on the basis of other ECHR rights.
- Applications for further leave to remain from applicants granted discretionary leave following refusal of asylum or humanitarian protection in which the applicant claims that refusal to grant further leave to remain would breach her/his ECHR right (except Article 3 claims, which are fee exempt).
- Applications for further discretionary leave made by victims of trafficking or slavery who have had a positive conclusive grounds decision from a competent authority of the national referral mechanism (NRM), have already accrued 30 months' discretionary leave and are seeking to extend it for reasons related to trafficking or slavery.

To benefit from the fee waiver policy, you must show that any one or more of the following apply:

- you are destitute, meaning that you cannot meet your essential living needs or that you are unable to obtain adequate accommodation; *or*
- you are at risk of imminent destitution; *or*

- your income is not sufficient to meet a child's particular and additional needs; *or*
- you are faced with exceptional financial circumstances.

Immigration health surcharge

An additional charge, described as an 'immigration health surcharge' is charged by the Home Office in applications for limited leave to enter or remain. Exceptions include applications for:[5]

- indefinite leave to enter or remain;
- entry clearance for leave to enter for six months or less – eg, for visitors, fiancé(e)s and some prospective students;
- leave to enter or remain by a child under 18 who is being looked after by a local authority;
- leave to enter or remain based on protection grounds, including asylum, humanitarian protection and some human rights claims (not including stand-alone Article 8 claims);
- leave to remain on medical grounds under Article 3 of the ECHR;
- applications made solely under Article 3 of the ECHR for health reasons;
- leave to remain that relates to someone being identified as a victim of human trafficking;
- leave to remain outside the Immigration Rules with access to public funds under the Home Office policy known as the 'destitution domestic violence concession' (see p36).

The fee waiver application is an application for the waiver of the application fee, biometric enrolment fee and the immigration health surcharge. The standard immigration health surcharge is £470 per person per year of leave applied for by applicants aged under 18, students, applicants for leave to remain under the Youth Mobility Scheme (Tier 5) and each of their dependants. The standard immigration health surcharge is £624 a year per person per year of leave applied for by everyone else. It is payable with the application fee at the time of making the application.

For information on NHS healthcare, including charges and on who is exempt from them, see p589.

Section 3C extension of leave to remain

Section 3C of the Immigration Act 1971 operates to extend your leave to remain if the three conditions below are met. The exact section of section 3C that applies is important because it can affect your entitlement to benefits.

Your leave to remain is automatically extended, on the same conditions as before, while you wait for the Home Office to make a decision, if the following three conditions are met:[6]

- you have limited leave to remain and you apply to the Home Office to extend or vary your leave (section 3C(1)(a)); *and*
- your application is made 'in time' – ie, before your current leave expires (section 3C(1)(b)); *and*
- your current leave expires before a decision on the extension or variation application has been made (section 3C(1)(c)).

If the above conditions are satisfied and the Home Office refuses your application for leave to remain, your leave is further extended on the same conditions as before, if you have a right of appeal or administrative review (see below):

- section 3C(2)(b) extends your leave, during the period in which an appeal can be brought; *or*
- section 3(2)(c) extends your leave from the date that an in-time appeal is made, until it is concluded, and you have exhausted your appeal rights; *or*
- section 3(2)(ca) extends your leave from the date of a refusal of EU pre-settled or settled status during the period in which an appeal can be brought; *or*
- section 3(2)(cb) extends your leave from the time that an in-time appeal against a refusal of EU pre-settled status or settled status is made, until it is concluded, and you have exhausted your appeal rights; *or*
- section 3C(2)(d)(i) extends your leave during the period in which an application for administrative review can be sought; *or*
- section 3C(2)(d)(ii) extends your leave from the date that an in-time application for administrative review is made until it is decided.

For the way this can affect your entitlement to benefits see p86 and p92.

5. Appeals and other remedies

Appeals to the First-tier Tribunal

The First-tier Tribunal (Immigration and Asylum Chamber) is a judicial authority that is independent of the UK government.

Rights of appeal

Rights of appeal to the tribunal against immigration decisions are provided by statute. If you lodge an appeal, you are known as an 'appellant' and the Home Office is known as the 'respondent'. There are a limited number of Home Office decisions that can be appealed:

- refusal of a protection claim – ie, a claim for asylum or humanitarian protection;[7]
- refusal of a human rights claim, including applications within the Immigration Rules made on private and family life grounds;[8]
- revocation of protection (ie, refugee or humanitarian protection) status;[9]

- deprivation of British citizenship;[10]
- refusal of pre-settled or settled status under the European Union (EU) settlement scheme (provided the application was made on or after 31 January 2020).[11]

To get the appeal started, you must 'give notice of appeal' by submitting the correct appeal form to the Tribunal.

Appeal time limits

If you are outside the UK when entry clearance is refused, you must file your notice of appeal with the tribunal in the UK within 28 calendar days of receiving the decision.[12] Most decisions are given to you in person and the 28 days runs from the date decision is handed to you. If the decision is not handed to you in person, there is another 28 days for 'service' making a total 56 calendar days.

If you are in the UK when you receive a decision, you must give notice within 14 days of the date that the appeal is 'sent'. Generally, the date that a notice is sent must be taken from the covering letter, but if there is a postmark on the envelope or a later date on any of the paper work, that could be evidence of a later sending date.

Depending on the Home Office decision, if you are in the UK when you receive a decision, you may have to leave the UK before you can give notice of appeal. You then have 28 days after the date of departure to give notice of appeal.

In-country and out-of-country appeals

If you apply for entry clearance from outside the UK and you do not have leave to remain in the UK, you will normally remain outside the UK to file a notice of appeal with the tribunal and until the appeal is finally determined.

If you arrive at a UK port or are in the UK when you receive the decision, you will normally be able to submit your notice of appeal while still in the UK and will remain in the UK until the appeal is fully determined.

Certification

In certain circumstances, the Home Office has powers to 'certify' a case so that you cannot appeal the decision at all or until after you have you have left the UK.[13] Claims that may be certified include:

- a human rights claim in which it is shown that you can appeal from outside the UK without your human rights being breached;
- an asylum claim that is not arguable or is bound to fail;
- a claim that raises a reason to remain in the UK that could have been raised in an earlier appeal.

The Home Office decision to certify the case may itself be suitable for a challenge by judicial review (see p24).

Tribunal fees

For most appeals, a tribunal appeal fee is payable. This fee does not currently apply:

- if you are receiving asylum support; *or*
- if you are receiving legal aid; *or*
- if the Home Office waived the fees for the application that has been refused; *or*
- if you are a child being supported by a local authority; *or*
- if you are the parent of a child being supported by the local authority under social work powers to safeguard and promote the care of children in the area; *or*
- if you are appealing against the deprivation of your British citizenship; *or*
- if you are appealing against the revocation of your protection status; *or*
- if you are an European Economic Area (EEA), or the familiy member of an EEA, citizen and you are appealing against removal; *or*
- in asylum appeals in which the appellant is detained and the decision has been served by the detained asylum casework team.

Alternatively, you can apply to have the fee reduced if you receive certain benefits or have limited savings and are on a low income. If your appeal is allowed or dismissed in the First-tier Tribunal, you or the Home Office can appeal to the Upper Tribunal if there is an error of law that could have made a difference to the outcome. Appeals can progress from the Upper Tribunal to the Court of Appeal in England and Wales, the Court of Session in Scotland and, if it is a human rights appeal, to the European Court of Human Rights. If your appeal is allowed in the First-tier Tribunal and the Home Office does not make an onward appeal, the Home Office must then decide whether to grant leave and, if so, what type of leave should be granted.

Administrative review

When a Home Office decision cannot be appealed, you may be able to apply to the Home Office for an 'administrative review'.[14] The Immigration Rules specify which decisions can be subject to administrative review. Administrative review is carried out by the Home Office and not by an independent body. Decisions that can be subject to administrative review include:

- some entry clearance decisions; *and*
- some in-country decisions, including decisions on applications under the domestic violence rule; *and*
- some decisions to refuse or cancel leave to remain when a person arrives at the UK border.

If a decision has been made about you by the Home Office that cannot be appealed (see above), you may be able to apply to the Home Office for an administrative review. That is carried out internally by the Home Office, but not by the officer who made the initial decision. Examples of such decisions include a decision to refuse you entry clearance or to refuse you leave to enter or remain if you have not made an asylum, humanitarian protection or human rights claim. There is a fee of £80.

Administrative review time limits

Time limits run from the date on which you receive the 'notice of decision' (ie, the cover letter) that accompanies the written reasons.[15]

Time limits to apply for administrative review of decisions made before 31 January 2020 under Appendix EU[16] are:

- if you are in the UK and not detained, no more than 28 calendar days after you received the notice of decision; *or*
- if you are in UK immigration detention, no more than seven calendar days after you received the notice of decision; *or*
- if you are outside the UK, no more than 28 days after you received the decision.

Time limits for other eligible decisions are:

- if you are in the UK, no later than 14 calendar days after you received the decision; *or*
- if you are in immigration detention in the UK, no later than seven days after you received the decision; *or*
- if you are outside of the UK, no later than 28 after you received the decision; *or*
- if the decision is a grant of leave to remain, and you want to have the length and/or conditions reviewed, no later than 14 days after you received the biometric information document which sets out the length and conditions of leave granted.

Judicial review

Some Home Office and tribunal decisions can be challenged by judicial review, including:

- a decision that does not carry a right of appeal; *and*
- a decision to certify a case; *and*
- a decision that carries a right of administrative review; *and*
- an administrative review decision.

In England and Wales, judicial review applications in immigration matters are made to the Upper Tribunal and in some cases to the Administrative Court – eg, unlawful detention, refusal of British citizenship and trafficking decisions. In Scotland, judicial review claims are made to the Court of Session. Applications for judicial review are legally and procedurally complex, and you are strongly advised to seek professional immigration advice before beginning proceedings.

The Administrative Court and the Court of Session hear applications for immigration bail if they are also considering a judicial review claim of unlawful detention.

6. **Deportation and administrative removal**

'Deportation' is a procedure under which a person is removed from the UK and is excluded for at least 10 years, or for as long as the deportation order remains in force.

Automatic deportation

If you are not a British citizen and are convicted as an adult in the UK of an offence and are sentenced to 12 months or more in prison, the Home Office must make a deportation order unless an exception applies.[17]

Public good deportation

If you do not have the right of abode (see p16), the Home Office can decide to deport you (see above) for any reason if it considers your presence to be 'not conducive to the public good'.[18] The reasons are usually associated with a person's criminality and could range from convictions in the UK or elsewhere or serious criminal offences through persistent offending to police intelligence on criminal behaviour or threats to national security.

Family members of people facing deportation

The Home Office also has the power to deport your spouse or civil partner and children under 18,[19] but will not normally do so if they have indefinite leave to remain in their own right or are separated from you.[20]

Challenging deportation decisions

You will only have a right of appeal against a deportation decision if you raise an exception on asylum or human rights grounds. Otherwise the decision may be suitable for a judicial review challenge.

Administrative removal

Administrative removal is the procedure for removing someone who does not have leave to remain in the UK[21] – eg, because s/he is an illegal entrant or an overstayer. If you are removed, you may be banned from returning to the UK for a number of months or years, depending on whether you left the UK voluntarily or not and whether you left at the expense of the Home Office.

Notes

3. **British nationality**
   1 s11 BNA 1981
   2 s1 BNA 1981
   3 s2 BNA 1981

4. **Immigration and nationality applications**
   4 The Immigration and Nationality (Fees) Regulations 2016, No.226
   5 The Immigration (Health Charge) (Amendment) Order 2020, No.1086
   6 s3C IA 1971

5. **Appeals and other remedies**
   7 s82(1) NIAA 2002
   8 s82(1) NIAA 2002
   9 s82(1) NIAA 2002
   10 s40 BNA 1981
   11 The Immigration (Citizens' Rights Appeals) (EU Exit) Regulations 2020, No.61
   12 The Tribunal Procedure (First-tier Tribunal) (Immigration and Asylum Chamber) Rules 2014, No.2604 (as amended)
   13 ss94-99 NIAA 2002
   14 Appendix AR and Appendix AR (EU) IR
   15 para 34R(1) IR
   16 para 34R(1A) IR

6. **Deportation and administrative removal**
   17 ss32-39 UK Borders Act 2007
   18 s3(5) and (6) IA 1971
   19 s5 IA 1971
   20 para 365 IR
   21 s10 IAA 1999

Chapter 3

Leave to enter or remain

This chapter covers:

1. Leave to enter or remain

If you do not have the right of abode (see p16), you may be subject to immigration control and require 'permission' to enter or remain in the UK. This permission is known as 'leave'. You may have 'leave to enter', 'leave to remain', which are both time limited, or 'indefinite leave to remain'.

The Immigration Rules set out the circumstances in which leave to enter or remain can be granted for various purposes, including for study, employment and business, family connections, private life, long residence, human rights and asylum. The Immigration Rules also stipulate the duration of the leave and any conditions attached, the circumstances in which leave will be refused, curtailed or revoked, and the criteria for deporting people whose presence in the UK is considered to be against the public interest – eg, if someone has committed a serious criminal offence.

Changes to the Immigration Rules must be notified to parliament, but there does not need to be any debate before the changes take effect. The rules are currently extremely lengthy, complicated and difficult to navigate. That was recognised by the judiciary and the Law Commission and, in response, the Home Office is now redeveloping the rules. The Immigration Rules are available at gov.uk/guidance/immigration-rules. The website also contains policy guidance that explains the Immigration Rules. The explanation given in the guidance is not always followed by tribunals and courts, but the guidance must usually be followed by the Home Office.

Note: leave may also be granted outside the Immigration Rules (see p45).

Conditions of leave

Leave to enter or limited leave to remain in the UK may be granted with a limited number of conditions attached. If you breach the conditions attached to your leave, you may commit a criminal offence, your leave could be curtailed or revoked, and future applications for leave could be refused. You could also be detained and removed from the UK.

The conditions that may be attached to limited leave to remain include:

- a condition about where you live;
- a requirement to register with the police and/or report to the Home Office;
- restrictions on your taking employment or studying (see p30); *and/or*
- a condition preventing you from claiming 'public funds' as defined in the Immigration Rules.

Who is exempt from the usual conditions

Some people are exempt from some of the usual conditions attached to leave to enter and remain in the UK. The main categories of people who are exempt are seamen and women, aircrew, diplomats and members of the UK or visiting armed forces.[1]

Turkish nationals

The Turkish EC Association Agreement (ECAA) ceased to have effect in the UK on 31 December 2020. Under the ECAA, Turkish nationals could establish themselves in the UK for economic purposes, relying on the more favourable Immigration Rules in place on 1 January 1973, the date that the UK joined the European Community (EC).

The Home Office has introduced a five-year route to settlement (indefinite leave to remain) for these Turkish nationals and their family members, under Appendix ECAA of the Immigration Rules.

The scheme is open to Turkish nationals who applied for leave to remain under the ECAA before 11pm on 31 December 2020 and their applications were successful. Turkish business-persons, workers and their family members are eligible to apply for an extension of leave or for indefinite leave to remain. Partners who did not previously have leave in this category cannot apply and must consider an application under Appendix FM of the Immigration Rules. Dependent children younger than 21 years old can apply for entry clearance, leave to remain or indefinite leave to remain in this category. Children aged older than 21 cannot apply for entry clearance but can apply for an extension of leave or for indefinite leave to remain in this category only if they previously had leave in this category.

2. Time-limited leave

Leave may be granted for a limited period of time. Depending on the requirements in the Immigration Rules, you may be able to extended your leave to remain or 'switch' into another category. Not all types of leave can be extended or varied.

If you make a valid application to extend or vary your leave before it expires, that is known as an 'in-time' application. You will not then become an overstayer if your existing leave to remain expires before a decision is made on the extension or variation application. The law operates to extend your existing leave to remain, on the same conditions, until you have received a decision on the extension or variation application and, if refused, until you have exhausted your right to an administrative review or an appeal. See Chapter 2 for details of leave to remain under Section 3C Immigration Act 1971.

The Home Office published turnaround time for a decision on an application is six months. The most straightforward applications are often decided within the six-month period, but for some types of application decisions may take many months or even years.

If the application is refused, you may be able to challenge it with a right of appeal or administrative review. The Home Office has the power to 'certify' some asylum and human rights claims with the effect that there is either no appeal right or the appeal right cannot be exercised until after the person has left the UK.

3. Indefinite leave

Indefinite leave to enter or remain in the UK is leave without a time restriction. Indefinite leave is also known as 'settlement'.

There are no conditions (eg, on employment and claiming 'public funds' – see p31) attached to indefinite leave.[2] There is an exception to that if a sponsor gave an undertaking to support you if your application was successful. The sponsorship undertaking has the effect of preventing you from having recourse to public funds as defined in the Immigration Rules. If the applicant does have recourse to public funds, the sponsor may be liable to repay any benefits that s/he claims and could face criminal proceedings. This condition is not endorsed on the applicant's notice of decision or biometric residence permit. The applicant should know if a sponsorship undertaking was given but, if not, s/he may have to make enquiries with the Home Office.

Indefinite leave can lapse if you are absent from the UK for too long (see below). It can also be revoked (see below).

With indefinite leave, you can leave the UK and return without your leave lapsing if:

- you wish to return to settle in the UK; *and*
- you have indefinite leave to remain under the European Union (EU) settlement scheme, you have not been away from the UK for more than five years; *or*
- you have not been away from the UK for more than two years, unless there are special circumstances – eg, a previous long period of residence; *and*
- you did not receive any assistance from public funds towards the cost of leaving the UK. **Note:** 'public funds' in this context is the scheme that allows people to be reimbursed the costs of resettling in their country of origin. It does *not* refer to the fact that you may have claimed benefits and other public funds while in the UK (see p31).[3]

Indefinite leave may be revoked for reasons, including if:

- you become liable to deportation (see p25); *or*
- the leave was obtained by deception.

Note: if you are outside the UK and are granted indefinite leave to enter, your visa shows an 'expiry' or 'valid until' date. This is the date by which you must enter the UK. Upon entry, you automatically have indefinite leave to remain and this date becomes irrelevant.[4]

4. **Employment**

Certain types of leave are granted with a condition prohibiting employment. For example, visitors are usually prohibited from working in the UK. Other types of leave have conditions that limit the number of hours that you can work (eg, as a condition of leave to remain as a student), or for a specific period of employment or business activity. That may be described as 'authorised' work. The details of what is authorised can be found in the relevant government policy published on the Home Office website.

If you have leave for specific employment (eg, under the points-based system), you can only work in the employment or undertake the activity for which you were granted leave. You must apply to the Home Office for permission to change employment.

Employers must check that all new employees have the right to work in the UK and can be prosecuted for employing anyone who cannot lawfully work. You can also be individually prosecuted for working illegally, and you may also lose your leave to remain. The law on the employment of migrant workers has changed several times since this requirement was introduced (in 1997), and the checks an employer must make (or should have made) depend on the date the worker was first employed by the employer. Applying such checks can raise race discrimination issues. If you believe that you have been treated unfavourably by an employer or potential employer, you should seek advice from an employment and discrimination specialist.

Note: in England and Wales since 1 December 2014, some landlords must check whether you have the right to live in the UK before letting a property to you. This includes landlords who take in lodgers or sublet property.

5. Recourse to public funds

In most categories within the Immigration Rules, when you apply for limited leave to enter or remain you have to show that you can maintain and accommodate yourself and your dependants without recourse to 'public funds'. In most categories within the Immigration Rules, a grant of limited leave to enter or remain has a condition that prohibits you from having recourse to public funds.

This condition now affects most grants of limited leave to enter or remain for family or private life reasons granted under Article 8 of the European Convention on Human Rights (see p43). The condition is notified in the decision and endorsed on the biometric residence permit as 'no public funds'. If you breach this condition, you may commit a criminal offence, your current leave could be curtailed or revoked, and future applications for leave could be refused. You could also be detained and removed from the UK and/or refused citizenship on character grounds.

What are public funds

'Public funds' for the purposes of the Immigration Rules are:[5]

- attendance allowance;
- carer's allowance;
- child benefit;
- child tax credit;
- council tax benefit (now abolished);
- council tax reduction;
- disability living allowance;
- income-related employment and support allowance;
- housing benefit;
- income support;
- income-based jobseeker's allowance;
- pension credit;
- personal independence payment;
- severe disablement allowance;
- social fund payments;

- universal credit;
- working tax credit;
- homelessness assistance and housing provided under specific provisions;
- local welfare assistance (except the Discretionary Assistance Fund for Wales).

The restriction on public funds only applies to those public funds listed in the Immigration Rules. Any other state support that is not in the list above, is not restricted. This means that you may be able to access other forms of public funding, including legal aid, education, assistance from local authority social services departments (social work departments in Scotland) and social security benefits not listed above. NHS services are also not public funds under this definition, but they are restricted (see p589).

Note: in certain cases, you can still claim benefits defined as public funds without breaching the condition not to have recourse to public funds (see p96).

Applications to have 'no recourse to public funds' condition removed

If you have been granted leave to remain, which is subject to a 'no recourse to public funds' condition, and your circumstances change (eg, you have a baby and/or are unable to continue working, or you have become unable to support yourself), you may be able to make a 'change of conditions' application. Home Office guidance states that you can apply to have the no recourse to public funds condition removed, if:

- your financial circumstances have changed since being given permission to stay in the UK and you are no longer able to provide food or housing for yourself or your family; *or*
- your child is at risk because of your very low income; *or*
- you had financial problems when you first applied but you did not provide evidence of this and you now want to provide this evidence.

You can only make this application if you have been granted leave to remain:

- as a partner or parent or on private life grounds on the five-year or the 10-year route to settlement; *or*
- on human rights grounds.

Home Office policy is to remove the no recourse to public funds condition if:

- you are destitute; *or*
- there are particularly compelling reasons relating to the welfare of your child on account of your very low income; *or*
- there are exceptional circumstances in your case relating to your financial circumstances; *or*
- you are at risk of becoming destitute.

You are considered destitute if:

- you do not have adequate accommodation or any means of obtaining it (whether or not your other essential living needs are met); *or*
- you have adequate accommodation or the means of obtaining it, but cannot meet your other essential living needs; *or*
- you are at risk of destitution if either or both of the above are imminent.

Note: if you are on a five-year route to settlement and you apply to lift a no recourse to public funds condition, that will result in your being transferred to a 10-year route to settlement.

6. Sponsoring family members

Who is a sponsor

A sponsor is a British citizen, a person with the right of abode, a settled person or a person with refugee status or humanitarian protection. A sponsor supports another person (an applicant) to come to join her/him or remain with her/him in the UK. The Immigration Rules define a sponsor as the person in relation to whom you are seeking leave to enter or remain as a spouse, fiancé/e, civil partner, proposed civil partner, unmarried partner (including same-sex partner) or dependent relative.

A sponsor must usually demonstrate that s/he can maintain and support you in the UK without recourse to public funds. Parents must fulfil a similar role in the case of child applicants.[6] Support by third parties is permitted for some types of application,[7] but not for most 'family' applications.

Financial requirements

For most family applications, the sponsor must have a minimum specified annual income.[8] The amount increases depending on the number of applicants a person wishes to sponsor, including children and other dependants. A sponsor who is getting attendance allowance (AA), disability living allowance (DLA), personal independence payment (PIP), carer's allowance, industrial injuries disablement benefit and certain military and veteran payments does not have to have the specified minimum income.

If the sponsor has more than a certain amount of savings, these can be used to make up any shortfall in her/his annual income.

Your own income and savings can be taken into account if you are already in the UK with permission to work. If you are outside the UK, your income, savings and prospective income, and (in most cases) any support from a third party, are all disregarded.

Adequate maintenance

For leave to be granted under other parts of the Immigration Rules, including some family cases, you must show that you can, and will, be maintained adequately without recourse to public funds. Whether or not there is adequate maintenance depends on the number of applicants and dependants and the nature of the income. To be adequate, the income of the family as a whole must be equal to or greater than the amount an equivalent family would receive from income support (IS) if all the family members were entitled to have recourse to public funds. The use of this benchmark has been justified as necessary to prevent immigrant families or communities having a lower standard of living in the UK than the poorest British citizens.[9] However, the minimum income requirement used in most other cases is significantly higher than that.

Note: support from third parties can be counted for some types of applications not made under Appendix FM of the Immigration Rules.[10]

AA, DLA and PIP claimed by a sponsor can be included when establishing whether a family's income is the same or higher than the IS amount.[11] It is arguable that the same approach should be applied to industrial injuries disablement benefit, and severe disablement allowance and its replacement employment and support allowance. Applicants and sponsors should obtain specialist advice if that might be an issue.

Adequate accommodation

In most cases, to be granted leave to enter or remain as a family member, a certain standard and/or type of accommodation must be available to you.

There must be adequate accommodation for you, your dependants and your sponsor, without you having recourse to public funds and which you and your family own or occupy exclusively.

The accommodation must not be overcrowded. The Housing Act 1985 contains statutory definitions of overcrowding. Accommodation is considered overcrowded if two people aged 10 years or older of the opposite sex (other than husband and wife or unmarried partners) have to sleep in the same room, or if the number of people sleeping in the accommodation exceeds that permitted in the Act, which specifies the number of people for a given number of rooms or given floor area.

The Immigration Rules often require that the accommodation must be owned or occupied 'exclusively' by the family unit concerned. This means that you, your sponsor and your dependants must have exclusive use of bedrooms but you can share other rooms, such as the kitchen, bathroom and living-room, with other people.[12]

If your circumstances change

If you had to satisfy maintenance or accommodation requirements under the Immigration Rules before your leave was granted, your leave may be curtailed and/or a further application refused if you or your sponsor do not continue to meet these requirements throughout the period of leave granted.[13] **Note:** that only applies with limited leave to remain and not with applications for indefinite leave to remain if your leave is subject to a time limit – ie, that does not apply with indefinite leave to enter or remain (see p29). The Home Office might discover that your circumstances have changed if, for example, you or your sponsor make a claim for social security benefits.

If you have been issued with a biometric residence permit, you are required to inform the Home Office, as soon as possible, if you know or suspect that a change in circumstances means that you no longer meet the requirements for leave to remain.

If you think that a change of circumstances may affect your entitlement to leave to remain, you should get specialist advice urgently.

See p36 if a qualifying relationship has ended because of domestic violence.

Maintenance undertakings

A sponsor may be asked to give a written undertaking to be responsible for your maintenance and accommodation, or your care, for the period of leave applied for and any further period of leave to remain.[14] Undertakings are often requested for:

- dependent relatives, although not for children under 16 years coming for settlement;
- students relying on a private individual in the UK.

The benefit authorities sometimes mistakenly assume that every person referred to as a 'sponsor' will have given such an undertaking, but this is not the case. The definition of 'sponsor' is wider than that and not all sponsors are required to give a written undertaking.

If you have been granted leave to enter or remain as a result of a maintenance undertaking, you are excluded from claiming benefits.[15] If you subsequently claim benefit while in the UK, your sponsor may be required to pay back the value of the benefit claimed.[16] This restriction applies until you have been in the UK for five years after the date of the undertaking or the date of entry. If your sponsor dies, the undertaking ends immediately.

A maintenance undertaking may be enforceable, whether or not it is not formally drafted.[17] In one case, a formal declaration that a sponsor was able and willing to maintain and accommodate was held not to amount to an undertaking, because it did not include a promise to support.[18]

Unlike the condition not to have recourse to public funds, a maintenance undertaking is not stated on papers that notify a grant of leave or on the biometric residence permit.

Leave to remain as a partner on the five-year route to settlement

If you meet all the requirements of the Immigration Rules, you can be granted entry clearance for 33 months or leave to enter or remain for 30 months as the spouse, civil partner or unmarried partner of a:

- British citizen; *or*
- settled person; *or*
- member of HM Forces with four years' service; *or*
- holder of refugee status or humanitarian protection. This route is not the 'family reunion' route available to those partners and children who were in the sponsor's family before s/he left their country to claim asylum. See Chapter 4 for family reunion.

This leave is granted with a condition prohibiting recourse to public funds. When you have completed five years in this category, you can apply for indefinite leave to remain.

7. Domestic violence and bereavement

If the partner you joined dies[19] or your relationship breaks down because of domestic violence or abuse while you have leave in this category, you may be able to apply for indefinite leave to remain even though you have not completed five years in this category.[20] The domestic violence application can be made after leave to remain has expired as long as your relationship broke down before your leave expired.

If you need to claim public funds, you can make an application under the destitution domestic violence concession.[21] The application is made on an application form that can be emailed to the Home Office. The Home Office makes a very quick decision, often on the same day. If successful, you will be granted discretionary leave to remain for three months with recourse to public funds. The Home Office then expects you to make the full application for indefinite leave to remain as a victim of domestic violence within those three months.

8. The points-based system

On 2 December 2020, the Home Office introduced a new points-based system for people who wish to work or study in the UK. It appears to be truly points-based with some attributes attracting 'tradable' points.

The categories are named:

- student visa;
- skilled worker route;
- global talent route;
- graduate route (from summer 2021);
- intra-company transfer;
- other:
  - start-up and innovators;
  - health and care visa;
  - creative route;
  - sporting route;
  - seasonal workers;
  - Youth Mobility Scheme.

Notes

1. **Leave to enter or remain**
   1 s8 IA 1971

3. **Indefinite leave**
   2 s3(3)(a) IA 1971
   3 paras 18-19 IR
   4 See UKVI policy guidance ECB9.4, at gov.uk/government/publications/entry-clearance-vignettes-ecb09

5. **Recourse to public funds**
   5 para 6 IR

6. **Sponsoring family members**
   6 para 297 and Appendix FM IR
   7 *Mahad (previously referred to as AM) (Ethiopia) v Entry Clearance Officer* [2009] UKSC 16
   8 Appendix FM IR
   9 *KA (Pakistan)* [2006] UKAIT 00065; approved in *AM (Ethiopia) and Others and Another v Entry Clearance Officer* [2008] EWCA Civ 1082
   10 *Mahad (previously referred to as AM) (Ethiopia) v Entry Clearance Officer* [2009] UKSC 16
   11 *MK (Somalia) v Entry Clearance Officer* [2007] EWCA Civ 1521
   12 Ch8, s1, annex F IDI. This includes information on the minimum size of a room and a table showing the maximum number of people allowed for any specific number of rooms.
   13 paras 322(4)-23 IR
   14 para 35 IR
   15 s115(9)(c) IAA 1999
   16 para 35 IR; ss78, 105 and 106 SSAA 1992

17 *R (Begum)* [2003] *The Times*, 4 December 2003
18 *Ahmed v SSWP* [2005] EWCA Civ 535

7. Domestic violence and bereavement
19 Section BPILR Appendix FM Immigration Rules
20 paras 289A-C IR
21 gov.uk/government/publications/application-for-benefits-for-visa-holder-domestic-violence

Chapter 4

Asylum and human rights

This chapter covers:

1. Asylum seekers

Applying for asylum

If you apply for recognition as a refugee or as a person requiring protection from return to the country of your nationality or former habitual residence, you will be known as an 'asylum seeker'.[1]

Protection claims to the Home Office can be made on one or more of the following grounds:

- under the Refugee Convention (see p12); *or*
- under Article 3 of the European Convention on Human Rights (see p12). This prescribes that no one shall be subjected to torture or to inhuman or degrading treatment or punishment; *or*
- under the Qualification Directive (see p12).

The most common other European Convention on Human Rights Article raised in immigration cases is Article 8, which protects a person's right to enjoy private and family life without unnecessary or disproportionate interference (see p43).

'Temporary protection' is a separate and specific category of leave introduced by the Qualification Directive. It is intended to be given to people following a declaration by the European Union (EU) Council in recognition of a mass influx of displaced people. However, there have been no declarations since the directive came into force.

The definition of an asylum seeker for the purpose of support and accommodation (see p481) is limited to people who have applied under the Refugee Convention and/or Article 3 of the Human Rights Convention, so an application based only on Article 8 does not make someone an asylum seeker for asylum support purposes.[2] However, in certain situations, the Home Office can provide accommodation to people who are subject to immigration control who are not asylum seekers (see p507).

An asylum seeker may have applied for asylum at a port of entry before passing through passport control, or from inside the UK, having entered illegally or with leave for a different purpose under the Immigration Rules.

Note: if you delay making an in-country asylum application, your entitlement to asylum support may be affected (see p481).

If your asylum application is refused or withdrawn, and you have no further appeal rights, you may be able to make a fresh application (see p46).

Detention and removal

If you have leave to remain in another category when you claim asylum, you may be permitted to retain that leave, or the Home Office may curtail your leave. If you do not have leave to remain when you claim asylum, you are an illegal entrant or an overstayer and are, therefore, liable to be detained.

Many asylum seekers are given immigration bail, but a significant number are detained while their application is considered, in the expectation that their application will be considered quickly and they can then be quickly removed from the UK if refused.

A refused asylum seeker can be detained without time limit if the purpose of the detention is removal from the UK and there is some prospect that this will be imminent. People in immigration detention can seek advice or assistance from specialist immigration providers and Bail for Immigration Detainees (biduk.org), which specialises in immigration detention.

Permission to work

If you have not received a decision on your asylum claim after one year, and the delay is not your fault, you can apply to the Home Office for permission to work.[3]

If granted permission, the jobs that you can do are restricted to those on a 'shortage occupation list' that comprises, with some exceptions, mainly high-skilled occupations. This list can change depending on the demands of the UK labour market.

2. Refugee leave and humanitarian protection

If you are an asylum seeker who is recognised by the Home Office as a refugee or as being in need of humanitarian protection, you are granted refugee leave or humanitarian protection leave respectively.

Refugees and humanitarian protection

A **'refugee'** is someone who, owing to a well-founded fear of being persecuted because of race, religion, nationality, membership of a particular social group or political opinion, is outside the country of her/his nationality, and is unable to or, owing to such fear, is unwilling to avail her/himself of the protection of that country.

A person in need of **'humanitarian protection'** is someone who does not qualify as a refugee, but there are substantial grounds for believing that if s/he were returned to her/his country of origin, s/he would face a real risk of suffering serious harm. A person could, for example, face a risk of serious harm for reasons other than race, religion, nationality, membership of a particular social group or political opinion.

If you are granted refugee status or humanitarian protection the Home Office usually grants five years' leave to remain, with the option of applying for indefinite leave shortly before this leave expires. If you are granted human rights protection, you can be given 2.5 years' leave to remain if you meet the requirements of the Immigration Rules or up to 2.5 years discretionary leave if you do not. This is a 10-year route to settlement.

Refugee leave and humanitarian protection leave can be reviewed and revoked, or not extended, if:

- your actions bring you within the scope of the 1951 Refugee Convention 'cessation clauses' – eg, if you travel back to your home country without a reasonable explanation;[4] *or*
- there is a 'significant or non-temporary' change in the conditions in your country of origin (or part of the country), making it safe to return and a formal declaration of the change is made by the responsible state authority.

Family reunion

If you have refugee status or humanitarian protection, you can sponsor your spouse, civil partner, unmarried and/or same-sex partner and dependent children under 18 to come to the UK. The family member making the application must have been part of your family unit before you left the country to claim asylum. That is known as 'family reunion'. There are no minimum income or maintenance and accommodation requirements that must be met.

Successful family reunion applicants are granted leave to remain in line with your leave, but that is not recognition of the applicants as refugees or holders of humanitarian protection. The leave granted will expire at the same time as yours, and, therefore, may be limited leave of up to five years or indefinite leave.[5]

Family members who become part of your family unit after you fled your country must meet the usual immigration rules, including the minimum income and/or maintenance and accommodation requirements. Their leave may also be subject to a condition prohibiting recourse to public funds (see p31).

Exclusions

You can be excluded from refugee status or humanitarian protection status if:

- you have committed a crime against peace, a war crime, a crime against humanity or a serious non-political crime outside the UK before being admitted; *or*
- you are guilty of acts that are contrary to the purposes and principles of the United Nations. That could include being involved in terrorism or encouraging others to commit terrorist acts.

Your protection application can be 'certified' if you have committed a serious offence – eg, if you have been sentenced to 24 months (for refugee status) or 12 months (for humanitarian protection) in prison.

Article 3 of theEuropean Convention on Human Rights protects people from torture, inhuman and degrading treatment and cruel and unusual punishment. If you are excluded from refugee status or humanitarian protection but would face Article 3-type treatment in your home country, the Home Office cannot return you and may grant you a form of discretionary leave, known as restricted leave (see p45).

3. Stateless people

A stateless person is defined by international law as someone who is 'not considered a national by any state under the operation of its law'.[6] On 6 April 2013, the UK introduced a provision in the Immigration Rules to recognise and grant leave to remain to certain stateless people.[7] Before this date, stateless people could obtain travel documents but could not obtain leave. If you are recognised as stateless in the UK, you can still obtain a stateless person's travel document.

4. Leave for human rights and compassionate reasons

Leave granted for Article 8 of the European Convention on Human Rights grounds

Article 8 of the European Convention on Human Rights sets out the right to respect for your private and family life. That is not an absolute right and, in certain circumstances, the Home Office can interfere with this right. You may be able to rely on Article 8 to resist removal and gain leave to remain if you have family in the UK and/or have lived in the UK for some time and developed ties here.

Before 9 July 2012, leave to remain given for Article 8 reasons was granted outside the Immigration Rules and was called **'discretionary leave'** (see below).

Since 9 July 2012, the Immigration Rules have set out the circumstances in which the Home Office will grant leave to remain for private and family life reasons. This includes leave to remain for parents and partners who do not meet the requirements of minimum income, immigration status or English language.

If you have private and family life grounds but do not meet the requirements of the Immigration Rules, you can seek specialist advice on applying outside the Immigration Rules on human rights grounds.

From 9 July 2012, leave is given for periods of no longer than 30 months, potentially leading to indefinite leave after 10 continuous years. That is twice the length of time in which a family member can become eligible for settlement under other parts of the Immigration Rules. Home Office policy is to grant leave subject to a 'no recourse to public funds' condition, unless you raised exceptional circumstances in your application. It is possible to apply for this condition to be lifted if there has been a change in your circumstances, or if the circumstances were not known to the Home Office at the time the leave was granted.[8] Home Office policy is that 'exceptional circumstances' apply when a person is destitute or is a parent on a low income and there are particularly compelling reasons relating to the welfare of her/his child.[9]

Note: if you are a carer or a sibling of a British citizen child, you may be able to apply for leave to remain on Article 8 grounds.

Discretionary leave

Discretionary leave is granted:

- in medical cases. The threshold for leave on this basis is high: you must be seriously ill and face a real risk of being exposed to a serious, rapid and irreversible decline in your health, which would result in 'intense suffering', due to the absence of appropriate treatment were you to be removed from the UK;[10] *or*

- if returning you would breach the European Convention on Human Rights – eg, if the government of the country to which you would be returned would flagrantly deny your rights to a fair trial under Article 6 of the Convention or would deny your rights to enjoy family and private life; *or*
- in other exceptional circumstances specified in Home Office enforcement policies; *or*
- to a victim of trafficking within the meaning of Article 4 of the Council of Europe Convention on Action Against Trafficking in Human Beings where your circumstances are so compelling that it is considered appropriate to grant some form of leave; *or*
- to a refused asylum seeker, but it is considered appropriate to grant leave; *or*
- under transitional arrangements, if you have previously been granted discretionary leave.

People granted discretionary leave are able to work and claim public funds. Discretionary leave should not be granted with a condition prohibiting recourse to public funds.

Discretionary leave is normally granted for a period of 30 months, with the possibility of further extension periods of 30 months. When you have had discretionary leave for 10 continuous years, you can apply for indefinite leave to remain, unless you do not satisfy the indefinite leave rules – eg, because of a criminal conviction or a recent out-of-court settlement such as a caution or for a county court debt.

The previous policy was normally to grant discretionary leave for three years, with the possibility of being able to apply to extend this leave, and to grant indefinite leave to remain after six continuous years. If you were granted discretionary leave before 9 July 2012, pursuant to an asylum refusal, you may benefit from the previous policy and be able to apply for indefinite leave to remain after six years of discretionary leave. An exception applies to discretionary leave granted before 9 July 2012 pursuant to exclusion from refugee status or humanitarian protection on grounds of criminality. In this case, the restricted leave policy now applies (see below).

When you apply for an extension of discretionary leave or for indefinite leave to remain, the Home Office 'actively reviews' your case and will only grant leave if there have been no significant changes or criminality.

Unaccompanied children

In the case of an unaccompanied child whose claim for asylum has been refused, limited leave may be granted within the Immigration Rules for up to 30 months or until the child is 17 and a half, whichever is the shorter period.[11] It is important to recognise that a grant of limited leave under this rule operates as a refusal of the asylum claim, and the child should be assisted to access specialist legal advice on whether or not to appeal this refusal, at the time of the decision. At the expiry of this limited leave, if the child wishes to remain in the UK, s/he must make an application for further leave to remain and this application could be granted or refused.

Section 67 of the Immigration Act 2016 required the UK government to relocate to the UK and support a limited number of unaccompanied children who were living in other countries in Europe and who appeared likely to be eligible for refugee leave or humanitarian protection leave if allowed to apply for that in the UK. Leave to remain can be granted if they are subsequently refused refugee leave or humanitarian protection leave or if this was revoked on review (by which time the person may no longer be a child or may not be an unaccompanied child).

Restricted leave

If you are excluded from refugee status or humanitarian protection (see p41) for the reasons outlined on p42, but you cannot be removed from the UK for human rights reasons (eg, because you face a risk of torture on return), you may be granted restricted leave.

Restricted leave is usually only granted for a maximum of six months at a time, with restrictions:

- on your employment or occupation in the UK;
- on where you can live;
- requiring you to report to the Home Office or the police at regular intervals;
- prohibiting your studying at an educational institution; *and*
- prohibiting your doing voluntary work with children and/or vulnerable adults.

If you knowingly fail to comply with any restrictions imposed, you may commit a criminal offence.

If you have restricted leave and you depart from the UK and common travel area, your leave will lapse; if you want to return to the UK, you will need to make a fresh application.

Exceptional leave

Exceptional leave was replaced by humanitarian protection and discretionary leave in 2003. It was granted for similar reasons but also under blanket policies to applicants from countries experiencing civil or military upheaval.

Leave outside the Immigration Rules

You may be given leave outside the Immigration Rules in special or unusual situations that would not otherwise be covered, including in Article 8 cases (see p43).

The Home Office has a discretion to grant leave to remain outside the Immigration Rules for compassionate reasons. This leave will be subject to a 'no recourse to public funds' condition, unless there are exceptional circumstances described on p43.

5. Fresh applications

If you are a refused asylum seeker, you can be removed from the UK if you have used up all your appeal rights and are without leave to remain, or you have abandoned or withdrawn your asylum claim. Under the Immigration Rules, you may make 'further submissions' if there are new facts, fresh evidence, a change in the country of return or a change in the law.

The Home Office will decide whether the application should be granted or refused. If it is refused, the Home Office will then decide whether the further submissions amount to a 'fresh claim' – ie, a claim that includes significantly different material from the previous one, that is arguable and could succeed in front of a tribunal judge. If the Home Office accepts that it amounts to a fresh claim, a refusal will carry a right of appeal. If not, the only remedy is judicial review.

If you are a refused asylum seeker and you have made further submissions, you are entitled to claim asylum support while the submissions are being considered (see Chapter 21).

Notes

1. **Asylum seekers**
   1 s94(1) IAA 1999
   2 s94(1) IAA 1999
   3 Art 11 EU Dir 2003/9; paras 360-61 IR

2. **Refugee leave and humanitarian protection**
   4 Art 1C(1)-(6) 1951 UN Convention Relating to the Status of Refugees
   5 Part 11, paras 352A-FJ IR and policy instructions

3. **Stateless people**
   6 1954 UN Convention Relating to the Status of Stateless Persons
   7 Part 14 IR

4. **Leave for human rights and compassionate reasons**
   8 See UKVI, *Request for a Change of Conditions of Leave Granted on the Basis of Family or Private Life,* April 2015, available at gov.uk/government/publications/application-for-change-of-conditions-of-leave-to-allow-access-to-public-funds-if-your-circumstances-change
   9 The policy is contained in the IDI, 'Family Life (as a Partner or Parent)' FM 1.0a, and 'Partner and ECHR Article 8 Guidance', FM 8.0, which has been amended on several occasions.
   10 *Paposhvili v Belgium* (Application No. 41738/10) [2016] ECHR 1113, 13 December 2016
   11 para 352ZC IR

Chapter 5

European Economic Area nationals and their families

This chapter covers:

1. The European Economic Area member states

The European Economic Area

The **'European Economic Area'** (EEA) comprises the 27 member states of the European Union (EU) plus the European Free Trade Association (EFTA) countries.

The current member states of the EU are: Austria, Belgium, Bulgaria, Croatia, Cyprus, Czech Republic, Denmark, Estonia, Finland, France, Germany, Greece, Hungary, Ireland, Italy, Latvia, Lithuania, Luxembourg, Malta, Netherlands, Poland, Portugal, Romania, Slovenia, Slovakia, Spain and Sweden.

The EFTA countries are: Norway, Liechtenstein and Iceland.

Switzerland has bilateral agreements with the EU and UK, which provide for Swiss nationals to have similar rights to EEA nationals within the EEA and UK. References to EEA nationals in this *Handbook* therefore include Swiss nationals.

The UK ceased to be an EEA member state when we left the EU on 31 January 2020. This was followed by a transition period during which EEA Regulations continued to apply, which ended on 31 December 2020.

2. **Overview of immigration law changes since Brexit**

Prior to the UK ending its membership of the European Union (EU), the rights of European Economic Area (EEA) nationals and their family members living in the UK came from European law, which was largely reproduced in domestic law in the Immigration (European Economic Area) Regulations 2016 (the 'EEA Regulations') and European caselaw. These rights were based purely on the person's circumstances, and applications were not required unless an EEA national or her/his direct family member needed to evidence her/his free movement residence rights in the UK. Extended family members and unmarried partners could also take advantage of these rights, although an application was required first.

The UK formally left the EU on 31 January 2020, in a separation known as 'Brexit'. Following Brexit, a new immigration scheme was developed for EEA nationals and their family members to remain in the UK. This is known as the European Union Settlement Scheme (EUSS) and it is contained in Appendix EU of the Immigration Rules. EEA nationals and their family members have to actively make applications to the EUSS; it does not confer automatic rights.

Following Brexit, a 'transition period' was created during which time EU law continued to apply. The transition period ran from 1 February 2020 to 31 December 2020. During the transition period, EEA nationals and their family members could continue to rely on their free movement rights under the EEA Regulations, and they could also make applications to the EUSS and rely on grants of leave under this scheme. Free movement for EEA nationals also continued to apply during the transition period, and EEA nationals and their family members could continue to move to the UK based on their EEA rights up until 11pm on 31 December 2020 when the transition period ended.

The transition period finished on 31 December 2020. With this, free movement rights for EEA nationals and their family members ended.

The UK is now in a 'grace period', which is expected to last from 1 January 2021 to 30 June 2021. EEA nationals already living in the UK before 31 December 2020, and their family members, need to apply to the EUSS no later than 30 June 2021 if they wish to stay here after the end of the grace period.

During the grace period, EEA nationals who have not yet applied to the EUSS, or who have applied but are waiting to receive their status, may be able to continue to rely on their right to reside under the EEA Regulations only if they had a right to reside on 31 December 2020.

EEA nationals arriving from 1 January 2021 will not be able to gain status under the EUSS, unless they come to the UK to join an EEA family member who was already resident here before 31 December 2020. Instead, they will need to enter the UK under one of the various categories of the Immigration Rules just as non-EEA nationals would.

All these changes mean that it might be helpful to think of EEA nationals and family members as being split into the three immigration categories:

- those already resident before 31 December 2020 and who have already obtained status under the EUSS (see p55);
- those already resident before 31 December 2020 who have not yet obtained status under the EUSS but who need to apply by 30 June 2021 (see p55);
- those arriving from 1 January 2021 who are unable to apply to the EUSS and must use general immigration provisions, unless they are joining an EEA family member who was already resident prior to 31 December 2020 (see p57).

The documentation issued to EEA nationals and their family members has changed due to Brexit and many immigration statuses are now electronic (see p61).

The rules on deporting EEA nationals have also changed due to Brexit (see p61).

3. European Union Settlement Scheme

The European Union Settlement Scheme (EUSS) is the system of immigration control for European Economic Area (EEA) nationals and their family members who wish to remain in the UK after Brexit. It is set out in Appendix EU of the Immigration Rules, and clarified in supporting Home Office caseworker guidance. Applications are mandatory, and the deadline to apply is 30 June 2021.

Who should apply to the European Union Settlement Scheme?

It is mandatory for all EEA nationals and their family members who wish to remain in the UK to apply for leave to remain under the EUSS.

Direct family members of EEA nationals are defined in much the same way as under the EEA Regulations (see Chapter 12). Direct family members include spouses, civil partners, children and grandchildren under the age of 21, and dependent parents and grandparents. Family members need to evidence their relationship with the EEA national but are not required to have held residence documentation issued under the EEA Regulations. Extended family members, including durable partners (for example those who can show that their relationship is durable because they have cohabited for two years, for example) and dependent adult relatives are also included in the definition of a family member but only if they already hold or obtain a residence permit under the EEA

Regulations.[1] See Chapter 12 for a detailed explanation of extended family members (p223).

A recent change allows the family members of Northern Irish citizens to also apply to the EUSS, provided that the Northern Irish person is either/both a British citizen or Irish citizen, that s/he was born in Northern Ireland, and that at the time of her/his birth at least one of her/his parents was either/both a British citizen or Irish citizen or was otherwise entitled to reside in Northern Ireland without any residence restrictions.

British nationals, including EEA nationals with dual British citizenship, do not need to apply. Similarly, those who already hold indefinite leave to remain do not need to apply, though they can if they want to. Settled status may be helpful for those who already hold indefinite leave to remain as it allows additional protection from loss of leave due to absence; regular indefinite leave to remain allows the holder to be outside the UK for two years without losing her/his leave, while settled status allows the holder to be outside the UK for five years without losing her/his leave.

Irish nationals do not need to apply, though they can do if they wish. Non-EEA family members of Irish nationals do need to apply.

EEA nationals and their family members who hold permanent residence are required to apply to the EUSS. Permanent residence rights will cease at the end of the grace period on 30 June 2021, unless the holder is waiting for a pending EUSS application to be decided.

Applications are normally made online and are free of charge. Each member of the family needs to make her/his own application, though the applications of children can be linked to their parents. A smartphone app is used to check the applicant's identity and to scan passports or EEA national identity cards. Those without a passport or ID card are currently required to telephone the Home Office's EU Settlement Resolution Centre to request a paper application form. In addition, those applying on the basis of derivative rights are required to request paper application forms from the Home Office.

Applications are compulsory for EEA nationals and their family members to be able to stay in the UK. If you do not apply, you will become an overstayer after the deadline of 30 June 2021. This may mean losing the right to work, along with all other residency rights, and could result in removal from the UK. There are limited situations where late applications may be accepted (see p57) but relying on these provisions is not advised.

EEA nationals and their family members who have lived in the UK prior to 31 December 2020 can apply to the EUSS. These EEA nationals can also bring their family members to the UK under the EUSS after this date, but only if the family relationship existed by 31 December 2020. For EEA nationals arriving after the end of the transition period, and family relationships formed after this date, see below.

Leave under the European Union Settled Status Scheme

Applicants to the EUSS will receive either indefinite leave to remain (known as 'settled status') or limited leave to remain (known as 'pre-settled status').

These statuses are based on the length of residence in the UK. Unlike the EEA Regulations, it is not necessary for you to have held a free movement right to reside (eg, as a worker); you simply need to have been physically present in the UK. This means that some people will be able to gain rights under the EUSS who did not have free movement residence rights under the EEA Regulations.

Both 'settled' and 'pre-settled' status are subject to suitability criteria (see p53).

When you apply to the EUSS, you are asked whether you wish to apply for 'settled' or 'pre-settled' status. If you have lived in the UK for five years or more, it is important that you request 'settled status', as this provides greater rights.

Eligibility for settled status

EEA nationals and their family members are eligible for 'settled status' if they have lived in the UK continuously for five consecutive years or more. For your residence to be considered continuous, you must not have been outside the UK for more than six months within any one year, though you may be absent for up to one year for 'important reasons' – eg, pregnancy, childbirth, serious illness, study, vocational training or an overseas posting.[2] In addition, absences of any length for compulsory military service are disregarded and do not break the continuity of residence.[3]

You can rely on any consecutive five-year period of residence, not just the most recent five years.[4] However, you are prevented from relying on a past period of residence if you have been absent from the UK for more than five years since the period of residence you wish to rely upon.[5] In addition, you must not have been excluded or deported since the period of residence you wish to rely upon.[6]

Applications for 'settled status' are subject to suitability criteria (see p53).

If you are granted 'settled status', you will hold indefinite leave to remain.

When a parent is granted settled status, her/his child can also be granted 'settled status' even if the child has not yet lived in the UK for five years (though the child will need to make his/her own application).[7] If you already held permanent residence at the time your child was born inside the UK, the child will be born British and, therefore, will not need to apply to the EUSS and can instead simply apply for a British passport.[8] Once you hold 'settled status', any future children you have inside the UK will be born British.[9]

Once granted, 'settled status' can be lost if you remain outside the UK for more than five consecutive years. This is more generous that the usual two-year absence allowed for indefinite leave to remain. Settled status can also be lost due to serious offending (please see p61), or if it was obtained based on false representations or fraudulent documents.

Some applicants can be granted 'settled status' with less than five years' residence, including EEA nationals who have stopped work in certain circumstances and their family members, and the family members of certain EEA nationals who have died.[10] In these cases, the same requirements apply as for those who can obtain permanent residence with less than five years' residence under the EEA Regulations. See Chapter 12 for details.

Eligibility for pre-settled status

EEA nationals and their family members who have lived in the UK for less than five years can receive limited leave to remain, known as 'pre-settled status'. You can rely on a residence of any length under five years, though the period of residence must have begun before 11pm on 31 December 2020.[11]

Applications for pre-settled status are subject to suitability criteria (see p53).

When you are granted pre-settled status, you receive a grant of five years of limited leave to remain. Once you have reached five years of residence overall (including your period of residence in the UK prior to receiving pre-settled status), you can apply for settled status.

Example

Lenka is a Polish national. She arrives in the UK in January 2017 and receives 'pre-settled status' in January 2020 which is valid for five years. She can apply for 'settled status' in January 2022 and does not need to wait for her 'pre-settled status' to expire in January 2025.

Note: it is crucial for people with pre-settled status to actively apply for settled status when they reach five years of continuous residence. Pre-settled status does not automatically convert to settled status, and those who fail to apply risk becoming overstayers when their pre-settled status expires.

If you hold pre-settled status and wish to later progress to settled status, you must be careful not to break the continuity of your residence through being outside the UK for more than six months at a time, except for important reasons (see p51). This is because settled status requires five years of *continuous* residence.

In addition, Appendix EU requires that for people with pre-settled status to progress to settled status they must continue to meet the eligibility criteria that they met at the time of their pre-settled status application.[12] This means that if you were granted pre-settled status as an EEA national, but you have since lost your EEA nationality, you are not expected to be eligible for settled status when you reach five years of residence. Similarly, if you receive pre-settled status as the family member of an EEA national, but the relationship then ends or the EEA national leaves the UK before s/he obtains five years of residence, you are not expected to be able to progress to settled status unless you can meet the requirements for a 'retained right of residence' (eg, through divorce – see

Chapter 12).[13] There is also an exception for those granted pre-settled status on the basis of dependency as a child, parent or other relative, who will not need to evidence that they remain dependent to progress to settled status.[14]

Pre-settled status can be lost if you are outside of the UK for two years or more. In addition, 'pre-settled status' may be curtailed in cases of deception, on the basis of serious offending (see p61), or if you no longer meet the requirements, though the Home Office has discretion in such cases.

Suitability

The EUSS contains suitability criteria that restrict who can be granted status on the basis of criminality, deception and exclusion.

An application must be refused on grounds of suitability where there is a current deportation decision or order, or whether there is a current exclusion decision or order.[15]

An application may be refused on grounds of suitability if there is a live removal decision under the EEA Regulations, or if false evidence or information has been submitted.[16]

Certain criminal convictions may trigger suitability concerns. These include:

- any length of imprisonment within the last five years;
- imprisonment for a period of 12 months or more for a single offence at any time;
- for those who have lived in the UK less than five years, three or more convictions (whether or not imprisoned) within the last three years;
- previous involvement in serious deception.[17]

If your application triggers suitability concerns for any of the above reasons, your application will be referred from the Home Office's EUSS team to Immigration Enforcement. Immigration Enforcement will then consider whether the matter is serious enough to trigger deportation proceedings. If the suitability concern is not of such a severity as to warrant deportation (see below), then status should be granted.

Applicants over the age of 18 are required to disclose previous criminal convictions, although spent convictions do not need to be disclosed. In addition, the Home Office will run a criminal record check on all applicants over the age of 10. If you fail to disclose criminal convictions, there is a risk this may trigger suitability concerns on the basis of deception.

Where you have a pending prosecution (ie, you have been charged with a criminal offence but not yet been tried), the Home Office may put your application on hold until the matter has been concluded. The Home Office should consider proportionality and whether the offence is serious enough to trigger suitability concerns.[18]

Retained rights and the European Union Settlement Scheme

The EUSS allows people who have a 'retained right of residence' under the EEA Regulations to make an application for settled or pre-settled status under the scheme. There are specific requirements for retained rights of residence, including for the family member of an EEA national when the EEA national has died or ended the marriage or civil partnership through divorce. These are broadly the same under the EUSS as under the EEA Regulations; see Chapter 12 for a full discussion of retained rights of residence.

Note: the EUSS has a slightly broader definition of retained residence rights and allows applications for cases in which a variety of family relationships have broken down to due to domestic abuse (rather than just the breakdown of marriage or civil partnership). If the case relates to the breakdown of a marriage or civil partnership, the EUSS focuses on the date that the marriage or civil partnership is terminated by court order, which is the date that a person becomes a family member who has retained the right of residence. By contrast, in the EEA Regulations the important date is the date of initiation of proceedings for divorce (or termination of civil partnership).

These applications can be complex, so if you think you are eligible to make an application because you hold a retained right, seek specialist advice.

Derivative rights and the European Union Settlement Scheme

The EUSS also allows people who have a 'derivative right of residence' under the EEA Regulations to make an application for settled or pre-settled status under the scheme.

Derivative rights include the rights to reside as the carer of certain EEA national children and as the carer of certain British children. You can apply to the EUSS if you have a derivative right to reside (see p233). However, these applications can be complex and you should get specialist immigration advice.

A key change under the EUSS for carers with derivative rights is that they can access settled status (indefinite leave to remain) after five years of residence; they could not progress to permanent residence under the EEA Regulations.

As under the EEA Regulations, under the EUSS there is a significant barrier to recognition as a *Zambrano* carer (primary carers of British citizens –children or dependent adults). Home Office guidance currently states that to receive settled or pre-settled status as a *Zambrano* carer, you must either already have had this right recognised under the EEA Regulations or have exhausted all options in making a family or private life application under Appendix FM of the Immigration Rules. At the time of writing, this point is in the process of being challenged. See AskCPAG.org.uk and CPAG's *Welfare Rights Bulletin* for updates.

Family members of British citizens under the European Union Settlement Scheme (Surinder Singh cases)

Certain family members of British citizens can gain status under the EUSS. This is based on the EEA right to reside of non-EEA citizen family members of British citizens, returning to the UK after exercising treaty rights in an EEA member state. This is known as the 'Surinder Singh' route and can apply when, for example, a British citizen has lived and worked in another EU country with a non-EEA family member and then seeks to return to the UK with her/him. See p224 for a full explanation of the requirements.

Specific deadlines to return to the UK currently apply to EUSS applications from the family members of British citizens, which vary from the normal deadlines set out above. At present, if the British citizen was already in a relationship with a spouse, civil partner or durable partner before 31 January 2020, s/he can return to the UK under the EUSS until 29 March 2022.[19] If the relationship began after 31 January 2020 and before 31 December 2020, however, s/he must have returned to the UK before 31 December 2020 to be eligible for status under the EUSS.

Note: there have already been several changes to Appendix EU relating to these cases, and it is possible that further changes may be made and that these deadlines may change. These applications are complex. Seek specialist advice if you are making an application.

Note: the family members of Northern Irish citizens can apply to the EUSS using the main route for family members (see p50).

4. Resident before 31 December 2020 and leave obtained under European Union Settlement Scheme

People who were living in the UK before 31 December 2020 and who have already obtained 'settled' or 'pre-settled status' under the European Union Settlement Scheme (EUSS) are lawfully present in the UK. They can continue to live, work and study here. See above.

5. Resident before 31 December 2020 and no leave under European Union Settlement Scheme

European Economic Area (EEA) free movement rights ended on 31 December 2020. However, the UK has provided a 'grace period' from 1 January 2021 to

30 June 2021 during which time EEA nationals can continue to apply to the European Union Settlement Scheme (EUSS). In addition, in some circumstances they can continue to rely on EEA free movement rights during this period.

European Economic Area nationals and family members who had a right to reside on 31 December 2020

If you had a right to reside under the EEA Regulations on 31 December 2020 (please see Chapter 12 for a full explanation of rights to reside) and have not yet obtained status under the EUSS, you will be able to continue to rely on this (or another) right to reside to be lawfully present throughout the 'grace period' up until 30 June 2021. That is based on The Citizens' Rights (Application Deadline and Temporary Protection) (EU Exit) Regulations 2020, which provide for the protections of the EEA Regulations to continue to apply to EEA nationals and their family members throughout the grace period. However, these protections only apply if the person was lawfully resident under the EEA Regulations on 31 December 2020.

EEA nationals and their family members who had a right to reside on 31 December 2020 and who continue to have some form of right to reside during the grace period will continue to be lawfully present throughout the grace period. They should, however, apply to the EUSS before 30 June 2021 to ensure they do not lose their right to remain in the UK.

European Economic Area nationals and family members without a right to reside on 31 December 2020

If you did not have a right to reside under the EEA Regulations on 31 December 2020 (see Chapter 12 for a full explanation of rights to reside), you will not technically be lawfully present in the UK from 1 January 2021 onwards. However, you will still be able to apply to the EUSS to obtain lawful status in the UK.

Despite drafting the Temporary Protection Regulations in such a way so as to exclude people who did not have a right to reside on 31 December 2020 from lawful residence during the grace period, it does not appear that the government will take any enforcement action during this period. Its online guidance for employers currently states that employers should not ask employees whether they hold status under the EUSS until after 1 July 2021.

EEA nationals who did not have a right to reside under the EEA Regulations on 31 December 2020, such as self-sufficient people and students without comprehensive sickness insurance and people out of work who do not have jobseeker or retained worker status, are strongly advised to apply to the EUSS as soon as possible to minimise the chance of enforcement action being taken against them. In any event, they should apply no later than 30 June 2021.

European Economic Area nationals and family members who have not applied to European Union Settlement Scheme by 30 June 2021

The deadline to apply to the EUSS for EEA nationals (and those family members who were already resident in the UK by 31 December 2020) is 30 June 2021. After this date, if you have not applied you will be unlawfully present in the UK. You will lose the right to work, to rent, to hold bank accounts and other rights, and you may be removed from the UK.

If you apply to the EUSS before 30 June 2021 but have not yet received a decision from the Home Office by this date, if you had a right to reside under the EEA Regs on 31 December 2020, you can continue to have the same or a different right to reside under the EEA Regulations until your application to the Home Office (including any appeals against a refusal) is determined. If you did not have a right to reside on 31 December 2020, at the time of writing it appears that you will not be lawfully present while you wait for your decision. However, once you are granted status under the EUSS, you will have lawful immigration status in the UK.

In limited circumstances, it is possible to make a late application to the EUSS after 30 June 2021. For a late application to be accepted, the applicant must have 'reasonable grounds' for his/her late application and s/he must apply within a 'reasonable' time period. At the time of writing, it is not yet known what will amount to reasonable grounds or a reasonable time period, and you are strongly advised to apply before the 30 June 2021. If you have missed the deadline you should seek urgent immigration advice from a qualified advisor.

6. Arriving from 1 January 2021

European Economic Area nationals newly arriving from 1 January 2021 who are not joining family already resident in the UK

European Economic Area (EEA) nationals coming to live in the UK for the first time from 1 January 2021 onwards will not be able to apply to the European Union Setllement Scheme (EUSS) (unless they are joining family already resident here – see below).

If EEA nationals want to visit the UK, they can obtain six months' limited leave as a visitor on arrival. This status will be automatically generated when they enter the UK through airport passport e-gates and they will not be provided with any documentation. Like any other person granted leave to enter as a visitor, they will not have the right to work and will be subject to a 'no recourse to public funds' restriction.

EEA nationals who want to live in the UK from 1 January 2021 will need to apply for leave to remain using one of the existing immigration routes open to non-EEA nationals. See Chapter 3.

Family members arriving from 1 January 2021 to join European Economic Area nationals already resident here

EEA nationals already resident in the UK before 31 December 2020 will still be able to bring their family members to the UK after this date. That applies to both family members who are EEA nationals and family members who are non-EEA nationals. There are two potential options for family members to come to the UK in this way: EUSS family permits and EUSS travel permits.

European Union Settlement Scheme family permits

A family member of an EEA national may be eligible for an EU Settlement Scheme Family Permit if the EEA national wishing to bring the family member was resident in the UK before 31 December 2020 and if the EEA national either holds status under EUSS or would be eligible for this if s/he applied.

To be eligible as a family member, you must not have been resident in the UK before 31 December 2020, and your family relationship with the EEA national must have been established before this date. These provisions apply to direct family members and also to durable partners (see above). For durable partners, the relationship must have been durable before 31 December 2020 and the partner either must not have yet moved to the UK, or have ended a previous period of residence in the UK – eg, through absence.

Once you have obtained the family permit, newly arriving family members will need to travel to the UK within six months, either accompanying or joining the EEA national. For family permit applications made after 1 July 2021, the EEA national the family is accompanying or joining must already hold status under the EUSS.

After your arrival, you will need to make an application to the EU Settlement Scheme. Those arriving before 31 March 2021 must apply to the EUSS by 30 June 2021, and family members arriving after that date must apply to the EUSS within three months of their arrival date.

If an EEA family member has already arrived in the UK as a visitor (using the passport e-gates), s/he will not be able to apply for a family permit while inside the UK and will need to leave the UK before making her/his application.

It is anticipated that these requirements may vary after the end of the grace period. See AskCPAG.org.uk for updates.

European Union Settlement Scheme travel permits

Alternatively, family members travelling to join a resident EEA national in the UK can apply for an EU Settlement Scheme travel permit. The travel permit should be used if the family member had already held a residence document under the EEA

Regulations but that document has been lost or stolen. Once granted, you will need to travel to the UK within six months, and then make an application to the EU Settlement Scheme on arrival as above.

It is anticipated that these requirements may vary after the end of the grace period. See AskCPAG.org.uk for updates.

7. Frontier workers

Frontier workers are European Economic Area nationals who live in one country and work in another.

Frontier workers before 31 December 2020

Before 31 December 2020, it was straightforward for an EEA national to work in the UK while living in another country, because EEA nationals had a right of admission to the UK under European Union (EU)free movement law as implemented in the UK by the Immigration (European Economic Area) Regulations 2016. EEA nationals could cross the border into the UK simply by showing their passport or national identity card.

Frontier workers from 1 January 2021

EEA nationals who were cross-border working in the UK before 31 December 2020 may be able to access frontier worker rights under the Citizens' Rights (Frontier Workers) (EU Exit) Regulations 2020 (the Frontier Workers Regulations) through a 'frontier worker permit'. Though there is currently no deadline to apply for a frontier worker permit, this permit will be needed to avoid travel problems for frontier workers from 30 June 2021 onwards.

A person will be eligible for a frontier worker permit if s/he meets certain conditions, which must have been met:

- immediately before 11pm on 31 December 2020; *and*
- continuously since then.

The conditions are that the person is:

- an EEA national; *and*
- not primarily resident in the UK, which means:
  - s/he has been present in the UK for less than 180 days in the previous 12 months; *or*
  - s/he has returned to her/his country of residence at least once in the previous six months; *or*
  - s/he has returned to her/his country of residence at least twice in the previous 12 months; *and*

- a worker or self-employed person in the UK, or a person with retained worker or self-employed status. A person retains worker or self-employed status in certain situations such as being temporarily unable to work due to illness or accident, which are set out in regulation 4 of the Frontier Worker's Regulations.

If a person meets these conditions (both before 31 December 2020 and continuously since), s/he is entitled to apply for and be issued a frontier worker permit. S/he will then have a right of admission to the UK when s/he produces a valid identity document and a valid frontier worker permit.[20]

How to apply for a frontier worker permit

Applications are made online and similarly to the EU Settlement Scheme, can be made via a smartphone app. Applications are free of charg,e, and can be made both inside and outside the UK. There is currently no deadline to apply for a frontier worker permit. However, you should apply as soon as possible to avoid difficulties cross-border working after 30 June 2021.

What does a frontier worker permit provide

Frontier worker permits are valid for five years, with the exception of frontier worker permits granted on the basis of retained residence rights, which are valid for two years.

Frontier worker permits do not provide a route to settlement in the UK.

A frontier worker permit gives a right of admission to the UK rather than leave to enter : it is a right to be admitted, rather than a permission. A person who has a right of admission to the UK as a frontier worker, and from 30 June 2021 who holds a frontier worker permit, does not require leave to enter or remain the UK for the duration of their permit.

EU Settlement Scheme or frontier worker permit

Before applying for a frontier worker permit it is important to check if you might be able to meet the requirements to make an application under the EU Settlement Scheme (EUSS) instead. EUSS provides a clear route to settlement, so is preferable for people who wish to remain in the UK long term. EUSS requires at least six months of residence per year, so frontier workers may meet EUSS requirements if their absences from the UK do not total more than six months per year.

In particular, frontier workers who have spent more than six months per year inside the UK may wish to consider taking the EUSS route. See p49 for a detailed explanation of who is eligible for settled and pre-settled status.

Family members

A frontier worker's family members cannot obtain a frontier worker permit. However, family members of frontier workers can apply to the EU Settlement Scheme (EUSS) instead.

If the frontier worker's family member is already resident in the UK, then the family member can apply to the EUSS on the basis of his/her relationship with the frontier worker. **Note**: the frontier worker does not need to be eligible under the EUSS themselves for a family member to use this route, it is sufficient that the worker meets the requirements for a frontier worker permit.

Alternatively, if the frontier worker's family member is outside the UK then s/he can apply for an EUSS family permit to come to the UK to join the frontier worker (see p57).

8. Documentation under the European Union Settlement Scheme

Most European Economic Area (EEA) nationals who are granted settled or pre-settled status are not given any physical evidence of their status. Instead, you will receive an email confirming your grant of status and containing a 16-digit reference number. The status holder can login to the government's status-checking website (gov.uk/view-prove-immigration-status), using the email address and the details of the passport or ID card connected to his/her status. This website allows you to generate a share code to provide to employers, landlords and others to prove your status.

Non-EEA family members of EEA nationals will usually receive biometric residence permits (BRPs) confirming her/his status under the European Settlement Scheme (EUSS). However, if the family member already held a BRP under the EEA Regulations, s/he will normally keep this BRP and will not be issued with a new one under the EUSS until her/his EEA Regulations BRP expires.

As many people have only a digital status under EUSS, it is vital to update the Home Office when a passport/ID card is renewed or when the connected phone number or email address changes.

9. Deportation

The rules for deporting European Economic Area (EEA) nationals and their family members changed on 1 January 2021. For any offences committed before 11pm on 31 December 2020, the more generous rights provided by the EEA Regulations apply. For offences committed after this time, the new stricter deportation rules apply.

Deportation rules for offences conducted before 31 December 2020

EEA nationals and their family members who commit criminal offences prior to 31 December 2020 can only be deported from the UK for public policy, public security or public health reasons.[21]

A decision made on public policy, public security or public health grounds must:

- not be taken for the economic benefit of the UK; *and*
- be 'proportionate'; *and*
- be based exclusively on the conduct of the individual concerned, which must represent a genuine, present and sufficiently serious threat, affecting one of the fundamental interests of society; *and*
- be for reasons that relate to your case in particular, rather than being intended to deter others; *and*
- not be justified by a person's previous criminal convictions alone; *and*
- only be made after taking into account the person's age, state of health, family and economic situation, her/his length of residence in the UK, her/his social and cultural integration in the UK, and the extent of her/his links with her/his country of origin.

EEA nationals and family members with five years' continuous lawful residence cannot be deported unless there are 'serious' grounds of public policy or public security.[22] An EEA national who has resided in the UK for 10 years cannot be excluded or removed except on imperative grounds of public security.[23] Similarly, an EEA national aged under 18 cannot be excluded or removed unless it is in her/his best interests or her/his removal is imperative on grounds of public security.[24]

Both settled and pre-settled status can be removed if they were obtained fraudulently. Pre-settled status can also be lost if a person ceases to meet the requirements and removal of the status is considered to be proportionate.

Deportation rules for offences conducted after 31 December 2020

For conduct committed from 1 January 2021 onwards, EEA nationals and family members can be deported if it is considered to be conducive to the public good.

This is a much harsher threshold than the above. It is the same deportation test which applies to other non-EEA immigration routes in the UK. See Chapter 2 for further details of specific deportation criteria based on the conducive to the public good test.

Notes

3. European Union Settlement Scheme

1 Please note, durable partners arriving in the UK after 1 January 2020 require a family permit but do not need to have held status under the EEA Regulations. See Section 6 below for further information.
2 Appendix EU Annex 1, definition 'Continuous qualifying period', IR
3 Appendix EU Annex 1, definition 'Continuous qualifying period', IR
4 Home Office, caseworker guidance, *EU Settlement Scheme: EU, other EEA and Swiss citizens and their family members*, version 3.0, 8 November 2019, p34
5 Home Office, caseworker guidance, *EU Settlement Scheme: EU, other EEA and Swiss citizens and their family members*, version 3.0, 8 November 2019, p34
6 Home Office, caseworker guidance, *EU Settlement Scheme: EU, other EEA and Swiss citizens and their family members*, version 3.0, 8 November 2019, p34
7 Appendix EU EU11(7) IR
8 s1(1)(b) BNA 1981
9 s1(1)(b) BNA 1981
10 Appendix EU EU11(4),(5) and (6) IR
11 Appendix EU Annex 1, definition 'Continuous qualifying period', IR
12 Appendix EU EU4 IR
13 See Appendix EU Annex 1, definition 'Family member who has retained the right of residence'. **Note**: Appendix EU provides that where EEA and non-EEA spouses separate, from the time that they initiate divorce proceedings the EEA national is treated as being resident. This means that if the EEA national leaves the UK before the divorce is finalised, the non-EEA's continuity of residence should not be affected. Also note that the Home Office has extended discretion which may be considered in cases of domestic abuse, etc.
14 Appendix EU EU4 IR
15 Appendix EU EU15 IR
16 Appendix EU EU16 IR
17 Home Office, caseworker guidance, *EU Settlement Scheme: suitability requirements*, version 2.0, 11 December 2019, p 13
18 Home Office, caseworker guidance, *EU Settlement Scheme: suitability requirements*, version 2.0, 11 December 2019, p 25
19 Appendix EU Annex 1, definitions 'Qualifying British citizen' and 'Family member of a qualifying British citizen', IR

7. Frontier workers

20 Regulation 6, the Citizens' Rights (Frontier Workers) (EU Exit) Regulations 2020

9. Deportation

21 Reg 19(5) I(EEA) Regs
22 Reg 21(3) I(EEA) Regs
23 Reg 21(4)(b) I(EEA) Regs
24 Reg 21(4)(b) I(EEA) Regs

Chapter 6

Checking your immigration status

This chapter covers:

1. Introduction

This chapter explains how to check your immigration status to establish your entitlement to social security benefits.

You can usually identify your immigration status in the UK from your biometric residence permit, your passport and any endorsements in it by the UK immigration authorities (eg, stamps, stickers or vignettes), from a grant of status letter from the Home Office, or through an online status checker.

Note: your status (or nationality) may have changed since your passport, endorsement or card was issued, or you may not hold any of these, including if the item has been lost or stolen.

If your immigration status is uncertain, you should contact a specialist adviser. A list of advisers and organisations is included in Appendix 2.

Note: anyone who gives immigration advice must be professionally regulated. For further details, see p7.

2. British nationals and people with the right of abode

If you are a British national, you can apply to HM Passport Office for a **UK passport** (see Appendix 6, Figure 1). However, not all British nationals have been issued with a passport and your British nationality does not depend on your being a passport holder.

All British nationals, not just British citizens, can apply for a UK passport and it is important to distinguish between the different types of British nationality when checking your immigration status (see p15). Your passport specifies the type of British nationality you have. Holders of UK passports who have the right of abode in the UK are described as: 'British citizens or British subjects with the right of abode in the UK'.

Note: UK passports may also be issued to people whose right of abode is awaiting verification. The passport contains the endorsement: 'The holder's status under the Immigration Act 1971 has not yet been determined.'

If you have been granted British citizenship after applying to register or naturalise as a British citizen, you will have been issued with a certificate confirming this (see Appendix 6, Figure 2).

If you have the right of abode in the UK and are also a national of another Commonwealth country, you may have a **certificate of entitlement** endorsed in a passport issued by that country (see Appendix 6, Figure 3).

Although rare, a **certificate of patriality** issued under the Immigration Act 1971, and which was valid immediately before 1 January 1983, is regarded as a certificate of entitlement unless the holder no longer has the right of abode – eg, if you have renounced this, or if there has been independence legislation.[1]

Some people with the right of abode in the UK may hold a **confirmation of 'right of abode' document**. This was a non-statutory document issued for a brief period before the commencement of the Immigration Act 1988 to dual nationals with the right of abode who had opted to travel on non-British passports.

If you do not hold a passport or certificate confirming your British citizenship or right of abode, you may be able to prove that you have this status in some other way – eg, by producing a birth certificate showing that you were born in the UK before 1983. If your claim to British citizenship or the right of abode is complicated, you may need to prove descent from your parents and/or grandparents, and/or marriage to a person and that person's place of birth, ancestry and/or nationality status at specific times. If this applies to you, it may be helpful to get specialist immigration advice to check your citizenship and/or right of abode.

3. People with leave to enter or remain

Entry clearance confirming leave to enter

Entry clearance is endorsed by a sticker (known as a '**vignette**') placed in your passport or travel document, or by data stored digitally in an identity card and government database (see p68).

The vignette endorsement may be designated as a visa, entry clearance, EU Settlement Scheme family permit or an EEA family permit, which will no longer be valid or issued after 30 June 2021.

Two types of vignette are now issued. The type of vignette depends on the type of entry clearance you are given. Both include a photograph of the holder (see Appendix 6, Figure 9). Older versions look similar, but without a photograph (see Appendix 6, Figure 8). Even older ones comprise a smaller sticker, signed and date-stamped by an official (similar to the leave to remain endorsement vignette shown in Appendix 6, Figure 8).

Accompanying dependants whose details were included in the main applicant's passport might have received their own vignettes, fixed in the main applicant's passport.

Entry clearance granting you leave to enter allows you to enter the UK at a port without having to demonstrate that you satisfy the requirements of the Immigration Rules (unless you commit an act of fraud or there is a material change in circumstances). The vignette endorsement is usually date-stamped on entry (see Appendix 6, Figure 10) and confirms that you have been granted leave to enter the UK, often for the remaining period of validity stated on the vignette.

In some circumstances, an immigration officer can vary or extend your leave on your arrival in the UK.

The date the entry clearance first becomes valid is usually the same as the date of authorisation. As the holder, you may present yourself for initial entry under the entry clearance at any time during its validity. However, entry clearance officers have the discretion to defer the date the entry clearance first becomes valid for up to three months after authorisation if, for example, you wish to delay travelling to the UK.

If you are granted entry clearance, you may travel to, and remain in, the UK for the purpose for which it was granted. You may be able to travel in and out of the UK repeatedly, provided your entry clearance remains valid. However, if entry clearance has been authorised for multiple journeys to the UK of a fixed duration (eg, under the visitor category of the Immigration Rules), the duration of each visit is limited to a maximum of six months. This limitation is stated on the vignette under the heading 'duration of stay'.

If you have been granted indefinite leave to enter the UK, your visa shows an 'expiry' or 'valid until' date. This is the date by when the entry clearance needs to be presented to enter the UK for the first time, after which you have indefinite leave and the date becomes irrelevant.[2]

If you have presented the entry clearance at a port, there should be an ink stamp showing where and on which date that occurred. The date when the entry clearance was presented is the date when the entry clearance took effect as indefinite leave.

If you are granted entry clearance with a vignette for leave to enter on certain conditions (eg, as a student on condition that you do not work except in authorised employment and do not have recourse to public funds), these should be stated on the endorsement (see Appendix 6, Figure 9). However, if you have been granted entry clearance for leave to enter on the basis of a maintenance undertaking (see p35), the reference on the vignette may be the name of the family member whom you are joining and there may be no indication that a maintenance undertaking has been given.

Leave to enter without entry clearance

Nationals of some countries cannot enter the UK for any purpose without first obtaining entry clearance (visa nationals). Others can apply at the port of entry for leave to enter for some of the purposes provided for under the Immigration Rules.

It is sometimes difficult to identify the purpose for which an endorsement of leave to enter has been given if someone made an application at the port of entry. If limited leave has been granted, the endorsement may be an **ink stamp**, stating the duration of the leave period for which leave is granted and the conditions (if any) attached to the leave (see Appendix 6, Figure 8). Each stamped endorsement by an immigration officer granting leave to someone without entry clearance should be accompanied by a rectangular date stamp, showing when the leave was granted. Since 1 January 2020, EU and non-visa nationals may have entered the UK through a passport Passport eGate, in which case their status may be held electronically as an eVisa. That is also referred to as digital-only status.

The example shown in Appendix 6, Figure 8 is the endorsement usually made in the passport of someone given leave to enter at a port of entry as a visitor or student on a short course (of six months or less). The endorsement shows that leave has been granted on condition that the holder does not engage in any employment or have recourse to public funds.

If you are returning to the UK and already have indefinite leave to enter or remain, you may simply be given a date stamp on being readmitted.

If you leave the UK and return during a period of leave that has been given for more than six months, an immigration officer may endorse a grant of leave to enter with the same conditions, using an ink stamp stating this.[3]

If you are, or were, a Commonwealth citizen and you entered the UK before the Immigration Act 1971 came into force, you may have received an ink stamp on entry with no conditions attached. You are known as 'freely landed'. You may have been treated as having been given indefinite leave to enter or remain when the 1971 Act came into force and might have retained this status by remaining resident in the UK (see p29).

Leave to remain granted in the UK

The UK **residence permit** replaced all former stamp and ink endorsements for permission to stay in the UK for longer than six months. The permit is a vignette, similar in appearance to that used to endorse entry clearance (see p66), and includes a photograph of the holder (see Appendix 6, Figure 8).

Previously, leave may have been endorsed using a smaller vignette sticker or by a rectangular stamp accompanied by a pentagonal date stamp (see Appendix 6,

Figure 8).

If you were granted leave to remain on certain conditions (eg, as a student on condition that you do not work except in authorised employment and do not have recourse to public funds), these should be stated on the permit (see Appendix 6, Figure 9). However, if you were granted leave to remain on the basis of a maintenance undertaking (see p35), this is not stated on the permit.

Biometric residence permits

Biometric residence permit cards for foreign nationals are now replacing the vignette (sticker) endorsements and other UK immigration status documents (see Appendix 6, Figure 5). You are issued with one as an alternative to having a sticker or ink stamp endorsement placed in your passport, which is not endorsed with your immigration status at all.

A biometric residence permit is a plastic card, the same size as a debit or credit card, which bears the holder's photograph, name, date of birth, nationality and immigration status. An electronic chip attached to the card holds digitised biometric details, including fingerprints, a facial image and biographical information (including name, and date and place of birth).

The card also shows details of your immigration status and entitlements in the UK, including what kind of leave you have and whether you can work. A database holds a record of the biometrics of every person to whom a card has been issued, so these can be cross-checked.

If you have the new identity card, you may need to inform the Home Office of specified changes in your circumstances. If you fail to do so, you may face prosecution or other sanctions (see p35).

Leave extended for an application, appeal or administrative review

Limited leave is automatically extended beyond the date it is due to expire if you make a valid application to extend or vary your leave before this date.[4] Leave extended in this way continues on the same conditions as before, until a decision is made by the Home Office. If the Home Office refuses your application, and you make an in-time appeal, your leave continues until any in-country appeal rights or rights to administrative review are exhausted. The same conditions attached to your original leave continue to apply during the extension (apart from the time limit).

If the Home Office refuses your application, and you make an in-time appeal, your leave continues until any in-country appeal rights or rights to administrative review are exhausted. The same conditions attached to your original leave continue to apply during the extension (apart from the time limit). It is not completely clear whether you are defined as a 'person subject to immigration control' and therefore excluded from most benefits during the time when you are appealing or seeking an administrative review (see p92).

The Home Office can take a long time to decide applications, and appeals against refusals to vary or to extend leave can take longer still, so you may have your leave extended in this way for many months, or even years. Also, if the result of the administrative review is significantly different or additional reasons are given for upholding the decision, you may apply for a further review that, if done in time, extends your leave even further. Your passport or biometric residence permit, if you had one when you applied, may be retained during this time. For these reasons, it can be difficult to show that your leave is ongoing. The Home Office may acknowledge a valid application for leave with a letter but does not always do so. However, the Home Office offers to confirm specifically that you have ongoing leave if you request that. There is a helpline for employers, prospective employers and prospective landlords: the number for this service is available from the Home Office website.

Travel and status documents issued to non-UK nationals

Where necessary, leave to enter or leave to remain may have been endorsed on an **immigration status document** (which is simply an A4-sized piece of paper) – eg, because your passport was not available when your leave was granted. Refugee leave and humanitarian protection are never endorsed in a passport issued by the holder's government, because the use of such a passport is considered to be an indication that you are happy to be protected by the government that issued it, which would be incompatible with having asylum in the UK (see Appendix 6, Figure 4).

Refugees are entitled to a **Refugee Convention travel document** (coloured blue), which is similar in format to a passport (see Appendix 6, Figure 11).

A dependant of a refugee or person with humanitarian protection may be granted entry clearance on the basis of refugee family reunion on a standard **'Uniform Format Form' (UFF)**, if s/he has no passport or cannot obtain one. The previous version, **a GV3 document**, had an endorsement stating: 'visa family reunion – sponsor'. The sponsor referred to is the relative with refugee status who the dependant is joining in the UK. This endorsement can confuse benefit decision makers who wrongly assume that a maintenance undertaking has been given (see p114).

If you are recognised as stateless under the terms of the 1954 United Nations Convention Relating to the Status of Stateless Persons, you are entitled to a **stateless person's document** (coloured red).

If you have indefinite leave but were not recognised as a refugee, or you were granted exceptional leave, discretionary leave or humanitarian protection, you can apply for a **certificate of travel** (coloured black). However, to qualify for such a document, usually you must have applied to your national authorities (if they have a presence in the UK) for a passport or travel document and been formally and unreasonably refused one in writing.

4. People without leave

If you have entered the UK without permission or remained in the UK after your limited leave to enter or remain has expired, you may have committed a criminal offence and could be arrested and detained for removal from the UK. This also applies if you have remained in the UK after you have been refused further leave or had your leave revoked or curtailed and any appeal rights have been exhausted. Any conditions attached to the limited leave that has expired or been revoked or curtailed cease to apply.

If you are in the UK without leave and come to the attention of the Home Office, you are likely to be served with a **notice** informing you that you are liable to be removed from the UK, and explaining why (see Appendix 6, Figure 12). You may also be detained or given immigration bail (see p14). If so, you should have been issued with a notice informing you of this and of any conditions attached.

If further leave has been refused, a line may be drawn through the previous endorsement of leave in your passport. A decision refusing leave to enter at a port may be endorsed by a crossed-through ink date stamp.

You must be notified of any immigration decision in writing. Sending a notice to your last known address or the address of a representative (eg, a solicitor or other regulated person) might be sufficient, so you may not necessarily be aware of a decision concerning you. Get specialist advice if you are in any doubt.

5. Long-term residents and the 'Windrush generation'

Significant restrictive changes to immigration law in the UK came into force on 1 January 1973, under the Immigration Act 1971. Most people who were settled in the UK at that time without any time restriction on their leave retained their right to remain indefinitely, but many of these people do not hold a current passport or other document to show that they have this right.

If you are a Commonwealth citizen settled in the UK before 1 January 1973 (known as the 'Windrush generation') and were still in the UK on this date, you can be assumed to have had no time restriction on your right to be in the UK. The Home Office has confirmed this in recent announcements, but this has yet to be tested.

If you are a Commonwealth citizen who arrived in the UK on or after 1 January 1973 and you have been given leave to enter or remain in the UK (including indefinite leave), you have a right to stay in the UK for as long as your leave remains valid.

Spouses and children of Commonwealth citizens who were settled in the UK on 1 January 1973 were admitted to the UK with indefinite leave if they arrived at any time between 1 January 1973 and 1 August 1988, or after 1 August 1988 on a visa that was applied for before 1 August 1988.

Note: indefinite leave can be lost if:

- you are absent from the UK for over two years (for Commonwealth citizens, this only applies after 1 August 1988 – absences of any duration between 1 January 1973 and 1 August 1988 do not matter); *or*
- a deportation order (see p25) has been made against you. However, if you are a Commonwealth citizen, you may be exempt from deportation if you were living in the UK on 1 January 1973 and you have lived in the UK for at least the last five years immediately before deportation is considered (excluding any period of imprisonment of six months or more).

The Windrush Compensation Scheme

The Windrush Compensation Scheme is designed to assist people of any nationality who have lived in the UK for a long time, but who do not have the documents to prove this. The following people can apply for nationality or immigration documents under the scheme:

- a Commonwealth citizen who settled in the UK before 1 January 1973 or has right of abode;
- a child of a Commonwealth citizen who settled before 1 January 1973, where the child was in the UK or arrived in the UK before the age of 18;
- a person of any nationality who settled in the UK before 31 December 1988 and is settled in the UK.

The Windrush Compensation Scheme exists to compensate those who have suffered losses because they could not produce documentation to establish immigration status. This might be because they lost a job or were refused employment or have been denied housing, benefits or NHS care free of charge.

The Home Office has announced that it will:

- waive the citizenship fee and some of the usual requirements for anyone of the 'Windrush generation' who wishes to apply for citizenship;
- ensure that those who made their lives here but who have now retired to their country of origin are able to return to the UK – the cost of any fees associated with this process will be waived;
- set up a new independent scheme to compensate people who have suffered loss;
- establish a new customer contact centre for anyone affected to get appropriate advice;
- ensure that people who arrived after 1973 but before 1 August 1988 can also access the dedicated Windrush team so they can access the support and assistance needed to establish their right to be in the UK;
- assist those who contact the dedicated Windrush team to obtain evidence of their residence in the UK, including employment and health records.

Note:

- The law in this area is complicated and the Home Office has, for many years, been unreasonable and hostile in its approach to long-term residents without documentation, including applying an unreasonably high standard of proof in cases and only backing down when challenged through the courts.
- A criminal offending history can lead to deportation action being taken, even if someone has been lawfully resident in the UK for many years.
- If the Home Office decides that someone does not have a right to be in the UK, s/he is at risk of arrest, indefinite detention and enforced removal from the UK.
- If possible, obtain legal advice and assistance before contacting the Home Office.
- Government cuts and high demand mean that legal aid may not be available, even if you are eligible.

6. **Asylum seekers**

People who have applied for refugee or humanitarian protection leave or other forms of international protection are commonly called 'asylum seekers' (see p39).

Since 2002, the Home Office has issued asylum seekers with an **application registration card** (ARC) (see Appendix 6, Figure 8). The ARC may state whether you have any dependants or permission to work.

If you claim asylum at a port of entry or if you do not have leave to remain and you claim asylum in-country, you may be given immigration bail (temporary admission before 15 January 2018) as an alternative to immigration detention until your application is decided. If you have been detained, you might have subsequently been granted immigration bail. If you have any of these types of status, you should have been issued with a notice informing you of this and of any conditions (see Appendix 6, Figure 13). See p14 for further information.

If you apply for asylum when you have leave to enter or remain for another purpose, you can apply for your leave to be extended until a decision is made by the Home Office and, if the application is refused, any appeal rights are exhausted.

7. European Economic Area nationals

EEA nationals and their family members, who had a right to reside before the end of the Brexit transition period at 11pm on 31 December 2020, had a right to apply to the Home Office for, and be issued with, certain documents. These documents were declaratory of the right to reside and those rights existed whether not you held one of these documents. See Chapter 5 for further details.

Under the European Union Settlement Scheme

If you are an EEA national or the family member of an EEA national, you may have been granted leave to remain, known as pre-settled status, or indefinite leave to remain, known as settled status, under the EU Settlement Scheme. Please see Chapter 5 for further details.

For EEA nationals, these forms of status are currently granted electronically. Usually, you will receive an email confirming your grant of leave and containing a 16-digit reference number. This reference number acts as an electronic token, which can be used on the Home Office's website to view and confirm the grant of leave.[5] You will be given a 'share code', which proves your status to others.

The correspondence confirming a grant of 'settled status' or 'pre-settled status' under the EU Settlement Scheme makes it clear that the grant email (or letter in the case of paper applications) itself is not valid proof of leave to remain under the scheme. To view or prove your immigration status and to obtain a share code, you will need to go to the website and input details of the identity document you used when you applied (your passport, national identity card, or biometric residence card or permit) and your date of birth. You will also need access to the mobile number or email address you used when you applied as you will be sent a code for logging in.

For non-EEA family members of EEA nationals, if you already hold a biometric residence permit under the EEA Regulations, that will not be replaced until it expires and you will need to confirm your grant of leave under the EU Settlement Scheme online in the same way as EEA nationals. However, if you do not yet hold a biometric residence permit under the EEA Regulations, you will receive a new biometric residence permit confirming your EU Settlement Scheme grant.

Note: EEA nationals and their family members who live in the UK before 31 December 2020 have until the current deadline of 30 June 2021 to apply to the

EU Settlement Scheme and, therefore, are not required to hold either 'settled status' or 'pre-settled status' (or the associated documentation) in the meantime. However, from 30 June 2021 it will become essential to hold either of these forms of status, and you risk being an overstayer if you do not (see p52).

Under the Immigration Rules

As set out on p57, EEA nationals and their family members who arrive in the UK from 1 January 2021 will be required to apply for, and hold leave to remain under the Immigration Rules.

8. Passport issues

Leaving the UK

Embarkation from (leaving) the UK is endorsed by a triangular ink stamp in the embarking person's passport (see Appendix 6, Figure 14). This practice was suspended in March 1998, but then reintroduced in 2015.

New or lost passports

If you have been granted leave to enter or remain that has been endorsed in a passport that has expired or been lost before your leave is due to expire, the expiry or loss of the passport does not affect your leave. This is most common for people granted indefinite leave – eg, if you had your leave endorsed in your passport, but this has now expired and your new passport is not endorsed.

In this situation, you can apply for confirmation of your status. This now takes the form of a biometric residence permit card (see p68).

Illegible passport stamps

Problems may arise if an endorsement on a passport is either unclear or illegible, or if you required leave and your passport was not endorsed on your last entry.

If your passport has been endorsed illegibly, you may be deemed to have been granted leave to enter for six months with a condition prohibiting employment,[6] or, if you arrived in the UK before 10 July 1998, to have been given indefinite leave to enter the UK.[7] If you required leave to enter the UK, but your passport was not endorsed on entry, you may be considered an illegal entrant.[8] You should obtain specialist advice. See also p70.

Note: certain documents, such as a passport that indicates that you have indefinite leave to remain, must be current in order to demonstrate that you have a right to work in the UK. Other documents, such as a UK passport, can demonstrate a right to work if they are either current or if they have expired.[9]

Notes

2. **British nationals and people with the right of abode**
   1 s39(8) BNA 1981

3. **People with leave to enter or remain**
   2 See UKVI policy guidance ECB9.4, at gov.uk/government/publications/entry-clearance-vignettes-ecb09
   3 s3(3)(b) IA 1971
   4 s3C IA 1971

7. **European Economic Area nationals**
   5 gov.uk/view-prove-immigration-status

8. **Passport issues**
   6 Sch 2 para 6(1) IA 1971, as amended
   7 Sch 2 para 6(1) IA 1971, prior to amendment and as interpreted by the courts
   8 *Rehal v SSHD* [1989] Imm AR 576
   9 The Immigration (Restrictions on Employment) (Codes of Practice and Amendment) Order 2014, No.1183 and Home Office guidance, *An Employer's Guide to Right to Work Checks* at gov.uk/government/publications/right-to-work-checks-employers-guide, updated 21 December 2020

Part 3

Benefits and immigration status

Chapter 7

People subject to immigration control

This chapter covers:

You should consult this chapter, together with Chapter 8, if you, your partner and children are *not* all British or Irish citizens.

Since the end of the transition period (11pm, 31 December 2020), the immigration status restrictions on benefits were extended to apply not only to many non-European Economic Area (EEA) nationals but also to many EEA nationals.

If you, your partner, your parent or your child have applied for asylum in the UK, you should also check Chapter 9.

1. Introduction

Entitlement to most benefits and tax credits depends on your immigration status. The immigration status of your partner can also affect how much you are paid. In addition, it is important to know the immigration status of any partner or child included in your claim, because if s/he has leave that is subject to the condition that s/he has no recourse to public funds, her/his right to remain in the UK could be jeopardised if you are paid an additional amount for her/him. This chapter provides an overview of how immigration status affects your benefit and tax credit entitlement and how a benefit claim can affect your partner's or child's right to remain in the UK.

If you are defined as a 'person subject to immigration control', the general rule is that you are excluded from most benefits and tax credits. However, there are limited exceptions. This chapter explains who is defined as a 'person subject to immigration control'. The relevant benefits, the exempt groups and the rules on how your benefits are affected if your partner or child is a 'person subject to immigration control' are covered in Chapter 8.

If you applied for asylum in the UK and have been granted refugee leave, humanitarian protection or discretionary leave to be in the UK, more generous benefit rules can apply (see Chapter 9).

In addition to immigration status restrictions, most benefits also have presence and residence conditions, which you must satisfy. See Part 4 for more details.

If your immigration status excludes you from benefits and consequently you do not have any, or enough, income to live on, you may be entitled to other forms of state support (eg, asylum support, or, support from your local authority), particularly if you are a child, or you have a child or you have care needs. See Chapter 21 and Chapter 25.

2. How and why to check the effect of immigration status on benefits

It is important to know your immigration status, and that of anyone included in your claim, before making a claim for a benefit because:

- your immigration status may mean that you come within the definition of a 'person subject to immigration control'. In most cases, this means that you are excluded from many benefits, but there are limited exceptions;
- your immigration status can mean that you satisfy, or are exempt from, the residence or presence requirements for the benefit you want to claim;
- your partner's immigration status may affect whether or not you can be paid benefit for her/him;
- if your benefit includes an increased amount for someone included in your claim, this can affect her/his right to remain in the UK if her/his leave is subject to a no recourse to public funds condition.

If you are not a British or Irish citizen or if anyone you could include in your claim is not a British or Irish citizen, work through the following steps.

- **Step one:** be clear about your immigration status and that of anyone you could include in your claim. See Chapter 6 for an overivew. However, if you are unsure about your immigration status, get specialist immigration advice before making any benefit claims (see p7).
- **Step two:** check whether you are defined as a 'person subject to immigration control' (see p81). If you are not, your immigration status does not exclude you from benefit entitlement, but you must still satisfy any rules on residence and presence. If you have a partner or child who is subject to immigration control, see p104 for how your benefit, and in some circumstances their right to remain in the UK, can be affected.

- **Step three:** if you are defined as a 'person subject to immigration control', check whether the benefit you want to claim is one that excludes people subject to immigration control (see p95). If not, your immigration status does not exclude you from entitlement to that benefit, but you must still satisfy any rules on residence and presence.
- **Step four:** if the benefit you want to claim is one from which people subject to immigration control are generally excluded, check whether you come into an exempt group. These vary between the different benefits (see p96). If you are exempt, you must still satisfy all the other conditions of entitlement, including the residence and presence requirements.
- **Step five:** if you cannot claim the benefit you want, but you have a partner who may be able to include you in her/his claim, see p104.
- **Step six:** if you, or a member of your family, have leave to enter or remain in the UK that is subject to a no recourse to public funds condition, check whether any benefits claim could breach this condition because that could jeopardise your (or her/his) current or future immigration status (see p87).
- **Step seven:** if you are not entitled to any, or enough, benefits, check whether you can obtain alternative state support – eg, asylum support (if you are an asylum seeker or are dependent on an asylum seeker) or support under the Children Act or Children (Scotland) Act (if you are a child or are responsible for a child). See Chapter 21.

3. Who is a 'person subject to immigration control'

Most people, apart from British citizens, are subject to immigration control. However, for benefit and tax credit purposes, the term 'person subject to immigration control' has a specific meaning, given below. It is this meaning that is referred to when the phrase 'person subject to immigration control' is used in this *Handbook*.

For benefit and tax credit purposes, you are defined as a **'person subject to immigration control'** if you:[1]

- require leave to enter or remain in the UK but do not have it (see p85); *or*
- have leave to enter or remain in the UK that is subject to a condition that you do not have recourse to 'public funds' (see p87); *or*
- have leave to enter or remain in the UK, given as a result of a maintenance undertaking (see p90); *or*
- have leave to remain in the UK solely because you are appealing against a refusal to vary your previous leave (see p92).

Examples of circumstances in which you are *not* a person subject to immigration control include:

- if you are a British or Irish citizen. British and Irish citizens do not require leave to enter or remain in the UK;
- if you have refugee leave or humanitarian protection. For the duration of your leave you are not defined as a person subject to immigration control. If you apply for indefinite leave to remain *before* your refugee leave or humanitarian protection expires, your leave is extended until your application is decided (see p86);
- if you have leave to enter or remain in the UK under the European Union Settlement Scheme (EUSS – see p49) you are *not* defined as a person subject to imigration control for the duration of that leave.[2] The only potential exception is if the last bullet point of the definition applies, but that could only apply at the end of a five-year period of limited leave (therefore, the earliest it can apply is 2023) and arguably does not apply to appeals under the EUSS (see p92). Otherwise, you are not defined as a person subject to immigration control and are not excluded on that basis from the benefits listed on p95. However, if you have pre-settled status and are claiming a benefit requiring a right to reside, see p153 and p158;
- you are a non-European Economic Area (EEA) national and you are in a protected group that can have a free movement right to reside after 31 December 2020 *and* you currently have a free movement right to reside. For further details including the duration for which these rules can apply, see below;
- you are an EEA national and you are in a protected group that can have a free movement right to reside after 31 December 2020. For further details, including the duration for which these rules can apply, see below.

Note: Until the end of the transition period (11pm, 31 December 2020), EEA nationals (see p47 for the list of EEA states) could not be defined as a person subject to immigration control because the definition only applied to non-EEA nationals. Since 31 December 2020, if you are an EEA national, you need to check whether you are defined as a person subject to immigration control – *unless* you fall into one of the protected groups list below. If one of these apply, you cannot be a person subject to immigration control during the periods stated because transitional rules continue to limit the definition of a person subject to immigration control to only non-EEA nationals.[3] You are also not defined as a person subject to immigration control if you have pre-settled status or settled status under the EU Settlement Scheme, for the duration of that leave (unless the fourth bullet point of the above definition applies to you); see also the third bullet point above. You are also not defined as a person subject to immigration control if you are a frontier worker (see p256) because you do not require leave to enter or remain in the UK.[4] However, you are required to obtain a frontier worker permit by 30 June 2021 (see p59).

Even if *you* are not defined as a person subject to immigration control, you still need to check whether this definition applies to your partner or child.

Protected groups that can have free movement residence rights

If you have a European free movement right to reside in the UK, you do not require leave to enter or remain in the UK and are, therefore, not defined as a 'person subject to immigration control'. However, since the end of the transition period (31 December 2020), whether you are an EEA or non-EEA national, you can only have a free movement right to reside while you are in a protected group.

The protected groups and the rules that are relevant to determining whether you are a defined as a person subject to immigration control are summarised below.

If you are a **non-EEA national**, you do not require leave to enter or remain in the UK if:

- you are in one of the protected groups below; *and*
- you currently have a free movement right to reside.

If both the above points apply, you do not require leave to enter or remain, and you cannot be refused benefits on the basis of your immigration status even if, for example, you have been given leave to enter or remain that is subject to a condition that you do not have recourse to public funds, or which has been given as a result of a maintenance undertaking. Conditions attached to any leave you have (eg, that you do not have recourse to public funds) do not have any effect while you have a right to reside under the EEA Regulations.[5]

If you are an **EEA national**, you are not defined as a person subject to immigration control if you are in one of the protected groups below *whether or not* you currently have a free movement right to reside. That is because while one of these groups applies to you, transitional rules limit the definition of person subject to immigration control to only non-EEA nationals.[6] However, to be entitled to one of the benefits that requires a right to reside, you will *also* need to currently have a free movement right to reside.

You are in a **protected group** if:[7]

- **between 31 December 2020 and 30 June 2021:** on 31 December 2020 you had a free movement right to reside (see note below), and on that date you did not have, and since then you have not had, leave under the EU Settlement Scheme; *or*
- **beyond 30 June 2021:** you were in the group above and on or before 30 June 2021 you applied for leave under EU Settlement Scheme and that application (or appeal against a refusal) has not been finally determined, withdrawn or abandoned; *or*
- **between 31 December 2020 and 30 June 2021:** you are defined as the 'relevant family member' (see p168) of a person who on 31 December 2020 had a free movement right to reside and did not have leave under the EU

Settlement Scheme, and you currently do not have leave under the EU Settlement Scheme.

Note:
- For an overview of who can have a European free movement right to reside see p166.
- You can be *treated as* having had a free movement right to reside on 31 December 2020, if you previously had a free movement right to reside in the UK and on that date you were absent from the UK, but your absence was in circumstance that does not break your continuity of residence - eg: if that absence, together with any other absences in the one year period, were less than six months in total (see p250).[8]
- If you previously had a permanent right to reside in the UK and since then you lost this right to reside due to being absent from the UK for more than two years, you are *treated as* having a permanent right to reside on 31 December 2020 if on that date you had been absent from the UK for a period of more than two, but less than five years, and immediately before leaving the UK you had a permanent right to reside in the UK.[9]
- Having limited leave granted under the EU Settlement Scheme (also known as pre-settled status) is also a protected group that enables you to have a free movement right to reside (see p168). That is not listed above because if you have pre-settled status that by itself means you are not defined a person subject to immigration control (unless you have limited leave solely because you are appealing against a refusal to vary this leave). If you have pre-settled status and you want to claim a benefit that requires a right to reside see p151.

As a non-EEA national, the free movement rights to reside you are most likely to have had on 31 December 2020 and/or have currently are:
- as the 'family member' of an EEA national who has a relevant free movmement right to reside (eg, as a worker – see p218);
- in limited circumstances, you may have retained a right to reside as a former family member (see p228);
- a permanent right to reside (see p244 and third bullet in the note above).
- a deriative right to reside (eg, as the primary carer of an EEA worker's child who is in education – see p233). **Note**: if you are the primary carer of a British citizen who is in the UK, and it is necessary for you to have a right to reside in the UK so that s/he can continue to reside within the EU (often referred to as a *'Zambrano carer'*),although you do not require leave and are, therefore, not defined as a person subject to immigration control, you are still excluded from benefits that require a right to reside (other than a very limited exception for child benefit and child tax credit), because this particular right to reside does not satisfy the right to reside requirement (see p151). However, you are not excluded from other benefits that do not require a right to reside, such as

personal independence payment (PIP) and carer's allowance (CA).[10] If the British citizen is a child, you may also be able to get support under the Children Act 1989 (or Children (Scotland) Act 1995) from your local authority (see p589). If you are a primary carer of a dependent British citizen, get specialist immigration advice as it may be possible for you to obtain leave to remain that would give you access to benefits.

You require leave to enter or remain, but do not have it

If you require leave to enter or remain in the UK but do not have leave, you are 'a person subject to immigration control'[11] *unless* you are an EEA national and in one of the protected groups listed above.

You require leave to enter or remain in the UK *unless* you are:

- a British or Irish citizen; *or*
- a person with the right of abode (see p16); *or*
- an EEA national in the UK as a frontier worker (from 1 July 2021, you will need to hold a valid frontier worker permit – see p59);[12] *or*
- (**until at least 30 June 2021**) a non-EEA national who is in a protected group that can have a free movement right to reside *and* you have such a right to reside (see above).

Unless you are in one of the groups above, you require leave to enter or remain in the UK. For more information on when leave to enter or remain is granted, see Chapter 3.

Examples of when you require leave to enter or remain but do not have leave include if:

- you are an asylum seeker on immigration bail (before 15 January 2018, you would have had 'temporary admission' – see p14); *or*
- you have overstayed your limited leave to remain – ie, you did not apply for further leave before your period of leave expired. **Note:** if you apply for further leave on the same or a different basis before your current leave expires, your leave is extended from the date it would have expired until your application is decided, and, therefore, you are *not* someone who requires leave but does not have it (see 'Extension of leave' on p86); *or*
- you have entered the UK without either leave to enter or a European free movement right to enter, and since then you have not obtained any leave to remain; *or*
- you previously had a European free movement right of residence (see below), but that has now ceased, and you have not obtained leave under the EU Settlement Scheme nor any other leave to remain; *or*
- you are subject to a deportation order.

Note:

- If you came to live in the UK before 1 January 1973, and you are, or were, a Commonwealth citizen, or you came before 1 August 1988 and are now British or have a right of abode or indefinite leave, you may be entitled to compensation from the Home Office Windrush Compensation Scheme[13] if you, or your relative, experienced losses, including loss of benefits, due to lack of documentary evidence of your status (see also p70). DWP guidance states that payments under this scheme, or the previous Windrush Exceptional Payments Scheme, should be disregarded for all means-tested benefits 'on an extra-statutory basis'.[14] **Note**: the council tax reduction regulations have been amended to disregard these payments as income and capital. Also, interest on payments made under the compenation scheme are ignored as income for tax credits for 52 weeks.[15] If you have previously had a claim for benefits refused or terminated due to your lack of documents, you may still be able to challenge that decision.[16]
- There are close links between the benefit authorities and the Home Office. Making a claim for benefit could alert the Home Office to your presence and status in the UK. If you need immigration leave but do not have any, or you are unsure of your immigration status, get specialist immigration advice before making a claim for benefits or being included in someone else's claim (see Appendix 2).

Extension of leave

If you have time-limited leave to enter or remain in the UK and you make a valid application for a further period of leave, on the same or a different basis, *before* your current leave expires, your current leave is extended beyond the date it was due to expire, and until your application is decided or withdrawn (but it may be cancelled in certain circumstances, such as if you breach a condition attached to the leave).[17] If your leave has been extended, you continue to have the same benefit entitlements as you had previously (see examples below). If the extension of your leave means that you continue to be entitled to benefits, you **must** notify the relevant benefit authority. You should provide evidence that you made your application for leave before your previous leave expired, and explain that your leave has been extended under section 3C of the Immigration Act 1971 and, therefore, your benefit entitlements continue. It can also be helpful to refer the decision maker to the relevant part of the decision makers' guidance that confirms this.[18] **Note**: if you have an award of PIP, attendance allowance (AA) or disability allowance (DLA) that is due to end on the date your original grant of leave expires, you will need to request a supersession of that decision on the basis that your leave has been extended and you continue to satisfy all the other conditions of entitlement. Alternatively, submit a renewal claim before your current award ends (see CPAG's *Welfare Benefits and Tax Credits Handbook* for further details).

Examples

Olabisi had been receiving universal credit (UC) for several months. She had discretionary leave (with no conditions attached) that was due to expire on 31 January 2021. On 15 January 2021, she submitted a valid application for a further period of discretionary leave, and she is still waiting for a decision from the Home Office. Her leave is extended, and Olabisi continues not to be defined as a person subject to immigration control and continues to be entitled to UC until the Home Office decides her application. However, because the Department for Work and Pensions (DWP) already had on record that Olabisi's discretionary leave was due to expire on 31 January 2021, it terminated her UC and notified her of its decision that she was not entitled to UC from 1 February 2021 because she had become a person subject to immigration control. Olabisi requested a mandatory reconsideration of this decision, provided a copy of the Home Office email confirming the date she applied for further leave, explained that her leave had, therefore, been automatically extended under section 3C of the Immigration Act 1971, and referred to the relevant UC guidance confirming this extension.[19] The DWP revised its decision and Olabisi's UC was put back into payment.

Azeez had leave to remain in the UK as the spouse of a British woman. His leave was subject to a no recourse to public funds condition (see below) and was due to expire on 31 January 2021. On 15 January 2021, he submitted a valid application for indefinite leave to remain, and he is still waiting for a decision. His leave is extended and continues to be subject to the no recourse to public funds condition. Consequently, Azeez continues to be defined as a person subject to immigration control and continues to be excluded from the benefits listed on p95 (unless he is in a relevant exempt group – see p96).

Note: if your application for further leave is refused, you may have a right to appeal (or seek an administrative review) against the refusal from within the UK. The time limits are very short (generally 14 days or less) so get immigration advice immediately. If your leave had already been extended while your application to the Home Office was pending, your leave is further extended while an appeal (or administrative review) can be brought, and extended further while any such appeal (or administrative review) is pending. For information on whether you then become a person subject to immigration control, see p92.

Your leave has a 'no recourse to public funds' condition

You are a 'person subject to immigration control' if you have leave to enter or remain in the UK that is subject to the condition that you do not have recourse to public funds.[20]

Most people admitted to the UK with time-limited leave given for a particular purpose, such as spouses/civil partners, students or visitors, are given leave to stay on condition that they do not have recourse to public funds. If you are an EEA national who enters the UK on this basis after 31 December 2020 (see p57). Increasingly, this condition is also being added to those given time-limited leave to remain for other reasons, such as family ties, so you should always check whether your leave is subject to this condition.

People granted refugee leave, humanitarian protection (see p41), leave under family reunion provisions (see p41), leave granted under the EU Settlement Scheme, or, in most cases, discretionary leave (see p43) do not have a no recourse to public funds condition attached to their leave.

Indefinite leave (see p29) is never given with this condition attached.[21] However, if you have been granted indefinite leave as a result of someone undertaking to maintain and accommodate you, you come under the definition of a 'person subject to immigration control' (see p90).

Public funds

'Public funds' are defined in the Immigration Rules as:[22]

- AA;
- CA;
- child benefit;
- CTC
- council tax benefit (now abolished);
- council tax reduction;
- DLA;
- income-related employment and support allowance (ESA);
- homelessness assistance and housing provided under specific provisions;
- housing benefit (HB);
- income support;
- income-based jobseeker's allowance (JSA);
- local welfare assistance (except the Discretionary Assistance Fund for Wales);
- pension credit;
- PIP;
- severe disablement allowance;
- social fund payments;
- UC;
- working tax credit.

Only the above benefits, tax credits and other assistance listed in the Immigration Rules are public funds. If you receive any other benefit or assistance, you do not breach any no recourse to public funds condition attached to your leave.

If you have recourse to public funds when your leave prohibits that, you have breached a condition of your leave. This breach may affect your right to remain in the UK. You could have your leave curtailed, be liable to be deported, have further leave refused and/or be prosecuted for committing a criminal offence.[23]

If your leave is subject to a no recourse to public funds condition, you are defined as a 'person subject to immigration control' and the benefit rules exclude you from entitlement to the above benefits.

However, if you are within an exempt group (which vary according to benefit – see Chapter 8), the rules for that benefit do not then exclude you and you can claim that benefit. If you receive one of the above benefits (except council tax reduction), because you come within a relevant exempt group, you are *not* regarded as having recourse to public funds under the Immigration Rules and so have not breached that condition of your leave.[24] If you receive council tax reduction as a result of being exempt, you still count as having recourse to public funds. That is because the council tax reduction regulations are not referred to by the part of the Immigration Rules that disregards entitlements due to being in an exempt group.[25] Get specialist immigration advice before claiming council tax reduction (see Appendix 2).

If your leave is subject to a no recourse to public funds condition, you are regarded as having recourse to public funds if someone else's benefit is increased because of your presence.[26] For example, if the amount of your partner's HB is greater because you are included in her/his claim, that counts as recourse to public funds. This means, if your leave is subject to a no recourse to public funds condition, you have breached that condition, which could jeopardise your current or future immigration status (see p31). Get specialist immigration advice before someone makes a claim that includes extra benefit because of your presence (see Appendix 2).

Note: if your leave is subject to a no recourse to public funds condition and you are, or are likely to become, destitute, seek immigration advice about applying to the Home Office to have that condition removed (see p32).

Domestic violence

If you were granted leave to enter or remain in the UK as a spouse, civil partner or partner, but that relationship has broken down because of domestic violence, you may be able to apply for leave to remain under the 'destitution domestic violence' concession (see p36). This leave lasts for three months and is not subject to any condition that you do not have recourse to public funds. During this period of leave, you are not defined as a 'person subject to immigration control' and can, therefore, claim all benefits, subject to the normal conditions of entitlement.[27] **Note:** having this type of leave means you are exempt from the habitual residence test for means-tested benefits (see p142) and the requirement to have been living in the UK for the past three months for child benefit and CTC (see p129); during your period of leave, you have a right to reside that satisfies that requirement for all benefits that have it (see p151).

If you apply for indefinite leave (under what is commonly known as the 'domestic violence rule'[28]) before the three-month period of concessionary leave expires, your leave is extended while the Home Office decides your application.[29] You continue not to be a person subject to immigration control and continue to be entitled to benefits.[30] You need to notify the relevant benefit authority that you have applied for indefinite leave before your previous leave expired, and provide evidence of this (see p86).

If you do not apply for indefinite leave by the end of the three months, you become someone who requires leave but does not have it and, therefore, once again a person subject to immigration control. If you are claiming any of the benefits listed on p95, your entitlement ceases unless you are in one of the exempt groups listed on p96.

Your leave is given as a result of a maintenance undertaking

If you have leave to enter or remain in the UK given as a result of a maintenance undertaking, you are a 'person subject to immigration control'.[31]

Maintenance undertaking

A **'maintenance undertaking'** is a written undertaking given by another person, under the Immigration Rules, to be responsible for your maintenance and accommodation.[32]

There are specific Home Office forms on which an undertaking can be given. However, no official form need be used, provided the undertaking is sufficiently formal and definite.[33] The document must contain a promise or agreement that the other person will maintain and accommodate you in the future. If it merely contains a statement about her/his present abilities and intentions, that does not amount to an undertaking.[34]

Your leave is considered to be 'as a result of a maintenance undertaking' if this was a factor in granting leave. It does not need to have been the only, or even a major, factor.[35] However, if the maintenance undertaking was not relevant to your being granted leave, the fact that the undertaking exists does not make you a person subject to immigration control.

If it is unclear whether or not your leave was granted as a result of a maintenance undertaking, the onus is on the benefit authority to prove that leave was granted on that basis.[36] If your leave has been granted outside the Immigration Rules, the causal connection between the leave and the undertaking cannot be inferred.[37]

If you are in doubt about whether you have leave given as a result of an undertaking, get specialist immigration advice (see Appendix 2).

Consequences for your sponsor if you claim benefits

If you have leave to enter or remain as a result of a maintenance undertaking and you claim benefits, the person/s who signed the undertaking to maintain and accommodate you could be asked to repay any UC, IS, income-based JSA or income-related ESA paid to you. However, in practice, this rarely happens because the rules for these benefits exclude people with this form of leave from entitlement for the first five years (unless the person/s who gave the undertaking has/have died – see p97).

The DWP can only recover UC or IS paid to you from the person who gave the undertaking in certain circumstances.[38] Recovery is through the family court (in Scotland, the sheriff court).

The DWP can also prosecute someone for failure to maintain you if that results in UC, IS, income-based JSA, or income-related ESA being paid.[39]

As the DWP can recover benefit or to take court action, if the DWP asks you about an undertaking, get independent advice (see Appendix 2).

Sponsors

People who have been given leave to enter or remain as the result of a maintenance undertaking are often referred to as **'sponsored people'**, and those giving the undertakings as **'sponsors'**. This terminology is used by the benefit authorities, including in their guidance to decision makers. However, the term 'sponsor' is also used in connection with other types of leave, and that can lead to confusion and errors in decision making. For example, the word occurs in the Immigration Rules in relation to those seeking leave to enter or remain on the basis of their relationship to their partner (see p33),[40] and people commonly describe themselves as having been 'sponsored' by their partner when they are granted such leave. The Upper Tribunal has provided a helpful discussion of this confusion.[41]

Another common area of confusion is when a family member of someone with refugee leave or humanitarian protection is given leave to enter or remain under the family reunion provisions (see p114). Although the person with refugee leave or humanitarian protection is not required to provide a maintenance undertaking, the confusion arises because the Home Office policy on family reunion and the entry visa given to the family member uses the word 'sponsor'.

You only come within this definition of a person subject to immigration control if you have been given leave to enter or remain *as a result* of an undertaking. However, if you have been given time-limited leave to enter or remain because, for example, you were 'sponsored' by your spouse/civil partner, your leave is subject to a no recourse to public funds condition and you come within the second group of people subject to immigration control (see p87).

If you only have leave to remain because you are appealing

You are a 'person subject to immigration control' if you have leave to enter or remain only because your leave has been extended while you appeal against a decision to vary, or refuse to vary, your leave (see p68).[42]

If you have time-limited leave (see p66), and you apply for a further period of leave, on the same or a different basis, *before* your existing leave expires, your current leave is extended beyond the date it was due to expire and until your application is decided by the Home Office (see p86).[43]

If your leave had been extended as above and your application is then refused, you may be entitled to appeal (or seek an administrative review) against the refusal from within the UK. If so, your leave is further extended during the short time period in which an appeal (or review) can be brought, and you continue to have the same type of leave during the short time period in which you can do bring an appeal (or review).[44]

If you appeal (or seek a review) within the time limit, your leave is extended until the appeal or review is dealt with.[45] You continue to have the same type of leave, subject to the same conditions, while your appeal (or review) is pending.

However, during the time when your leave is extended, initially because you are within the period when you can appeal and subsequently, once you have appealed, because your appeal is pending, you are defined as a 'person subject to immigration control'.[46]

It is strongly arguable that you are not a person subject to immigration control during the time when you can request an appeal against a refusal of leave under the EU Settlement Scheme, or an administrative review, or while you have requested either, and it is pending.[47]

Most of the DWP guidance does not include this category of people within their summary of the definition of a person subject to immigration control.[48] However, HM Revenue and Customs does include this category as part of the definition in its tax credit and child benefit guidance.[49] **Note:** at the time of writing, none of the guidance had been updated to include EEA nationals as potentially falling within the definition.

In practice, your entitlement to benefit is only affected by your being a person subject to immigration control while your appeal against a decision on varying your leave is pending, if your original leave was *not* subject to a no recourse to public funds condition. Although an example of such leave includes limited leave granted under the EU Settlement Scheme (also known as pre-settled status), grants of this leave only began to be issued in 2018 and are for five years, which means they will not expire until 2023 at the earliest (and see also the argument above that these rules do not apply when appealing against a refusal of leave under the EU Settlement Scheme). If your original leave *was* subject to a no recourse to public funds condition, you were already a person subject to immigration control and an extension of your leave simply means that you carry on being so.

Example

Banu is an Iranian national who was granted 30 months' discretionary leave in the UK without any public funds condition attached. She is not a person subject to immigration control and so has full access to benefits during the period of her leave. Just before her discretionary leave expires, she applies for a further period of discretionary leave. Her original leave is extended while her application is pending. The Home Office refuses her application and, because she has a right to appeal against this decision from within the UK, Banu appeals immediately. Her discretionary leave is further extended while the appeal is pending. She is now a person subject to immigration control since she has leave only because she is appealing and, therefore, her entitlement to benefits ends.

Notes

3. **Who is a 'person subject to immigration control'**

1 s115(9) IAA 1999
2 para 10120 CBTM wrongly lists someone with pre-settled status as a person subject to immigration control.
3 Regs 3(4)-(6), 4(2) and (5)-(8) and 12(1)(i) CR(ADTP) Regs; DMG Memo 26/20 paras 36,37 and 41; ADM 30/20, paras 36, 37 and 41
4 Reg 5 CR(FW) Regs; ADM Memo 33/20 para 45; DMG Memo 29/20, para 45
5 Reg 43 and Sch 3 para 1 I(EEA) Regs; paras C1050 and C2012 ADM; Vol 2 Ch 7 Part 1 para 070838 DMG
6 Regs 3(4)-(6), 4(2) and (5)-(8) and 12(1)(i) CR(ADTP) Regs; DMG Memo 26/20, paras 36, 37 and 41; ADM 30/20, paras 36, 37 and 41
7 Regs 3(4)-(6), 4(2) and (5)-(8) CR(ADTP) Regs
8 Reg 3(5)(b) and 4(6)(c) CR(ADTP) Regs; Reg 3 I(EEA) Regs
9 Regs 3(5)(c) and 4(5)(d) CR(ADTP) Regs
10 See, for example, *DM v SSWP (PIP)* [2019] UKUT 26 (AAC)
11 s115(9)(a) IAA 1999
12 Regs 1(2)(b) and (4), 5 and 6 CR(FW) Regs; DMG Memo 29/20, paras 45 and 49; ADM Memo 33/20, paras 45 and 49
13 gov.uk/apply-windrush-compensation-scheme
14 HB Adjudication Circular A8/2019
15 Regs 10(2)(f) and 19 (table 6, para 24) TC(DCI) Regs
16 See, for example, HB Circular A8/2019 on the process for revising housing benefit decisions.
17 s3C IA 1971
18 Vol 2, Part 3 para 073192 DMG; paras C1679 and C2017 ADM; TCM 0290150 (Step 8)
19 para C1679 ADM
20 s115(9)(b) IAA 1999
21 s3(1) IA 1971
22 para 6.2 IR
23 s24(1)(b)(ii) IA 1971
24 para 6.2, notes under 'public funds' definition, IR
25 para 6.2, notes under 'public funds' definition, IR
26 para 6.2, notes under 'public funds' definition, IR
27 Confirmed in Vol 2 Part 3 paras 073181-84 DMG and paras C1674-77 ADM
28 paras 289A-C IR
29 s3C IA 1971
30 Confirmed in Vol 2 Part 3 para 073183 DMG and para C1676 ADM; HB/CTB U4/2012; TCM 0290150 Step 9
31 s115(9)(c) IAA 1999

32 s115(10) IAA 1999
33 *R (Begum) v Social Security Commissioner* [2003] EWHC 3380 (Admin); CIS/2474/1999; CIS/2816/2002 and CIS/47/2002
34 *Ahmed v SSWP* [2005] EWCA Civ 535; CIS/426/2003
35 CIS/3508/2001
36 R(PC) 1/09
37 R(PC) 1/09; *SJ v SSWP (SPC)* [2015] UKUT 505 (AAC), reported as [2016] AACR 17
38 s106 SSAA 1992
39 s105 SSAA 1992
40 para 6.2, notes under 'public funds' definition, IR
41 *OO v SSWP (SPC)* [2013] UKUT 335 (AAC)
42 s115(9)(d) IAA 1999; s3C(1) and (2)(b) and (c) IA 1971; *EE v City of Cardiff (HB)* [2018] UKUT 418 (AAC)
43 s3C(1) and (2)(a) IA 1971
44 s3C(1) and (2)(b), (ca) and (d) IA 1971
45 s3C(1) and (2) (c), (cb) and (d) IA 1971
46 s115(9)(d) IAA 1999 refers to leave continuing while you appeal because of the rule in Sch 4 para 17. Sch 4 para 17 was repealed by NIAA 2002, which also inserted s3C into IA 1971. In *EE v City of Cardiff (HB)* [2018] UKUT 418 (AAC) it was held that s17(2) IA 1978 requires that the reference in s115(9)(d) must be read as a reference to Sch 4 para 17 re-enacted as 3C(1) and (2)(b) and (c) IA 1971. See also *GO v HMRC (CHB)* [2018] UKUT 328 (AAC).
47 As s3(c)(2)(ca), (cb) and (d) do not re-enact Sch 4 para 17 IAA 1999 and were not inserted until 31 January 2020 for (ca) and (cb) and 20 October 2014 for (d).
48 See, for example, Vol 2 para 070833 DMG and paras C1041 and C2006 ADM
49 See, for example, TCTM 02102 and para 10120 CBTM (**note:** this wrongly includes those with pre-settled status).

Chapter 8

People subject to immigration control and benefits

This chapter covers:

1. Benefits and tax credits affected by immigration status (below)
2. People subject to immigration control who can be entitled (p96)
3. Partners and children who are subject to immigration control (p104)

Before using the information in this chapter, check whether you, your partner or child are a 'person subject to immigration control'. This is explained in Chapter 7.

1. Benefits and tax credits affected by immigration status

The general rule is that if you are defined as a 'person subject to immigration control' (see p81), you are excluded from council tax reduction[1] (see p575) and the following benefits and tax credits:[2]

- attendance allowance;
- carer's allowance;
- child benefit;
- child disability payment (expected to be introduced in Scotland in 2021);[3]
- child tax credit;
- disability living allowance;
- contributory employment and support allowance (ESA) in youth;[4]
- funeral support payments (in Scotland);[5]
- income-related ESA;
- housing benefit;
- incapacity benefit in youth;[6]
- income support;
- income-based jobseeker's allowance (JSA);
- pension credit;
- personal independence payment;

- severe disablement allowance;
- social fund payments;
- universal credit;
- working tax credit.

However, there are limited exceptions which mean that some people who are subject to immigration control can claim means-tested benefits (see below), some non-means-tested benefits (see p98), tax credits (see p102) and social fund payments (see p103).

Even if cannot claim yourself, a family member may be able to claim a benefit that includes an amount for you, or you might be able to make a joint claim (see p104).

Claiming other benefits

If you are a 'person subject to immigration control', you are only excluded from the benefits and tax credits listed above; you are not excluded from claiming other benefits.

For example, if you have paid sufficient national insurance contributions, you can claim any of the contributory benefits – eg, retirement pension, contribution-based JSA and contributory ESA. (**Note:** if you have worked and paid contributions in a European Economic Area country and you are covered by the European Union co-ordination rules (see p355), or in a country with which the UK has a relevant reciprocal agreement (see p397), these contributions may be taken into account when working out your UK benefit entitlement.)

You are also not excluded from benefits that depend on previous employment – eg, maternity allowance (MA) or industrial injuries benefits. You are also not excluded from some of the Scottish benefits – eg, young carer grant, Scottish child payment or a Best Start grant. You may also be able to get help from your local welfare assistance scheme (see p579).

2. People subject to immigration control who can be entitled

Some people who are defined as a 'person subject to immigration control' are not excluded from claiming the benefits and tax credits on p95. The exempt groups vary between the different categories of benefits and tax credits, so being exempt for one category does not necessarily mean you can receive a benefit in a different category.

Note: if your leave prohibits you from having recourse to public funds (see p31), you can still claim any benefit to which you are entitled on the basis of being in an exempt group (but not council tax reduction), even though these benefits (except employment and support allowance (ESA) in youth and incapacity benefit (IB) in youth) are defined as 'public funds'. This is because the Immigration Rules do not regard you as having recourse to public funds if you are entitled because you are in an exempt group (see p87).[7]

Means-tested benefits

Being a person subject to immigration control does not exclude you from getting universal credit (UC), income support (IS), income-based jobseeker's allowance (JSA), income-related ESA, pension credit and housing benefit if:[8]

- your leave is on the basis of a maintenance undertaking (see p90) and the person who gave the undertaking (often referred to as your 'sponsor') has died. If the undertaking was given by more than one person, they must all have died;[9]
- your leave is on the basis of a maintenance undertaking and you have been resident in the UK for five years (see below);
- (except UC claimed from 1 January 2021) you are a national of Turkey or North Macedonia or a European Economic Area (EEA) country (*except* Bulgaria, Liechtenstein, Lithuania, Romania or Slovenia), and lawfully present in the UK (see below).

Your leave is on the basis of a maintenance undertaking and you have been resident for five years

You are not excluded from the above means-tested benefits on the basis of being a person subject to immigration control if you have:[10]

- leave to enter or remain given as a result of a maintenance undertaking (see p90); *and*
- been resident in the UK for at least five years since either the date the undertaking was given or the date when you came to the UK, whichever is later.

If you go abroad during the five years, you may still count as resident in the UK during your absence. This depends on the duration and circumstances of your absence (see p130).[11] If your absence abroad is such that you cease to be resident in the UK, you can add together periods of residence either side of the gaps in order to meet the five-year rule.[12]

Nationals of Turkey, North Macedonia and most European countries

You are not excluded from the above means-tested benefits, *except* UC (see below) on the basis of being defined as a person subject to immigration control if you are:[13]

- a national of a country that has ratified either the European Convention on Social and Medical Assistance or the European Social Charter (1961). This applies to all the EEA countries (*except* Bulgaria, Liechtenstein, Lithuania,

Romania or Slovenia), as well as the non-EEA countries of Turkey and North Macedonia; *and*
- lawfully present in the UK. You satisfy this if you currently have leave to enter or remain in the UK.

Note:
- UC was excluded from the benefits covered by this exempt group from 1 January 2021.[14] However, if your claim or award began before 1 January 2021 this exempt group continues to apply, such that your entitlement continues.[15] It may be arguable that this exclusion is unlawful on the basis that UC should, like the other means-tested benefits, be defined as 'social assistance' under these agreements and therefore lawfully present nationals of the countries that have ratified these agreements should not be excluded due to being a 'person subject to immigration control' from UC, in addition to not being excluded from the other means-tested benefits.[16]
- You are also not excluded from council tax reduction by your immigration status if you come into this category.[17] However, if your leave is subject to a no recourse to public funds condition and you receive council tax reduction as a result of being in this category, this counts as having recourse to public funds and so breaches the condition of your leave. That is because the council tax reduction regulations are not referred to by the part of the Immigration Rules that disregards entitlements due to being in an exempt group.[18]
- You must satisfy all the other conditions of entitlement, including having a right to reside (see p151). **Note:** if you are an asylum seeker and have been given immigration bail, although you are 'lawfully present' in the UK, the courts have held you not to have a right to reside.[19]

Non-means-tested benefits

If you are in any of the exempt groups below, being defined as a person subject to immigration control does not exclude you from getting the following non-means-tested, non-contributory benefits:[20]
- attendance allowance (AA);
- child benefit;
- disability living allowance (DLA);
- ESA in youth;
- funeral support payments (in Scotland);
- IB for incapacity in youth;
- personal independence payment (PIP);
- severe disablement allowance.

You are not excluded if:
- your leave is as a result of a maintenance undertaking (see p90);[21]

- you are a national of Algeria, Morocco, San Marino, Tunisia or Turkey (see below);
- (AA, DLA, PIP and child benefit only) you are covered by a reciprocal agreement (see p100);
- (in limited circumstances) you are a family member of an EEA national (see p101).

Note:
- It is expected that the above exempt groups will also apply to child disability payment (expected to be introduced in Scotland in 2021).[22] However, at the time of writing the necessary amending legislation had not been published.[23]
- Your entitlement to benefit still depends on your satisfying all the other conditions of entitlement, including those on presence and residence (see Part 4).

Nationals of Algeria, Morocco, San Marino, Tunisia and Turkey

You are not excluded from one of the non-means-tested benefits listed above on the basis of being defined as a person subject to immigration control, if you:[24]
- are a national of Morocco, San Marino, Tunisia or Turkey (or Algeria if you made your claim before 1 January 2021 – see below) *and* you are either currently lawfully working (see below) in Great Britain, or you have ceased lawfully working for a reason such as pregnancy, childcare, illness or accident, or because you have reached retirement age;[25] *or*
- you are living with a member of your family (see p361) covered by the above bullet point.

Until 1 January 2021, this protection was due to your being covered by European Union (EU) Association and Co-operation Agreements (see p408). However, after the transition period ended at 11pm on 31 December 2020, these agreements ceased to have direct effect in the UK, except provisions mean if you claimed before 1 January 2021, you continue to be entitled as if the agreements were still in force.[26]

The UK has negotiated Trade and Continuity Agreements with the above countries that include broadly similar protections and took effect from 1 January 2021. If you claim on or after 1 January 2021, the protection from being excluded as a person subject to immigration control only applies if you are covered by one of these replacement agreements (see bullets above), which have been reached with all the above countries except, at the time of writing, **Algeria**. If you, or the family member you are living with, are a national of Algeria and need to claim one of these benefits, check if a new agreement has been concluded.

If you claim **child benefit** on or after 1 January 2021 and you are a national of Morocco, San Marino, Tunisia or Turkey, the regulations state you are not excluded on the basis of being a person subject to immigration control (simply by being a national of one of those countries).[27] However, HM Revenues and Customs (HMRC) do not accept that the regulations have this effect (although they accept this regulation does not require you or your family member to be lawfully working), and stated they intend to amend the regulation.[28] At the time of writing, DWP guidance was unclear, the explantory notes to the amending regulations were unclear, and HMRC guidance had not been updated.[29] **Note:** you also need to satisfy all the other conditions of entitlement for child benefit, including having a right to reside (see p157).

Note: at the time of writing the UK had signed, but not implemented, a Partnership, Trade and Co-operation Agreement with **Albania**, which was understood to include provisions on family benefits that could enable you to be entitled to child benefit despite being a person subject to immigration control.[30] Get upto date advice if this could affect you.

Lawfully working

'Lawfully working' was interpreted in relation to the EU Association and Co-operation Agreements as being an 'insured person' under the EU co-ordination rules (see p355).[31] In broad terms, this means that you must have been insured by having paid (or been credited with) national insurance (NI) contributions.[32] However, this does not necessarily apply to the Trade and Continuity Agreements. In practice, it is likely that you will only be accepted as lawfully working if your work does not breach any work restrictions attached to your leave or, if you are an asylum seeker, you have permission to work from the Home Office.

You are covered by a reciprocal agreement

You are not excluded from claiming AA, DLA, PIP or child benefit (but none of the other non-means-tested benefits listed on p98) on the basis of being a person subject to immigration control if you are covered by a reciprocal agreement the UK has with another country.[33] At the time of writing, only Denmark, Germany and Norway had agreements in relation to AA and DLA, and the necessary amendments to include PIP had not been made to individual agreements. However, you may be able to claim child benefit if you are covered by the relevant agreement with Austria, Barbados, Belgium, Canada, Denmark, Finland, France, Germany, Israel, Mauritius, New Zealand, Norway, Portugal, Spain and Sweden or former Yugoslavia (Bosnia-Herzegovina, Croatia, Kosovo, North Macedonia, Montenegro, Serbia and Slovenia[34]).

Note: at the time of writing, it was expected that the UK would negotiate new agreements, or update exisiting agreements, with EEA countries to take affect in 2021 – see AskCPAG.org.uk and CPAG's *Welfare Rights Bulletin*.

See Appendix 5 for a list of the countires that have reciprocal agreements and p397 for more information on them.

You are a member of a family of a European Economic Area national

In limited circumstances, you are not excluded from the above non-means-tested benefits on the basis of being a person subject to immigration control if you are a member of a family of an EEA national.[35]

From the end of the transition period (11pm, 31 December 2020), this exempt group no longer exists[36] *unless* (until at least 30 June 2021) you are in one of the three protected groups that can continue to use free movement rights listed on p83.[37] However, if you are an EEA national, see the note below.

The regulations refer to 'a member of a family of a national of a state contracting party to the Agreement on the EEA.' The relevant states are the EEA states.

It is strongly arguable that no additional conditions should be placed on who counts as an 'EEA national'. Similarly *'member of a family'* is not defined in the regulations and it is, therefore, arguable that the term should be given its ordinary everyday meaning and include, for example, a sister, uncle and a partner who is not a spouse or civil partner.

However, at the end of 2019, the benefit authorities, and particularly HMRC, had begun to interpret this exempt group as only applying to a 'family member' as defined in EU law (see p218) and only applying to EEA nationals with a right to reside in the UK as a qualified person (see p171). Furthermore, the Home Office also changed its guidance in June 2020 to take a similarly narrow interpretation.[38] Consequently, although there are arguments that the definition of this exempt group should be the ordinary, everyday meaning, these arguments should not be pursued if you have leave that is subject to a 'no recourse to public funds' condition, because any benefits paid would not be disregarded by the Home Office and would breach that condition.

Note:

- If you are an **EEA national** and you are in one of the protected groups that can continue to use free movement rights, you are not defined as a 'person subject to immigration control' (see p83) and, therefore, are not excluded from benefits on this basis and, therefore, do not need to consider whether this, or any other, exempt group applies.
- If you are a **non-EEA national** and you are in one of the protected groups that can continue to use free movement rights, *and* you are defined as a 'family member' (see p220) of an EEA national who has a European free movement right to reside in the UK (eg, as a worker) you are not defined as a 'person subject to immigration control' (see p83). Even if you have been granted immigration leave that is subject to a 'no recourse to public funds' condition, this condition does not have any effect while you have a right to reside under the EEA Regulations – eg, as the family member of an EEA worker.[39]
- For further information, including caselaw, on this exempt group see the 11th edition of this *Handbook* pp86-88.

Tax credits

Being a person subject to immigration control does not exclude you from getting child tax credit (CTC) or working tax credit (WTC) if:[40]

- your leave is on the basis of a maintenance undertaking (see p90) and the person who gave the undertaking (often referred to as your 'sponsor') has died. If the undertaking was given by more than one person, they must all have died;[41]
- your leave is on the basis of a maintenance undertaking and you have been resident in the UK for five years (see below);
- (for WTC) you are a national of an EEA state (*except* Bulgaria, Liechtenstein, Lithuania, Romania or Slovenia), or Turkey or North Macedonia and lawfully present in the UK (see below);
- (for CTC) you are a national of Algeria, Morocco, San Marino, Tunisia or Turkey and lawfully working in the UK (see p103).

Note: if you are a person subject to immigration control, but your partner is not (or s/he is in one of the above exempt groups), you can receive tax credits on the basis of a joint claim (see p107).

Your leave is on the basis of a maintenance undertaking and you have been resident for five years

You are not excluded from CTC or WTC on the basis of being a person subject to immigration control if you have:[42]

- leave to enter or remain given as a result of a maintenance undertaking (see p90); *and*
- been resident in the UK for at least five years since either the date the undertaking was given or the date when you came to the UK, whichever is later.

If you go abroad during the five years, you may still count as resident in the UK during your absence. This depends on the duration and circumstances of your absence (see p130).[43] If your absence abroad is such that you cease to be resident in the UK, you can add together periods of residence either side of the gaps in order to meet the five-year rule.[44]

Nationals of Turkey, North Macedonia and most European countries

You are not excluded from WTC on the basis of being a person subject to immigration control, if you are:[45]

- a national of a country that has ratified either the European Convention on Social and Medical Assistance or the European Social Charter (1961). This applies to all the EEA countires (*except* Bulgaria, Liechtenstein, Lithuania, Romania or Slovenia), as well as the non-EEA countries of Turkey and North Macedonia; *and*

- lawfully present. You satisfy this if you currently have leave to enter or remain in the UK.

Note: you must still satisfy all the other conditions of entitlement, including working a sufficient number of hours to count as working 'full time', under the WTC rules.

Asylum seekers with temporary admission in the UK (see p14) have been accepted as 'lawfully present',[46] and this should also be accepted if you are an asylum seeker with immigration bail. However, to be entitled to WTC you must work sufficient hours and so you will only benefit from this provision if you have obtained, and work in accordance with, permission from the Home Office (see p40).

Nationals of Algeria, Morocco, San Marino, Tunisia and Turkey

You are not excluded from CTC on the basis of being a person subject to immigration control if you are a national of Morocco, San Marino, Tunisia or Turkey (or Algeria if you made your claim before 1 January 2021[47]), and:[48]

- you are currently lawfully working in the UK (see p100); *or*
- have ceased lawfully working for a reason such as pregnancy, childcare, illness or accident, or because you have reached retirement age;[49]
- are the family member of either of the above and you are legally resident in the UK.

For further details on the agreements with these countries, see p408.

Social fund and other payments

You are not excluded from social fund payments on the basis of being a person subject to immigration control if you are in one of the exempt groups for either means-tested benefits (see p97) or non-means-tested benefits (see p98).[50]

You must meet the other conditions of entitlement, including (except for winter fuel payments) being in receipt of a qualifying benefit. What counts as a qualifying benefit varies for different social fund payments but is broadly the means-tested benefits and, in some circumstances, tax credits. See CPAG's *Welfare Benefits and Tax Credits Handbook* for details.

Note:

- In Scotland, social fund funeral expenses payments and Sure Start maternity grants have been replaced by funeral support payments and Best Start grants. You are excluded from a **funeral support payment** if you are a person subject to immigration control unless you are in one of the exempt groups for non-means-tested benefits (see p98).[51] There are no immigration status requirements for **Best Start grants.**[52]

- In England, if you are responsible for the costs of a funeral of a child aged under 18 or a stillborn baby, you may be entitled to a **children's funeral fund payment** – there are no immigration status (or residence) requirements.[53]

3. Partners and children who are subject to immigration control

Some benefits and tax credits have special rules that apply if your partner or child who lives with you is a 'person subject to immigration control'. These rules vary, so check the rules for the benefit or tax credit you want to claim.

Means-tested benefits

Universal credit

If you live with your **partner** and claim universal credit (UC), you are generally required to make a joint claim. If your partner is a 'person subject to immigration control' and is not in one of the exempt groups who can get UC listed on p97, your joint claim is treated as a claim for UC as a single person and:[54]

- your award is based on the maximum amount for a single person;[55]
- your partner's income and capital are taken into account;[56]
- your partner does not need to accept a claimant commitment or comply with any work-related requirements because s/he is not a UC claimant;[57]
- your partner is not classed as a non-dependant and therefore no deduction (ie, 'housing costs contribution') is made from your UC;[58]
- if you are under 35, your partner does not prevent your rent being restricted to the one-bedroom shared accommodation rate;[59]
- if you have a child, your partner does not affect your being 'responsible' for her/him (so you are entitled to a child element, and, if you are receiving education, that does not exclude you from UC) nor being her/his 'responsible carer', when determining your work-related requirements;[60]
- the couple rate of the earnings threshold applies for determining when no work-related requirements apply to you, and in calculating any self-employed 'minimum income floor' that may apply if you are self-employed (**note**: the 'minimum income floor' does not apply to your partner if s/he is self-employed).[61]

These claims described above do not include additional amounts for your partner. Therefore, if her/his leave is subject to a no recourse to public funds condition, your claim for UC does not breach this condition because it does not result in your receiving increased public funds as a result of her/his presence (see p87). If your UC claim as a single person includes a housing costs element, in almost all circumstances this will not be higher as a result of your partner's presence because s/he is not a claimant and therefore ignored in the housing costs calculation.[62] However, if you and your partner are joint tenants, her/his share of the rent is used to calculate your housing costs element.[63] If this results in an additional amount of housing costs being paid as a result of your partner's presence, your claim will breach any no recourse to public funds condition attached to her/his partner's leave. However, the only scenario that CPAG is aware of in which this can arise is if you and your partner are joint tenants with one or more other joint tenants, because then the share of the rent used to calculate your housing costs is greater due to the presence of your partner. If you have concerns about breaching any condition attached to your partner's leave, get specialist immigration advice before making a claim (see Appendix 2).

Note:

- If you have reached pension age and your partner is under pension age, but you cannot make a joint claim for UC because s/he is excluded as a 'person subject to immigration control', your claim is *not* treated as a single claim for UC. Instead, you can claim pension credit (PC) and housing benefit (HB) and you are treated as a single person for these claims.[64]
- If you are living in temporary or supported accommodation, you cannot claim the UC housing costs element, but can claim HB to help with your rent alongside claiming the other elements of UC. The rules for HB in this situation are the same as for other HB claims: any partner or child is included in your HB claim and award, regardless of her/his immigration status. If this results in more HB being paid as a result of her/his presence, your HB claim will breach any no recourse to public funds condition attached to her/his leave (see p106).

You can include any **child** for whom you are responsible in your UC claim, regardless of the child's immigration status (subject to the 'two-child limit'). However, if your child's leave is subject to a no recourse to public funds condition, receipt of UC elements for her/him breaches this condition and could affect her/his current or future right to remain in the UK. Get specialist immigration advice before making a claim (see Appendix 2).

Income support, income-based jobseeker's allowance and income-related employment and support allowance

If your **partner** is a person subject to immigration control (see p81), s/he is included in your claim for income support (IS), income-based jobseeker's allowance (JSA), including if you are a joint-claim couple, or income-related employment and support allowance (ESA). However, you are only paid a personal allowance at the single person's rate, unless s/he comes into one of the exempt groups that can get the means-tested benefits on p97, in which case you are paid at the couple rate.[65]

In all cases, your partner is still treated as part of your household and part of your claim. Therefore, her/his work, income and capital can all affect your benefit entitlement. Her/his presence also means you cannot be entitled to IS as a lone parent. Similarly, unless your partner receives a qualifying benefit or is severely sight impaired or blind, her/his presence might mean that you are not entitled to a severe disability premium.

Premiums are payable if either you or your partner satisfy the qualifying conditions and should be paid at the couple rate.

If your partner's leave to enter or remain in the UK is subject to the condition that s/he does not have recourse to public funds, be aware that receiving the couple rate of a premium breaches this condition and could affect her/his right to remain in the UK (see p87). Obtain specialist immigration advice before claiming the benefit that would result in the premium being paid.

Pension credit

If your **partner** is a person subject to immigration control (irrespective of whether or not s/he is in one of the exempt groups listed on p97), s/he is treated as not being part of your household for PC.[66] This means that you are paid as a single person and your partner's income and capital do not affect your claim. It also means that if s/he is under pension age, you can claim PC and HB (rather than UC) and you are treated as a single person for both PC and HB.[67]

If you would otherwise be entitled to the additional amount for severe disability, your partner's presence may mean that you are not entitled to it, as the DWP regards her/him as 'normally residing with' you for this purpose (unless s/he is disregarded under separate rules – eg, if s/he is blind or receives a qualifying benefit).[68]

You can include any **child** for whom you are responsible in your PC claim, regardless of the child's immigration status. However, if the child's leave is subject to a no recourse to public funds condition, receipt of PC amounts for her/him will breach that condition and could affect her/his right to remain in the UK (see p87). Get specialist immigration advice before making a claim.

Housing benefit

If your partner is a person subject to immigration control, s/he is included in your HB claim and your applicable amount includes the couple rate of the personal allowance and any premiums to which either of you are entitled.

However, the exception, when your HB claim is treated as a single claim, is if you have reached pension age and your partner is under pension age, but you cannot make a joint claim for UC because s/he is excluded as a 'person subject to immigration control' (and not in one of the exempt groups on p97).[69]

If a child for whom you are responsible is a person subject to immigration control, s/he is included in your claim and (subject to the 'two-child limit') your applicable amount includes a personal allowance for her/him, together with any premiums for which s/he qualifies.

Other than when the above exception applies, if your partner's and/or child's leave is subject to a no recourse to public funds condition and you claim HB, this could result in additional public funds being paid as a result of her/his presence. This breaches that condition of her/his leave and could affect her/his current or future right to remain in the UK (see p87). Obtain specialist immigration advice before making a claim (see Appendix 2).

Council tax reduction (see p575) is also defined as public funds, so if your council tax reduction is greater (eg, because you lose a single person's discount) as a result of the presence of someone whose leave is subject to a no recourse to public funds condition, that person's current or future right to remain in the UK could be affected. Get specialist immigration advice before making a claim (see Appendix 2).

Non-means-tested benefits

Non-means-tested benefits that are either contributory or based on employment are not affected by your or your partner's or child's immigration status.

If your own immigration status does not exclude you from **child benefit**, you can claim for any child for whom you are responsible, regardless of the child's immigration status. However, if your child has leave which is subject to a no recourse to public funds condition, a claim for child benefit will result in additional public funds being paid as a result of her/his presence and this will breach that condition. This could affect her/his current or future right to remain in the UK (see p87). Get specialist immigration advice before making a claim.

If your child is not a person subject to immigration control, or s/he is but s/he comes into one of the exempt groups on p98, s/he can claim **disability living allowance** (or **child disability payment** in Scotland, once introduced), even if you are a person subject to immigration control.

S/he must still satisfy all the other conditions of entitlement, including the residence and presence rules (see Part 4).

Tax credits

If your **partner** is a person subject to immigration control and you are not (or you are but are in one of the exempt groups on p102), your joint claim for tax credits is treated as if your partner were not subject to immigration control. You are therefore entitled to working tax credit (WTC) and child tax credit (CTC).[70] However, unless you or your partner are responsible for a child, or your partner is a national of an EEA country (except Bulgaria, Liechtenstein, Lithuania, Romania or Slovenia), North Macedonia or Turkey and is lawfully present in the UK, your WTC does not include the couple element.[71]

There are no immigration status conditions for **children**. Any child for whom you are responsible is included in your claim and your WTC and/or (subject to the 'two-child limit') CTC includes amounts for her/him, provided you meet all the conditions of entitlement, including, for example, that the child normally lives with you.

If you are not a person subject to immigration control, but your partner is because her/his leave is subject to a no recourse to public funds condition, s/he is not regarded as having such recourse by making a joint tax credits claim with you. This means that you and your partner can make the joint claim without it affecting her/his right to remain in the UK. If such a joint claim includes a child whose leave is subject to a no recourse to public funds condition, any tax credits awarded in respect of her/him are also not regarded as having had recourse.[72]

However, if your claim for CTC or WTC is not a joint claim as described above (ie, it is a single claim or a joint claim but neither you nor your partner are a person subject to immigration control) and it includes an amount for a child whose leave is subject to a no recourse to public funds condition, this breaches that condition and could affect her/his right to remain in the UK (see p87). Get specialist immigration advice before making a claim (see Appendix 2).

Note: it is only possible to make a new claim for tax credits in very limited circumstances. See CPAG's *WelfareBenefits and Tax Credits Handbook* for who can still make a new claim, and see the 2018/19 edition of this *Handbook* for how your partner's immigration status affects a new claim.

Notes

1. **Benefits and tax credits affected by immigration status**

1 Reg 13 CTRS(PR)E Regs; reg 19 CTR(SPC)S Regs; reg 19 CTR(S) Regs; reg 29 CTRSPR(W) Regs; Sch para 20 CTRS(DS)W Regs
2 s115(1) IAA 1999; reg 3(1) TC(Imm) Regs
3 Reg 5(1)(c) DACYP(S) Regs (draft)
4 Reg 11(1)(b) ESA Regs; reg 12(1)(b) ESA Regs 2013
5 Reg 9(5) FEA(S) Regs
6 Reg 16(1)(b) SS(IB) Regs

2. **People subject to immigration control who can be entitled**

7 para 6.2, notes under 'public funds' definition, IR
8 Reg 2(1)-(1A) and Sch Part 1 SS(IA)CA Regs; Vol 2 Ch 7, para 070835 DMG; para C1060 ADM
9 Reg 2(1)-(1A) and Sch Part 1 para 3 SS(IA)CA Regs
10 Reg 2(1)-(1A) and Sch Part 1 para 3 SS(IA)CA Regs
11 CPC/1035/2005
12 R(IS) 2/02
13 Reg 2(1)-(1A) and Sch Part 1 para 4 SS(IA)CA Regs, confirmed in *OD v SSWP (JSA)* [2015] UKUT 438 (AAC); ADM Memo 29/20, paras 36-41; DMG Memo 25/20, paras 41-46
14 Reg 2(2)(a) SSCBCTC(A) Regs
15 Reg 1(2) SSCBCTC(A) Regs

16 See justification for exclusion in Explanatory Memo to SSCBCTC(A) Regs, para 7.8.
17 Reg 13(1A) CTRS(PR)E Regs; reg 19(2) CTR(S) Regs; reg 19(2) CTR(SPC)S Regs; reg 29(2) CTRSPR(W) Regs; Sch para 20(2) CTRS(DS)W Regs
18 para 6.2, notes under 'public funds' definition, IR
19 *Szoma v SSWP* [2005] UKHL 64, reported as R(IS) 2/06; *Yesiloz v London Borough of Camden* [2009] EWCA Civ 415. The case concerned an asylum seeker with temporary admission, which was replaced by immigration bail on 15 January 2018, but the same arguments are likely to apply.
20 Reg 2(2), (3) and (4)(b) and Sch Part 2 SS(IA)CA Regs; reg 2(1)(a)(ib) SS(AA) Regs; reg 9(1)(ia) SS(ICA) Regs; reg 16(d)(ii) SS(PIP) Regs; reg 2(1)(a)(ib) SS(DLA) Regs; reg 11(1)(b) and (3) ESA Regs; reg 12(1)(b) and (3) ESA Regs 2013; reg 16(1)(b) and (5) SS(IB) Regs; reg 9(5) FEA(S) Regs; reg 7(7) CA(YCG)(S) Regs; Vol 2 Ch 7, para 070836 DMG; para 10140 CBTM
21 Reg 2 and Sch Part 2 para 4 SS(IA)CA Regs
22 Suggested by reference to s115(3) in reg 5(1)(c) DACYP(S) Regs (draft)
23 Changes are needed to reg 2 SS(IA)CA Regs.
24 Reg 2 and Sch Part II para 2 SS(IA)CA Regs; Vol 2 para 070836 DMG; para 10140 CBTM; DMG Memo 25/20, paras 40 and 46; ADM Memo 29/20, paras 35 and 41
25 *Krid v Caisse Nationale d'Assurance Vieillesse des Travailleurs Salariés (CNAVTS)*, C-103/94 [1995], para 26
26 Reg 1(3) SSCBCTC(A) Regs
27 Reg 2(3A) and Sch Part II para 2 SS(IA)CA Regs
28 Email from HMRC
29 DMG Memo 25/20, para 46 and ADM Memo 29/20, para 41; Explanatory Memo to SSCBCTC(A) Regs; para 10140 CBTM
30 Partnership, Trade and Cooperation Agreement between UK and Albania – signed 5 February 2021
31 *Sürül v Bundesanstalt für Arbeit*, C-262/96 [1999]
32 *Sürül v Bundesanstalt für Arbeit*, C-262/96 [1999], in particular paras 85-86 and 93
33 Reg 2(3) SS(IA)CA Regs; para 10140 CBTM
34 FANIII(Y)O
35 Reg 2 and Sch Part 2 para 1 SS(IA)CA Regs; Vol 2 para 070836 DMG; para 10140 CBTM
36 Reg 57 ISSC Regs
37 Regs 3(4)-(6), 4(2) and (5)-(8) and 12(1)(q) CR(ADTP) Regs
38 Home Office guidance, *Public Funds*, v15.0, 12 June 2020, pp21-2
39 Reg 43 and Sch 3 para 1 I(EEA) Regs; paras C1050 and C2012 ADM; Vol 2 Ch 7 Part 1 para 070838 DMG
40 Reg 3(1) TC(Imm) Regs
41 Reg 3(1) TC(Imm) Regs, case 2
42 Reg 3(1) TC(Imm) Regs, case 1
43 CPC/1035/2005
44 R(IS) 2/02
45 Reg 3(1) TC(Imm) Regs, case 4
46 *Szoma v SSWP* [2005] UKHL 64, reported as R(IS) 2/06, and see *Yesiloz v London Borough of Camden* [2009] EWCA Civ 415
47 Reg 3(1) TC(Imm) Regs, case 5 para (a)
48 Reg 3(1) TC(Imm) Regs, case 5
49 *Krid v Caisse Nationale d'Assurance Vieillesse des Travailleurs Salariés (CNAVTS)*, C-103/94 [1995] ECR I-00719, para 26
50 Reg 2 SS(IA)CA Regs
51 Reg 9(f) FEA(S) Regs
52 EYA(BSG)(S) Regs
53 The Social Fund (Children's Funeral Fund for England) Regulations 2019, No.1064; ADM Memo 13/19 and DMG Memo 10/19

3. **Partners and children who are subject to immigration control**

54 ss3 and 4(1)(c) and (2) WRA 2012; Reg 3(3) UC Regs; reg 9 UC,PIP,JSA&ESA(C&P) Regs
55 Regs 3(3) and 36(3) UC Regs and, for housing costs, see Schs 4 and 5 UC Regs
56 Regs 18(2) and 22(3) UC Regs
57 ss3 and 4(1)(e) WRA 2012; reg 3(3) UC Regs; reg 9(1) UC,PIP,JSA&ESA(C&P) Regs
58 Sch 4 para 9(2)(b) UC Regs
59 Sch 4 paras 27 and 28 UC Regs
60 ss4(1)(d) and 19(6) WRA 2012; regs 4, 14(1)(c), 24 and 86 UC Regs
61 s39 WRA 2012; regs 62(1), (3) and (4) and 90(3) UC Regs; para H4077 ADM
62 S/he must be a claimant to be defined as a joint renter or joint owner-occupier: Schs 4 para 1 and 5 para 1 UC Regs.

63 Sch 4 paras 6, 24 and 35 UC Regs
64 Art 7(1),(2)(a) and (b) and (3)(b) WRA(No.31)O; HB Circular A9/2019, paras 15-17; DMG Memo 7/19 para 12
65 **IS** Reg 21(3) and Sch 7 para 16A IS Regs
JSA Reg 85(4) and Sch 5 para 13A JSA Regs
ESA Reg 69 and Sch 5 para 10 ESA Regs
66 Reg 5(1)(h) SPC Regs
67 Confirmed in HB Circular A9/2019, paras 15-17 and DMG Memo 7/19 para 12
68 Sch 1 paras 1(1)(a)(ii) and 2 SPC Regs; Vol 13, para 78946 DMG
69 Art 7(1),(2)(a) and (b) and (3)(b) WRA(No.31); HB Circular A9/2019, paras 15-17; DMG Memo 7/19 para 12
70 Reg 3(2) TC(Imm) Regs
71 Reg 11(4) and (5) WTC(EMR) Regs
72 para 6.2 notes under 'public funds' definition IR. The TC(Imm) Regs are made under s42 TCA 2002.

Chapter 9

Asylum seekers and refugees

This chapter covers:

This chapter explains some of the specific benefit and tax credit rules that apply to asylum seekers and to people granted leave, such as refugee leave, humanitarian protection or discretionary leave, as a result of an asylum application. It also covers the rules on integration loans available to people granted refugee leave or humanitarian protection and their dependants. For more information about these categories of leave, see Chapter 4.

1. Asylum seekers

You are referred to as an '**asylum seeker**' while you are waiting for a Home Office decision on your application for refugee status (see p39).

If you are seeking asylum in the UK, you will generally be a 'person subject to immigration control' (someone who requires, but does not have, leave – see p85). You are, therefore, excluded from the social security benefits listed on p95, unless you are in one of the exempt groups (see p96).

However, you are not a person subject to immigration control if you already have leave on some other basis (provided that leave is not subject to a 'no recourse to public funds' condition and was not given as the result of a maintenance undertaking) or, until at least 30 June 2021, if you are in one of the protected groups that can have a free movement right to reside and you are are either a European Economic Area (EEA) national, or you *have* such a free movement right to reside (see p83).

If benefit can be paid for you, either because you are not excluded from making a claim or because your partner can include you in her/his claim, that does not affect your asylum application. You can receive any benefit defined as a 'public fund' (see p88) because asylum seekers are *not* subject to a no recourse to public funds condition. If you receive public funds, this does not affect the outcome of your asylum application.

You are exempt from the national insurance (NI) number requirement (see p443) if (as is generally the case for asylum seekers) you require leave but do not have it and you are included in your partner's benefit claim or you make a joint tax credit claim with her/him, and you do not already have an NI number.

If you are excluded from claiming social security benefits because you are a person subject to immigration control, you may be entitled to alternative forms of state support, including asylum support from the Home Office if you are destitute.

If you are not eligible for asylum support or benefits, ask your local authority for help. If you have children, you may be eligible for support under the Children Act 1989 or Children (Scotland) Act 1995 (see p511). You may be able to get assistance from your local authority under one or more of the community care provisions, particularly if you have additional needs as a result of your age, health or disability (see p509). You may also be entitled to help from your local welfare assistance scheme (see p579).

See Chapter 21 for details of the support available for asylum seekers.

Note: asylum support for essential living needs is not taken into account for universal credit (UC). It is only disregarded for income support (IS), income-based jobseeker's allowance (JSA) and income-related employment and support allowance (ESA) if it counts as 'income in kind'. If your partner claims housing benefit (HB), asylum support for essential living needs is taken into account as income unless your partner also receives UC, IS, income-based JSA, income-related ESA or pension credit, as these benefits 'passport' your partner onto maximum HB so all of your and your partner's other income is ignored.[1]

However, any social security benefit your partner receives is taken into account as income when calculating your asylum support, unless you can show that benefit cannot reasonably be expected to be available to you – eg, a disability benefit paid to your partner (see p520).

2. Benefits and tax credits for people granted leave following an asylum application

If, following your asylum application, you are granted leave that is not subject to the condition that you do not have recourse to public funds, you are no longer a 'person subject to immigration control'. For example, if you are granted refugee leave, humanitarian protection or (except in rare cases when a no recourse to public funds condition has been attached) discretionary leave, you are not a person subject to immigration control during that period of leave. You are no longer excluded from the benefits listed on p95 and can claim all benefits and tax credits, provided you meet the usual conditions of entitlement.

However, if you are granted leave that is subject to the condition that you do not have recourse to public funds, you come within the definition of a 'person subject to immigration control' (see p87) and you are excluded from the benefits listed on p95, unless you are exempt (see p96). If this applies, get immigration advice as it may be possible for this condition to be removed (see p43).

Guidance summarising how to claim benefits once you are granted leave is available online and includes information on the documents you should take to your first interview with Jobcentre Plus.[2]

Note:

- If you are granted refugee leave, humanitarian protection or discretionary leave, you are exempt from the habitual residence test (see p142). If you have been granted refugee leave in the last eight weeks or under the 'gateway protection scheme', Department for Work and Pensions (DWP) policy is to fast-track your claim (see p140).
- If you are granted refugee leave or humanitarian protection, you can be joined by certain family members under family reunion provisions (see p41).
- If you, or the family member who you have joined under the family reunion provisions, have been granted refugee leave or humanitarian protection, you are exempt from the 'past presence test' for personal independence payment, disability living allowance, child disability payment, attendance allowance and carer's allowance (see p282).
- If you are granted refugee leave, you may be able to claim child benefit, guardian's allowance, child tax credit (CTC) and working tax credit (WTC) backdated to the date of your asylum application (see p115).
- If you are granted refugee leave or humanitarian protection, you are *not* excluded from a Sure Start maternity grant (or if in Scotland, you should not receive a lower Best Start grant) on the basis that you already have a child under 16 who was a member of your family before you came to the UK – eg, if you arrived in the UK with your first child and then give birth to your second child in the UK.[3]
- If you are attending a part-time course to learn English and claim universal credit (UC), the course must be compatible with your work-related requirements.[4] Therefore, if you are subject to all work-related requirements, you must show that you meet these despite being on a part-time course, including that you are able and willing immediately to attend an interview and take up paid work. If your work coach agrees that studying English is part of your 'voluntary work preparation', the hours spent attending your course can be deducted from your work search requirements.[5]
- If you are granted refugee leave or humanitarian protection, you may be eligible for an integration loan (see p116).

- If you have been receiving asylum support, this stops (and if you were provided with accommodation, you are required to leave) 28 days after you are granted leave (see p483). You should claim benefits as soon as you can – you do not need to wait until the asylum support stops. **Note:** asylum support is not taken into account as income for UC.[6] It is also not taken into account as income for housing benefit (HB) if you are also claiming UC or pension credit, as these benefits 'passport' you onto maximum HB so all your, and any partner's, income is ignored.[7] If you do not receive a passporting benefit your asylum support does count as income for HB. You do not need to wait to claim benefits until you have a national insurance (NI) number (see p445).[8]

Family reunion

If you have been granted refugee leave or humanitarian protection, certain family members may join you under the family reunion rules (see p41).

A family member who comes to the UK and is given leave under these provisions is not a 'person subject to immigration control' for the duration of that leave and can claim all benefits, provided s/he meets the usual rules of entitlement.

However, sometimes the benefit authorities decide that your family member is a person subject to immigration control on the basis that her/his Home Office documents describe you as her/his 'sponsor' and they wrongly conclude from this that s/he has been given leave as a result of a maintenance undertaking (see p90).

This is incorrect. No undertaking is required for your family member to join you in the UK and DWP guidance states this clearly (although it incorrectly states the family member will have indefinite leave).[9]

If you are a family member with leave in the UK under the family reunion provisions and you are refused benefits or tax credits because the decision maker decides you are a person subject to immigration control, challenge the decision and refer the decision maker to the DWP guidance.

In Scotland, you can claim a Scottish Welfare Fund family reunion crisis grant from your local authority if your family member(s) have been granted leave to enter the UK to join you under the family reunion provisions. You can apply before they arrive (see p579).

Note: if you are joining a family member in the UK but not under the family reunion provisions,you may be a 'person subject to immigration control' (see p81) – eg, if you previously applied for asylum in an EEA country and were transferred to the UK before the end of 2020 under the 'Dublin III Regulation'[10] to have your application considered by the Home Office and you are in the UK as someone who requires leave but does not have it.

Backdating child benefit and tax credits

If you have been granted refugee leave or 'section 67 leave' as a relocated child (see p44) (not humanitarian protection or discretionary leave), you can claim child benefit, guardian's allowance and tax credits backdated to the date of your asylum application.[11] If you made more than one asylum application, these benefits can be backdated to date of the first application, if the basis of the asylum applications remained the same. If refugee leave was granted as a result of events that only occurred after the first asylum application, then these benefits would only be backdated to the date of the asylum application made after these new events.[12] **Note**: at the time of writing, HM Revenue and Customs (HMRC) guidance stating child benefit is only payable from the date of the successful asylum applicaton was being challenged.

Note: there is no provision to pay backdated UC.

You must claim backdated child benefit (and any guardian's allowance) within three months, and tax credits within one month, of receiving the Home Office letter granting you leave as a refugee or section 67 leave as a relocated child.[13] If the Home Office letter is sent to a solicitor acting for you, the three- or one-month period starts from the date your solicitor receives the letter.[14]

If you were a dependent on your partner's asylum application, and s/he has now been granted refugee leave, and you have also been granted refugee leave, your partner must be the child benefit claimant to get it backdated.

These backdating rules apply to a person who has *both* claimed asylum and been granted refugee leave (or section 67 leave).[15] Consequently, if you were a dependant on your partner's asylum application, and s/he has now been granted refugee leave, your partner should be the child benefit claimant for the claim to be backdated. However, if you were a dependant on your partner's asylum application, you were also granted refugee leave, you made the child benefit claim and HMRC refused the claim on the basis that you were not the asylum applicant, you should challenge that decision on the basis that the words 'person who has claimed asylum' are not defined and must be interpreted as including a dependant on the asylum claim to be consistent with the policy intention. This argument was recently accepted by the Upper Tribunal.[16]

The amount of tax credits paid is reduced by the amount of asylum support you received for your essential living needs over the period (see below).

The amount of child benefit and guardian's allowance paid is not reduced by any asylum support you may have received.

Backdating tax credits

In practice, it is hard to claim backdated tax credits. You can only claim if you applied for asylum on or before 31 January 2019, because that was the final day that a claim for tax credits could be made before UC was introduced. That is because your tax credits claim is treated as having been made on the date of your asylum application,[17] and if a claim for tax credits has been made by the above date, the legislation that abolishes tax credits is treated as not having come into force.[18] Under the special backdating rules for refugees, your claim is then treated as having been renewed each April.[19] If successful, your claim can continue until you claim UC.

A further barrier is that the amount of tax credits paid is reduced by the amount of asylum support you received for your essential living needs over the period.[20] In many cases, the total amount of asylum support paid for essential living needs is more than the amount of tax credits and, therefore, cancels out any entitlement over the backdated period. However, if you did not receive asylum support or your tax credit entitlement exceeds the amount of asylum support paid (eg, if you worked sufficient hours to qualify for WTC), you can be entitled to an amount of backdated tax credits. **Note:** an argument that the reduction should only be for the amounts of asylum support paid in respect of children was rejected by the Upper Tribunal,[21] but a further judicial review challenge is being made by CPAG.[22]

Note: it can be extremely difficult to get HMRC to accept your claim for backdated tax credits. You should, therefore, telephone HMRC as soon as possible after receiving the Home Office letter granting you refugee leave and always within the one-month time limit. Be clear that you are making a claim and ask HMRC to take all the information required for your claim to be accepted.[23] On the same day, submit a completed claim form and covering letter referring to your telephone claim. HMRC can accept a claim by telephone (the suggested method[24]) or letter, but your claim must contain all the information required and must satisfy the NI number requirement (see p444).[25] For a copy of the claim form, the steps to take if HMRC refuses to accept your claim, details of current legal challenges and how to ensure you can benefit if any are successful, see cpag.org.uk/welfare-rights/judicial-review/judicial-review-pre-action-letters/refugees-inc-hrt-issues and ask an advice centre to help you.

3. Integration loans

Integration loans are interest-free loans to assist people who have recently been granted either refugee status or humanitarian protection to integrate into UK society.

The minimum amount of a loan is £100 and there is no fixed maximum amount.[26]

Note: before applying for an integration loan, which has to be repaid, you may want to get advice from local refugee services on charitable and other assistance. You may also be entitled to help from your local welfare assistance scheme (see p579). Depending on your local scheme, you may be able to apply for grants or items such as furniture, but be aware that many local authorities do not give cash and some require the assistance to be repaid.

Applications

You must be eligible to apply for an integration loan and must make a valid application. Whether or not you are awarded a loan is at the discretion of the decision maker.

You are eligible to apply for an integration loan if you:[27]

- have been granted refugee leave, humanitarian protection (see p41) or leave to enter or remain as a dependant of someone with either refugee leave or humanitarian protection after 11 June 2007;
- are aged 18 or over;
- have not previously had an integration loan; *and*
- are capable of repaying the loan.

You should apply by completing the form on the gov.uk website. If fully completed, this ensures your application is valid.[28]

To be valid, the application must contain:[29]

- your full name;
- any other names you have used;
- your date of birth;
- your address;
- your telephone number (if you have one);
- your email address (if you have one);
- evidence about your leave to remain and your age;
- your national insurance number;
- details of your (and any dependants') income, assets, liabilities and outgoings;
- confirmation of whether any member of your household has applied for or received an integration loan; *and*
- the amount requested.

When deciding whether to give you a loan, the decision maker must take into account:[30]

- the length of time since your leave was granted;
- your financial position – ie, your income, assets, liabilities and outgoings;
- your likely ability to repay the loan;
- what you intend to use the loan for; *and*
- the total available budget for loans.

Although the legislation does not specify which intended uses of a loan are more likely to be accepted, the application form provides the following headings for you to set amounts against, and guidance to decision makers confirms that these examples of 'integration needs' can be accepted (if they cannot be met through assistance available from Jobcentre Plus):[31]

- help with housing, including:
  - deposits for rented accommodation;

  - rent payments;
  - house-moving expenses;
  - essential items;
- help with finding work, including:
  - travel expenses to attend interviews;
  - work clothing/equipment;
  - initial childcare costs;
  - subsistence while training;
- help with education, including:
  - the cost of a training programme;
  - requalification/professional qualification.

There is space on the form for other needs that would assist your integration. However, the guidance states that a loan should normally be refused for:[32]
- non-essential items;
- domestic assistance and respite care;
- mobility items;
- general living expenses (including utility bills);
- council tax payments;
- medical items;
- cars, including driving lessons and a licence, unless this is essential for your employment;
- repayment of debts;
- airfares for dependants to join you in the UK.

It is helpful to read the guidance before making your application, as it covers examples of factors that can be relevant. For example, in addition to how long you have been in the UK, your financial independence can also be relevant – your application may be considered weaker if you have been working and living independently in the UK for some time before you apply than if you were not working or living independently – eg, if you have been receiving asylum support. The guidance also states that decision makers can take your 'character' into account – eg, a loan will usually be refused if you have been convicted of an offence.

Decisions, payment and repayments

After you have applied for a loan, you should be sent a written decision stating:[33]
- whether the application was valid;
- if so, whether a loan will be made;
- if so, the amount, conditions and terms of repayment; *and*
- the deadline for responding to say whether you wish to take the loan.

If you are entitled to a loan, a loan agreement should be attached to the decision letter, which you can sign and return to the decision maker. Usually, you must do this within 14 days of being sent the decision. If you are unhappy with the decision, either because you were refused a loan or offered a smaller amount than you need, you can ask for a reconsideration, which is carried out by a different decision maker. Your request for a reconsideration must be received within 14 days of the date on the decision letter.[34] There is no right to an independent appeal.

If the Home Office decides that you are entitled to an integration loan, it passes your details to the Department for Work and Pensions (DWP), which then pays the loan, normally directly into your bank account, and manages your repayments.

Integration loans are recovered through direct deductions from benefits in the same way as for other third-party debts.[35] The rate of recovery and the start date of deductions should be notified to you. See CPAG's *Welfare Benefits and Tax Credits Handbook* for further details about deductions from benefit.

If direct deductions from your benefit are not possible (eg, because you do not receive a relevant benefit), you should be notified when repayments will begin, and the method, amount and frequency of these.

If your circumstances change, you can ask the DWP to revise the terms of recovery. These should be notified to you in writing.[36]

Notes

1. **Asylum seekers**

1 **UC** Reg 66 UC Regs
IS Sch 9 para 21 IS Regs
JSA Sch 7 para 22 JSA Regs
ESA Sch 8 para 22 ESA Regs
HB Sch 5 paras 4 and 23 HB Regs; regs 25 and 26 HB(SPC) Regs

2. **Benefits and tax credits for people granted leave following an asylum application**

2 gov.uk/government/publications/claiming-universal-credit-and-other-benefits-if-you-are-a-refugee; gov.uk/government/publications/refugees-guidance-about-benefits-and-pensions
3 *SK and LL v SSWP* [2020] UKUT 145 (AAC); ADM Memo 32/20 and DMG Memo 28/20
4 Reg 12(4) UC Regs
5 Reg 95(4) UC Regs
6 Reg 66 UC Regs
7 Sch 5 paras 4 and 23 HB Regs; regs 25 and 26 HB(SPC) Regs

8 gov.uk/government/publications/claiming-universal-credit-and-other-benefits-if-you-are-a-refugee; gov.uk/government/publications/refugees-guidance-about-benefits-and-pensions
9 Vol 2, para 070709 DMG
10 EU Reg 604/2013 – note this ceased to apply after 31 December 2020
11 **CB/GA** Reg 6(2)(d) and (e) CB&GA(Admin) Regs
TC Regs 3(4)-(10) and 4 TC(Imm) Regs
12 *FK v HMRC* [2009] UKUT 134 (AAC)
13 **CB/GA** Reg 6(2)(d) CB&GA(Admin) Regs
TC Reg 3(5) TC(Imm) Regs
14 *Tkachuk v SSWP* [2007] EWCA Civ 515; CIS/3797/2003
15 Reg 6(2)(d) and (e) CB&GA(Admin) Regs
16 CSF/33/2020
17 Reg 3(6)(a) TC(Imm) Regs
18 Art 3 WRA(No.32)O
19 Reg 3(6)(b) TC(Imm) Regs
20 Reg 3(9) TC(Imm) Regs
21 **CTC**/3692/2008
22 CO/2410/2020
23 Reg 5(2)(b) TC(CN) Regs; see also *MR v HMRC (TC)* [2018] UKUT 238 (AAC)
24 gov.uk/claim-tax-credits/backdate-a-claim
25 Reg 5 TC(CN) Regs

3. **Integration loans**
26 UKVI, *Integration Loans Policy Guidance*, para 6.2, available at gov.uk/government/publications/integration-loans-policy-guidance-process; UKVI, *Integration Loan Application Form Guidance*, April 2020
27 Reg 4 ILRFO Regs
28 gov.uk/refugee-integration-loan
29 Reg 5 and Sch ILRFO Regs
30 Reg 6 ILRFO Regs
31 UKVI, *Integration Loans Policy Guidance*, para 9, available at gov.uk/government/publications/integration-loans-policy-guidance-process
32 UKVI, *Integration Loans Policy Guidance*, para 9.3, available at gov.uk/government/publications/integration-loans-policy-guidance-process
33 Reg 8(1) ILRFO Regs
34 UKVI, *Integration Loans Policy Guidance*, available at gov.uk/government/publications/integration-loans-policy-guidance-process; Part 12
35 Reg 9(1) and (3) ILRFO Regs; Sch 9 para 1 SS(C&P) Regs; Sch 6 para 12 UC,PIP,JSA&ESA(C&P) Regs
36 Reg 10 ILRFO Regs

Part 4

Asylum and human rights

Chapter 10

Residence and presence rules: overview

This chapter covers:

This chapter describes the different residence and presence conditions that apply when you make a claim for benefits and tax credits in the UK. The two most well known conditions are the habitual residence test and the right to reside requirement, which are covered in more detail in Chapter 11. The groups of people who have a right to reside are covered in Chapter 12. The residence and presence requirements for individual benefits and tax credits are covered in Chapter 13.

If you are not a British or Irish citizen, first check Part 3 to see whether your immigration status means you are excluded from benefits as a 'person subject to immigration control'. If you are not excluded, you must still satisfy the residence and presence conditions described in this chapter.

If you live with a partner or child who is not British or Irish, check whether her/his immigration status affects your benefits. If her/his immigration leave is subject to a 'no recourse to public funds' condition, check whether any claim you make could affect her/his right to stay in the UK (see p104).

If you, or a member of your family included in your claim, go abroad (either temporarily or to stay), see Part 5 for the ways this affects your benefits and tax credits.

1. Introduction

There are residence and presence conditions for the following benefits and tax credits:

- attendance allowance;
- bereavement support payment;
- Best Start grant (in Scotland);
- carer's allowance;
- child benefit;
- child disability payment (expected in Scotland in 2021);
- child tax credit;
- child winter heating allowance (in Scotland);
- disability living allowance;
- contributory employment and support allowance (ESA) in youth;
- funeral support payments (in Scotland);
- income-related ESA;
- guardian's allowance;
- housing benefit (residence conditions only, except during an absence from your home);
- incapacity benefit (IB) for incapacity in youth;
- income support;
- income-based jobseeker's allowance (JSA);
- pension credit;
- personal independence payment;
- category D retirement pension;
- Scottish child payment (in Scotland);
- severe disablement allowance;
- social fund payments;
- universal credit;
- working tax credit;
- young carer grant (in Scotland).

There are presence conditions for the following benefits:

- contributory ESA;
- IB;
- industrial injuries benefit;
- contribution-based JSA;
- maternity allowance;
- retirement pensions;
- severe disablement allowance.

Council tax reduction also has residence conditions (see p575).

There are no residence or presence requirements for widowed parent's allowance and for statutory sick pay, statutory maternity pay, statutory adoption pay, statutory paternity pay or statutory shared parental pay paid by your employer.

The residence and presence conditions vary between the different benefits and tax credits. If you satisfy the rules for one, you do not necessarily satisfy the rules for another.

The way in which the different residence and presence conditions affect your entitlement to benefit is set out in the UK benefits and tax credits legislation. Depending on the benefit or tax credit, you may be required to satisfy tests for:

- presence;
- past presence;
- 'living in' for three months;
- residence;
- ordinary residence;
- habitual residence;
- the right to reside.

However, these can be modified by the following.

- European Union (EU) co-ordination rules. If you are covered by particular co-ordination rules (see p355), they can help you get benefits in the UK – eg, by exempting you from certain past presence requirements or by enabling you to count certain periods of residence (or employment, or insurance) in (depending on whihc rules apply) an European Economic Area (EEA), or EU, country, or Ireland (under the princple of 'aggregation' see p383). However, in limited circumstances they can also exclude you from entitlement if the UK is not the 'competent state' to pay that benefit (see p369). These rules can also allow certain benefits to be paid when you go to an EEA country (or EU or Ireland) (this is known as the benefit being 'exported'), and the rules for each benefit are covered in Chapter 15. **Note:** the EU co-ordination rules are different from EU free movement residence rights, which can enable you to satisfy the right to reside requirement. In general, you do not need to know whether you are covered by the co-ordination rules to know whether you have a free movement right to reside, but you may need to know if you have a right to reside to know if you are covered by the co-ordination rules (see p356). The details of the EU co-ordination rules, including when and how they apply and how this has been affected by the UK leaving the EU, are covered in Chapter 16, and the main ways they can assist with the residence and presence tests, or affect your entitlement in other ways, are highlighted for each benefit in Chapter 13.
- International agreements, including reciprocal agreements. There are reciprocal agreements between Great Britain and Northern Ireland, and between the UK and some EEA and non-EEA countries. If these apply, they can

help you to qualify for benefits and tax credits if you have recently moved between Great Britain and Northern Ireland, or if you have come to the UK or gone abroad. They operate in similar ways to the EU co-ordination rules and, in general, apply only when the EU co-ordination rules cannot assist you. There are also international agreements between EU and non-EU countries, which can also have similar effects (see Chapter 17).

Note: you must also check *where* you are required to satisfy a particular residence or presence test. This varies for different benefits and tax credits, and can be Scotland, England and Wales, Great Britain, the UK, the 'common travel area' (ie, the UK, Ireland, the Channel Islands and the Isle of Man) or the EEA. In this *Handbook* all references to the EEA are to be read as including Swtizerland. The EEA states are listed on p47.

2. Presence

Most benefits and tax credits have rules about presence and absence. You must usually be present in Great Britain (UK for tax credits) at the time you make your claim and then continue to be present. There are specific rules that allow you to be treated as present during some temporary absences (see p308) and the European Union (EU) co-ordination rules can also mean that the requirement to be present in Great Britain does not apply if you are staying or living in a European Economic Area, or EU state, or Ireland (depending on which co-ordination rules apply). These exceptions vary between the different benefits and tax credits, and are covered in Chapter 14 and 15.

To satisfy the presence requirement, you must show that you are physically present in Great Britain. For a benefit authority to disqualify you from benefit on the basis that you were absent from Great Britain, it must show you were absent throughout that day.[1] For further details on the meaning of presence and absence, see p307.

Other than child disability payment (which is expected to require presence in the common travel area – see p280), Scottish benefits require residence, or ordinary residence, rather than presence.

3. Past presence

The following benefits have a past presence requirement:
- attendance allowance;
- carer's allowance;

- child disability payment (expected in Scotland in 2021);
- disability living allowance;
- personal independence payment.

In addition to being present at the time you make your claim for the above benefits, you must also have been present (or treated as present – see p329) in Great Britain (the common travel area for child disability payment) for 104 weeks out of the past 156 weeks (shorter periods if you are a child) before you become entitled. However, there are exceptions when either no past presence, or a shorter period, is required.

There is a shorter past presence test of 26 weeks in the last 52 weeks for severe disablement allowance (SDA), employment and support allowance (ESA) in youth and incapacity benefit (IB) in youth. However, these are very rarely relevant now as you cannot make a new claim for these benefits. Most SDA and IB awards have been converted to ESA, and once you have satisfied the past presence test, you do not need to do so again while you are in the same period of limited capability for work or incapacity for work.

If you are covered by the European Union co-ordination rules (see p355), depending on the benefit, you may be exempt from the past presence requirement or you may be able to add certain periods of residence in a European Economic Area country to your period of presence in Great Britain (under the 'aggregation principle' – see p383).

For more details of the past presence test, including exceptions and shorter periods for children, see p280.

4. **Living in for three months**

You must have been living for the past three months in:

- the common travel area (the UK, Ireland, Channel Islands and the Isle of Man) in order to satisfy the habitual residence test for income-based jobseeker's allowance (JSA) (see below); *or*
- the UK for child benefit and child tax credit (CTC) (see p129).

The phrase 'living in' is not defined in the regulations and should, therefore, be given its ordinary, everyday meaning. It does not have the same meaning as 'presence' and you may satisfy this condition despite having been temporarily absent. 'Living in' also does not have the same meaning as habitual residence.[2] The Upper Tribunal held that a man continued to be 'living in' the UK despite a 15-month temporary absence while he was abroad travelling.[3]

When deciding whether your absence means that you stopped 'living in' the UK/common travel area, the following factors are relevant:[4]

- the reasons for your absence;

- the intended, and actual, length of your absence;
- the duration and connectedness (including your family ties, work, education, bank account and GP) of your previous residence in the UK/common travel area and whether any of these connections were maintained while you were abroad;
- whether you maintained your accommodation in the UK/common travel area while you were abroad; *and*
- the nature of your accommodation abroad.

For child benefit and CTC only, if you return to the UK after a specific temporary absence, you are exempt from this requirement (see p129). See p308 for more information about temporary absences.

If you are covered by the European Union (EU) co-ordination rules (see p349) and have moved to the UK from a European Economic Area (EEA) country, you may be able to use periods of residence there to satisfy this condition (under the 'aggregation principle' – see p383). **Note:** although this is confirmed in guidance to child benefit and CTC decision makers,[5] it is arguable that the guidance is overly restrictive as it suggests that this only applies if your residence would satisfy an entitlement condition to a 'family benefit' in the other country, which would only be the case in Croatia, Cyprus, Denmark and Hungary.

Income-based jobseeker's allowance

To satisfy the habitual residence test (see p139) for income-based JSA, you must have been living in the common travel area for the past three months (in addition to having a right to reside and being habitually resident 'in fact').[6] This requirement does not apply if:

- you are exempt from the habitual residence test (see p142);
- at any time during the last three months you have worked abroad and paid class 1 or 2 national insurance (NI) contributions, or been posted abroad as a Crown servant or while a member of HM forces. **Note:** in November 2015, the government said that this also applied to family members of HM forces, but the legislation has never been amended.[7]

Note:

- You can now only make a new claim for income-based JSA in very limited circumstances. See CPAG's *Welfare Benefits and Tax Credits Handbook*.
- You cannot make an 'advance claim' for income-based JSA to start on a future date when you will have lived in the common travel area for three months because the rules do not allow your claim to be treated as having been made on a future date if you do not satisfy the habitual residence test.[8]
- An argument that this requirement is unlawful if you have moved from an EEA country was recently dismissed by the Upper Tribunal – see p98 of the 10th edition of this *Handbook*.[9]

Child benefit and child tax credit

To be treated as present in Great Britain for child benefit, and present in the UK for CTC, you must have been living in the UK for three months, ending on the first day of your entitlement.[10] This requirement does not apply if you:[11]

- are an EEA national who is a 'worker' in the UK (see p189), including if you have retained that status (see p201);
- are an EEA national who is a self-employed person in the UK (see p196), including if you have retained that status (see p201);
- are a non-EEA national who would be classed as a worker or self-employed person if you were an EEA national;
- are a family member of someone in any of the above three groups;
- are a refugee (see below if you are a family member of a refugee);
- have been granted humanitarian protection (see below if you are a family member of a person granted humanitarian protection);
- you have been granted 'section 67 leave' as a relocated unaccompanied child (see p44);
- have leave granted outside the Immigration Rules with no restriction on accessing public funds;
- have been granted leave to remain in the UK under the 'destitution domestic violence' concession, pending an application for indefinite leave to remain under the 'domestic violence rule' (see p89);
- have leave under the displaced persons provisions;
- have been deported or otherwise legally removed from another country to the UK;[12]
- are returning to the UK after a period working abroad and, other than for last three months of your absence, you were paying UK class 1 or class 2 NI contributions;
- are returning to the UK after an absence of less than 52 weeks and either:
  - before departing the UK you were ordinarily resident for three months; *or*
  - you were covered by the rules that treat you as present during a temporary absence for eight or 12 weeks during payment of child benefit (see p327) or CTC (see p340).

If you are not covered by one of the above exemptions, you must satisfy the requirement to have been living in the UK for three months. However, see p127 for ways that you may be able to include time spent outside the UK.

Family members of refugees

If you are the family member of a refugee or a person with humanitarian protection and have leave on the basis that you joined her/him under the family reunion provisions (see p41), your leave does not mean you are exempt from the requirement to have been living in the UK for three months. You are therefore not entitled to child benefit and CTC until you have been living in the UK for three months.

In practice, HM Revenue and Customs does not always require such claimants to have been living in the UK for three months. However, if your claim is refused on this basis, you may be able to argue that this is unlawful discrimination. In a case involving the past presence test for disability living allowance, the Upper Tribunal held that the requirement was unlawful, not only for a claimant with leave as a refugee but also for a claimant with leave as a family member of a refugee (and the subsequent guidance and amending regulations also cover dependent family members of someone with humanitarian protection – see p282).[13] Obtain specialist advice if you want to challenge a refusal of benefit on this basis, and also submit new claims for child benefit and/or CTC as soon as you have been living in the UK for three months.

5. **Residence**

The requirement to be simply 'resident', rather than 'ordinarily resident' or 'habitually resident', is only a condition for:

- category D retirement pension – resident in Great Britain (see p252);
- carer's allowance supplement – resident in Scotland (see p280); *and*
- child winter heating assistance – resident in Scotland (see p293).

However, it is a necessary part of being ordinarily resident (see p131) or habitually resident (see p135).

Residence is more than a physical presence in a country and you can be resident without being present – eg, if you are abroad on holiday. Similarly, you can be present without being resident.

To be resident in a country, you must be seen to be making your home there for the time being; it need not be your only home, nor a permanent one.[14] You can remain resident during a temporary absence, depending on the duration and circumstances of your absence.[15] Your intentions to return, your accommodation, and where your family and your personal belongings are can all be relevant. It is possible to be resident in two countries at once.[16]

Note:

- You must 'reside in Scotland' to use the universal credit payment options that only apply in Scotland. In general, this applies if your address has a postcode in Scotland.[17]
- You are required to be 'living in' England or Wales for a funeral expenses payment (see p292) and a Sure Start maternity grant (see p294). The phrase 'living in' is not defined and, therefore, should have its ordinary, everyday meaning (see p127), which is arguably similar to 'resident'.

Children

The only benefits that can be claimed by a child under 16 that have residence requirements are disability living allowance (DLA), housing benefit (HB) and child benefit. For DLA and HB, the claimant must be habitually resident. For child benefit, the claimant must be ordinarily resident and have a right to reside.

Although children are covered by the same rules as for adults, in order to decide whether or not they satisfy the residence requirement,[18] in practice, a child's ordinary or habitual residence is usually decided by looking at the residence of her/his parent(s) or person(s) with parental responsibility (in Scotland, parental rights and responsibilities) for her/him. A child who lives with that person usually has the same ordinary or habitual residence as her/him, so a child who joins a parent (or person with parental responsibility) may become ordinarily and habitually resident almost immediately.[19] If there is only one person with parental responsibility, the child usually has the same ordinary and habitual residence as her/him.[20]

However, the Upper Tribunal has held that a non-European Economic Area national child was not ordinarily resident because he had overstayed his immigration leave and was therefore not lawfully resident, despite the child living with his mother who was both lawfully and ordinarily resident (see p135).[21]

Whether or not a child has a right to reside is determined in the same way as it is for an adult. So if a child under 16 is claiming child benefit, s/he (but not the child s/he is responsible for) must have a right to reside. If a child under 16 is claiming HB, s/he must have a right to reside in order to satisfy the habitual residence test.

6. **Ordinary residence**

The following benefits and tax credits have a requirement to be ordinarily resident in Great Britain (or in the UK for child benefit, tax credits and social fund funeral payments, or Scotland for Scottish benefits):

- bereavement support payment;
- Best Start grant (in Scotland);
- child benefit;
- child disability payment (expected in Scotland in 2021);
- child tax credit (CTC);
- employment and support allowance in youth;
- funeral support payments (in Scotland);
- incapacity benefit in youth;
- category D retirement pension;
- Scottish child payment (in Scotland);
- severe disablement allowance;

- social fund funeral payments and winter fuel payments;
- working tax credit (WTC);
- young carer grant (in Scotland).

There are some limited exceptions to the requirement to be ordinarily resident and also the European Union (EU) co-ordination rules may assist you in satisfying it. The exceptions and assistance provided by the co-ordination rules vary between the different benefits and are covered in Chapter 13.

In practice, claims are rarely refused on the basis of ordinary residence.

You cannot be ordinarily resident without being resident (see p130).

The term 'ordinary residence' is not defined in the legislation, but caselaw has confirmed:

- the words should have their natural and ordinary meaning;[22]
- you are ordinarily resident in a country if you have a home there that you have adopted for a settled purpose and where you live for the time being (whether for a short or long duration);[23]
- subsequent events can be taken into account if they cast light on whether you were ordinarily resident on the date of your benefit claim;[24]
- ordinary residence can start on arrival (see below);
- a person in the country for a temporary purpose can be ordinarily resident in that country (see below);
- in general, your residence must be voluntary for you to be ordinarily resident (see p133);
- ordinary residence can continue during absences abroad, but leaving to settle abroad usually ends ordinary residence (see p134);
- it is possible for a person to be ordinarily resident in more than one place or country;[25]
- a person who lives in the country but has no fixed abode can be ordinarily resident;[26]
- ordinary residence is different from the concept of 'domicile'.[27]

Ordinary residence on arrival

Ordinary residence can begin immediately on arrival in Great Britain (or the UK, or Scotland, for the relevant benefits).[28] In a family law case, a man who separated from his wife in one country (where he had lived and worked for three years) and went to live at his parents' house in another was found to become immediately ordinarily resident there. The Court of Appeal held that, where there is evidence that a person intends to make a place her/his home for an indefinite period, s/he is ordinarily resident when s/he arrives there.[29] In another case, a court decided that a woman returning from Australia after some months there had never lost her ordinary residence in England. However, if she had, she would have become ordinarily resident again when the boat embarked from Australia.[30] In a case involving students, they had to show that they were ordinarily resident within a few weeks of first arriving in the UK, and it was not argued that they could not be ordinarily resident because they had only just come to Great Britain.[31]

Ordinary residence while here for a temporary purpose

To be ordinarily resident in Great Britain (or the UK or Scotland), you do not have to intend, or be able, to live here permanently.

You should be ordinarily resident if you are living here 'for settled purposes as part of the regular order of [your] life for the time being whether of short or long duration'. The purpose can be for a limited period – eg, 'education, business or profession, employment, health, family, or merely love of the place'.[32]

If you are in the UK solely for business purposes, you can still be ordinarily resident here.[33] You may have several different reasons for a single stay – eg, to visit relatives, get medical advice, attend religious ceremonies and sort out personal affairs.[34]

The reason must be a settled one. This does not mean that the reason has to be long-standing,[35] but there must be evidence of it. The benefit authorities should consider how long you are likely to reside in the UK. If you intend to live here for the time being, they should accept your intention as sufficient, unless it is clearly unlikely that you are going to be able to stay. The benefit authorities should not make a deep examination of your long-term intentions.[36] The type of accommodation you occupy may be relevant.[37] If you have made regular visits to the UK, this may also be relevant.[38]

Involuntary residence

Ordinary residence generally requires that you have '*voluntarily* adopted' to live somewhere with a settled purpose.[39] Therefore, a person who is held in a place against her/his will is not usually ordinarily resident there. It can be arguable that if you were taken out of the country against your will (eg, as a child or for a forced marriage), you should be ordinarily resident on your return. However, if you are in the country because of circumstances that limit or remove your choice, this does not necessarily prevent you from being ordinarily resident here.

In practice, the question of determining ordinary residence if you lack the capacity to 'voluntarily adopt' your place of residence rarely arises when determining entitlement to benefits and tax credits. However, it is more common when trying to determine local authority responsibility for providing support, and so the principles established in that caselaw can be relevant. Depending on the facts, if you lack capacity you can be held to be ordinarily resident where the person who makes decisions on your behalf resides, if that is where you are based, or alternatively, where your residence is sufficiently settled (omitting the criteria for it to be 'voluntarily adopted').[40]

Deportation to the UK does not prevent you from becoming ordinarily resident here.[41] The issue is whether your residence is part of your settled purpose. If you have decided to live in the UK, it does not matter if the reason for your decision is because you were deported here. For the purposes of tax credits and child benefit, you are treated as ordinarily resident if you are in the UK as a result of deportation or having been otherwise legally removed from another country.[42]

Absence abroad

You may cease to be ordinarily resident if you go abroad. This depends on all the facts of your situation, including:

- your stated intentions when you go abroad and whether these are followed by your subsequent actions;
- why you go abroad;
- how long you stay abroad;
- what connections you keep with the country – eg, accommodation, furniture and other possessions, and visits back.[43]

If you decide to move abroad for the foreseeable future, you usually stop being ordinarily resident in Great Britain (or the UK, or Scotland) on the day you leave.[44] There can be exceptions, which depend on your circumstances, including if your plans are clearly impractical and you return to the UK very quickly.

If your absence abroad is part of your normal pattern of life, your ordinary residence may not be affected.[45] This can apply if you are out of the UK for half, or even most, of the year – eg, if you spend each summer in the UK and the winter abroad, you may still be ordinarily resident in the UK.[46]

If your absence abroad is extraordinary or temporary and you intend to return to Great Britain (or the UK or Scotland), your ordinary residence may not be affected.[47] Your subsequent actions can strengthen the relevance of your intentions – eg, if you intended to return to the UK and by the time of the decision you have, in fact, returned.[48]

However, if despite intending to return, you are away from the UK for a long time and do not keep strong connections with the UK, you may lose your ordinary residence. In one case, a citizen of the UK and colonies lived in the UK for over four years and then returned to Kenya for two years and five months because her business here failed and there was a business opportunity in Kenya. She intended to make enough money to support herself on her return to the UK. Her parents and parents-in-law remained in the UK. It was decided that she had lost her ordinary residence during her absence.[49]

In deciding whether an absence affects your ordinary residence, the decision maker must consider all your circumstances. Every absence is unique, and you should provide full details of all your circumstances including:

- why you wish to go abroad;

- how long you intend to be abroad; *and*
- what you intend to do while you are abroad.

Each of these considerations must be taken into account, and it is your responsibility to demonstrate that your absence will be temporary.[50]

Note: in addition to affecting your ordinary residence, an absence may also affect your benefit entitlement if it means you cease to satisfy other residence or presence requirements for the benefit or tax credit you are claiming (see p307), or if it means you cease to be treated as a couple (see p310).

Legal residence

It may be arguable that whether or not residence must be lawful to count as ordinary residence, depends on the context. However, caselaw suggests that if this entails entitlement to a state benefit, the residence must be lawful.[51] This approach was applied recently to exclude from disability living allowance (DLA) a non-European Economic Area (EEA) national child who had overstayed his immigration leave in the UK, on the basis that he was not ordinarily resident.[52] (**Note:** ordinary residence ceased to be a requirement for DLA, attendance allowance and carer's allowance, for claims made on or after 8 April 2013.)

You may be affected by this if you are a non-EEA national defined as a 'person subject to immigration control' because you require leave and do not have it (see p85), but you are not excluded from benefits on this basis because you are in an exempt group. See p102 for the exempt groups for tax credits, p98 for child benefit and p103 for social fund payments. The requirement for residence to be lawful could also affect your entitlement to category D retirement pension (see p252).

Note: if you require leave but do not have it, but are entitled to tax credits because you are making a joint claim with a partner who is not excluded by her/his immigration status, HM Revenue and Customs sometimes appears to treat the provision that allows the immigration status of one partner to be ignored in a joint claim as overriding the requirement for that partner to be ordinarily resident (if interpreted as requiring the residence to be lawful) and as overriding the right to reside requirement for CTC (see p107).

7. Habitual residence

The following benefits and tax credits have a habitual residence requirement:

- attendance allowance;
- Best Start grant (in Scotland – only in limited circumstances – see p294);
- carer's allowance;
- child disability payment (expected in Scotland in 2021);
- disability living allowance;

- income-related employment and support allowance;
- housing benefit;
- income support;
- income-based jobseeker's allowance;
- pension credit;
- personal independence payment;
- universal credit;
- young carer grant (in Scotland).

You must satisfy (or be exempt from) the habitual residence test to get the above benefits. See Chapter 11 for details.

Note:

- You are also excluded from council tax reduction if you do not satisfy (and are not exempt from) the habitual residence requirement (see p577).[53]
- You may be entitled to a winter fuel payment from the social fund if, instead of being ordinarily resident in Great Britain, you are habitually resident in one of the listed European Economic Area (EEA) countries (see p293).
- You may be entitled to child winter heating assistance if, instead of being resident in Scotland, you are habitually resident in one of the listed EEA countries (see p293).

8. The right to reside

The following benefits and tax credits have a right to reside requirement:

- child benefit;
- child tax credit (CTC);
- income-related employment and support allowance;
- housing benefit;
- income support;
- income-based jobseeker's allowance;
- pension credit;
- universal credit.

The right to reside requirement for all the above benefits, other than child benefit and CTC, is part of the habitual residence test. To be entitled to the above benefits, you must satisfy the right to reside requirement, unless, for the means-tested benefits only, you are exempt from the habitual residence test (see p139).

You are also excluded from council tax reduction if you do not satisfy the right to reside requirement (see p577).[54]

See Chapter 11 for details of the habitual residence test and the right to reside requirement, Chapter 12 for who has a right to reside, and Chapter 13 for the residence and presence requirements for each benefit.

Notes

2. **Presence**
   1 R(S) 1/66

4. **Living in for three months**
   2 *CL v SSWP* [2020] UKUT 146 (AAC), paras 34-39
   3 *TC v SSWP (JSA)* [2017] UKUT 222 (AAC)
   4 *AEKM v Department for Communities (JSA)* [2016] NICom 80, paras 21, 46-48 and 61; *TC v SSWP (JSA)* [2017] UKUT 222 (AAC), paras 21, 27 (which adopts this case into British caselaw) and 32-38
   5 TCTM 02035; para 10025 CBTM
   6 Reg 85A(2) JSA Regs
   7 Reg 85A(2A) JSA Regs; 'Changes to jobseeker's allowance to benefit armed forces families', announced 1 November 2015 on gov.uk
   8 Reg 13(9) SS(C&P) Regs
   9 *CL v SSWP* [2020] UKUT 146 (AAC)
   10 **CB** Reg 23(5) CB Regs
   CTC Reg 3(6) TC(R) Regs
   11 **CB** Reg 23(6) CB Regs
   CTC Reg 3(7) TC(R) Regs
   12 **CB** Reg 23(3) CB Regs
   CTC Reg 3(3) TC(R) Regs
   13 *MM and IS v SSWP (DLA)* [2016] UKUT 149 (AAC); Vol 2 Ch 7, para 071716 DMG; Ch C2, para C2027 ADM; regs 2, 6, 7 and 14 Social Security (Miscellaneous Amendments No.4) Regulations 2017, No.1015

5. **Residence**
   14 R(IS) 6/96, para 19; R(P) 2/67
   15 CPC/1035/2005; see also *TC v SSWP (JSA)* [2017] UKUT 222 (AAC)
   16 R(IS) 9/99, para 10
   17 The Universal Credit (Claims and Payments) (Scotland) Regulations 2017, No.227
   18 *Re A (A Minor) (Abduction: Child's Objections)* [1994] 2 FLR 126: on habitual residence, but also applies to ordinary residence.
   19 *Re M (Minors) (Residence Order: Jurisdiction)* [1993] 1 FLR 495
   20 *Re J (A Minor) (Abduction: Custody Rights)* [1990] 2 AC 562, p578
   21 *MS v SSWP (DLA)* [2016] UKUT 42 (AAC)

6. **Ordinary residence**
   22 *Levene v Inland Revenue Commissioners* [1928] AC 217; R(M) 1/85
   23 *R v Barnet London Borough Council ex parte Shah* [1983] 2 AC 309
   24 *Arthur v HMRC* [2017] EWCA Civ 1756
   25 *IRC v Lysaght* [1928] AC 234; *Britto v SSHD* [1984] Imm AR 93; R(P) 1/01; CIS/1691/2004; *GC v HMRC (TC)* [2014] UKUT 251 (AAC)
   26 *Levene v Inland Revenue Commissioners* [1928] AC 217
   27 *R v Barnet London Borough Council ex parte Shah* [1983] 2 AC 309
   28 R(F) 1/62
   29 *Macrae v Macrae* [1949] 2 All ER 34. The countries were Scotland and England, which are separate for family law purposes. In R(IS) 6/96, para 27, the commissioner doubted the correctness of *Macrae* because he considered it used a test very close to the 'real home' test rejected in *Shah*. He does not seem to have heard any argument about this; *Macrae* was cited in *Shah* and was not one of the cases mentioned there as wrong: pp342-43.
   30 *Lewis v Lewis* [1956] 1 All ER 375
   31 *R v Barnet London Borough Council ex parte Shah* [1982] QB 688, p717E
   32 *R v Barnet London Borough Council ex parte Shah* [1983] 2 AC 309, p344; see also *Arthur v HMRC* [2017] EWCA Civ 1756, in particular paras 16 and 32
   33 *Inland Revenue Commissioners v Lysaght* [1928] AC 234; *AA v SSWP (IS)* [2013] UKUT 406 (AAC)
   34 *Levene v Inland Revenue Commissioners* [1928] AC 217, HL; *GC v HMRC (TC)* [2014] UKUT 251 (AAC)
   35 *Macrae v Macrae* [1949] 2 All ER 34
   36 *R v Barnet London Borough Council ex parte Shah* [1983] 2 AC 309
   37 R(F) 1/82; R(F) 1/62; R(P) 1/62; R(P) 4/54
   38 *GC v HMRC (TC)* [2014] UKUT 251 (AAC)
   39 *R v Barnet London Borough Council ex parte Shah* [1983] 2 AC 309

40 *R Waltham Forest LBC ex parte Vale*, unreported, 11 February 1985; but see also *R (Cornwall Council) SSH and another* [2015] UKSC 46
41 *Gout v Cimitian* [1922] 1 AC 105
42 **TC** Reg 3(3) TC(R) Regs
CB Reg 23(3) CB Regs
43 R(F) 1/62; R(M) 1/85; *Britto v SSHD* [1984] Imm AR 93
44 *Hopkins v Hopkins* [1951]; *R v Hussain* [1971] 56 Crim App R 165; *R v IAT ex parte Ng* [1986] Imm AR 23 (QBD); *Al Habtoor v Fotheringham* [2001] EWCA Civ 186
45 *R v Barnet London Borough Council ex parte Shah* [1983] 2 AC 309
46 *Levene v Inland Revenue Commissioners* [1928] AC 217; *Inland Revenue Commissioners v Lysaght* [1928] AC 234; *AA v SSWP (IS)* [2013] UKUT 406 (AAC)
47 *R v Barnet London Borough Council ex parte Shah* [1983] 2 AC 309, p342D
48 *R v IAT Ex parte Siggins* [1985] Imm AR 14
49 *SSHD v Haria* [1986] Imm AR 165
50 *Chief Adjudication Officer v Ahmed and Others*, 16 March 1994 (CA), reported as R(S) 1/96
51 *R v Barnet London Borough Council ex parte Shah* [1983] 2 AC 309, Lord Scarman – comments obiter; *Mark v Mark* [2005] UKHL 42, para 36 ; *MS v SSWP (DLA)* [2016] UKUT 42 (AAC)
52 *MS v SSWP (DLA)* [2016] UKUT 42 (AAC)

7. **Habitual residence**
53 Reg 12 CTRS(PR)E Regs; reg 16 CTR(SPC)S Regs; reg 16 CTR(S) Regs; reg 28 CTRSPR(W) Regs; Sch para 19 CTRS(DS)W Regs

8. **The right to reside**
54 Reg 12 CTRS(PR)E Regs; reg 16 CTR(SPC)S Regs; reg 16 CTR(S) Regs; reg 28 CTRSPR(W) Regs; Sch para 19 CTRS(DS)W Regs

Chapter 11

Habitual residence and the right to reside

This chapter covers:
1. The habitual residence test (below)
2. 'Habitual residence in fact' (p146)
3. The right to reside (p151)

This chapter explains how the habitual residence test and the right to reside requirement apply to the various benefits and tax credits, and how you can show habitual residence. For information on who has a right to reside, see Chapter 12.

1. The habitual residence test

The habitual residence test applies to the following benefits:
- attendance allowance (AA);
- Best Start grant (in Scotland, in limited circumstances – see p294);
- carer's allowance (CA);
- child disability payment (expected in Scotland in 2021);
- disability living allowance (DLA);
- income-related employment and support allowance (ESA);
- housing benefit (HB);
- income support (IS);
- income-based jobseeker's allowance (JSA);
- pension credit (PC);
- personal independence payment (PIP);
- universal credit (UC);
- young carer grant (in Scotland).

To be entitled to one of the above benefits, you must satisfy, or be exempt from, the habitual residence test for that benefit. The habitual residence test and the groups of people exempt from the test vary depending on the benefit you are claiming (see below).

Note:

- In this *Handbook* all references to the European Economic Area (EEA) are to be read as including Switzerland. The EEA countries are listed on p47.
- The habitual residence test only applies to the claimant(s). For further details on what this means for different benefits, see p141.
- Whether or not you satisfy, or are exempt from, the habitual residence test is a decision that must be made on the 'balance of probabilities' (see p456).
- You are also excluded from council tax reduction (see p575) if you do not satisfy (and are not exempt from) the habitual residence test.[1]
- You may be entitled to a winter fuel payment from the social fund if, instead of being ordinarily resident in Great Britain, you are habitually resident in one of the listed EEA countries (see p293).
- You may be entitled to child winter heating assistance if, instead of being resident in Scotland, you are habitually resident in one of the listed EEA countries (see p280).

Satisfying the habitual residence test for each benefit

To satisfy the habitual residence test for **means-tested benefits** you must:

- be 'habitually resident in fact' in the common travel area (the UK, Ireland, Channel Islands and Isle of Man) (see p146); *and*
- have a right to reside in the common travel area that is not excluded for the benefit you want to claim (see p151); *and*
- (for income-based JSA only) have been living in the common travel area for the past three months (see p127).

However, if you are exempt from the habitual residence test for means-tested benefits (see p142), you are treated as satisfying all parts of the test.

To satisfy the habitual residence test for **AA, DLA, PIP, CA**, and, it is expected, **child disability payment (CDP)**, you must be 'habitually resident in fact' (see p146) in the common travel area, *unless*:

- you are exempt from this requirement (see p142); *or*
- you are covered by the main European Union (EU) co-ordination rules (or fo CDP the UK-Ireland Protocol) (see p355), and you are 'habitually resident in fact' in an EEA country (Ireland if relying on the Protocol) (see p285).

However, to disapply the past presence test on the basis that you are covered by the EU co-ordination rules and have a genuine and sufficient link to the UK (or, for child disability payment, Scotland), you must be 'habitually resident in fact' in Great Britain (or, for child disability payment, the common travel area), or an EEA country if you are making a new claim there, or continuing to be paid an exisiting award, while covered by the EU co-ordination rules (see p282).

To satisfy the habitual residence test for a **young carer grant**, unless you are exempt (see p142), you must be 'habitually resident in fact' (see p146) in the UK, Channel Islands, Isle of Man, or the EEA see p280.

You only need to satisfy the habitual residence test for a **Best Start grant** if you are aged under 20 and neither you nor your partner receive a 'qualifying benefit' (a means-tested benefit or tax credits). Unless you are exempt (see p142), you must be 'habitually resident in fact' (see p146) in the UK, Channel Islands, Isle of Man, or, if you have leave under the EU Settlement Scheme or a specified free movement residence right, the EEA (see p294).

If you are exempt from the habitual residence test for the benefit you want to claim, your residence should not be examined further. Provided you meet the other conditions of entitlement, you are eligible for benefit. However, in practice, the decision maker may not consider whether you are exempt, so make this clear, particularly if you might not otherwise be accepted as satisfying the test – eg, because you have only recently arrived in the common travel area.

The Department for Work and Pensions (DWP) sometimes develops policies varying the usual procedures for specific groups. For example, internal guidance states that if, when you make your new claim, you can provide evidence that you have come to the UK under the 'gateway protection programme' or 'vulnerable person relocation scheme', or you have been granted leave as a refugee in the last eight weeks, a shorter habitual residence test applies (because you are clearly exempt) and your claim is fast-tracked.[2]

Who does the habitual residence test apply to

The habitual residence test applies to the benefit claimant.

If you have a partner living with you and you claim **UC**, you must make a joint claim and both of you must satisfy, or be exempt from, the habitual residence test. If your partner fails the test, see below.

For **other means-tested benefits** (except income-based JSA claimed as a joint-claim couple – see p142), only one partner in a couple claims the benefit. If that partner satisfies, or is exempt from, the habitual residence test, you are paid as a couple. You and your partner should therefore consider which one of you should make the claim.

However, if you have reached pension age and your partner is under pension age but is not entitled to UC because s/he fails the habitual residence test (and, therefore, you cannot make a joint claim for UC with your partner), you are treated as a single person for any claim you make for PC and/or HB.[3]

For **AA, DLA, PIP, CA, child disability payment, young carer grant** and (if you are under 20 and not getting a qualifying benefit) **Best Start grants**, the habitual residence test applies to the claimant.

The habitual residence test does not apply to any child included in your claim.

Couples claiming universal credit

If you live with your partner and claim UC, you are generally required to make a joint claim, and you and your partner must both satisfy, or be exempt from, the habitual residence test.

If you satisfy or are exempt from the habitual residence test, but your partner fails it, your joint claim is treated as a claim for UC as a single person and:[4]

- the maximum amount of UC is that for a single person;[5]
- your partner does not have to accept a claimant commitment or comply with any work-related requirements because s/he is not a claimant;[6]
- your partner's income and capital are taken into account in calculating your UC award;[7]
- your partner is not classed as a 'non-dependant' and therefore no deduction (ie, 'housing costs contribution') is made from your UC;[8]
- if you are under 35, your partner does not prevent your rent being restricted to the one-bedroom shared accommodation rate;[9]
- if you have a child, your partner does not affect your being 'responsible' for her/him (so you are entitled to a child element, and, if you are receiving education, that does not exclude you from UC) nor being her/his 'responsible carer' – eg, when determining your work-related requirements;[10]
- the couple rate of the earnings threshold applies for determining when no work-related requirements apply to you, and for any self-employed 'minimum income floor'.[11]

Note: if you have reached pension age and your partner is under pension age but is not entitled to UC because s/he fails the habitual residence test, your claim is *not* treated as a single claim for UC. Instead, you must claim PC and HB and you are treated as a single person for each of these claims.[12]

Joint-claim jobseeker's allowance

If you are a member of a 'joint-claim couple' for income-based JSA (see CPAG's *Welfare Benefits and Tax Credits Handbook* for what this means) and either you or your partner do not satisfy, or you are not exempt from, the habitual residence test, you do not need to make a joint claim. The partner who is habitually resident can claim income-based JSA for both of you.[13] You are paid as a couple.

Who is exempt from the habitual residence test

You are exempt from the habitual residence test for **means-tested benefits**, if you:[14]

- are a refugee. If you are a family member of a refugee, see below;
- have humanitarian protection. If you are a family member of someone with humanitarian protection, see below;
- have discretionary leave;
- have destitution domestic violence concession leave (see p36);

- have temporary protection granted under the displaced persons' provisions;
- have been deported, expelled or legally removed from another country to the UK and you are not a 'person subject to immigration control' (see p81);
- are an EEA national and are a 'worker' (see p189), including if you retain this status (see p201);
- are an EEA national and are a self-employed person (see p196), including if you retain this status (see p201);
- are the family member (see p218), other than an extended family member, of someone in either of the above two bullet points;
- are an EEA national and a 'frontier worker' (see p256);
- have pre-settled status and you are a family member (see p220), other than an 'extended family member', of someone in the above bullet point;
- have pre-settled status, and you are a family member, other than an extended family member, of a 'relevant person of Northern Ireland' (see p152) and s/he would be a worker or self-employed person if s/he were are an EEA national;[15]
- are an EEA national with a permanent right to reside acquired in less than five years – eg, certain former workers or self-employed people who have retired or are permanently incapacitated, and their family members (see p253);
- (for income-related ESA only) are being transferred from an award of IS which was transitionally protected from the requirement to have a right to reside (see p155);
- (for HB only) receive IS, income-related ESA or PC;[16]
- (for HB only) receive income-based JSA and either:
  - you have a right to reside other than one that is excluded for HB (see p152); *or*
  - you have been receiving both HB and income-based JSA since 31 March 2014. Your exemption on this basis ends when either you cease to be entitled to that income-based JSA or you make a new claim for HB.[17]

You are exempt from the requirement to be habitually resident **for ayoung carer grant** if you are in one of the first six bullet points listed above.[18]

You are exempt from the requirement to be habitually resident for a **Best Start grant** if you or your partner are receiving a 'qualifying benefit' (a means-tested benefit or tax credits) or you are in one of the first six bullet points listed above.[19]

For **AA**, **DLA**, **PIP**, **CA** and **child disability payment**, you are only exempt from the requirement to be 'habitually resident in fact' in the common travel area, if you are treated as being habitually resident (as well as treated as being present, and for child disability payment, ordinarily resident) because you are abroad in your capacity as a serving member of the forces (or, for child disability payment, a civil servant), or are living with someone who is abroad as a serving member of the forces (or civil servant) and you are the spouse, civil partner, (or for child disability payment only, living together as if married / civil partners), son, stepson, daughter, stepdaughter, or (except for child disability payment) father, stepfather, mother, stepmother mother-in-law or father-in-law of that person, and, for CDP only, you can demonstrate a 'genuine and sufficient link' to Scotland (see p283).[20]

Family members of refugees and those with humanitarian protection

If you are the family member of a refugee or someone with humanitarian protection and you have leave on the basis that you joined her/him under the family reunion provisions (see p41), your leave does not mean you are exempt from the habitual residence test. You are therefore not entitled to means-tested benefits until you have established your habitual residence, and for income-based JSA, until you have been living in the common travel area for three months.

This exclusion from benefits is arguably unlawful discrimination. In a case involving the past presence test for DLA, the Upper Tribunal held that the requirement was unlawful, not only for a claimant with leave as a refugee but also for a claimant with leave as a family member of a refugee. When the regulations were amended, equivalent rights were also extended to dependent family members of someone with humanitarian protection (see p282). If you have leave on this basis and are refused a means-tested benefit for failing the habitual residence test, challenge the decision and get specialist advice to argue that this is unlawful discrimination.

Note: if you live with your partner and claim UC, both of you must satisfy, or be exempt from, the habitual residence test. If only your partner does so, your joint claim is treated as a claim made by your partner as a single person (see p142).[21]

If you fail the habitual residence test

If you do not satisfy, and are not exempt from, the habitual residence test, you are not entitled to UC, IS, income-based JSA, income-related ESA, PC, HB, AA, DLA, PIP, CA, child disability payment, young carer grant or (if the test applies to you) a Best Start grant.

- For UC and PC , you are treated as not present in Great Britain.[22]
- For IS, income-based JSA, income-related ESA and HB, you are classed as a 'person from abroad'. This means for IS, income-based JSA and income-related ESA, you have an applicable amount of nil,[23] and for HB you are treated as not liable for rent.[24]
- For AA, DLA, PIP, CA, child disability payment, young carer grant and a Best Start grant, you have failed to meet the prescribed residence requirements.[25]

Have you been refused benefit?

1. If you are refused benefit because you have failed the habitual residence test, consider challenging this decision. See CPAG's *Welfare Benefits and Tax Credits Handbook* for information on how to do so. You may want to contact a local advice agency for help with this.

2. While you are challenging the decision, make another claim. If this is refused, also challenge this decision and make another claim, and so on. That is because when the decision refusing your initial claim is looked at again, the decision maker (or First-tier Tribunal) cannot take into account circumstances that did not exist at the time the original decision was made.[26] So, if the decision maker (or tribunal) considers that you were not habitually resident at the time benefit was originally refused, but you are now (eg, because you have now been resident for an appreciable period of time), s/he cannot take this into account when looking again at the original decision. However, if by the date of the decision on your second or subsequent claim, you had, for example, completed an appreciable period of residence or rented accommodation (evidence of settled intention to reside), s/he can take this into account. The benefit authority may say that you cannot make another claim while your appeal (or request to have the first decision looked at again) is pending. That is not the case.[27] It may help to refer to the fact that when amending regulations were introduced, the Secretary of State in 2007 said in his report that 'it needs to be emphasised that neither the fact that a person's claim for benefit has been disallowed on the grounds that the habitual residence test has not been satisfied, nor the fact that there is an outstanding appeal against that decision, prevents that individual from making a fresh claim for benefit.'[28]

3. The decision maker should consider whether you satisfy, or are exempt from, the habitual residence test on your date of claim and, if not, on each day from then until the date s/he makes the decision.[29]

4. Check whether you are exempt from the habitual residence test for the benefit you are claiming (see p142).

5. Establish which part of the test the decision maker says you have failed (if you are exempt, you do not have to satisfy *any* part).

6. If you are claiming a means-tested benefit and the decision maker considers you do not have a right to reside, check Chapter 12 for the ways in which you can have a right to reside.

7. If you have claimed income-based JSA and the decision maker considers that you have not lived in the common travel area for the past three months, see p127.

8. If the decision maker considers you not to be 'habitually resident in fact', see below.

9. The local authority must make its own decision on HB and not just follow a DWP decision that you are not habitually resident. See p142 for who is exempt and p459 for the relevance of decisions on other benefit claims.[30]

10. If you have been receiving IS, HB, child tax credit (CTC) and/or working tax credit (WTC) and you make a claim for UC which the DWP refuses on the basis that you fail the habitual residence test, this does not terminate your award of your previous benefit. An existing award of one of these benefits only ends if you have claimed UC and the DWP is satisfied that you meet the first four of the basic conditions for UC.[31] One of these conditions is that you be in Great Britain, and if you fail the habitual residence test you are treated as not in Great Britain.[32] Therefore, a decision that you fail the habitual residence test means the DWP is *not* satisfied that you meet the condition of being in Great Britain

and so your award of IS, HB, CTC or WTC should continue while you challenge the refusal to award you UC.

11. If you made a joint claim for UC and your partner has satisfied, or is exempt from, the habitual residence test but you have been found not to be habitually resident, your joint claim is treated as a claim by your partner as a single person. S/he is not paid benefit for you, but your income and capital are taken into account (see p142). S/he can continue to be paid UC while you challenge the decision on your entitlement.

12. Although the onus of proof is on the benefit authority to establish that you are *not* habitually resident, produce as much evidence as possible to show that you *are*. All decisions should be made on the balance of probabilities. See Chapter 20 for more information on evidence.

2. 'Habitual residence in fact'

There is no definition of 'habitual residence' in the regulations. However, there is a considerable amount of caselaw on its meaning and certain principles have emerged from this. To count as 'habitually resident in fact' in the required area for the benefit you are claiming (see note below):

- you must be resident (see below);
- your residence must be voluntary (see p147);
- you must have a settled intention to make that area your home for the time being (see p147);
- in most cases, you must have resided in that area for an 'appreciable period of time' (see p148). **Note:** this is not a fixed period and there are some exceptions.

Most disputes about whether someone is 'habitually resident in fact' concern the last two bullet points.

The decision about whether or not you are habitually resident is a factual question and must be made on the 'balance of probabilities'. You should always provide as much evidence as you can about all your circumstances that are relevant to your habitual residence. Ultimately, the burden of proof lies with the benefit authority to show that you are *not* habitually resident, but it is always better to show that you are habitually resident, rather than rely on this 'burden of proof'.[33] See Chapter 20 for more information about providing evidence.

Note: the area in which you need to be 'habitually resident in fact' depends on the benefit you are claiming (see p140).

Residence

You cannot be habitually resident in the required area (see p140) unless you are actually resident there. It is not enough to intend to reside there in the future.[34] For information on residence, see p130.

Voluntary residence

You cannot be 'habitually resident in fact' unless your residence is voluntary.[35] In practice, this is rarely a barrier to your being found habitually resident in fact. However, it could be relevant if you are returning to live in the required area (see p140) after having been taken or kept away against your will (see p149). **Note:** if you have been deported, expelled or otherwise legally removed from another country to the UK and you are not a 'person subject to immigration control' (see p81), you are exempt from the habitual residence test for means-tested benefits (see p142).

Settled intention

For your residence to become habitual, you must have a settled intention to reside in the required area (see p140). This is not determined just by your declaring your intention, but depends on the evidence about all the factors that are relevant to it.[36]

Your settled intention to reside does not need to be permanent; it is enough that you intend to make the required area your home for the time being.

Do you have a settled intention?

The following factors are relevant when determining whether or not you have a settled intention.

1. Your reasons for moving. If there is one or more clear reason why you have moved to the required area (such as a family breakdown, a desire to study there or an offer of employment), this helps to show your settled intention.
2. The steps you took to prepare for moving – eg, the plans you made beforehand about where you would live, enquiries about work, making arrangements for your children to attend school, contacting people you know and settling your affairs in the country you were leaving, such as closing bank accounts, disposing of property and ending a tenancy.
3. The strength of your ties to the required area compared with your ties to other places (this is sometimes called your 'centre of interests') – eg, whether you are joining family or friends, whether you have registered with a doctor or joined any clubs or associations, whether your children are in school, whether you have begun a course of study, whether you have transferred your bank account, or whether you have rented accommodation. Similarly, if you have these sort of ties outside the required area, this may indicate a weaker settled intention.
4. The viability of your continued residence is a relevant factor, but not an additional requirement. This means that you do not need to separately show that you could survive without claiming the benefits to which the habitual residence test applies.[37] The viability of your residence is simply one factor that can be taken into account when considering whether you have a settled intention to reside,[38] and therefore you can be accepted as habitually resident in fact even though you have very few or no resources.

5. Your current immigration status and your future options. For example, obtaining limited leave (also know as pre-settled status) under the European Union (EU) Settlement Scheme and the option this gives you to obtain indefinite leave (also known as settled status) in future is evidence of a settled intention to reside in the UK.

As with the requirement to be resident (see p130), you must be seen to be making a home in the required area, but it need not be your only home or a permanent one.[39] Therefore, a long-standing intention to move outside the required area (eg, when debts are paid) does not prevent you from being habitually resident.[40]

Events after you claim benefit or receive a decision may confirm that your intention was always to reside in the UK – eg, if you are refused benefit because the Department for Work and Pensions (DWP) does not accept that you have a settled intention to stay in the UK, the fact that you are still here by the time of the appeal hearing may help show that you always intended to reside here.[41]

There is a close connection between 'settled intention' and 'appreciable period': the stronger your settled intention, the shorter the period you need to reside in order to count as 'habitually resident in fact'.[42]

Appreciable period

In most cases, you do not count as 'habitually resident in fact' until you have resided in the required area (see p140) for an 'an appreciable period of time'.[43]

However, your appreciable period is reduced or may not apply at all if you are:

- a returning resident in certain circumstances (see below); *and/or*
- covered by the main EU co-ordination rules (see p150).

There is no fixed period of time that amounts to an appreciable period and it depends on your circumstances.[44] Benefit authorities must not set a standard minimum period of residence, and any such policy should be challenged by judicial review. There is extensive caselaw on what constitutes an appreciable period of residence. Periods of between one and three months are frequently cited,[45] but decision makers should not put too much weight on any one decision, nor should any general rule about a specific time period be derived from it.[46]

Your appreciable period can include visits to prepare for settled residence made before that residence is taken up.[47]

The stronger your settled intention to make your home in the common travel area for the time being, the shorter your period of actual residence need be before you can be accepted as habitually resident in fact (and vice versa).[48]

Advance claims

You can claim carer's allowance, disability living allowance (DLA), attendance allowance (AA) or personal independence payment (PIP) in advance if in the next three months (six months for AA) you will have been resident for an appreciable period and so be 'habitually resident in fact'.[49] However, in practice, this is only relevant if, from that future date, you will satisfy, or be exempt from, the past presence test (see p280).

It is expected you will be able to make an advance claim for child disability payment if you are likely to satisfy the residence and presence requirements, including being habitually resident, within the next 13 weeks.[50]

Your claim for a Best Start grant can be treated as having been made up to 10 days after the date it was received if the decision maker considers you would only be entitled from that later date.[51]

You cannot make an advance claim for a young carer grant and you must therefore satisfy, or be exempt from, the habitual residence test on the day of your application.[52]

You cannot make an advance claim for income support, income-based jobseeker's allowance (JSA), income-related employment and support allowance (ESA), pension credit (PC) or housing benefit for a future date when you will have been resident for an appreciable period because the rules prevent your claim from being treated as made on a future date if you do not satisfy the habitual residence test.[53]

This exclusion does not apply to universal credit (UC), but you can only make a UC claim in advance if the DWP considers you will be entitled within the next month and you are in a group accepted by the DWP.[54] DWP guidance states this is limited to prisoners and care leavers.[55]

Returning residents

If you were living in the required area (see p139) in the past and you return to that area, you may count as 'habitually resident in fact' either immediately on your return or after a much shorter period of residence than would otherwise be the case.[56]

Are you a returning resident?

If you are a returning resident, you should consider the following issues.[57]

1. Were you habitually resident when you were previously in the area?
2. If so, did you cease to be habitually resident when you went abroad either immediately on departure or while you were abroad?
3. If so, when did you resume habitual residence? This may involve deciding when you resumed residence, and then when that residence became 'habitual'.

If you never stopped being habitually resident in fact, you continue to be habitually resident on your return. This could apply if you only went abroad for a short period – eg, for a short holiday. It could also apply if you were abroad for an extended holiday.[58] Similarly, it can apply if your absence abroad was only ever intended to be for a temporary period. For example, in one case, a man was held not to have ceased to be habitually resident on his return from a two-year Voluntary Service Overseas placement, during which time he had given up his tenancy in the UK and put his possessions in storage.[59] It may also apply if your absence abroad was involuntary. Guidance to decision makers states that people who leave, or remain away from, the UK because of a forced marriage are not considered to have lost their habitual residence as they were abroad through no fault of their own. They are therefore considered to be habitually resident from the date of their claim.[60]

If you have ceased to count as habitually resident in fact while abroad, whether or not you need to complete a further period of residence here on your return before you can resume your habitual residence depends on the following.[61]

- The circumstances in which your earlier habitual residence was lost. If you went abroad for a temporary or conditional reason and/or you stayed away longer because of circumstances beyond your control, you may be more likely to be found habitually resident immediately on your return.
- The links between you and the required area while abroad. This could include retaining property, bank accounts and membership of organisations, maintaining contact with family and friends and making visits back to the common travel area (their frequency, length and purpose are all relevant).
- The circumstances of your return. Evidence of your settled intention is relevant (see p147).

In two cases that were heard jointly, a commissioner applied the above factors and found both claimants to be habitually resident on the day of their return.[62]

Even if you are not able to resume your previous habitual residence immediately on your return, you may still be able to argue that your previous habitual residence here is a factor that reduces the period of time that counts as an appreciable period of actual residence.

If you are covered by the European Union co-ordination rules

If you are covered by the main EU co-ordination rules (see p355), the period of time you must be resident before you can be found to be 'habitually resident in fact' can be shorter than otherwise might be required, and can be outweighed by other factors that show you are habitually resident. The co-ordination rules can only assist you in this way if you are claiming a 'special non-contributory benefit' (see p367) – ie:

- income-based JSA;
- income-related ESA;
- PC;
- DLA mobility component;
- PIP mobility component;[63]
- child disability payment mobility component (expected in Scotland in 2021).

The main co-ordination rules state that you are entitled to 'special non-contributory benefits' in the member state in which you are 'resident'[64] and define 'residence' as the place where you 'habitually reside' (see p371).[65]

The Court of Justice of the European Union (CJEU) has held that when deciding where someone habitually resides, her/his length of residence in the member state cannot be regarded as an intrinsic element of the concept of residence. The case concerned a British national who lived in the UK until he was 23 and then moved to France, where he worked for 14 years until he was made redundant. He returned to the UK and was refused benefit on the basis of not having completed an appreciable period of actual residence. The CJEU held that the claimant, who was covered by the EU co-ordination rules and was claiming a special non-contributory benefit, could not be deemed not to be habitually resident merely because the period of residence completed was too short.[66] Although the case concerned a returning resident, subsequent caselaw confirms that the principle applies to any claimant covered by the EU co-ordination rules.[67] So, while 'duration and continuity of presence' is one of the factors that should be considered when determining where you habitually reside, it is only one factor and can be outweighed by others. Therefore, you cannot be denied income-based JSA, income-related ESA, PC, DLA mobility component, PIP mobility component or, it is expected, child disability payment mobility component, solely because you have not completed an 'appreciable period' of actual residence in the common travel area.

3. The right to reside

The right to reside requirement applies to:

- child benefit;
- child tax credit (CTC);
- income-related employment and support allowance (ESA);
- housing benefit (HB);
- income support (IS);
- income-based jobseeker's allowance (JSA);
- pension credit (PC);
- universal credit (UC).

You are also excluded from council tax reduction (see p575) if you do not have a right to reside.[68]

The residence rights that are specifically excluded vary among the different benefits, so you must check that your right to reside is not one that is excluded for the benefit you are claiming. It may also be relevant to check whether that benefit requires you to have a right to reside in the UK or if you can satisfy the requirement with a right to reside in another part of the common travel area (the UK, Ireland, Channel Islands and Isle of Man).

The details of the right to reside requirement for the above benefits are covered in this section. For details of the circumstances in which you have a right to reside see Chapter 12, but if you have limited leave under the European Union (EU) Settlement Scheme (also known as pre-settled status), see p153 and p158.

Note: If you have been claiming benefits in the UK since 2004, there are transitional rules that can mean you do not need a right to reside for the benefit you want to claim (see p155 for means-tested benefits and p159 for child benefit and CTC).

Who does the right to reside test apply to

The right to reside test only applies to the claimant.

For means-tested benefits, other than UC , if your partner does not have a right to reside, you can still include her/him in your claim and you are still paid as a couple (see p141).

For UC, if your partner does not have a right to reside, see p142.

If you are claiming income-based JSA as a 'joint-claim couple' and your partner does not have a right to reside, see p142.

If you are receiving CTC on the basis of a joint claim, both you and your partner must have a right to reside (see p296). If your partner ceases to have a right to reside, your entitlement to CTC ends. Unless you are in one of the very limited circumstances in which you can make a new claim for CTC, you must claim UC (see p142).

The right to reside requirement does not apply to any child included in your claim.

Means-tested benefits

The right to reside requirement for means-tested benefits is part of the habitual residence test (see p139). Therefore, check whether you are exempt from the habitual residence test – if so, you do not need to demonstrate your right to reside (see p142). If you are not exempt from the habitual residence test, in addition to having a right to reside, you must also be 'habitually resident in fact' (see p146) and, for income-based JSA, have lived in the common travel area for the past three months (see p127).

The type of residence right you need

To satisfy the right to reside requirement for UC, IS, income-based JSA, income-related ESA, PC and HB, you must have a right to reside in the common travel area (ie, the UK, Ireland, Channel Islands and Isle of Man), *other than:*[69]

- limited leave granted under the EU Settlement Scheme (also known as pre-settled status – see p52) unless you are the family member (other than an extended family member) of:
  - a relevant person of Northern Ireland (see below) who *would* have a free movement right to reside (other than one listed here) *if* s/he were are a European Economic Area (EEA) national; *or*
  - a frontier worker (see p256). If that applies,you are exempt from the habitual residence test (see p142).

However, this exclusion of pre-settled status has just been held to be unlawful (see first bullet point in the note below);

- limited leave to enter as the holder of an EU Settlement Scheme family permit or travel permit (see p58). See third bullet point in the note below;
- as an EEA national with an initial right of residence during your first three months in the UK if you arrived before the end of 2020 (see p181);
- as a family member of someone in the bullet point above;
- as the 'primary carer' of a British citizen who is dependent on you and would have to leave the EU if you left the UK (see p240). **Note:** to date, all legal challenges to this exclusion have failed;[70]
- (except for income-based JSA) as an EEA jobseeker (see below);
- (except for income-based JSA) as a family member of an EEA jobseeker. **Note:** this exclusion does not apply if you are a former family member of a jobseeker and you have retained your right to reside (see p155).

Note:

- The inclusion of pre-settled status as an excluded right to reside in each of the means-tested benefit regulations has, at the time of writing, just been held to be unlawful. If you have pre-settled status, see below.
- If you have one of the above rights to reside, you are only excluded if it is your *only* right to reside. If you have any other right to reside that is not listed above, you satisfy the requirement.
- If you have limited leave to enter as the holder of an EU Settlement Scheme family permit or travel permit although this leave does not satisfy the right to reside requirement, check whether you are in a protected group that can have a free movement right to reside as a 'relevant family member' (see p168), and whether you have such a free movement right (see p171).
- to be entitled to council tax reduction, you must have a non-excluded right to reside and the exclusions vary between England and Wales and Scotland (see p577).

Pre-settled status

If you have limited leave granted under the EU Settlement Scheme (also known as 'pre-settled status') (see p52), you may be able to satisfy the right to reside requirement for means-tested benefits in one or more ways. The Department for

Work and Pensions (DWP) is most likely to accept this if the right to reside you have is one that the regulations do not exclude. Therefore, to obtain benefit as quickly as possible, it is helpful to work through the following steps, because the legislation for Steps 1 to 4 is not in dispute.

Step 1: Are you an Irish citizen? If you are, your citizenship satisfies the right to reside requirement, and that is not altered by your having pre-settled status (see p163).

Step 2: Do you have a free movement right to reside? Having pre-settled status means you are in one of the protected groups (see p168) that can have a free movement right to reside (see p171). If you have such a right to reside, other than one listed above, you satisfy the right to reside requirement for the means-tested benefit(s) you want to claim. That is confirmed in guidance.[71]

Step 3: Are you the family member of a frontier worker? If you are the family member (see p220), other than an extended family member, of an EEA frontier worker (see p256), and you have pre-settled status, you are exempt from the habitual residence test (see p142).

Step 4: Are you the family member of a 'relevant person of Northern Ireland' (see below), other than an extended family member, who *would* have a free movement right to reside under the EEA Regulations (see p171) (other than one listed above) *if* s/he were are an EEA national? If that applies, the regulations for each of the means-tested benefits do not exclude you.[72]

A **'relevant person of Northern Ireland'** is defined as a British or Irish citizen who was born in Northern Ireland and at the time of her/his birth at least one of her/his parents was a British or Irish citizen or had the right to reside in Northern Ireland without time limit.[73]

Step 5: If you have pre-settled status but no other non-excluded right to reside, you will need to check the latest legal position. At the time of writing, the regulations for each of the means-tested benefits listed pre-settled status as an excluded right to reside.[74] However, on 18 December 2020, the Court of Appeal held, in relation to two EU national UC claimants, that this exclusion was unlawful.[75] The court quashed the relevant provisions in each of the means-tested benefit regulations but the effect of that quashing order has been delayed until a further appeal to the Supreme Court has been determined. At the time of writing, the Supreme Court was due to hear the appeal 18-19 May 2021. Therefore, it is extremely unlikely that the DWP will accept that your pre-settled status satisfies the right to reside test for a means-tested benefit. The DWP should 'stay' ('sist' in Scotland) (delay making a decision on) your claim or reconsideration request until the judgement from the Supreme Court is known. Guidance to decision makers that the quashing of the regulations does not affect claims made from 1 January 2021, and so such claims should not be 'stayed', is wrong and should not be followed.[76] Note, there may be further delays because a question of whether it is lawful to exclude pre-settled status as a qualifying right to reside under Northern Ireland's UC regulations, has been referred to the CJEU.[77]

If you have pre-settled staus, but no other non-excluded right to reside, you should make a claim for the relevant means-tested benefit and challenge any refusals. For more details, see cpag.org.uk/welfare-rights/legal-test-cases/current-test-cases/eu-pre-settled-status.

Jobseekers

If your only right to reside is as an EEA jobseeker, you do not satisfy the right to reside test for any of the means-tested benefits except income-based JSA (and child benefit and CTC).

If you are excluded from UC, but your partner has a right to reside (other than one which is excluded), your joint claim for UC is treated as a UC claim by your partner as a single person (see p142).

Note:

- Challenges to the exclusion from HB of those whose only right to reside is as an EEA jobseeker have failed.[78]
- It is arguable that UC is a benefit designed to facilitate access to the labour market, and that it is therefore unlawful to exclude someone whose only right to reside is as a jobseeker.[79] However, the Court of Appeal has rejected this argument in relation to income-related ESA (see p182).[80]

Family members of jobseekers

If your only right to reside is as a family member (see p218) of an EEA jobseeker, that does not satisfy the right to reside requirement for any of the means-tested benefits except income-based JSA, but does satisfy the requirement for child benefit and CTC.

If you previously had a right to reside as a family member of an EEA jobseeker and you retain that because the EEA jobseeker has died or no longer lives in the UK or your marriage or civil partnership to her/him has been terminated, your retained right to reside satisfies the right to reside requirement for *all* means-tested benefits, as well as child benefit and CTC. That was confirmed by the Court of Session in Scotland.[81] For further details on former family members who can retain their residence rights, see p228.

If you have been getting benefit since April 2004

You do not need a right to reside to be entitled to any of the means-tested benefits, except UC, if you have been receiving any combination of the following benefits continuously since 30 April 2004:[82]

- council tax benefit (until it was abolished from 1 April 2013);
- income-related ESA (only from 31 October 2011 – see p156);
- HB;
- IS;
- income-based JSA;
- PC.

This transitional protection means you do not need a right to reside in order to continue to receive that benefit, or to be entitled to one of these benefits if you are able to make a new claim for it, provided the periods of entitlement have been continuous since 30 April 2004.

UC is not covered by this transitional protection. If you are an EEA national, have been residing in the UK since 2004 and now need to claim UC but do not have a right to reside, in most cases you will be entitled to obtain indefinite leave to remain under the EU Settlement Scheme (also known as settled status) (see p51). This leave satisfies the right to reside requirement for all benefits that have that requirement from the date the leave is granted. See Appendix 2 if you need advice about applying under the EU Settlement Scheme, or want advice on your other immigration options.

The rules on transitional protection did not apply to income-related ESA when ESA was introduced – it was only added from 31 October 2011. In addition, you could make a new claim for income-related ESA without needing a right to reside if it was linked by a gap of less than 12 weeks to a previous award of income-related ESA that was part of a continuous period of entitlement to the above benefits going back to 30 April 2004. **Note:** the latter rules would only enable you to make a new claim for income-related ESA if you are in one of the very limited groups that can still do so – eg, until 27 January 2021, if you or your partner have been receiving severe disability premium in the last month and continue to satisfy the conditions for that benefit.

For transitional protection to apply, you must have been the claimant throughout the whole period of continuous entitlement, rather than a partner, child or parent of a claimant.[83]

If you were entitled to IS on the grounds of disability or incapacity for work and were reassessed and transferred to income-related ESA, you were exempt from the habitual residence test on the date of transfer.[84]

The benefit authorities rarely check, or even ask, whether you have transitional protection. So, if you have been receiving one or more of the above benefits since 30 April 2004, you should always make this clear when you make your claim, and provide evidence.[85]

Example

Astrid is Swedish and came to the UK in January 2004. She had health problems and claimed IS on grounds of incapacity while living with friends. In 2008, she moved into a bedsit and claimed HB. In 2012, Astrid's IS was converted to income-related ESA. Astrid has now reached pension age and claims PC.

Astrid did not need to satisfy the right to reside requirement for any of these benefit claims because she had been in receipt of one or more of the relevant benefits for every day since 30 April 2004.

If Astrid were younger and needed to claim UC, rather than PC, she would not have transitional protection. She would not be entitled to UC as she does not have a right to reside.

However, if she obtained indefinite leave to remain under the EU Settlement Scheme (also known as settled status), she would have a right to reside that would enable her to be entitled to UC from the date the leave is granted.

Child benefit and child tax credit

For child benefit and CTC, the right to reside requirement is part of the presence test. This also requires you to be ordinarily resident (see p131) in the UK and to have lived in the UK for the past three months (see p127).

If you do not have a right to reside, you are treated as not present in the UK and therefore not entitled to child benefit or CTC.[86]

The type of residence right you need

To satisfy the right to reside requirement for child benefit and CTC, you must have a right to reside in the UK, other than:[87]

- as the primary carer of a British citizen who is dependent on you and who would have to leave the EU if you left the UK (see p240). However, you are not excluded on this basis if you are working in the UK and a national of Morocco, San Marino, Tunisia or Turkey (or Algeria if you made your claim before 1 January 2021[88]), because you are covered by agreements that provide for equal treatment in relation to family benefits that, therefore, override this exclusion (see p99).[89] To date, all other legal challenges to this exclusion have failed;[90]
- limited leave granted under the EU Settlement Scheme (also known as pre-settled status) (see p57), but see below for exceptions and an argument that this exclusion is unlawful;
- limited leave to enter as the holder of an EU Settlement Scheme family permit or travel permit (see p58). **Note:** check whether you are in a protected group that can have a free movement right to reside as a 'relevant family member' (see p168), and whether you have such a free movement right (see p171).

Note:

- If you have one of the above rights to reside, you are only excluded if that is your *only* right to reside. If you have any other right to reside that is not listed above, you satisfy the requirement.
- If you are not entitled to child benefit for a child living with you because you do not have a non-excluded right to reside, someone else who contributes to the cost of that child may be able to claim child benefit instead. To be entitled, s/he must contribute at least the amount of child benefit that would be payable for the child.[91] See CPAG's *Welfare Benefits and Tax Credits Handbook* for further details.
- The Court of Justice of the European Union has dismissed an application from the European Commission to declare the right to reside test for child benefit and CTC unlawful.[92] The Court of Appeal in Northern Ireland has also held

that the right to reside requirement for child benefit is not unlawful.[93] See p381 for more information.

Pre-settled status

The child benefit and CTC regulations list pre-settled status as an excluded right to reside that does not, by itself, satisfy that requirement for either benefit. However, if you have pre-settled status you may be able to satisfy the right to reside requirement for child benefit and CTC in one or more ways. HM Revenues and Custom (HMRC) is most likely to accept that if the right to reside you have is one that the regulations do not exclude (Steps 1–3). Therefore, to obtain benefit as quickly as possible, it is helpful to work through the following steps.

Step 1: Are you an Irish citizen? If you are, your citizenship satisfies the right to reside requirement, and that is not altered by your having pre-settled status (see p163).

Step 2: Do you have a free movement right to reside? Having pre-settled status means you are in one of the protected groups (see p168) that can have a free movement right to reside (see p171), and if you have such a right to reside, other than the one in the last bullet point listed above, that satisfies the right to reside requirement for child benefit and CTC.

Step 3: Are you the family member (see p220), other than an extended family member, **of a 'relevant person of Northern Ireland'** (see p153) who would have a free movement right to reside under the EEA Regulations (see p171) if s/he were are an EEA national? If that applies, the regulations for child benefit and CTC do not exclude you on the basis of your pre-settled status.[94]

Step 4: If you have pre-settled status but no other non-excluded right to reside, the regulations exclude this right to reside. However, the Court of Appeal held this exclusion to be unlawful for means-tested benefits. The DWP's appeal against this was, at the time of writing, due to be heard by the Supreme Court on 18-19 May 2021 (see 'step 5' on p153).[95] The same argument applies to an EU national with pre-settled status claiming child benefit and CTC, but is extremely unlikely to be accepted by HMRC until the Supreme Court judgement is known. If your child benefit or CTC is refused or termiated, because HMRC do not accept that pre-settled status is a non-excluded right to reside, challenge this decision on the basis that the Court of Appeal held this exclusion was unlawful and ordered that the relevant part of the means-tested benefit regulations be quashed. The details of your challenge will depend on the latest legal position, and are more complex if you are not an EU national. For further details, links to the Court of Appeal judgment and Order, together with the latest information, and advice on what to do, see cpag.org.uk/welfare-rights/legal-test-cases/current-test-cases/eu-pre-settled-status.

If you have been getting benefit since April 2004

The right to reside requirement only applies to child benefit and CTC claims made on or after 1 May 2004.[96]

If you are still receiving the same award of child benefit that began before 1 May 2004, you do not need a right to reside.

If you have been claiming CTC since before 1 May 2004, you also do not need a right to reside to continue to receive it. Although the tax credit rules treat you as making a new claim each year when you respond to your annual declaration (or when you receive a notice saying you will be treated as having made a declaration), this renewal claim does not require a right to reside.[97]

Note: in future you will be required to claim UC, either after a change in your circumstances or when the DWP transfers CTC claimants to UC. You will need a right to reside to be entitled to UC. If you are an EEA national, or a family member or carer of an EEA national, and you obtain indefinite leave to remain under the EU Settlement Scheme (also known as settled status) (see p51), that satisfies the right to reside requirement for UC from the date the leave is granted. Get immigration advice before applying to the EU Settlement Scheme if you are not an EEA national, or if you have any criminal convictions – see Appendix 2.

Notes

1. **The habitual residence test**

1 Sch para 21 CTRS(DS)E Regs; reg 12 CTRS(PR)E Regs; reg 16 CTR(SPC)S Regs; reg 16 CTR(S) Regs; reg 28 CTRSPR(W) Regs; Sch para 19 CTRS(DS)W Regs
2 See *Refugees and asylum seekers*rightsnet.org.uk/universal-credit-guidance; see also House of Commons, *Hansard,* answer to Written Question 238412, 2 April 2019
3 Art 7(2)(b) and (3)(b) WRA(No.31)O; HB Circular A9/2019, paras 15-17; Memo DMG 07/19, para 12
4 ss3 and 4(1)(c) and (2) WRA 2012; regs 3(3) and 9 UC Regs
5 Regs 3(3) and 36(3) UC Regs
6 ss3 and 4(1)(e) WRA 2012; reg 3(3) UC Regs; reg 9 UC,PIP,JSA&ESA(C&P) Regs
7 Regs 3(3), 18(2) and 22(3) UC Regs
8 Sch 4 para 9(2)(b) UC Regs
9 Sch 4 paras 27 and 28 UC Regs
10 ss4(1)(d) and 19(6) WRA 2012; regs 4, 14(1)(c), 24 and 86 UC Regs
11 Regs 62(3) and (4) and 90 UC Regs
12 Art 7(2)(b) and (3)(b) WRA(No.31)O; HB Circular A9/2019, paras 15-17; Memo DMG 07/19, para 12
13 Reg 3E(1) and (2)(d) JSA Regs
14 **UC** Reg 9(4) UC Regs
IS Reg 21AA(4) IS Regs
JSA Reg 85A(4) JSA Regs
ESA Reg 70(4) ESA Regs
PC Reg 2(4) SPC Regs
HB Reg 10(3B) HB Regs; reg 10(4A) HB(SPC) Regs
15 See also ADM Memo 19/20 and DMG Memo 17/20
16 Reg 10(3B)(k) HB Regs; reg 10(4A)(k) HB(SPC) Regs; *LB Hillingdon v MJ and Another (HB)* [2009] UKUT 151 (AAC)
17 Reg 3 HB(HR)A Regs
18 Reg 8(2) CA(YCG)(S) Regs

19 Sch 2 para 4(1)(b) and (2) and Sch 3 para 3(1)(b) and (2) and Sch 4 para 4(1)(b) and(2) EYA(BSG)(S) Regs
20 **AA** Reg 2(2) and (3A) SS(AA) Regs
DLA Reg 2(2) and (3A) SS(DLA) Regs
PIP Regs 19 and 20 SS(PIP) Regs
CA Reg 9(3) SS(ICA) Regs
CDP Reg 5(6)-(7) DACYP(S) Regs (draft)
21 Regs 3(3), 18(2), 22(3) and 36(3) UC Regs; reg 9 UC,PIP,JSA&ESA(C&P) Regs
22 **UC** Reg 9 UC Regs
PC Reg 2 SPC Regs
23 **IS** Regs 21 and 21AA and Sch 7 para 17 IS Regs
JSA Regs 85 and 85A and Sch 5 para 14 JSA Regs
ESA Regs 69 and 70 and Sch 5 para 11 ESA Regs
24 Reg 10(1) HB Regs; reg 10(1) HB(SPC) Regs
25 **AA** s64(1) SSCBA 1992; reg 2(1) SS(AA) Regs
DLA s71(6) SSCBA 1992; reg 2(1) SS(DLA) Regs
PIP s77(3) WRA 2012; reg 16 SS(PIP) Regs
CA s70(4) SSCBA 1992; reg 9(1) SS(ICA) Regs
YCG reg 8 CA(YCG)(S)Regs
BSG Sch 2 para 1(c) and para 4 EYA(BSG)(S)Regs
CDP Reg 5 DACYP(S) Regs (draft)
26 Reg 3(9) SS&CS(DA) Regs; reg(5)(2) UC,PIP,JSA&ESA(DA) Regs; s12(8)(b) SSA 1998
27 s8(2) SSA 1998
28 Statement by the Secretary of State for Work and Pensions given as part of Cm 7073, May 2007, para 20, available at gov.uk/government/uploads/system/uploads/attachment_data/file/243307/7073.pdf
29 See, for example, *GE v SSWP (ESA)* [2017] UKUT 145 (AAC), reported as [2017] AACR 34, paras 52-58; and *SSWP v KK (JSA)* [2019] UKUT 313 (AAC), para 8
30 Confirmed in *EP v SSWP (JSA)* [2016] UKUT 445 (AAC), paras 24-25
31 Reg 8 UC(TP) Regs; s4(1)(a)-(d) WRA 2012
32 Reg 9 UC Regs

2. **'Habitual residence in fact'**
33 R(IS) 6/96, para 15
34 CIS/15927/1996
35 *R v Barnet London Borough Council ex parte Shah* [1983] 2 AC 309, p342; *Cameron v Cameron* [1996] SLT 306; R(IS) 9/99
36 *Nessa v Chief Adjudication Officer* [1999] UKHL 41
37 CIS/4474/2003, paras 15-16
38 R(IS) 2/00, para 28, followed in CIS/1459/1996 and CIS/16097/1996
39 R(IS) 6/96, para 19
40 *M v M(Abduction: England and Scotland)* [1997] 2 FLR 263
41 R(IS) 2/00, para 30
42 CJSA/1223/2006; R(IS) 7/06; CIS/1304/97 and CJSA/5394/98, paras 29-31
43 *Nessa v Chief Adjudication Officer* [1999] UKHL 41, reported in R(IS) 2/00
44 *Nessa v Chief Adjudication Officer* [1999] UKHL 41, reported in R(IS) 2/00; *Cameron v Cameron* [1996] SLT 306
45 CIS/4474/2003; R(IS) 7/06
46 CIS/1972/2003; CIS/2559/2005
47 *Nessa v Chief Adjudication Officer* [1999] UKHL 41, reported in R(IS) 2/00, para 26
48 CJSA/1223/2006; R(IS) 7/06; CIS/1304/97 and CJSA/5394/98, paras 29-31
49 **AA** s65(6) SSCBA 1992
CA Reg 13 SS(C&P) Regs
DLA Reg 13A(1) SS(C&P) Regs
PIP Reg 33(1) UC,PIP,JSA&ESA(C&P) Regs
50 Reg 24, DACYP(S) Regs (draft)
51 Reg 4 EYA(BSG)(S) Regs
52 Reg 8 CA(YCG)(S) Regs
53 **IS/JSA/ESA** Reg 13(9) SS(C&P) Regs
PC Reg 13D(4) SS(C&P) Regs
HB Reg 83(10) HB Regs; reg 64(11) HB(SPC) Regs
54 Reg 32 UC,PIP,JSA&ESA(C&P) Regs
55 para A2048 ADM
56 *Nessa v Chief Adjudication Officer* [1999] UKHL 41, reported in R(IS) 2/00
57 CIS/1304/1997 and CJSA/5394/1998, para 11
58 *TC v SSWP (JSA)* [2017] UKUT 222 (AAC)
59 *KS v SSWP (SPC)* [2010] UKUT 156 (AAC)
60 **HB**/CTB Circular A22/2010, paras 11-12
61 CIS/1304/97 and CJSA/5394/98, paras 34-38
62 CIS/1304/97 and CJSA/5394/98, paras 40-41
63 *SSWP v DS* [2019] UKUT 238 (AAC); Ch C2 para C2097 and Appendix 1 para 4 ADM
64 Art 70(4) EU Reg 883/04
65 Art 1(j) EU Reg 883/04

66 *Swaddling v Chief Adjudication Officer*, C-90/97 [1999] ECR I-01075
67 R(IS) 3/00

3. **The right to reside**
68 Reg 12 CTRS(PR)E Regs; reg 16 CTR(SPC)S Regs; reg 16 CTR(S) Regs; reg 28 CTRSPR(W) Regs; Sch para 19 CTRS(DS)W Regs
69 **UC** Reg 9(3) UC Regs
IS Reg 21AA(3) IS Regs
JSA Reg 85A(3) JSA Regs
ESA Reg 70(3) ESA Regs
PC Reg 2(3) SPC Regs
HB Reg 10(3A) HB Regs; Reg 10(4) HB(SPC) Regs
70 Most recently *R (on the application of HC) v SSWP and Others* [2017] UKSC 73
71 ADM Memo 29/20 paras 24 and 87-114; DMG Memo 25/20 paras 23-35 and 92-119
72 **UC** Reg 9(3A) UC Regs
IS Reg 21AA(3B) IS Regs
JSA Reg 85A(3B) JSA Regs
ESA Reg 70(3B) ESA Regs
PC Reg 2(3B) SPC Regs
HB Reg 10(3AB) HB Regs; reg 10(4ZB)HB(SPC) Regs
confirmed in ADM Memo 19/20 and DMG Memo 17/20
73 Appendix EU, Annex 1, IR; see also ADM Memo 19/20 para 10 and DMG Memo 17/20 para 10
74 **UC** Reg 9(3)(c)(i) UC Regs
IS Reg 21AA(3A)(a) IS Regs
JSA Reg 85A(3A)(a) JSA Regs
ESA Reg 70(3A)(a) ESA Regs
PC Reg 2(3A)(a) SPC Regs
HB Reg 10(3AA)(a) HB Regs; reg 10(4ZA)(a)HB(SPC) Regs
75 *Fratila and Tanase v SSWP* [2020] EWCA Civ 1741
76 ADM Memo 2/21; DMG Memo 1/21
77 C-709/20 *Department for Communities (NI)* referred 30 December 2020
78 Most recently, *Stach v Department for Communities and DWP* [2018] NIQB 93
79 *Vatsouras (C-22/08) and Koupatantze (C-23/08) v Arbeitsgemeinschaft (ARGE) Nurnberg* 900 [2009] ECR I-04585
80 *Alhashem v SSWP* [2016] EWCA Civ 395
81 *Slezak v SSWP* [2017] CSIH 4, reported as [2017] AACR 21
82 Reg 6(1) SS(HR)A Regs, preserved by reg 11(2) SS(PA)A Regs
83 CIS/1096/2007
84 Reg 70(4)(l) ESA Regs; reg 10A ESA(TP)(EA) Regs
85 For a recent example, see *AP v SSWP* [2018] UKUT 307 (AAC)
86 **CB** s146 SSCBA 1992; reg 23(4) CB Regs
CTC s3(3) TCA 2002; reg 3(5) TC(R) Regs
87 **CB** Reg 23(4) CB Regs
CTC Reg 3(5) TC(R) Regs
88 **CB** Regs 23(4A)(a) CB Regs
CTC Reg 3(5A)(a) TC(R) Regs
89 **CB** Regs 1(3) and 23(4)(b) and (4A) CB Regs
CTC Reg 3(5)(b)(ii), and (5A) and (12) TC(R) Regs
HMRC v HEH and SSWP (TC and CHB) [2018] UKUT 237 (AAC)
90 Most recently, *R (on the application of HC) v SSWP and Others* [2017] UKSC 73
91 s143(1)(b) SSCBA 1992
92 *European Commission v UK*, C-308/14 [2016]
93 *Commissioners for HMRC v Aiga Spiridonova*, 13/115948
94 **CB** Regs 1(3) and 23(4B) CB Regs
CTC Reg 3(5B) and (11) TC(R) Regs
95 *Fratila and Tanase v SSWP* [2020] EWCA Civ 1741
96 **CB** Reg 23(4) CB Regs
CTC Reg 3(5)(a) TC(R) Regs
97 Reg 3(5)(a) TC(R) Regs

Chapter 12

Who has a right to reside

This chapter covers:

This chapter explains who has a right to reside. For information on the benefits and tax credits that require a right to reside, details of the requirement for each and the types of residency rights that are specifically excluded, see p151.

The right to reside requirement is only one of the residence and presence conditions that must be satisfied for some benefits and tax credits. For all the residence and presence rules for each benefit, see Chapter 13.

If you, your partner and child are *not* all British or Irish citizens, you also need to check whether your benefit entitlements are affected by being defined as a 'person subject to immigration control' (see Chapters 7 and 8).

1. Introduction

Whether or not you have a right to reside depends on your nationality, immigration status and your other particular circumstances, and also on the nationality, immigration status and other circumstances of your family members and certain people for whom you care. You may have more than one right of residence, or you may not have any.

Any residence right is sufficient to satisfy the right to reside requirement, unless it is specifically excluded for the particular benefit you want to claim (see p152 and p157).

The residence rights of some people are more complicated than others. In general, if you are a European Economic Area (EEA) national (see p47) and you began residing in the UK before 11pm on 31 December 2020, or if you are a family member or primary carer of such an EEA national, your residence rights are more complex. The majority of this chapter therefore covers the rights of these groups.

Note: In this *Handbook* all references to the EEA are to be read as including Swtizerland. The EEA countries are listed on p47.

2. British, Irish and Commonwealth citizens

British citizens have an automatic right of residence in the UK under UK law and, therefore, do not require leave to enter or remain in the UK.

British citizens do not automatically confer residence rights on their family members. If you are not a British citizen, but you are, and have been since before 31 December 2020, a family member of a British citizen or a dual British/European Economic Area (EEA) citizen, or the primary carer of a British citizen, you may, in limited circumstances, have a European free movement right to reside (see p171).

If you are a Commonwealth citizen and have been a long-term resident in the UK (eg, if you are part of the 'Windrush generation'), you may have a right of residence on the basis of having the right of abode (see p16), indefinite leave or British citizenship. If you are unsure of your status, or do not have documents to prove it, get immigration advice before contacting the Home Office as this is a complex area (see Appendix 2).

Irish citizens

If you are an Irish citizen, you have an automatic right to reside in the UK and do not require leave to enter or remain in the UK (unless you are subject to a deportation or exclusion order).[1] As an Irish citizen, you are not required to obtain leave under the European Union (EU) Settlement Scheme (see p57), but you can if you began residing in the UK before 31 December 2020 and you wish to do so, for example, to make it easier for a family member to also get leave.

If you are the family member of an Irish citizen in the UK, your free movement residence rights as a family member depend on the Irish citizen having a relevant right to reside in the same way as family members of other EEA nationals (see p218). You need to obtain leave under the EU Settlement Scheme before the deadline of 30 June 2021 (see p57).

3. Changes due to the UK leaving the European Union

The UK left the European Union (EU) on 31 January 2020. In accordance with the Withdrawal Agreements, the UK's departure was followed by the transition period until 11pm on 31 December 2020 (see below). During this period, the European free movement residence rights described in this chapter continued to apply in the UK until the end of the transition period, alongside the residence rights provided to EEA nationals, or the family members or primary carers of European Economic Area (EEA) nationals, who obtained leave under the EU Settlement Scheme (see below).

At the end of the transition period, European free movement rights were, in general, ended within UK law.[2] That included revoking the EEA Regulations, which were the main domestic legislation providing free movement residence rights in UK law. However, these regulations continue to have effect if you are covered by one of the protected groups that can use free movement rights (see p168).

Transition period

The transition period (also called the 'implementation period') was the period from the UK leaving the EU at 11pm on 31 January 2020 to 11pm on 31 December 2020.[3] During the transition period, in general, EU legislation and caselaw, as well as all EU-derived law (eg, the EEA Regulations) continued to have effect the day after the UK's departure from the EU as it did the day before.[4] During the transition period, all references to the EU or EEA were treated as if they included references to the UK, and references to an EEA national or EU citizen were treated as if they included references to a UK national.[5] However, note that British citizens only had European free movement residence rights in limited circumstances (see p171).

If you are an EEA national already living in the UK by the end of the transition period, or the family member of such an EEA national, or you lived in the UK with a derivative right to reside in the UK before the end of the transition period, you can apply for leave under the EU Settlement Scheme and you must do so by the deadline of 30 June 2021 (see below). Also check whether you are in a protected group that can have free movement residence rights after the end of the transition period (see p168). For a summary of the relevant law on free movement after the end of the transition period, see p174.

If you are an EEA national arriving after the end of the transition period, unless you are joining your family member who is an EEA national living in the UK before that period ended, you will need leave to enter or remain in the UK. If you enter the UK as a visitor, you will be granted six months' time-limited leave that is subject to a 'no recourse to public funds' condition. If you want to enter the UK other than as a visitor, you will need to obtain leave under the same rules as non-EEA nationals (see p57). Your benefit entitlements will depend primarily on your immigration status, and whether you are defined as a 'person subject to immigration control' (see p81) and, if you are, whether you are covered by an exempt group for the benefit you want to claim (see Chapter 8). To check your right to reside, see p166.

For information on how the law on free movement residence rights operates after the UK left the EU, and after the end of the transition period, see p174.

Note: the UK leaving the EU and the ending of the transition period also affects the EU co-ordination rules (see p350).

European Union Settlement Scheme

If you are an EEA national and began residing in the UK before 11pm on 31 December 2020, or you are the family member of such an EEA national, or you are a non-EEA national and have been residing in the UK (before the end of the transition period) with a derivative right to reside, you may be able to apply for leave under the EU Settlement Scheme (see p49). You must apply by the deadline of 30 June 2021.[6] The Withdrawal Agreements require the UK to admit applications after this deadline if there are reasonable grounds for the deadline being missed,[7] but at the time of writing the guidance on that had not been finalised, and you should not rely on your application being admitted late. The deadline for applications can be different if you were, and remain, the family member of an EEA national already living in the UK by the end of the transition period, and you joined her/him in the UK after this date – eg, you have entered with an EU Settlement Scheme family permit or EU Settlement Scheme travel permit (see p58).

If you have indefinite leave to enter or remain granted under the EU Settlement Scheme (also known as **settled status**), this satisfies the right to reside requirement for all benefits that have this requirement.

If you have limited leave to enter or remain granted under the EU Settlement Scheme (also known as **pre-settled status**), at the time of writing, the regulations listed this as an excluded right to reside for all benefits with that requirement. Although the Court of Appeal has held that this exclusion is unlawful for EU nationals claiming mean-tested benefits, the effect of that decision was delayed pending the outcome of the Department for Work and Pensions' (DWP's) further appeal to the Supreme Court.

Therefore, you should always provide evidence of a non-excluded free movement right to reside if possible (note your pre-settled status means you are in a protected group that can have a free movement right to reside – see p168). For details of the legal challenge, other exemptions and the steps to work through, see p152 for means-tested benefits and p157 for child benefit and child tax credit.

If you have been granted limited leave granted on the basis that you hold a valid **EU Settlement Scheme family permit** or **EU Settlement Scheme travel permit** (see p58), that does not satisfy the right to reside requirement for all benefits that have this requirement. However, check whether you are in a protected group that can have a free movement right to reside on the basis of being a 'relevant family member' of an EEA national who on 31 December 2020 had a free movement right to reside under the EEA Regulations and did not have leave under the EU Settlement Scheme (see p168), and check whether you currently have a free movement right to reside (see p171), other than one that is excluded for the benefit you want to claim (see p151).

If you are granted indefinite or limited leave under the EU Settlement Scheme, or leave on the basis that you hold a valid EU Settlement Scheme family permit or travel permit, in most cases you are not issued with a physical document (unless, for example, you are a non-EEA national family member of an EEA national and did not already have a biometric residence permit when you applied). Instead, you confirm your settled or pre-settled status by accessing your online profile. You can get a 'share code' to allow others, including the DWP, HM Revenue and Customs or local authority, to view your status online.[8]

Alternatively, you can provide the benefit authority with a copy of the Home Office document emailed to you when you were granted leave under the EU Settlment Scheme. Although this is not proof of status by itself, the decision maker should accept this as supporting evidence and can then verify your status directly with the Home Office.

4. European and non-European nationals

Whether you are a European Economic Area (EEA) national or a non-EEA national, the following overview applies to you from 1 January 2021.

If you are a British or Irish citizen you have a right to reside in the UK (see p163).

If you are *not* a British citizen, you have a right to reside if either:

- you are within a period of leave to enter or remain granted under UK immigration law. Any type of leave gives you a right to reside that satisfies the right to reside requirement for all benefits that have this requirement *except:*

  - limited leave to enter or remain granted under the European Union (EU) Settlement Scheme (also known as pre-settled status) (see above); *or*
  - limited leave to enter or remain granted on the basis you hold a valid EU Settlement Scheme family permit or EU Settlement Scheme travel permit (see above);
- you are in one of the protected groups that can have a free movement right to reside (see below) *and* you have a free movement right to reside (see p171). To claim a benefit that requires a right to reside, you need to have a free movement right to reside that is not excluded for the benefit you want to claim (see p152 and p157).

If you are within a period of immigration leave, you have a right to reside throughout the duration of that leave. However, check the following points about how the type of leave you have may affect your entitlement to benefits.

- If you have limited leave granted under the EU Settlement Scheme (also known as pre-settled status), at the time of writing, although the regulations listed that as an excluded right to reside for all benefits with that requirement, the Court of Appeal had held that this status was itself a qualifying right to reside for EU citizens claiming means-tested benefits, and that the exclusion in those regulations is unlawful. However, due to the effect of this decision being delayed and the Department for Work and Pensions seeking to challenge it, you should always provide evidence of a non-excluded free movement right to reside if possible. For details, other exemptions and the steps to work through, see p152 for means-tested benefits, and p157 for child benefit and child tax credit.
- If you have limited leave granted on the basis that you hold a valid EU Settlement Scheme family permit or travel permit (see p58), that is an excluded right to reside for each of the benefits that require a right to reside. However, if you are a 'relevant family member' of an EEA national who on 31 December 2020 had a free movement right to reside under the EEA Regulations and did not have leave under the EU Settlement Scheme, you are in a protected group that has a free movement right to reside (see below). If you have such a right (see p171), that will satisfy the right to reside requirement for the benefits that require it, provided your free movement right is not excluded for the benefit you want to claim (see p152 and p157).
- If you have indefinite leave granted under the EU Settlement Scheme (also known as **settled status**), that satisifies the right to reside requirement for all benefits that require it.
- If you have time-limited leave that has been granted subject to a 'no recourse to public funds' condition, or if you have indefinite leave granted as the result of a maintenance undertaking, you are defined as a 'person subject to immigration control' (see p81) and, unless you are in an exempt group, you are excluded from benefits on this basis (see Chapter 8).

- If you have refugee leave or humanitarian protection, you have a right to reside that satisfies the requirement for all benefits that require it, and you are not defined as a 'person subject to immigration control'. Furthermore, you are exempt from some of the residence and presence requirements that can mean you are entitled to benefits more quickly (see p112).
- **Note:** the Court of Appeal has held that having temporary admission as an asylum seeker does *not* give you a right to reside in the UK and this is likely to apply also to immigration bail (which has replaced temporary admission).[9]

5. Protected groups that can have European free movement residence rights

Since the end of the transition period (11pm on 31 December 2020), you can only have a free movement right to reside if you are in one of the protected groups below. If you are in one of these groups, the European Economic Area (EEA) Regulations continue to be available to you, for the purpose of claiming benefits, despite their having been revoked more generally as part of the ending of free movement rights within UK law at the end of the transition period.

If you need a free movement right to reside to claim a benefit that requires you to have a right to reside, you need to check whether:

- you are in one of the four protected groups below; *and*
- you have a free movement right to reside (see p171), other than one that is excluded for the benefit you want to claim (see p151).

You are in a protected group, if:[10]

- you have limited leave granted under the European Union (EU) Settlement Scheme (also known as pre-settled status). **Note:** the Court of Appeal recently held that pre-settled status was itself a qualifying right to reside for EU citizens claiming means-tested benefits. However, due to the implementation of this decision being delayed until the Department for Work and Pensions' (DWP's) further appeal to the Supreme Court has been determined, you should always provide evidence of a free movement right to reside (other than one that is excluded for the benefit you want to claim), if possible. For details and other exemptions, see p152 for means-tested benefits and p157 for child benefit and child tax credit; *or*
- (between 31 December 2020 and 30 June 2021) on 31 December 2020 you had a free movement right to reside (see notes below for when you can be *treated as* having this), and on that date you did not have, and have not since had, leave under the EU Settlement Scheme; *or*
- (beyond 30 June 2021) you were in the group above and on or before 30 June 2021, you applied for leave under EU Settlement Scheme and that application

(or appeal against a refusal) has not been finally determined, withdrawn or abandoned; *or*

- (between 31 December 2020 and 30 June 2021) you are defined as the 'relevant family member' (see below) of a person who, on 31 December 2020, had a free movement right to reside and, on that date, did not have leave under the EU Settlement Scheme, and you do not have leave under the EU Settlement Scheme.

Note the following about the last three protected groups.

- You can be *treated as* having had a free movement right to reside on 31 December 2020, if you previously had a free movement right to reside in the UK and on that date you were absent from the UK, but your absence was in circumstances that does not break your continuity of residence – eg, if that absence, together with any other absences in the last 12-month period, was less than six months in total – (see p250).[11]
- If you previously had a permanent right to reside in the UK and since then you lost this right to reside due to being absent from the UK for more than two years (see p255), you are *treated as* having a permanent right to reside on 31 December 2020 if on that date you had been absent from the UK for a period of more than two but less than five years, and immediately before leaving the UK you had a permanent right to reside in the UK.[12]
- If you are an EEA national in one of the last three protected groups above, you cannot be defined as a 'person subject to immigration control', even if you do not have a free movement right to reside.[13]
- If you are in the second or third protected group above, note that the free movement right to reside you had on 31 December 2020 can be the same as, or different from, the free movement right to reside that you have when you claim benefits (see the first example below).
- The regulations define you as a 'relevant person' if you are in the second or fourth protected group above.[14]
- As with all evidence of your benefit entitlement, you should provide sufficient evidence that you (or the person that you are a 'relevant family member' of) had a free movement right to reside on 31 December 2020 if you can. If you cannot, however, you should ask the benefit authority to make its own investigations (eg, by checking HM Revenue and Customs records), and you should provide sufficient information to enable the benefit authority to do so (see p460).[15]

You are a **'relevant family member'** of a person ('P') if:[16]

- on 31 December 2020 you were a 'family member' (see p218) of P. That includes if you were an 'extended family member' and you held, and continue to hold, a valid residence document issued under the EEA Regulations (see p465); *or*

- on 31 December 2020 you were P's durable partner (whether or not you hold a valid residence document issued under the EEA Regulations – see note below); *or*
- you became a 'family member' as defined under the EEA Regulations after 31 December 2020 due to being an extended family member on that date and at a later date being issued with a valid residence document under the EEA Regulations (see p465); *or*
- you are the spouse or civil partner of P and P is a Swiss national; *or*
- you are P's child and either:
  - the other parent is in the second or fourth of the protected groups on p168, or has leave granted under the EU Settlement Scheme, or is a British citizen; *or*
  - you were born or adopted after 31 December 2020, and P is either an EEA or Swiss national living in the UK (or a British citizen living in an EEA state or Switzerland), with a right to reside in that state, since before 31 December 2020, and P has sole or joint custody of you.[17]

Note: Although you are defined as a 'relevant family member' if you were a durable partner of a relevant person on 31 December 2020 even if you did not have a valid residence document issued under the EEA Regulations on that date, this only enables you to be in a protected group that can *potentially* have a free movement right to reside. To actually have a right to reside under those regulations as a family member, you will need to have a residence document issued under the EEA Regulations, and in most cases that had to be applied for by 31 December 2020 (see p223). If you have not been issued with the necessary residence document, being in a protected group by being a relevant family member will only assist you if you have *another* right to reside under the regulations. See the second example below.

Examples

Natalia is a Lithuanian national and moved to the UK on 24 December 2020 with her three-year-old son. After a couple of weeks, she starts looking for work and on 1 February 2021 she starts a part-time job working 20 hours aweek in a warehouse. By 28 February 2021, she has exhausted her savings and as her wage is too low to support her and her son, she claims universal credit (UC) and child benefit. She is entitled to both benefits. This is because, on 31 December 2020, she did not have leave under the EU Settlement Scheme and she had an initial right to reside under the EEA Regulations (see p181). Natalia is, therefore, in the second protected group on p168 , so the EEA Regulations continue to be available to her until 30 June 2021. By the date she claims UC and child benefit, she has a right to reside as a worker (see p189), and also as a worker she is exempt from the child benefit requirement to have been living in the UK for three months (see p127).

On 28 June 2021, Natalia applies to the EU Settlement Scheme, but is not granted pre-settled status until 1 August 2021. She can continue to receive UC and child benefit on the basis of her right to reside as a worker as the EEA Regulations continue to apply to her: for the period until 1 August because she is in the third protected group above, and from 1 August 2021 due to being in the first protected group above.

Felix is an Austrian national who has been living in the UK with his Slovakian girlfirend Katrin since 2018. On 31 December 2020, neither had applied to the EU Settlement Scheme. On that date, Katrin was working full time and had a right to reside as a worker. Therefore, in January 2021 she is in the second protected group above. Felix is in the fourth protected group above because he is the durable partner of Katrin and, therefore, a 'relevant family member' of someone who on 31 December 2020 had a free movement right to reside under the EEA Regulations and did not have leave under the EU Settlement Scheme. However, that does not give him a right to reside under the EEA Regulations, so to be treated as Katrin's 'family member' (and thereby have a right to reside as the family member of a worker), he would need to have been issued with a residence document under the EEA Regulations that remain in force, and he has not. In February 2021, Felix begins working as a self-employed carpenter and, because he is in a protected group, this self-employment gives him a right to reside under the EEA Regulations as a self-employed person. This means that when the couple need to claim UC in March 2021, due to Katrin being made redundant that month, they can be paid as a couple because each is in a protected group and each has a qualifying free movement right to reside at the time they wish to claim UC: Felix as a self-employed person (see p196) and Katrin because of her retained worker status (on the basis that she is involuntarily unemployed and registered as a jobseeker – see p202).

6. European free movement residence rights

Since 11pm on 31 December 2020, you can only have a free movement right to reside if you are in a protected group. Therefore, you first need to check whether you are covered by one of these groups for the period of your benefit claim.

If you *are* in a protected group, then the European Economic Area (EEA) Regulations continue to be available to you for specific purposes, including claiming benefits, despite their having been revoked more generally as part of the ending of free movement within UK law (see p164).

If you are in a protected group, you may have European free movement residence rights if you are:

- an EEA national; *or*
- a family member of an EEA national (that does not include a British citizen, except in limited circumstances – see below) who has a right to reside. You do not need to be an EEA national yourself; *or*
- someone who was previously in the above group; *or*
- the primary carer of certain EEA nationals (or certain British citizens).

Whether or not you have European free movement residence rights also depends on other factors set out in the relevant sections of this chapter.

Note: references to EEA nationals in this chapter should be read as *not* including **British citizens**, unless otherwise stated. That also applied throughout the transition period that followed the UK's departure from the European Union (EU). During this transition period, which ended at 11pm on 31 December 2020, EU law continued to apply in the UK, references to the EEA or EU were treated as if they included references to the UK and references to EEA nationals or EU citizens are treated as if they included British citizens. However, for the purpose of European free movement residence rights, British citizens were *not* included in references to EEA nationals.[18]

If you are a British citizen, you always have a right to reside in the UK under UK law. However, British citizens do not generally give free movement residence rights to their family members, except in limited circumstances. If you are the family member of a British citizen (including if you have dual citizenship), see p224. If you are the primary carer of a British citizen, see p233.

For a list of EEA member states, see p47.

In general, **Swiss nationals** have the same residence rights as EEA nationals, so references to EEA nationals in this *Handbook* include Swiss nationals.

Croatian, A2 and A8 nationals may have their current free movement residence rights affected by certain restrictions that applied in the past. For a list of these countries and details of the restrictions, see p176.

Checklist

Since 11pm on 31 December 2020, you can only have a European free movement right to reside if:

- you are an EEA national, or a family member of an EEA national or you have a derivative right to reside (in most cases by being a carer of an EEA national or child of an EEA national); *and*
- you are in one of the protected groups that can use free movement residence rights to be entitled to benefits (see p168).

Unless you have limited leave granted under the EU Settlement Scheme (also known as pre-settled status), whether you are in a protected group will depend on you (or the person that you are a 'relevant family member' of – see p219) having had a free movement right to reside on 31 December 2020. Therefore you may need to check both:

- whether you (or the person you are a 'relevant family member' of) had a free movement right to reside on 31 December 2020; *and*
- whether you have a free movement right to reside when you claim benefit (and for the duration of your claim).

You can work through the following checklist to check either or both of the above. You will also need to check the details of each right to reside that may apply to ensure the relevant requirements are satisfied.

Note: if you need to have had a free movement right to reside on 31 December 2020 in order for you to come within a protected group, the free movement right to reside that you had on that date does *not* need to be the same free movement right to reside that subsequently enables you to claim benefit (see the first example on p170).

In relation to the relevant time (see above), check the following.

- **Step one:** are you an EEA national and did you begin residing in the UK in the last three months of 2020, or on 31 December 2020 were you the family member of such an EEA national? This initial right of residence (see p181) does not satisfy the right to reside requirement for means-tested benefits, but, if you had this **initial right to reside** on 31 December 2020, you may be in one of the protected groups that can use free movement residence rights (see p168).
- **Step two:** are you an EEA national with a right to reside as a **'qualified person'**?[19] That is, you are in the UK as a:
  - jobseeker (see p182);
  - worker (see p189), including if you have retained this status (see p201);
  - self-employed person (see p196), including if you have retained this status (see p201); *or*
  - self-sufficient person, including a self-sufficient student (see p211).
- **Step three:** are you a **'family member'** (see p218) of someone covered in Step two? You have this right to reside whether you are an EEA or non-EEA national. In limited circumstances, you may have a right to reside if you were the family member of someone in Step two but s/he has now died, left the UK or your marriage or civil partnership has been terminated (see p228).
- **Step four:** do you have a **permanent right of residence** (see p244)? That is normally after five years of 'legal residence' in the UK (which can include periods with a right to reside under Steps one, two or three above) but can sometimes be acquired before five years.
- **Step five:** do you have a **'derivative' right to reside** through someone else's right to reside but not as her/his family member? That covers certain children and certain primary carers (see p233).

Note:

- If you have been granted indefinite leave under the EU Settlement Scheme (also known as **settled status**) (see p49), that gives you a right to reside from the date that leave was granted, which satisfies the right to reside requirement for all benefits that have that requirement. However, as the leave is not retrospective, it does not give you a right to reside for any period before the date it was granted.

- If you have been granted limited leave under the EU Settlement Scheme (also referred to as **pre-settled status**) (see p49), for the duration of this leave you are in a protected group that can continue to have free movement residence rights under the EEA Regulations (see p168). Note also that, at the time of writing, the Court of Appeal had held that pre-settled status was itself a qualifying right to reside for EU citizens claiming means-tested benefits. However, due to delays in this decision being implemented and the Department for Work and Pensions seeking to challenge it further, you should always provide evidence of a non-excluded free movement right to reside if possible. For details and other exemptions, see p152 for means-tested benefits and p157 for child benefit and child tax credit.
- If you have limited leave granted on the basis that you hold an **EU Settlement Scheme family permit** or an **EU Settlement Scheme travel permit** (see p58), that does *not* satisfy the right to reside requirement for any of the benefits that require it. However, if you are a 'relevant family member' of an EEA national who on 31 December 2020 had a free movement right to reside under the EEA Regulations and did not have leave under the EU Settlement Scheme, you are in a protected group that has a free movement right to reside (see p168). You will need a free movement right that is not excluded for the benefit you want to claim (see p152 and p157).
- You can have more than one European free movement right to reside at a time – eg, you may be a self-employed person and also the family member of someone with a permanent right of residence.[20]
- If you are a **Croatian, A2 or A8 national**, a family member (see p220) of a Croatian, A2 or A8 national, or if you are the primary carer of a child of a Croatian, A2 or A8 national and may have a derivative right to reside (see p233), see p176 for the additional restrictions that can affect your right to reside.

Legal sources of European free movement residence rights

The UK left the EU at 11pm on 31 January 2020, and from this date, in accordance with the Withdrawal Agreements, there was a transition period until 11pm on 31 December 2020 (see p164). During this time, EU law and EU-derived law, such as the EEA Regulations (see below), continued to apply as they did before the UK left the EU.[21]

At the end of the transition period, EU law was converted into UK law, and together with EU-derived law, continues to apply in the UK as it did on 31 December 2020.[22] However, from this date, this retained law could be amended or revoked.

The law on European free movement rights was, in general, revoked within UK law from 11pm on 31 December 2020.[23] However, the Withdrawal Agreements provide protections for EEA nationals already living in the UK, and British citizens living in EEA states, before the end of the transition period, and the family members of each.[24] New regulations are intended to reproduce these protections, and if you are in one of the protected groups, you can have free movement residence rights. For details of these protected groups, including the duration of the protection, see p168. Questions about the interpretation of these protections can be referred to the Court of Justice of the European Union (CJEU) for up to eight years from the end of the transition period.[25] If the protected rights were not already provided for in UK legislation, new legislation must do so – eg, to provide for the rights of 'frontier workers' (see p256).

In practice, for the purposes of establishing benefit entitlement on the basis of a European free movement right, either during a period before the end of the transition period or, if you are in one of the protected groups, after the end of the transition period, the starting point is the EEA Regulations. However, these regulations must be interpreted in accordance with not only the Withdrawal Agreements but also the, now retained, EU law that they are intended to implement. If this retained law is not significantly modified, then its interpretation must be in accordance with EU legal principles and CJEU caselaw decided before the end of the transition period, and *may* have regard to new EU law, decided or passed after 31 December 2020. However, specified courts may depart from CJEU caselaw.[26] These specified courts include the Supreme Court, the level of courts below this, including the Court of Appeal, and equivalent-level courts across the UK.[27] If the retained law *is* modified, it is interpreted in accordance with EU caselaw (decided before the end of the transition period) and EU legal principles, *only* if doing so is consistent with the intention of the modifications.[28]

Whether the retained law is modified or not, it must implement the rights and protections contained in the Withdrawal Agreements.

The main EU legislation that continues to be relevant in determining European free movement residence rights of EEA nationals, their family members and those with derivative residence rights comes from the EU treaties, in particular the **Treaty on the Functioning of the European Union** (TFEU), or the EEA agreement that provides similar rights for Norway, Iceland and Liechtenstein.

The rights provided by the TFEU include the right of EU nationals to move and reside freely within the EU. However, this right is subject to limitations and conditions set out in the TFEU and in other legislation that give effect to the treaty.[29] This means that people covered by the TFEU must satisfy certain conditions to have a right of residence. The most important secondary legislation that sets out residence rights and the conditions that must be satisfied is **EU Directive 2004/38**. This brings together most rights of residence under EU law into one piece of legislation and replaces many earlier directives and regulations, which previously set out EU residence rights. Directive 2004/38 has been in force since 30 April 2006 and was extended from 1 March 2009 to cover nationals of Norway, Iceland and Liechtenstein.[30] **Note:** while the EU Directive is the most important source of residence rights for EEA nationals and their family members, it is not the only one – eg, some derivative rights of residence (see p233) stem from other EU legislation.[31]

Swiss nationals and their family members are covered by a separate agreement that provides similar rights.[32]

The Immigration (European Economic Area) Regulations 2016, referred to in this *Handbook* as the '**EEA Regulations**', reproduce in UK law most of the residence rights contained in EU Directive 2004/38 and some provided directly under TFEU and other provisions of EU law. The EEA Regulations apply to all EEA nationals (but not British citizens – see p163) and Swiss nationals.[33] The current EEA Regulations replaced very similar regulations from 1 February 2017.[34] **Note:** the EEA Regulations were, in general, revoked from the end of the transition period. However they continue to be available if you are are in a protected group listed on p168.[35]

7. Croatian, A2 and A8 nationals

Since the end of the transition period at 11pm on 31 December 2020, you can only have a free movement right to reside while you are in one of the protected groups (see p168). If you are in one of the protected groups, or for a period before the end of the transition period, your free movement residence rights could be affected by additional restrictions that previously applied to nationals of the countries listed below.

Croatia, A2 and A8 states

Croatia joined the European Union (EU) on 1 July 2013.

Restrictions applied until 30 June 2018.

The A2 states are: Bulgaria and Romania.

These states joined the EU on 1 January 2007.

Restrictions applied until 31 December 2013.

The A8 states are: Czech Republic, Estonia, Hungary, Latvia, Lithuania, Poland, Slovakia and Slovenia.

These states joined the EU on 1 May 2004.

Restrictions applied until 30 April 2009.

The treaties under which the above 'accession' states joined the EU allowed existing member states, including, at the relevant dates, the UK, to restrict accession nationals' access to their labour markets, and their residence rights as workers and jobseekers. The duration of these restrictions was limited to five years from the date the states joined the EU, but could be extended for a further two years if certain conditions were met. The UK government imposed the restrictions for five years and then extended them for A8 and A2 nationals for an additional two years. However, this extension of restrictions for A8 nationals from 1 May 2009 to 30 April 2011 has been held to be unlawful by the Supreme Court.[36] This means that, retrospectively, A8 nationals were not subject to restrictions during this two-year period.[37]

Although the restrictions on Croatian, A2 and A8 nationals ended some years ago, you need to know what the restrictions were if the free movement residence rights you, or your family member, had during the relevant period of restriction affects the free movement residence rights:

- you had before the end of the transition period (31 December 2020); *or*
- you had on 31 December 2020 (as this could determine whether you are in a protected group who can have a free movement right to reside after that date – see p168); *or*
- the person that you are the 'relevant family member' of, had on 31 December 2020 (because this could determine whether you are in a protected group that can have a free movement right to reside after that date – see p168).

In particular, the restrictions may be relevant if you are seeking to establishing permanent residence and you, or your family member whose free movement residence rights you need to rely on, are a Croatian, A2 or A8 national. The restrictions can also be relevant in determining whether you have a derivative right to reside as the primary carer of a child in education when the child's parent is a Croatian, A2 or A8 national who has worked in the UK (see p235).

Note: these restrictions do not affect your eligibility to apply for leave under the EU Settlement Scheme (see p165).

Restrictions on employment and residence rights

Between 1 July 2013 and 30 June 2018 (if you are a Croatian national) or between 1 January 2007 and 31 December 2013 (if you are an A2 national), unless you were in one of the exempt groups listed on p178, you must have obtained an 'accession worker authorisation document' (in most cases, an accession worker registration certificate if you are Croatian, or an accession worker card if you are an A2 national, specifying the employer you could work for) before taking up employment, and then have worked in accordance with it.[38] Your residence rights were restricted as follows.[39]

- You did not have a right to reside as a jobseeker.
- You were only defined as a 'worker' if you had an accession worker authorisation document and worked in accordance with it.
- You could not retain your 'worker' status when you stopped work in the ways other workers could (see p201).

If you are an A8 national, between 1 May 2004 and 30 April 2009, unless you were in one of the exempt groups listed on p179, you had to work for an 'authorised employer'.[40] In general, this meant you had to register each job you took with the

Worker Registration Scheme (but see p180 for the precise meaning, because that can affect your residence rights). Your residence rights were restricted as follows.[41]

- You did not have a right to reside as a jobseeker.
- You were only defined as a 'worker' if you were working for an 'authorised employer' (see p181).
- You could not retain your 'worker' status when you stopped work in the ways other workers could (see p201).[42] However, if you lost your job within the first month of employment, you could retain your status in these ways until the end of the month. **Note:** the Court of Justice of the European Union held that the exclusion of an A8 national subject to restrictions from retaining worker status was not unlawful.[43]

The restrictions do not affect other residence rights you may have or had as a European Economic Area (EEA) national – eg, as a self-employed or self-sufficient person.[44] The Upper Tribunal has also held that the restrictions were not imposed on A8 nationals to limit their rights to permanent residence in less than five years and so periods of unregistered employment can count for this purpose (see p253).[45]

Other rights under EU law (eg, under the EU co-ordination rules covered in Chapter 16) were not affected.

Croatian and A2 nationals who were exempt from restrictions

Between 1 July 2013 and 30 June 2018 (if you are a Croatian national) or between 1 January 2007 and 31 December 2013 (if you are an A2 national), you were subject to worker authorisation and had additional restrictions on your residence rights (see above), *unless* you:[46]

- had on 30 June 2013 (Croatian) or 31 December 2006 (A2) leave to enter or remain with no restriction on employment;
- were 'legally working' (see p180) in the UK for 12 months without breaks of more than 30 days (in total), up to and including 31 December 2006 (A2) or 30 June 2013 (Croatian);[47]
- had 'legally worked' for 12 months (beginning before or after 31 December 2006 (A2) or 30 June 2013 (Croatian)), disregarding any breaks of less than 30 days (in total);[48]
- were a posted worker – ie, you were working in the UK providing services on behalf of an employer who was not established in the UK;
- were a member of a diplomatic mission (or the family member of such a person) or a person otherwise entitled to diplomatic immunity;
- had dual nationality with the UK or another (non-A2/Croatian) EEA state;
- were the spouse/civil partner (or, Croatian only, unmarried or same-sex partner) of a UK national or of a person with indefinite leave to enter or remain (see p29[49]) in the UK;

- were the spouse/civil partner (or, Croatian only, unmarried or same-sex partner) or child under 18 of a person with leave to enter or remain in the UK that allowed employment;
- had a permanent right of residence (see p244);
- were a student with a registration certificate that stated that you could not work more than 20 hours a week (unless it was part of vocational training or during vacations) and you complied with this. If the certificate confirmed you could work during the four months after the course ended, the exemption continued for this period;
- were a family member of an EEA national who had a right to reside, unless the EEA national was an A2 (or, if you are Croatian, a Croatian) national subject to worker authorisation (or, A2 only, the only reason s/he was not an A2 national subject to worker authorisation is because s/he was covered by the bullet point below);
- were a family member of an A2 (or, if you are Croatian, a Croatian) national subject to worker authorisation who had a right to reside (for an A2 national only, as a worker, student, self-employed or self-sufficient person). If you are a Croatian national (or an A2 national relying on an A2 worker), you were a 'family member' if you were the descendant and either under 21 or dependent, the spouse/civil partner, or (Croatians only) the unmarried or same-sex partner;
- were a 'highly skilled person' – ie, you:[50]
  - met the points-based criteria in the Immigration Rules for entering the UK on this basis; *or*
  - had a qualification at degree level or higher in the UK, or Higher National Diploma in Scotland and, within 12 months of this award, you applied for a registration certificate confirming your unconditional access to the labour market.

A8 nationals who were exempt from restrictions

Between 1 May 2004 and 30 April 2009, if you are an A8 national, you were defined as 'requiring registration' and so any work you did had to be for 'an authorised employer' (see p180) and your residence rights were restricted (see p177) *unless* you:[51]

- had leave to enter or remain on 30 April 2004 which had no restriction on employment;
- were 'legally working' (see below) in the UK for 12 months, without breaks of more than 30 days (in total), up to and including 30 April 2004 (see also note below);[52]
- had 'legally worked' in the UK for 12 months (beginning before or after 30 April 2004), disregarding any breaks of less than 30 days (in total);[53]
- were the spouse/civil partner or child under 18 of a person with leave to enter or remain in the UK that allowed employment;

- had dual nationality with the UK and another (non-A2/A8) EEA state or Switzerland;
- were a family member of another EEA or Swiss national who had a right to reside under the EEA Regulations (other than an A2/A8 national subject to registration/authorisation if her/his only right to reside was for the first three months in the UK);
- were the member of a diplomatic mission (or the family member of such a person) or a person otherwise entitled to diplomatic immunity;
- were a posted worker – ie, you were working in the UK providing services on behalf of an employer who was not established in the UK.

Note: the Upper Tribunal held that an A8 national who was not in one of the above exempt groups could be treated as if he were if the outcome would otherwise be 'disproportionate'. It ruled that it would be disproportionate to disregard the man's years of work and subsequent involuntary unemployment just because he failed to satisfy the second bullet above because he was abroad (albeit still employed in the UK) on 30 April 2004 and had then failed to register his employment under the Worker Registration Scheme (as he believed he did not need to). The Upper Tribunal accepted that he had therefore acquired a permanent right to reside.[54]

Legally working

The phrase 'legally working' has a specific meaning and only refers to employment: periods of self-employment do not count as 'legally working' for the purpose of exempting you from restrictions.

If you are a Croatian or A2 national, you were 'legally working' before the restrictions ended (see p176) if:[55]

- you were working in accordance with your worker authorisation document; *or*
- you were working during a period when you were in one of the exempt groups on p178 (other than posted workers); *or*
- the work was done before 1 July 2013 (for Croatian nationals) or before 1 January 2007 (for A2 nationals), either in accordance with any leave you had under the Immigration Act 1971 or when you did not require leave (except work done with permission from the Home Office while you were an asylum seeker[56]).

If you are an A8 national, you were 'legally working' before the restrictions ended (see p176) if:[57]

- you were working for an authorised employer (see below); *or*
- you were working during a period when you were in one of the exempt groups listed above (other than if you were the spouse/civil partner or child of a person whose leave to enter or remain in the UK allowed employment); *or*

- the work was done before 1 May 2004 either in accordance with any leave you had under the Immigration Act 1971 or when you did not require leave (except work done with permission from the Home Office while you were an asylum seeker[58]).

Authorised employer for A8 nationals

If you were an A8 national subject to restrictions, you were defined as working for an **'authorised employer'** if:[59]

- you were within the first month of employment; *or*
- you applied for a worker's registration certificate under the Worker Registration Scheme within the first month of work, but did not yet have a certificate or refusal; *or*
- you had a valid worker's registration certificate issued under the Worker Registration Scheme for that employer; *or*
- you had been 'legally working' for that employer since 30 April 2004; *or*
- you began work at an agricultural camp between 1 May 2004 and 31 December 2004, and before 1 May 2004 you had been issued with leave under the Immigration Act 1971 as a seasonal worker at such a camp.

If you applied for a registration certificate after the first month of work, you only counted as working for an authorised employer from the date it was issued.[60]

Note: the Upper Tribunal has held that the restrictions on A8 nationals had not been imposed to limit their rights to permanent residence in less than five years and so all periods of employment count for this purpose, even if they were not for an authorised employer (see p253).[61]

If you were a Croatian, A2 or A8 national subject to restrictions and your employment ended, you stopped legally working, stopped being a 'worker' and, unless you were exempt, you could not retain your worker status. However, if you were still under a contract of employment, you continued to be legally working and a worker – eg, if you were on maternity leave, holiday leave, sick leave or compassionate leave (including if the leave was unpaid).[62]

If you need to provide evidence that your employment gave you worker status, in most cases you will need to show it was in accordance with your worker authorisation document (if you are a Croatian or A2 national), or that (beyond the first month) it was registered under the Worker Registration Scheme, if you are an A8 national. For details of how to obtain this evidence if you do not have it, see p472.

8. **Initial right of residence**

Until the end of the transition period at 11 pm on 31 December 2020, all European Economic Area (EEA) nationals had a right to enter the UK.[63] If you are an EEA national and you entered the UK before the end of the transition period, you also have or had an initial right of residence for the first three months of your stay, provided you hold or held a valid identity card or passport.[64] You have or had this initial residence right whether or not you are or were working or seeking work, subject to your not becoming an unreasonable burden on the UK's social assistance system.[65]

You also have or had a right of residence if you are or were a family member (see p218) of an EEA national who has or had this initial right of residence for three months (whether or not *you* are an EEA national) provided you hold or held a valid passport.[66]

Note: you can have another residence right (eg, as a family member of a worker and/or as a jobseeker) in addition to your initial right of residence – ie, you do not have to wait for the three months to end before you have another residence right.

If your *only* right of residence is on the basis of your (or your family member's) initial three-month right of residence, that does not satisfy the right to reside requirement for any of the means-tested benefits because it is one of the excluded residence rights for those benefits (see p152). However:

- if, on 31 December 2020, you (or the person you are a 'relevant family member' of – see p168) had this right to reside and, on that date, did not have leave granted under the European Union (EU) Settlement Scheme, you are (until at least 30 June 2021) in one of the protected groups that can use free movement residence rights. If you are an EEA national, these protections also mean that you cannot be defined as a 'person subject to immigration control' (see p81). For further details, including the duration of these protections, see p168;
- if you have *another* residence right during your initial three months in the UK, you can satisfy the right to reside requirement for means-tested benefits, provided it is not another excluded right to reside;
- if your *only* right of residence is on the basis of your (or your family member's) initial three-month right of residence, that satisfies the right to reside requirement for child benefit and child tax credit (CTC). However, in practice, you are unlikely to qualify for child benefit or CTC during this period because, unless you are exempt, you must have been living in the UK for the past three months (see p127);
- you can count a period during which this is your only right of residence as part of the continuous five-year period required for permanent residence (see p245).

9. Jobseekers

Since the end of the transition period at 11pm on 31 December 2020, you can only have a free movement right to reside, including as a jobseeker (or family member of a jobseeker), while you are in one of the protected groups that can have these rights (see p168).

If you are in one of the protected groups, or for a period before the end of the transition period, you may have a right to reside as a 'jobseeker' if you are a European Economic Area (EEA) national looking for work in the UK (see below).

You may also have a right to reside if you are a family member (see p218) of a jobseeker. However, these residence rights only satisfy the right to reside requirement for child benefit, child tax credit (CTC) and income-based jobseeker's allowance (JSA) (see p188). You may have difficulty claiming these benefits over the longer term solely on the basis of your right to reside as a jobseeker because of evidence requirements (see p184).

You should therefore always check whether you have a right of residence on some other basis.

Note:

- If you had a right to reside as a jobseeker (or family member of a jobseeker) on 31 December 2020, and on that date, you did not have leave granted under the European Union (EU) Settlement Scheme, you are (until at least 30 June 2021) in one of the protected groups that can use free movement residence rights. If you are an EEA national, these protections also mean that you cannot be defined as a 'person subject to immigration control' (see p81). For further details, including the duration of these protections, see p168.
- If you have previously been a 'worker' (see p189) or a self-employed person (see p196) and are now looking for work, in addition to having a right to reside as a jobseeker, you may also have a right to reside as someone who has retained her/his worker or self-employed status (see p201). Either option satisfies the right to reside requirement for all benefits.
- Periods when you have a right to reside as a jobseeker count towards the five years required for permanent residency (see p245), which then satisfies the right to reside requirement for all benefits.

Who has a right to reside as a jobseeker

If you are in one of the protected groups that can have a free movement right to reside after the end of the transition period at 11pm 31 December 2020 (see p168), or during an earlier period, you have a right to reside as a jobseeker if you are an EEA national and:[67]

- you are in the UK and you can provide evidence that you are seeking employment and have a 'genuine chance of being engaged' (for details on when latter requirement applies, see p184). **Note**: (under the EEA Regulations only) after 91 days, this evidence must be 'compelling' (see p184); *and*
- (rarely required by the benefit authorities) you entered the UK to seek employment, or (under the EEA Regulations only) you are present in the UK seeking employment immediately after having a right to reside as a worker

(except if you retained worker status while involuntarily unemployed – see p202), a student or a self-sufficient person.

If you previously had a right to reside as a jobseeker for 91 days, or you retained either worker or self-employed status while involuntarily unemployed (see p202) for at least six months, in order to have a right to reside as a jobseeker under the EEA Regulations (unless you have been absent from the UK continuously for at least 12 months since having either residence right), you must:[68]

- provide 'compelling' evidence (see below) that you are seeking employment and have a genuine chance of being engaged from the start of your current period of residence as a jobseeker; *and*
- (rarely required by the benefit authorities) have since had an absence from the UK.

Note: if you are refused benefit because of a requirement that is in the EEA Regulations only, you may be able to challenge the decision on the basis that these regulations should be interpreted in accordance with EU caselaw and legal principles (see p174) and the regulations cannot interpret the category of jobseeker more narrowly than the Court of Justice of the European Union (CJEU).[69]

Croatian, A2 and A8 nationals

If you are a Croatian, A2 or A8 national, you did not have a right to reside as a jobseeker during the period of restrictions, if these restrictions applied to you (see p176).[70] **Note:** the extension of the restrictions on A8 nationals from 30 April 2009 to 30 April 2011 has been held to be unlawful.[71] This means that if you are an A8 national, retrospectively, you were not excluded from having had a right to reside as a jobseeker during this two-year period.

For how long do you have a right to reside as a jobseeker

There is no time limit on how long you can have a right to reside as a jobseeker. It continues for as long as you can provide the required evidence that you are continuing to seek work and have a genuine chance of being engaged.[72] However, under the EEA Regulations, in order to continue to have a right to reside as a jobseeker for longer than 91 days, this evidence must be 'compelling' (see below).

Providing evidence

To have a right to reside as a jobseeker, you must provide evidence that you are seeking employment and have a genuine chance of being engaged. See below for the type of employment you must be looking for and have a genuine chance of obtaining and when you must show this genuine chance.

Under the EEA Regulations (but not under EU law), this evidence must be 'compelling':[73]

- in order to continue to have a right to reside as a jobseeker for more than 91 days;
- from the start of your period of residence as a jobseeker (but see note below) if you previously:
  - had a right to reside as a jobseeker for a total of 91 days; *or*
  - retained worker or self-employed status while involuntarily unemployed (see p202) for at least six months.

Note:
- If you have had an absence from the UK for a continuous period of at least 12 months, on your return you can have 91 days with a right to reside as a jobseeker before your evidence must be compelling.[74]
- If you previously had a right to reside as a jobseeker for at least 91 days, or you retained worker or self-employed status for at least six months, the EEA Regulations require you to have been absent from the UK before you can have a period with a right to reside as a jobseeker.[75] However, the benefit authorities have not been enforcing this requirement, except in very rare cases.

Providing compelling evidence: the 'genuine prospects of work test'

The **'genuine prospects of work test'** is a term used by the benefit authorities, including in their guidance. It refers to the above requirement in the EEA Regulations for the evidence that you are continuing to seek work and have a genuine chance of being engaged to be 'compelling' after 91 days as a jobseeker.

Note: new guidance confirms this test no longer applies to those retaining worker or self-employed status on the basis of being involuntarily unemployed for longer than six months (see p202).[76]

Although the terms and the detail of the guidance emphasise the need for evidence that you have a 'genuine chance of being engaged' over the need for evidence that you are continuing to seek work, the EEA Regulations require both.

If you are asked to provide compelling evidence to satisfy the 'genuine prospects of work test', or you are told that you have failed to do so, note the following.

1. Check whether this test should be applied to you. If you have a right to reside other than as a jobseeker, this test does not apply to you at any point.[77] You can continue to receive the benefit or tax credit you are claiming for as long as your other residency right continues. However, this is frequently overlooked. If you have another right to reside, make sure the Department for Work and Pensions (DWP) or HM Revenue and Customs (HMRC) is aware of this and make it clear that your other right to reside means that the test should not be applied to you. **Note:** if you are claiming benefit while working part time, provided this work gives you worker (see p189) or self-employed status (see p196), the guidance to decision makers confirms that you are not subject to the test.[78]

2. Check whether the test has been applied to you at the right time. If your only right to reside is as a jobseeker, it applies after 91 days.[79] However, if you previously had a right to reside as a jobseeker for 91 days, the test will be applied to you from the first day of this current period of residence as a jobseeker, unless since then you have had an absence from

the UK of a continuous period of 12 months. Although you are required to provide compelling evidence after 91 days of having a right to reside as a jobseeker, the DWP tends to follow guidance stating that only periods of entitlement to income-based or contribution-based JSA count towards the 91 days.[80] This guidance also states that certain periods can be disregarded when calculating the 91-day period, including up to 13 weeks when you are treated as being available for work because you have experienced domestic violence, periods of temporary absence when you are treated as being in Great Britain (see p318) and periods of sickness.[81]

3. The term 'compelling' is not defined in the legislation and, therefore, should have its ordinary, everyday meaning. The Upper Tribunal held that the requirement to provide 'compelling' evidence means you are required to provide evidence that shows, on the balance of probabilities, that you are seeking employment and have a genuine chance of being engaged and that to require a higher standard of proof is contrary to EU law.[82] In a different case, the Upper Tribunal held that when determining whether you have a genuine chance of being engaged, a period of six months or more seeking employment without success is a relevant factor to be taken into account, but only one among others.[83]

4. Whether you have a genuine chance of being engaged requires looking forward, and so future events are also relevant.[84] Provide evidence of any qualifications and experience you expect to get in the near future. If you have appealed against a decision that you have not provided compelling evidence, the tribunal can draw conclusions from events that occurred after the time of the decision about circumstances at or before that time. For example, obtaining a job six weeks after the decision is evidence of your chance of being engaged on the date of the decision.[85] **Note:** the CJEU recently held that a jobseeker cannot be required to show a genuine chance of being engaged until after a 'reasonable period', which could be six months.[86]

5. In rare circumstances, if you have an offer of a job that you cannot take up immediately, but which is being held open for you and is due to start in less than three months, you may have a right to reside as a 'worker' (see p189).

6. DWP guidance to decision makers includes lists of examples of relevant evidence.[87] This guidance wrongly emphasizes the need for there to have been a change in your circumstances for your evidence to be accepted as compelling; the Upper Tribunal has held that a change of circumstances is just one factor to take into account. If the limited way in which the guidance is framed caused the decision maker to fail to ask all the relevant questions about your evidence and you appeal, the First-tier Tribunal may need to ask a broader range of questions.[88]

7. The introduction of universal credit (UC) has greatly reduced the relevance of this requirement for benefit claimants who are jobseekers. That is because a right to reside as a jobeeker only satisfies the right to reside requirement for income-based JSA (and most of these claims have now been terminated), child benefit and CTC. In practice, HMRC only requires compelling evidence from jobseekers claiming child benefit and CTC claims occasionally, and if HMRC does so, it should clearly request the evidence required from you.[89]

8. For further details, see p161 and pp178–181 of the 11th edition of this *Handbook*.

Employment you must seek and have a genuine chance of obtaining

In order to have a right to reside as a jobseeker, you must be looking for and have a genuine chance of obtaining employment that would count as sufficient for you to be a 'worker' (see p190) if you obtained it. The CJEU recently held that a jobseeker cannot be required to show a genuine chance of being engaged until after a 'reasonable period', which could be six months.[90] **Note:** if you are only looking for work on a self-employed basis because you are establishing yourself as self-employed, you may have a right of residence as a self-employed person (see p196).

In most cases, you should be accepted as seeking employment and having a genuine chance of being engaged if you are 'signing on' and provide evidence that you are actively seeking and available for work for JSA or national insurance (NI) credits, or that you satisfy the work search and work availability requirements if you come under the UC system.

There are only be a few unusual circumstances in which you would satisfy these conditions and not be accepted as having a genuine chance of being engaged.[91] If the decision maker decides you do not have a genuine chance of being engaged, argue that your case is not one of these rare cases. It may help to look in detail at the requirements that you already satisfy. For example, if you have placed restrictions on your availability, but because you can still show you have reasonable prospects of securing employment, these have been accepted for the purpose of your JSA claim, you may be able to argue that it is irrational to decide that you do not have a genuine chance of being engaged. This argument was discussed at the Upper Tribunal, but it was accepted that it did not apply in any of the cases in question, and so no decision was required.[92]

There is no change to the type of work you must be seeking and have a genuine chance of obtaining after 91 days, when you are required to provide compelling evidence of this (see above).

If you have not claimed jobseeker's allowance

You do not need to have claimed or be receiving JSA in order to have a right to reside as a jobseeker: you must simply be an EEA national and provide evidence that you are seeking employment and have a genuine chance of being engaged.[93]

The most straightforward way of demonstrating that you meet these requirements is to claim contribution-based JSA on the basis that you satisfy the work search and work availability requirements, or NI credits on the basis of unemployment.

However, if you are not eligible for benefit or NI credits, or you are waiting for a decision on your claim, or you have not made a claim, you can still have a right to reside as a jobseeker if you provide evidence you are seeking employment and have a genuine chance of being engaged. This could be relevant, for example, if you want to claim child benefit or you want to count the period towards the continuous five years required for permanent residence (see p245).

Benefit entitlement

Although having right to reside as a jobseeker only satisfies the right to reside requirement for three benefits (see below), having this right to reside in the past can also assist with current entitlement to other benefits, if:

- you had a right to reside as a jobseeker (or family member of a jobseeker) on 31 December 2020, because that can mean that you are (until at least 30 June 2021) in a protected group that can have *other* free movement rights, and, if you are an EEA national, not be defined as a 'person subject to immigration control'. For further details, including the duration of these protections, see p168; *or*
- you had a right to reside as a jobseeker in the past as part of a period of five years of residing in the UK with free movement residence rights and therefore have a permanent right to reside (see p245). If you had this permanent right to reside on 31 December 2020 (or had lost it due to being absent from the UK for more than two years, but your absence was less than five years on that date), that can mean you are in a protected group, as above.

If you have a right to reside as a jobseeker, this satisfies the right to reside requirement for:

- child benefit;
- income-based JSA; *and*
- CTC.

In addition to having a right to reside:

- for child benefit and CTC, you must also have been living in the UK for the three months prior to your claim, unless you are exempt from this requirement (see p127);
- for income-based JSA, in order to satisfy the habitual residence test you must be accepted as 'habitually resident in fact' (see p146) and must have been living in the common travel area for the three months prior to your claim (see p127).

However, in almost all circumstances, you cannot make a new claim for CTC or income-based JSA and must claim UC instead.

If you have a right to reside as a jobseeker, this does *not* satisfy the right to reside requirement for:

- UC;
- housing benefit (HB) (but see below);
- income support;
- income-related employment and support allowance (ESA);
- pension credit.

You must therefore have another right to reside to get one of the above benefits (other than another excluded right to reside – see p152).

Jobseekers have more limited benefit entitlement than most other groups with European free movement residence rights under EU law. Under EU Directive 2004/38, the UK is not obliged to provide entitlement to social assistance to those with a right to reside as a jobseeker.[94] However, it is required to give EEA jobseekers who have established real links with the UK labour market equal access to the financial benefits that are intended to facilitate access to that labour market as British citizens.[95]

Note: the CJEU has held that financial benefits intended to facilitate access to the UK labour market must be made available to EEA jobseekers on an equal basis to British citizens.[96] It may be arguable that UC is a benefit designed to facilitate access to the labour market, and that it is therefore unlawful to exclude someone whose only right to reside is as a jobseeker. However, the Court of Appeal rejected this argument in relation to income-related ESA as that benefit was held not to be one designed to facilitate access to the labour market and therefore excluding access to it was not unlawful.[97]

Housing benefit

If you have a right to reside as a jobseeker, this does not satisfy the right to reside requirement for HB.[98]

However, you are exempt from the habitual residence test for HB (see p142) if you are receiving income-based JSA and either you:

- have a right to reside other than one that is excluded for HB (see p152); *or*
- have been receiving both HB and income-based JSA since 31 March 2014. Your exemption on this basis ends when either you cease to be entitled to that income-based JSA or you make a new claim for HB.[99]

10. **Workers**

Since the end of the transition period at 11pm on 31 December 2020, you can only have a free movement right to reside, including as a worker (or family member of a worker), while you are in one of the protected groups that can have these rights (see p168).

If you are in one of the protected groups, or for a period before the end of the transition period, you may have a right to reside as a 'worker' if you are a European Economic Area (EEA) national working in the UK (see below). You may also have a right to reside if you are a family member (see p218) of a worker. Once you have established worker status, it is important to be clear when you cease to be a worker (see p195). In limited circumstances, you can retain your worker status after you stop being a worker (see p201).

If you have a right to reside as a worker, as someone who has retained worker status, or as the family member of a worker, your right to reside satisfies the right to reside requirement for all benefits.

If you had a right to reside as a worker (or family member of a worker) on 31 December 2020, and on that date, you did not have leave granted under the European Union (EU) Settlement Scheme, you are (until at least 30 June 2021) in one of the protected groups that can use free movement residence rights. If you are an EEA national, these protections also mean that you cannot be defined as a 'person subject to immigration control' (see p81). For further details, including the duration of these protections, see p168.

Who has a right to reside as a worker

If you are in one of the protected groups that can have a free movement right to reside after the end of the transition period at 11pm on 31 December 2020 (see p168), or during an earlier period, you have a right to reside as a worker if you are an EEA national in the UK and:[100]

- you are in an employment relationship (see p192); *and*
- the work you do entails activities that are 'genuine and effective', rather than 'marginal and ancillary' (see p194).

The EEA Regulations cross-refer to EU law for the meaning of 'worker'.[101] However, the term 'worker' is not defined in EU legislation. Instead, the above conditions, and their meaning, have been established through EU caselaw, and this caselaw must be used to interpret the concept (see p174).

The reason why you moved to the UK is irrelevant provided you meet the above conditions.[102] For example, if your main intention in coming to the UK was to study, that is not relevant when determining whether you are a worker.[103]

Your motives for seeking employment can be taken into account when determining whether you are pursuing activity as an employed person. However, once it is established that you are, your motives are irrelevant.

Note:

- If you have been a worker, you do not necessarily lose this status just because you stop working. For more information on when you cease being a worker, see p195, and for the circumstances in which you can retain your worker status, see p201.
- If you are an EEA national and on 31 December 2020, and continuously since then, you have been working in the UK while 'not primarily resident in the UK', you may have rights as a 'frontier worker' (see p256). These rights include being exempt from the habitual residence test for means-tested benefits (see p142).

Croatian, A2 and A8 nationals

If you are a Croatian or A2 national and during the period of restrictions (1 July 2013 to 30 June 2018 for Croatian, and 1 January 2007 to 31 December 2013 for A2, nationals) you were subject to worker authorisation, you did not have a right to reside as a worker unless you held an accession worker authorisation document and worked in accordance with it (see p180).[104]

If you were an A8 national and during the period of restrictions (1 May 2004 to 30 April 2009) you were required to register your work, you did not have a right to reside as a worker unless you were working for an 'authorised employer' (see p180).[105] The extension of restrictions on A8 nationals from 30 April 2009 to 30 April 2011 has been held to be unlawful (see p176).[106] This means that you can retrospectively be accepted as having had worker status during this period, even if this would not have been accepted at the time because you were not working for an 'authorised employer'.[107]

Guidance to decision makers

Decision makers are advised to follow a two-stage process when determining whether you are, or were, a worker (or self-employed).[108] Although this guidance is not legally binding, it is helpful to know its content either to offset potential problems before your claim is decided or to challenge an incorrect decision more effectively.

The guidance advises decision makers first to establish whether your average gross earnings reach a minimum earnings threshold equal to the level at which you start to pay national insurance contributions. This is £183 a week (£792 a month) in 2020/21 and will be £184 a week (£797 a month) in 2021/22. If your average gross earnings were at least this amount for a continuous period of three months immediately before you claim benefit, you are automatically accepted as a worker (or self-employed).

If your earnings did not meet this threshold, the guidance is clear that, in all cases, decision makers should then take into account all your circumstances in relation to the criteria set out below to establish whether your activity was genuine and effective, rather than marginal and ancillary, to determine whether you are (or were) a worker (or self-employed).[109]

You should not be told that you are not a worker (or self-employed) just because you have not met the minimum earnings threshold for three months. It may be useful to refer the decision maker or First-tier Tribunal to a recent Upper Tribunal decision, which held that a local authority was wrong to decide that a housing benefit claimant had ceased to be self-employed when her earnings decreased below the minimum earnings threshold, and that this error was due to the local authority failing to apply the second part of the guidance and take into account of all of the circumstances of her self-employment.[110]

Employment relationship

You count as being in an 'employment relationship' if you:[111]

- provide services;
- receive remuneration in return for those services (see below);
- perform your work under the direction of another person (see below).

The services you provide must entail activities that are 'genuine and effective' as opposed to 'marginal and ancillary' (see p194).

Although, in general, your employment must have started for you to be a worker, you may be a worker if you have moved to the UK to take up a job offer and it is not possible for you to begin work immediately but the offer is being held open for you.[112]

What counts as remuneration

In order to be a worker, you must receive 'remuneration' in return for the services you provide.

If you do voluntary work and receive payments for expenses, you are not a worker.[113] This is because the payments you receive are not provided in return for the services you perform, but rather to compensate you for the expenses you have incurred in providing them.

You can still count as a worker if the remuneration you receive is in the form of payment in kind rather than, or in addition to, money.[114]

Working under the direction of another person

To count as a worker, you must perform the services for, and under the direction of, someone else – ie, there must be someone who can tell you how to do the work. If you provide services in return for remuneration and you are not under the direction of another person, you count as self-employed (see p196) rather than a worker.[115]

If you are taxed as a self-employed person, this by itself does not prevent you from being in an employment relationship, although it is a relevant factor. For example, many people who work in the construction industry and pay tax as subcontractors under the Construction Industry Scheme provide services in return for payment and work under the direction of another person. They are therefore workers and not self-employed.

It does not matter whether the person or organisation that provides the remuneration is the same as the person or organisation to whom you provide services.[116]

'Cash in hand', agency and 'trafficked' work

You count as being in an employment relationship if you provide services in return for renumeration under the direction of another person. This is not affected by the fact that:

- you are paid 'cash in hand'. The concept of 'worker' is an economic status, rather than a legal one.[117] However, you must still provide evidence of your employment;
- you were 'trafficked' into the work. Even if you could get discretionary leave to remain in the UK as a result of the trafficking (which would mean you were exempt from the habitual residence test for means-tested benefits – see p142), that does not prevent you from having a free movement right to reside as a worker on the basis of your work.[118] You still need to provide evidence of your employment;
- you did not declare the work to the Department for Work and Pensions at the time.[119] This is likely to be most relevant when you are relying on past periods of employment;
- the person or organisation to whom you provide the services is different from the person or organisation that pays you for these – eg, if you are 'employed' by an employment agency.[120] However, the activities entailed in your provision of services must still be accepted as genuine and effective rather than marginal and ancillary (see below and, in particular p195, regarding the regularity of the work). There is nothing inherent in working for an agency that would exclude your activities from being genuine and effective and that depends on the facts of each case.[121]

Example

Nora is a Hungarian national working as a nurse 'employed' by an employment agency. The payment she receives is via the agency, but the services are provided to a private care home. The care home has a contractual relationship with the agency, rather than with Nora, and it pays the agency. Nora still counts as a worker because she is providing services and doing so in return for remuneration, even though there is a separation between the care home where she provides the services and the agency that pays her.

For your worker status to be accepted, you must provide evidence of your employment and this may be harder to do in some of the circumstances above, such as if you are paid cash in hand or you were trafficked into the work. The benefit authority must take your own account of your work into account as evidence, unless it is self-contradictory or inherently improbable (see p456). If you have provided details of your employment to another government agency and these have been accepted (eg, to the police as part of an investigation of trafficking), a record of these should be accepted as relevant evidence when determining whether you have worker status.[122] See Chapter 20 for more information on evidence requirements and p470 for evidence of your work.

'Genuine and effective', not 'marginal and ancillary'

You only have a right to reside as a worker if the services you provide entail activities that are 'genuine and effective', as opposed to those that are on such a small scale as to be regarded as 'marginal and ancillary'.[123]

When deciding this, the decision maker must assess, as a whole, all the circumstances of your case.[124] See p191 for details of the guidance issued to decision makers. Relevant factors that must be considered include:

- the number of hours you work;
- the duration of your employment;
- the level of earnings;
- whether the work is regular or erratic;
- other employment rights;
- whether the work is 'marginal and ancillary' – ie, is insignificant in scale, is not for the economic benefit of the employer or is just a small part of a more substantial relationship between you and the employer.

Number of hours worked

The number of hours you work in a given period is a relevant factor when determining whether your work is genuine and effective. There is no minimum number of hours you must work. Provided other factors indicate that the work is genuine and effective, even work for a few hours a week can count as genuine and effective.

In one case, the Court of Justice of the European Union (CJEU) held that, after an overall assessment of the employment relationship, the possibility could not be ruled out that someone who worked only 5.5 hours a week could be a worker.[125] However, in most circumstances, you must work for more than 5.5 hours a week for your activity to be accepted as genuine and effective. In one case, someone working as an au pair for 13 hours a week for £35 per week plus board and lodging, for a duration of 5.5 weeks, was held to be a worker.[126]

The duration of the employment

The duration of the employment is a relevant factor to consider when deciding whether or not your work is genuine and effective. However, it is not conclusive, so if your work only lasts a short time, this fact by itself cannot exclude you from being a worker.[127]

Provided other factors indicate that the work you do is genuine and effective, even very short periods of work can still be sufficient to mean you have worker status while doing this work. In one case, the Court of Appeal found that someone was a worker during employment that was (and was always known to be) of two weeks' duration.[128] Although a short duration of employment that was fixed from the outset may not prevent you from being a worker,[129] work that is curtailed prematurely may be more likely to be considered to be genuine and effective.[130] The CJEU recently held that employment of two weeks' duration, which was not a fixed-term contract but which ended because of involuntary unemployment, meant the person had acquired worker status that was then retained for six months because he had registered as a jobseeker (see p202).[131]

Level of earnings

If your earnings are very low, this may be a factor that indicates that your work is not genuine and effective. However, low earnings cannot, by themselves, prevent you from being a worker. Even if your earnings are so low that they do not meet your needs and you supplement them by claiming means-tested benefits, this does not prevent you from being a worker.[132]

Note: your earnings can include non-monetary payments in kind (see p192).

Irregular or erratic work

If you are in an employment relationship in which you are only occasionally called upon to work, this may indicate that your work is not genuine and effective. However, the decision maker must always look at all your circumstances. There is nothing inherent in an 'on-call' or 'zero-hour' contract that prevents you from being a worker; it depends on the work you do.[133] Similarly, there is nothing inherent in doing temporary work for an agency that prevents you from being a worker. If the work is regular, rather than intermittent, and for a prolonged period or with a high likelihood of further work being obtained, you may be a worker.[134]

Other employment rights

If you have a right in your contract of employment (eg, to paid holidays or sick pay), or you are a member of a trade union recognised by your employer, these are factors that may indicate that your employment is genuine and effective.[135]

Work not for an economic purpose or part of a wider relationship

Work may count as 'marginal' or 'ancillary' if it is done as part of another relationship which is more significant – eg, if a lodger performs a small task for her/his landlord as part of the terms of her/his tenancy.[136]

Work does not count as 'genuine and effective' if its main purpose is not for the economic benefit of the employer – eg, if the work is a means of rehabilitation to enable people with health problems to reintegrate into the labour market. Similarly, fostering children or caring for a person with disabilities have been held not to be economic activities and receipt of a fostering allowance or carer's allowance does not count as remuneration in a commercial sense.[137]

When you cease to be a worker

You only cease to be a worker when the employment relationship (see p192) ends. While you are still under a contract of employment, you continue to be a worker. You are therefore still a worker if you are a woman on maternity leave (including unpaid maternity leave), or if you are on holiday, sick or compassionate leave (including if it is unpaid).[138] Similarly, you are still a worker during periods when you have been furloughed.

If you have ceased to be a worker, you may retain your worker status in certain circumstances (see p201).

Benefit entitlement

If you have a right to reside as a worker, or as a family member (see p218) of a worker, this satisfies the right to reside requirement for all benefits that have such a requirement (see p151). You are also exempt from the habitual residence test for means-tested benefits (see p142) and therefore do not need to be 'habitually resident in fact' (see p146). You are also exempt from the requirement to have been living in the UK for the past three months for child benefit and child tax credit, see p129.

Your current entitlement to benefits can be assisted if you had a right to reside as a worker, or as a family member of a worker, in the past – specifically:

- on 31 December 2020, because this can mean that you are (until at least 30 June 2021) in a protected group that can have free movement rights, and, if you are an EEA national, not be defined as a 'person subject to immigration control' (see p81). For further details, including the duration of these protections (see p168); *or*
- as part of a period of five years of residing in the UK with free movement residence rights which enabled you to acquire a permanent right to reside (see p244). If you had this permanent right to reside on 31 December 2020 (or had lost it due to being absent from the UK for more than two years, but your absence was less than five years on that date), that can mean you are in a protected group as above.

See p470 for information on providing evidence of work.

11. Self-employed people

Since the end of the transition period at 11pm on 31 December 2020, you can only have a free movement right to reside, including as a self-employed person (or family member of a self-employed person), while you are in one of the protected groups that can have these rights (see p168).

If you are in one of the protected groups, or for a period before the end of the transition period, you may have a right to reside as a 'self-employed person' if you are a European Economic Area (EEA) national undertaking self-employed activity in the UK. You may also have a right to reside if you are a family member (see p218) of a self-employed person. Once you have established your status as a self-employed person, it is important to be clear when you cease to be self-employed (see p199). In limited circumstances, you can retain your status as a self-employed person after you cease self-employed activity (see p201).

If you have a right to reside as a self-employed person, as someone who has retained status as a self-employed person, or as a family member of a self-employed person, your right to reside satisfies the right to reside requirement for all benefits.

If you had a right to reside as a self-employed person (or family member of a self-employed person) on 31 December 2020, and on that date, you did not have leave granted under the European Union (EU) Settlement Scheme, you are (until at least 30 June 2021) in one of the protected groups that can use free movement residence rights. If you are an EEA national, these protections also mean that you cannot be defined as a 'person subject to immigration control' (see p81). For further details, including the duration of these protections, see p168.

Who has a right to reside as a self-employed person

If you are in one of the protected groups that can have a free movement right to reside after the end of the transition period at 11pm on 31 December 2020 (see p168), or during an earlier period, you have a right to reside as a self-employed person if you are an EEA national in the UK and:[139]

- you provide services;
- you receive remuneration in return for those services (see p192);
- you do not perform your work under the direction of another person (see p192); *and*
- the work you do entails activities that are 'genuine and effective', rather than 'marginal and ancillary' (see p194).

The EEA Regulations cross-refer to EU law for the meaning of 'self-employed person'.[140] However, the term 'self-employed person' is not defined in EU legislation. Instead the above requirements, and their meaning, have been established through EU caselaw, and this caselaw must be used to interpret the concept (see p174).

The meanings of the above conditions are the same as they are for workers. The main difference between the definition of a self-employed person and a worker is that the work a self-employed person does is not done under the direction of another person.

Whether or not you satisfy these requirements depends on all your circumstances. For example, in one case, the Upper Tribunal held that someone selling the *Big Issue* was self-employed, as the activities involved were 'genuine and effective'.[141] A subsequent case held that someone selling the *Big Issue* was not self-employed, as his activities were not genuine and effective (although this decision was largely due to there being insufficient evidence for the whole period and, arguably, the tribunal did not consider all the relevant circumstances adequately).[142] Recently, the Upper Tribunal has held that the First-tier Tribunal had not made an error of law in finding that someone selling the *Big Issue* was not self-employed because her activities were not genuine and effective. It held that the First-tier Tribunal *had* considered all the relevant factors and not, for example, just looked at the person's low level of earnings.[143]

Fostering children and caring for a person with disabilities have both been held not to be self-employment because they are not economic activities and the fostering allowance or carer's allowance received is not remuneration in a commercial sense.[144]

Decision makers are advised in guidance to follow a two-stage process when determining whether you are, or were, self-employed (or a worker).[145] Although this guidance is not legally binding, it is helpful to know its content either to pre-empt potential problems before your claim is decided or to challenge an incorrect decision more effectively (see p191).

Note: if you are an EEA national and on 31 December 2020, and continuously since then, you have been self-employed in the UK while 'not primarily resident in the UK' you may have rights as a 'frontier worker' (see p256), including being exempt from the habitual residence test for means-tested benefits (see p59).

Croatian, A2 and A8 nationals

If you are a Croatian, A2 or A8 national and were self-employed during the relevant period of restrictions (see p176), your residence rights as a self-employed person were exactly the same as for nationals of any other EEA country – there were no restrictions for self-employed people.

When you become and cease to be self-employed

Whether you have become self-employed or you have ceased to be self-employed can be harder to determine than whether you have become a worker or you have ceased to be a worker. Unlike a person who is employed, a person who is self-employed does not have a contract of employment that starts and ends on a particular date. You may count as self-employed when you are setting yourself up to work as a self-employed person and continue to count as self-employed, despite the fact that you have no work coming in for the time being.

When you become self-employed

The EEA Regulations define you as a self-employed person if you are established in the UK in order to pursue activity as a self-employed person within the meaning of (or, for period until 31 December 2020, 'in accordance with'[146]) Article 49 of the Treaty on the Functioning of the European Union.[147] The treaty prohibits restrictions on the freedom of establishment, including 'the right to take up and pursue activities as a self-employed person and to set up and manage undertakings'.[148]

However, you must have more than an intention to pursue self-employed activity, and you must provide evidence of the steps you have taken or the ways in which you have set yourself up as self-employed.[149] Exactly what steps you must take depends on your particular circumstances. It helps if you have registered with HM Revenue and Customs (HMRC) as self-employed. However, if you have not registered, this does not necessarily mean you are not self-employed.[150]

Relevant steps include:

- advertising your services;
- researching opportunities to find customers;
- setting up your accounts;
- registering with HMRC as self-employed for purposes of national insurance contributions and taxes;
- obtaining equipment required for the work you intend to do;
- setting up a website for your business.

The above steps are only examples; you do not have to take any of these particular steps, but the more steps you have taken, the more likely it is that you will be accepted as having a right to reside as a self-employed person.

Note: if you are told that you do not have residence rights as a self-employed person until you have been earning money from your self-employed activity for three months, and/or earning a certain amount of money, this is incorrect. It is likely to be based on an incorrect interpretation of decision makers' guidance (see p191).

For more information on evidence of self-employment, see p470.

When you cease to be self-employed

If you have stopped all your self-employed activity and do not intend to resume that activity, it is clear that you have ceased to be a self-employed person. However, some situations are less clear – eg, if you are in a temporary lull, you can continue to be a self-employed person despite having no current work. Whether you continue to be a self-employed person during a period when you have little or no work depends on your particular circumstances and the evidence you provide.[151]

Factors that are relevant in determining whether or not you have ceased self-employment include:[152]

- the amount of work you have coming in;
- steps you are taking to find new work;
- whether you are continuing to market your services;
- whether you are developing your business in new directions;
- whether you are maintaining your accounts;
- if you were entitled to a payment from the Self-Employment Income Support Scheme (payable if your self-employed income had been reduced due to your

activity, capacity or demand being due to the coronavirus pandemic, and entitlement requiring a declaration that you intended to continue trading);
- your motives and intentions.

Which factors are relevant depends on the nature of your self-employment and all your circumstances. However, the more factors that show you are still undertaking self-employed activity, the stronger your argument that you have not ceased to be a self-employed person.

If you have ceased to be self-employed, you may be able to retain your self-employed status in certain circumstances (see p201).

Pregnancy

If you are working on a self-employed basis and you become pregnant, you can continue to count as self-employed during your maternity period when you do no self-employed work, provided you intend to resume your self-employment at the end of your maternity period.[153] The Upper Tribunal, in two linked cases, emphasised the need for careful fact finding to establish whether self-employment is maintained during maternity leave. This includes establishing whether the self-employment was 'genuine and effective' before the start of maternity leave and what steps are being taken to maintain that self-employment, taking into account all the circumstances, even if little, or no, actual work is done. Only one of the women in these cases was found, due to her particular circumstances, to have maintained her self-employed status during her maternity period.[154] The question of whether the other woman could *retain* her self-employed status, taking into account European caselaw on retaining worker status when stopping work because of late pregnancy,[155] was referred to the Court of Justice of the European Union, which held that she did (see p208).[156]

Benefit entitlement

If you have a right to reside as a self-employed person, or as a family member (see p218) of a self-employed person, this satisfies the right to reside requirement for all benefits that have such a requirement (see p151). You are also exempt from the habitual residence test for means-tested benefits (see p142), and therefore do not need to be 'habitually resident in fact' (see p146). You are also exempt from the requirement to have been living in the UK for the past three months for child benefit and child tax credit (see p129).

Your current entitlement to benefits can be assisted if you had a right to reside as a self-employed person, or as a family member of a self-employed person, in the past – specifically:
- on 31 December 2020, because this can mean that you are (until at least 30 June 2021) in a protected group that can have free movement rights, and, if you are an EEA national, not be defined as a 'person subject to immigration

control' (see p81). For further details, including the duration of these protections (see p168); *or*

- as part of a period of five years of residing in the UK with free movement residence rights that enabled you to acquire a permanent right to reside (see p244). If you had this permanent right to reside on 31 December 2020 (or had lost it due to being absent from the UK for more than two years, but your absence was less than five years on that date), that can mean you are in a protected group as above.

See p470 for information on providing evidence of self-employment.

12. Retaining worker or self-employed status

Since the end of the transition period at 11pm on 31 December 2020, you can only have a free movement right to reside, including retained worker or self-employed status (or as the family member of either), while you are in one of the protected groups that can have these rights (see p168).

If you are in one of the protected groups, or for a period before the end of the transition period, you can retain the status of 'worker' or 'self-employed', even though you are no longer working, if:[157]

- you are involuntarily unemployed and registered as a jobseeker (see p202);
- you are undertaking vocational training (see p206);
- you are temporarily unable to work because of an illness or accident (see p206);
- you are unable to work because you are in the late stages of pregnancy or have just given birth (see note below).[158]

Before arguing that you have retained your worker or self-employed status, check whether you have actually ceased to be a worker (see p195) or self-employed (see p199). For example, if you are off work on unpaid sick leave but you can return to your job when you are better, you are still a worker and so do not need to argue that you have retained your worker status. Similarly, you may still count as self-employed if you are in a temporary period with little or no work.

Note:

- If you had retained worker or self-employed status (or you were the family member of an European Economic Area, EEA, national who had that status) on 31 December 2020, and on that date, you (and, if you were the family member, s/he) did not have leave granted under the European Union (EU) Settlement Scheme, you are (until at least 30 June 2021) in one of the protected groups that can use free movement residence rights. If you are an EEA national, these protections also mean that you cannot be defined as a 'person subject to immigration control' (see p81). For further details, including the duration of these protections (see p168).

- If you are retaining your worker or self-employed status on the basis of the last bullet point above, either on 31 December 2020 as the basis of your being in a protected group or since that date, see the note on p208.
- Following a decision by the Court of Justice of the European Union (CJEU) that a self-employed man could retain his self-employed status when he was involuntarily unemployed and registered as a jobseeker,[159] the EEA Regulations were amended from 24 July 2018 to include the right of self-employed people to retain their status in the same circumstances as workers. If these circumstances applied to you before 24 July 2018, you can rely on the CJEU judgment.[160]
- It may also be possible to argue that you can retain your worker or self-employed status in other circumstances to those listed above. The CJEU has held that EU Directive 2004/38 does not provide an exhaustive list of such circumstances.[161] However, the Upper Tribunal held that a man who had been required, for a temporary period, to stop work to care for his children did not retain his worker status.[162]

Croatian, A2 and A8 nationals

If you are a Croatian or A2 or A8 national who was subject to restrictions (see p177), you could not retain your worker status during the relevant period of restrictions in the ways described in this section. However, if you were an A8 national subject to restrictions and you stopped working during the first month of employment, you could retain your worker status in the ways described in this section for the remainder of that month.[163]

The extension of the restrictions on A8 nationals from 30 April 2009 to 30 April 2011 has now been held to be unlawful (see p176).[164] This means that if you would have been accepted as having retained your worker status during these two years were it not for your being subject to restrictions at that time, you can retrospectively be accepted as having retained your worker status during this period.[165]

If you are a Croatian, A2 or A8 national and were self-employed during the relevant periods of restrictions, you could retain your self-employed status in exactly the same way as nationals of any other EEA country – there were no restrictions on retaining self-employed status.

You are involuntarily unemployed and registered as a jobseeker

You retain your status as a worker or self-employed person if you:[166]
- are recorded as involuntarily unemployed (see below); *and*
- have registered yourself as a jobseeker with the relevant employment office (see p204); *and*

- provide evidence that you are seeking employment (or, to retain self-employed status, seeking either employment or self-employment).

In addition to the above, the EEA Regulations contain requirements that are very rarely enforced by benefit authorities that in order to:[167]

- retain your worker or self-employed status beyond six months, your evidence that you are continuing to seek employment (or, to retain self-employed status, continuing to seek either employment or self-employment) must be 'compelling' (see p204); *and*
- retain worker status:
  - you must have entered the UK in order to seek employment; *or*
  - you must be present in the UK seeking employment immediately after having a right to reside as a worker (except if you retained your worker status on this basis), a student or a self-sufficient person; *and*
- retain self-employed status:
  - you must have entered the UK as a self-employed person or in order to seek self-employment; *or*
  - you must be present in the UK seeking self-employment immediately after having a right to reside as a self-employed person (except if you retained your self-employed status on this basis), a student or self-sufficient person.

Involuntary unemployment

You are 'involuntarily unemployed' if you are seeking and are available to take up employment (or self-employment, to retain your status as a self-employed person). This depends on your remaining in the labour market. The circumstances in which you left your last job, or ceased your self-employment, including whether you did so voluntarily, are relevant in determining whether you have remained in the labour market. However, they are just one factor and all your actions and circumstances, both at the time of leaving, or ceasing, work and since then, must also be taken into account.[168]

Example

Karl is German. He was working at a food processing factory for seven months. The shift times changed recently, which meant that when he was on late shifts he had to catch three buses to get home from work. He found this commute exhausting and asked his employer if he could just do the early shift when the bus connections were better. His employer said that all employees must work both early and late shifts, so Karl handed in his notice. Even while working his notice, Karl looked for other alternative work closer to home. He did not find any, but now his job has ended he spends more time contacting potential employers. Karl counts as involuntarily unemployed, despite the fact that he left his previous employment voluntarily.

Most of the caselaw covers the circumstances in which you are involuntarily unemployed for the purpose of retaining worker status because it was decided before the CJEU confirmed that self-employed people can also retain their status on this basis (see p201). However, in the case in which this was confirmed, the CJEU accepted that the man's self-employed activity had ceased because of a lack of work due to the economic downturn, and as this was due to reasons beyond his control, it was 'involuntary unemployment'.[169] More recently, the Upper Tribunal accepted the concession from the Department for Work and Pensions (DWP) that the principles established in caselaw also apply to retaining self-employed status and held that a self-employed driver who lacked the means to obtain a reliable vehicle was involuntarily unemployed.[170]

Registering as a jobseeker

You must register as a jobseeker with the 'relevant employment office'. In the UK, this is Jobcentre Plus.

The best way to register as a jobseeker is to claim universal credit (UC) on the basis that you are searching, and are available, for work and/or jobseeker's allowance (JSA), and show that you continue to satisfy the work search and work availability requirements (or the requirements to be available for and actively seeking work for JSA). Be clear when completing the habitual residence test for UC that you are currently seeking work. If you are not entitled to benefit, contact the job centre and claim national insurance credits on the basis of unemployment. You do not need to receive UC or JSA in order to be registered as a jobseeker.

You may also satisfy the requirement to register as a jobseeker if you claim a benefit that does not require you to look for work (eg, UC while you are the responsible carer of a child under three or pension credit (PC)) and you declare to the job centre in the course of making your claim that you are looking for work – eg, you provide a written statement as part of your habitual residence test.[171] You must provide evidence of your work search. **Note:** this way of registering as a jobseeker is only relevant for retaining your worker or self-employed status and claiming benefit on the basis of having a right to reside as a worker or self-employed person. It does not enable you to claim benefits, such as UC or PC, if your only right to reside is as a jobseeker (as this is an excluded right to reside for those benefits – see p152).

If there was a gap between when your work ended and when you registered as a jobseeker, see p209.

For how long can you retain worker or self-employed status

The length of time you can retain your worker or self-employed status while involuntarily unemployed depends on whether or not you have already been employed or self-employed in the UK for more than a year.

If you were employed or self-employed for more than a year, you can retain your worker or self-employed status on this basis indefinitely, until there is an event that indicates that you have entirely withdrawn from the labour market.[172] Receipt of maternity allowance by a woman who remained registered with employment agencies has been held *not* to be such an event.[173]

You need not have been employed in one continuous job. Also, small gaps between jobs (eg, around two weeks) do not necessarily mean that you were not employed for more than a year.[174] The same principles should also apply to small gaps in self-employed activity.

Although the EEA Regulations state that, to retain your worker or self-employed status on this basis for longer than a continuous period of six months, you must provide 'compelling' evidence of continuing to seek work, new guidance confirms this no longer applies in practice.[175] If your benefit is refused or terminated due to your not being accepted as retaining your status beyond six months, you will need to set out why that is wrong, as summarised below.

Until 31 December 2020, the EEA Regulations also required that, in addition to providing evidence that you were seeking work, you also provided evidence of having a 'genuine chance of being engaged' and that after six months your evidence of both had to be 'compelling' (a requirement referred to by the DWP as the 'genuine prospects of work' test). However, in February 2020 the Upper Tribunal held that the requirement to provide evidence of having a 'genuine chance of being engaged' went beyond what was required under EU law and was, therefore, unlawful.[176] The regulations were then amended to omit this requirement, but note that for earlier periods you can rely on the Upper Tribunal decision. However, the Upper Tribunal also held that the requirements to retain status while involuntarily unemployed do not change at all after six months.[177] New guidance confirms the DWP's acceptance of this and states that the 'genuine prospects of work' test no longer applies to those retaining worker or self-employed status while involuntarily unemployed.[178]

If you were employed for less than a year, the EEA Regulations limit the period during which you can retain your worker or self-employed status while involuntarily unemployed to a maximum of six months.[179] The EU Directive allows you to retain worker status for no less than six months.[180] The CJEU held that worker status could be retained for six months following employment of two weeks' duration, which was not a fixed-term contract and that ended due to involuntary unemployment, provided the person registered as a jobseeker.[181] Applying this decision, the Upper Tribunal recently held that a First-tier Tribunal had been wrong to decide that a man who became involuntarily unemployed could not retain his self-employed status because he had been self-employed for less than a year.[182]

Once you can no longer retain your worker or self-employed status on this basis, you may have a right to reside as a jobseeker (see p182). If so, note that under the the EEA Regulations, you must:[183]

- have a period of absence from the UK (although the benefit authorities have not been enforcing this requirement, except in a few cases); *and*

- (unless your absence was for at least 12 continuous months) provide 'compelling' evidence of seeking employment and having a genuine chance of being engaged from the start of your period of residence as a jobseeker (see p184).

Note: having a right to reside as a jobseeker only satisfies the right to reside requirement for child benefit, child tax credit (CTC) and income-based JSA, but may assist in either if you had this right on 31 December 2020, if it means you are in one of the protected groups that can have a free movement residence right (see p168), and/or may assist you to obtain a permanent right reside after five years of residing with a free movement right to reside in the UK (see p245).

You have started vocational training

You retain your worker or self-employed status, if you have either:[184]

- started vocational training related to your previous employment or, to retain self-employment, related to your previous occupation; *or*
- started vocational training and you are 'involuntarily unemployed' (see p203). This applies if you have to retrain in order to find work that is reasonably equivalent to your former employment.[185]

In general, you should be able to argue that any training or study that can assist you in obtaining employment counts as vocational training. This can include a course leading to a qualification for a particular profession, trade or employment or a course that provides the necessary training or skills.[186] A course can be vocational for you even if it is not vocational for someone else – eg, a photography course if you want to work as a photographer.

Training related to your previous employment or occupation

If you are not involuntarily unemployed, your vocational training must be related to your previous employment for you to retain your worker status or related to your previous occupation for you to retain your self-employed status. For this to apply, there must be a relationship between the purpose of your studies and your previous occupational activity.[187] The decision maker must take into account all your previous occupational activity in the UK, not just your most recent employment.[188] If you consider that the course you are pursuing is related to any of your previous employment in the UK, explain this relationship in detail to the decision maker and provide evidence.

You are temporarily unable to work because of an illness or accident

You can retain your worker or self-employed status if you are temporarily unable to work as a result of an illness or accident.[189]

Always check if you have actually ceased to be a worker (see p195) or self-employed (see p199). For example, if you are off work on unpaid sick leave but you can return to your job when you are better, you are still a worker and so do not need to argue that you have retained your worker status.

As a result of an illness or accident

To retain your worker or self-employed status on this basis, your inability to work must be as a result of an illness or accident.

The test of your inability to work is unrelated to any test in the benefits system – eg, you do not need to show you have 'limited capability for work' or that you are 'incapable of work'. Instead, the test is whether you can be fairly described as unable to do the work you were doing or, if it follows a period in which you were seeking work, the sort of work you were seeking.[190]

You do not need to have claimed a benefit payable on grounds of illness or disability, such as employment and support allowance, or any benefit at all, to retain your right to reside as a worker on this basis.[191] However, if you *have* received benefit paid on the basis of your illness or disability, this is evidence of your inability to work for that period. Otherwise, you need to provide other evidence of your inability to work, such as a medical certificate from your GP.

Your inability to work must be caused by your own illness or accident – eg, you cannot retain your worker status if you are unable to work because you are looking after a child who is ill.[192]

Temporary inability to work

Your inability to work must be temporary. This simply means not permanent.[193] It is your inability to work that must be temporary not your health condition, so you can retain your worker or self-employed status on the basis of a permanent illness or effect of an accident if this fluctuates and causes temporary periods when you are unable to work.[194]

You are considered temporarily unable to work if, taking into account all the available evidence, there is a realistic prospect of your being able to work again and re-enter the labour market.[195]

Note: if there is no reasonable prospect of your being able undertake *any* work again (whether the same as, or different to, the work you did previously), then you cannot *retain* your worker or self-employed status. However, you may have acquired a permanent right to reside on the basis of your permanent incapacity (see p253).

You are pregnant or have recently given birth

If you have established worker or self-employed status and you are now not working because you are pregnant or have recently given birth, you may still count as a worker or as self-employed, or you may be able to retain your worker or self-employed status.

You do not cease to be a worker while you are still under a contract of employment (see p195). You are therefore still a worker while on maternity leave, whether or not it is paid. **Note:** this also applied to Croatian, A2 and A8 nationals who established worker status during the period of restrictions (see p176).[196]

You can remain a self-employed person if you intend to resume your self-employment after your maternity period. This depends on whether you can show that you have remained engaged in genuine and effective self-employed activity, even though you are not working while in your maternity period (see p199).[197]

If you have ceased to be a worker or self-employed, you may retain your worker or self-employed status if you have a pregnancy-related illness that prevents you from working on the basis that you are temporarily unable to work because of an illness or accident (see p206).[198] You can also retain your worker or self-employed status on this basis if you have another illness, unrelated to your pregnancy, that results in your being temporarily unable to work. **Note:** pregnancy itself does not mean you are temporarily unable to work because of an illness or accident.[199]

Stopping work during the late stages of pregnancy or after childbirth

You retain your worker or self-employed status if you stop work (or stop seeking work if you retained your worker or self-employed status while involuntarily unemployed – see p202) because of the physical constraints of the late stages of pregnancy and the aftermath of childbirth, provided you intend to start work again (or start seeking work and thereby retain your worker or self-employed status while involuntarily unemployed) within a 'reasonable period' after the birth of your child.[200]

The Upper Tribunal has held that, in most cases, a 'reasonable period' is 52 weeks, although this may differ if your circumstances are unusual.[201] The Upper Tribunal also held that, in most cases, your 'reasonable period', and therefore the period during which you retain your worker or self-employed status on this basis, starts 11 weeks before your due date. However, in exceptional cases, it could be earlier if the physical constraints of your pregnancy require you to stop work (or to stop seeking work if you have retained worker or self-employed status) sooner, and you can provide evidence of this – eg, if you have a multiple pregnancy or if you can no longer carry out particular requirements of your work.[202]

Note: the CJEU has only recently held that a self-employed woman must retain her status on this basis if her circumstances are comparable to those of a worker who retains her worker status on this basis. The principles established in caselaw concerning the retention of worker status on this basis also apply to retaining self-employed status.[203]

If you intend to work again within a 'reasonable period', you should always make this clear to the decision maker. You should still be accepted as retaining worker or self-employed status on this basis unless you state that you have absolutely no intention of returning to work under any circumstances.[204]

Note: if you are relying on your retained worker or self-employed status on this basis either on 31 December 2020 as the basis of your being in a protected group that can have a free movement right to reside after that date (see p168), or since that date as the right to reside that entitles you to benefit, the benefit authorities may not accept you had, or have, this right to reside. That is because the protections that enable you to use a free movmement right to reside after the end of the transition period specifically refer to free movemement rights under the EEA Regulations and this free movement right is based on European caselaw that has never been included in the EEA Regulations. If your claim for benefit is refused on this basis, challenge that decision and get specialist advice. It is strongly arguable that this free movement right to reside should be accepted. Firstly, it is arguable that while the above circumstances apply to you, you have a right to reside as a worker within the meaning of Article 45 of the Treaty on the Functioning of the European Union (TFEU), or as a self-employed person within the meaning of Article 49 of the TFEU, which is how these terms are defined in the EEA Regulations.[205] Secondly, the protections contained within the EU Withdrawal Agreements applied to all EEA nationals who had *any* European free movement residence right at the end of the transition period and continued to reside in the UK thereafter.[206]

If the basis on which you retain your worker or self-employed status changes

You can continue to retain your worker or self-employed status if you are in one of the groups on p201 and move into another category.[207]

Example

Nikolas is Greek. He worked for 13 months in a hotel. The hotel was losing money and Nikolas was made redundant. He claimed income-based JSA. Five months later, Nikolas became depressed and was unable to carry on looking for work. He claimed UC on the basis of being too ill to work. Nikolas is entitled to UC because he has retained his right to reside as a worker – initially, as someone who was involuntarily unemployed and who had registered as a jobseeker, and then because of his temporary inability to work as a result of his illness.

There is no limit to the number of times you can change the basis on which you retain worker or self-employed status. However, if you lose your worker or self-employed status, you cannot regain it without undertaking further employment or self-employment that gives you worker or self-employed status.

Gaps

If you cease to be a worker or self-employed and do not retain that status, you cannot regain it again. To be a worker or self-employed in the future, you must acquire that status afresh. However, if there is just a gap between your having worker or self-employed status and your being covered by one of the groups that can retain that status on p201, you may not have lost that status. This depends on all your circumstances, including the length of the gap.

Several Upper Tribunal decisions have confirmed that a gap between your employment ending and your registering as a jobseeker while involuntarily unemployed does not necessarily mean that you lose your worker status. The same principles should apply to any gap between your self-employed activity ceasing and your registering as a jobseeker. These decisions have held that the significance of a gap depends on whether the length of the gap, and the reasons for it, indicate that you have left the labour market.[208] If the delay is for more than a few days, all your circumstances (including the reasons for the gap and what you did during that time) should be considered to establish whether there are reasonable grounds for the delay, so that it is not considered an 'undue delay'. The longer the gap, the more compelling the reasons must be.[209]

Arguably, you should be able to retain your worker or self-employed status if there is a gap between your ceasing work and your being temporarily unable to work because of an illness or accident, since there is no requirement for the illness or accident to be the reason for your ceasing work. You do not need to have been receiving any benefit while you were temporarily unable to work, so if there was a delay before you claimed benefit, this does not necessarily mean there was a gap between your being a worker or self-employed and retaining your worker or self-employed status on the basis of your temporary inability to work.[210]

Example

Rita is a Portuguese national who came to the UK a year ago and began full-time work in a restaurant. After eight months she was injured in a cycling accident and so left her job. She did not claim any benefits as she lived with her partner who supported her. She has just separated from her partner and has made a single claim for UC, as she is still unable to work because of her injuries. Rita provides the DWP with a medical certificate that confirms her inability to work since the date of her accident. She satisfies the right to reside requirement for UC as she retains her worker status because she is temporarily unable to work as a result of her accident. There is no gap between her retaining her worker status on this basis and her last day of employment.

You can also retain your worker or self-employed status during a short gap between two different bases on which you can retain that status. Whether the gap is relevant also depends on your circumstances, the bases you are switching between, the length of the gap and your actions during it.

Benefit entitlement

If you retain your worker or self-employed status, this satisfies the right to reside requirement for all benefits that have such a requirement (see p151).

If you are a family member (see p218) of someone who retains her/his worker or self-employed status, your residence rights are the same as if you were the family member of someone who is a worker or someone who is self-employed, and, therefore, you satisfy the right to reside requirement for all the benefits that have this requirement.

If you retain worker or self-employed status (or you are a family member of someone who does), you are also exempt from the habitual residence test for means-tested benefits (see p142), and therefore do not need to be 'habitually resident in fact' (see p146). You are also exempt from the requirement to have been living in the UK for the past three months for child benefit and, if you are in one of the limited circumstances in which you can make a new claim, CTC (see p129).

Your current entitlement to benefits can be assisted if you had retained worker or self-employed status, or were a family member of someone who had either, in the past – specifically:

- on 31 December 2020, because this can mean that you are (until at least 30 June 2021) in a protected group that can have free movement rights, and, if you are an EEA national, not be defined as a 'person subject to immigration control' (see p81). For further details, including the duration of these protections, see p168; *or*
- as part of a period of five years of residing in the UK with free movement residence rights which enabled you to acquire a permanent right to reside (see p244). If you had this permanent right to reside on 31 December 2020 (or had lost it due to being absent from the UK for more than two years, but your absence was less than five years on that date), that can mean you are in a protected group, as above.

13. Self-sufficient people and students

Since the end of the transition period at 11pm on 31 December 2020, you can only have a free movement right to reside, including as a self-sufficient person (or as the family member of a self-sufficient person), while you are in one of the protected groups that can have these rights (see p168).

If you are in one of the protected groups, or for a period before the end of the transition period, you have a right of residence as a self-sufficient person if you are a European Economic Area (EEA) national and you, and any family members who do not have an independent right to reside, have:[211]

- sufficient resources (see p213) not to become a burden on the social assistance system of the UK during your period of residence (see p214); *and*
- comprehensive sickness insurance cover in the UK (see p214).

You have a right to reside as a student if you are an EEA national and:[212]
- you are enrolled as a student in a government-accredited college;
- you provide an assurance that you have sufficient resources (see p213) for yourself, and any family members who do not have an independent right to reside, not to become a burden on the UK social assistance system during your intended period of residence (see p214);
- you, and any family members who do not have an independent right to reside, have comprehensive sickness insurance cover in the UK (see p214).

Because the requirements to have a right to reside for students and self-sufficient people are very similar, this chapter refers to those who have a right to reside as a student as 'self-sufficient students'. The specific differences that apply to students are on p216.

You can also have a right to reside if you are a family member of a self-sufficient person or self-sufficient student.

If you had a right to reside as a self-sufficient person (or family member of a self-sufficient person) on 31 December 2020, and on that date, you did not have leave granted under the European Union (EU) Settlement Scheme, you are (until at least 30 June 2021) in one of the protected groups that can use free movement residence rights. If you are an EEA national, these protections also mean that you cannot be defined as a 'person subject to immigration control' (see p81). For further details, including the duration of these protections, see p168.

Periods when you have a right to reside as a self-sufficient person or student, or a family member of either, count as periods of having 'resided legally' for acquiring permanent residence after five years (see p245).

Croatian, A2 and A8 nationals

If you are a Croatian, A2 or A8 national, your residence rights as a self-sufficient person or self-sufficient student during the relevant period of restrictions were the same as other EEA nationals – ie, there were no restrictions for self-sufficient people.

Note: certain students were exempt from the restrictions that applied to Croatian and A2 nationals. You were not subject to worker authorisation if you were a student with a registration certificate which stated that you could not work more than 20 hours a week (unless it was part of vocational training or during vacations) and you complied with this. If the certificate confirmed that you could work during the four months after the course finished, the exemption continued for this period (see p178).

If this applied to you and you worked no more than 20 hours a week, you may have had a right to reside as a 'worker' (see p189). In addition, you counted as 'legally working' and, after a year of legally working (see p180), you were no longer subject to worker authorisation.

If you were employed during the relevant period of restrictions, but your work was not in accordance with your worker authorisation document (or, if you are an A8 national, for an 'authorised employer'), you cannot rely on those earnings as your resources for the purpose of having a right to reside as a self-sufficient person.[213]

For further details of the restrictions that previously applied to Croatian, A2 and A8 nationals, see p176.

Sufficient resources

Your resources must be 'sufficient' to avoid you, and any family member whose right to reside depends on her/his being your family member, becoming a burden on the social assistance system of the UK (see below).[214] The government cannot set a fixed amount that it regards as 'sufficient' and must take your personal situation into account.[215]

Your resources are 'sufficient' if they:[216]

- are more than the maximum level you (and your family) can have to be eligible for 'social assistance' (see below); *or*
- are not more than that level, but the decision maker considers that they are sufficient, taking into account your personal circumstances (and those of any family member whose right to reside depends on their being your family member).

The 'maximum level' is the equivalent of your means-tested benefit applicable, or maximum, amount, including any premiums or elements. Your resources also include your accommodation, so if your resources are more than your applicable, or maximum, amount plus your rent, they should be sufficient. You may also be self-sufficient if your resources are more than your applicable, or maximum, amount and you are provided with free and stable accommodation by friends or family.[217]

You do not need to own the resources that make you self-sufficient. It is enough if you have access to them – eg, if you are supported by someone else.[218]

The source of the resources does not matter.[219] However, you cannot rely on your earnings from your employment in the UK to give you self-sufficient status.[220] (In most circumstances, this does not matter as your employment means you have a right to reside as a 'worker', but it is relevant if, for example, you did not have worker status because you did not satisfy the additional conditions imposed on you as a Croatian, A2 or A8 national – see p176). However, if you are employed and have worker status in an EEA state, but you live in UK, you can rely on your earnings to have a right to reside as a self-sufficient person in the state in the UK.[221] You can also rely on the earnings of your non-EEA national spouse/civil partner.[222] An EEA national child can rely on the earnings of her/his non-EEA parent, even if that parent's employment in an EEA country is unlawful due to a lack of residence card and work permit.[223]

Not a burden on the social assistance system

You count as self-sufficient if you have sufficient resources 'not to become a burden on the social assistance system of the UK during your period of residence'.

'Burden' has been held to be an 'unreasonable burden'.[224]

The 'social assistance system of the UK' includes all means-tested benefits.[225] In its guidance, the Department for Work and Pensions does not include child tax credit (CTC), but lists all the means-tested benefits (although in the universal credit (UC) guidance, only UC and pension credit (PC) are listed).[226]

You must not be automatically regarded as not self-sufficient just because you make a claim for a means-tested benefit. Although a claim could indicate that you do not have sufficient resources to avoid becoming an unreasonable burden on the social assistance system of the UK, the decision maker must carry out an assessment of the specific burden that awarding you the benefit you have claimed would make on the system as a whole. This assessment must take all your circumstances into account, including the likely duration of your claim,[227] at the point you make your claim for benefit on the basis of your right to reside as a self-sufficient person – you do not need to have had sufficient resources at the start of your period of residence. However, from the point the assessment is carried out, you must show sufficient resources for your intended period of residence, including for five years if permanent residence is sought.[228] **Note:** the Upper Tribunal held that the 'open-ended' nature of a claim for PC was a factor in deciding that claim represented an 'unreasonable burden' and so the claimant did not therefore have a right to reside as a self-sufficient person.[229] However, it is arguable that the tribunal should have limited the assessment period to five years, since she would then have had a permanent right to reside.

Although you should always provide any evidence you have that shows that the award of benefit would not mean you would become an 'unreasonable burden', the onus is on the decision maker to prove the specific burden that would be caused by an award (see p457).[230]

Comprehensive sickness insurance

To have a right of residence as a self-sufficient person, in addition to having sufficient resources (see p213), you must also have comprehensive sickness insurance cover in the UK.

This requirement is satisfied if you have private health insurance.[231]

It is also satisfied if the UK can be reimbursed by an EEA state for any NHS costs you incur while in the UK.[232] That usually applies if you are covered by the

European Union co-ordination rules (see p355) and an EEA state continues to be your 'competent state' (see p369) – eg, if you are:

- resident in the UK, but you are working or self-employed in an EEA state;
- resident in the UK, you receive a pension from an EEA state, you do not also receive a pension from the UK, and you are not working or self-employed in the UK (see p374);[233]
- living temporarily in the UK (eg, you are a student on a course in the UK) and during your stay in the UK you are entitled to health treatment in an EEA state because you are insured there.[234]

In these circumstances, you may have been issued with a European health insurance card (EHIC) (and/or an S1 card) by the country in which you were last insured. However, this does not, in itself, confirm that you have comprehensive sickness insurance cover in the UK. As with other residence documents (see p465), the card only confirms your rights on the date it was issued; it does not mean you retain those rights if your circumstances change and the UK becomes your competent state. For example, if your presence in the UK ceases to be a 'stay' and you become 'resident' (see p371), holding an EHIC does not mean you have comprehensive sickness insurance because the UK will no longer be able to be reimbursed for NHS costs by the state that issued the EHIC.[235]

The question of whether being covered by the common travel area reciprocal agreement regarding healthcare costs satisfies the requirement for comprehensive sickness insurance cover has been referred to the Court of Justice of the European Union (CJEU).[236] The same reference also asks whether it is lawful to require all relevant family members to satisfy this requirement for the purpose of the primary carer of a self-sufficient child having a derivative right to reside (see p240).

Access to NHS treatment where the UK bears this cost does not satisfy the requirement to have comprehensive sickness insurance cover in the UK.[237] However, the European Commission considers this to be unlawful and, in October 2020, began infringement proceedings requiring the UK to amend the relevant rules.[238] Note the European Commission can bring such proceedings within four years of the transition period ending on 31 December 2020, and any resulting judgment from the CJEU remains binding in the UK (see p174).[239]

If you have sickness insurance cover but it is not 'comprehensive', you may be able to argue that it is disproportionate for the benefit authority to insist on this requirement being met if it is the only barrier to your having a right to reside as a self-sufficient person.[240]

Arguments that it is disproportionate to insist on this requirement when you do not have *any* sickness insurance have, so far, failed.[241]

If you have difficulty satisfying the requirement to have comprehensive sickness insurance cover, get specialist advice.

Self-sufficient students

You have a right to reside as a self-sufficient student if you are an EEA national and:[242]

- you are enrolled as a student in a government-accredited establishment for the principal purpose of following a course of study (including vocational training); *and*
- you provide an assurance that you have sufficient resources for yourself, and any family members (see below) who do not have an independent right of residence, not to become a burden on the UK social assistance system during your intended period of residence (see below); *and*
- you, and any family members who do not have an independent right of residence, have comprehensive sickness insurance (see above).

The conditions for having a right of residence as a student are very similar to those for a self-sufficient person. The only differences are as follows.

- To have the right to reside as a self-sufficient student, you must be enrolled on a course of study.[243]
- The requirement to have sufficient resources is met by providing an assurance that you have 'sufficient resources'.[244] The assessment of what counts as 'sufficient resources' is the same as for a self-sufficient person (see p213) and it is not clear what practical difference it makes to provide an assurance of this. Although you may be more easily accepted as having a right to reside if you provide an assurance of your resources at the start of your studies, this does not prevent you from losing your right of residence if your circumstances change. However, such a loss is never automatic and always depends on your circumstances.[245] Also, if you are only likely to need to claim benefits on a temporary basis, depending on the length of your course, it may be easier to argue that your claim does not amount to an unreasonable burden on the social assistance system of the UK (see p214).
- The definition of family member is different (see below).

Family members

Family member of a self-sufficient student

You are the '**family member**' of a self-sufficient student (once s/he has been in the UK for three months) if you are:[246]

- her/his spouse or civil partner; *or*
- her/his dependent child (regardless of your age); *or*
- the dependent child (regardless of your age) of the student's spouse or civil partner.

The above definition of family member is narrower than that which generally applies (see p220), and only applies if the student does not have another right to reside that can confer a right of residence on you.

If you are the parent/grandparent of a self-sufficient student who has been in the UK for at least three months, or a parent/grandparent of her/his spouse or civil partner, you may be able to be treated as a family member on the basis of being an extended family member if you have the relevant documentation (see p223).[247]

This means that when assessing whether you have sufficient resources, you do not need to take account of anyone who does not come within this definition of family member after you have lived in the UK for three months – eg, your resources do not need to be sufficient for your non-dependent children under 21 or dependent parent living in the UK.

Benefit entitlement

If you have a right to reside as a self-sufficient person, a self-sufficient student, or family member of either, that satisfies the right to reside requirement for all benefits that have such a requirement (see p151).

The most common way in which periods of residence as a self-sufficient person or student (or family member of either) can assist you to access benefits that require a right to reside, is when such periods are in the past (see below). That is because, during your period of self-sufficiency, your resources often exclude you from means-tested benefits. However, if they do not, it cannot automatically be decided that you are not self-sufficient just because you have claimed a means-tested benefit (see p214). **Note:** during your period of residence as a self-sufficient person you may be entitled to child benefit, from which your resources never exclude you, and CTC, for which your resources can be be greater than for other means-tested benefits.

Your current entitlement to benefits can be assisted if you had a right to reside as a self-sufficient person, a family member of a self-sufficient person, or as a student or family member of a student, in the past – specifically:

- on 31 December 2020, because this can mean that you are (until at least 30 June 2021) in a protected group that can have free movement rights, and, if you are an EEA national, not be defined as a 'person subject to immigration control' (see p81). For further details, including the duration of these protections, see p168; *or*
- as part of a period of five years of residing in the UK with free movement residence rights which enabled you to acquire a permanent right to reside (see p244). If you had this permanent right to reside on 31 December 2020 (or had lost it due to being absent from the UK for more than two years, but your absence was less than five years on that date), this can mean you are in a protected group, as above.

14. Family members of European Economic Area nationals

Since the end of the transition period at 11pm on 31 December 2020, you can only have a free movement right to reside, including as a family member of a European Economic Area (EEA) national with one of the residence rights listed below, while you are in one of the protected groups that can have these rights (see p168).

If you are in one of the protected groups, or for a period before the end of the transition period, you have a right to reside if you are a 'family member' (see p220) of an EEA national who has:[248]

- a right to reside as a 'qualified person' – ie, a:[249]
  - jobseeker (see p182);
  - worker (see p189), including if s/he has retained this status (see p201);
  - self-employed person (see p196), including if s/he has retained this status (see p201);
  - self-sufficient person, including a self-sufficient student (see p211); *or*
- a permanent right of residence (see p244); *or*
- an initial right to reside (see p181).

You have this right to reside as a family member of an EEA national with one of the free movement residence rights listed above, whether or not you are an EEA national yourself.

You have a right to reside for as long as the EEA national has one of the above residence rights and for as long as you remain her/his family member. In general, if s/he ceases to have a relevant right to reside or if you cease to be her/his family member, your right to reside ends. However, there are some limited circumstances in which you can continue to have residence rights as a former family member (see p228).

Note: British citizens only give residence rights to their family members in limited circumstances (see p224).

The type of right to reside you have depends on the type of right to reside your family member has. If you only have a right to reside as the family member of a jobseeker or person with an initial right to reside, that does not satisfy the right to reside requirement for most benefits (see p231). However, if you had either residence right on 31 December 2020, that can mean you are in a protected group that can have free movement rights (see first bullet point below), and periods with either residence right count towards the five years required for permanent residency (see p245), which then satisfies the right to reside requirement for all benefits.

Note:

- If you had a right to reside as a family member of an EEA national with one of the residence rights listed above on 31 December 2020, and on that date, you did not have leave granted under the European Union (EU) Settlement Scheme, you are (until at least 30 June 2021) in one of the protected groups that can use free movement residence rights. If you are an EEA national, these protections also mean that you cannot be defined as a 'person subject to immigration control' (see p81). For further details, including the duration of these protections, see p168.
- If you are the family member of an EEA national who was living in the UK before the end of the transition period, and you were her/his family member on 31 December 2020, for information on whether the leave you have or can obtain under the EU Settlement Scheme, satisfies the right to reside requirement, see p165.

Protected groups that can use free movement residence rights

Since the end of the transition period at 11pm on 31 December 2020, you can only have any free movement right to reside, including as a family member of an EEA national with one of the residence rights listed above, while you are in one of the protected groups that can have these rights. These are explained on p168. Some additional points that are specific to family members are covered below.

If you do not have limited leave granted under the EU Settlement Scheme (also known as pre-settled status), then whether or not you are in a protected group will depend on whether you, or, if you are reliant on being a 'relevant family member' of another person, whether s/he, on 31 December 2020:

- had a free movement right to reside; *and*
- did not have leave under the EU Settlement Scheme on that date.

Note: the definition of 'relevant family member' (see p169) is wider than the definition of 'family member' (see p220).

The specific requirements can be complicated for family members, so you need to check carefully which requirements you, and which requirements the person you are a family member of, need to satisfy, and at which date(s). For example:

- if, on 31 December 2020, you were the **'family member'** (see p220) of an EEA national who had one of the free movement residence rights above and you do not have leave granted under the EU Settlement Scheme, then you are in a protected group because on that date *you* had a free movement right to reside under the EEA Regulations. This applies *whether or not* the EEA national had leave granted under the EU Settlement Scheme on that date. Therefore, free moveement residence rights continue to be available to you until 30 June 2021, and thereafter if by that date you have applied to the EU Settlement

Scheme and your application (or appeal against a refusal) has not yet been finally determined;

- if the above did not apply to you, but you are a **'relevant family member'** (see p168) of an EEA national who on 31 December 2020 had a free movement right to reside, this will mean you are in a protected group (until at least 30 June 2020) *provided* you do not have leave under the EU Settlement Scheme *and* the person you are the 'relevant family member' of, did not have such leave on 31 December 2020. That coulld apply if, for example, you arrived in the UK after the end of the transition period, or if on 31 December 2020, you were in the UK and a durable partner of an EEA worker, but had not been issued a residence document under the EEA Regulations – see the second example on p171.

Croatian, A2 and A8 nationals

If you are a Croatian, A2 or A8 national and during the relevant period of restrictions you were a family member of an EEA national with one of the residence rights listed above, you have a right to reside in the same way as family members of other EEA nationals. In addition, this may mean that you were exempt from the restrictions (see p178 for Croatian and A2 nationals and p179 for A8 nationals). However, if you are relying on the past residence rights of your family member who is a Croatian, A2 or A8 national, note that these may have been affected by these restrictions.

For further details of the restrictions that previously applied to Croatian, A2 and A8 nationals, see p176.

Who is a family member

If you are in one of the protected groups that can have a free movement right to reside after the end of the transition period at 11pm on 31 December 2020 (see p168), or during an earlier period, you have a right to reside as a family member of an EEA national who has a relevant free movement right to reside (see p218), if you come within the definition of 'family member' below.

Family member

You are a 'family member' of an EEA national if you are her/his:[250]

- spouse or civil partner;
- child, grandchild or great-grandchild (or the child, grandchild or great-grandchild of her/his spouse or civil partner) and you are under 21;
- child, grandchild or great-grandchild (or the child, grandchild or great-grandchild of her/his spouse or civil partner) and you are dependent on her/him;
- parent, grandparent or great-grandparent (or the parent, grandparent or great-grandparent of her/his spouse/civil partner) and you are dependent on her/him.

If you are not covered by the above definition, you can be *treated as* a family member and have residence rights on that basis if:

- you are an 'extended family member'; *and*
- you have been issued with an EEA family permit, a registration certificate or a residence card under the EEA Regulations (see p465). If you do not have this documentation, or it no longer remains in force, you are not treated as a family member.[251]

For the meaning of 'extended family member' and information on the required residence documents, see p223.

Note:

- A wider definition of 'relevant family member' is used to determine which family members of EEA nationals in the UK before the end of the transition period (31 December 2020) can be in a protected group that can use free movement rights after the end of the transition period. For details of the definition and the protections, including their duration, see p168.
- A narrower definition applies to family members of students (see p216).

Spouses and civil partners

Spouses and civil partners are family members. If you are not married to, or in a civil partnership with, your partner, see p223.

You remain a spouse or civil partner if you have separated, including while you are in the process of getting divorced or dissolving a civil partnership. It is only once you are legally divorced (ie, in the UK, when the *decree nisi* is given) or the civil partnership has been legally terminated that you cease to count as the spouse or civil partner of the other person.[252]

If your marriage or civil partnership has been terminated (or if your spouse/civil partner dies or leaves the UK), in certain circumstances, you may continue to have a right to reside (see p228).

Aged under 21

You count as a family member of a person if you are her/his child (or grandchild or great-grandchild), or a child of her/his spouse/civil partner, and you are aged under 21.

You do not need to show that you are dependent on the person in order to count as her/his family member. Therefore, you do not need to live with her/him or show you are receiving support from her/him, and it is irrelevant whether you do or not.[253]

Example

Greta is a Lithuanian national aged 18. On 29 December 2020, Greta moved to the UK and rented a flat in Portsmouth. In February 2021, she claims universal credit (UC). At that time, Greta is in a protected group that can have a free movement right to reside, because on 31 December 2020 she had a free movement right to reside under the EEA Regulations because she had an initial right to reside (see p181) and she had not been granted leave under the EU Settlement Scheme. Greta's initial right to reside does not entitle her to UC because it is an excluded right to reside (see p152), but she also has a right to reside as the family member of a worker. That is becuase Greta's father, who is also Lithuanian, is working full time in Glasgow. Greta does not receive any support from him, but is defined as his family member because she is his daughter and is aged under 21. Greta's right to reside as the family member of a worker means she is exempt from the habitual residence test for UC (see p142). It also means she can be entitled to child benefit because she satisfies the right to reside requirement and is exempt from the requirement to have been living in the UK for three months (see p127).

For information on providing evidence of your age, see p469.

Dependent

In some situations, to count as a family member of someone, you must be dependent on that person – eg, if you are her/his parent or grandparent, or child aged 21 or older.

'Dependence' is not defined in the legislation, but caselaw has established a number of principles.[254]

There are only three things you must show in order to establish that you are dependent on a person.

- You receive support from her/him.
- The support you receive is 'material'. If the person is providing you with financial help, paying your bills, buying you food or providing your meals, providing you with accommodation or caring for you because you are ill or disabled, this all counts as 'material support'. Translation, emotional and social support do not count.[255]
- The support *contributes to* the 'basic necessities of life'. It is not necessary for this to be your only source of support.

It is irrelevant if there are alternative sources of support, including savings or potential employment, available to you, either in your country of origin or in the UK.[256]

If you only became dependent on the EEA national in the UK, this does not prevent you from being classed as a family member. It is sufficient that you are dependent at the point when your claim for benefit is decided.[257] (**Note**: if you are an extended family member on the basis of dependency/member of household, you must have been dependent on/member of the household of the EEA national in the country you have come from – see below.)

You can be dependent on someone even if you receive benefit, and your dependency should be considered independently of any benefit you claim. A decision maker should not make the 'circular' decision that that you are not entitled because awarding you a benefit that depends on your residence rights as a dependent family member would mean you would to cease to be dependent. Whether you are dependent while receiving a benefit depends on whether or not your evidence shows the three things listed above.[258]

Extended family members

If you do not come within the definition of 'family member' on p220, but you have a partner or relative in the UK who is an EEA national with a relevant right to reside (see p218), you can be *treated as* a family member, and therefore have residence rights on that basis, if you:[259]

- are an 'extended family member' (see below); *and*
- have been issued with an EEA family permit, a registration certificate or a residence card under the EEA Regulations and it remains in force. If you do not have this documentation, or it no longer remains in force, you are *not* treated as a family member.[260] In most cases you must have applied for this residence document before the end of the transition period (11pm on 31 December 2020). The exception is that you may be granted a family permit to enter the UK if on 31 December 2020 you were a partner, in a durable relationship, of an EEA national who had a free movement right to reside and who did not have leave under the EU Settlement Scheme. For details of these documents, see p465.

Extended family member

You are an '**extended family member**' of an EEA national if s/he is your:[261]

- partner and you are in a durable relationship[262] with her/him (or you are the child, under 18, of the partner); *or*
- non-adoptive legal guardian (under the law of the country in which the guardianship order was granted), you are under 18, dependent on her/him and have lived with her/him since s/he became your legal guardian;[263] *or*
- relative and:
- you have serious health problems that require her/his (or her/his spouse or civil partner's) day-to-day care;[264] *or*
- you were dependent on her/him (or you were a member of her/his household) in another country and you accompanied or joined her/him in the UK (or you wish to join her/him in the UK) and you continue to be dependent on her/him (or to be a member of her/his household).[265] Your previous connection does not need to have been the same as it is now – eg, you may have been a member of her/his household before coming to the UK and then be dependent on her/him on your arrival;[266] *or*
- you would meet the requirements (other than those relating to entry clearance) of the Immigration Rules for indefinite leave as her/his dependent relative.

The term 'dependent' is not defined in the legislation and its meaning is the same as that for a family member (see p222).

Before 1 February 2017, you were also defined as an extended family member if you were a relative of the EEA national's spouse or civil partner and:

- you had serious health problems that required her/his care. The spouse or civil partner of this category was then added back into the definition from 15 August 2019 following a judgment of the Court of Justice of the European Union (CJEU);[267] *or*
- you were previously dependent on her/him (or you were a member of her/his household) in another country and you accompanied or joined her/him in the UK (or you wished to join her/him in the UK) and you continued to be dependent on her/him (or to be a member of her/his household).

If you were issued with a residence document on this basis, you continue to be defined as an extended family member, provided you have been continuously resident in the UK since 1 February 2017.[268]

Family members of British citizens

Even before European free movement rights were ended in UK law at the end of the transition period (11pm on 31 December 2020), British citizens did not generally give free movement residence rights to their family members. That is because, in most cases, an EEA national could only confer European free movement residence rights on her/his family members if s/he had moved to, or was residing in, a different EEA country to the one of which s/he is a national.[269] However, in the limited circumstances covered below, a British citizen could confer a free movement right to reside on family members. These rights continue to apply if you are in one of the protected groups that can have a free movement right to reside (see p168).

If you are in one of the protected groups, or for a period before the end of the transition period, a British citizen can confer a right of residence on you if you are her/his family member if:

- s/he is residing, or immediately before returning to the UK, did reside, with a right to reside as a worker, self-employed person, self-sufficient person or self-sufficient student, or a permanent right to reside, in an EEA state and you resided there with her/him as her/his family member. On her/his return to the UK, s/he can confer a right to reside on you (see below);
- s/he is self-employed and carries out some of her/his business activities in an EEA state (see p227);
- s/he is a dual British/EEA citizen (see p227).

In addition, you may have a right to reside in the following circumstances.

- You may have a right to reside if you have obtained leave under the EU Settlement Scheme (see p49). If you have indefinite leave (also known as settled status) that satisfies the right to reside requirement for benefits (see p166). If you have limited leave under the EU Settlement Scheme (also known as pre-settled status), see p153 for means-tested benefits and p158 for child benefit and child tax credit.

- If you are the primary carer of a British citizen who would not be able to continue to live anywhere in the EEA if you were required to leave the UK, you may have a 'derivative right to reside' (see p240). **Note:** having a derivative right to reside is different from having a right to reside as a family member (see p233).
- If you are joining your family member who is British, and you have been given leave by the Home Office (eg, as a spouse or civil partner), you have a right to reside during that period of leave. That is under domestic immigration law and is not a European free movement right. See Part 2 for more information on immigration law. If your leave is subject to a condition that you do not have recourse to public funds, you are defined as a 'person subject to immigration control' (see p87) and excluded from all the benefits listed on p95, unless you are exempt (see p96).

The British citizen has resided in another state

If you are a family member (see p220) of a British citizen, you have a right to reside as her/his family member if:[270]

- s/he is residing, or immediately before returning to the UK, did reside, in an EEA state with a right to reside as a worker, self-employed person, self-sufficient person, self-sufficient student or a permanent right to reside; *and*
- you are or were residing as a family member (including as an 'extended family member'[271]) with her/him in that state, your family life was created or strengthened there, and your residence there together was 'genuine' (see below).

On returning to the UK together, the British citizen confers a free movement right to reside on you.

Note: if you returned to the UK together after 31 December 2020, and the above bullet points applied to you on that date, you are in a protected group (until at least 30 June 2021). That is because the wording of the regulations applies while you were residing in an EEA state *and* on your joint return to the UK (and, therefore, you had a right to reside under the EEA Regulations on 31 December 2020, despite being out of the UK).[272] For details of the protected groups, including their duration, see p168.

You do not have a right to reside on this basis if you only became the British citizen's family member after s/he returned to the UK.[273]

The EEA Regulations have interpreted these rights more restrictively than the CJEU, and some of these restrictions have recently been confirmed to be unlawful by the Upper Tribunal. Amendments have been made to the regulations, but for periods before these amendments you can rely directly on the Upper Tribunal decisions and the CJEU caselaw to which they refer. For information on the continuing requirement to interpret free movement residence rights in accordance with CJEU caselaw, see p174.

Until 11 pm on 31 December 2020, the EEA Regulations only gave you a right to reside as a family member of a British citizen while s/he had a right to reside in the UK under the regulations in the same ways as EEA nationals (with minor easements).

From this date, the EEA Regulations were amended such that the British citizen is *treated as* satisfying any requirement to be a 'qualified person' (see p172).[274] This amendment followed an Upper Tribunal decision and earlier caselaw from the CJEU, which held that an EEA national who had been a worker in a different EEA state and then returned to her/his own state did not need to be undertaking an economic activity in her/his own state in order for her/his family member to have a right to reside.[275]

If you were an 'extended family member' of a British citizen in the EEA state, the EEA Regulations require you to have been lawfully resident in that state.[276] This does not necessarily mean you had been granted the relevant EEA residence document by that state; your residence may instead have been lawful under domestic immigration law.[277]

The British citizen's and your residency in the EEA state must have been '**genuine**', which has been held to mean real, substantive or effective, and more than mere physical presence.[278] The EEA Regulations list the following as being relevant when considering whether residence is 'genuine':

- the length of your joint residence in the EEA state;
- the nature and quality of your joint accommodation in the EEA state and whether it was the British citizen's principal residence;
- the degree of your and the British citizen's integration in the EEA state;
- whether the residence in the EEA state was your first lawful residence in the EU.

Until 11 pm on 31 December 2020, the EEA Regulations also required the British citizen to have transferred her/his 'centre of life' to the EEA state. From this date, the EEA Regulations were amended following an Upper Tribunal decision confirming that this was not a requirement under EU law.[279] **Note:** when considering whether residence was genuine, the CJEU has focused on whether residence enabled the creation or strengthening of family life in that state and whether the conditions for the relevant residence right were satisfied.[280]

The EEA Regulations exclude you from having a right to reside on the basis of being a family member of a British citizen who has resided in an EEA country if you are a non-EEA national and the purpose of your residence in the EEA state was to circumvent the immigration laws.[281]

The British citizen lives in the UK and carries out activities in another state

Until the end of the transition period (11pm on 31 December 2020), if you were the family member (see p220) of a British citizen who was employed or self-employed in the UK and whose business involved her/him undertaking some activities in an EEA state, you could have a right of residence, depending on your circumstances. This right was not covered in the EEA Regulations or the EU Directive 2004/38 but was confirmed by the CJEU as coming directly from the Treaty on the Functioning of the European Union (TFEU). The cases concerned a non-EEA spouse of a British citizen providing services in EEA countries from a business in the UK,[282] and a non-EEA family member of a Dutch national residing in the Netherlands but working in another EEA country.[283] If you began living in the UK as the family member of a British citzen, in these circumstances, before the end of the transition period, you may be able to obtain leave under the EU Settlement Scheme. If you are a non-EEA national, however, you should get immigration advice before applying, because your application could be complex and you may also have other immigration options. If you are granted indefinite leave under the EU Settlement Scheme (also known as settled status), that satisfies the right to reside requirement for all benefits that have that requirement. If you are granted limited leave (also known as pre-settled status), see p153 and p158.

The British citizen also has citizenship of a European Economic Area state

If you are the family member of a British citizen who also has citizenship of an EEA state, you may have a right to reside in the same circumstances as if you were the family member of an EEA national, provided that before acquiring British citizenship s/he had a free movement right to reside as either a 'qualified person' (see p171) or a permanent right to reside (see p244).

These rights are not provided under EU Directive 2004/38 as that does not apply to British citizens living in the UK, including citizens of EEA states who only acquired British citizenship after moving to the UK, and so it cannot provide rights to that person's family member. Instead they are provided by the TFEU, as confirmed by the CJEU, which held that an EEA national who moved to the UK, resided here as a worker, acquired permanent residence and then dual British nationality, continued to have citizenship rights under the TFEU, including the right to build a family life with the non-EEA national she subsequently married.[284] Consequently, the CJEU held that her spouse had a right to reside in the UK on conditions which must not be stricter than those that would apply to a family member of another EEA national.[285] The nationality of the family member does not affect these rights and they apply equally to EEA or non-EEA family members.[286]

The EEA Regulations were amended on 24 July 2018 following this decision, but interpret the rights more restrictively (see below). If you do not have a right to reside under the EEA Regulations, you may be able to rely on the above CJEU judgment. Challenge any refusal of benefit if this is not accepted and get specialist advice.

If you are the family member of a dual British/EEA citizen, you can have a right to reside under the EEA Regulations provided s/he had a right to reside as a national of a state that was at that time an EEA state,[287] either as a qualified person or a permanent right to reside (or was a family member of an EEA national with either) before s/he became a British citizen.[288] If s/he currently has a right to reside as a qualified person, s/he must have had such a right at the time of acquiring British citizenship, and continuously since then, for you to have a right to reside as her/his family member. If you are a non-EEA national, s/he must have had a right to reside as a qualified person or a permanent right to reside in the UK under the EEA Regulations at the time s/he acquired British citizenship.[289]

Note: although these rights have only been included in the EEA Regulations since 24 July 2018, they are treated as if they were in force before this date.[290] Similarly, the CJEU judgment confirms rights that previously existed.[291] This means you may be able to rely on these rights to acquire permanent residence and to challenge earlier decisions refusing you benefit.

In an earlier case, the CJEU held that a dual British/EEA state citizen did not have rights under EU law as she had never moved between EEA states, but had lived all her life in the UK. Therefore, she could not confer any residence rights on her family members.[292]

Following this judgment, the definition of 'EEA national' in the EEA Regulations was amended to exclude anyone who was also a British citizen.[293] Although this definition was amended again from 24 July 2018, the recent amendments do not treat family members of dual British/ EEA citizens the same as family members of EEA citizens in all circumstances. You may therefore need to rely on the limited transitional protection that was given to family members of dual nationals who had residence rights before 16 October 2012, when family members of dual British/EEA nationals did have the same rights as family members of EEA nationals.[294] If you had such a right to reside before this date, it continues in limited circumstances.[295] See p1604 of the 2013/14 edition of CPAG's *Welfare Benefits and Tax Credits Handbook* for details.

Former family members who retain their right to reside

In general, if you are the family member of an EEA national who confers a right to reside on you, your right to reside ceases if s/he:

- is no longer your family member (see p220); *or*
- no longer has a relevant right to reside.

However, you can *retain* your right to reside in certain circumstances. Whether or not these apply to you depends on the type of right to reside your family member has. **Note:** several of these circumstances may mean that you have other residence rights that could be easier to prove or may apply instead (see p231).

When you may retain your right to reside

You may retain your right to reside if the EEA national who confers this right on you dies or leaves the UK, or if your marriage or civil partnership to her/him is terminated. These rights are in EU Directive 2004/38 but are not exactly reproduced in the EEA Regulations (see below). The decision maker is more likely to accept that you retain your right to reside if you satisfy the requirements of the EEA Regulations, so you should check these requirements first. If you cannot satisfy these, check whether you satisfy the requirements of the EU Directive (see p230), because the EEA Regulations should be implementing these (see p174). **Note:** under the EEA Regulations, you can count periods of residence spent as a former family member who retains her/his right of residence towards the five years of residence required for permanent residence (see p245).

European Economic Area Regulations

If you are in one of the protected groups (see p168) that can have a free movement right to reside after the end of the transition period (11pm on 31 December 2020) or for a period before that date, you retain your right to reside under the EEA Regulations if you are a family member of a 'qualified person' (see p172) or a person with a permanent right to reside (see p244) and:[296]

- that person dies and you are:
  - not an EEA national, but if you were you would be a worker, or a self-employed or self-sufficient person (or you are the family member of such a non-EEA national) and you resided in the UK with a right to reside under the EEA Regulations for at least a year immediately before s/he died; *or*
  - her/his child or grandchild (or the child or grandchild of her/his spouse or civil partner) and you were in education (see p237) immediately before her/his death and you remain in education; *or*
  - a parent with custody of a child in the previous bullet point; *or*
- that person leaves the UK and you are:
  - her/his child or grandchild (or the child or grandchild of her/his spouse or civil partner) and you were in education (see p237) immediately before s/he left the UK and you remain in education; *or*
  - a parent with custody of a child in the previous bullet point; *or*
- your marriage or civil partnership to that person is terminated, and s/he was a qualified person (or had a permanent right to reside) at least until the termination proceedings began,[297] and you are not an EEA national, but if you were, you would be a worker or a self-employed or self-sufficient person (or you are the family member of such a non-EEA national), and you were residing in the UK with a right to reside under the EEA Regulations at the date of the termination and:

- the marriage/civil partnership had lasted for at least three years with you both residing in the UK for at least one of those years; *or*
- you have custody of the qualified person's child; *or*
- you have a right of access to the qualified person's child which a court has said must take place in the UK; *or*
- your continued right of residence in the UK is warranted by particularly difficult circumstances, such as your (or another family member's) being subject to domestic violence during the period of the marriage/civil partnership. Your rights are not retained in this way if your spouse or civil partner left the UK before the termination proceedings began.[298]

You have a right to reside on this basis for as long as the conditions apply to you,[299] until you can acquire a permanent right of residence (see p244).[300] For details on using periods with this residence right to acquire permanent residency, see p248.

European Union Directive 2004/38

If you do not satisfy the requirements of the EEA Regulations above, but you satisfy the requirements of the EU Directive 2004/38 below, you can argue that the EEA Regulations should be treated as if the requirements were the same. For more information on the continued relevance of EU Directive for interpreting rights under the EEA Regulations after the end of the transition period, see p174.

You can retain your right to reside under EU Directive 2004/38 if you are a family member of an EEA national who has a right to reside as a worker, self-employed or self-sufficient person, or as a self-sufficient student and:

- the EEA national dies and you have lived in the UK as her/his family member for at least a year before her/his death and you are a non-EEA national;[301] *or*
- the EEA national leaves the UK and you are:[302]
  - her/his child, grandchild or great-grandchild and in education; *or*
  - the parent with custody of a child in education; *or*
- your marriage or civil partnership to the EEA national is terminated, and s/he had a right to reside as a worker, self-employed or self-sufficient person, or as a self-sufficient student at least until the termination proceedings began,[303] and:[304]
  - before the termination proceedings were started, the marriage/civil partnership had lasted for at least three years with you both residing in the UK for at least one of these years. Your rights are not retained in this way if your spouse or civil partner left the UK before the termination proceedings began;[305] *or*
  - you have custody of her/his child; *or*
  - you have a right of access to her/his child, which a court has said must take place in the UK; *or*

- your continued right of residence in the UK is warranted by particularly difficult circumstances, such as your being subject to domestic violence during the period of the marriage/civil partnership. Your rights are not retained in this way if your spouse or civil partner left the UK before the termination proceedings began.[306]

It may be arguable that if you are an EEA national, you can retain your right to reside in each of the three circumstances above without needing to satisfy any other conditions.[307] However, two Upper Tribunal decisions rejected this interpretation and took the view that the provisions in the Directive just confirm that any independent residence rights that an EEA national may have had are not affected by the above changes.[308] It is arguable that these parts of each decision are not legally binding as each case failed on other grounds, but they will be persuasive until further caselaw decides the issue.

Periods when you have retained your right to reside as a former family member are not, on their own, sufficient to enable you to acquire a permanent right of residence after five years, because you are also required to show that you are a worker, or a self-employed or a self-sufficient person, or you are the family member of such a person.[309]

Other residence rights

If you are covered by any of the circumstances that enable you to retain your right to reside as a family member, under either the EEA Regulations or the EU Directive, or if your circumstances are similar but you do not fit within these rules, check whether similar rights could apply to you. The main ones that might apply are the following.

- If you have had a right to reside in the UK as the family member of an EEA national who has conferred a right to reside on you for five years, you may have a permanent right to reside (see p245).
- If you were the family member of an EEA national who has died and s/he was a worker or a self-employed person, you may have a permanent right to reside (see p253).
- If you are the child of a worker and you are in education, or you are the primary carer of such a child, you may have a 'derivative right to reside' (see p233).

Benefit entitlement

Whether your right to reside as the family member of an EEA national satisfies the right to reside requirement depends on:

- the type of free movement right to reside the EEA national has; *and*
- the benefit you want to claim.

Your right to reside is the equivalent of the EEA national's right to reside. This means the following.

- If on 31 December 2020, you were the 'relevant family member' (a term that is wider than 'family member' on p220) of an EEA national who, on that date, had *any* free movement right to reside, that can mean you are (until at least 30 June 2021) in a protected group that can have free movement residence rights, and, if you are an EEA national, not be defined as a 'person subject to immigration control' (see p81). For further details, including the duration of these protections, see p168.
- If you are the family member of a worker or self-employed person, you have the same residence rights as if you were a worker or a self-employed person yourself. That satisfies the right to reside requirement for all benefits that have such a requirement (see p151). You are also exempt from the habitual residence test for means-tested benefits (see p142), and therefore do not need to be 'habitually resident in fact' (see p146).
- If you are the family member of a self-sufficient person or self-sufficient student, you have the same residence rights as if you were a self-sufficient person or student yourself. That satisfies the right to reside requirement for all benefits that have such a requirement (see p151).
- If your only right to reside is as the family member of an EEA national who has a right to reside as a jobseeker, you have the same residence rights as if you were a jobseeker yourself. If this is your only right to reside, that does not satisfy the right to reside requirement for any of the means-tested benefits (except income-based jobseeker's allowance – see p152).
- If you are the family member of an EEA national who has an initial right of residence for three months, you have an equivalent right to reside. If this is your only right to reside, that does not satisfy the right to reside requirement for any of the means-tested benefits (see p152).
- If you are the family member of an EEA national who has a permanent right of residence, your right to reside satisfies the right to reside requirement for all benefits that have such a requirement (see p151). However, you only have a permanent right to reside yourself (and are exempt from the habitual residence test – see p142), if you are the family member of an EEA national who acquired this permanent residency in less than five years (see p253). **Note:** if you had this permanent right to reside on 31 December 2020 (or had lost it due to being absent from the UK for more than two years, but your absence was less than five years on that date), that can mean you are in a protected group, as in the first bullet above.
- If you have a right to reside as a former family member (see p228), your right to reside satisfies the right to reside requirement for all benefits that have such a requirement (see p151).

15. **Derivative residence rights**

Since the end of the transition period at 11pm on 31 December 2020, you can only have a free movement right to reside, including a derivative right to reside, while you are in one of the protected groups that can have these rights (see p168).

You may be able to 'derive' a right to reside from someone with a right to reside without being her/his family member. These rights are not listed in European Union (EU) Directive 2004/38, but are based on other provisions of EU law, as interpreted by caselaw. The European Economic Area (EEA) Regulations list these rights as 'derivative rights of residence'. However, they interpret them more narrowly and impose some additional conditions. If these mean you do not have a right to reside, you can rely on the rights confirmed by the EU caselaw.

Note:

- If you had a derivative right to reside on 31 December 2020, and on that date, you did not have leave granted under the EU Settlement Scheme, you are (until at least 30 June 2021) in one of the protected groups that can use free movement residence rights. If you are an EEA national, these protections also mean that you cannot be defined as a 'person subject to immigration control' (see p81). For further details, including the duration of these protections, see p168.
- You cannot count periods when you have a derivative right to reside towards the five years of residence required for permanent residency (see p245).
- Some of the circumstances below are similar to those that enable you to retain a right to reside if you are a former family member of an EEA national who conferred a right to reside on you and who has now died or left the UK, or your marriage or civil partnership to her/him has been terminated (see p228). Check whether this may apply to you because it may make it easier to have your residence rights accepted by the benefit authorities and, in certain circumstances, you can count periods with a right to reside as a former family member towards the five years required for permanent residence.
- If you do not fit into any of the groups below, but your circumstances are similar, it may still be arguable that you have a right to reside (see p242).
- If you are a non-EEA national and you have a derivative right to reside or you are a family member of an EEA national in the UK, you may be able to obtain leave to remain under the EU Settlement Scheme (see p49). If you have indefinite leave (also known as as settled status), that satifies the right to reside requirement for those benefits that have it (see p151). If you have limited leave under the EU Settlement Scheme (also known as pre-settled status), this means you are in a protected group that can have a free movement right to reside and, in most cases, this will satisfy the right to reside requirement if you have a derivative right to reside, or if you are a family member of an EEA national with a right to reside (see p218). For further details, exceptions and details of the

Court of Appeal judgment that held that the regulations listing pre-settled status as an excluded right to reside are unlawful, see, for means-tested benefits, p153 and, for child benefit and CTC, p158.

Who has a derivative right to reside

If you are in one of the protected groups (see p168), or for a period before the end of the transition period (11pm on 31 December 2020), you have a derivative right to reside if you are not an 'exempt person' (see below) and you are:[310]

- the child of an EEA national who was a 'worker' in the UK (see p189) while you were living in the UK, and you are currently in education (see p236);[311] *or*
- the primary carer of a child in the above bullet point and the child would be unable to continue her/his education in the UK if you left the UK for an indefinite period (see p238);[312] *or*
- the primary carer of a self-sufficient child who is an EEA national, who would be unable to remain in the UK if you left for an indefinite period (see p240);[313] *or*
- the primary carer of a British citizen residing in the UK who would be unable to reside in the UK or an EEA state if you left the UK for an indefinite period (see p240).[314] **Note:** this right to reside does not satisfy the right to reside requirement for any of the benefits that have this requirement, except for child benefit and child tax credit in limited circumstances, if you are a national of Algeria, Morocco, San Marino, Tunisia or Turkey (see p157); *or*
- aged under 18 and your primary carer is covered by either the second, third or fourth bullet points above and s/he would be prevented from residing in the UK if you left the UK for an indefinite period, and you do not have leave to enter or remain in the UK (other than under the EU Settlement Scheme) (see p241).

Who is an 'exempt person'

Under the EEA Regulations, you are excluded from having a derivative right to reside if you are an 'exempt person'.[315] You are an 'exempt person' if you have a right to reside:[316]

- under any other provision of the EEA Regulations. If this other right to reside is excluded for the benefit you want to claim (eg, as a jobseeker, or an initial right to reside if you are claiming a means-tested benefit), see below;
- as a British citizen or as a Commonwealth citizen with a right of abode;
- as a person with indefinite leave (other than under the EU Settlement Scheme); *or*
- under provisions that exempt certain people from the requirement to have leave – eg, specified aircrew and diplomats.

Have you been refused universal credit on the basis that you are an exempt person?

If you have a derivative right to reside as the primary carer of a worker's child in education, and the Department for Work and Pensions (DWP) refuses your claim for universal credit (UC), or another means-tested benefit, on the grounds that you do not have this derivative right to reside because you have a right to reside as an EEA jobseeker and are therefore an 'exempt person', you should challenge the decision.

1. You can only have a right to reside as a jobseeker if you are looking for work. If you are not looking for work and your claimant commitment does not require you to satisfy the work search and work availability requirements, you do not have a right to reside as a jobseeker and so you are not excluded from having a derivative right to reside. This would apply, for example, if you are the responsible carer of a child under three years old, if you have limited capability for work or (for 13 weeks) if you have experienced domestic violence. For details of the work-related requirements for UC, see CPAG's *Welfare Benefits and Tax Credits Handbook.*

2. If your claimant commitment requires you to search for and be available for work, your right to reside as a jobseeker means you are an 'exempt person' under the EEA Regulations. However, this exclusion is arguably unlawful as the EEA Regulations must be interpreted in accordance with the EU law they are intended to implement (see p174), and there is no requirement in EU law that to access subsistence benefits on the basis of this derivative right to reside you must not have *another* right to reside. The Court of Justice of the European Union (CJEU) recently confirmed this and held that a similar exclusion in German law was unlawful.[317] If you are the primary carer of a worker's child in education, the UK is required to encourage all efforts to enable that child to attend her/his education under the best possible conditions.[318] It is arguable that excluding you as a primary carer who is also a jobseeker from having a derivative right to reside under the EEA Regulations, and so excluding you from UC, infringes this requirement.[319] This argument was already being accepted by First-tier Tribunals in several appeals, without the DWP seeking to appeal the decisions, and the recent CJEU case adds considerable weight to the argument.

3. At the time of writing, the Upper Tribunal was considering a case in which the claimant had been refused UC on the basis that she did not have a derivative right to reside because she was an 'exempt person'.[320] See AskCPAG.org.uk and CPAG's *Welfare Rights Bulletin* for updates.

Croatian, A2 and A8 nationals

The rules about derivative residence rights applied to Croatian, A2 and A8 nationals during the relevant period of restrictions in exactly the same way as for other EEA nationals. However, if you are deriving your right to reside from being a worker's child in education, the primary carer of such a child, or a child of such a primary carer, the restrictions that applied to workers could affect you, because they affected who could have 'worker' status.

If a Croatian or A2 national was subject to restrictions (see p177), the work s/he did only gave her/him worker status if it was done in accordance with her/his worker authorisation document. Therefore, if you are the child of a Croatian or A2 national and you are in education, or you are the primary carer of such a child, the work done by the parent must have been done in accordance with a worker authorisation document for it to enable you to have a derivative right to reside.[321]

If an A8 national was subject to restrictions (see p177), the work s/he did during the period of restrictions (see p176) only gave her/him worker status if it was done for an 'authorised employer' (see p180). Therefore, if you are the child of an A8 national and you are in education, or you are the primary carer of such a child, the work done by the parent must have been for an 'authorised employer' for you to have a derivative right to reside. This includes a period when the parent had a valid worker's registration certificate for her/his employer, but s/he did not complete 12 months of working for an 'authorised employer'.[322] It also includes a period in which the parent was in her/his first month of employment, since the first month of any employment, even if it was never registered, counted as working for an 'authorised employer', provided s/he satisfied the requirements of being a worker, including that the work was accepted as 'genuine and effective' (see p190).[323]

For further details of the restrictions that previously applied to Croatian, A2 and A8 nationals, see p176.

Worker's child in education

A child has a right to reside if:[324]

- s/he was living in the UK at a time when one of her/his parents (or the parent's spouse or civil partner) had a right to reside in the UK as a worker (see p237); *and*
- s/he is now in education (see below).

The purpose of this right of residence is to enable a child to take up her/his right to be educated in the EEA state where her/his (step-)parent is (or has been) employed if the child is also living in that state.[325] For this right to education to be effective, the child must have a right of residence as long as s/he is in education. As the child's right of residence continues until s/he has *completed* her/his education (see below), there is no upper age limit. This *Handbook* refers to a 'child' in education, because s/he must have been a child when the education began.[326]

There must have been a common period when the child was in the UK and one of her/his parents (or step-parents) was a worker in the UK.[327] A child is not considered to have been in the UK before s/he is born.[328] However, if a woman with worker status stops work because of the physical constraints of the late stages of pregnancy or aftermath of childbirth, she can retain worker status (see p207). If this applies, once the child is born, it is arguable that s/he is then the child of a worker (see p237).

The (step-)parent does not need to have continued to be a worker, or have been in the UK, when the child started school or at any time since then.[329]

It is the child's parent, or her/his parent's spouse or civil partner, who must have been an EEA worker in the UK while the child was also in the UK.[330] A child does not have this type of right to reside if the EEA worker is her/his grandparent,[331] her/his parent's partner (rather than spouse or civil partner),[332] or her/his non-parent legal guardian.[333] However, it may be arguable that the question of which rights are conferred on a child by her/his legal guardian should be reconsidered following a recent judgment of the CJEU, which held that a child is the 'extended family member' of her/his non-adoptive legal guardian (see p223).[334]

Note: The Court of Appeal held that you cannot have a right to reside on this basis if your parent was a self-employed EEA national rather than a worker.[335] However, it may be arguable that the Withdrawal Agreements provide for a right to reside on this basis.[336] The DWP accept this if the parent had been a 'frontier worker' in the UK on the basis of being self-employed person (or worker) (see p256), and the guidance confirming this notes it as an example of a new right to reside provided by the Withdrawal Agreement.[337]

Who is 'in education'

Caselaw has confirmed that the definition of '**education**' excludes nursery education,[338] and that a child's rights begin when s/he starts compulsory education at around the age of five (and excludes preschool)[339] or when s/he starts school in reception class, despite being under five years old.[340]

The definition in the EEA Regulations excludes nursery education, but does not exclude education received before the compulsory school age if this is equivalent to the education received at or after the compulsory school age.[341]

Differences in Scotland may affect when residence rights begin. Although there is no reception class in Scotland, it may still be arguable that a child can be 'in education' when s/he is approaching age five. Furthermore, as the Scottish Curriculum for Excellence starts at the age of three, it maybe arguable that a child in Scotland can be in education well before the age of five.

Residence rights apply to the child and her/his primary carer until at least the age of 'majority' while the child remains in education. The *child's* residence rights can continue beyond this age until s/he has completed her/his education. This includes all forms of education, whether vocational or general, and can include university courses. Whether or not the residence rights of the child's *primary carer* continue after the child reaches the age of majority depends on whether the child continues to need her/his presence or care to continue and complete her/his education.[342]

Who is a 'worker'

The child's parent or step-parent who was employed in the UK must have been an EEA national to enable her/him to have had a right to reside as a worker.

The EEA Regulations state that, for this purpose, 'worker' does not include a jobseeker or someone who retains her/his worker status (see p201).[343] It is arguable that the latter exclusion is wrong. The EU regulation that gives a child the right to be educated in a state does so for the child of a national of one EEA state 'who is or has been employed' in another EEA state.[344] Caselaw confirms that a child has a right to reside if s/he is now in education and was in the EEA state during a time when one of her/his parents was exercising rights of residence in that state as a 'worker' or a 'migrant worker'.[345] It appears from the wording of EU Directive 2004/38 that a person who retains her/his status as a worker resides in a country as a 'migrant worker', as s/he has equivalent rights to 'workers', provided s/he satisfies the conditions for retaining worker status. Also, family members of someone who has retained her/his status as a worker have residence rights equivalent to those of family members of workers.

Absence of the child from the UK

A child may lose her/his right to reside as a worker's child in education if s/he leaves the UK but then returns. However, this depends on all the circumstances. DWP guidance suggests that a child may lose this right to reside if s/he has become habitually resident in another EEA state for a substantial period, but not if the absence from the UK is just temporary.[346] However, it may be arguable that what matters is whether the child's studies undertaken on her/his return are a continuation of her/his earlier education. The CJEU has held that a worker's child in education continued to have his rights, despite an absence during which the child went back to his country of origin, because he returned to continue his studies which he could not pursue in his own country.[347]

Primary carer of a worker's child in education

You have a derivative right to reside under the EEA Regulations if you:[348]

- are the 'primary carer' (see below) of a child of a worker who is in education; *and*
- the child would be unable to continue to be educated in the UK if you were required to leave (see p239).

The basis of this right builds on the residence rights of the child, which are necessary in order to be educated in the country where her/his parent is, or was, employed.[349] It is assumed that the child needs an adult to look after her/him and, consequently, her/his primary carer must also have a right of residence.[350] Your rights as the primary carer continue until the child reaches at least the age of majority, and beyond that if s/he continues to need your presence and care in order to pursue and complete her/his education (see p237).[351]

You can have a right to reside as the primary carer of a worker's child in education if you were that worker or if the worker was someone else.

Neither you nor the child need be self-sufficient in order to have residence rights.[352]

Your nationality (other than if you are British, because you would then be an 'exempt person' – see p234 – so you would not need a derivative residence right) and the nationality of the child do not affect this right of residence.[353] However, the child's parent (or step-parent) who had the right to reside as a worker must be an EEA national.

If the child in education is British, that does not prevent you from having a derivative right to reside as her/his primary carer, provided s/he is the child of an EEA worker. Although the EEA Regulations define the child as an 'exempt person' (see p234), that only prevents her/him from having a derivative right to reside under those regulations; it does not prevent you from having a derivative right to reside as her/his primary carer.[354]

Note: The Court of Appeal held that you cannot have a right to reside on this basis if the parent of the child in education was a self-employed EEA national rather than a worker.[355] However, it may be arguable that the Withdrawal Agreements provide a right to reside if you are the primary carer of a child in education if one of her/his parents had, during a common period when the child was in the UK, been a self-employed EEA national in the UK.[356] The DWP accepts this if the parent had been a 'frontier worker' in the UK on the basis of being self-employed person (or worker) (see p256), and the guidance confirming this notes it as an example of a new right to reside provided by the Withdrawal Agreement.[357]

Who is a primary carer

You are a 'primary carer' of someone if you are her/his direct relative or legal guardian, and either you:[358]

- have primary responsibility for that person's care; *or*
- share equally the responsibility for that person's care with one other person (see p234).

Note: if you do not come within the above definition of 'primary carer', you may be able to argue that you have rights based on EU caselaw (see p233) – eg, if you are the primary carer of someone who is dependent on you, but you are not her/his direct relative or legal guardian.

You are not regarded as someone's primary carer solely on the basis of a financial contribution you make towards her/his care.[359]

Is the child dependent on you

The decision of whether or not a child would be unable to continue her/his education or remain in the UK, or, if British, whether s/he would be unable to reside in the EEA, if you were to leave the UK, must take account, in the best interests of the child, of all her/his specific circumstances.[360]

If you share equally the responsibility of caring with another person, the question of whether the child would be unable to continue her/his education or remain in the UK, or the British citizen would be unable to reside in the EEA, must be decided on the basis that you would both leave the UK, unless the person with whom you share the care has already acquired a derivative right to reside before the responsibility for care became shared.[361]

Primary carer of a child who is self-sufficient

You have a derivative right to reside under the EEA Regulations if:[362]

- you are the 'primary carer' (see above) of a child under 18 who is residing in the UK as a self-sufficient person (see p211); *and*
- the child would be unable to remain in the UK if you were required to leave (see above).

The basis of this right of residence is to make effective the rights of the child, as it is assumed that s/he needs an adult to look after her/him and so her/his primary carer must also have a right of residence.[363]

Note: the EEA Regulations treat the primary carer as a family member of the child. Therefore, the child's resources must be sufficient for both you and her/him (see p213 for what counts as sufficient) and you must both have comprehensive sickness insurance cover (see p214).[364] However, the question of whether it is lawful to require all relevant family members to have comprehensive sickness insurance has been referred to the CJEU.[365]

Your nationality does not affect this right of residence. However, the child must be an EEA national to have a right to reside as a self-sufficient person.

Primary carer of a British citizen

You have a derivative right to reside under the EEA Regulations if you:[366]

- are the 'primary carer' (see p239) of a British citizen who is residing in the UK; *and*
- the British citizen would be unable to reside in the UK or an EEA state if you left the UK for an indefinite period (see p239). Other than in exceptional circumstances, this residence right only applies to non-EEA nationals.

This right of residence is based on the right provided by Article 20 of the Treaty on the Functioning of the European Union (TFEU) for all nationals of EU member states to be citizens of the EU, and for every EU citizen to have the right to move and reside freely within the EU. If an EU citizen is dependent on another person who is a non-EEA national to make this right effective, the non-EEA national as the EU citizen's primary carer must be given a right of residence.[367] However, the EEA Regulations only provide these rights when the dependent person is British. If you are the primary carer of an EEA national who is not British, you can rely directly on EU law, but as these arguments can be complex you should get specialist advice.

Note: in most cases when this right to reside applies, the British citizen is a dependent child, but, in exceptional cases, could be a dependent adult.[368]

Having a right to reside on the basis of being the primary carer of a British citizen only entitles you to child benefit and child tax credit (CTC) if you (or the family member you are living with) are a national of Algeria, Morocco, San Marino, Tunisia or Turkey and you (or s/he) are lawfully working in the UK (see p408). Otherwise, having a right to reside on the basis of being the primary carer of a British citizen does not enable you to be entitled to any benefit that requires a right to reside, because that is listed as an excluded right of residence in each of the benefit and tax credit regulations (see p151). However, it does mean that you are not defined as a 'person subject to immigration control' (see p85). You may therefore be able to claim attendance allowance, disability living allowance (DLA), personal independence payment and carer's allowance, provided you meet all the other presence and residence requirements (see p280). You may also be entitled to working tax credit (WTC), since you have a right to work.

Note: if this is your only right of residence, you should obtain specialist immigration advice on the type(s) of immigration leave you can apply for, and which would be best in your circumstances. You may be entitled to immigration leave on the basis of your right to family life (see p43). If this leave is granted without the condition that you have no recourse to public funds, you are not excluded from benefits, as you are not defined as a 'person subject to immigration control' (see p81) and you have a non-excluded right to reside (see p166). You may be entitled to leave under the EU Settlement Scheme (see p49). This leave is always granted without any public funds conditions. If you are granted indefinite leave under the EU Settlement Scheme (also known as settled status), that satisfies the right to reside requirement for benefits. If you are granted pre-settled status, note that the Court of Appeal held that pre-settled status was itself a qualifying right to reside and quashed the regulations that list it as an excluded right to reside for means-tested benefits. However, due to delays in this decision being implemented, the DWP seeking to challenge it further, and the argument relating specifically to EU citizens, the benefit authorities may not accept that pre-settled status is a qualifying right to reside. For details of all excluded residence rights and steps to follow if you have pre-settled status, see p152 for means-tested benefits and, for child benefit and CTC, see p157.

Child of a primary carer

You have a derivative right to reside under the EEA Regulations if:[369]

- you are aged under 18 and your primary carer has a derivative right to reside as the primary carer of:
  - a worker's child in education (see p236); *or*

- a child under 18 who is residing in the UK as a self-sufficient person (see p240); *or*
- a British citizen who would be unable to reside in the UK or an EEA state if the primary carer left the UK (see above); *and*

- you do not have leave to enter or remain in the UK (other than under the EU Settlement Scheme); *and*
- your primary carer would be prevented from residing in the UK if you left the UK for an indefinite period.

The basis of this right of residence is to make effective the rights of the primary carer and the other child for whom s/he is caring. Your nationality does not affect this right of residence.

Example

Veronika is a Czech national and has lived in the UK since 2016. She is aged 16, has learning difficulties and is eight months pregnant. She has stopped attending school. Veronika's mother last worked in the UK in 2017 when she stopped work to care for Veronika's grandfather. She has a right to reside as the primary carer of Patrik, Veronika's younger brother who is nine years old and in school. Veronika has a derivative right to reside because her mother has to look after her, and if Veronika left the UK, so too would her mother. This right to reside enables Veronika to be entitled to UC on the basis of her pregnancy. When Veronika's baby is born, she will be able to claim child benefit and continue to get UC as she will be responsible for a child.

Other derivative rights

It is arguable that you may have a right to reside if your circumstances do not exactly fit the criteria for the derivative rights on p234, but they are similar and the legal principles underlying derivative residence rights could be applied. For example, you may be able to argue that you have a right to reside in the following situations.

- You are the primary carer of a worker's child who is under school age. Such a child has a clear right to reside as the family member of a worker and it may be arguable that you must have a right to reside to make the child's right effective. However, the Upper Tribunal held that the primary carer does not have right to reside in this situation.[370]
- You are the primary carer of a child who has a permanent right to reside. The same principles that apply to give other primary carers residence rights arguably apply if the child has permanent residence – ie, to make effective the rights of the child.
- You are aged under 21 (but not under 18) and/or are dependent on a primary carer with a derivative right to reside and s/he would be prevented from

residing in the UK if you left the UK for an indefinite period, and you do not have leave to enter or remain in the UK. The EEA Regulations only give a derivative right to reside in this situation if you are under 18.[371]

- You are the child of a self-employed person in education, or you are the primary carer of such a child. The Court of Appeal held that you cannot have a right to reside on this basis and permission to appeal to the Supreme Court was refused.[372] However, it may be arguable that the Withdrawal Agreements do provide for residence rights on this basis.[373] The DWP accept that you can have an equivalent right to reside while you are in education if you had been in the UK while your parent had been a 'frontier worker' in the UK on the basis of being *either* a worker or self-employed person (see p256), and the guidance confirming that notes it as an example of a new right to reside.[374]

There may be other circumstances in which you need a right to reside to make effective someone else's residence rights. The strength of your argument always depends on your circumstances and those of the other relevant people.

Benefit entitlement

If you have a derivative right to reside (other than on the basis of being the primary carer of a British citizen – see below), this satisfies the right to reside requirement for any of the benefits or tax credits to which that requirement applies (see p151).

If your right to reside is on the basis of your being the primary carer of a British citizen, this is specifically excluded for each of the benefits and tax credits that have a right to reside requirement (see p151). To date, all legal challenges to this general exclusion have failed. However, the Upper Tribunal held that a Moroccan national, whose only right to reside in the UK was as the primary carer of a British citizen, was entitled to child benefit and CTC as she was lawfully working in the UK and therefore covered by the association agreement between the EU and Morocco. This provides for equal treatment in relation to family benefits and therefore she could not be excluded from these benefits by the UK benefit regulations.[375] For details of these agreements, see p408.

If you had a derivative right to reside in the past, note:

- if you had a derivative right to reside on 31 December 2020, that can mean that you are (until at least 30 June 2021) in a protected group that can have free movement rights, and, if you are an EEA national, not defined as a 'person subject to immigration control' (see p81). For further details, including the duration of these protections, see p168;
- the period of time when you have a derivative right to reside does not count towards the five years of residence required for permanent residence (see below). If you have lived in the UK for five years, check whether you can obtain indefinite leave to remain in the UK under the EU Settlement Scheme (also

known as settled status) as this requires actual residence, not residence with a right to reside (see p49).

16. **Permanent right to reside**

Note: since the end of the transition period at 11pm on 31 December 2020, you can only have a free movement right to reside, including a permanent right to reside, while you are in one of the protected groups that can have these rights.

If you are in one of the protected groups (see below and p168), or for a period before the end of the transition period, you can have a permanent right to reside if you have resided in the UK with a free movement right to reside (other than a derivative right to reside) for a continuous period of five years, disregarding certain gaps, or in certain limited circumstances, after a shorter period of time (see p253).

Once you have a permanent right to reside, you do not need to satisfy any ongoing conditions[376] (eg, you do not also need to be a worker) and this right of residence satisfies the right to reside requirement for all the benefits that have such a requirement.

Other than in exceptional circumstances, you only lose your permanent right of residence if you are absent from the UK for more than two consecutive years, but note also the second bullet point below (see p255).[377]

The main information on the protected groups, including their duration, is on p168. Below are some additional points on rules about both the protected groups and permanent residence.

- You are in a protected group that can have a free movement right to reside (until at least 30 June 2021), if on 31 December 2020, you did not have leave granted under the European Union (EU) Settlement Scheme, and either:[378]
  - you had a permanent right to reside on that date; *or*
  - you are *treated as* having permanent right to reside on that date if you had lost a previously acquired permanent right to reside due to being absent for more than two years, but your absence on 31 December 2020 was less than five years; *or*
  - you are a 'relevant family member' (see p169) of a European Economic Area (EEA) national who was in either of the above groups.
- If you are an EEA national covered by the above protected group, this also means that (until at least 30 June 2021), you cannot be defined as a 'person subject to immigration control' (see p81).
- If you have pre-settled status, you are in a different protected group that can have a free movement right to reside. It may be easier for you to obtain a permanent right to reside, because the quality of residence required for some of the five years may be easier to satisfy (see p245). However, note also that, at the time of writing, the Court of Appeal had just held that pre-settled status

was itself a qualifying right to reside for EU citizens claiming means-tested benefits – see p153 (and for child benefit and CTC, see p157).

- Check whether you can obtain indefinite leave under the EU Settlement Scheme (also known as settled status), as the criteria includes that you either have resided in the UK for five years (not necessarily with a right to reside, but if you are not an EEA national you will need to have been a family member of an EEA national or had a derivative right to reside) *or* you are an EEA national and satisfy the criteria for obtaining this leave after less than five years which are broadly the same as those to acquire permanent residence in less than five years (or you were the family member of such an EEA national at the relevant time). For information on the criteria for settled status, see p51.
- From the date you are granted settled status, you have a right to reside that satisfies the right to reside requirement for all the benefits that have it. However, this does not in itself provide anyone defined as your family member with a right to reside, although s/he may be able to obtain her/his own grant of settled status. In contrast, anyone defined as your family member (see p218) *does* have a right to reside if you have a permanent right to reside.

Permanent residence after five years

If you are in one of the protected groups (see above), or for a period before the end of the transition period (31 December 2020), you have a permanent right to reside if you have 'resided legally' (see below) for a continuous period of five years (see p250).[379]

You can have permanent residence whether you are an EEA national or non-EEA national, provided you satisfy the criteria. However, if you are a non-EEA national, there are fewer ways in which you count as having resided legally (see p248). If you are a Croatian, A2 or A8 national, additional restrictions may affect you during the years after your country joined the EU and you can only count periods of residence in the UK before your country joined the EU in limited circumstances (see p249).

Resided legally

The precise quality of residence that you are required to have had for a continuous period of five years in the UK may vary depending on the legislation you are relying on. In most cases, it makes no difference, and so the phrase 'resided legally' is used in this section. However, check the quality of residence you are required to have in case this could affect your rights.[380]

- For periods before the end of the transition period (11pm on 31 December 2020), and after that date if you are in a protected group *other than* having pre-settled status, EEA Regulations require you to have resided 'in accordance with these regulations' (or previous regulations).
- For periods after the end of the transition period, while you have pre-settled status, the EEA Regulations are amended such that you are required to have

resided 'lawfully'. This could potentially include periods when you did not have a free movement right to reside, but, for example, did have pre-settled status.

EU Directive 2004/38 requires you to have resided 'legally'. This means that you must have had a residence right under the Directive or under any of the earlier EU legislation that it replaced. You count as residing legally during periods when you have a free movement right to reside:[381]

- as a worker (see p189), including if you have retained this status (see p201);
- as a self-employed person (see p196), including if you have retained this status (see p201);
- as a self-sufficient person, including a self-sufficient student (see p211);
- as a family member of any of the above (see p247);
- (EEA Regulations only) as a jobseeker, or family member of a jobseeker, since 30 April 2006 (see p247); *or*
- (EEA Regulations only) based on your, or your family member's, initial right of residence, since 30 April 2006 (see p247).

Most periods when you have a free movement residence right, other than a derivative right to reside, can count, but periods with rights other than those above can be more complicated.

Note: if you have lived in the UK for five years, even if you did not have a right to reside for all, or any of that period, check whether you can obtain indefinite leave to remain in the UK under the EU Settlement Scheme (also known as settled status). That only requires actual residence, not residence with a right to reside (see p49). From the date you are granted settled status, you have a right to reside that satisfies the right to reside requirement for all the benefits that have that requirement. However, it does not in itself provide your family members with a right to reside, but each may be able to obtain her/his own grant of settled status. In contrast, anyone defined as your family member does have a right to reside if you have a permanent right to reside (see p218).

Periods before 30 April 2006

The right of permanent residence was only introduced on 30 April 2006 when the EU Directive 2004/38 and the EEA Regulations 2006 came into force. However, you can still count periods when you had a right of residence before 30 April 2006 towards the required five years, if your residence was on the basis of one or more of those points listed above (other than the last two bullet points: jobseeker or initial right to reside, or as a family member of an EEA national with either).

If you completed five years' legal residence before 30 April 2006 and then had a gap of less than two years when you were either out of the UK or residing in the UK but not 'residing legally', this does not affect your acquiring permanent residency.[382] If you completed five years' legal residence and then had a gap of two or more years when you were not residing in accordance with the EEA Regulations, see p252. If you completed five years' legal residence and were then absent from the UK for more than two continuous years, you lost your right of permanent residence (see p255).

Jobseekers

You can count periods when you had a right to reside as a jobseeker (see p182), or as a family member of a jobseeker, from 30 April 2006 towards your five years of 'residing in accordance with the EEA Regulations'.[383] You cannot count periods before this date, as jobseekers did not have a right to reside under earlier regulations. If you need to rely on periods when you were seeking work before 30 April 2006, check whether you had another residence right at that time – eg, if you retained worker status.

Guidance to decision makers confirms that if you have had a right to reside as a jobseeker, including if you have been awarded income-based jobseeker's allowance (JSA) on the basis of this right to reside for a continuous period of five years, this is sufficient for you to acquire permanent residence.[384] It further states that if your JSA is disallowed, the continuity of your legal residence is broken.[385] This is not necessarily correct, as you can have a right to reside as a jobseeker without receiving JSA (see p187).[386] The guidance also confirms that a period when your income-based JSA is not paid because of a sanction does not affect your continuity of residence as a jobseeker.[387]

Note: periods when your only right of residence was as a jobseeker, or as a family member of a jobseeker, do not count as 'residing legally' under the EU Directive.[388] However, this is rarely a problem in practice since you can count such periods under the EEA Regulations.

Initial right of residence

You can count periods after 30 April 2006 when you had an initial right of residence for the first three months after your arrival in the UK (see p181), or as the family member of someone with an initial right of residence, towards your five years of residing in accordance with the EEA Regulations.[389] (You cannot count such periods under the EU Directive.[390]) There was no initial right of residence before 30 April 2006.

Family members

You can count periods when you have a right to reside as the family member (see p220) of a 'qualified person' (see p172) towards your five years of 'residing legally', including if you are an 'extended family member' with the relevant residence document.[391]

If you are the family member of a person who has acquired permanent residency after residing legally in the UK for five years, you have a right to reside for as long as you remain her/his family member.[392] Under the EEA Regulations, you can also use periods as a family member of a person with a permanent right of residence towards your five years of residing in accordance with those regulations, and so acquire a permanent right of residence yourself.[393] This is in addition to any other periods when you have a right to reside through being a family member of an EEA national with a right to reside – eg, as a worker (see p245).

Note:

- If you are a non-EEA national, see below.
- If you are the family member of a person who has acquired permanent residency in less than five years, you may have permanent residency yourself (see p253).

Former family members

In certain circumstances, you can count periods since 30 April 2006 when you retained a right to reside as a former family member under the EEA Regulations towards your five years of residence required for permanent residence. If you are a non-EEA national, you must have a right to reside as a former family member at the end of your five-year period to acquire a permanent right to reside under the EEA Regulations.[394]

The circumstances in which your retained right to reside as a former family member count towards your five years are if you are also a worker or a self-employed or self-sufficient person, or the family member of such a person.[395] However, if you were the child of the qualified person and were in education immediately before the qualified person died or left the UK, or you were the parent with custody of such a child, you do not have to meet this additional requirement.[396]

For further details on retaining your residence rights as a former family member, see p228.

Non-European Economic Area nationals

Periods when you are in the UK with leave to enter or remain do not count as periods of 'residing legally' under the EU Directive. They also do not count under the EEA Regulations as they are not periods in which you resided in accordance with those regulations and so do not count towards the five years required for permanent residency.[397]

If you are a non-EEA national, you cannot have a right of residence as a worker, self-employed person, person who retains either of these statuses, a self-sufficient person or a self-sufficient student. However, you can have a right of residence as the family member of an EEA national who is in one of these groups.

In practice, therefore, the only ways you can obtain a permanent right of residence after five years of residing legally is by either:

- residing for a five-year period as the family member of an EEA national who is legally residing; *or*

- retaining the right as a former family member on the basis of either the death of your spouse or civil partner or the termination of your marriage or civil partnership (see p230).[398]

Note:
- If you are the family member of a dual British/EEA citizen, you can only acquire a permanent right to reside as her/his family member under the EEA Regulations if, at the time s/he acquired British citizenship, s/he was either a 'qualified person' (see p172) or had a permanent right to reside under those regulations.[399]
- In limited circumstances, you can also acquire a right of permanent residence in less than five years if you are the family member of an EEA national who has acquired a permanent right of residence in less than five years (see p253).

Croatian, A2 and A8 nationals

If you are a Croatian, A2 or A8 national, you can acquire permanent residency after five years of residing legally in the same way as any other EEA national. However, note the following.

- If you are relying on periods when you were subject to additional restrictions on your residence rights, these may affect whether you had a right to reside as a jobseeker or a worker, or retained worker status (see p176). **Note:** the Court of Appeal has held that the restrictions on A8 nationals ended on 30 April 2009 and their extension to 30 April 2011 was unlawful.[400] This means that if at the time you would not have had a right to reside as a jobseeker, a worker or retained your worker status during this two-year period because of the restrictions, you can retrospectively be accepted as having had these residence rights and count this period as one when you were residing legally.
- The Upper Tribunal held that it was 'disproportionate' to disregard the years of work by an A8 national and his subsequent involuntary unemployment, just because he had not complied with the restrictions, and accepted that he had acquired permanent residency (see p179).[401]
- If you are relying on periods when you were living in the UK before your country joined the EU, you do not count as having resided legally just on the basis that you had leave to enter or remain in the UK. However, you count as residing legally if:[402]
  - you had leave to enter or remain in the UK; *and*
  - you would have had a right of residence as a worker, self-employed person, person who retains one of those statuses, a self-sufficient person or self-sufficient student, except for the fact that you were not an EU national at the time.

Derivative right to reside

Periods when you have resided with a derivative right to reside (see p233) do not count as periods of residing legally, and so you cannot count them towards your five years for the purposes of acquiring permanent residency under either the EEA Regulations or the EU Directive.[403]

Continuity of residence

You acquire permanent residency when you have been 'residing legally' (see p245) for a continuous period of five years.[404] However, the continuity of your residence is not affected by certain absences from the UK (see below). It is also arguable that the continuity of your residence is not affected by certain gaps during the five years when you were in the UK, but did not count as 'residing legally' (see p251).

Note: if one of the absences below applied to you on 31 December 2020, you are *treated* as residing in the UK for the purpose of determining whether you are in a protected group that can (until at least 30 June 2021) have a free movement right to reside. For details of these protections, including their duration, see p168.[405]

Absence from the UK

Temporary absences from the UK do not affect the continuity of your residence if:[406]

- they add up to less than six months a year in total;
- it is one absence of up to 12 consecutive months for important reasons – eg, pregnancy and childbirth, serious illness, study or vocational training, or a posting abroad. If you have one absence of up to 12 months for a similar important reason, it should also not affect the continuity of your residence;[407] *or*
- they are for compulsory military service.

If you have one or more of the above temporary absences from the UK, you can count the time spent abroad as part of your five continuous years.[408] However, you are likely to need to make this argument to the benefit authority, as guidance to decision makers only refers to earlier caselaw that held that time spent abroad during a temporary absence does *not* count towards your five continuous years.[409] In support of your argument, note that the guidance is not legally binding and that the approach of the most recent caselaw (each heard by a two-judge panel rather than a single commissioner) should be followed. The Upper Tribunal summarised these alternative approaches, noting that the most recent caselaw has held that the absences abroad counted towards the five years.[410]

Example

Botond is a Hungarian national. In July 2015, he came to the UK and began working as a self-employed carpenter. His business was declining, so he stopped his self-employment in August 2019 and returned to Hungary. Botond was then offered employment in the UK, and he returned to take this up in January 2020. However, in February 2021, Botond left work to care for his British girlfiend and claimed universal credit (UC) as her carer. Botond satisfied the right to reside right requirement for UC as he was in a protected group that could have a free movement right to reside on 31 December 2020 he had a right to reside as a worker and did not have leave under the EU Settlement Scheme – see p168) *and* when he claimed UC he had a permanent right to reside as he had legally resided in the UK for a continuous period of five years, including the five months he was in Hungary. In March 2021, Botond applied for settled status under the EU Settlement Scheme and that was granted in April 2021.

Your continuity of residence is broken if you are subject to a deportation or exclusion order, or you are removed from the UK.[411]

Gaps while in the UK

Between the periods when you are residing legally in the UK, you may have one or more temporary periods when you remain in the UK, but you are not 'residing legally'. These periods are not covered in the EU Directive or the EEA Regulations, but have been considered by caselaw.[412]

You may be able to argue that the continuity of your residence is not affected by such a gap, on the grounds that if continuity is not affected by your being abroad for certain periods, it should also not be affected by equivalent periods when you remain in the UK but do not count as residing legally.[413] This argument was rejected by the Court of Appeal which held that acquiring a permanent right of residence depends on continuous residence with a qualifying status.[414] However, it is arguable that the Court of Appeal did not adequately consider all the arguments and relevant caselaw, and also that the decision only applies in cases where the facts are comparable to the ones in that case, which concerned a non-EEA national who could not provide evidence of five years' residence as a dependent family member.[415] Since this decision, the Upper Tribunal stated that the legislation on continuity should be interpreted as requiring continuity of residence, not necessarily continuity of having 'resided legally', provided the total period of having 'legally resided' is at least five years.[416] However, a more recent Upper Tribunal decision held that the previous Upper Tribunal decision was decided without referring to the Court of Appeal's decision and that the latter interpretation should be followed.[417]

It is, therefore, important to identify a right to reside in any potential gaps in your five years if possible. You should also check whether you can obtain indefinite leave to remain under the EU Settlement Scheme (also known as 'settled status'), but note that this leave only gives you a right to reside from the date it is granted (see p49).

Guidance to decision makers states that you can have a cumulative gap of up to 30 days in any 12-month period between periods of residence on different bases – eg, a gap between having a right to reside as a self-employed person and then as a worker. However, it goes on to state that a gap between two periods of the same type of residence (eg, as a jobseeker) breaks the continuity of residence.[418] The guidance gives no legal basis for this and, as guidance, it is not legally binding.

The guidance also correctly notes that if you have been given a benefit sanction, the continuity of your residence is not affected.[419] However, it also states that if your UC or JSA is disallowed, the continuity of your legal residence is broken.[420] This is not necessarily correct, as you can have a right to reside as a jobseeker, or with worker status retained while involuntarily unemployed and registered as a jobseeker, without receiving UC or JSA (see p187 and p204).[421]

If you stopped work to care for someone, you may be able to argue that you retained your worker or self-employed status (see p201).

If the gap was while you were in prison, this generally interrupts the continuity of your residence and you cannot count the time spent in prison towards your five years.[422] The Court of Justice of the European Union (CJEU) found that taking time spent in prison into account when calculating the five years is contrary to the EU Directive's aim of strengthening social cohesion. This aim was a key factor behind establishing the right of permanent residency and was also the reason why permanent residency depends not just on the duration, but also the quality of residence, relating to the level of integration in the member state. Receiving a prison sentence shows a person's non-compliance with the values of that state.[423]

This approach suggests that other gaps in your five-year period should be treated differently, particularly if they do not call into question your level of integration in the UK – eg, periods when you temporarily ceased to be a worker or self-employed because you were caring for someone. Being detained in a secure mental health unit does not break continuity of residence.[424]

Note: if you were in prison on 31 December 2020, it is likely that the benefit authorities will not accept that you had a free movement right to reside on that date for the purpose of determining whether you are in a protected group that can (until at least 30 June 2021) have a free movement right to reside.[425] For details of these protections, including their duration, see p168. If you are refused benefit on this basis, challenge the decision and seek specialist advice.

Gaps after five years

If you have a gap, during which you were in the UK but not residing in accordance with the current or previous regulations, of at least two continuous years after a five-year period during which you resided either:[426]

- in accordance with previous regulations (see p245) – ie, before the current regulations came into force on 1 February 2017; *or*
- before the country of which you are a national joined the EU (see p249),

you cannot count those periods of residence under the EEA Regulations.

However, it is arguable that discounting these periods of residence, which would otherwise result in permanent residence, is not compatible with EU law: the EU

Directive is clear that permanent residence is only lost if you are absent from the UK for more than two consecutive years (see p255).[427] The CJEU has held that a gap of less than two years which follows the five-year period does not affect the acquisition of permanent residence.[428] However, this does not necessarily mean that a gap of more than two years does affect it. In addition, the CJEU judgment concerned periods wholly before the right of permanent residence existed (ie, before 30 April 2006), whereas the exclusion in the EEA Regulations also covers periods since then. For residence before 30 April 2006, see p246.

Permanent residence in less than five years

If you are in one of the protected groups (see p168), or for a period before the end of the transition period (31 December 2020), you can, in the circumstances below, acquire a permanent right of residence in less than five years.

You have a permanent right to reside if you:[429]

- were a worker (see p189) or self-employed person (see p196) and at the time you cease working, you:
  - had reached pension age, or (workers only) had taken early retirement,[430] and you either:
    - had a spouse or civil partner who is a British citizen (or who lost that nationality by marrying you); *or*
    - had worked in the UK for the preceding year and resided in the UK continuously (see p255) for more than three years. Under the EEA Regulations, this residence must have been immediately before you stopped working; *or*
  - stopped your activity as a worker or self-employed person in the UK because of a permanent incapacity (see below) and:
    - you had a spouse or civil partner who is a British citizen (or who lost that nationality by marrying you); *or*
    - you had resided in the UK continuously (see p255) for more than two years; *or*
    - the incapacity was as a result of an accident at work or occupational disease that resulted in benefit entitlement – eg, industrial injuries disablement benefit; *or*
  - you are a worker or self-employed in another EEA country while residing in the UK and returning, as a rule, at least once a week, following (under the EEA Regulations immediately following) three years of continuous employment or self-employment, and residence, in the UK; *or*
- are the family member of a worker or self-employed person in any of the above groups and satisfy other conditions (see p255); *or*
- are the family member of a worker or self-employed person who died while still working and who did not acquire a permanent right of residence as a result of being in one of the above groups and:

- s/he had resided (see p255) in the UK for two years; *or*
- the death resulted from an accident at work or an occupational disease; *or*
- (EU Directive only) you lost your UK nationality as a result of marrying her/him.

Note: these circumstances can enable you to obtain indefinite leave to remain under the EU Settlement Scheme (also referred to as 'settled status') in less than five years (see p49).

Permanent incapacity

'Permanent incapacity' is the opposite of temporary incapacity.[431]

If your incapacity is not permanent, you may be able to retain your worker or self-employed status on the basis that you are temporarily unable to work due to illness or accident (see p207).

What can be treated as a period of work

If the basis on which you acquire a permanent right to reside in less than five years requires you to have worked for a period of time, in addition to the periods when you are actually working, the following are treated as periods of activity as a worker or self-employed person:[432]

- periods when you were not working for reasons not of your making;
- periods when you were not working because of an illness or accident;
- periods of involuntary unemployment (see p203) recorded by the relevant employment office – ie, Jobcentre Plus. **Note:** the EEA Regulations limit this basis to workers, but it is strongly arguable it should also apply to self-employed persons given the CJEU caselaw confirming that self-employed people as well as workers can retain status on this basis (see p202).

Under the EEA Regulations, you must meet the requirements for retaining worker status during these periods (see p201). If you are a Croatian, A2 or A8 national, the EEA Regulations also require you to have complied with the additional restrictions that affected whether you could have, or retain, worker status in order to count periods as periods of work (see p176).[433] However, the Upper Tribunal has held that the UK did not impose restrictions on the right of A8 nationals to permanent residence in under five years and, therefore, periods of employment count for this purpose, even if they did not comply with the restrictions – eg, if your work was not registered under the Worker Registration Scheme.[434]

Note: if you retire or become permanently incapable of work while you are in one of the above situations, since you are treated as being in a period of activity as a worker or self-employed person, provided you satisfy the other requirements, you can acquire permanent residence on that basis. This approach was followed by the Court of Appeal, which held that a permanent right to reside can still be acquired, if permanent incapacity is preceded by temporary incapacity rather than actual employment, provided the person has resided in the UK (see below) for more than two years at the date the incapacity became permanent.[435]

Residing in the UK

Some of the ways in which you can acquire permanent residence in less than five years require you to have resided in the UK continuously for specified periods. Whether or not you satisfy this can be affected by the way the phrase 'resided in the UK continuously' is interpreted.

The Supreme Court has held that to acquire permanent residency in less than five years following retirement, 'residence' means 'factual residence', rather than the 'legal residence' required for acquiring permanent residence after five years[436] and that earlier caselaw that interpreted 'residence' as 'legal residence' should not be followed.[437] In a subsequent case, the Upper Tribunal has held that this meaning of 'residence' also applies for acquiring permanent residence in less than five years following permanent incapacity.[438]

It is also arguable that when calculating the period of your continuous residence, certain absences should not affect your continuity of residence in the same way as for acquiring permanent residence after five years (see p250).

Family members

You acquire permanent residence in less than five years if you are living in the UK and are the family member (see p220) of someone who has acquired a permanent right to reside under the first bullet point on p253. The requirements of the EU Directive and the EEA Regulations differ on the circumstances in which you have this right to reside.

- **Under the EU Directive,** you must 'reside with' the family member in the UK. You do not have to live with the person; it is sufficient that you are living in the UK now.[439] You do not have to have lived in the UK for the same period as her/him, and you do not need to have been her/his family member throughout this time.[440]
- **Under the EEA Regulations, since 1 February 2017,** you must have had a right to reside on the basis of being her/his family member at the point s/he ceased activity as a worker or self-employed person.[441]

If you are refused benefit on the grounds that you do not satisfy the EEA Regulations but you do satisfy the EU Directive, you should challenge the decision on the basis that you have a right to reside under the Directive.

Loss of permanent right to reside

Once you have a permanent right to reside (either because you have resided legally in the UK for five years or under the rules that enable you to acquire permanent residence in less than five years), you only lose this right if you are absent from the UK for more than two consecutive years.[442]

Note:

- You are *treated as* having a permanent right to reside in the UK on 31 December 2020 for the purpose of being in a protected group that can have a free movement right to reside after that date, if you had lost your previous permanent right to reside due to being absent from the UK for more than two years, but on that date your absence was less than five years.[443] For further details of these protections, including their duration, see p168.
- In exceptional circumstances, your residence rights can be revoked or cancelled on grounds of public policy, public security or public health (see p61).[444] If you are told this has happened or will happen to you, get specialist immigration advice immediately.

Benefit entitlement

If you have a permanent right to reside, this satisfies the right to reside requirement for all the benefits that have this requirement (see p151).

If you acquired a permanent right to reside in less than five years, you are exempt from the habitual residence test for means-tested benefits (see p142), and therefore do not need to be 'habitually resident in fact' (see p146).

If you had this permanent right to reside on 31 December 2020 (or had lost it due to being absent from the UK for more than two years, but your absence was less than five years on that date), this can mean you are (until at least 30 June 2021) in a protected group that can have free movement rights, and, if you are an EEA national, not be defined as a 'person subject to immigration control' (see p81). For further details, including the duration of these protections, see p168.

To claim benefit on the basis of your permanent residence, you must provide evidence of this. It may help you to refer to decision makers' guidance, including sections on evidence, if this supports your situation.[445] You should always provide as much documentary evidence that you satisfy the conditions for permanent residence as you can. However, if you are unable, for example, to prove you worked for a relevant period, the decision maker should use additional records available to her/him – eg, national insurance contribution records.[446] This is covered in more detail on p460. For more information on evidence, see Chapter 20.

17. Frontier worker

You may have rights (see below) as a frontier worker in the UK if you are a European Economic Area (EEA) national and on 31 December 2020, and continuously since then, you have been 'not primarily resident in the UK' (see below), and either:[447]

- a worker in the UK (see p189); *or*
- a self-employed person in the UK (see p196); *or*
- you have retained your worker or self-employed status (see p201).

You are treated as '**not primarily resident in the UK**'if you have either:[448]

- been present in the UK for less than 180 days in the last 12 months; *or*
- returned to your country of residence at least once in the last six months, or at least twice in the last 12 months, unless there are exceptional reasons for your not doing so.

The rights that you have as a frontier worker include rights to means-tested benefits without nationality-based discrimination.[449] Consequently, if you are a frontier worker, or if you have been granted limited leave under the European Union (EU) Settlement Scheme (also known as 'pre-settled status') and you are a family member of a frontier worker, you are exempt from the habitual residence test for all means-tested benefits (see p142). **Note:** you still have to satisfy all the other conditions of entitlement, including the requirement to be present in Great Britain (other than for specified temporary absences – see p314).[450]

If you are the child of a frontier worker, you have a right to reside in the UK to complete your education. Your primary carer also has a right to reside until you reach the age of majority, or if you continue to need a primary carer beyond then, until you complete your education. These rights are similar to the derivative residence rights that the child of a worker in education, and her/his primary carer, can have (see p236). However, a significant difference is that while only children of *workers* in education (and their primary carer's children) can have a derivative right to reside under the EEA Regulations, a child in education (and her/his primary carer) can have this right to reside if her/his parent is a frontier worker on the basis of being a worker or a self-employed person.[451]

Note: separate regulations prevent you from claiming UC, if you are (or, for a joint claim, you and your partner are both) a 'frontier worker'. For the purpose of this exclusion 'frontier worker' is defined as a person 'in Great Britain' for the purpose of UC,[452] but who does not reside in the UK (other than a crown servant, or member of the forces posted, overseas) who does not reside in the UK.[453] If you are excluded from claiming UC on this basis, you may be able to make new claim for the legacy means-tested benefits and tax credits.

18. Other European freedom of movement residence rights

Until the end of the transition period (11pm 31 December 2020), if you did not have a right to reside in the UK under the European Economic Area (EEA) Regulations or on EU Directive 2004/38, it was possible in limited circumstances to argue that despite not meeting all of the specific conditions required in those pieces of legislation, you still had a right to reside by applying principles that have been accepted in other cases.

In particular, it has been accepted that you may have residence rights directly from the Treaty on the Functioning of the European Union, if these are necessary for someone else's rights not to be infringed.[454] For example, for a British citizen not to be deterred from moving freely and working in an EEA country, it may be necessary for her/his family members to have a right to reside if they accompany her/him on her/his return to the UK (see p224).[455] In other cases, it has been accepted that you can have a right to reside to make another person's EU citizenship meaningful – eg, a British child may require her/his primary carer to have a right to reside (see p240).[456]

It may be possible to argue that despite not meeting every requirement, you should still have a right to reside if this would be 'proportionate' in your circumstances. See p179 for an example of when this argument was accepted in relation to an A8 national who had not fully complied with his employment restrictions and p214 for an example of this argument in relation to the need to have comprehensive sickness insurance cover in order to have a right to reside as a self-sufficient person. However, arguments based on this proportionality principle are complex and have been held not to apply, except possibly in exceptional circumstances.[457]

To make such arguments for any period after the transition period, you must be in one of the protected groups that can have a right to reside after that date (see p168 and p174), and you should get specialist advice.

Notes

2. **British, Irish and Commonwealth citizens**
 1 s3ZA IA 1971

3. **Changes due to the UK leaving the European Union**
 2 s1 and Sch 1 ISSCA 2020; reg 4 ISSCA(C) Regs
 3 Arts 2(e), 126 and 127 WA 2019; ss1A, 1B, 8A and Sch 2 part 1A EU(W)A 2018;
 4 ss 1A and 1B EU(W)A 2018
 5 s1B(3)(d) and (e) EU(W)A 2018
 6 Reg 2 CR(ADTP) Regs, and articles of the Withdrawal Agreements cited
 7 Art 18(d) WA 2019; 17(1)(d) UK-EFTA Agreement; Art 16(1)(d) UK-Swiss Agreement
 8 gov.uk/view-prove-immigration-status

4. **European and non-European nationals**
 9 *Yesiloz v LB Camden and Another* [2009] EWCA Civ 415

5. **Protected groups that can have European free movement residence rights**
 10 Regs 3 and 4 CR(ADTP) Regs; reg 83 and Sch 4 paras 1-4 ISSC Regs; ADM Memo 29/20, paras 24 and 87-114; DMG Memo 25/20, paras 23-35 and 92-119; ADM Memo 30/20; DMG Memo 26/20
 11 Reg 3(5)(b) and 4(6)(c) CR(ADTP) Regs; reg 3 I(EEA) Regs
 12 Regs 3(5)(c) and 4(5)(d) CR(ADTP) Regs
 13 Regs 3(4)-(6), 4(2) and (5)-(8) and 12(1)(i) CR(ADTP) Regs
 14 Reg 3(6) CR(ADTP) Regs; ADM Memo 30/20, para 10; DMG Memo 26/20, para 10
 15 Reg 13 CR(ADTP) Regs; *Kerr v DSDNI* [2004] UKHL 23, paras 62-69; ADM Memo 30/20, para 42; DMG Memo 26/20, para 42
 16 Regs 3(6) CR(ADTP) Regs; ADM Memo 30/20, para 9; DMG Memo 26/20, para 9
 17 Reg 3(6)(g)(iii) and (iv) CR(ADTP) Regs and provisions of the Withdrawal Agreements cited

6. **European free movement residence rights**
 18 This approach was taken in the I(EEA) Regs: see reg 2(1), definition of 'EEA national', I(EEA) Regs.
 19 Regs 6 and 14(1) I(EEA) Regs. The term 'qualified person' appears in these regulations, but is not used in the EU Directive, although the same groups of people are covered: Arts 7 and 14 EU Dir 2004/38.
 20 See, for example, *SSWP v JB (JSA)* [2011] UKUT 96 (AAC)
 21 ss1A and 1B EU(W)A 2018
 22 ss2-5 EU(W)A 2018
 23 s1 and Sch 1 ISSCA 2020; reg 4 ISSCA(C) Regs
 24 Part 2, WA 2019; Part 2, UK-EFTA Agreement; UK Swiss Agreement
 25 Art 158, WA 2019
 26 s6 EU(W)A 2018
 27 s6 EU(W)A 2018; The European Union (Withdrawal) Act 2018 (Relevant Court) (Retained EU Case Law) Regulations 2020, No.1525
 28 s6 EU(W)A 2018
 29 Arts 20 and 21 TFEU
 30 EEA Joint Committee Decision No.158/2007
 31 EU Reg 492/2011
 32 *Agreement between the European Community and its Member States, of the one part, and the Swiss Confederation, of the other, on the free movement of persons,* Cmd 5639, 21 June 1999 (in force on 1 June 2002)
 33 Reg 2(1) I(EEA) Regs
 34 Reg 1(2) I(EEA) Regs – except reg 9, which was replaced from 25 November 2016
 35

7. **Croatian, A2 and A8 nationals**

36 *SSWP v Gubeladze* [2019] UKSC 31 dismissed the SSWP's appeal from *SSWP v Gubeladze* [2017] EWCA Civ 1751, which had dismissed the SSWP's appeal from *TG v SSWP (PC)* [2015] UKUT 50 (AAC); see also DMG Memo 11/19 and ADM Memo 14/19.
37 See, for example, *AM v SSWP (ESA)* [2019] UKUT 215 (AAC) and *SSWP v KK (JSA)* [2019] UKUT 313 (AAC)
38 **Croatia** Reg 8 AC(IWA) Regs
A2 Reg 9 A(IWA) Regs
39 **Croatia** Regs 4 and 5 AC(IWA) Regs
A2 Reg 6 A(IWA) Regs; reg 7B I(EEA) Regs 2006, as saved by reg 45 and Sch 4 para 2 I(EEA) Regs
40 Reg 7 A(IWR) Regs
41 Reg 5 A(IWR) Regs; reg 7A I(EEA) Regs 2006, as saved by reg 45 and Sch 4 para 2 I(EEA) Regs
42 The CJEU has held that excluding an A8 national subject to restrictions from retaining worker status is not unlawful: *Prefeta v SSWP*, C-618/16 [2018].
43 *Prefeta v SSWP*, C-618/16 [2018]
44 CIS/1042/2008; *SSWP v JB* [2011] UKUT 96 (AAC)
45 *NZ v SSWP (ESA) (Third interim decision)* [2017] UKUT 360 (AAC); see also *SSWP v NZ (ESA) (Final decision)* [2019] UKUT 250 (AAC)
46 Reg 2 AC(IWA) Regs; reg 2 A(IWA) Regs; *OB v SSWP (ESA)* [2017] UKUT 255 (AAC)
47 *SSWP v LM (ESA) (Interim decision)* [2017] UKUT 485 (AAC), paras 20-21, which confirms that reg 2(8) A(IWR) Regs requires you to have been legally working at the beginning and end of the 12-month period.
48 *SSWP v LM (ESA) (Interim decision)* [2017] UKUT 485 (AAC), paras 20-21, which confirms that reg 2(8) A(IWR) Regs requires you to have been legally working at the beginning and end of the 12-month period.
49 s33(2A) IA 1971
50 Reg 3 AC(IWA) Regs; reg 4 A(IWA) Regs
51 Reg 2 A(IWR) Regs
52 *SSWP v LM (ESA) (Interim decision)* [2017] UKUT 485 (AAC), paras 20-21, which confirms that reg 2(8) A(IWR) Regs requires you to have been legally working at the beginning and end of the 12-month period.
53 *SSWP v LM (ESA) (Interim decision)* [2017] UKUT 485 (AAC), paras 20-21, which confirms that reg 2(8) A(IWR) Regs requires you to have been legally working at the beginning and end of the 12-month period.
54 *JK v SSWP (SPC)* [2017] UKUT 179 (AAC); see also *SSWP v LM (ESA) (Interim decision)* [2017] UKUT 485 (AAC), paras 22-24
55 Reg 2(5) AC(IWA) Regs; reg 2(12) A(IWA) Regs
56 *Miskovic and Another v SSWP* [2011] EWCA Civ 16
57 Reg 2(7) A(IWR) Regs
58 *Miskovic and Another v SSWP* [2011] EWCA Civ 16
59 Reg 7 A(IWR) Regs
60 *SSWP v ZA* [2009] UKUT 294 (AAC); *Szpak v SSWP* [2013] EWCA Civ 46
61 *NZ v SSWP (ESA) (Third interim decision)* [2017] UKUT 360 (AAC)
62 *BS v SSWP* [2009] UKUT 16 (AAC)

8. **Initial right of residence**

63 Reg 11 I(EEA) Regs
64 Reg 13(1) I(EEA) Regs; Art 6(1) EU Dir 2004/38
65 Reg 13(3) I(EEA) Regs; Art 14(1) EU Dir 2004/38
66 Reg 13(2) I(EEA) Regs; Art 6(2) EU Dir 2004/38

9. **Jobseekers**

67 Art 45 TFEU; Art 14 EU Dir 2004/38; *The Queen v Immigration Appeal Tribunal, ex parte Antonissen*, C-292/89 [1991] ECR I-00745; reg 6 I(EEA) Regs
68 Reg 6(1) and (8)-(10) I(EEA) Regs
69 Art 45 TFEU; *The Queen v Immigration Appeal Tribunal, ex parte Antonissen*, C-292/89 [1991] ECR I-00745
70 **Croatia** Reg 5 AC(IWA) Regs
A2 Reg 6 A(IWA) Regs
A8 Regs 4(2) and (4) and 5(2) A(IWR) Regs
71 *SSWP v Gubeladze* [2017] EWCA Civ 1751 dismissed the SSWP's appeal from *TG v SSWP (PC)* [2015] UKUT 50 (AAC).
72 *The Queen v Immigration Appeal Tribunal, ex parte Antonissen*, C-292/89 [1991] ECR I-00745, para 21; confirmed in *SSWP v MB (JSA) (and linked cases)* [2016] UKUT 372 (AAC), reported as [2017] AACR 6, para 49
73 Reg 6 I(EEA) Regs
74 Reg 6(8) I(EEA) Regs
75 Reg 6(1), (8) and (9) I(EEA) Regs
76 ADM Memo 31/20, paras 11 and 14; DMG Memo 27/20, paras 11 and 14

77 Confirmed in Vol 2 Ch 7, para 073080 DMG
78 Vol 2 Ch 7, para 073120 DMG
79 Reg 6(1) and (5)-(8) I(EEA) Regs
80 Vol 2 Ch 7, para 073107 DMG
81 Vol 2 Ch 7, para 073108 DMG
82 *KS v SSWP* [2016] UKUT 269 (AAC) and ECJ caselaw cited; Vol 2 Ch 7, paras 073096-073100 DMG
83 *SSWP v MB (JSA) (and linked cases)* [2016] UKUT 372 (AAC), reported as [2017] AACR 6, paras 49-60, especially paras 49 and 57
84 *SSWP v MB (JSA) (and linked cases)* [2016] UKUT 372 (AAC), reported as [2017] AACR 6, para 47
85 *OS v SSWP (JSA)* [2017] UKUT 107 (AAC), paras 5-7 and caselaw cited
86 *G.M.A. v État beige* C-710/19 [2020]
87 Vol 2 Ch 7, paras 073099-073100 DMG
88 *SSWP v MB (JSA) (and linked cases)* [2016] UKUT 372 (AAC), reported as [2017] AACR 6, paras 61, 91 and 127
89 *DD v HMRC and SSWP (CB)* [2020] UKUT 66 (AAC)
90 CH/3314/2005; *G.M.A. v État beige* C-710/19 [2020]
91 R(IS) 8/08, para 6; *SSWP v MB (JSA) (and linked cases)* [2016] UKUT 372 (AAC), reported as [2017] AACR 6, in particular paras 32-33; CIS 1951/2008, para 21; see also *Shabani v SSHD (EEA – jobseekers; nursery education)* [2013] UKUT 315 (IAC)
92 s7 JSA 1995; reg 8 JSA Regs; This argument was discussed in *SSWP v MB (JSA) (and linked cases)* [2016] UKUT 372 (AAC), reported as [2017] AACR 6, paras 63-79. However, it did not apply in any of the cases in question and so no decision was required.
93 *The Queen v Immigration Appeal Tribunal, ex parte Antonissen*, C-292/89 [1991] ECR I-00745, para 21; R(IS) 8/08, para 5; *GE v SSWP (ESA)* [2017] UKUT 145 (AAC), reported as [2017] AACR 34, para 46; see also *Cardiff CC v HM (HB)* [2019] UKUT 271 (AAC), paras 6 and 18, and *SSWP v KK (JSA)* [2019] UKUT 313 (AAC), para 9
94 Art 24(2) EU Dir 2004/38; see also *Jobcentre Berlin Neukölln v Alimanovic*, C-67/14 [2015]; *Vestische Arbeit Jobcenter Kreis Recklinghausen v García-Nieto*, C-299/14 [2016]
95 *Vatsouras and Koupatantze v Arbeitsgemeinschaft Nürnberg*, C-23/08 [2009] ECR I-04585, paras 40 and 45
96 *Vatsouras and Koupatantze v Arbeitsgemeinschaft Nürnberg*, C-23/08 [2009] ECR I-04585, para 40
97 *Alhashem v SSWP* [2016] EWCA Civ 395. The case is not being appealed further.
98 The exclusion of jobseekers from HB was held not to be unlawful in *Stach v The Department for Communities and DWP* [2018] NIQB 93.
99 Reg 3 HB(HR)A Regs

10. **Workers**

100 Regs 4(1)(a), 6(1) and 14(1) I(EEA) Regs; Arts 7(1)(a) and 14(2) EU Dir 2004/38; Art 45 TFEU
101 Reg 4(1)(a) I(EEA) Regs
102 *Levin v Staatssecretaris van Justitie*, C-53/81 [1982] ECR I-1035
103 *LN v Styrelsen for Videregßende Uddannelser og Uddannelsesstøtte*, C-46/12 [2013] ECR
104 **Croatia** Reg 5 AC(IWA) Regs
A2 Reg 6 A(IWA) Regs
105 Reg 5(2) A(IWR) Regs
106 *SSWP v Gubeladze* [2019] UKSC 31 dismissed the SSWP's appeal from *SSWP v Gubeladze* [2017] EWCA Civ 1751, which had dismissed the SSWP's appeal from *TG v SSWP (PC)* [2015] UKUT 50 (AAC).
107 See, for example, *AM v SSWP (ESA)* [2019] UKUT 215 (AAC)
108 Vol 2 Ch 7, paras 073031-58 DMG; paras C1480-C1506 ADM; HB A3/2014; HMRC, *Child Benefit and Child Tax Credit: right to reside establishing whether an EEA national is/was a worker or a self-employed person under EU law*, February 2014
109 Vol 2 Ch 7, para 073040 DMG; para C1489 ADM; HB A3/2014 para 15; HMRC, *Child Benefit and Child Tax Credit: right to reside establishing whether an EEA national is/was a worker or a self-employed person under EU law*, February 2014, para 7
110 *RF v LB Lambeth* [2019] UKUT 52 (AAC); see also *CC v HMRC and SSWP (CB)* [2020] UKUT 66 (AAC), para 26
111 *Raulinv Minister van Onderwijs en Wetenschappen*, C-357/89 [1992] ECR I-01027, para 10
112 *SSWP v RR (IS)* [2013] UKUT 21 (AAC), reported as [2013] AACR 20
113 CIS/868/2008; CIS/1837/2006; see also *VW v SSWP (PC)* [2014] UKUT 573 (AAC)
114 *Steymann v Staatssecretaris van Justitie*, C-196/87 [1988] ECR I-06159; R(IS) 12/98

115 *Jany v Staatssecretaris van Justitie*, C-268/99 [2001] ECR I-08615, para 34
116 *SSWP v KP (JSA)* [2011] UKUT 241 (AAC); *SSWP v MM (IS)* [2015] UKUT 128 (AAC), paras 31 and 36
117 *Bettray v Staatssecretaris van Justitie*, C-344/87 [1989] ECR I-01621, para 16; *JA v SSWP (ESA)* [2012] UKUT 122 (AAC); *EP v SSWP (JSA)* [2016] UKUT 445 (AAC), para 21
118 *EP v SSWP (JSA)* [2016] UKUT 445 (AAC), para 22
119 *Barry v London Borough of Southwark* [2008] EWCA Civ 1440, para 45; *NE v SSWP* [2009] UKUT 38 (AAC), para 4
120 *Bettray v Staatssecretaris van Justitie*, C-344/87 [1989] ECR I-01621; *SSWP v KP (JSA)* [2011] UKUT 241 (AAC)
121 *NE v SSWP* [2009] UKUT 38 (AAC), para 9; *SSWP v MM (IS)* [2015] UKUT 128 (AAC), paras 31 and 36
122 *EP v SSWP (JSA)* [2016] UKUT 445 (AAC), para 21
123 *Levin v Staatssecretaris van Justitie*, C-53/81 [1982] ECR I-01035, para 17
124 *Ninni-Orasche v Bundesminister für Wissenschaft, Verkehr und Kunst*, C-413/01 [2003] ECR I-13187, para 27
125 *Genc v Land Berlin*, C-14/09 [2010] ECR I-00931
126 R(IS) 12/98
127 *Ninni-Orasche v Bundesminister für Wissenschaft, Verkehr und Kunst*, C-413/01 [2003] ECR I-13187, para 25
128 *Barry v London Borough of Southwark* [2008] EWCA Civ 1440
129 *Ninni-Orasche v Bundesminister für Wissenschaft, Verkehr und Kunst*, C-413/01 [2003] ECR I-13187, para 19
130 In *NE v SSWP* [2009] UKUT 38 (AAC), para 9; R(IS) 12/98
131 *Tarola v Minister for Social Protection*, C-483/17 [2019]
132 *Vatsouras and Koupantze v Arbeitsgemeinschaft (ARGE) Nürnberg 900* [2009] C-22/08 and C-23/08 [2009] ECR I-04585, paras 27-28 and caselaw cited
133 *Raulin v Minister van Onderwijs en Wetenschappen*, C-357/89 [1992] ECR I-01027
134 *NE v SSWP* [2009] UKUT 38 (AAC); CIS/1793/2007; *SSWP v MM (IS)* [2015] UKUT 128 (AAC)
135 *Genc v Land Berlin*, C-14/09 [2010] ECR I-00931
136 *Barry v London Borough of Southwark* [2008] EWCA Civ 1440, para 20
137 *SSWP v SY (IS)* [2012] UKUT 233 (AAC); *JR v SSWP (IS)* [2014] UKUT 154 (AAC); *JR v Leeds City Council (HB)* [2014] UKUT 154 (AAC)
138 *BS v SSWP* [2009] UKUT 16 (AAC); CIS/4237/2007

11. **Self-employed people**

139 Reg 4(1)(b) and 6(1)(c) I(EEA) Regs; Art 7(1)(a) EU Dir 2004/38; Art 49 TFEU; *Aldona Malgorzata Jany and Others v Staatssecretaris van Justitie*, C-268/99 [2001] ECR I-08615
140 Reg 4(1)(b) I(EEA)Regs
141 *Bristol City Council v FV (HB)* [2011] UKUT 494 (AAC)
142 *HMRC v IT (CTC)* [2016] UKUT 252 (AAC), paras 25-28
143 *DV v SSWP* [2017] UKUT 155 (AAC)
144 *SSWP v SY (IS)* [2012] UKUT 233 (AAC); *JR v SSWP (IS)* [2014] UKUT 154 (AAC); *JR v Leeds City Council (HB)* [2014] UKUT 154 (AAC)
145 Vol 2 Ch 7, paras 073031-58 DMG; HB A3/2014; HMRC, *Child Benefit and Child Tax Credit: right to reside establishing whether an EEA national is/was a worker or a self-employed person under EU law*, February 2014
146 Amended by reg 5(c) CR(ADTP) Regs and Sch 4 para 4(c) ISSC Regs
147 Reg 4(1)(b) I(EEA) Regs – until 31 December 2020
148 Art 49 TFEU; R(IS) 6/00
149 R(IS) 6/00, para 31
150 *TG v SSWP* [2009] UKUT 58 (AAC), para 5
151 *SSWP v JS (IS)* [2010] UKUT 240 (AAC), paras 5 and 8; *RJ v SSWP (JSA)* [2011] UKUT 477 (AAC), paras 9 and 17; *HMRC v HD (Interim decision) and HMRC v GP* [2017] UKUT 11 (AAC)
152 *SSWP v JS (IS)* [2010] UKUT 240 (AAC), para 5; Vol 2 Ch 7, para 072842 DMG; para C1452 ADM
153 CIS/1042/2008
154 *HMRC v HD (Interim decision) and HMRC v GP* [2017] UKUT 11 (AAC); see also *HMRC v HD (CHB)(Second interim decision)* [2018] UKUT 148 (AAC), paras 2 and 3
155 *Saint Prix v SSWP*, C-507/12 [2014]
156 *HMRC v HD (CHB) (Second interim decision)* [2018] UKUT 148 (AAC); *HMRC v Dakneviciute*, C-544/18 [2019]

12. **Retaining worker or self-employed status**

157 Art 7(3) EU Dir 2004/38; *Gusa v Minister for Social Protection (Ireland),* C-442/16 [2017]; reg 6 I(EEA) Regs
158 *Saint Prix v SSWP,* C-507/12 [2014]; *HMRC v Dakneviciute,* C-544/18 [2019]
159 *Gusa v Minister for Social Protection (Ireland),* C-442/16 [2017]
160 See, for example, *SB v SSWP (UC)* [2019] UKUT 219 (AAC)
161 *Saint Prix v SSWP,* C-507/12 [2014], paras 31 and 38; *Tarola v Minister for Social Protection,* C-483/17 [2019], para 26; *HMRC v Dakneviciute,* C-544/18 [2019], para 28; see also *Gusa v Minister for Social Protection (Ireland),* C-442/16 [2017] Attorney General Opinion, 26 July 2017, paras 67-79
162 *JS v SSWP (IS)* [2019] UKUT 135 (AAC)
163 Reg 5(4) A(IWR) Regs; reg 7A(4) I(EEA) Regs 2006, as saved by reg 45 and Sch 4 para 2 I(EEA) Regs
164 *SSWP v Gubeladze* [2019] UKSC 31 dismissed the SSWP's appeal from *SSWP v Gubeladze* [2017] EWCA Civ 1751, which had dismissed the SSWP's appeal from *TG v SSWP (PC)* [2015] UKUT 50 (AAC).
165 See, for example, *AM v SSWP (ESA)* [2019] UKUT 215 (AAC)
166 Art 7(3)(b) and (c) EU Dir 2004/38; *Gusa v Minister for Social Protection (Ireland),* C-442/16 [2017]; reg 6(2)(b) and (c), (3), (4)(b) and (c) and (4A) I(EEA) Regs
167 Reg 6(2)(b) and (c), (3), (4)(b) and (c) and (4A)-(7) I(EEA) Regs
168 CH/3314/2005, para 11; confirmed in *SSWP v EM (IS)* [2009] UKUT 146 (AAC), para 10; *SSWP v MK* [2013] UKUT 163 (AAC), paras 44-47; *SB v SSWP (UC)* [2019] UKUT 219 (AAC), paras 8-13
169 *Gusa v Minister for Social Protection (Ireland),* C-442/16 [2017], paras 17 and 31
170 *SB v SSWP (UC)* [2019] UKUT 219 (AAC), paras 8-13
171 *SSWP v Elmi* [2011] EWCA Civ 1403; paras 072826-27 DMG
172 Art 7(3)(b) EU Dir 2004/38; *SSWP v MM (IS)* [2015] UKUT 128 (AAC), paras 53-54; *KH v Bury MBC and SSWP* [2020] UKUT 50 (AAC), paras 40-43
173 *SSWP v MM (IS)* [2015] UKUT 128 (AAC), paras 53-58
174 *SSWP v MM (IS)* [2015] UKUT 128 (AAC), paras 45-46
175 Reg 6(1)(e), (2)(b), (4)(b), (4C) and (7) I(EEA) Regs; ADM Memo 31/20, paras 11 and 14; DMG Memo 27/20, paras 11 and 14
176 *KH v Bury MBC and SSWP* [2020] UKUT 50 (AAC), especially paras 39-44 and 67
177 *KH v Bury MBC and SSWP* [2020] UKUT 50 (AAC), paras 4, 26, 36, 39 and 67
178 ADM Memo 31/20, paras 11 and 14; DMG Memo 27/20, paras 11 and 14
179 Reg 6(1), (2)(c), (3), (4)(c) and (4A) I(EEA) Regs
180 Art 7(3)(c) EU Dir 2004/38
181 *Tarola v Minister for Social Protection,* C-483/17 [2019]
182 *SB v SSWP (UC)* [2019] UKUT 219 (AAC)
183 Reg 6(1) and (7)-(10) I(EEA) Regs
184 Art 7(3)(d) EU Dir 2004/38; reg 6(1), (2)(d) and (e) and (4)(d) and (e) I(EEA)Regs
185 *SSWP v EM (IS)* [2009] UKUT 146 (AAC), para 10; see also *OB v SSWP (ESA)* [2017] UKUT 255 (AAC), para 32
186 *Brown v Secretary of State for Scotland,* C-197/86 [1988] ECR I-03205
187 *Lair v Universität Hannover,* C-39/86 [1988] ECR I-03161, para 37
188 *Raulin v Minister van Onderwijs en Wetenschappen,* C-357/89 [1992] ECR I-01027, paras 18 and 19
189 Art 7(3)(a) EU Dir 2004/38; reg 6(2)(a) and (4)(a) I(EEA) Regs
190 CIS/4304/2007, para 35
191 *HK V SSWP (ESA)* [2017] UKUT 421 (AAC)
192 CIS/3182/2005
193 *SSHD v FB* [2010] UKUT 447 (IAC), para 23; *LM v HMRC (CHB)* [2016] UKUT 389 (AAC); *SSWP v LM (ESA)* [2017] UKUT 485 (AAC), paras 31-34
194 CIS/3890/2005
195 *De Brito v SSHD* [2012] EWCA Civ 709; *Konodyba v Royal Borough of Kensington and Chelsea* [2012] EWCA Civ 982; *Samin v Westminster CC* [2012] EWCA Civ 1468 (this part of the decision was not in dispute in the further appeal to the Supreme Court); *LM v HMRC (CHB)* [2016] UKUT 389 (AAC); *SSWP v LM (ESA)* [2017] UKUT 485 (AAC), paras 31-34
196 CIS/4237/2007
197 CIS/1042/2008; *HMRC v HD (Interim decision) and HMRC v GP* [2017] UKUT 11 (AAC); see also *HMRC v HD (CHB) (Second interim decision)* [2018] UKUT 148 (AAC), para 2
198 CIS/731/2007
199 CIS/4010/2006

200 *Saint Prix v SSWP*, C-507/12 [2014]; *SSWP v SFF and others* [2015] UKUT 502 (AAC), reported as [2016] AACR 16; *HMRC v Dakneviciute*, C-544/18 [2019]
201 *SSWP v SFF and Others* [2015] UKUT 502 (AAC), reported as [2016] AACR 16, para 35; confirmed in Vol 2 Ch 7, paras 073224 and 073230 DMG and para C1521 ADM
202 *SSWP v SFF and others* [2015] UKUT 502 (AAC), reported as [2016] AACR 16, para 26; *Weldemichael and Another v SSHD* [2015] UKUT 540 (IAC), paras 22-23
203 *HMRC v Dakneviciute*, C-544/18 [2019], paras 39-42; Vol 2 Ch 7, paras 073214-5 DMG; para C1528-9 ADM
204 *SSWP v SFF and Others* [2015] UKUT 502 (AAC), reported as [2016] AACR 16, paras 24 and 25
205 Reg 4(1)(a) and (b) I(EEA)Regs; *Saint Prix v SSWP*, C-507/12 [2014], especially paras 37, 38 and 47; *HMRC v Dakneviciute*, C-544/18 [2019], especially paras 31, 34 and 41
206 Art 10, WA 2019; Art 9, UK-EFTA Agreement; Art 10, UK-Swiss Agreement
207 CIS/4304/2007, para 34; *SSWP v IR* [2009] UKUT 11 (AAC); *SSWP v SFF and Others* [2015] UKUT 502 (AAC), reported as [2016] AACR 16, para 40; *GE v SSWP (ESA)* [2017] UKUT 145 (AAC), reported as [2017] AACR 34, para 41
208 CIS/1934/2006; *SSWP v IR (IS)* [2009] UKUT 11 (AAC)
209 *SSWP v MK* [2013] UKUT 163 (AAC); *VP v SSWP (JSA)* [2014] UKUT 32 (AAC), reported as [2014] AACR 25, paras 56-61; *SSWP v MM (IS)* [2015] UKUT 128 (AAC), paras 47-52; *SSWP v LM (Interim decision) (ESA)* [2017] 485 (AAC), para 23; *FT v LB Islington and SSWP (HB)* [2015] UKUT 121 (AAC); *KH v Bury MBC and SSWP* [2020] UKUT 50 (AAC)
210 *HK V SSWP (ESA)* [2017] UKUT 421 (AAC), para 7

13. **Self-sufficient people and students**

211 Art 7(1) EU Dir 2004/38; regs 4(1)(c) and (2)-(4), 6(1) and 14(1) I(EEA) Regs
212 Art 7(1) EU Dir 2004/38; regs 4(1)(d) and (2)-(4), 6(1) and 14(1) I(EEA) Regs
213 *VP v SSWP (JSA)* [2014] UKUT 32 (AAC), reported as [2014] AACR 25, paras 88-97
214 Reg 4 I(EEA)Regs
215 Art 8(4) EU Dir 2004/38
216 Reg 4 I(EEA) Regs
217 *SG v Tameside MBC (HB)* [2010] UKUT 243 (AAC)
218 *Zhu and Chen v SSHD*, C-200/02 [2004] ECR I-09925; *AMS v SSWP (PC)* [2017] UKUT 48 (AAC), para 62
219 *Commission of the European Communities v Kingdom of Belgium*, C-408/03 [2006] ECR I-02647; *Zhu and Chen v SSHD*, C-200/02 [2004] ECR I-09925
220 *VP v SSWP (JSA)* [2014] UKUT 32 (AAC), reported as [2014] AACR 25, paras 88-97
221 *VP v SSWP (JSA)* [2014] UKUT 32 (AAC), reported as [2014] AACR 25, para 94
222 *Singh and Others v Minister of Justice and Equality*, C-218/14 [2015]
223 *Bajratari v SSWP*, C-93/18 [2019]
224 *Pensionsversicherungsanstalt v Brey*, C-140/12 [2013], paras 54-57
225 CH/1400/2006; *SG v Tameside MBC (HB)* [2010] UKUT 243 (AAC); *Pensionsversicherungsanstalt v Brey*, C-140/12 [2013]
226 Vol 2 Ch 7, para 073244 DMG; para C1729 ADM
227 *Pensionsversicherungsanstalt v Brey*, C-140/12 [2013], paras 64 and 75-78; *AMS v SSWP (PC)* [2017] UKUT 48 (AAC)
228 *VP v SSWP (JSA)* [2014] UKUT 32 (AAC), reported as [2014] AACR 25, paras 77, 84 and 94
229 *AMS v SSWP (PC) (Final decision)* [2017] UKUT 381 (AAC), reported as [2018] AACR 27; see also *HK v SSWP (PC)* [2020] UKUT 73 (AAC), para 41
230 See, for example, confirmation of this in relation to evidence of collective impact: *AMS v SSWP (PC) (Final decision)* [2017] UKUT 381 (AAC), reported as [2018] AACR 27, para 23
231 *W (China) and Another v SSHD* [2006] EWCA Civ 1494
232 *SG v Tameside MBC (HB)* [2010] UKUT 243 (AAC); *VP v SSWP (JSA)* [2014] UKUT 32 (AAC), reported as [2014] AACR 25; *SSWP v HH (SPC)* [2015] UKUT 583 (AAC); Vol 2 Ch 7, para 073246 DMG; para C1730 ADM
233 *SSWP v HH (SPC)* [2015] UKUT 583 (AAC); *AMS v SSWP (PC) (Final decision)* [2017] UKUT 381 (AAC), reported as [2018] AACR 27, paras 2 and 4-5; Vol 2 Ch 7, para 073246 DMG; para C1730 ADM
234 Arts 1(j) and (k) and 19 EU Reg 883/2004; *I v Health Services Executive*, C-255/13 [2014], para 59

235 *SSWP v GS (PC)* [2016] UKUT 394 (AAC), reported as [2017] AACR 7, paras 13-40; Vol 2 Ch 7, para 073246 DMG; para C1730 ADM; see also Decision S1 of 12 June 2009 of the Administrative Commission for the Co-ordination of Social Security Systems, C-106/08 [2010]
236 *VI v HMRC* C-247/20, following *Ahmad v SSHD* [2014] EWCA Civ 988 para 53
237 *FK (Kenya) v SSHD* [2010] EWCA Civ 1302; *VP v SSWP (JSA)* [2014] UKUT 32 (AAC), reported as [2014] AACR 25; *SSWP v LL (SPC)* [2014] UKUT 136 (AAC); *Ahmad v SSHD* [2014] EWCA Civ 988; see also *Cardiff CC v HM (HB)* [2019] UKUT 271 (AAC), para 19
238 European Commission press release, 30 October 2020 (ec.europa.eu/commission/presscorner); see also pending case *A v Latvijas Republikas Veselibas ministrija*, C-535/19
239 Art 87 WA 2019
240 *Baumbast and R v SSHD*, C-413/99 [2002] ECR I-07091
241 *KS v SSWP* [2016] UKUT 269 (AAC), para 6; *SSWP v GS (PC)* [2016] UKUT 394 (AAC), reported as [2017] AACR 7, paras 42-46R; *B v SSWP* [2017] UKUT 472 (AAC), paras 72-73; see also *Cardiff CC v HM (HB)* [2019] UKUT 271 (AAC), para 19
242 Art 7(1) EU Dir 2004/38; regs 4(1)(d) and (2)-(5), 6(1) and 14(1) I(EEA) Regs
243 Reg 4(1)(d)(i) I(EEA) Regs
244 Reg 4(1)(d)(iii) I(EEA) Regs
245 *Grzelczyk v Centre Public d'aide Sociale d'Ottignies-Louvain-la-Neuve*, C-184/99 [2001] ECR I-06193
246 Art 7(4) EU Dir 2004/38; reg 7(2) I(EEA) Regs
247 Art 7(4) EU Dir 2004/38

14. **Family members of European Economic Area nationals**

248 Arts 6(2) and 7(1)(d) and (2) EU Dir 2004/38; *Clauder*, C-E-4/11 [2011] EFTACR 216, para 43; regs 13(2) and 14(2) I(EEA) Regs
249 Regs 6 and 14(1) I(EEA) Regs. The same groups are covered in Arts 7 and 14 EU Dir 2004/38, although the term 'qualified person' is not used.
250 Art 2(2) EU Dir 2004/38; reg 7(1) I(EEA) Regs
251 Reg 7(3) I(EEA) Regs; CPC/3588/2006; *SS v SSWP (ESA)* [2011] UKUT 8 (AAC); *SSWP v LZ (SPC)* [2014] UKUT 147 (AAC); *Macastena v SSHD* [2018] EWCA Civ 1558; *SSHD v Aibangbee* [2019] EWCA Civ 339; *MW v SSWP (UC)* [2019] UKUT 184 (AAC)
252 *Aissatou Diatta v Land Berlin*, C-267/83 [1985] ECR I-00567
253 CF/1863/2007
254 CIS/2100/2007, which considers the findings of *Centre Public d'Aide Sociale de Courcelles v Lebon*, 316/85 [1987] ECR I-02811, *Zhu and Chen v SSHD*, C-200/02 [2004] ECR I-09925 and *Jia v Migrationsverket*, C-1/05 [2007] ECR I-00001; *SSWP v MB (JSA) (and linked cases)* [2016] UKUT 372 (AAC), paras 132-39
255 *SSWP v MF (SPC)* [2018] UKUT 179 (AAC)
256 *Reyes v Migrationsverket*, C-423/12 [2014]; *Centre Publique d'Aide Social de Courcelles v Lebon* C-316/85 [1987] ECR 02811; *ECO v Lim (EEA dependency)* [2013] UKUT 437 (IAC)
257 *Pedro v SSWP* [2009] EWCA Civ 1358. Arguably, this remains good law despite the assumptions made in *Reyes v Migrationsverket*, C-423/12 [2014].
258 *Centre Publique d'Aide Social de Courcelles v Lebon*, C-316/85 [1987] ECR I-02811, para 20; *SSWP v MB (JSA) (and linked cases)* [2016] UKUT 372 (AAC), reported as [2017] AACR 6, paras 132-39
259 Reg 7(3) I(EEA) Regs; CPC/3588/2006; *SS v SSWP (ESA)* [2011] UKUT 8 (AAC); *SSWP v LZ (SPC)* [2014] UKUT 147 (AAC); *Macastena v SSHD* [2018] EWCA Civ 1558; *SSHD v Aibangbee* [2019] EWCA Civ 339; *MW v SSWP (UC)* [2019] UKUT 184 (AAC); *AM v SSWP and CC Swansea Council* [2019] UKUT 361 (AAC), paras 19-21
260 Reg 7(3) I(EEA) Regs; CPC/3588/2006; *SS v SSWP (ESA)* [2011] UKUT 8 (AAC); *SSWP v LZ (SPC)* [2014] UKUT 147 (AAC); *Macastena v SSHD* [2018] EWCA Civ 1558; *SSHD v Aibangbee* [2019] EWCA Civ 339; *MW v SSWP (UC)* [2019] UKUT 184 (AAC); *AM v SSWP and CC Swansea Council* [2019] UKUT 361 (AAC), paras 19-21
261 Reg 7(3) and 8 I(EEA) Regs; the same groups are covered in Art 3 EU Dir 2004/38, but the term is not used.
262 See CIS/612/2008 for discussion of the meaning of 'durable relationship'.
263 *SM v ECO, UKVI*, C-129/18 [2019]

264 *TR (reg 8(3) EEA Regs 2006) Sri Lanka* [2008] UKAIT 4
265 *SSHD v Rahman and Others*, C-83/11 [2012]; *Oboh and Others v SSHD* [2013] EWCA Civ 1525; *Soares v SSHD* [2013] EWCA Civ 575; *AA (Algeria) v SSHD* [2014] EWCA Civ 1741
266 *Dauhoo (EEA Regs – Reg 8(2)) v SSHD* [2012] UKUT 79 (IAC)
267 *SM v ECO, UKVI*, C-129/18 [2019]; reg 2(5)(c), I(EEA)A Regs 2019
268 Reg 8(7) I(EEA) Regs; see also *Soares v SSHD* [2013] EWCA Civ 575, in particular para 26; *SSHD v Rahman and Others*, C-83/11 [2012]; Recital 6 and Art 3(2) EU Dir 2004/38
269 Art 3(1) EU Dir 2004/38
270 Regs 1, 7(4) and Reg 9 I(EEA) Regs since 1 February 2017 and reg 4 and Sch 5 I(EEA) Regs for prior period from 25 November 2016; Art 21(1) TFEU; Arts 7(1) and (2) and 16(1) and (2) EU Dir 2004/38; *R v IAT and Singh ex parte SSHD*, C-370/90 [1992] ECR I-04265; *Minister voor Vreemdelingenzaken en Integratie v Eind*, C-291/05 [2007] ECR I-10719; *O and B v Minister voor Immigratie, Intergratie en Asiel*, C-456/12 [2014]; *Coman and Others v Inspectoratul General pentru Imigrari and Others*, C-673/16 [2018]
271 *SSHD v Banger*, C-89/17 [2018]
272 Reg 9 I(EEA) Regs; Reg 5(h) CR(ADTP) Regs; Sch 4 para 4(h) ISSC Regs
273 Confirmed in *B v SSWP* [2017] UKUT 472 (AAC), which reviews the relevant caselaw.
274 Reg 5(h) CR(ADTP) Regs; Sch 3 para 6(h) and Sch 4 para 4(h) ISSC Regs
275 *HK v SSWP (SPC)* [2020] UKUT 73 (AAC); *Minister voor Vreemdelingenzaken en Integratie v Eind*, C-291/05 [2007] ECR I-10719, para 45. The case relates to an earlier EU regulation, but the same reasoning applies to Art 7(2) EU Dir 2004/38. For an additional summary of *Eind*, see *B v SSWP* [2017] UKUT 472 (AAC), paras 33-39. See also DMG Memo 21/20 and ADM Memo 24/20.
276 Reg 9(1A) and (2)(d) I(EEA) Regs
277 *SSHD v Christy* [2018] EWCA Civ 2378
278 *O and B v Minister voor Immigratie, Integratie en Asiel*, C-456/12 [2014]; *ZA (Reg 9 EEA Regs; abuse of rights) Afghanistan* [2019] UKUT 281 (IAC), para 75; *VW v SSWP (PC)* [2014] UKUT 573 (AAC)
279 *ZA (Reg 9 EEA Regs; abuse of rights) Afghanistan* [2019] UKUT 281 (IAC)
280 *O and B v Minister voor Immigratie, Intergratie en Asiel*, C-456/12 [2014], in particular paras 51-56
281 Reg 9(4) I(EEA) Regs
282 *Mary Carpenter v SSHD*, C-60/00 [2002] ECR I-06279, para 46; *S and G v Minister voor Immigratie, Integratie en Asiel*, C-457/12 [2014]
283 *S and G v Minister voor Immigratie, Integratie en Asiel*, C-457/12 [2014]
284 Art 21(1) TFEU
285 *Lounes v SSHD*, C-165/16 [2017]
286 *AS v SSWP (UC)* [2018] UKUT 260 (AAC); *ODS v SSWP (UC)* [2019] UKUT 192 (AAC)
287 *Kovacevic (British citizen – Art 21 TFEU) Croatia* [2018] UKUT 273 (IAC)
288 Reg 2(1) I(EEA) Regs
289 Reg 9(A) I(EEA) Regs; reg 5(I) CR(ADTP) Regs; Sch 3 para 6(1)(i) and Sch 4 para 4(i) ISSC Regs
290 Reg 3 I(EEA)A Regs 2018
291 *Lounes v SSHD*, C-165/16 [2017]; *AS v SSWP (UC)* [2018] UKUT 260 (AAC); *ODS v SSWP (UC)* [2019] UKUT 192 (AAC); *Kovacevic (British citizen – Art 21 TFEU) Croatia* [2018] UKUT 273 (IAC)
292 *McCarthy v SSHD*, C-434-09 [2011] ECR I-03375
293 Reg 2(1) I(EEA) Regs
294 *AA v SSWP* [2009] UKUT 249 (AAC); *HG v SSWP (SPC)* [2011] UKUT 382 (AAC)
295 Sch 3 I(EEA)A Regs 2012 up to, and Sch 6 para 9 I(EEA) Regs since, 1 February 2017; reg 10(e) CR(ADTP) Regs
296 Regs 10 and 14(3) I(EEA) Regs; reg 5(j) CR(ADTP) Regs; sch 3 para 6(1)(j) and Sch 4 para 4(j) ISSC Regs
297 *Baigazieva v SSHD* [2018] EWCA Civ 1088
298 *SSHD v NA*, C-115/15 [2016]; reg 10(5)(b) I(EEA) Regs
299 Reg 14(3) I(EEA) Regs
300 Reg 10(8) and (9) I(EEA) Regs; *MK v SSWP (ESA)* [2020] 235 (AAC), para 11
301 Art 12 EU Dir 2004/38
302 Art 12 EU Dir 2004/38
303 *Baigazieva v SSHD* [2018] EWCA Civ 1088
304 Art 13 EU Dir 2004/38
305 *Singh and Others v Minister of Justice and Equality*, C-218-14 [2015]
306 *SSHD v NA*, C-115/15 [2016]
307 Arts 12(1) and 13(1) EU Dir 2004/38
308 *JP v SSWP (ESA)* [2018] UKUT 161 (AAC), paras 12-21; *GA v SSWP (SPC)* [2018] UKUT 172 (AAC), paras 27-44

309 Arts 12, 13 and 18 EU Dir 2004/38; *Ziolkowski and Szeja*, joined cases C-424/10 and C-425/10 [2011] ECR I-14035, para 44

15. **Derivative residence rights**

310 Reg 16 I(EEA) Regs
311 See also *London Borough of Harrow v Ibrahim and SSHD*, C-310/08 [2010] ECR I-01065; *Teixeira v London Borough of Lambeth and SSHD*, C-480/08 [2010] ECR I-01107; *GBC Echternach and A Moritz v Minister van Onderwijs en Wetenschappen*, joined cases 389/87 and 390/87 [1989] ECR I-00723; *Baumbast and R v SSHD*, C-413/99 [2002] ECR I-07091
312 See also *London Borough of Harrow v Ibrahim and SSHD*, C-310/08 [2010] ECR I-01065; *Teixeira v London Borough of Lambeth and SSHD*, C-480/08 [2010] ECR I-01107; *GBC Echternach and A Moritz v Minister van Onderwijs en Wetenschappen*, joined cases 389/87 and 390/87 [1989] ECR 00723; *Baumbast and R v SSHD*, C-413/99 [2002] ECR I-07091
313 See also *Zhu and Chen v SSHD*, C-200/02 [2004] ECR I-09925; *SSHD v NA*, C-115/15 [2016]
314 See also *Zambrano v ONEm*, C-34/09 [2011] ECR I-01177; *Dereci and Others v Bundesministerium für Inneres*, C-256/11 [2011] ECR I-11315
315 Reg 16(1) I(EEA) Regs
316 Reg 16(7)(c) I(EEA) Regs
317 *JD v Jobcenter Krefeld* C-181/19 [2020], especially paras 64, 71 and 79; see also *Fratila and Tanase v SSWP* [2020] EWCA Civ 1741, especially paras 42-55
318 Art 10 EU Reg 492/2011 (before 1 June 2012, Art 12 EC Reg 1612/68 was in identical terms). See the emphasis on the state's duties in*MA v Department for Social Development (JSA)*[2011] NICom 205, para 13. See also comment in *HK v SSWP* [2017] UKUT 421 (AAC), para 10, which was cited in support in *AV v SSWP (UC)* CUC1190/2019, paras 6-10
319 See the emphasis on the state's duties in *MA v Department for Social Development (JSA)* [2011] NICom 205, para 13.
320 **UC**/1035/2019
321 *HMRC v IT (CTC)* [2016] UKUT 252 (AAC)
322 *SSWP v JS (IS)* [2010] UKUT 347
323 *DJ v SSWP* [2013] UKUT 113 (AAC)
324 Reg 16(3) I(EEA) Regs
325 Art 10 EU Reg 492/2011 (before 1 June 2012, Art 12 EC Reg 1612/68 was in identical terms)
326 *Baumbast and R v SSHD*, C-413/99 [2002] ECR I-07091
327 *Bolton MBC v HY (HB)* [2018] UKUT 103 (AAC), reported as [2018] AACR 31, and caselaw cited
328 *Brown v The Secretary of State for Scotland*, C-197/86 [1988] ECR I-03205
329 *Teixeira v LB Lambeth and SSHD*, C-480/08 [2010] ECR I-01107, para 74; *Baumbast and R v SSHD*, C-413/99 [2002] ECR I-07091, para 63; *SSHD v NA*, C-115/15 [2016]
330 *Baumbast and R v SSHD*, C-413/99 [2002] ECR I-07091, para 57; *Alarape and Tijani (Article 12, EC Reg 1612/68) Nigeria* [2011] UKUT 413 (IAC), paras 28-29
331 *JS v SSWP (ESA)* [2016] UKUT 314 (AAC)
332 *IP v SSWP (IS)* [2015] UKUT 691 (AAC)
333 *MS v SSWP (IS)* [2016] UKUT 348 (AAC)
334 *SM v ECO, UKVI*, C-129/18 [2019]
335 *Hrabkova v SSWP* [2017] EWCA Civ 794 – permission to appeal to UKSC refused
336 Arts 24(1)(h) and (2) and 25(1)(b) and (2) WA 2019; Arts 23(1)(h) and (2) and 24(1)(b) and (2) UK-EFTA Agreement
337 ADM Memo 33/20, para 53; DMG Memo 29/20, para 53
338 CIS/3960/2007
339 *SSWP v IM (IS)* [2011] UKUT 231 (AAC), paras 17 and 28
340 *Shabani v SSHD* [2013] UKUT 315 (IAC)
341 Reg 16(7)(a) I(EEA) Regs
342 Art 10 EU Reg 492/2011; *Landesamt für Ausbildungsförderung Nordrhein-Westfalen v Lubor Gaal*, C-7/94 [1995] ECR I-1031, paras 24 and 25; *Teixeira v LB Lambeth and SSHD*, C-480/08 [2010] ECR I-01107, paras 76-87; *Alarape and Tijani v SSHD*, C-529/11 [2013], paras 24, 25 and 31
343 Reg 16(7)(b) I(EEA)Regs
344 Reg 10 EU Reg 492/2011 (before 1 June 2012, Art 12 EC Reg 1612/68 was in identical terms)
345 *London Borough of Harrow v Ibrahim and SSHD*, C-310/08 [2010] ECR I-01065; *Teixeira v London Borough of Lambeth and SSHD*, C-480/08 [2010] ECR I-01107; *Baumbast and R v SSHD*, C-413/99 [2002] ECR I-07091; *SSWP v Czop* and *SSWP v Punakova*, joined cases, C-147/11 and C-148/11 [2012]; *Landesamt für Ausbildungsförderung Nordrhein-Westfalen v Lubor Gaal*, C-7/94 [1995] ECR I-01031

346 Vol 2 Ch 7, para 073401 DMG
347 *Echternach and Moritz v Netherlands Minister for Education and Science*, joined cases 389/87 and 390/87 [1989] ECR I-00723, paras 18-23
348 Reg 16(1) and (4) I(EEA) Regs
349 Art 10 EU Reg 492/2011 (before 1 June 2012, Art 12 EC Reg 1612/68 was in identical terms)
350 *Baumbast and R v SSHD*, C-413/99 [2002] ECR I-07091
351 *Teixeira v LB Lambeth and SSHD*, C-480/08 [2010] ECR I-01107, paras 84-86; *Alarape and Tijani v SSHD*, C-529/11 [2013]
352 *Teixeira v LB Lambeth and SSHD*, C-480/08 [2010] ECR I-01107, para 3
353 *Baumbast and R v SSHD*, C-413/99 [2002] ECR I-07091, para 75; see also *SSWP v RR (IS)* [2013] UKUT 21 (AAC), reported as [2013] AACR 20, paras 75-76
354 Reg 16(1),(3),(4) and (7)(c) I(EEA) Regs
355 *Hrabkova v SSWP* [2017] EWCA Civ 794 – permission to appeal to UKSC refused
356 Arts 24(1)(h) and (2) and 25(1)(b) and (2) WA 2019; Arts 23(1)(h) and (2) and 24(1)(b) and (2) UK-EFTA Agreement
357 ADM Memo 33/20 para 53; DMG Memo 29/20 para 53
358 Reg 16(8) I(EEA) Regs
359 Reg 16(11) I(EEA) Regs
360 *Chavez-Vilchez and Others v Raad van bestuur van de Sociale verzekeringsbank*, C-133/15 [2017]; Vol 2 Ch7, paras 073385 and 073389 DMG; paras C1829 and C1833 ADM; see also *Patel and Shah v SSHD* [2019] UKSC 59
361 Reg 16(8)-(10) I(EEA) Regs; *MA v Department for Social Development (JSA)* [2011] NICom 205, para 13; Vol 2 Ch7, paras 073386 and 073403 DMG; paras C1830-1 and C1834 ADM
362 Regs 4(c) and 16(1) and (2) I(EEA) Regs
363 *Zhu and Chen v SSHD*, C-200/02 [2004] ECR I-09925; see also *Alokpa and Moudoulou v Ministre du Travail, de l'Emploi et de l'Immigration*, C-86/12 [2013], paras 27-29; *SSHD v NA*, C-115/15 [2016]; *Bajratari v SSHD*, C-93/18, AG Opinion, 19 June 2019
364 Reg 4(3) and (5) I(EEA) Regs; DMG Memo 24/16, para 13
365 *VI v HMRC* C-247/20
366 Reg 16(1) and (5) I(EEA) Regs
367 *Zambrano v ONEm*, C-34/09 [2011] ECR I-01177; *Dereci and Others v Bundesministerium für Inneres*, C-256/11 [2011] ECR I-11315
368 *A v Belgium* C-82/16 [2018]; *Patel and Shah v SSHD* [2019] UKSC 59; see, for example, *DM v SSWP (PIP)* [2019] UKUT 26 (AAC)
369 Reg 16(1) and (6) I(EEA) Regs
370 *AM v SSWP and CC Swansea Council* [2019] UKUT 361 (AAC), paras 49-64
371 Reg 16(6) I(EEA) Regs
372 *Hrabkova v SSWP* [2017] EWCA Civ 794
373 Arts 24(1)(h) and (2) and 25(1)(b) and (2) WA 2019; Arts 23(1)(h) and (2) and 24(1)(b) and (2) UK-EFTA Agreement
374 ADM Memo 33/20 para 53; DMG Memo 29/20 para 53
375 *HMRC v HEH and SSWP (TC and CHB)* [2018] UKUT 237 (AAC)

16. **Permanent right to reside**

376 Art 16(1) EU Dir 2004/38
377 Art 16(4) EU Dir 2004/38; reg 15(3) I(EEA) Regs
378 Regs 3(5) and (6) and 4(2) and (6) CR(ADTP) Regs
379 Art 16(1) and (2) EU Dir 2004/38; reg 15(1) I(EEA) Regs
380 Art 16(1) and (2) EU Dir 2004/38; reg 15(1)(a) and (b) and Sch 6 para 8 I(EEA) Regs; reg 6(e) CR(ADTP) Regs; Sch 4 para 4(m) ISSC Regs
381 Arts 7 and 16(1) and (2) EU Dir 2004/38; regs 6, 7, 14 and 15 I(EEA) Regs; *Ziolkowski and Szeja v Land Berlin*, joined cases C-424/10 and C-425/10 [2011] ECR I-14035
382 *SSWP v Lassal*, C-162/09 [2010] ECR I-09217; *SSWP v Dias*, C-325/09 [2011] ECR I-06387; Sch 6 para 8(4) I(EEA) Regs
383 Regs 6(1)(a), 7, 14(1) and (2) and 15(1) and Sch 6 para 8 I(EEA) Regs; *GE v SSWP (ESA)* [2017] UKUT 145 (AAC), reported as [2017] AACR 34
384 Vol 2 Ch 7, para 073428 DMG; para C1807 ADM; HB Circular A8/15, para 19
385 Vol 2 Ch 7, para 073443 DMG; HB Circular A8/15, para 27
386 *GE v SSWP (ESA)* [2017] UKUT 145 (AAC), reported as [2017] AACR 34, para 46
387 Vol 2 Ch 7, para 073442 DMG; HB Circular A8/15, para 26
388 *Ziolkowski and Szeja*, joined cases C-424/10 and C-425/10 [2011] ECR, I-14035
389 Regs 13 and 15(1) I(EEA) Regs; *GE v SSWP (ESA)* [2017] UKUT 145 (AAC), reported as [2017] AACR 34

390 *Ziolkowski and Szeja*, joined cases C-424/10 and C-425/10 [2011] ECR I-14035; *GE v SSWP (ESA)* [2017] UKUT 145 (AAC), reported as [2017] AACR 34, paras 59-66
391 *Macastena v SSHD* [2018] EWCA Civ 1558; *SSHD v Aibangbee* [2019] EWCA Civ 339; *MW v SSWP (UC)* [2019] UKUT 184 (AAC)
392 Reg 14(2) I(EEA) Regs; *Clauder*, C-E-4/11 [2011] EFTACR 216, para 43
393 Regs 14(2) and 15(1)(a) and (b) I(EEA) Regs
394 Reg 15(1)(f) I(EEA) Regs
395 Reg 10(6) I(EEA) Regs; Arts 12, 13 and 18 EU Dir 2004/38; *Ziolkowski and Szeja*, joined cases C-424/10 and C-425/10 [2011] ECR I-14035
396 Reg 10(3) and (4) I(EEA) Regs
397 *Ziolkowski and Szeja*, joined cases C-424/10 and C-425/10 [2011] ECR I-14035
398 Arts 12(2), 13(2) and 18 EU Dir 2004/38
399 Reg 9A(3) and (4) I(EEA) Regs
400 *SSWP v Gubeladze* [2019] UKSC 31 dismissed the SSWP's appeal from *SSWP v Gubeladze* [2017] EWCA Civ 1751, which had dismissed the SSWP's appeal from *TG v SSWP (PC)* [2015] UKUT 50 (AAC).
401 *JK v SSWP (SPC)* [2017] UKUT 179 (AAC); see also *SSWP v LM (ESA) (Interim decision)* [2017] UKUT 485 (AAC), paras 22-24
402 *Ziolkowski and Szeja*, joined cases C-424/10 and C-425/10 [2011] ECR I-14035; Sch 6, para 8(1) and (3) I(EEA) Regs; *SSWP v LS (IS)* [2012] UKUT 207 (AAC)
403 *Oakfor and Others v SSHD* [2011] EWCA Civ 499; *Alarape and Tijani v SSHD*, C-529/11 [2013]; *Bee and Another v SSHD* [2013] UKUT 83 (IAC); reg 15(2) I(EEA) Regs
404 Art 16(1) EU Dir 2004/38; reg 15(1) I(EEA) Regs
405 Regs 3(5)(b) & 4(6)(c) CR(ADTP) Regs; reg 3 I(EEA) Regs
406 Art 16(3) EU Dir 2004/38; reg 3 I(EEA) Regs
407 *Babajanov v SSHD* [2013] UKUT 513 (IAC)
408 *Idezuna v SSHD* [2011] UKUT 474 (IAC); *Babajanov v SSHD* [2013] UKUT 513 (IAC)
409 Vol 2 Ch 7, paras 073360 and 073417 DMG; para C1796 ADM; HB Circular A8/2015, para 7; CIS/2258/08
410 *OB v SSWP (ESA)* [2017] UKUT 255 (AAC), para 28
411 Reg 3(3) I(EEA) Regs; Sch 3 para 6(1)(b) and Sch 4 para 4(b) ISSC Regs
412 *OB v SSWP (ESA)* [2017] UKUT 255 (AAC), paras 29-30 and 34; see also *AP v SSWP (IS)* [2018] UKUT 307 (AAC), paras 15-18, and *ODS v SSWP (UC)* [2019] UKUT 192 (AAC), para 22
413 Following *SSWP v Dias*, C-325/09 [2011] ECR I-06387; see also *Saint Prix v SSWP*, C-507/12 [2014], paras 45 and 46, and *HMRC v Dakneviciute*, C-544/18 [2019], para 40
414 *SSHD v Ojo* [2015] EWCA Civ 1301, para 20
415 For example, there is no discussion of *Saint Prix v SSWP*, C-507/12 [2014], paras 45 and 46.
416 *OB v SSWP (ESA)* [2017] UKUT 255 (AAC), paras 29-30 and 34; see also *AP v SSWP (IS)* [2018] UKUT 307 (AAC), paras 15-18, and *ODS v SSWP (UC)* [2019] 192 (AAC), para 22
417 *Cardiff CC v HM (HB)* [2019] UKUT 271 (AAC)
418 Vol 2 Ch 7, paras 073433-35 DMG; paras C1812-14 ADM; HB Circular A8/2015, paras 20-22
419 Vol 2 Ch 7, para 073442 DMG; para C1820 ADM; HB Circular A8/15, para 26
420 Vol 2 Ch 7, para 073443 DMG; para C1821 ADM; HB Circular A8/15, para 27
421 *GE v SSWP (ESA)* [2017] UKUT 145 (AAC), reported as [2017] AACR 34, para 46; *SSWP v WN (rule 17)* [2018] UKUT 268 (AAC)
422 *Onuekwere v SSHD*, C-378/12 [2014]; reg 3(1), (3)(a) and (4) I(EEA) Regs - but see *SSHD v MG*, C-400/12 [2014] and Art 28(3) EU Dir 2004/38
423 *Onuekwere v SSHD*, C-378/12 [2014], paras 24-26
424 *SSHD v JO (Qualified person – hospital order – effect) Slovakia* [2012] UKUT 237 (IAC)
425 Regs 3(5)(b) and 4(6)(c) CR(ADTP) Regs; reg 3(3)(a) and (4) I(EEA) Regs
426 Sch 6 para 8(4) I(EEA) Regs
427 Art 16(4) EU Dir 2004/38
428 *SSWP v Dias*, C-325/09 [2011] ECR I-06387; see also *SSWP v Lassal*, C-162/09 [2010] ECR I-09217
429 Regs 5 and 15 I(EEA) Regs; Art 17 EU Dir 2004/38
430 *JP v SSWP (ESA)* [2018] UKUT 161 (AAC), paras 2, 4, 23-40 and 24

431 *SSHD v FB* [2010] UKUT 447 (IAC), para 23; *LM v HMRC (CHB)* [2016] UKUT 389 (AAC); *SSWP v LM (ESA)* [2017] UKUT 485 (AAC); see also *BL v SSWP (ESA)* [2019] UKUT 364 (AAC), paras 20-23
432 Reg 5(7) I(EEA) Regs; Art 17(1) EU Dir 2004/38
433 Regs 5(7) and 6(2) I(EEA) Regs; regs 7A(3) and 7B(3) I(EEA) Regs 2006, as saved by reg 45 and Sch 4 para 2 I(EEA) Regs
434 *NZ v SSWP (ESA) (Third interim decision)* [2017] UKUT 360 (AAC); see also *SSWP v NZ (ESA) (Final decision)* [2019] UKUT 250 (AAC)
435 *De Brito v SSHD* [2012] EWCA Civ 709
436 *SSWP v Gubeladze* [2019] UKSC 31; see also *AT v Pensionsversicherungsanstalt* C-32/19 [2020]
437 *ID v SSWP (IS)* [2011] UKUT 401 (AAC), paras 17 and 18
438 *SSWP v NZ (ESA) (Final decision)* [2019] UKUT 250 (AAC)
439 *PM (EEA – spouse – 'residing with') Turkey* [2011] UKUT 89 (IAC)
440 Art 17(3) EU Dir 2004/38; see also *RM (Zimbabwe) v SSHD* [2013] EWCA Civ 775, para 56 – cited in *TG v SSWP (PC)* [2015] UKUT 50 (AAC), para 33, and *JP v SSWP (ESA)* [2018] UKUT 161 (AAC), paras 5 (footnote 1) and 42; paras 62-64 of the AG's Opinion in *Givane*, C-257/00 [2003] ECR I-00345, although the ECJ did not address the issue itself.
441 Reg 15(1)(d) I(EEA) Regs
442 Art 16(4) EU Dir 2004/38; reg 15(3) I(EEA) Regs – note that the words 'only' and 'consecutive' were removed from these regulations from 1 February 2017, but EU law has not changed and should be followed.
443 Regs 3(5)(c) and 4(6)(d) CR(ADTP) Regs
444 Part 4 I(EEA) Regs
445 Vol 2 Ch 7, paras 073350-68 and 073414-43 DMG; paras C1750-77 and C1793-824 ADM; HB Circular A8/2015
446 Vol 2 Ch 7, paras 073429-32 DMG; para C1810 ADM

17. **Frontier worker**

447 Regs 3 and 4 CR(FW) Regs; Arts 45 and 49 TFEU; Arts 24 and 25 WA 2019; Arts 23 and 24 UK-EFTA Agreement; Arts 20 and 23 UK Swiss Agreement; ADM Memo 33/20; DMG Memo 29/20
448 Regs 3(3) CR(FW) Regs
449 Arts 24 and 25 WA 2019; Arts 23 and 24 UK-EFTA Agreement; Arts 20 and 23 UK Swiss Agreement; Arts 45 and 49 TFEU; EU Reg 492/2011
450 ADM Memo 33/20, para 51; DMG Memo 29/20, para 51
451 Arts 24(1)(h) and (2) and 25(1)(b) and (2) WA 2019; Arts 23(1)(h) and (2) and 24(1)(b) and (2) UK-EFTA Agreement; EU Reg 492/2011; ADM Memo 33/20 para, 35 and 53; DMG Memo 29/20, para 35 and 53
452 s4(1)(c) WRA 2012
453 Arts 1(3) and 4(11) WRA 2012(No.32)O

18. **Other European freedom of movement residence rights**

454 Arts 20 and 21 TFEU
455 For discussion of this principle of deterrence, see *B v SSWP* [2017] UKUT 472 (AAC), paras 25-29, 39, 49 and 62-63.
456 *Sanneh v SSWP (and linked cases)* [2015] EWCA Civ 49, paras 6-7 and 71-3; see also *LO v SSWP (IS)* [2017] UKUT 440 (AAC)
457 *Mirga v SSWP* [2016] UKSC 1; see also *MM v SSWP (ESA)* [2017] UKUT 437 (AAC); *LO v SSWP (IS)* [2017] UKUT 440 (AAC); *JS v SSWP (IS)* [2019] UKUT 135 (AAC)

Chapter 13

Residence and presence: rules for individual benefits

This chapter covers:

This chapter explains the residence and presence rules for each benefit. It also covers how you may be assisted by the European Union (EU) co-ordination rules. Further information on the different residence and presence tests is in Chapter 10, further information on the habitual residence and right to reside tests is in Chapter 11, and further information on the EU co-ordination rules is in Chapter 16. This chapter does not explain the rules on being paid while you are abroad. These are covered in Part 5.

1. Means-tested benefits

To be entitled to **universal credit (UC), income support (IS), income-based jobseeker's allowance (JSA), income-related employment and support allowance (ESA), housing benefit (HB) and pension credit (PC)**, you (and your partner for joint-claim JSA or UC) must:

- (except for HB – see below) be present in Great Britain (see p126);[1] *and*
- satisfy the habitual residence test (see p139), unless you are exempt (see p142).[2]

To satisfy the habitual residence test for these benefits, you must:

- be 'habitually resident in fact' in the common travel area (the UK, Ireland, Channel Islands and the Isle of Man);
- have a right to reside in the common travel area (but see p155 if you have been receiving benefit since April 2004);
- (income-based JSA only) have been living in the common travel area for the past three months (see p127).

Although there is no requirement to be present in Great Britain to be entitled to HB, the HB rules on occupying your home have the same effect and mean that you can cease to be entitled if you go abroad.[3] However, in certain circumstances you are treated as occupying your home while you are temporarily absent from your home and outside Great Britain, and your entitlement can therefore continue while you are abroad for limited periods (see p310).

For the means-tested benefits other than HB, in certain circumstances you are treated as present in Great Britain during a temporary absence, so you can continue to receive these benefits while you are abroad for limited periods (see p314).

For all means-tested benefits, the habitual residence test applies to the claimant.

If you live with a partner and claim UC or joint-claim JSA, the habitual residence test applies to both of you, as you are both claimants.

If you satisfy the habitual residence test but your partner does not:
- for UC if you are both under pension age, your joint claim is treated as a claim for UC as a single person, but your partner's income and capital are taken into account (see p142);
- for UC if you have reached pension age and your partner is under pension age, your claim is not treated as a single claim for UC. Instead, you can claim PC and HB and you are treated as a single person for each of these claims (see p142);
- for joint-claim JSA, you do not need to make a joint claim and are still paid as a couple (see p142).

Note:
- To be entitled to the carer element in UC, you must satisfy all the conditions of entitlement to carer's allowance (except the earnings limit), including the past presence test (see p280).[4]
- If you are receiving HB, IS, child tax credit (CTC) or working tax credit (WTC) and claim UC and the Department for Work and Pensions (DWP) decides you do not satisfy the above residence or presence tests, this does *not* terminate your existing award of any of these four benefits. You can therefore continue

to receive HB, IS, CTC or WTC while you challenge the decision that you are not entitled to UC (see the 10th bullet point on p145).[5]

If your partner is abroad

If your partner is abroad, the effect this has on your benefit depends on whether the separation is permanent or, if temporary, whether you still count as members of the same household.

If you separate permanently (ie, you do not intend to resume living together), you no longer count as a couple and must claim as a single person.[6] Your partner's income and capital no longer affect your benefit.

If you are still regarded as a couple, your partner's absence abroad can affect your benefit in two ways.

- At some point, you will cease to be paid an amount of benefit for your partner.
- Your partner's capital and income can continue to affect your entitlement.

If you and your partner are living apart temporarily, you continue to count as a couple because you are still treated as members of the same household, unless:[7]

- **for UC**, you have been separated (or expect to be separated) for more than six months;
- **for IS, income-based JSA, income-related ESA, PC and HB**, you are likely to be separated for more than 52 weeks. However, you still count as a couple if you are unlikely to be separated for 'substantially' longer than 52 weeks and there are exceptional circumstances, such as a stay in hospital, or if you have no control over the length of the absence;
- **for IS, income-based JSA, income-related ESA and PC**, you or your partner are detained in custody or in a high-security psychiatric hospital, or are on temporary release, or are living permanently in a care home.

Your partner's absence is from *you*, not from the family home, so these rules can apply even if your partner has never lived in your current home, and your former household need not have been in this country.[8] However, you must have been living with your partner in the same household before you can be treated as continuing to be members of that household.[9]

If the question of whether you or your partner intend to resume living together is relevant, your intention must be 'unqualified'. This means that it must not depend on a factor over which you have no control – eg, the right of entry to the UK being granted by the Home Office[10] or the offer of a suitable job.[11]

If you still count as a couple, you may be able to continue to receive an amount of benefit for your partner while s/he is abroad for a limited period. The rules vary between the different means-tested benefits (see Chapter 15).

Once you stop being paid for your partner because these rules do not apply, or at the end of the limited period:

- **for UC**, you cease to be entitled as joint claimants and must notify the DWP. Your award is based on the maximum amount for a single person, but your

partner's income and capital are taken into account until you have been, or you expect to be, apart for six months (as then you cease to be treated as a couple).[12] **Note:**
  - if your partner's absence abroad means s/he is no longer habitually resident in the common travel area, s/he is treated as no longer present. Your joint claim is then treated as if you had claimed UC as a single person for the purpose of being paid a sinlge person's allowances, but your partner's income and capital are taken into account until you have been, or you expect to be, apart for six months (as then you cease to be treated as a couple). Once you cease to be treated as a couple you are treated as having claimed as a single person;[13]
  - if you are claiming UC jointly with your partner who is under pension age and you have reached pension age, once s/he stops being treated as present in the UK or ceases to be habitually resident in the common travel area, you stop being entitled to UC. Instead you can claim PC and HB, and you are treated as a single person for each of these claims;[14]
- **for IS, income-based JSA, income-related ESA and HB**, your applicable amount no longer includes an amount for your partner. However, your partner's capital, income and work are still taken into account as s/he is still treated as part of your household;[15]
- **for PC**, you are paid as a single person. Your partner's income and capital are ignored because s/he is no longer treated as part of your household.[16]

Note: if you have reached pension age and your partner is under pension age and you cease to be paid PC or HB for your partner because s/he is abroad, when s/he returns you will need to make a joint claim for UC. However note that if your partner fails the habitual residence test, you will not be entitled to UC, but you can instead need to claim PC and HB, and you are treated as a single person for each of these claims (see p142).[17]

If your child is abroad

If you have a child who is abroad, the effect this has on your benefit depends on whether, for **UC and PC**, you are still treated responsible for him/her, or for the **other means-tested benefits**, s/he is still treated as being part of your household, despite temporarily living away from you.

If your child ceases to be included in your claim, you are no longer paid benefit for her/him. Other aspects of your benefit entitlement may also be affected if you no longer have a child included in your claim – eg, your work-related requirements may change or the number of bedrooms you are allowed in your UC housing costs or HB calculation may change. For further details, see CPAG's *Welfare Benefits and Tax Credits Handbook.*

For UC, you cease to be responsible for a child if s/he is absent from your household and the absence exceeds, or is expected to exceed, one month, or, in limited circumstances, two or six months (see p316).[18]

For PC, you cease to be responsible for a child if s/he is, or expected to be, absent from Great Britain for four weeks, or in limited circumstances, eight or 26 weeks (see p324).[19]

For the **other means-tested benefits**, s/he ceases to be treated as part of your household if:[20]

- **for IS, JSA, ESA and HB**, s/he is not living with you and:
  - has no intention of resuming living with you; *or*
  - is likely to be absent for more than 52 weeks, unless there are exceptional circumstances, such as being in hospital, or if you have no control over the length of absence and the absence is unlikely to be substantially longer than 52 weeks;
- **for IS, JSA and ESA**, s/he is not living with you and has been abroad for more than:
  - four weeks; *or*
  - eight weeks (26 weeks for ESA) to get medical treatment;
- there are other reasons that are not related to residence or presence, such as being fostered. See CPAG's *Welfare Benefits and Tax Credits Handbook* for more information.

For IS or income-based JSA, once your child stops being treated as part of your household, s/he is no longer included in your applicable amount. If s/he returns to your household, you must claim CTC (or UC) for her/him instead.[21] See p318 for IS and p320 for income-based JSA.

Note: you can only be paid means-tested benefits and CTC for your third and subsequent child in limited circumstances (due to the 'two-child limit'). These include (for UC and HB) certain transitional rules which may no longer apply if your child returns from abroad after payments for her/him (or your claim) ended because s/he was no longer part of your household. (HB is always paid for a child for whom you receive a CTC element.)

For HB, UC, IS and income-based JSA, if you have adopted a child or s/he has been placed with you for adoption, this is generally an exception that means you can be paid for the child even if s/he is your third or subsequent child. However, this does not apply if you adopted the child under the law of another country before the adoption under UK law.[22]

The rules on the 'two-child limit' and the exceptions vary between the benefits. Check the details of the benefit you are claiming in CPAG's *Welfare Benefits and Tax Credits Handbook.*

European Union co-ordination rules

If you are covered by the main European Union (EU) co-ordination rules (seep355), these can assist you to satisfy the habitual residence test for **PC** and, if you are in one of the very limited groups not required to claim UC, **income-based JSA** and **income-related ESA**, sooner. That is because you cannot be denied benefit solely on the basis that your length of actual residence is too short, since the period of your residence is only one relevant factor in determining whether you are 'habitually resident in fact' and can be outweighed by others (see p150).[23]

UC, IS and HB are not covered by the main EU co-ordination rules and neither the UK-EU Protocol nor the UK-Ireland Convention can assist you to be entitled to any of the means-tested benefits (see p363). However other equal treatment provisions of EU law may assist (see p382).

Reciprocal agreements

Most means-tested benefits are not covered by reciprocal agreements. One exception is the agreement between Great Britain and Northern Ireland which, since 6 April 2016, has covered income-related ESA (as well as contributory ESA), and since 27 November 2016, has covered income-based JSA (as well as contribution-based JSA),[24] and from 24 July 2020 covers UC.[25]

If you moved to Great Britain from Northern Ireland (or vice versa) while claiming ESA before 6 April 2016, the DWP policy was to make an extra-statutory payment to cover any loss of income-related ESA (or contributory ESA) that resulted from having to make a new claim. See p399 for further details.

2. Bereavement benefits

To be entitled to bereavement support payment, you must be ordinarily resident (see p131) in Great Britain (or Sark – see p405) on the date your spouse or civil partner died.[26]

You do not need to satisfy any residence or presence rules to be entitled to widowed parent's allowance.

European Union co-ordination rules

Since the end of the transition period (31 December 2020), you may be covered by the main European Union (EU) co-ordination rules or similar co-ordination rules contained in the new UK-EU Protocol, or, for situations involving the UK and Ireland only, the UK-Ireland Convention. If you are covered by any of these co-ordination rules (see p355), and the UK is your 'competent state' (see p369):[27]

- you can, if necessary, rely on national insurance contributions paid by your late spouse or civil partner in one or more European Economic Area (EEA) countries (EU if relying on the UK-EU Protocol), or Ireland if you are relying on the UK-Ireland Convention, to calculate your entitlement to bereavement benefits (under the 'aggregation principle' – see p383); *and*

- the bereavement support payment requirement to be ordinarily resident in Great Britain on the date your spouse or civil partner died does not apply if you were resident in an EEA country (EU country/Ireland)on that date.

If you have moved to the UK from an EEA state (EU state/Ireland) that was paying you a bereavement benefit, you may be able to continue to receive this (referred to as 'exporting' the benefit – see p385) if that state remains the competent state to pay that benefit.

Reciprocal and other international agreements

If your late spouse or civil partner lived and worked in a country with which the UK has a reciprocal agreement (see p397), periods of insurance paid in that country can count towards your bereavement benefit entitlement.

If the agreement treats you as being present in the UK while in the other country and you were ordinarily resident in that country on the date your spouse or civil partner died, you are treated as ordinarily resident in Great Britain on that date.[28]

Guidance lists the relevant countries.[29]

Note: the reciprocal agreements were amended to include, from 6 April 2017, bereavement support payment.[30]

If your late spouse or civil partner was covered by an international agreement between the EU and another country, you may be able to count periods of insurance s/he paid in the relevant country towards your bereavement benefit entitlement (see p408).

For more information on reciprocal and other international agreements, see Chapter 17.

---

3. Child benefit, Scottish child payment and guardian's allowance

Child benefit

To be entitled to child benefit, you and your child(ren) must be present in Great Britain (see p126).[31]

You are treated as not present and, therefore, not eligible for child benefit if:[32]

- you are not ordinarily resident in the UK (see p131); *or*
- you do not have a right to reside in the UK (see p151); *or*
- you have not been living in the UK for the three months prior to your claim, unless you are exempt (see p127).

Note: you do not need to have a right to reside if you claimed child benefit before 1 May 2004 and you have been receiving it continuously since that date (see p159).

You are treated as present if you are:[33]

- a Crown servant posted overseas and:
  - you are, or immediately before your posting abroad you were, ordinarily resident in the UK; *or*
  - immediately before your posting you were in the UK in connection with that posting; *or*
- the partner of a Crown servant posted overseas and in the same country as her/him, or temporarily absent from that country under the same exceptions that enable child benefit to continue during a temporary absence from Great Britain (see p327); *or*
- a person who is in the UK as a result of your being deported or legally removed from another country.

You and/or your child can be treated as present for limited periods during a temporary absence (see p327).

While you are treated as present, you continue to satisfy that condition of entitlement. This means that you can continue to receive child benefit if it is already being paid and you can also make a fresh claim during your, or your child's, absence. If you, or your child, spend longer abroad than the permitted periods (see p327), you (or s/he) cease to satisfy the presence condition and your entitlement to child benefit ends.

Note: if you or your child are treated as present, you must satisfy all the other conditions of entitlement including, if your child is not living with you, contributing to the costs of her/him at least the amount of child benefit that would be payable for her/him.[34]

Scottish child payment

To be entitled to a Scottish child payment, you must be ordinarily resident (see p131) in Scotland.[35]

Guardian's allowance

Entitlement to guardian's allowance depends on entitlement to child benefit, so you must meet the above conditions for child benefit. In addition, at least one of the child's parents must have:[36]

- been born in the UK or a European Economic Area (EEA) country; *or*
- spent a total of 52 weeks in any two-year period in Great Britain at some time after reaching the age of 16.

In order to satisfy the second condition above, you are treated as being present in Great Britain during any absence abroad which is due to your employment as a serving member of the forces, an airman or airwoman, mariner or continental shelf worker.

European Union co-ordination rules

Since the end of the transition period (31 December 2020), you may be covered by the main European Union (EU) co-ordination rules or, for situations involving the UK and Ireland only, the UK-Ireland Convention. If you are not covered by either, but you are covered by the new UK-EU Protocol, that will not assist you in the ways below because it does not cover family benefits.

If you are covered by the main EU co-ordination rules, or, for situations involving the UK and Ireland only, the UK-Ireland Convention (see p355), you may be able to:

- use certain periods of residence in another EEA country (Ireland if relying on the Convention) to satisfy the child benefit requirement to have been 'living in' the UK for the past three months (under the 'aggregation principle' – see p383). For further information, including on HM Revenue and Customs guidance that suggests this only applies to residence in four EEA countries, see p284;
- use time spent in an EEA country (Ireland if relying on the Convention) to satisfy the guardian's allowance requirement to have spent 52 weeks in any two-year period in Great Britain (under the 'aggregation principle' – see p383). It may also be arguable that this condition should not apply to you if you are covered by the co-ordination rules and have a 'genuine and sufficient link to the UK' (see p283);[37]
- be paid for a child resident in an EEA country (Ireland if relying on the Convention) without her/his needing to satisfy the UK rules on temporary absences. However, you must still satisfy all the other conditions of entitlement, including contributing to the costs of the child an amount at least equal to the amount of child benefit payable for that child;[38]
- continue to receive a family benefit from an EEA state (Ireland if relying on the Convention) if you were receiving it before you moved to the UK (referred to as 'exporting' the benefit – see p385) and that state continues to be the 'competent state' to pay that benefit (see p369).

Child benefit and guardian's allowance are categorised, and arguably Scottish child payment should be categorised, as 'family benefits' under the main EU co-ordination rules. For more details on 'family benefits', see p386.

Reciprocal and other international agreements

If you are covered by a reciprocal agreement, that may allow periods of residence and/or presence in the other country to be treated as residence and/or presence in Great Britain in order to be entitled to child benefit and guardian's allowance.

Arguably, it could also enable you to to use periods of residence in the other country to satisfy the requirement for child benefit to have been living in the UK for the past three months. For more information on reciprocal agreements, see p406.

Israel also has an agreement with the EU that can assist in ways that are similar to the EU co-ordination rules (see above). For more information on this agreement with Israel, see p410.

4. Disability and carers' benefits

For attendance allowance (AA), disability living allowance (DLA), personal independence payment (PIP) and carer's allowance (CA), you must:[39]

- be present in Great Britain at the time of your claim;
- have been present in Great Britain for at least 104 weeks in the last 156 weeks (the 'past presence test'). See p126, but also the rules for children below and the exceptions below;
- be habitually resident in the common travel area (see p139).

For AA, DLA, PIP and CA, you are treated as being present and habitually resident, if you:[40]

- are abroad as a serving member of the armed forces; *or*
- are living with someone who is abroad as a serving member of the armed forces and s/he is your spouse, civil partner, son, stepson, daughter, stepdaughter, father, stepfather, father-in-law, mother, stepmother or mother-in-law.

If the **DLA claimant is a child under 16**, the past presence requirement is reduced. For a baby under six months old, the 104 weeks is reduced to 13 weeks, and that continues to apply until the child is 12 months old. For a child claiming DLA when aged six months to 36 months old, the 104 weeks is reduced to 26 weeks. The Upper Tribunal has recently held that increasing the duration of the past presence test in 2013, for children aged three to 16, was unlawful and that the previous requirement to have been present for 26 weeks out of the last 52 must be treated as continuing for claimants in this age group.[41] Challenges that the past presence requirement for a child breaches public sector equality duties have, to date, failed.[42] **Note**: a child's residence, but *not* her/his presence or past presence, is generally determined by the residence of the person responsible for her/him (see p130).

To be entitled to the **carer's allowance supplement**, you must be in receipt of CA and resident (see p130) in Scotland on the qualifying date.[43]

To qualify for a **young carer grant**, on the day of your application you must be:[44]

- ordinarily resident in Scotland; *and*

- habitually resident in the UK, Channel Islands, Isle of Man, or the European Economic Area (EAA) (see p140) or be exempt from this requirement (see p142).

If you are under 19, in receipt of the higher rate of the DLA, or child disability payment, care component and either resident in, or have a genuine and sufficient link to, Scotland you may be entitled to **child winter heating assistance** (see p293).

For child disability payment (expected to be introduced in Scotland in 2021) it is expected you must:[45]
- be present in the common travel area (the UK, Ireland, Channel Islands and Isle of Man) at the time of your claim;
- have been present in the common travel area for at least 26 weeks in the last 52 weeks (the 'past presence test'). The 26 weeks is reduced to 13 for children younger than three years old, in the same way as for DLA. See p130, but also the exceptions below;
- be habitually resident in the common travel area (see p139);
- be ordinarily resident in Scotland.

For child disability payment, you are treated as being present, ordinarily resident and habitually resident if you can demonstrate a genuine and sufficient link to Scotland (see p283) and you:[46]
- are abroad as a serving member of the armed forces or civil servant; *or*
- are living with someone in the bullet above and you are her/his spouse, civil partner, (or you are lving together as if you were either), child, stepchild, or child in care.

For child winter heating assistance (for those under 19 and in receipt of the higher rate of the DLA care component), on any day in the qualifying week you must be:[47]
- resident (see p130) in Scotland; *or*
- habitually resident (see p146) in an EEA state (other than Cyprus, France, Greece, Malta, Portugal or Spain) or Switzerland *and* have a 'genuine and sufficient link to Scotland' (see p283).

For **employment and support allowance (ESA) in youth, incapacity benefit (IB) in youth and severe disablement allowance (SDA)**, you must:[48]
- be present in Great Britain at the time of your claim (see p126);
- have been present in Great Britain for not less than 26 weeks in the last 52 weeks (the 'past presence' test – see p127);
- be ordinarily resident in Great Britain (see p131).

For ESA in youth, IB in youth and SDA, once you satisfy these tests, you do not need to do so again while you are in the same period of limited capability for work or incapacity for work.[49]

When you can be treated as present

You are treated as being present during certain absences (see p329). Any period when you are treated as present can be counted to satisfy both the presence and the past presence tests.

Exceptions to the past presence test

For **AA, DLA and PIP** (and, it is expected, **child disability payment**[50]) the 104-week (or 26-week or 13-week) past presence test does not apply if you are terminally ill.[51] The definition of 'terminal illness' is the same as applies for other purposes for these benefits – ie, that you have a progressive disease and your death as a result of that disease can reasonably be expected within six months.[52]

If you have been granted refugee leave or humanitarian protection, or you have leave as the dependent family member of someone who has such leave (eg, because you joined her/him under the family reunion provisions – see p41), you are exempt from the past presence test.[53] That is not always picked up by the Department for Work and Pensions (DWP) when you make your claim, so make sure the DWP is aware that the past presence test does not apply to you.

For **child disability payment**, it is expected that if you do not satisfy the past presence test, but will within 13 weeks, your claim may be treated as an advance claim, and decided from the date you satisfy this requirement.[54]

European Union co-ordination rules

Since the end of the transition period (31 December 2020), you may be covered by the main European Union (EU) co-ordination rules or, for situations involving the UK and Ireland only, the UK-Ireland Convention. If you are not covered by either, but you are covered by the new UK-EU Protocol, that will not assist you in the ways below because it does not cover disability and carer's benefits.

If you are covered (see p355) by the main EU co-ordination rules or, for situations involving the UK and Ireland only, the UK-Ireland Convention:

- you are not entitled to AA, DLA care component, the daily living component of PIP, CA, (or, it is expected, the care component of child disability payment[55])' or for claims made while resident in an EEA state, young carer's grant or carer's allowance supplement *unless* the UK is your 'competent state' (see p369).[56] That might not be the case if you (or your family member who brings you within the co-ordination rules) receive a contributory benefit (classed as a 'pension') paid by an EEA state (Ireland if relying on the Convention), or your family member is working in an EEA country (Ireland if relying on the Convention) (see p374);

- you may be able to claim AA, DLA, PIP, CA, and, it is expected, child disability payment, more quickly, either because the past presence test does not apply to you (see below) or because periods of residence in an EEA state (Ireland if relying on the Convention) can be used to satisfy the test (under the 'aggregation principle' – see p284);
- you may be able to make a new claim for AA, DLA care component, the daily living component of PIP, CA, young carer's grant and carer's allowance supplement (and, it is expected, the care component of child disability payment) if you live in an EEA country (see p285);
- you may be entitled to the mobility component of PIP or DLA (and child disability payment, expected in Scotland in 2021) sooner than you would otherwise be (see p286);
- if you have moved to the UK from an EEA state, you may continue to receive a sickness or invalidity benefit from that state or, if you are relying on the Convention, if you have moved from Ireland you may continue to receive a sickness, invalidity or long-term care benefit (referred to as 'exporting' the benefit – see p385), if that state (Ireland) continues to be the competent state to pay that benefit (see p369).

When the past presence test does not apply

The past presence test does not apply to AA, DLA, PIP, CA and, it is expected, child disability payment (in Scotland), if:[57]

- you are covered by the main EU co-ordination rules (or, for child disability payment only, the agreement between the UK and Gibraltar – see p400) (see p355); *and*
- you are habitually resident in Great Britain (the UK, for child disability payment); *and*
- you can demonstrate 'a genuine and sufficient link' to the UK (to Scotland, for child disability payment) – see below.

Note:

- The DWP interprets 'habitual residence' in this context in the same way as 'residence' is interpreted under the EU co-ordination rules (see p371).[58]
- You may be able to make a new claim if you are habitually resident in an EEA country (see p285).

Genuine and sufficient link

The phrase **'genuine and sufficient link to the UK'** (for Scottish benefits see note below) is not defined in regulations, but comes from a case decided by the Court of Justice of the European Union (CJEU).[59] The way this phrase is interpreted must therefore be consistent with this judgment.

Although the regulations require you to demonstrate a 'genuine and sufficient link to the UK *social security system*', the Court of Appeal has held that the last three words must be disregarded as they are not authorised by the CJEU's judgment.[60]

The circumstances that applied in the CJEU case and which were held to have amounted to a 'genuine and sufficient link to the UK' are relevant, but they are not exhaustive. Many factors can be relevant to determining whether you have a genuine and sufficient link to the UK, depending on your circumstances and the benefit you are claiming, and include:[61]

- whether you have worked in the UK;
- whether you have spent a significant part of your life in the UK;
- whether you are receiving a UK contributory benefit;
- evidence of your motives, intentions and expectations;
- if you are claiming a disability benefit, whether your carer would be entitled to CA;
- whether you are dependent on a family member who has worked in the UK and/or receives a UK contributory benefit. 'Family member' in this context is not limited to the definition of 'member of the family' in the co-ordination rules (see p361). The Upper Tribunal has held that a child claiming DLA had a 'genuine and sufficient link to the UK ' on the basis that he was dependent on his sister who had worked in the UK for at least five years.[62] This principle that your link can be established through someone else's link to the UK was also accepted by the Court of Appeal in a subsequent case.[63]

The Upper Tribunal has held that your presence in Great Britain is also a factor, and the closer your period of presence comes to satisfying the two-year past presence requirement, the more significance should be attached to this factor. This part of the decision did not need to be addressed by the Court of Appeal, which merely noted that it is highly unlikely that presence alone would ever be the sole factor demonstrating a 'genuine and sufficient link' to the UK.[64]

Note: the requirement to demonstrate a **'genuine and sufficient link to Scotland'**, for specific elements of the residence and presence requirements for child disability payment, child winter heating assistance (see p280 for both), carer's allowance supplement and young carer grant (see p285 for both), must be interpreted in a way consistent with the caselaw referred to above, but in relation to Scotland. For child disability payment, carer's allowance supplement and young carer's grant, the regulations state that a link is sufficient if not granting that benefit would be incompatible with the relevant co-ordination rules that apply.[65]

When the co-ordination rules can help you satisfy the past presence test

If you are covered by the main EU co-ordination rules, or the UK-Ireland Convention (see p355), you may be able to satisfy the past presence test by adding certain periods of residence in an EEA state (Ireland if relying on the Convention) to periods of presence in Great Britain (or, for child disability payment, the UK) (under the 'aggregation principle').[66] If possible, provide evidence to show the decision maker (or tribunal) that you are exempt from the test due to your 'genuine and sufficient link' to the UK (or, for child disability payment, Scotland) *and* that you satisfy the past presence test by aggregating your residence in an EEA state with your presence in Great Britain (or, for child disability payment, Scotland), in case one is not accepted.

Note: the Upper Tribunal has held that 'mere residence' in an EEA country cannot be aggregated in order to satisfy the past presence test under the main EU co-ordination rules and only periods of residence during which you were 'insured' can be aggregated under the UK-Ireland Convention.[67] For further details on the aggregation principle, see p383.

Making a new claim while living in another European Economic Area state

If you are living in an EEA state, you can make a new claim (or continue to be paid an existing award – see p330) for **AA, DLA care component, the daily living component of PIP, CA** or, it is expected, **child disability payment** care component, without needing to satisfy the usual habitual residence, presence and past presence (and, for child disability payment only, ordinary residence) requirements if the UK is your 'competent state' (see p369),[68] and:[69]

- you are covered by the main EU co-ordination rules (or, for child disability payment, the UK-Ireland Convention or the agreement between the UK and Gibraltar – see p400) (see p355); *and*
- you are habitually resident in an EEA state (or Gibraltar if relying on the agreement with Gibraltar, and Ireland if relying on the UK-Ireland Convention, for child disability payment); *and*
- you can demonstrate a 'genuine and sufficient link' to the UK (to Scotland, for child disability payment) (see p283).

You can make a new claim (including for a backdated period if you *would have* been entitled had these rules been in force at the time) for **carer's allowance supplement** or **young carer's grant** without needing to satisfy the requirement to be resident or ordinarily resident in Scotland if:[70]

- you have a 'genuine and sufficient link' to Scotland (see p283); *and*
- the UK is your 'competent state' to pay this benefit; *and*
- you are either:
  - resident in an EEA state and covered by the main EU co-ordination rules (see p355); *or*
  - resident in Ireland and covered by the UK-Ireland Convention (see p358); *or*
  - resident in Gibraltar and covered by the agreement between the UK and Gibraltar (see p400).

Disability and carer's benefits are not covered by the UK-EU Protocol at all.

Mobility component

You are only entitled to the mobility component of DLA or PIP or child disability payment if you are habitually resident in the UK. That is because, under the main EU co-ordination rules, DLA mobility component is listed as, and PIP mobility component is accepted as, and it is expected that child disability payment mobility payment will be treated as, a special non-contributory benefit and therefore not 'exportable' (see p367).[71] You can only be paid these in the state where you are resident, which means where you 'habitually reside'.[72]

The UK-Ireland Convention does not cover these mobility components at all.

If you are covered by the main EU co-ordination rules (see p355), these can still assist you to be entitled to the DLA or PIP or child disability payment mobility component sooner than you would otherwise be because:

- the past presence test does not apply to you if you are covered by the rules on p283; *and*
- you cannot be found to be not habitually resident and denied benefit solely on the basis that you have not been actually resident for an 'appreciable period' of time. Your length of actual residence is only one relevant factor in determining whether you are 'habitually resident in fact' and can be outweighed by other factors (see p150).

Reciprocal agreements

At the time of writing, the UK had reciprocal agreements in relation to the disability and carer's benefits with few countries and, other than the agreement between Northern Ireland and Great Britain, none had been updated to include PIP. See Appendix 5 for a list of the countries that have reciprocal agreements and p397 for more information on those agreements. However, the agreement between the UK and Gibraltar can assist with claims for young carer's grant, carer's allowance supplement and child disability payment (see p400).

At the time of writing, the UK government was seeking to negotiate new agreements, or update existing agreements, to replace or supplement arrangements that were previously in place due to membership of the EU.

The reciprocal agreement between Northern Ireland and Great Britain provides for periods of residence and presence in one territory to count as residence and presence in the other territory for the purpose of entitlement to AA, DLA, PIP and CA.[73]

5. Industrial injuries benefits

Industrial injuries benefits are:

- industrial injuries disablement benefit;
- reduced earnings allowance;

- retirement allowance;
- constant attendance allowance;
- exceptionally severe disablement allowance.

To be entitled to any of these benefits, you must have been:
- in Great Britain when the accident at work happened;[74] *or*
- engaged in Great Britain in the employment that caused the disease (even if you have also been engaged outside Great Britain in that employment);[75] *or*
- paying UK national insurance (NI) contributions, either at class 1 rate or at class 2 rate as a volunteer development worker when the accident at work happened or you contracted the disease. Benefit is not payable until you return to Great Britain.[76]

There are exceptions to these rules, which mean you can qualify for benefit in respect of an accident which happens, or a disease which is contracted, outside Great Britain while you are:[77]
- employed as a mariner or airman or airwoman;
- employed as an apprentice pilot on board a ship or vessel;
- on board an aircraft on a test flight starting in Great Britain in the course of your employment.

In these cases, there are also more generous rules for defining when accidents arise 'out of and in the course of' your employment, and for complying with time limits under the benefit rules.[78]

European Union co-ordination rules

Since the end of the transition period (31 December 2020), you may be covered by the main European Union (EU) co-ordination rules (which cover the UK and European Economic Area states) or similar co-ordination rules contained in the new UK–EU Protocol (which cover the UK and EU states), or, for situations involving the UK and Ireland only, the UK–Ireland Convention (see p355). If you are covered by any of these co-ordination rules, you can, if necessary, rely on periods of employment and NI paid in member states to qualify for industrial injuries benefits in the UK (under the 'aggregation principle' – see p383).

Industrial injuries benefits are classed as 'benefits for accidents at work and occupational diseases' under the co-ordination rules (see p363).

If you have an accident while travelling abroad in another member state, that can be deemed, under the co-ordination rules, to have occurred in the state liable to pay benefits for accidents at work and occupational diseases. If one state determines that you have had an accident or contracted a disease, that should be accepted by the state liable to pay benefit in respect of that accident or disease. These outcomes are achieved under the principle of equal treatment of facts or events (see p382).[79]

If you have worked in two or more member states in jobs that gave you a prescribed industrial disease, you get benefit from the state in which you last did work that, by its nature, is likely to cause that disease and which recognises that disease under its industrial injuries scheme.[80] If you make your claim to the state that does not have responsibility under this rule, your claim and all supporting evidence must be forwarded to the relevant institution in the correct state without delay.[81]

Reciprocal agreements

The UK has reciprocal agreements with several countries that cover industrial injuries benefits. The agreements determine which country is responsible for determining and paying your entitlement, and if and how you can combine injuries or take account of new accidents or diseases. For more information, see p404.

6. Contribution-based jobseeker's allowance and contributory employment and support allowance

To be entitled to contribution-based jobseeker's allowance (JSA) or contributory employment and support allowance (ESA), you must be in Great Britain.[82] The rules about when you can be paid during a temporary absence abroad are covered on p318 for JSA and p321 for ESA. There are no residence conditions, unless you are claiming contributory ESA in youth (see p280).

Note: looking for work abroad does not count towards satisfying the JSA requirement that you be 'actively seeking employment'.[83]

European Union co-ordination rules

Contribution-based jobseeker's allowance

Since the end of the transition period (31 December 2020), you may be covered by the main European Union (EU) co-ordination rules, which cover the UK and European Economic Area (EEA) states, or similar co-ordination rules contained in the new UK–EU Protocol, which cover the UK and EU states, or, for situations involving the UK and Ireland only, the UK–Ireland Convention (see p355).

If you are covered by any of these co-ordination rules, you can, if necessary, rely on the equivalent of national insurance (NI) contributions paid in a member state to entitle you to contribution-based JSA in the UK (under the 'aggregation principle' – see p383). However, in most cases, because it is an unemployment benefit, you can only aggregate your contributions if your most recent period of paying or being credited with those contributions was in the UK.[84] See p384 for more details.

If you are coming to, or returning to, the UK to look for work and you are covered by the main EU co-ordination rules and have been insured in an EEA state (and obtain a U2 form authorising you to export your unemployment benefit), or if you are covered by the UK-Ireland Convention and have been insured in Ireland, you may be able to continue to receive (referred to as 'exporting') that state's unemployment benefit for up to three months, if:[85]

- you were getting that unemployment benefit immediately before coming to the UK;
- you have been registered as available for work for four weeks (or less if the other state's rules allow) in the other state;
- you claim JSA within seven days after you were last registered in the other state; *and*
- you meet the relevant jobseeking requirements for JSA.

The three months can be extended to a maximum of six months if the state from which you are claiming the unemployment benefit agrees.[86]

You cannot 'export' unemployment benefit under the UK–EU Protocol.[87]

For general information on 'exporting' benefits, see p385.

Contributory employment and support allowance

If you are covered by the any of the EU co-ordination rules (see p355), you can, if necessary, rely on the equivalent of NI contributions paid in an EEA state (Ireland if relying on the UK-Ireland Convention) to entitle you to contributory ESA in the UK (under the 'aggregation principle' – see p383).

If you are covered by any of the EU co-ordination rules (see p355) and have moved to the UK from an EEA state (Ireland if relying on the UK-Ireland Convention), you may be able to continue to receive a sickness or (unless you are only covered by the Protocol) an invalidity benefit from that state (referred to as 'exporting' the benefit – see p385) if that state continues to be your 'competent state' for paying that benefit (see p369).

Reciprocal and other international agreements

If you have lived and worked in a country with which the UK has a reciprocal agreement (see p397), you may be able to count periods of insurance paid in that country towards your entitlement to contribution-based JSA or contributory ESA in the UK if the agreement covers you and that benefit. Similarly, if you are covered by another type of international agreement between the EU and another country, you may be able to do the same (see p408).

Although most reciprocal agreements do not cover income-based JSA or ESA (see p404), the reciprocal agreement between Northern Ireland and Great Britain was extended to cover income-based JSA (as well as contribution-based JSA) from

27 November 2016 (see p399) and contributory ESA (as well as income-related ESA) from 6 April 2016.[88] If you moved from Northern Ireland to Great Britain or vice versa while claiming ESA before this date, the Department for Work and Pensions policy was to make extra-statutory payments to cover any loss arising from having to make a new claim. If you were receiving extra-statutory payments on this basis up to 27 November 2016, and do not satisfy the contributory conditions for entitlement to contributory ESA, you are treated as satisfying those conditions and as having made a claim for ESA from 27 November 2016 and your period of limited capability for work is treated as continuous (see p399).[89]

7. Maternity allowance

Entitlement to maternity allowance (MA) is based on past employment. In general, you must have been employed or self-employed in Great Britain.[90] However, you can count weeks during which you were employed abroad before you returned to Great Britain if, through out the whole period of your absence, you remained ordinarily resident in Great Britain and you paid, or would have been liable to pay were it not for a reciprocal agreement, class 1 national insurance contributions.[91]

There are no residence requirements for MA. However, in general you are disqualified if you are absent from Great Britain.[92] See p336 for the rules allowing you to be paid during a temporary absence.

European Union co-ordination rules

Since the end of the transition period (31 December 2020), you may be covered by the main European Union (EU) co-ordination rules, which cover the UK and European Economic Area states, or similar co-ordination rules contained in the new UK-EU Protocol, which cover the UK and EU states, or, for situations involving the UK and Ireland only, the UK-Ireland Convention.

If you are covered by any of these co-ordination rules (see p355) and the UK is your competent state (see p369), you can, if necessary, rely on periods of employment or self-employment in one or more member states to satisfy the employment and earnings conditions to qualify for MA in the UK (under the 'aggregation principle' – see p383).

If you are covered by any of the EU co-ordination rules (see p355) and have moved to the UK from another member state, you may be able to continue to receive a maternity or paternity benefit from that other state (referred to as 'exporting' the benefit – see p385) if that state continues to be your 'competent state' for paying that benefit (see p369).

8. Retirement pensions

Retirement pensions, other than a category D retirement pension, do not have any residence or presence conditions. They can be paid without time limit, whether or not you are present in Great Britain. However, going abroad can mean you are not paid the annual uprating, can be relevant to decisions on deferring your retirement and can prevent you from 'de-retiring' while you are abroad (see p338).[93]

To be entitled to a category D retirement pension, you must have been:[94]

- resident in Great Britain for at least 10 years in any continuous period of 20 years ending on or after your 80th birthday; *and*
- ordinarily resident (see p131) in Great Britain on either:
  - your 80th birthday; *or*
  - the date on which you claimed the category D pension, if later.

European Union co-ordination rules

Since the end of the transition period (31 December 2020), you may be covered by the main European Union (EU) co-ordination rules, which cover the UK and European Economic Area (EEA) states, or similar co-ordination rules contained in the new UK-EU Protocol, which covers the UK and EU states, or, for situations involving the UK and Ireland only, the UK-Ireland Convention.

If you are covered by any of these co-ordination rules (see p355), you can, if necessary, rely on the equivalent of national insurance (NI) contributions paid in the member states (see note below) to calculate your entitlement to retirement pensions in the UK; and you can count certain periods of residence in EEA countries to meet the residence requirement for a category D pension (under the 'aggregation principle' – see p383).

Your award may be reduced to reflect the proportion of years of contributions paid, or periods of residence completed, in the UK out of the total years of contributions paid or periods of residence completed in all member states.[95]

The requirement to be ordinarily resident for a category D retirement pension may not apply to you if you are covered by the EU co-ordination rules and you can show that you have a 'genuine and sufficient link to the UK' (see p283).[96]

If you move to the UK from an EEA state, you can continue to receive an old age pension if you were receiving it before you moved (referred to as 'exporting' the pension – see p385), and it will be uprated as normal, if the state that pays the pension continues to be the competent state to pay that benefit (see p369).

Note: although the main co-ordination rules were, in general, revoked in UK law from the end of the transition period, and now only apply to those covered by the Withdrawal Agreement protections (see p355), the provisions relating to aggregation of NI contributions for entitlement to, and uprating of, UK retirement pensions were saved and continue to apply.[97] The UK–EU Protocol also contains these rules on aggregation and uprating exported old age pensions, but the protocol does not cover Iceland, Norway, Liechtenstein or Switzerland. At the time of writing, it was understood that the UK government was negotiating with these four countries to agree, for the rules specifically on old age pensions, to continue to also apply to these states.[98]

Reciprocal and other international agreements

If you have lived and worked in a country with which the UK has a reciprocal agreement (see p397), you may be able to count periods of residence or insurance paid in that country towards your UK retirement pension entitlement. For further information on reciprocal agreements and retirement pensions, see p405.

Similarly, if you are covered by another international agreement between the EU and another country, you may be able to do the same (see p408).

9. Social fund and other payments

Funeral payments

To qualify for a **funeral expenses payment** from the social fund you must live in England and Wales,[99] and to qualify for a **funeral support payment** you must be ordinarily resident (see p131) in Scotland at the date you make your application.[100] For either benefit, you must also satisfy the conditions below.

- The person who has died must have been ordinarily resident (see p131) in the UK at the date of her/his death (this does not apply for funeral support payment if s/he was a still-born child).[101]
- The funeral must usually take place in the UK. However, it can take place in a European Economic Area (EEA) country or the UK if you or your partner :[102]
  - are an EEA national with a right to reside as a 'worker' (see p189), or self-employed person (see p196), including if you have retained either status (see p201);
  - have a right to reside as a family member (other than an 'extended family member') of one of the above (see p218);
  - a have a permanent right of residence acquired in less than five years, or her/his family member (see p253);
  - (funeral support payment only) have limited leave (pre-settled status) or indefinite leave (settled status) granted under the European Union (EU) Settlement Scheme (see p49);
  - arguably, are a person with any other free movement right of residence in the UK (see below).

Note:
- Since the end of the transition period (11pm on 31 December 2020), you can only have one of the free movement residence rights listed above if you are in a protected group (see p168).
- It is arguable that you can also qualify for a funeral expenses payment for a funeral held in an EEA state if you have *any* free movement right to reside in the UK. That is because the relevant law on residence rights has developed since the above rules were introduced and now covers additional groups of EEA nationals and their family members. The above rules were introduced following a case in which the Court of Justice of the European Union (CJEU) held that requiring a funeral to be in the UK was unlawfully discriminatory against EU migrant workers.[103] Arguably, the same applies to other groups who can now have free movement residence rights but who are not listed in the funeral payment regulations – eg, people who have a permanent right of residence following five years of legal residence in the UK. For the continuing relevance of EU caselaw, see p174.[104]

To qualify for a **children's funeral fund payment**, the funeral must take place in England on or after 23 July 2019, and be for a child aged under 18 or stillborn. There are are no residence (or immigration status) requirements.[105]

Winter fuel payments

To qualify for a **winter fuel payment** from the social fund, you must be ordinarily resident (see p131) in Great Britain on any day in the qualifying week.[106]

The qualifying week

The '**qualifying week**' is the week beginning on the third Monday in September before the winter you want to be paid for.

To qualify for **child winter heating assistance** if you are under 19 and in receipt of the higher rate of the disabilty living allowance, or child disability payment, care component, on any day in the qualifying week, you must be:[107]
- resident (see p130) in Scotland; *or*
- habitually resident (see p146) in an EEA state (other than Cyprus, France, Greece, Malta, Portugal or Spain) *and* have a 'genuine and sufficient link' to Scotland (see p283). If that applies, you need to claim using a specific form.[108]

European Union co-ordination rules

You are not required to be ordinarily resident in Great Britain to be entitled to a winter fuel payment if, on any day in the qualifying week, you are:[109]
- covered by the main EU co-ordination rules (see p355);

- habitually resident in an EEA country (other than Cyprus, France, Gibraltar, Greece, Malta, Portugal or Spain); *and*
- can demonstrate a 'genuine and sufficient link to the UK ' (see p283).

Winter fuel payments are not covered by the UK-EU Protocol or the UK-Ireland Convention.[110]

Was your application for a winter fuel payment refused before September 2013?

The EU rules were only included in the UK regulations from 16 September 2013. However, they are based on a judgment of the CJEU, dated 21 July 2011.[111] If you had your winter fuel payment refused because, at the relevant time, you were not ordinarily resident in Great Britain, but you satisfied the above rules, you can request that the decision be revised. The Department for Work and Pensions (DWP) will revise its decision on the grounds of official error if it was made on or after 21 July 2011.[112] If the decision was made before this date, the DWP's position is that it can only be revised if another ground for revision is available.[113] For a discussion of similar issues in relation to previous refusals of disability benefits, see p333.

Maternity grant payments

To qualify for a **Sure Start maternity grant** from the social fund, you must live in England or Wales.[114]

To qualify for a **Best Start grant**, you must be ordinarily resident in Scotland.[115] In addition, if neither you nor your partner receive a qualifying benefit (a means-tested benefit or tax credits), but you qualify for a grant because you are aged under 20, you must also satisfy one of the following:[116]

- you are habitually resident (see p140) in the UK, Channel Islands or Isle of Man; *or*
- you, or your partner, are habitually resident in the EEA *and* have a right to reside in the UK either as a qualified person or a family member (other than an extended family member) of a qualified person or a permanent right to reside (see p171), or have limited leave (pre-settled status) or indefinite leave (settled status) under the EU Settlement Scheme; *or*
- you are exempt from this habitual residence test (see p142).

10. **Tax credits**

You can only make a new claim for tax credits in very limited circumstances (see *CPAG's Welfare Benefits and Tax Credits Handbook)*. If you can make a new claim for tax credits, you must satisfy the residence and presence rules below. If you are already entitled to tax credits, you must continue to satisfy these to continue to be entitled. **Note:** if you already have an award of one type of tax credit and you become entitled to the other, this is treated as a change of circumstances and a new claim is not required.

To be entitled to **child tax credit** (CTC), you (and your partner in a joint claim) must:[117]

- be present in the UK (see p124); *and*
- be ordinarily resident in the UK (see p131); *and*
- have a right to reside in the UK (see p151); *and*
- have been living in the UK for the three months prior to your claim (unless you are exempt – see p127).

To be entitled to **working tax credit** (WTC), you (and your partner in a joint claim) must be:[118]

- present in the UK (see p126); *and*
- ordinarily resident in the UK (see p131).

There are, however, some exceptions.[119]

- There are several groups of people who are exempt from the requirement to have been living in the UK for three months prior to the date of your CTC claim (see p127).
- You do not need to have a right to reside for CTC if you claimed CTC before 1 May 2004 and you have been receiving it since then (see p159).
- You are treated as ordinarily resident in the UK for CTC and WTC and, for CTC, you are not required to have been living in the UK for the past three months, if you have been deported or otherwise legally removed from another country to the UK.
- You are treated as ordinarily resident in the UK for WTC if you have a free movement right to reside (see p171). However, in practice, being accepted as ordinarily resident is rarely a problem.
- You can be treated as present for either eight or 12 weeks during a temporary absence, or while you or your partner are a Crown servant posted overseas (see p340). While you are treated as present, you continue to satisfy the conditions of entitlement to tax credits. This means that you can continue to receive tax credits that are already being paid and can make a renewal claim during your absence. If you spend longer abroad than the permitted periods, you cease to satisfy the presence condition and your tax credit entitlement ends.

You can be entitled to the childcare element of WTC if your childcare is provided outside the UK if either:[120]

- it is provided in an European Economic Area (EEA) country and is regulated by the relevant authorities of that country;[121] *or*
- you are are employed by the Ministry of Defence and the childcare is regulated in accordance with the requirements of the Department for Education.

Note:
- If you are a self-employed EEA national, the definition of 'self-employed' for WTC purposes[122] is different from, and does not affect, the meaning of 'self-employed' for the purpose of having a right to reside that satisfies that requirement for CTC (see p196).
- If you are responsible for a child but do not have a right to reside and so are not entitled to CTC, the number of hours you need to work to be entitled to WTC is still determined on the basis that you are responsible for a child.[123] If HM Revenue and Customs (HMRC) tells you that you are not entitled to WTC unless you work 30 hours because you do not receive CTC, that is wrong.

Being absent (other than while you are treated as present), ceasing to be ordinarily resident or losing your right to reside are all changes that you must notify to HMRC within one month. Failure to do so may result in your being overpaid and/or being given a penalty.

Couples and children

If you are a member of a couple and are entitled on the basis of a joint tax credit claim, you must both satisfy the residence requirements. Your entitlement to tax credits as a couple ends if either you or your partner:
- are abroad for longer than a permitted temporary absence of eight or 12 weeks (see p340);
- (for CTC only) lose the right to reside;
- cease to be ordinarily resident.

Note: in most cases, the person who continues to satisfy the residence rules cannot make a new single claim for CTC and/or WTC, but may be entitled to universal credit instead. For the limited exceptions, see CPAG's *Welfare Benefits and Tax Credits Handbook*.

If you or your partner are abroad (even for a permitted temporary absence of less than eight or 12 weeks) and you (or s/he) were the only partner in full-time work, you may lose entitlement to WTC if the requirement to be in full-time work is no longer satisfied.

If at any point HMRC considers that you and your partner have separated and this is likely to be permanent, your entitlement to tax credits on the basis of your joint claim ends.[124]

You have a duty to notify HMRC of any of the above changes within one month of their taking place. Failure to do so may result in your being overpaid or being given a penalty.

There are no presence or residence requirements for any child in your claim, but you must be responsible for her/him. You count as being responsible if the child normally lives with you or, if there are competing claims, you have main responsibility for her/him.[125]

If your partner or child is a non-EEA national, also check the rules in Part 3. In particular, see p107 if:

- your child is a non-EEA national with leave that is subject to a no recourse to public funds condition; *and/or*
- your partner is a non-EEA national who does not have leave to enter or remain in the UK and does not have a right to reside.

You can only be paid CTC for your third and subsequent child in limited circumstances (due to the 'two-child limit'). These include if the child was born before 6 April 2017 or if an exception applies. One exception is if you have adopted the child or s/he has been placed with you for adoption. However, this exception does not apply if you adopted the child under the law of another country before the adoption under UK law.[126] For details of the 'two-child limit' rule, including the exceptions, see CPAG's *Welfare Benefits and Tax Credits Handbook*.

European Union co-ordination rules

Since the end of the transition period (31 December 2020), you may be covered by the main European Union (EU) co-ordination rules or similar co-ordination rules contained in the new UK-EU Protocol, or, for situations involving the UK and Ireland only, the UK-Ireland Convention. However, the UK-EU Protocol does not apply to CTC or WTC.

CTC is classed as a 'family benefit' under the main co-ordination rules and the UK-Ireland Convention. If you are covered by either (see p355), you may be able to be paid CTC for a partner or child resident in an EEA country (or in Ireland if relying on the Convention). However, you still have to satisfy all the other conditions for CTC, including that the child is 'normally living with' you.[127] For more details on the payment of family benefits, see p386.

WTC is not covered by any of the EU co-ordination rules. Therefore, if your partner is in Ireland or another EEA country, although you may be entitled to CTC on the basis of a joint claim, you are only entitled to WTC on the basis of a single claim.[128] In this case, or if you are a single claimant entitled to claim for a child in an EEA country, your CTC claim is decided in accordance with the EU co-ordination rules, but your WTC claim is decided solely under UK legislation. If you or your partner are working in an EEA country but live in the UK and therefore remain present and ordinarily resident in the UK, this work can count for the purposes of your WTC claim.[129]

In any of the circumstances above, your claim(s) is likely to be deemed 'complex' and processed by the 'international team' at HMRC. If you experience difficulties, you can refer to guidance for decision makers on how these claims should be administered,[130] and get an advice agency to help.

Although the co-ordination rules do not apply to WTC, other provisions of EU law mean that you cannot be refused the childcare element of WTC:

- if your partner receives a benefit from an EEA state that is substantially similar to a UK benefit that is accepted as evidence of incapacity (see p382).[131] Since the Upper Tribunal held this to be the case, the WTC regulations have been amended;[132]
- in respect of childcare costs solely because the childcare provider is located in an EEA state.[133] Since the Northern Irish commissioners held this to be the case, the WTC regulations have been amended.[134]

Notes

1. **Means-tested benefits**

1 **UC** s4(1)(c) WRA 2012
IS s124(1) SSCBA 1992
JSA s1(2)(i) JSA 1995
ESA s1(3)(d) WRA 2007
PC s1(2)(a) SPCA 2002

2 **UC** Reg 9 UC Regs
IS Regs 21-21AA IS Regs
JSA Regs 85-85A JSA Regs
ESA Regs 69-70 ESA Regs
HB Reg 10 HB Regs; reg 10 HB(SPC) Regs
PC Reg 2 SPC Regs

3 s130(1)(a) SSCBA 1992; reg 7 HB Regs; reg 7 HB(SPC) Regs

4 Reg 30 UC Regs; para F6203 ADM

5 s4(1)(a)-(d) WRA 2012; reg 9 UC Regs; reg 8 UC(TP) Regs

6 **UC** Reg 3(6) UC Regs
IS Reg 16(2)(a) IS Regs
JSA Reg 78(2)(a) JSA Regs
ESA Reg 156(3)(a) ESA Regs
PC Reg 5(1)(a)(i) SPC Regs
HB Reg 21(2)(a) HB Regs; reg 21(2)(a) HB(SPC) Regs

7 **UC** Reg 3(6) UC Regs
IS Reg 16(1)-(3) IS Regs
JSA Reg 78(1)-(3) JSA Regs
ESA Reg 156(1)-(4) ESA Regs
PC Reg 5 SPC Regs
HB Reg 21(1) and (2) HB Regs; reg 21(1) and (2) HB(SPC) Regs

8 CIS/508/1992

9 *Broxtowe Borough Council v CS(HB)* [2014] UKUT 186 (AAC)

10 CIS/508/1992; CIS/13805/1996

11 CIS/484/1993

12 Regs 3(3) and (6), 18(2), 22(3) and 36(3) UC Regs; Reg 9(1) UC,PIP,JSA&ESA(C&P) Regs

13 Regs 3(3) 9, 18(2), 22(3) and 36(3) UC Regs; reg 9(1) and (6) UC,PIP,JSA&ESA(C&P) Regs

14 Art 7(2)(b) and (3)(b) WRA(No.31)O ; HB Circular A9/2019, paras 15-17; DMG Memo 7/19, para 12

15 **IS** Regs 4, 16 and 21 and Sch 7 paras 11 and 11A IS Regs
JSA Regs 78 and 85 and Sch 5 paras 10 and 11 JSA Regs
ESA Reg 156 and Sch 5 paras 6 and 7 ESA Regs
HB Reg 21 HB Regs; reg 21 HB(SPC) Regs

16 Regs 3-5 SPC Regs

17 s4(1A) SPCA 2002; Arts 4(2), 6(2)(a), 7(1), (2)(a) and (b) and (3)(b) and 8 WRA(No.31)O; HB Circular A9/2019; DMG Memo 7/19

18 Reg 4(7) UC Regs

19 Sch IIA para 7 SPC Regs;

20 **IS** Reg 16 IS Regs
JSA Reg 78 JSA Regs
ESA Reg 156 ESA Regs
HB Reg 21 HB Regs; reg 21 HB(SPC) Regs

21 Reg 1(4B) and (8B) SS(WTCCTC)(CA) Regs

22 **UC** Sch 12 para 3 UC Regs; ADM Memo 10/17, paras 15 and 29
IS/JSA Regs 5 and 6 The Social Security (Restrictions on Amounts for Children and Qualifying Young Persons) Amendment Regulations 2017, No.376; Sch 12 para 3 UC Regs; DMG Memo 10/17, paras 13, 14 and 26
HB Reg 22 HB Regs; reg 22 HB(SPC) Regs
23 *Swaddling v Chief Adjudication Officer*, C-90/97 [1999] ECR I-01075
24 SS(NIRA) Regs; SS(GBRA)(NI) Regs; SS(NIRA)(A) Regs; SS(GBRA)(A)NI Regs
25 **UC** SS(NIRA) Regs; see also ADM Memo 18/20

2. **Bereavement benefits**
26 s30(1) PA 2014 – Sark is the only 'specified territory'.
27 Arts 5, 6, 7, 42 and 43 EU Reg 883/04; Arts 5, 6, 7 and 43 UK-IC; Arts SSC 6, 7, 8, 37 and 38 UK-EUP
28 Sch 1 para 4 The Social Security (Reciprocal Agreements) Order 2017, No.159; DMG Vol 2 Ch 7 Part 6 para 077080-83
29 DMG Vol 2 Ch 7 Part 6 para 077110-24
30 The Social Security (Reciprocal Agreements) Order 2017, No.159; SS(NIRA)(A) Regs; SS(GBRA)(A)NI Regs

3. **Child benefit, Scottish child payment and guardian's allowance**
31 s146 SSCBA 1992
32 Reg 23 CB Regs
33 Regs 23, 30 and 31 CB Regs
34 s143(1)(b) SSCBA 1992
35 Regs 18(d) and 19(2)(c), The Scottish Child Payment Regulations 2020, No.351
36 Reg 9 GA(Gen) Regs
37 *Stewart v SSWP*, C-503/09 [2011] ECR I-06497; *SSWP v JG (IS)* [2013] UKUT 298 (AAC); *SSWP v Garland* [2014] EWCA Civ 1550
38 s143(1)(b) SSCBA 1992; *RK v HMRC (CHB)* [2015] UKUT 357 (AAC); *JL v HMRC (CHB)* [2017] UKUT 193 (AAC)

4. **Disability and carers' benefits**
39 **AA** Reg 2 SS(AA) Regs
DLA Reg 2 SS(DLA) Regs
PIP Reg 16 SS(PIP) Regs
CA Reg 9 SS(ICA) Regs
CDP Reg 4(1)(d) and (2)(a) and (b) DACYP(S) Regs (draft)
40 **AA** Reg 2(2) and (3A) SS(AA) Regs
DLA Reg 2(2) and (3A) SS(DLA) Regs
PIP Regs 19 and 20 SS(PIP) Regs
CA Reg 9(3) SS(ICA) Regs
41 *TS (by TS) v SSWP (DLA); EK (by MK) v SSWP (DLA)* [2020] UKUT 284 (AAC) – the DWP are not appealing
42 *FM v SSWP (DLA)*[2017] UKUT 380 (AAC), reported as [2019] AACR 8; *TS (by TS) v SSWP (DLA); EK (by MK) v SSWP (DLA)* [2020] UKUT 284 (AAC)
43 s81 SS(S)A 2018
44 Reg 8 CA(YCG)(S) Regs
45 Reg 5(1)(e), (2) and (3) DACYP(S) Regs (draft)
46 Reg 5(6) and (7) DACYP(S) Regs (draft)
47 Reg 4(1)(c) and Sch The Winter Heating Assistance for Children and Young People (Scotland) Regulations 2020
48 **ESA** Reg 11 ESA Regs; reg 12 ESA Regs 2013
IB Reg 16 SS(IB) Regs
SDA Reg 3 SS(SDA) Regs
49 **ESA** Reg 11(4) ESA Regs; reg 12(4) ESA Regs 2013
IB Reg 16(6) SS(IB) Regs
SDA Reg 3(3) SS(SDA) Regs
50 Reg 5(10) DACYP(S) Regs (draft)
51 **AA** Reg 2(3) SS(AA) Regs
DLA Reg 2(4) SS(DLA) Regs
PIP Reg 21 SS(PIP) Regs
52 **AA** s35(2C) SSA 1975
DLA s66(2) SSCBA 1992
PIP s82(4) WRA 2012
53 **AA** Reg 2C SS(AA) Regs
DLA Reg 2C SS(DLA) Regs
PIP Reg 23A SS(PIP) Regs
CA Reg 9C SS(ICA) Regs
CDP Reg 5(10) DACYP(S) Regs (draft)
MM and IS v SSWP (DLA) [2016] UKUT 149 (AAC)
54 Reg 24 DACYP(S) Regs (draft)
55 Regs 5(4), 8 and 9 DACYP(S) Regs (draft)
56 ss65(7), 70(4A) and 72(7B) SSCBA 1992; s84 WRA 2012; s81(2A) and (9)-(15) SS(S)A; reg 8(3)-(10) CA(YCG)(S) Regs; Art 16 UK-IC

57 **AA** Reg 2A SS(AA) Regs
DLA Reg 2A SS(DLA) Regs
PIP Reg 22 SS(PIP) Regs
CA Reg 9A SS(ICA) Regs
CDP Regs 8 DACYP(S) Regs (draft)
58 *SSWP v MM and BK v SSWP* [2016] UKUT 547 (AAC), para 33; Art 1(j) EU Reg 883/04; Art 11 EU Reg 987/09
59 *Stewart v SSWP*, C-503/09 [2011] ECR I-06497
60 *Kavanagh and Another v SSWP* [2019] EWCA Civ 272, para 68 – see also para 32: the DWP dropped this part of its appeal against *SSWP v MM and BK v SSWP* [2016] UKUT 547 (AAC), paras 28-31. See also ADM Memo 11/19 and DMG Memo 8/19
61 *Stewart v SSWP*, C-503/09 [2011] ECR I-06497; *Kavanagh and Another v SSWP* [2019] EWCA Civ 272; *SSWP v JG (IS)* [2013] UKUT 298 (AAC); *SSWP v Garland* [2014] EWCA Civ 1550
62 *PB v SSWP(DLA)* [2016] UKUT 280 (AAC)
63 *Kavanagh and Another v SSWP* [2019] EWCA Civ 272
64 *SSWP v MM and BK v SSWP* [2016] UKUT 547 (AAC), para 32; *Kavanagh and Another v SSWP* [2019] EWCA Civ 272, paras 86-90
65 **CDP** regs 5, 7 and 9
CAS s81(2A) and (9)-(15) SS(S)A 2018
YCG reg 8(3)-(10) CA(YCG)(S) Regs
66 Art 6 and Annex XI UK entry para 2 EU Reg 883/04; Art 6 UK-IC
67 *SSWP v MM and BK v SSWP* [2016] UKUT 547 (AAC), paras 18-27 and 35. The challenge to this part of the decision was dropped – see *Kavanagh and Another v SSWP* [2019] EWCA Civ 272, paras 30-31; Art 19 UK-IC.
68 ss65(7), 70(4A) and 72(7B) SSCBA 1992; s84 WRA 2012; regs 5(4) and 9 DACYP(S) Regs (draft)
69 **AA** Reg 2B SS(AA) Regs
DLA Reg 2B SS(DLA) Regs
PIP Reg 23 SS(PIP) Regs
CA Reg 9B SS(ICA) Regs
CDP Regs 5(4) and 9 DACYP(S) Regs (draft)
All see also DMG Memo 16/20, paras 14 and 18-21 and ADM Memo 17/20, paras 14 and 18-21
70 **CAS** s81(2A) and (9)-(15) SS(S)A 2018
YCG reg 8(3)-(10) CA(YCG)(S) Regs
71 *Bartlett and Others v SSWP*, C-537/09 [2011] ECR I-03417; *SSWP v DS* [2019] UKUT 238 (AAC); para C2097 and Appendix 1 para 4 ADM
72 Arts 1(j) and 70 EU Reg 883/04; *Swaddling v Adjudication Officer*, C-90/97 [1999]
73 Sch para 2(1) SS(NIRA) Regs; Sch para 2(1) SS(GBRA)(NI) Regs

5. **Industrial injuries benefits**
74 s94(5) SSCBA 1992
75 Reg 14 SS(IIPD) Regs
76 Reg 10C(5) and (6) SSB(PA) Regs
77 Reg 2 SS(II)(AB) Regs; reg 2 SS(II)(MB) Regs
78 Regs 3, 4, 6 and 8 SS(II)(MB) Regs; regs 3 and 6 SS(II)(AB) Regs
79 Art 5 EU Reg 883/04; Art 5 UK-IC; Art SSC 6 UK-EUP
80 Art 38 EU Reg 883/04; Art 36 EU Reg 987/09; *SSWP v OF (by MF) (II)* [2011] UKUT 448 (AAC); Art SSC 33 UK-EUP
81 Art 36(2) EU Reg 987/09; Art SSC 33 UK-EUP

6. **Contribution-based jobseeker's allowance and contributory employment and support allowance**
82 **JSA** s1(2)(i) JSA 1995
ESA ss1(3)(d) and 18(4)(a) WRA 2007
83 *GP v SSWP (JSA)* [2015] UKUT 476 (AAC), reported as [2016] AACR 14
84 Art 61(2) EU Reg 883/04; Art 21(1) and (2) UK-IC; Art SSC 56 UK-EUP
85 Art 64 EU Reg 883/04; Arts 7 and 21 UK-IC
86 Art 64(3) EU Reg 883/04; Art 21(4(c) UK-IC
87 Art 3(1) and (4) and 8 UK-EUP
88 SS(NIRA) Regs; SS(GBRA)(NI) Regs
89 Sch Arts 2A-2B SS(NIRA) Regs; Sch Arts 2A-2B SS(GBRA)(NI) Regs; see also DMG Memo 1/17, paras 4-7

7. **Maternity allowance**
90 s2(1) and s35(1) SSCBA 1992
91 The Social Security (Maternity Allowance) (Work Abroad) Regulations 1987, No.417; Vol 2 Ch 7, paras 075570-73 DMG
92 s113(1) SSCBA 1992

8. **Retirement pensions**
93 s113 SSCBA 1992; reg 4(1) SSB(PA) Regs
94 Reg 10 SS(WB&RP) Regs
95 Art 52 EU Reg 883/04; for example, see Vol 2, para 075771 DMG; Art 26 UK-IC; Art SSC 47 UK-EUP

96 *Stewart v SSWP*, C-503/09 [2011] ECR, I-06497; *SSWP v Garland* [2014] EWCA Civ 1550, paras 14 and 28
97 Reg 9 The Social Security Co-ordination (Revocation of Retained Direct EU Legislation and Related Amendments) (EU Exit) Regulations 2020, No.1508
98 para 7.12 Explanatory Memo to The Social Security Co-ordination (Revocation of Retained Direct EU Legislation and Related Amendments) (EU Exit) Regulations 2020, No.1508

9. **Social fund and other payments**
99 Reg 7(9A) SFM&FE Regs
100 Reg 9(1) FEA(S) Regs
101 **FEP** Reg 7(5) SFM&FE Regs
FSP Reg 9(2)(a) and (6) FEA(S) Regs
102 **FEP** Reg 7(9) and (10) SFM&FE Regs
FSP Reg 9(2)(b),(3) and FEA(S) Regs
103 *O'Flynn v Adjudication Officer*, C-237/94 [1996] ECR I-02617; R(IS) 4/98
104 Art 24 EU Dir 2004/38
105 The Social Fund (Children's Funeral Fund for England) Regulations 2019, No.1064
106 Reg 2 SFWFP Regs
107 Reg 4(1)(c) and Sch The Winter Heating Assistance for Children and Young People (Scotland) Regulations 2020, No.352
108 mygov.scot/child-winter-heating-assistance-for-children-who-no-longer-live-in-scotland
109 Reg 2 SFWFP Regs
110 Art SSC 3(4) UK-EUP; Art 3 UK-IC
111 *Stewart v SSWP*, C-503/09 [2011] ECR I-06497
112 Reg 3(5)(a) SS&CS(DA) Regs; para 73245 and Vol 2 Part 6 Appendix 1, para 10 DMG
113 Vol 2 Part 6 Appendix 1, para 11 DMG
114 Reg 5(6) SFM&FE Regs
115 Sch 2 para 4(1)(a), Sch 3 para 3(1)(a) and Sch 4 para 4(1)(a) EYA(BSG)(S) Regs
116 Sch 2 para 4(1)(b) and (2), Sch 3 para 3(1)(b) and (2) and Sch 4 para 4(1)(b) and(2) EYA(BSG)(S) Regs

10. **Tax credits**
117 s3(3) TCA 2002; reg 3(1) and (5) TC(R) Regs
118 s3(3) TCA 2002; reg 3(1) TC(R) Regs
119 Reg 3 TC(R) Regs
120 Reg 14(2)(d) WTC(EMR) Regs; HMRC leaflet WTC5, *WTC: help with the costs of childcare,* 2019, p8
121 For periods before 21 March 2019, see *NB v HMRC (TC)* [2016] NICom 47
122 Reg 2(1) WTC(EMR) Regs
123 Regs 2(2) and 4 (2nd condition) WTC(EMR) Regs
124 s3(5A) TCA 2002
125 s8(2) TCA 2002; reg 3(1) CTC Regs
126 Reg 11(2) CTC Regs
127 *RI v HMRC (TC)* [2019] UKUT 306 (AAC);
128 CCM 20090, 20160, 20170 and 20260; TCTM 09374 and 09376
129 TCM 0288580; see also *GC v CHMRC (TC)* [2014] UKUT 251 (AAC)
130 CCM 20000
131 *AS v HMRC* [2017] UKUT 361 (AAC)
132 Reg 13(6)(K) WTC(EMR) Regs
133 *NB v HMRC (TC)* [2016] NICom 47; Art 56 TFEU
134 Reg 14(2)(d) WTC(EMR) Regs

Part 5

Benefits while abroad

Chapter 14

Going abroad

This chapter covers:

This chapter provides an overview of the way your entitlement to benefits and tax credits is affected if you, or a member of your family for whom you claim, go abroad. The specific information about individual benefits and tax credits is in Chapter 15.

1. Introduction

Most benefits and tax credits are affected if you, or your partner or child, go abroad. The rules vary between different benefits and tax credits. Some can always be paid abroad, some can only be paid in certain circumstances and for limited periods, and some benefits have rules affecting the amount that can be paid if you are abroad.

Note: some benefits are affected if you leave Great Britain and others are affected if you leave the UK.

Your entitlement while you, or your partner or child, are abroad depends on the following factors:

- the benefit or tax credit you are claiming (see Chapter 15);
- the reason for going abroad;
- whether the absence is temporary or permanent;
- the length of time the absence will last;
- the country to which you are, or s/he is, going;
- whether you are covered by any of the European Union (EU) co-ordination rules, and if so, which rules;
- whether you are covered by a reciprocal agreement the UK has with the country you, or your partner or child, are going to.

In addition to the above factors, other changes that occur indirectly as a consequence of your being abroad can also affect your entitlement – eg, if your income changes, or you cease to count as being in full-time work for the benefit or tax credit you are claiming. Further details on the way these other changes affect your entitlement are covered in CPAG's *Welfare Benefits and Tax Credits Handbook*.

Before you go abroad

If you are thinking about going abroad, check how your entitlement will be affected well in advance of your departure, because that could affect your decisions, including on the duration of your absence. It also ensures you have sufficient time to take any necessary action before you leave. Notify the benefit authority(ies) that pays your benefit before you leave, providing details of your destination, purpose and expected duration of your absence abroad. If it is possible for you get your UK benefit paid abroad, you should give the relevant benefit authority as much notice as possible, because it may be very slow in making these arrangements.

To see how going abroad affects your entitlement, check which rules apply (see below) and then check the rules for the specific benefit or tax credit you are claiming (see Chapter 15).

If you might want to claim a benefit from the country you are going to, it is worth checking what the conditions of entitlement are, as you might want to take relevant documents with you – eg, a statement of the national insurance contributions you have paid, which you can obtain from HM Revenues and Customs, or proof of your past employment. **Note:** check whether claiming a benefit in another country could affect your entitlement to benefits paid abroad by the UK – eg, if you claim a benefit in a European Economic Area (EEA) country, this could mean that the UK is no longer the 'competent state' responsible for paying a different benefit to you in that country (see p369).

Which rules apply

Your entitlement to UK benefits or tax credits while you, or a family member, are abroad can be affected by three different sets of rules.

- **The UK benefit and tax credit legislation** contains rules about how absence from the UK affects entitlement (see below). Check these rules first. If you can be paid the benefits you want when you or your family member are outside Great Britain (or the UK for tax credits) under these rules, you do not generally need to check the other rules. However, if you want to be paid a disability or carer's benefit when you go to an EEA country and you are covered by the EU co-ordination rules, check whether these affect your entitlement.
- If you or your family member go to an EEA country (listed on p47), even if you are not entitled under UK legislation, you may be able to receive UK benefits if the **EU co-ordination rules** apply to you (not all the rules apply in all the EEA countries) (see p355).

- **Reciprocal agreements** exist between the UK and some other countries (see p313). These can assist in similar ways to the EU co-ordination rules and, in general, only apply if the EU co-ordination rules do not help you. There are also reciprocal agreements between Great Britain and Northern Ireland.

2. How your benefits and tax credits are affected

UK law

There are different ways in which the UK benefits and tax credits rules affect your entitlement when you (or your family member) go abroad. The main ways in which they result in your not receiving benefit (or not being paid for your family member) are *if*:

- during your (or her/his) absence, you (or s/he) stop meeting the requirement to:
  - be present in Great Britain, the UK or the common travel area ie, the UK, Ireland, Channel Islands and the Isle of Man (see below);
  - be ordinarily resident in Scotland or Great Britain or the UK (see p309);
  - be habitually resident in the common travel area (see p309); *or*
  - have a right to reside in the UK or common travel area (see p310);
- your partner's absence abroad means you no longer count as a couple (see p310);
- your child's absence abroad means s/he is no longer included in your claim (see p310);
- you stop being covered by the rules that allow you to receive housing costs for a certain period while you are absent from your home (see p310).

All of the above rules have exceptions. In particular, you can be treated as present in certain circumstances, provided (in most cases) your absence is temporary (see below).

Presence and absence

Most benefits require you to be present in Great Britain (the UK, for tax credits and the common travel area for child disability payment). You can be treated as present and, therefore, continue to be entitled to the benefit or tax credit, during a temporary absence in specified circumstances (see below). You are disqualified from entitlement to some benefits if you are absent from Great Britain (or the UK or common travel area), although there are exemptions.

Presence and absence

'Presence' means being physically present in Great Britain (or the UK or common travel area) and **'absence'** means 'not physically present'.

You count as present on the day you return from an absence. For many decades it has been accepted that you also count as present on the day you leave to go abroad. However, the Upper Tribunal recently held in a housing benefit (HB) case that the day you leave Great Britain counts as the first day of your absence. It is arguable that this decision only applies to HB, as its reasoning was partly based on the specific wording of the HB regulations. Departmwnt for Work and Pensions' guidance continues to state that both the day you leave and the day you return count as days of presence.[1]

Other than child disability payment, Scottish benefits require residence, or ordinary residence, rather than presence.

Temporary absence

You can be treated as present, and therefore entitled to most benefits and tax credits, during a temporary absence in specified circumstances. Your entitlement depends on:

- whether your absence counts as 'temporary' for the benefit or tax credit you are claiming (see below); *and*
- how long (if at all) the rules for that benefit or tax credit treat you as present while you are absent (see Chapter 15).

Temporary absence

For attendance allowance (AA), disability living allowance (DLA), personal independence payment (PIP), child disability payment, tax credits and (for the claimant's, but not the child's, absence) child benefit, you are **'temporarily absent'** from Great Britain (the UK, for tax credits) if, at the beginning of the period, your absence is unlikely to exceed 52 weeks.[2]

For all other benefits, temporary absence is not defined. It is your responsibility to demonstrate that your absence will be temporary, and you should therefore provide full details of why you are going abroad, how long you intend to be away and what you intend to do while you are abroad.[3] However, although your intentions are relevant, they are not decisive.[4] The nature of an absence can also change over time: if your absence is found to be temporary at the beginning of the period, it does not mean that it will always remain temporary. If your circumstances change while you are abroad (eg, you go abroad for one reason and decide to stay for a different purpose), your absence may no longer be regarded as temporary.[5] Although there is no set period for a temporary absence (except for tax credits, child benefit, AA, DLA, PIP and child disability payment), as a general rule, absences of more than 12 months are not considered to be temporary unless there are exceptional circumstances.[6] If the purpose of your trip abroad is obviously temporary (eg, for a holiday, to visit friends or relatives or for a particular course of medical treatment) and you buy a return ticket, your absence should be viewed as temporary.

If your absence counts as temporary for the benefit or tax credit you are claiming, you are entitled to receive the benefit or tax credit for a specified period. This period varies for each benefit or tax credit and according to your circumstances. Many of the rules that entitle you to benefit during a specified period only do so if certain circumstances apply, but some simply state a maximum period. See Chapter 15 for information on the specific benefit you are claiming.

Note: for many benefits and tax credits, your intended absence still counts as temporary even if it is longer than the maximum period for which the benefit or tax credit is payable.

Example

Mohsen receives PIP. He goes to visit family in Iran and buys a return ticket to come back after seven months. Mohsen is entitled to PIP for the first 13 weeks of his absence (the maximum period in these circumstances – see p329). Although his intended period of absence is longer than this maximum period, it is still a temporary absence.

Ordinary residence

In order to be entitled to some benefits and tax credits, you must be ordinarily resident in Great Britain (the UK, for child benefit and tax credits, and Scotland for most Scottish benefits). See p131 for a list of benefits and tax credits that require you to be ordinarily resident and an explanation of what 'ordinary residence' means. If, by going abroad, you cease to be ordinarily resident, your entitlement to any benefit or tax credit that requires you to be ordinarily resident ends. However, if your absence abroad is temporary and you intend to return to Great Britain (or the UK or Scotland), your ordinary residence is not usually affected.[7] Ceasing to be ordinarily resident is rarely the reason why your entitlement ends when you go abroad. It is more likely that your entitlement ends simply because you are absent (see p307). If you receive a decision that your entitlement to a benefit or tax credit has ended because you have ceased to be ordinarily resident, ask for the decision to be looked at again and get specialist advice.

Habitual residence

In order to be entitled to some benefits, you must be habitually resident in a specified area, or be exempt from this requirement. See p139 for which benefits require you to be habitually resident, an explanation of what this means, including the required area for each benefit, and who is exempt. If, by going abroad, you cease to be habitually resident, your entitlement to any benefit that requires you to be habitually resident ends. However, ceasing to be habitually resident will rarely be the reason why your entitlement ends, which is more likely to be simply due to your being absent (see p307) or, for HB, absent from your home (see p310). **Note:** if you need to make a new claim when you return from abroad, you will not usually have ceased to be habitually resident if your absence was temporary and you intended to return to the common travel area.[8] However, you may need to explain this to the decision maker.

Right to reside

In order to be entitled to some benefits and tax credits, you must have a right to reside in either the UK or the 'common travel area' (the UK, Ireland, Channel Islands and the Isle of Man). See p151 for which benefits and tax credits require a right to reside. If, by going abroad, you lose your right to reside, your entitlement to any benefit or tax credit that requires you to have a right to reside ends. However, an absence does not necessarily mean you lose your right to reside – it depends on your circumstances.

Couples and children living apart

There are general rules on when you continue to count as a couple despite living apart from your partner and when a child living elsewhere is still included in your claim. These rules are not specific to absences abroad, but if your partner or child is abroad, they can affect your entitlement.

If your partner goes abroad, this can affect your benefit or tax credit in the following ways.

- For tax credits and universal credit (UC), you may no longer be entitled to make a joint claim as a couple and may need to make a single claim.
- Depending on the circumstances, including the permanence or duration of your partner's absence, at some point you will stop being paid for your partner.
- Even if you are not paid for your partner, in some circumstances her/his income and capital can still affect your claim.

If your child goes abroad, depending on the circumstances, including the duration, s/he can stop being part of your claim. This can affect your entitlement – either you stop being paid for her/him or your entitlement ends altogether.

Note: you can only be paid means-tested benefits and child tax credit for your third and subsequent child in limited circumstances (due to the 'two-child limit'). These include (for UC and HB) certain transitional rules which may cease to apply when your child returns from abroad after payments for her/him, or your claim, ended because s/he was abroad. The rules and exceptions vary between the benefits, so check the details of the benefit you are claiming in CPAG's *Welfare Benefits and Tax Credits Handbook*.

For further details of the rules about couples and children for means-tested benefits, see p273, and for tax credits, see p296.

Absence from your home

If you are temporarily absent from the accommodation you normally occupy as your home, you can be treated as occupying it for a period. These rules apply to

HB and to housing costs in UC, income support (IS), income-based jobseeker's allowance (JSA), income-related employment and support allowance (ESA) and pension credit (PC). They mean you can continue to receive payments during your temporary absence.

The absence rules are not (except for HB) specific to your being outside Great Britain, but can still affect you if you are absent from your home when abroad. For further details, see CPAG's *Welfare Benefits and Tax Credits Handbook*.

A new period of absence starts if you return home, even for a short stay, and then leave again. A stay of at least 24 hours before you leave again may be enough.[9]

If you are temporarily absent from your home, you can continue to be paid **UC** housing costs for up to six months while you are absent for any reason. You are no longer treated as occupying your home once your absence has lasted, or is expected to last, longer than six months.[10] The main exception to this is if you are absent because of a fear of domestic violence, in which case you can be treated as occupying your home for up to 12 months.[11] However, your entitlement to UC may cease before six months if you are absent from your home because you are abroad (see p315).

If you are temporarily absent from home, have not rented out your home and intend to return to it, you can continue to be paid housing costs in your **IS, income-based JSA, income-related ESA or PC**. You can be paid for up to:

- **13 weeks** while you are absent, whatever the reason. You must be unlikely to be away for longer than this;[12]
- **52 weeks** in specific circumstances.[13] These include if you, your partner or child are in hospital, if you are undergoing or recovering from medical treatment, or if you are absent from home because of domestic violence. See CPAG's *Welfare Benefits and Tax Credits Handbook* for more details.

For **HB**, the above 13- or 52-week rule only applies if your absence is in Great Britain.[14]

If you are temporarily absent from home while abroad, have not rented out your home and intend to return to it, you can continue to be paid **HB** for up to:[15]

- **four weeks**, if you are absent outside Great Britain and the absence is not expected to exceed this;
- **eight weeks**, if the absence abroad is in connection with the death of your partner, your (or your partner's) close relative, or a child for whom you (or your partner) are responsible: the above four weeks are extended by up to four weeks if the decision maker considers it unreasonable for you to return within the first four weeks;
- **26 weeks in specific circumstances**. These include if you, your partner or child are in hospital, if you are undergoing or recovering from medical treatment, or if you are absent from home because of domestic violence. See CPAG's *Welfare Benefits and Tax Credits Handbook* for more details. Your

absence abroad must be unlikely to exceed (or in exceptional circumstances, substantially exceed) 26 weeks;
- **26 weeks,** if you are a member of HM forces posted overseas, a mariner or a continental shelf worker. Your absence abroad must be unlikely to exceed 26 weeks.

Note:
- When counting the period of absence for HB, the day of departure counts as a day of absence from Great Britain, but the day of return does not.[16]
- The 13- or 52-week period for which you can be paid HB while you are absent from your home but in Great Britain continues to run during any absence abroad. You may, therefore, be able to return to Britain and continue to be paid HB while absent from your home for the remainder of the 13- or 52-week period. However, if your entitlement has ended as a result of your absence abroad, you cannot qualify for HB again until you return home,[17] but note in most cases you will now need to claim UC instead of HB.
- HB guidance contains a useful table summarising when you can receive HB during different periods of absence, both in Great Britain and abroad.[18]
- If you have a European free movement European Economic Area (EEA) right to reside in the UK and go abroad to an EEA state, it may be arguable that the shorter period of time during which you remain entitled to HB while temporarily absent abroad is discriminatory under European Union (EU) law and should not apply (see p324).
- If you are temporarily absent from your home, you can continue to be entitled to council tax reduction in certain circumstances (see p578).

European Union co-ordination rules

If you go to an EEA country, you may be able to benefit from the EU co-ordination rules. If these apply to you, they can override the specific UK rules that prevent you from being entitled to benefit outside the UK and mean you can be paid your UK benefit in that EEA country for longer than would be the case under the UK rules described above. Since the end of the transition period (31 December 2020), there are three main sets of co-ordinating rules that may apply. The main EU co-ordination rules provide the greatest protections across the greatest number of benefits and all of the EEA countries, and the UK–Ireland Convention has similar rules but for situations involving the UK and Ireland only. The new UK-EU Protocol contains fewer protections and only covers the EU countries. For example, the main EU co-ordination rules can enable you to be paid some benefits for a family member living in an EEA country and the Convention provides the same in relation to a family member living in Ireland, but the Protocol does not cover family benefits. The rules you are covered by can be affected by your nationality, the country you are going to and other circumstances, including the date you moved (see p355).

See Chapter 15 for information on the individual benefits and tax credits and Chapter 16 for further information on the co-ordination rules.

Reciprocal and other international agreements

The UK has reciprocal agreements with several EEA and non-EEA countries. For a list of these and further information, see p397. In general, a reciprocal agreement only applies if the EU co-ordination rules do not assist you (see p401). They can also assist if you are moving between Great Britain and Northern Ireland or between the UK and the Channel Islands, the Isle of Man or Gibraltar. In addition, the EU and the Council of Europe have other agreements with some countries that can also affect your entitlement. See Chapter 17 for further information on all the agreements.

For more information on reciprocal agreements with EEA states since the UK left the EU, see p401.

Notes

2. **How your benefits and tax credits are affected**

1 R(S)1/66; *Slough BC v PK* [2019] UKUT 128 (AAC); Vol 2, para 070642 DMG; para C1122 ADM
2 **AA** Reg 2(3C) SS(AA) Regs
DLA Reg 2(3C) SS(DLA) Regs
PIP Reg 17(2) SS(PIP) Regs
CDP Reg 7(2)(a) DACYP(S) Regs (draft)
CB Reg 24(2) CB Regs
TC Reg 4(2) TC(R) Regs
3 *Chief Adjudication Officer v Ahmed and Others*, 16 March 1994, CA, reported as R(S) 1/96
4 *Chief Adjudication Officer v Ahmed and Others*, 16 March 1994, CA, reported as R(S) 1/96
5 R(S) 1/85
6 R(U) 16/62
7 *R v Barnet London Borough Council ex parte Shah* [1983] 2 AC 309, p342D
8 *KS v SSWP (SPC)* [2010] UKUT 156 (AAC)
9 *R v Penwith District Council ex parte Burt* [1988] 22 HLR 292 (QBD); para A3/3.460 GM
10 Sch 3 para 9(1) UC Regs
11 Sch 3 paras 6 and 9(3) UC Regs
12 **IS** Sch 3 para 3(10) IS Regs
JSA Sch 2 para 3(10) JSA Regs
ESA Sch 6 para 5(10) ESA Regs
PC Sch 2 para 4(10) SPC Regs
13 **IS** Sch 3 para 3(11)-(13) IS Regs
JSA Sch 2 para 3(11)-(13) JSA Regs
ESA Sch 6 para 5(11)-(13) ESA Regs
PC Sch 2 para 4(11)-(13) SPC Regs
14 Reg 7(13), (16), (17) and (18) HB Regs; reg 7(13), (16), (17) and (18) HB(SPC) Regs
15 Reg 7(13A)-(13G), (16), (17A)-(17D) and (18) HB Regs; reg 7(13A)-(13G), (16), (17A)-(17D) and (18) HB(SPC) Regs
16 *Slough BC v PK* [2019] UKUT 128 (AAC)
17 Reg 7(13B) and (17B) HB Regs; reg 7(13B) and (17B) HB(SPC) Regs
18 **HB** Circular A7/2016

Chapter 15

Going abroad: rules for individual benefits

This chapter covers:

This chapter explains the UK benefit and tax credit rules on being paid when either you or your family members are abroad. It also covers the ways in which the European Union (EU) co-ordination rules may affect whether you can be paid benefit. See Chapter 14 for an overview of how your entitlement is affected when you go abroad and see Chapters 16 and 17 for more details on the EU co-ordination rules and international agreements.

1. Means-tested benefits

You cannot usually receive means-tested benefits when you are abroad, because the rules for each benefit require you to be present in Great Britain (for housing benefit (HB) and council tax reduction, your absence from Great Britain affects whether you can be treated as occupying your home – see p324 for HB and p578 for council tax reduction). However, you can be treated as present (or as occupying your home for HB and council tax reduction) in certain circumstances. The rules differ between the different benefits.

Note: if you were receiving one of the legacy means-tested benefits and it stopped because you went abroad, when you return you will be unable to reclaim that benefit and must claim universal credit (UC) instead, *unless* you are in one of the limited circumstances that mean you can make a new claim for a legacy means-tested benefits – eg, if you live in temporary accommodation you must claim HB for help with your rent, in addition to any UC. For the full list of circumstances, see CPAG's *Welfare Benefits and Tax Credits Handbook*.

Universal credit

You cannot usually be paid UC if you (and your partner, if it is a joint claim) are not in Great Britain.[1] However, if you were entitled to UC immediately before leaving Great Britain and you are temporarily absent, you can continue to be entitled for:[2]

- **one month** if your absence is not expected to exceed, and does not exceed, one month; *or*
- **two months** if your absence is in connection with the death of your partner or child, or a close relative of yours (or of your partner or child), and it would be unreasonable for you to return to Great Britain within the first month. You are automatically exempt from the work search requirement and are treated as 'able and willing immediately to take up work' for six months following the death of your partner or child;[3]
- **six months** if your absence is not expected to exceed, and does not exceed, six months and you are a mariner or continental shelf worker; *or*
- **six months** if your absence is not expected to exceed, and does not exceed, six months and is solely in connection with the medically approved care, convalescence or treatment of you, your partner or child. You are automatically exempt from the work search requirement and are treated as 'able and willing immediately to take up work' during this period.[4]

Note:

- Since 24 July 2020, periods of temporary absence in Northern Ireland are ignored due to reciprocal arrangements between Great Britain and Northern Ireland that treat periods of presence and residence (and also employment) in one territory as having the same effect on UC as if it had occurred in the other territory.[5]
- To be entitled to the carer element in your UC while you are abroad, you must satisfy the rules for being paid carer's allowance abroad (see p329).
- The limited capability for work element was abolished for new UC claims from 3 April 2017. If your entitlement to UC ends because you are abroad, you cannot be entitled to this element in a future claim unless extremely limited circumstances apply. See CPAG's *Welfare Benefits and Tax Credits Handbook*.

If your partner is abroad

If you have a joint claim for UC and both you and your partner go abroad, your entitlement is not affected while one of the above situations applies to both of you. After this time, if you both remain abroad, your entitlement ends.

If you stay in Great Britain while your partner is abroad, her/his absence does not affect your entitlement during the one-, two- or six-month period if one of the above circumstances applies to her/him. After this time, unless your partner is in Northern Ireland (see note above), you cease to be entitled as joint claimants and your joint claim is treated as a claim by you as a single person.[6] However, if you and your partner have been, and expect to be, apart for less than six months you are still treated as a couple, so although you are awarded the elements for a single person, your partner's income and capital are taken into account.[7] Once you have been, or expect to be, apart for six months, you stop being treated as a couple[8] and your entitlement as a single person is unaffected by your absent partner.

If your partner's absence abroad means that s/he stops being habitually resident (including if s/he no longer has a right to reside) in the 'common travel area', s/he is treated as no longer present (see p144). Your joint claim is treated as a claim by you as a single person, but your partner's income and capital are taken into account (unless you are no longer being treated as a couple, as described above).[9]

If you have reached pension age, and your partner is under pension age, once her/his absence exceeds the periods above, your joint claim for UC is treated as a claim by you as a single person. However as a single person you are not entited to UC once you have reached pension age and therefore your entitlement to UC ends. From this date, you can claim pension credit (PC) and HB and you are treated as a single person for each of these claims.[10]

If your child is abroad

If your child is abroad (unless s/he is in Northern Ireland – see p315), you cease to be entitled for her/him if her/his absence is, or is expected to be, longer than the one-, two- or six-month periods allowed in the circumstances above. The circumstances must apply to your child.[11] **Note:** the rules that restrict payment of UC for your third or subsequent child in limited circumstances (the 'two-child limit') may affect you when your child returns. For further details, see p274.

European Union co-ordination rules

The Department for Work and Pensions (DWP) considers that UC is not a 'social security benefit' under the main European Union (EU) co-ordination rules or the UK-EU Protocol. The UK-Ireland Convention lists UC as 'social assistance' and the only co-ordinating rules that apply relate to the recovery of overpayments (see p368).

Therefore, none of these rules can assist you to be paid UC if you go to Ireland or another European Economic Area (EEA) country. You can only be paid under the UK rules above.

Income support

You cannot usually get income support (IS) if you are not in Great Britain.[12] However, if you were entitled to IS immediately before leaving Great Britain and you are temporarily absent, your entitlement can continue:[13]

- **indefinitely** if your absence is for NHS treatment at a hospital or other institution outside Great Britain;
- during the first **four weeks** of your absence, if it is unlikely to exceed 52 weeks and:
  - you are in Northern Ireland; *or*
  - you and your partner are both abroad and s/he satisfies the conditions for one of the pensioner premiums, a disability premium or a severe disability premium; *or*
  - you are entitled to statutory sick pay (SSP) and are abroad for the sole purpose of receiving treatment (see below) for the incapacity that entitles you to SSP; *or*
  - you have been (or are treated as) continuously entitled to SSP before you go abroad for 364 days (or 196 days if you are terminally ill or receiving the highest rate of disability living allowance care component, the enhanced rate of the daily living component of personal independence payment or armed forces independence payment). Two or more periods of entitlement to SSP are treated as continuous if the break between them is not more than 56 days each time; *or*
  - you are not:
    - entitled to SSP (unless you are covered by either group above); *or*
    - in 'relevant education'; *or*
    - involved in a trade dispute, or have returned to work for 15 days or less following the dispute; *or*
- during the first **eight weeks** of your absence, if it is unlikely to exceed 52 weeks and is solely in connection with arrangements made for the treatment (see below) of a disease or disablement of a child or qualifying young person (for whom you count as responsible under the IS rules).

'**Treatment**' must be carried out by, or under the supervision of, a person qualified to provide medical treatment, physiotherapy or similar treatment.

If you are entitled to housing costs in your IS, your temporary absence from your home can mean that you cease to be entitled to receive these (see p310).

Note: if your entitlement to IS ends because you go abroad, when you return, you cannot reclaim IS and must claim UC instead.

If your partner is abroad

If you are the IS claimant and you stay in Great Britain, your IS applicable amount includes an amount for your partner who is abroad for:[14]

- the first **four weeks**; *or*
- the first **eight weeks**, if s/he meets the conditions of the eight-week rule above.

If both you and your partner are abroad, your IS includes an amount for your partner for the first eight weeks if both of you meet the conditions of the eight-week rule above.[15]

After this four- or eight-week period, your benefit is reduced because your applicable amount is calculated as if you have no partner. However, your partner is still treated as being part of your household and, therefore, her/his work, income and capital affect your IS entitlement, unless you are no longer treated as a couple (see p310).[16]

If your child is abroad

If you were getting an amount in your IS for your child before s/he went abroad, you continue to be paid for her/him for:[17]

- the first **four weeks**; *or*
- the first **eight weeks**, if your child meets the conditions of the eight-week rule above.

After this four- or eight-week period, you are no longer paid IS for your child. When s/he returns to Great Britain, unless you have continued to be paid IS for another child, you will not be able to receive a personal allowance for her/him within your IS and will have to claim UC. (If you are already receiving IS for two or more children and your returning child was born after 6 April 2017, you may not be able to receive IS for her/him due to the 'two-child limit' – see p274.)

European Union co-ordination rules

IS is not covered by any of the EU co-ordination rules (except, to co-ordinate the recovery of overpayments, the UK-Ireland Convention — see p368). This means that these rules cannot assist you and if you go to an EEA country, you can only be paid under the UK rules above.

Income-based jobseeker's allowance

You cannot usually get jobseeker's allowance (JSA) if you are not in Great Britain.[18] However, if you are temporarily absent from Great Britain, both income-based and contribution-based JSA can continue to be paid:[19]

- **indefinitely** if you are entitled to JSA immediately before leaving Great Britain and your absence is for NHS treatment at a hospital or other institution outside Great Britain;

- for up to **four weeks** if you are entitled to JSA immediately before leaving Great Britain and:
  - your absence is unlikely to exceed 52 weeks, you continue to satisfy the conditions of entitlement and you are in Northern Ireland. **Note:** the reciprocal agreements between Great Britain and Northern Ireland can mean that after four weeks, the administration of your claim moves to Northern Ireland – you do not have to make a new claim[20] (see p399); *or*
  - your absence is unlikely to exceed 52 weeks, you continue to satisfy the conditions of entitlement and your partner is also abroad with you and satisfies the conditions for one of the pensioner premiums, a disability premium or a severe disability premium; *or*
  - you get a specified type of training allowance that means you do not have to satisfy the JSA jobseeking conditions;[21]
- for up to **eight weeks** if you are entitled to JSA immediately before leaving Great Britain and your absence is unlikely to exceed 52 weeks and is solely in connection with arrangements made for the treatment of a disease or disablement of a child or qualifying young person. The treatment must be carried out by, or under the supervision of, a person qualified to provide medical treatment, physiotherapy or similar treatment and you must count as responsible for the child or young person in the same way as for the similar rule on temporary absence for IS (see p317);
- for an absence of up to **seven days** if you are attending a job interview and you notified your work coach before you left (in writing if required). On your return, you must satisfy her/him that you attended the interview as stated;
- for an absence of up to **15 days** for the purpose of training as a member of the reserve forces.

You can be treated as available for work and actively seeking work during certain temporary absences abroad (these are similar to those listed above).[22] If you are getting contribution-based JSA under the UC system, you are exempt from the work search requirement and are treated as 'able and willing immediately to take up work' during these absences.[23] See CPAG's *Welfare Benefits and Tax Credits Handbook* for details.

If you are entitled to housing costs in your income-based JSA, your temporary absence from your home can mean that you cease to be entitled to receive these (see p310).

Note: if your entitlement to income-based JSA stops because you go abroad, when you return you cannot reclaim income-based JSA and must claim UC instead (unless you are in one of the limited circumstances when it is possible to make a new claim for income-based JSA).

Joint-claim jobseeker's allowance if your partner is abroad

If you are a member of a 'joint-claim couple' (see CPAG's *Welfare Benefits and Tax Credits Handbook* for what this means) and your partner is temporarily absent from Great Britain on the date you make your claim, you are paid as a couple for:[24]

- an absence of up to **seven days** if your partner is attending a job interview;
- up to **four weeks** if your partner is:
  - in Northern Ireland and her/his absence is unlikely to exceed 52 weeks; *or*
  - getting a specified type of training allowance that means s/he does not have to satisfy the JSA jobseeking conditions.

If you are a joint-claim couple and your partner goes abroad after you claimed JSA, and her/his absence is for NHS treatment at a hospital or other institution outside Great Britain, you are paid as a couple for up to four weeks.[25]

After this seven-day/four-week period, or from the date s/he leaves Great Britain if none of those circumstances apply, your JSA is reduced because your applicable amount is calculated as if you have no partner.[26] However, your partner is still treated as part of your household if s/he is abroad for treatment in the circumstances above. Therefore, her/his work, income and capital affects your joint-claim JSA entitlement, unless s/he stops being treated as part of your household for another reason (see p273).[27]

If your partner is no longer treated as part of your household, you can claim income-based JSA as a single person.

Income-based jobseeker's allowance if your partner is abroad

If you are the income-based JSA claimant and you stay in Great Britain, your applicable amount includes an amount for your partner while s/he is abroad for:[28]

- the first **four weeks** of a temporary absence; *or*
- the first **eight weeks** if your partner meets the conditions of the eight-week rule on p318.

If both you and your partner are abroad, your applicable amount includes an amount for your partner for the first eight weeks if both of you meet the conditions of the eight-week rule on p318.[29]

After this four- or eight-week period, your benefit is reduced because your applicable amount is calculated as if you have no partner. However, your partner is still treated as part of your household and, therefore, her/his work, income and capital affect your income-based JSA entitlement, unless you are no longer treated as a couple (see p273).[30]

Income-based jobseeker's allowance if your child is abroad

If you were getting JSA for your child before s/he went abroad, you can continue to be paid for her/him for:[31]

- the first **four weeks**; *or*

- the first **eight weeks** if your child meets the conditions of the eight-week rule on p319.

After this four- or eight-week period, the income-based JSA paid in respect of your child stops. When s/he returns to Great Britain, unless you have continued to be paid income-based JSA for another child, you cannot receive a personal allowance for her/him within your income-based JSA and you will have to claim UC. If you are already receiving income-based JSA for two or more children and your returning child was born after 6 April 2017, you may not be able to receive income-based JSA for her/him due to the 'two-child limit' (see p274).

European Union co-ordination rules

Income-based JSA is classed as a 'special non-contributory benefit' under the main EU co-ordination rules and the UK-EU Protocol (see p367) and 'social assistance' under the UK-Ireland Convention (see p368). This means that it cannot be 'exported' and, if you go to Ireland or another EEA country, the co-ordination rules cannot assist you, and you can only be paid income-based JSA abroad under the UK rules explained above.

However, each of the co-ordination rules may enable you to be paid contribution-based JSA for up to three months if you go to an EEA country (see p334).

Income-related employment and support allowance

You cannot usually get employment and support allowance (ESA) if you are not in Great Britain.[32] However, if you were entitled to ESA immediately before leaving Great Britain and you are temporarily absent, you can continue to be entitled to both income-related and contributory ESA:[33]

- **indefinitely** if:
  - your absence is for NHS treatment at a hospital or other institution outside Great Britain; *or*
  - you are living with your spouse, civil partner, son, daughter, stepson, stepdaughter, father, father-in-law, stepfather, mother, mother-in-law or stepmother who is a serving member of the armed forces;
- for the first **four weeks**, if your absence is unlikely to exceed 52 weeks;
- for the first **26 weeks**, if your absence is unlikely to exceed 52 weeks and is solely in connection with arrangements made for the treatment of:
  - your disease or disablement that is directly related to your limited capability for work which began before you left Great Britain; *or*
  - the disease or disablement of a dependent child who you are accompanying.

The treatment must be carried out by, or under the supervision of, a person qualified to provide medical treatment, physiotherapy or similar treatment.

If you are due to have a medical examination to assess your limited capability for work when you go abroad, you can ask for this to be carried out in the other country, or to be postponed until you return. If your request is refused and you go abroad and miss your medical, your ESA is terminated, unless it is accepted that you had a good cause for not attending. In deciding whether you had good cause, the decision maker must take all your circumstances into account, including the fact that you were outside Great Britain.[34] See CPAG's *Welfare Benefits and Tax Credits Handbook* for further details.

If you appeal against a decision on your limited capability for work-related activity while abroad, the tribunal should consider the hypothetical work-related activity that applies in the area of the UK where the tribunal hearing is held, unless you object. This area is usually Newcastle if you opt for a paper hearing.[35]

If you are entitled to housing costs in your income-related ESA, your temporary absence from your home can mean that you cease to be entitled to receive these (see p310).

Note: if your entitlement to income-related ESA stops because you go abroad, when you return, you cannot reclaim income-related ESA and must claim UC instead. If you *can* make a new claim for income-related ESA on your return, you are only entitled to the work-related activity component in limited circumstances. See CPAG's *Welfare Benefits and Tax Credits Handbook.*

If your partner is abroad

If you are the claimant, you stay in Great Britain and your partner goes abroad, your income-related ESA includes an amount for her/him for:[36]

- the first **four weeks**; *or*
- the first **26 weeks** if s/he is accompanying a child abroad for treatment and meets the conditions of the 26-week rule above.

If both you and your partner are abroad, your income-related ESA includes an amount for your partner for the first 26 weeks if both of you are accompanying a child abroad for treatment and you both meet the conditions of the 26-week rule above.[37]

After this four- or 26-week period, your benefit is reduced because your applicable amount is calculated as if you have no partner. However, your partner is still treated as part of your household and, therefore, her/his work, income and capital affect your income-related ESA entitlement, unless you are no longer treated as a couple (see p310).[38]

European Union co-ordination rules

Income-related ESA is listed under the main co-ordination rules and the UK-EU Protocol as a 'special non-contributory benefit' (see p367) and under the UK-Ireland Convention as 'social assistance'. This means that it cannot be 'exported' and, if you go to Ireland or another EEA country, the co-ordination rules cannot assist you, and you can only be paid income-related ESA abroad under the UK rules explained on p321.

However, each of the co-ordination rules may enable you to continue to be paid contributory ESA if you go to live in an EEA country, but note UK-EU Protocol only assists during assessment phase and only in EU states (see p334).

Reciprocal agreements

Reciprocal agreements have not been updated to include ESA (see p397), with the following exceptions.

- The reciprocal agreements between Northern Ireland and Great Britain have included ESA (both income-related and contributory) since 6 April 2016.[39] The purpose of these agreements is to ensure you do not lose out if you move from one territory to the other while claiming ESA. For more information on arrangements between Great Britain and Northern Ireland, including if you moved before 6 April 2016, see p399.
- If your award of contributory ESA was converted from an award of incapacity benefit (IB), it is covered by each of the agreements (with the exception of the Isle of Man, Israel and Switzerland) that cover IB (see Appendix 5).[40]

Pension credit

You cannot usually get PC if you are not in Great Britain.[41] However, if you were entitled to PC immediately before leaving Great Britain and you are temporarily absent, your entitlement can continue:[42]

- for up to **four weeks**, provided your absence is not expected to exceed that;
- for up to **eight weeks**, provided your absence is not expected to exceed that, the decision maker considers it unreasonable for you to return to Great Britain within four weeks and the absence is in connection with the death of:
  - your partner;
  - a child who normally lived with you; *or*
  - a close relative of you, your partner or child who normally lives with you;
- for up to **26 weeks**, provided your absence is not expected to exceed that and is solely in connection with medical treatment or medically approved convalescence or care as a result of medical treatment, for you, or your partner or a child who you are accompanying and who normally lives with you.

If you are entitled to housing costs in your PC, your temporary absence from home can mean that you cease to be entitled to receive these (see p310).

If your partner is abroad

If your partner is abroad and you are entitled to PC, either while in Great Britain or abroad because you are covered by the above rules, your PC only includes an amount for her/him if s/he is also covered by the above rules. After this, s/he is not treated as part of your household, you are paid as a single person and her/his income and capital do not affect your claim.[43]

Note: if your partner is under pension age and you stop being paid PC for her/him while s/he is abroad, on her/his return you cannot include her/him in your PC claim and you must make a joint claim for UC instead. However, if your partner fails the habitual residence test, you will not be entitled to UC, but can instead claim PC and HB, and you are treated as a single person for each of these claims.[44]

For further information about your partner going abroad, see p310.

If your child is abroad

If your child is temporarily absent from Great Britain, you continue to be entitled to an amount in your PC for her/him:[45]

- **for up to four weeks**, if her/his absence is not expected to exceed this; *or*
- **for up to eight weeks**, if her/his absence is not expected to exceed this and is in connection with the death of your partner, a child or qualifying young person who normally lives with you, or a close relative of hers/his, yours or your partner's, and the DWP considers it unreasonable for her/him to return to Great Britain within four weeks; *or*
- **for up to 26 weeks**, if her/his absence is not expected to exceed this and it is solely in connection with her/his or your or your partner's medical treatment, or medically approved convalescence.

European Union co-ordination rules

PC is classed as a 'special non-contributory benefit' under the main EU co-ordination rules and the UK-EU Protocol (see p367) and as 'social assistance' under the UK-Ireland Convention. This means that it cannot be 'exported' and, if you go to Ireland, an EU or an EEA country, the co-ordination rules cannot assist you. You can only be paid PC abroad under the UK rules.

Housing benefit

You cannot normally get HB if you are not in Great Britain due to the requirements for you to be occupying your home, except during certain temporary absences. The length of temporary absence you are allowed is shorter if you go abroad than if you were absent from your home but remained in Great Britain.[46]

Provided you meet the other conditions of entitlement, you have not rented out your home and you intend to return to it, you can continue to be paid HB when you are temporarily absent from Great Britain for:[47]

- **up to four weeks**, if your absence is not expected to exceed this;
- **up to eight weeks**, if the absence abroad is in connection with the death of your partner, your (or your partner's) close relative, or a child for whom you (or your partner) are responsible: the above four weeks are extended by up to

four weeks if the decision maker considers it unreasonable for you to return within the first four weeks;

- **up to 26 weeks in specific circumstances.** These include if you, your partner or child are in hospital, if you are undergoing or recovering from medical treatment, or if you are absent from home because of domestic violence. See CPAG's *Welfare Benefits and Tax Credits Handbook* for more details. Your absence abroad must be unlikely to exceed (or in exceptional circumstances, substantially exceed) 26 weeks;
- **26 weeks**, if you are a member of HM forces posted overseas, a mariner or a continental shelf worker. Your absence abroad must be unlikely to exceed 26 weeks.

Note:

- When counting the period of absence for HB, the day of departure counts as a day of absence from Great Britain, but the day of return does not.[48]
- Unless you are in one of the limited circumstances when you can make a new claim for HB (eg, if you are in temporary accommodation), if your entitlement to HB stops because you go abroad, when you return you cannot reclaim HB and must claim UC instead.
- DWP guidance states your HB can continue if you are unable to return from abroad within the periods above due to coronavirus pandemic travel restrictions, although there has been no change to the regulations.[49]
- If you have a European free movement right to reside in the UK (see p171) and you go abroad to an EEA country, it is arguable that the shorter period during which you can be entitled while abroad should not apply as it is indirect discrimination and potentially unlawful under EU law (see p381). The Court of Justice of the European Union accepted a similar argument in relation to funeral payments, ruling that requiring the funeral to take place in the UK unlawfully discriminated against EU migrant workers (see p292).[50]

For further details on the rules on absence from your home, see p310.

If your partner or child is abroad

Whether or not you have amounts included in your HB for your partner or child who is abroad depends on whether s/he is treated as part of your household (see p273 for partner and p274 for child). The amount of your HB may also depend on whether s/he is treated as occupying the home (see p310).

You can only be paid HB for your third or subsequent child in limited circumstances (due to the 'two-child limit'). These include if you have been receiving an amount for the child in your HB since 5 April 2017. However, these transitional rules may cease to apply when your child returns from abroad if payments for her/him, or your claim, stopped because s/he was abroad. For further details, see p274.

European Union co-ordination rules

HB is not covered by any of the EU co-ordination rules (see p368). This means that these rules cannot assist you. If you go to an EEA country, you can only be paid under the UK rules above.

2. Bereavement benefits

In general, bereavement benefits are payable while you are abroad. However, if you are receiving widowed parent's allowance because your spouse or civil partner died before 6 April 2017, your benefit is not uprated each year if, on the day before the annual uprating takes place, you have ceased to be 'ordinarily resident' (see p131) in Great Britain (unless you have gone to an European Economic Area (EEA) country and you are covered by the European Union (EU) co-ordination rules, or you can rely on a reciprocal agreement – see below).

You may be entitled to a bereavement support payment if you were ordinarily resident in Great Britain on the date your spouse or civil partner died. If you were abroad on that date, see p131 for whether your absence meant that you had ceased to be ordinarily resident.

European Union co-ordination rules

Bereavement benefits are classed as 'survivors' benefits' under each of the EU co-ordination rules (see p363) and are, therefore, fully 'exportable' (see p385). If you are covered by any of these rules (see p355) and the UK is your 'competent state' (see p369):[51]

- and you go to stay or live in an EEA country (or EU country if relying on the UK-EU Protocol, or Ireland if relying on the UK-Ireland Convention), you can be paid your bereavement support payment or widowed parent's allowance for as long as you would receive it if you remained in Great Britain, including any annual uprating; *and*
- for bereavement support payment, the requirement to be ordinarily resident in Great Britain on the date your spouse or civil partner died does not apply if you were resident in an EEA state (or EU state if relying on the Protocol, or Ireland if relying on the Convention) on that date.

Reciprocal agreements

If you are covered by a reciprocal agreement, this can assist in a similar way to the EU co-ordination rules (see above) in respect of the relevant country.[52] The reciprocal agreements were amended to include bereavement support payment from 6 April 2017.[53] For more information on reciprocal agreements, see Chapter 17.

3. Child benefit, Scottish child payment and guardian's allowance

Child benefit

You and your child can be treated as present in Great Britain and, therefore, you can continue to be entitled to child benefit for a limited period during a 'temporary absence' (see p308).

Provided you are 'ordinarily resident' (see p131), you are treated as present during a temporary absence for:[54]

- the first **eight weeks**; *or*
- the first **12 weeks** of any period of absence, or any extension to that period, which is in connection with:
  - the treatment of an illness or disability of you, your partner, a child for whom you are responsible, or another relative of yours or your partner's; *or*
  - the death of your partner, a child or qualifying young person for whom you or your partner are responsible, or another relative of yours or your partner's.

'Relative' means brother, sister, parent, grandparent, great-grandparent or child, grandchild or great-grandchild.[55]

Your child is treated as present during a temporary absence for:[56]

- the first **12 weeks** of any period of absence; *or*
- **any period** during which s/he is absent for the specific purpose of being treated for an illness or disability which began before her/his absence began; *or*
- **any period** when s/he is in Northern Ireland; *or*
- **any period** during which s/he is absent only because s/he is:
  - receiving full-time education at a school or college in a European Economic Area (EEA) country; *or*
  - engaged in an educational exchange or visit made with the written approval of the school or college s/he normally attends; *or*
  - a child who normally lives with a Crown servant posted overseas who is either in the same country as her/him or is absent from that country for one of the reasons in the two bullet points immediately above.[57]

If a child is born outside Great Britain during the eight- or 12-week period in which you were treated as present in Great Britain, s/he is treated as being in Great Britain for up to 12 weeks from the start of your absence.[58]

While you and your child are present, or treated as present, you satisfy that condition of entitlement. This means that you can continue to receive any child benefit already being paid and can also make a fresh claim during your, or her/his, absence. **Note:** if you or your child are treated as present, you must satisfy all the other conditions of entitlement including, if your child is not living with you, contributing at least the amount of child benefit that would be payable for the costs of that child.[59] For information on all the conditions of entitlement for child benefit, see CPAG's *Welfare Benefits and Tax Credits Handbook*.

Scottish child payment

You cease to be entitled to a Scottish child payment the week after you cease to be ordinarily resident in Scotland (see p131).[60]

Guardian's allowance

Entitlement to guardian's allowance generally depends on entitlement to child benefit, so you can be paid guardian's allowance abroad for the same period as child benefit (see p327). For the limited circumstances in which you can be entitled to guardian's allowance because you are *treated* as entitled to child benefit, including if you are receiving a family benefit from another country, see CPAG's *Welfare Benefits and Tax Credits Handbook*.

Your guardian's allowance is not uprated each year if you have ceased to be ordinarily resident (see p131) in Great Britain on the day before the annual uprating takes place,[61] unless you have gone to an EEA country and you are covered by the European Union (EU) co-ordination rules (see below) or you can rely on a reciprocal agreement.

European Union co-ordination rules

Since the end of the transition period (31 December 2020), you may be covered by the main EU co-ordination rules or, for situations involving the UK and Ireland only, the UK-Ireland Convention. If you are not covered by either but you are covered by the new UK-EU Protocol, that will not assist you in the ways below because it does not cover 'family benefits'.

Child benefit and guardian's allowance are listed under the UK-Ireland Convention and are categorised under the main EU co-ordination rules as 'family benefits' (see p363). It is strongly arguable that Scottish child payment should also be categorised as a 'family benefit'. If these rules apply to you (see p355) and the UK is your 'competent state' (see p369):

- you can be paid child benefit and guardian's allowance (and arguably Scottish child payment) for a child resident in an EEA country (Ireland if you are relying on the Convention). The child does not have to be in education. However, you must still satisfy all the other conditions of entitlement, including contributing to the costs of the child an amount at least equal to the amount of child benefit payable for her/him; *and/or*
- you can 'export' (continue to be paid) child benefit and guardian's allowance (and arguably Scottish child payment) if you go to stay or live in an EEA country (Ireland if you are relying on the Convention) and the UK continues to be your competent state (see p369), and your benefit is uprated in the normal way.

These rules can be complicated in certain circumstances – eg, if there is entitlement to family benefits in more than one state.

See p386 for more information on the payment of family benefits under the main EU co-ordination rules or the UK-Ireland Convention.

Reciprocal and other international agreements

If you are covered by a reciprocal agreement, this may enable periods of residence and/or presence in the other country to be treated as residence and/or presence in Great Britain in order to be entitled to child benefit and guardian's allowance. For more information on reciprocal agreements, see p406.

There are agreements with Israel that can assist in ways that are similar to the EU co-ordination rules (see above). For more information on these agreements with Israel, see p410.

4. Disability and carers' benefits

Provided you continue to be habitually resident (see p146), if you go abroad you are treated as being present in Great Britain (or in the common travel area, for child disability payment) and can continue to receive (or make a new claim for[62]) **attendance allowance (AA), disability living allowance (DLA), personal independence payment (PIP), carer's allowance (CA)**, and, it is expected, **child disability payment:**[63]

- (except CA) for the first **13 weeks** of a 'temporary absence' (see p308);
- (except CA) for the first **26 weeks** of a 'temporary absence' (see p308), if the absence is solely in connection with medical treatment for your illness or disability that began before you left Great Britain (common travel area for child disability payment);
- (for CA only) for up to **four weeks** if your absence is (and was when it began) for a temporary purpose and does not exceed four weeks. If you are not accompanied by the disabled person for whom you are caring, you must satisfy the rules that entitle you to CA during a break from caring. See CPAG's *Welfare Benefits and Tax Credits Handbook* for more information;
- (for CA only) if your absence is temporary and for the specific purpose of caring for a disabled person who is also absent from Great Britain and who continues to receive AA, DLA care component paid at the highest or middle rate, the daily living component of PIP, armed forces independence payment or constant attendance allowance;
- while you are abroad as an aircraft worker or mariner or continental shelf worker;
- while you are a serving member of the armed forces (or, for child disability payment, a civil servant), or you are living with someone who is abroad as a

serving member of the forces (or civil servant) and you are the spouse, civil partner, (or for child disability payment only, living together as if married / civil partners), son, stepson, daughter, stepdaughter, or (except for child disability payment) father, stepfather, mother, stepmother mother-in-law or father-in-law of that person, and, for CDP only, you can demonstrate a 'genuine and sufficient link' to Scotland. **Note:** you are also treated as habitually resident if you are in this group.

It is expected that **child disability payment** will *also* cease 13 weeks after you cease to be ordinarily resident in Scotland. Similarly DLA wil cease 13 weeks after you become ordinarily resident in Scotland, and you will then transfer onto the equivalent components and rate(s) of child disability payment without needing to make a claim.[64]

If your entitlement to **PIP** ended because you went abroad, the above rules did not apply for the whole period you were away and you return to Great Britain within 12 months, a new claim for PIP can be assessed on the basis of the information held about your last claim if your needs have not changed. The Department for Work and Pensions (DWP) refers to this as a 'rapid reclaim'.[65]

If you lose your entitlement to **CA**, you should still be eligible for a carer premium in your income support, income-based jobseeker's allowance, income-related employment and support allowance and housing benefit for a further period of eight weeks, provided you remain entitled to these benefits while you are away.[66] If you lose your entitlement to CA while you are abroad and the disabled person for whom you care is staying in the UK, s/he may be entitled to a severe disability premium in her/his benefit during your absence instead. For further information on premiums, see CPAG's *Welfare Benefits and Tax Credits Handbook*.

You can continue to be paid an **increase in your CA** for your spouse/civil partner or dependent adult while s/he is abroad if:[67]

- you are entitled to CA; *and*
- you are residing with her/him. **Note:** you can be treated as residing together during a temporary absence from each other.[68]

If you are under 19, in receipt of higher rate DLA, or child disability payment, care component and have a 'genuine and sufficient link' to Scotland while habitually resident in specific European Economic Area (EEA) countries, you may qualify for **child winter heating assistance** (see p293).

European Union co-ordination rules

Since the end of the transition period (31 December 2020), you may be covered by the main European Union (EU) co-ordination rules or, for situations involving the UK and Ireland only, the UK-Ireland Convention. If you are not covered by either but you are covered by the new UK-EU Protocol, that will not assist you in the ways below because it does not cover disability and carers' benefits.

Since April 2013, if you move to, and become habitually resident in, an EEA country (or, child disability payment only, Gibraltar), you can continue to be paid **AA, DLA care component, PIP daily living component** and **CA** (and, it is expected, **child disability payment care component**) without needing to satisfy the usual presence and residence requirements (see p280) if:[69]

- you are covered by the main EU co-ordination rules (or, for child disability payment, the UK-Ireland Convention or the agreement between the UK and Gibraltar – see p400) (see p355); *and*
- you are habitually resident in an EEA state (or for child disability payment, Gibraltar if relying on the agreement with Gibraltar, and Ireland if relying on the UK-Ireland Convention); *and*
- you can demonstrate a 'genuine and sufficient link' to the UK (to Scotland for child disability payment) (see p283).

Note: to continue to be paid your benefit, or to make a new claim (see p285), while the above bullets apply, the UK must be your 'competent state' to pay that benefit (see p369).[70] You can then continue to be paid for as long as the UK remains your competent state.

You can make a new claim (including for a backdated period if you would have been entitled if these rules been in force at the time) for **carer's allowance supplement** or **young carers' grant** without needing to satisfy the requirement to be resident or ordinarily resident in Scotland if:[71]

- you have a 'genuine and sufficient link to Scotland' (see p283); *and*
- the UK is your 'competent state' to pay this benefit; *and*
- you are either:
  - resident in an EEA state and covered by the main EU co-ordination rules (see p355); *or*
  - resident in Ireland and covered by the UK-Ireland Convention (see p358); or
  - resident in Gibraltar and covered by the agreement between the UK and Gibraltar (see p400).

Whether or not you could be paid in an EEA country **before April 2013** depends on the date your entitlement began, as AA, DLA and CA have been categorised in different ways under the co-ordination rules at different times.

Before 1 June 1992, AA, DLA and CA were classed as 'invalidity benefits' (see p363). If your entitlement began before this date, you can continue to be paid benefit in any EEA state.

From 1 June 1992, the UK government categorised AA, DLA and CA as 'special non-contributory benefits' (see p367). These are not 'exportable'. However, the Court of Justice of the European Union (CJEU) declared that this was wrong and that these benefits (except DLA mobility component) were 'sickness benefits'.[72]

This means they are 'exportable' and you should continue to receive the benefit if you are covered by the main EU co-ordination rules, for as long as the UK remains your competent state (see p371).[73] The CJEU has reconfirmed that DLA care component is a sickness, and not an invalidity, benefit.[74] It is expected that child disability payment care component will treated as a 'sickness benefit'.

Under the **main EU co-ordination rules, DLA mobility component** is listed as, **PIP mobility component** is accepted as, and **child disability payment mobility component** is expected to be treated as, a 'special non-contributory benefit' (see p367).[75] You can only be paid the mobility component in the state where you are resident under the co-ordination rules.[76] See p371 for details on where you are considered 'resident'.

The UK-Ireland Convention and UK-EU Protocol do not cover these mobility components at all.

You cannot make a new claim for DLA mobility component or PIP mobility component after you reach pension age and so if you lose your entitlement because you go abroad, you cannot re-establish this when you return to the UK if you have then reached pension age. The Upper Tribunal has held that this rule is *not* contrary to EU law in a case concerning a man who returned to the UK after living in France for several years.[77] **Note:** if you lose your entitlement to DLA or PIP because you went abroad and you reached pension age before your entitlement ended, you can become entitled again (including, if you were previously entitled, to the mobility component, despite being pension age or over), provided you make a renewal claim within 12 months of the previous award ending.[78] For further details on DLA and PIP entitlement criteria and the rules on renewal claims, see CPAG's *Welfare Benefits and Tax Credits Handbook*.

If you receive CA while in the UK and the main EU co-ordination rules apply to you (see p355), you may be able to continue to be paid an addition for an adult or child if s/he goes to stay or live in an EEA country. These additions count as 'family benefits' under the co-ordination rules (see p386).

Was your benefit stopped because you moved to another European Economic Area state on or after 8 March 2001?

If your AA, DLA care component or CA was stopped solely because you moved to an EEA state on or after 8 March 2001, this decision was wrong.[79]

The DWP can restore your entitlement and pay arrears from 18 October 2007 (or the date your payment was stopped, if this is later).[80] The DWP pays arrears from this date because this was when the CJEU decided these benefits had been wrongly categorised.

To get your entitlement restored and arrears paid for any period between 8 March 2001 and 18 October 2007, see p266 of the 10th edition of this *Handbook*.

Reciprocal agreements

Most reciprocal agreements do not cover disability and carers' benefits. However, the agreements with Guernsey, Jersey and the Isle of Man have provisions in relation to AA and DLA, and (Isle of Man only) CA. From 6 April 2016, the reciprocal arrangements between Great Britain and Northern Ireland provide for periods of presence and residence in Northern Ireland to count as presence and residence in Great Britain (and vice versa) for AA, DLA, PIP and carer's allowance.[81]

For general information on these agreements, see p399.

5. Industrial injuries benefits

Industrial injuries benefits are:

- disablement benefit;
- reduced earnings allowance (REA);
- retirement allowance;
- constant attendance allowance;
- exceptionally severe disablement allowance.

Disablement benefit and retirement allowance are not affected if you go abroad.[82]

Constant attendance allowance and exceptionally severe disablement allowance are payable for the first six months of a temporary absence, or a longer period that the Department for Work and Pensions (DWP) may allow.[83]

REA can be paid while you are temporarily absent abroad for the first three months (or longer if the DWP allows) if:[84]

- your absence from Great Britain is not in connection with employment, trade or business; *and*
- your claim was made before you left Great Britain; *and*
- you were entitled to REA before going abroad.

Note: REA has been abolished. If you break your claim, you may no longer be eligible for benefit.

European Union co-ordination rules

Industrial injuries benefits, with the exception of retirement allowance, are classed as 'benefits for accidents at work and occupational diseases' under each of the European Union (EU) co-ordination rules (see p363) and are, therefore, fully 'exportable'. If you are covered by these rules (see p355) and you go to stay or live in an European Economic Area country (EU country if relying on the UK-EU Protocol, or Ireland if relying on the UK-Ireland Convention), you can be paid without any time limit and the benefits will be fully uprated each year. See p385 for more details.

Reciprocal agreements

The UK has reciprocal agreements with several countries that cover industrial injuries benefits. These can enable you to continue to be paid benefit indefinitely when you go to a relevant country, and contain provisions for determining entitlement when more than one country is involved. For more information on reciprocal agreements covering industrial injuries benefits, see p404.

6. Contribution-based jobseeker's allowance and contributory employment and support allowance

You cannot usually get jobseeker's allowance (JSA) or employment and support allowance (ESA) if you are not in Great Britain.[85] However, contribution-based JSA can be paid when you are temporarily absent from Great Britain in the same circumstances as income-based JSA (see p318), and contributory ESA can be paid when you are temporarily absent from Great Britain in the same circumstances as income-related ESA (see p321).

European Union co-ordination rules

Since the end of the transition period (31 December 2020), you may be covered by the main European Union (EU) co-ordination rules or similar co-ordination rules contained in the new UK-EU Protocol, or, for situations involving the UK and Ireland only, the UK-Ireland Convention. The specific rules differ under each set of rules so you need to check which you are covered by (see p349).

Contribution-based jobseeker's allowance

Contribution-based JSA is classed as an unemployment benefit under each of these co-ordination rules (see p363). However, the **UK-EU Protocol** does not provide for unemployment benefits to be 'exported'.[86]

If you are covered by the main co-ordination rules or, if you are going to Ireland, the **UK-Ireland Convention** (see p355) and the UK is your 'competent state' (see p369, you can continue to be paid (referred to as 'exporting') contribution-based JSA for up to three months if:[87]

- you satisfied the conditions for contribution-based JSA before you left the UK for at least four weeks (in total, which need not be continuous[88]), unless the Department for Work and Pensions (DWP) authorised you to go abroad before then; *and*

- you register as unemployed in Ireland, if you are relying on the UK-Ireland Convention, or the European Economic Area (EEA) country you go to, within seven days, and comply with its procedures.

Contributory employment and support allowance

If you are covered by any of the the co-ordination rules (see p355) and the UK is your competent state (see p369), you may continue to be paid ('export') contributory ESA if you go to live in an EEA country (or in Ireland if you are relying on the UK-Ireland Convention).

Under each of the co-ordination rules, contributory ESA is classed as a 'sickness benefit' during the assessment phase, and an 'invalidity benefit' after the assessment phase.

Under the **main co-ordination rules**, invalidity benefits are fully 'exportable' and therefore you continue to receive your contributory ESA after the assessment phase if you move to an EEA state. If you have a long-term or permanent disability, it is arguable that contributory ESA during the assessment phase should be regarded as an 'invalidity benefit'.[89] Although 'sickness benefits' can be subject to limitations on exportability under the main co-ordination rules, in most cases they are exportable in similar circumstances and DWP guidance confirms you can continue to receive assessment phase ESA while staying temporarily in, or if you have moved to, an EEA county.[90]

If you are covered by the **UK-Ireland Convention**, you can continue to be paid your ESA during and after the assessment phase if you go to stay or live in Ireland.

Under the **UK-EU Protocol**, invalidity benefits are not exportable, which means if you go to stay or live in an EU country, you can only continue to be paid contributory ESA during the assessment phase.

If you can export your contributory ESA, it can continue to be paid while the UK remains your competent state. The DWP continues to assess your limited capability for work and your limited capability for work-related activity. However, any checks and medicals take place in the state in which you are living, with reports then sent to the DWP.[91]

If you appeal against a decision on your limited capability for work-related activity while abroad, the tribunal should consider the hypothetical work-related activity that applies in the area of the UK where the tribunal hearing is held, unless you object. This area is usually Newcastle if you opt for a paper hearing.[92]

Reciprocal agreements

If the country you are going to has a reciprocal agreement that covers contribution-based JSA (see Appendix 5), check whether you are covered by it. Such agreements can, for example, enable you to be paid a contribution-based benefit for a limited period and/or to use periods of employment completed, or national insurance contributions paid, in Great Britain to entitle you to unemployment benefits in the country you are going to. See p403 for further information.

Most reciprocal agreements do not cover contributory ESA (see p404). The exceptions are:

- the agreement with Northern Ireland, which, since 6 April 2016, covers contributory ESA (as well as income-related ESA);[93] *and*
- if your award of contributory ESA was converted from incapacity benefit (IB), it is covered by the agreements (except the Isle of Man, Israel and Switzerland) that cover IB (see Appendix 5).[94]

If you moved from Great Britain to Northern Ireland (or vice versa) while claiming ESA before 6 April 2016, the DWP policy was to make an extra-statutory payment to cover any loss of ESA that resulted from your having to make a new claim. If you were receiving extra-statutory payments on this basis up to 27 November 2016, and do not satisfy the contributory conditions for entitlement to contributory ESA, you are treated as satisfying those conditions and as having made a claim for ESA from 27 November 2016 and your period of limited capability for work is treated as continuous.[95] For further information on the arrangements between Northern Ireland and Great Britain, see p399.

7. Maternity allowance, incapacity benefit and severe disablement allowance

If you are temporarily absent from Great Britain, you can continue to be paid maternity allowance (MA), incapacity benefit (IB) and severe disablement allowance (SDA) if:[96]

- you are receiving attendance allowance (AA), disability living allowance (DLA), personal independence payment (PIP) or armed forces independence payment. For when AA, DLA or PIP can be paid abroad, see p329; *or*
- the Department for Work and Pensions (DWP) certifies that you should continue to be paid. You can then receive the benefit for the first 26 weeks of your temporary absence; *or*
- you are the spouse, civil partner, son, stepson, daughter, stepdaughter, father, stepfather, father-in-law, mother, stepmother or mother-in-law of a serving member of the armed forces and you are abroad only because you are living with her/him.

In addition:

- when you left Great Britain, you must have been continuously incapable of work for six months and have been continuously incapable since your departure; *or*

- your absence from Great Britain must be for the specific purpose of being treated for an incapacity which began before you left Great Britain; *or*
- for IB only, your incapacity for work is the result of a personal injury caused by an accident at work and your absence from Great Britain is for the specific purpose of receiving treatment for that injury.

If you are due to have a medical examination, this can be arranged abroad.

Note: most IB and SDA claims have been reassessed for transfer to employment and support allowance (ESA). If your award of IB or SDA is converted to contributory ESA, you do not need to resatisfy the national insurance (NI) contribution conditions. However, if you are getting IB or SDA and lose entitlement because you go abroad for more than 26 weeks, you do not requalify for IB or SDA on your return to Great Britain, and you can only get contributory ESA if you satisfy all the conditions of entitlement, including the NI contribution conditions. Losing entitlement because you go abroad could therefore result in a loss of potential future benefit.

You can continue to be paid an increase in your IB or SDA for your spouse/civil partner or dependent adult while s/he is abroad if you are residing with her/him.[97] **Note:** you can be treated as residing together during a temporary absence from each other.[98]

European Union co-ordination rules

Since the end of the transition period (31 December 2020), you may be covered by the main European Union (EU) co-ordination rules or similar co-ordination rules contained in the new UK-EU Protocol, or, for situations involving the UK and Ireland only, the UK-Ireland Convention. The specific rules differ under each set of rules so you need to check which you are covered by.

MA is classed as a 'maternity benefit' under each of the co-ordination rules (see p363). If these rules apply to you (see p355) and the UK continues to be your competent state to pay this benefit (see p369), you can be paid MA if you go to live or stay in an EEA country (EU country if relying on the protocol, or Ireland if relying on the convention).[99] See p385 for more details.

Long-term IB and SDA are classed as 'invalidity benefits' under the main EU co-ordination rules (see p363). If these rules apply to you (see p355) and the UK continues to be the 'competent state' to pay these benefits (see p369), you can 'export' (ie, continue to receive) your IB and SDA, including any uprating if you go to live in a European Economic Area (EEA) country.

The DWP continues to determine your incapacity for work, but any checks and medicals take place in the state in which you live and the reports are then sent to the paying state.[100]

If the main co-ordination rules apply to you and you remain in the UK, you may be able to continue to be paid an increase for an adult or child if s/he goes to stay or live in an EEA country. These increases are classified as 'family benefits'. See p386 for details about when you can receive these for a family member living abroad.

Reciprocal agreements

The UK has reciprocal agreements with several countries that cover incapacity, sickness and maternity benefits. If you are going to one of these countries, the agreement may enable you to continue to be paid benefit, make a new claim for MA or use NI contributions paid, or periods of employment completed, in the UK to qualify for benefit in the country you are going to. For more information on reciprocal agreements covering sickness and invalidity benefits, see p404, and for maternity benefits, see p404.

8. Retirement pensions

All retirement pensions are payable without any time limit while you are abroad.[101] However, if you are not ordinarily resident (see p131) in Great Britain:[102]

- on the day before the annual uprating takes place, your benefit is not uprated each year;
- when you claim state pension (for people who reach pension age on or after 6 April 2016) that you have deferred, the upratings that occurred while you were abroad are ignored when calculating both the deferral increase and rate payable;
- you cannot stop claiming ('de-retire') your 'old' retirement pension (for people who reached pension age before 6 April 2016) in order to accrue a deferral payment.[103]

The above does not apply if you go to a European Economic Area (EEA) state and you are covered by the European Union (EU) co-ordination rules, or you can rely on a reciprocal agreement (see below).

Although category D retirement pension is payable if you are abroad, you must meet the residence requirements at the date you make your claim (see p291).

If you live abroad, your retirement pension can be paid into a bank in either the country where you live or in the UK.

You can continue to be paid an increase in your category A retirement pension for your spouse/civil partner or dependent adult while s/he is abroad if:[104]

- you are entitled to the pension; *and*
- you are residing with her/him. You can be treated as residing together during a temporary absence from each other.[105]

European Union co-ordination rules

Since the end of the transition period (31 December 2020), you may be covered by the main EU co-ordination rules, which cover the UK and EEA states, or similar co-ordination rules contained in the new UK-EU Protocol, which covers the UK and EU states, or, for situations involving the UK and Ireland only, the UK-Ireland Convention.

Retirement pensions are classed as 'old age benefits' under each of the co-ordination rules (see p363). If you are covered by any of these rules (see p355), the UK is your 'competent state' (see p369) and you go to live in a member state:

- you can 'export' (ie, continue to be paid) your retirement pension without time limit;
- your retirement pension is paid at the same rate as if you were still in the UK, including your annual uprating; *and*
- you can opt to stop claiming your pension ('de-retire') in order to accrue a deferral payment while living in a member state.

Note: if you are relying on the UK-EU Protocol, that does not cover Iceland, Norway, Liechtenstein or Switzerland. At the time of writing, it was understood that the UK government was negotiating with these four countries to agree that the above rules on old age pensions can continue to also apply to these states in addition to the EU states (as is the case for those covered by the main co-ordination rules).

If you are covered by the **main EU co-ordination rules** and you remain in the UK, you may be able to continue to be paid an increase for an adult or child if s/he goes to stay or live in an EEA state. These increases count as 'family benefits' under these co-ordination rules. See p386 for more details.

Reciprocal agreements

If you are covered by a reciprocal agreement (see p397) that provides for uprating, you can continue to be paid your pension at the same rate as if you were still in the UK. **Note:** the agreements with Canada and New Zealand, and the former agreement with Australia, do not provide for uprating. For further information on reciprocal agreements and retirement pensions, see p405.

9. Statutory payments

There are no presence or residence rules for statutory sick pay (SSP), statutory maternity pay (SMP), statutory adoption pay (SAP), statutory paternity pay (SPP), statutory shared parental pay (SSPP) and statutory parental bereavement pay (SPBP). You remain entitled to these benefits if you go abroad, provided you meet the usual rules of entitlement, including those relating to being an employee.[106]

Although you are generally required to be employed in Great Britain to count as an 'employee', you count as an employee for the purpose of these benefits, even while employed abroad, in certain circumstances, including if:[107]

- your employer is required to pay secondary class 1 national insurance (NI) contributions for you; *or*
- you are a continental shelf worker or, in certain circumstances, an airman/woman or mariner; *or*
- you are employed in a European Economic Area (EEA) country and had you been employed in Great Britain you would be considered an employee, and the UK is the competent state under the European Union (EU) co-ordination rules (see p369).

Your employer is not required to pay you SSP, SMP, SAP, SPP, SSPP or SPBP if:[108]

- your employer is not legally required to pay employer's class 1 NI contributions (even if these contributions are, in fact, made) because, at the time they become payable, your employer:
  - is not resident or present in Great Britain; *and*
  - does not have (or is treated as not having) a place of business in Great Britain; *or*
- because of an international treaty or convention, your employer is exempt from the Social Security Acts, or they are not enforceable against your employer.

European Union co-ordination rules

The Department for Work and Pensions (DWP) considers that these statutory payments are treated as wages and not social security benefits under the main co-ordination rules,[109] and it is expected the same view will be taken under the UK-EU Protocol. It is arguable that SSP is a 'sickness benefit' and SMP, SAP, SSPB, SPP and SSPP are 'maternity/paternity benefits' under these EU co-ordination rules (see p363).[110] However, due to the absence of residence and presence requirements for these benefits, it is unlikely you would need to rely on that. The DWP accepts you can be paid all these statutory payments if you go to stay or live in an EEA state under the UK rules above.

The UK–Ireland Convention, however, has specific references to these statutory payments in order to prevent them being paid at the same time as Irish sickness, maternity, paternity or invalidity benefits.[111]

10. **Tax credits**

Provided you are ordinarily resident (see p131), you can be treated as being present and, therefore, entitled to child tax credit (CTC) and working tax credit (WTC) during a 'temporary absence' (see p308) for:[112]

- the first **eight weeks**; *or*
- the first **12 weeks** of any period of absence, or any extension to that period, which is in connection with:
  - the treatment of an illness or disability of you, your partner, a child for whom you are responsible, or another relative (see below) of either you or your partner; *or*
  - the death of your partner, a child or qualifying young person for whom you or your partner are responsible, or another relative (see below) of you or your partner.

'Relative' means brother, sister, parent, grandparent, grandchild or great-grandparent or child.[113]

You are also treated as present if you are:[114]

- a Crown servant posted overseas and:
  - you are, or immediately before your posting abroad you were, ordinarily resident in the UK; *or*
  - immediately before your posting you were in the UK in connection with that posting; *or*
- the partner of a Crown servant posted overseas and in the same country as her/him or temporarily absent from that country under the same exceptions that enable tax credits to continue during a temporary absence from Great Britain.

While you are treated as present in any of the above ways, you continue to satisfy that condition of entitlement. This means that you can continue to receive any tax credits that are already in payment, and can make a renewal claim during your absence. It also means that if you are receiving CTC or WTC and become entitled to the other, you can make a new claim for this during your absence (you are not required to claim universal credit (UC)).

If your childcare provider is located outside the UK, you can still be entitled to the childcare element of WTC (see p294).

Your tax credit entitlement ends if:

- you (or your partner, in a joint claim) spend longer abroad than the permitted temporary absence periods, as you cease to satisfy the presence condition; *or*
- you (or your partner, in a joint claim) cease to be ordinarily resident; *or*
- you are entitled to tax credits on the basis of a joint claim and you separate from your partner in circumstances in which the separation is likely to be permanent, as you cease to count as a couple.[115]

If your entitlement to tax credits on the basis of a joint claim ends, in almost all cases you cannot make a single claim, but may be able to claim UC instead. For the limited exceptions, see CPAG's *Welfare Benefits and Tax Credits Handbook*.

European Union co-ordination rules

Since the end of the transition period (31 December 2020), you may be covered by the main European Union (EU) co-ordination rules or similar co-ordination rules contained in the new UK-EU Protocol, or, for situations involving the UK and Ireland only, the UK-Ireland Convention. However, the UK-EU Protocol does not apply to CTC or WTC.

CTC is classed as a 'family benefit' under the main EU co-ordination rules and the UK-Ireland Convention (see p363). If either of these rules apply to you (see p355) and the UK is your 'competent state' (see p369), you can be paid CTC:

- if you go to stay or live in a European Economic Area (EEA) state (Ireland, if relying on the convention); *and/or*
- for a child resident in an EEA state (Ireland if relying on the convention) – provided you meet the other conditions of CTC, including that the child is 'normally living with' you.[116]

See p386 for more details on the payment of family benefits under the EU co-ordination rules.

WTC is not covered by any of the EU co-ordination rules. Therefore, if your partner is in an EEA country, although you may be able to make a joint claim for CTC as a couple, you can only be entitled to WTC on the basis of a single claim.[117]

If you or your partner are working in an EEA country but live in the UK and, therefore, remain present and ordinarily resident in the UK, this work can count for the purposes of your WTC claim.[118]

Notes

1. **Means-tested benefits**

1 ss3 and 4(1)(c) WRA 2012
2 Reg 11 UC Regs
3 Reg 99(1)-(3) UC Regs
4 Reg 99(1)-(3) UC Regs
5 Sch para 2, UC(NIRA) Regs; see also ADM Memo 18/20, para 3
6 Regs 3(3) UC Regs; reg 9(1)' UC,PIP,JSA&ESA(C&P) Regs
7 Regs 3, 18, 22 and 36 UC Regs
8 Reg 3(6) UC Regs
9 Regs 3(3), 9, 18(2), 22(3) and 36(3) UC Regs; reg 9(1) UC,PIP,JSA&ESA(C&P) Regs
10 Art 7(1), (2)(a) and (b) and (3)(b) WRA(No.31)O; HB Circular A9/2019, paras 15-17; DMG Memo 7/19, para 12
11 Reg 4(7) UC Regs
12 s124(1) SSCBA 1992
13 Reg 4 IS Regs
14 Reg 21 and Sch 7 paras 11 and 11A IS Regs
15 Reg 21 and Sch 7 para 11A IS Regs
16 Reg 16 IS Regs
17 Reg 16(5) IS Regs
18 s1(2)(i) JSA 1995
19 s21 and Sch 1 para 11 JSA 1995; reg 50 JSA Regs; reg 41 JSA Regs 2013

20 Sch para 2 SS(NIRA) Regs; Sch para 2 SS(GBRA)(NI) Regs
21 Regs 50(4) and 170 JSA Regs
22 Regs 14 and 19 JSA Regs
23 Reg 16 JSA Regs 2013
24 Regs 3E(1) and (2)(c), 50(6B), 86C and 170 and Sch 5A para 7 JSA Regs; Vol 4, paras 24146-49 DMG
25 Regs 3E(1) and (2)(c), 50(6B) and 86C JSA Regs
26 Regs 50(6B) and 78(1A) and (3)(c) and Sch 5A para 7 JSA Regs
27 Reg 78 JSA Regs
28 Reg 85 and Sch 5 paras 10 and 11 JSA Regs
29 Reg 85 and Sch 5 para 11 JSA Regs
30 Reg 78 JSA Regs
31 Reg 78(5) JSA Regs
32 ss1(3)(d) and 18(4)(a) WRA 2007
33 Regs 151-55 ESA Regs; regs 88-92 ESA Regs 2013
34 Reg 24 ESA Regs; reg 20 ESA Regs 2013
35 *BB v SSWP (ESA)* [2015] UKUT 545 (AAC); see also *KC and MC v SSWP (ESA)* [2017] UKUT 94 (AAC)
36 Regs 69 and 156 and Sch 5 paras 6 and 7 ESA Regs
37 Regs 69 and 156 and Sch 5 para 7 ESA Regs
38 Reg 156 ESA Regs
39 SS(NIRA) Regs; SS(GBRA)(NI) Regs
40 SS(RA)O
41 s1(2)(a) SPCA 2002
42 Regs 3 and 4 SPC Regs
43 Reg 5 SPC Regs
44 s4(1A) SPCA 2002; Arts 4(2), 6(2)(a), 7(1), (2)(a) and (b) and (3)(b) and 8 WRA(No.31)O; HB Circular A9/2019; DMG Memo 7/19
45 Sch IIA para 7 SPC Regs
46 s130(1)(a) SSCBA 1992; reg 7 HB Regs; reg 7 HB(SPC) Regs
47 reg 7 HB Regs; reg 7 HB(SPC) Regs
48 *Slough BC v PK* [2019] UKUT 128 (AAC)
49 LA Welfare Direct 6/2020 (updated 5 November 2020)
50 Art 18 TFEU; Art 24 EU Dir 2004/38; *O'Flynn v Adjudication Officer*, C-237/94 [1996] ECR I-02617; R(IS) 4/98

2. **Bereavement benefits**
51 Arts 5, 7, 42 and 43 EU Reg 883/04; Arts 5, 7 and 43 UK-IC; Arts 6, 8, 37 and 38 UK-EUP
52 Reg 5 SSB(PA) Regs
53 The Social Security (Reciprocal Agreements) Order 2017, No.159; SS(NIRA)(A) Regs; SS(GBRA)(A)NI Regs

3. **Child benefit, Scottish child payment and guardian's allowance**
54 Reg 24 CB Regs
55 Reg 24(1) CB Regs
56 Reg 21 CB Regs
57 Reg 32 CB Regs
58 Reg 21(2) CB Regs
59 s143(1)(b) SSCBA 1992
60 Reg 19, SCP Regs
61 Reg 5 SSB(PA) Regs

4. **Disability and carers' benefits**
62 Confirmed in ADM Memo 9/20 and DMG Memo 12/20
63 **AA** Reg 2(2), (3B) and (3C) SS(AA) Regs
DLA Reg 2(2), (3B) and (3C) SS(DLA) Regs
PIP Regs 17-20 SS(PIP) Regs
CA Reg 9(2) and (3) SS(ICA) Regs
CDP Regs 5(6)-(8) and 7 DACYP(S) Regs (draft)
64 regs 36 and 41 and Sch 1 part 3 DACYP(S) Regs (draft)
65 'Disability', House of Commons, *Hansard*, Written Statement, HCWS603, 20 April 2017; confirmed by emails to CPAG, November 2020
66 **IS** Sch 2 para 14ZA IS Regs
JSA Sch 1 para 17 JSA Regs
ESA Sch 4 para 8 ESA Regs
HB Sch 3 para 17 HB Regs
67 Reg 13 SSB(PA) Regs; Sch 2 para 7 SSB(Dep) Regs
68 Reg 2(4) SSB(PRT) Regs
69 **AA** Reg 2B SS(AA) Regs
DLA Reg 2B SS(DLA) Regs
PIP Reg 23 SS(PIP) Regs
CA Reg 9B SS(ICA) Regs
CDP Regs 5(4)-(5) and 9 DACYP(S) Regs (draft)
All – Art 7 EU Reg 883/04; see also ADM Memos 9/20 and 17/20, and DMG Memos 12/20 and 16/20
70 **AA** s65(7) SSCBA 1992
DLA s72(7B) SSCBA 1992
PIP s84 WRA 2012
CA s70(4A) SSCBA 1992
CDP Reg 9(2)(a)(ii) DACYP(S) Regs (draft)
All - see also ADM Memo 17/20 and DMG Memo 16/20
71 **CAS** s81(2A) and (9)-(15) SS(S)A 2018
YCG Regs 4(7), 8(3)-(10) and 12(1A) CA(YCG)(S) Regs
72 *Commission of the European Communities v European Parliament and Council of the European Union*, C-299/05 [2007], 18 October 2007

73 ss65(7), 70(4A) and 72(7B) SSCBA 1992; s84 WRA 2012
74 *SSWP v Tolley*, C-430/15 [2017]. This case relates to the old co-ordination rules, but on this point has been held to apply also to the current co-ordination rules: *LD v SSWP* [2017] UKUT 65 (AAC).
75 *Bartlett and Others v SSWP*,C-537/09 [2011]; see also *NG v SSWP(DLA)* [2012] UKUT 26 (AAC), reported as [2012] AACR; *SSWP v DS* [2019] UKUT 238 (AAC); para C2097 and Appendix 1 para 4 ADM
76 Art 70 EU Reg 883/04; *Swaddling v AO*, C-90/97 [1999]
77 *GS v SSWP (DLA)* [2015] UKUT 687 (AAC)
78 **DLA** Sch 1 paras 3 and 5 SS(DLA) Regs; Vol 10, para 61558 DMG
PIP Regs 15 and 26 SS(PIP) Regs; para P4082 ADM
79 *Commission of the European Communities v European Parliament and Council of the European Union*, C-299/05 [2007], 18 October 2007
80 Reg 6(35)-(37) SS(C&P) Regs; reg 7(9A) SS&CS(DA) Regs
81 Sch para 2(1), SS(NIRA) Regs; Sch para 2(1) SS(GBRA)(NI) Regs

5. Industrial injuries benefits
82 Reg 9(3) SSB(PA) Regs
83 Reg 9(4) SSB(PA) Regs
84 Reg 9(5) SSB(PA) Regs

6. Contribution-based jobseeker's allowance and contributory employment and support allowance
85 s1(2)(i) JSA 1995; ss1(3)(d) and 18(4)(a) WRA 2007
86 Arts SSC3(1) and (4) and SSC8 UK-EUP
87 Art 64 EU Reg 883/04; Arts 7 and 21 UK-IC
88 *Arbetsmarknadsstyrelsen v Rydergard*, C-215/00 [2002] ECR I-1817
89 *Stewart v SSWP*, C-503/09 [2011] ECR I-06497
90 paras C4142-3 ADM
91 Arts 5, 46 and 82 EU Reg 883/04; Arts 27, 46, 49 and 87 EU Reg 987/2009; Art 59(7) UK-IC; Art 63 UK-EUP
92 *BB v SSWP (ESA)* [2015] UKUT 545 (AAC); see also *KC and MC v SSWP (ESA)* [2017] UKUT 94 (AAC)
93 SS(NIRA) Regs; SS(GBRA)(NI) Regs
94 s179(3), (4) and (5) SSAA 1992; SS(RA)O
95 Sch Art 2A-2B SS(NIRA) Regs; Sch Art 2A-2B SS(GBRA)(NI) Regs

7. Maternity allowance, incapacity benefit and severe disablement allowance
96 Reg 2 SSB(PA) Regs
97 Reg 13 SSB(PA) Regs; reg 14 SS(IB-ID) Regs
98 Reg 2(4) SSB(PRT) Regs
99 Arts 7 and 21 EU Reg 883/04; Art 7 UK-IC; Art 8 UK-EUP
100 Arts 5, 46 and 82 EU Reg 883/04; Arts 27, 46, 49 and 87 EU Reg 987/2009

8. Retirement pensions
101 s113 SSCBA 1992; reg 4(1) SSB(PA) Regs
102 Regs 4(3) and 5 SSB(PA) Regs; ss18 and 20 PA 2014; regs 21-23 The State Pension Regulations 2015, No.173; for state pension, see DMG Memo 6/16
103 Reg 6 SSB(PA) Regs
104 Reg 13 SSB(PA) Regs; reg 10 SSB(Dep) Regs
105 Reg 2(4) SSB(PRT) Regs

9. Statutory payments
106 **SSP** Reg 10 SSP(MAPA) Regs
SMP Reg 2A SMP(PAM) Regs
SAP/SPP Reg 4 SPPSAP(PAM) Regs
SSPP Reg 6 SSPP(PAM) Regs
SPBP Reg 6 SPBP(PAM) Regs
107 **SSP** s163(1) SSCBA 1992; reg 16 SSP Regs; regs 5-10 SSP(MAPA) Regs
SMP s171(1) SSCBA 1992; regs 2, 2A, 5, 7 and 8 SMP(PAM) Regs
SAP/SPP ss171ZJ(2)-(3) and 171ZS(2)-(3) SSCBA 1992; regs 3, 4, 8 and 9 SPPSAP(PAM) Regs
SSPP s171ZZ4(2) SSCBA 1992; regs 5, 6, 7, 9, 10 SSPP(PAM) Regs
SPBP s171ZZ(14)(2)-(3) SSCBA 1992; regs 5-10 SPBP(PAM) Regs
108 **SSP** Reg 16(2) SSP Regs
SMP Reg 3 SMP(PAM) Regs; reg 17(3) SMP Regs
SAP/SPP Reg 2 SPPSAP(PAM) Regs; reg 32(3) SPPSAP(G) Regs; reg 24(4) ASPP(G) Regs
SSPP Reg 33(5) SSPP Regs; reg 4 SSPP(PAM) Regs
SPBP Reg 4 SPBP(PAM) Regs
109 See for example Vol2, Part 7, Ch1, para 070153 DMG

110 *Caisse nationale des prestations familiales v Hiddal and Bernard*, C-216/12 and C-217/12 held that a parental leave allowance was a family benefit under EU Reg 1408/71.
111 Arts 16 and 17 UK-IC

10. **Tax credits**
112 Reg 4 TC(R) Regs
113 Reg 2(1) TC(R) Regs
114 Regs 3, 5 and 6 TC(R) Regs
115 s3(5A) TCA 2002
116 s143(1)(b) SSCBA 1992; *RK v HMRC (CHB)* [2015] UKUT 357 (AAC), reported as [2016] AACR 4; *JL v HMRC (CHB)* [2017] UKUT 193 (AAC); *RI v HMRC (TC)* [2019] UKUT 306 (AAC)
117 CCM 20090, 20160 and 20170; TCTM 09374 and 09376
118 TCM 0288580; see also *GC v CHMRC (TC)* [2014] UKUT 251 (AAC)

Part 6

European co-ordination rules and international agreements

Chapter 16

European Union co-ordination rules

This chapter covers:

This chapter describes how European Union (EU) social security co-ordination rules can affect your entitlement to benefits, including helping you to satisfy the entitlement conditions for UK benefits and tax credits if you have moved from a European Economic Area (EEA) state to the UK, and to continue being paid, or make a new claim for, UK benefits and tax credits after you, or a member of your family, go to live in an EEA state.

The residence and presence conditions for the individual benefits that affect your entitlement while you are in Great Britain are covered in Part 4, and the rules that affect your entitlement to individual benefits if you go abroad are covered in Part 5.

If you are not a British or Irish citizen, check Part 3 first because your immigration status may exclude you from the benefit or tax credit you want to claim.

1. Introduction

The phrase 'European Union (EU) co-ordination rules' is used in this *Handbook* to refer to four different pieces, or collections, of legislation, which provide broadly similar social security rights, and require broadly similar conditions to be met. However, the rules contain important differences, in terms of which people and which European countries and which benefits, are covered by each, and the ways they affect benefit entitlements. These differences are covered in this chapter.

The specific rules that apply to you can depend on your nationality, the country you have moved to or from, the date you (or, in some cases, a member of your family) moved to or from the UK, and what you have been doing in the UK or another country. How you determine which rules apply to you is also covered in this chapter.

Note:

- In this *Handbook* all references to the EEA are to be read as including Switzerland. The European Economic Area (EEA) and EU states are listed on p47.
- The phrase '**member state**', when used in the context of the co-ordination rules in this *Handbook*, means those states covered by the specific rules being referred to. The **main co-ordination rules**, and the **old co-ordination rules**, cover the UK, all EEA states plus Switzerland, the **UK–EU Protocol covers** the UK and EU states, and the UK–Ireland Convention covers the UK and Ireland. In future, the UK–EU Protocol may be extended to cover Iceland, Liechtenstein, Norway and Switzerland – check for updates if this protocol could affect you.

The co-ordination rules can affect whether you qualify for benefits in the UK. In most cases, the co-ordination rules make it easier to satisfy the UK rules (eg, by enabling you to count periods of residence, insurance and employment in another member state) towards meeting the conditions of entitlement. However, in limited circumstances the co-ordination rules can prevent you from claiming a UK benefit – eg, if the UK is not the competent state to pay that benefit. For the ways the co-ordination rules can affect whether you qualify for individual UK benefits, see Chapter 13.

The co-ordination rules can also help you to be paid a UK benefit in another member state for longer than you would be able to do under UK law alone. See Chapter 15 for the ways the co-ordination rules can help you claim, or continue to receive, individual UK benefits if you or your member of your family are in an EEA country.

Overview

The original aim of the EU co-ordination rules was to secure and promote European freedom of movement, by ensuring that those covered by the rules do not lose out on social security protection because they move between EEA member states. The rules do not seek to harmonise the social security systems of individual states – their sole objective is to co-ordinate the different social security schemes.

Changes due to the UK leaving the European Union

The UK left the EU on 31 January 2020. However, the main EU co-ordination rules, and the European caselaw that has interpreted their meaning, together with other parts of EU law relating to European free movement, continued to apply to the UK as if it was still an EEA state until the end of the transition period.

Transition period

The transition period (also called the 'implementation period') was the period from the UK leaving the EU at 11pm on 31 January 2020 to 11pm on 31 December 2020.[1] During the transition period, in general, all EU, and EU-derived, legislation and caselaw, including the EU co-ordination rules, continued to have effect as before the UK left the EU.[2] For the purposes of the EU co-ordination rules, during the transition period, all references to the EEA were treated as if they included references to the UK, and any references to an EEA national or EU citizen were treated as if they included references to a UK national.[3]

From the end of the transition period, in general, the main EU co-ordination rules ceased to apply within UK law.[4] However, the Withdrawal Agreements provide protections for people in certain situations to continue to be able to use these co-ordination rules (see p356). For people not covered by these Withdrawal Agreement protections, a new UK–EU Protocol on Social Security may apply from the end of the transition period, providing more limited co-ordination of social security. For people moving between the UK and Ireland, a new bilateral agreement, the UK–Ireland Convention on Social Security, came into force from the end of the transition period and is intended to maintain broadly the same level of co-ordination as under the main co-ordination rules between these two countries.

From the end of the transition period, there are four sets of rules that may apply.

- The **main co-ordination rules**[5] can continue for EEA nationals and British citizens (and family members of either) covered by the **Withdrawal Agreement protections.** In broad terms, these protections may apply if, on 31 December 2020, your situation involved both an EEA state and the UK – eg, if on that date you were an EEA national living and working in the UK or a British citizen living and working in an EEA state. For people who remain covered by the main co-ordination rules, they apply as if the UK were still a member of the EEA.
- The **old co-ordination rules**[6] can continue for those covered by the **Withdrawal Agreement protections**, in limited circumstances, mainly for claims made before June 2012 and non-EEA (and non-British) nationals.
- A new **Social Security Protocol** was agreed between the UK and EU in December 2020. This protocol mirrors the structure of the main co-ordination rules (see p353), but only applies to the UK and EU states and provides more limited social security co-ordination after the end of the transition period for those not covered by Withdrawal Agreement protections.

- A new **UK–Ireland Convention on Social Security** was agreed in February 2019. This convention mirrors the structure of the main co-ordination rules (see p353) and broadly reproduces their principles and effects but is limited to the UK and Ireland and to specified benefits of each country. It was brought into force from the end of the transition period.[7]

For details on who is covered by each of the four sets of rules, see p355. For details of the benefits covered by each of the sets of rules, see p363. **Note:** the UK leaving the EU also affects residence rights – see p164.

How to check whether the co-ordination rules apply

To check whether and how the co-ordination rules apply to you, work through the following steps:

- **Step one:** check whether you are covered by Withdrawal Agreement protections (see p356).
- **Step two:** check which rules, if any, of the four sets of co-ordination rules (listed above)you are covered by. If you are covered by Withdrawal Agreement protections, it is likely to be the main co-ordination rules (see p357) but it could be the old co-ordination rules (see p359). If you are not covered by Withdrawal Agreement protections, check whether you are covered by the UK–EU Protocol (see p359). If your situation only involves the UK and Ireland, check whether you are (as well or instead) covered by the UK–Ireland Convention (see p358).
- **Step three:** check whether the particular benefit you want to claim is covered by the co-ordination rules, and into which category the benefit falls (see p363).
- **Step four:** check which state is the 'competent state' to pay the benefit you are claiming (see p369).
- **Step five:** check the principle you want to apply – eg, the aggregation principle or exporting benefits (see below for a list and links to each principle).
- **Step six:** check how that principle can affect your entitlement to an individual benefit while you are in the UK (see the section on 'EU co-ordination rules' at the end of each specific benefit in Chapter 13) or allows you to be paid that benefit when you or a member of your family are in a member state (see the section on 'EU co-ordination rules' at the end of each specific benefit in Chapter 15).

  Note:
- You may be entitled to benefit under UK social security legislation and not need to rely on co-ordination rules. Check the individual benefit rules in Chapter 13 if you want to be paid in the UK, or Chapter 15 if you want to be paid a benefit when you or a member of your family are in an EEA country.
- In many circumstances, the co-ordination rules can help you be entitled to benefit, or be paid benefit longer if you or a member of your family go abroad,

but they can also prevent you being entitled to some UK benefits – eg, if the UK is not your 'competent state'.

The co-ordination principles

The following principles are contained in the main co-ordination rules in relation to the EEA and UK, in the UK–EU Protocol in relation to the EU and UK, and in the UK–Ireland Convention, in relation to Ireland and the UK.

- **The single state principle.** You can generally only claim a particular category of benefit from one state at any one time. The state responsible for paying your benefit is referred to as the 'competent state' (see p369).
- **Equal treatment of people.** Discrimination on the grounds of nationality in terms of access to, or the rate of payment of, the benefits that are covered is prohibited (see p381).
- **Equal treatment of benefits, income, facts and events.** If receipt of a benefit, or a fact or an event, has a legal consequence in one state, this must be recognised in the same way by other member states (see p382).
- **Aggregation.** Periods of residence, insurance and employment in any of the member states can be used towards entitlement to benefit in another (see p383).
- **Exportability of certain benefits.** You can continue to be paid certain benefits abroad if you go to another of the states. These rules generally mean that you can be paid your UK benefit if you go to another member state for longer than under the UK rules (see p385).
- **Administrative co-operation.** Member states undertake to co-operate in the administration of the co-ordination rules.

There are exceptions to these general principles for specific categories of benefits and, in some cases, there are more detailed provisions on how the above principles should apply in certain circumstances

Legal sources of the co-ordination rules

The main co-ordination rules

Article 48 of the Treaty on the Functioning of the European Union (TFEU) requires the European Parliament and the Council of Ministers to make such rules in the field of social security:

> 'as are necessary to provide freedom of movement for workers; to this end, they shall make arrangements to secure for employed and self-employed migrant workers and their dependants:
> (a) aggregation, for the purpose of acquiring and retaining the right to benefit and of calculating the amount of benefit, of all periods taken into account under the laws of the several countries;
> (b) payment of benefits to persons resident in the territories of Member States.'

Under this article, the following further legislation has been made.

- **EU Regulation 883/2004** sets out the rules for co-ordinating the different social security systems of the various EU states. The structure of this regulation is as follows.
  - **Preamble.** This contains numbered 'recitals' that explain the purpose of the regulation and the principles it contains. These recitals can be used as an aid to interpret the subsequent articles.
  - **General Provisions.** Article 1 contains important definitions. Article 2 explains the 'personal scope' of the regulation (the people to whom it applies – see p355). Article 3 sets out the 'material scope' (the categories of benefits to which the regulation applies – see p363). Articles 4 to 10 contain the general principles of the regulation.
  - **Determination of the Legislation Applicable.** Articles 11 to 16 contain the general rules for working out which is the competent state (see p369).
  - **Special Provisions Concerning the Various Categories of Benefits.** Articles 17 to 70 contain more specific rules for different categories of benefits and are divided into chapters – one for each category of benefits.
  - **Administrative Commission and Advisory Committee.** Articles 71 to 75 establish organisations to oversee and implement the working of the regulation.
  - **Miscellaneous Provisions.** Articles 76 to 86 contain various rules on practical issues of administration.
  - **Transitional and Final Provisions.** Articles 87 to 91 provide for the implementation of the regulation and transitional measures.
  - **Annexes.** These contain further rules, most of which concern specific rules for individual member states.
- **EU Regulation 987/2009** contains procedures for implementing EU Regulation 883/2004.

The main co-ordination rules were converted into UK law from the end of the transition period (11pm, 31 December 2020).[8] In general, these rules were then immediately revoked and, therefore, ceased to apply to the UK from the end of the transition period.[9] However, for people covered by the **Withdrawal Agreement** protections (see p356), the co-ordination rules continue to form part of UK law and continue to apply in the same way as they did before the end of the transition period.[10] In addition, the provisions relating to aggregation of national insurance contributions for entitlement to, and uprating of, UK retirement pensions were saved and continue to apply.[11]

The old co-ordination rules

EU Regulation 883/2004 is the successor to **Regulation 1408/71**, which (together with its implementing regulation, EU Regulation 574/72) came into force on 1 April 1973 and is referred to in this *Handbook* as the **'old co-ordination rules'**. The current co-ordination rules build on these, taking into account developments in European caselaw and national legislation to modernise and simplify the rules and to extend their personal scope (see below).[12] However, the old co-ordination rules have not been repealed and continue to apply to limited groups of people (see p359). Since the majority of claims are now determined under the current co-ordination rules, this *Handbook* only covers current rules. For further information on the old co-ordination rules, see the 2012/13 edition of CPAG's *Welfare Benefits and Tax Credits Handbook*.

The UK–Ireland Convention on Social Security

The UK–Ireland Convention on Social Security was agreed in February 2019. It was brought into force from the end of the transition period (11pm on 31 December 2020).[13] The convention broadly mirrors the above structure of the main EU co-ordination rules and broadly reproduces their principles and effects but is limited to the UK and Ireland, to specified benefits of each country, and, in most cases, to nationals of each country.

The UK–EU Protocol on Social Security Co-ordination

The UK–EU Protocol on Social Security Co-ordination was agreed in December 2020 and forms part of the Trade and Co-operation Agreement between the UK and EU. The protocol was brought into force from the end of the transition period (11pm on 31 December 2020).[14] It broadly mirrors the above structure of the main EU co-ordination rules and broadly reproduces their principles and effects. However, the protocol is more limited. It only applies to the UK and EU states (not Iceland, Norway, Liechtenstein or Switzerland), covers fewer categories of benefits, and does not apply the principles to as many categories of benefits as the main co-ordination rules.

2. Who is covered

This *Handbook* refers to you being 'covered by the co-ordination rules' if you are covered by one of the sets of rules that co-ordinate the social security systems throughout the European Economic Area (EEA) and UK. However, there are four different sets of co-ordinating rules that could apply and it can be important to identify which, if any, you are covered by as some of the specific provisions are different. If more than one set of rules appears to apply to you, in general, you will be covered by the main co-ordinatuion rules (exceptions to this are noted when they arise). Check which rules apply by working through the following steps.

Step 1: are you covered by Withdrawal Agreement protections? These can apply if on (or in some circumstances, before) 31 December 2020, you were an EEA national living in the UK, or a British citizen living in an EEA country, or you are a member of the family of either. For the details of who is covered, see below. The Withdrawal Agreement protections mean the **main co-ordination rules** are available to you, so next you need to check whether you are covered by the main co-ordination rules (see p357). The Withdrawal Agreement protections can also mean that the **old co-ordination rules** are available to you. These rules could apply to you if either you have been receiving benefit under them since before June 2012, or you are a non-EEA (and non-British) national and, before the end of 2020, your circumstances involved both the UK and an EEA state. For details of the old co-ordination rules, see p359.

Step 2: are you covered by the UK–Ireland Convention? That can apply if you are (or you are a member of the family of) an Irish or British citizen, or a refugee, and live in either Ireland or the UK (see p358).

Step 3: are you covered by the UK–European Union (EU) Protocol? That can apply if you have only moved between the UK and the EU since the end of 2020, or if, for another reason, the other co-ordination rules do not apply (see p359).

Note: If you are covered by both the main co-ordination rules and the UK–Ireland Convention, you can rely on whichever is the more generous.[15]

Withdrawal Agreement protections

Since the end of the transition period, you can only be covered by the main co-ordination rules (or, in limited circumstances, the old co-ordination rules) if you covered by Withdrawal Agreement protections.

You have Withdrawal Agreement protections if, at the end of the transition period (31 December 2020), you were:[16]

- an EEA national 'subject to the legislation' (see p360) of the UK – eg, a Polish national working in the UK; *or*
- a UK national 'subject to the legislation' of an EEA state; *or*
- an EEA national 'subject to the legislation' of an EEA state while residing in the UK – eg, a French national living in the UK receiving a French social security benefit; *or*
- a UK national 'subject to the legislation' of the UK while residing in an EEA state; *or*
- a refugee or stateless person residing in the UK or an EEA state and 'subject to the legislation' of the UK or an EEA state; *or*
- a member of the family (see p361) or survivor of one of the above categories; *or*
- if none of the above apply, you are an EEA national with an EU free movement right to reside in the UK (see p171) or a UK national with an EU free movement right to reside in an EEA state; *or*
- a family member (see p220) of a person in the groups in the above bullet point.

Note:

- If one or more of the above groups applies to you, the main co-ordination rules (or, in limited circumstances, the old co-ordination rules) are potentially available to you. You, therefore, need to check whether you are covered by the main co-ordination rules (see below) (or, in limited circumstances, the old co-ordination rules – see p359). **Note:** although the criteria for who is covered by the main co-ordination rules are similar to the circumstances in the first six bullets above, the criteria are not exactly the same and will not apply in all cases.

- The Withdrawal Agreement protections continue to apply and, therefore, you can potentially be covered by the main co-ordination rules (or, in limited circumstances, the old co-ordination rules) for as long as:
  - (if you are covered by one of the last two bullets), you continue to have a free movement right to reside, or a right to work, as an EEA national in the UK, or a British citizen in an EEA country, or you continue to be a family member of a person who does;[17] *or*
  - (if you are covered by one of the first six bullets) you continue 'without interruption' to be in one of the situations listed[18] – eg, you continue to be an EEA national residing and working or claiming social security benefits in the UK or a British citizen residing and working or claiming social security benefits in an EEA country. Until new caselaw is established on the meaning of an 'interruption' to your situation, it may be relevant to refer to the caselaw on the meaning of the 'relevant situation remains unchanged', which can determine when the new co-ordination rules apply in place of the old (see p359). If you cease to be in one of the situations listed in the first six bullet points, but you are covered by one of the last two bullet points, the Withdrawal Agreement protections continue for as long as you have a free movement right to reside.
- Guidance produced jointly by the Department for Work and Pensions (DWP) and HM Revenue and Customs (and the Department of Health and Social Care) sets out examples of situations in which EEA and British citizens have Withdrawal Agreement protections. As this guidance was written in November 2020, it does not include references to the UK–EU Protocol (which was agreed on 24 December 2020), but does briefly cover the UK–Ireland Convention.[19]

Who is covered by the main co-ordination rules

Since the end of the transition period (31 December 2020 – see p350), you can only be covered by the main co-ordination rules if the Withdrawal Agreement protections apply to you (see above). If these protections apply to you, or for a period before the end of the transition period, you are covered by the main co-ordination rules if you fall within the range of people to whom they apply. That is known as the **'personal scope'** of these co-ordination rules.

In addition, your situation must involve either the UK and one or more EEA states or at least two EEA states. That generally means that you must have moved between an EEA state and the UK (or another EEA state), or you live in one and work in another, or you live in one and are the national of another.[20]

Note: Until the end of the transition period, the UK was treated as an EEA member state for the purpose of these co-ordination rules, and continues to be so treated for people covered by Withdrawal Agreement protections.

You are within the 'personal scope' of the main co-ordination rules if:[21]

- you are:
  - an EEA national; *or*
  - a British citizen; *or*
  - a refugee; *or*
  - a stateless person; *and*
- you are residing in the UK or an EEA state and you have been 'subject to the legislation of' one or more EEA states or the UK (see p360); *or*
- you are a member of the family (see p361) or a survivor of someone covered in the above bullet point. **Note:** the old co-ordination rules defined 'survivor' in terms of national legislation, so in the UK it meant a widow, widower or surviving civil partner.[22] However, there is no definition in the main co-ordination rules, so it might be possible to argue a wider meaning could apply.

If you are covered by the main co-ordination rules, check whether the benefit you are claiming or want to claim is covered by the co-ordination rules (see p363) and then check which state is the 'competent state' for that benefit (see p369).

Who is covered by the UK–Ireland Convention on Social Security

You are covered by the UK–Ireland Convention on Social Security if you come within the range of people to whom it applies. That is known as the **'personal scope'** of this convention.

In addition, your situation must involve both the UK and Ireland. That generally means that you have moved between the two states, or you live in one and work in the other, or you live in one and are the national of another.

You are within the 'personal scope' of the UK–Ireland Convention on Social Security, if:[23]

- you are:
  - an Irish citizen; *or*
  - a British citizen; *or*
  - a refugee; *or*
  - a stateless person; *and*
- you are residing in the UK or Ireland and you are or have been 'subject to the legislation of' the UK or Ireland (see p360); *or*
- you are a member of the family (see p361) or a survivor of someone covered in the above bullet point. 'Survivor' is defined as a surviving spouse or civil partner or child to whom a survivor's benefit or death grant is payable under Irish, or (not including for a child) UK, legislation.[24]

Note: If you are covered by both UK–Ireland Convention and the main co-ordination rules (which would require you to be covered by Withdrawal Agreement protections), you can rely on whichever is the more generous.[25]

Who is covered by the UK–EU Protocol

You are covered by the UK–EU Protocol if you are or have been 'subject to the legislation of' (see p360) the UK or an EU state, or you are the 'member of the family' (see p361) or survivor (not defined) of someone who has.[26]

In addition, your situation must involve either the UK and one or more EU states or at least two EU states. That generally means that you must have moved between an EU state and the UK (or another EU state), or you live in one and work in another, or you live in one but are the national of another.[27]

Note:

- You can be covered by the protocol regardless of your nationality. The protocol simply applies to 'persons, including stateless persons and refugees' who satisfy the above requirements.[28]
- The protocol is between the UK and the EU. Unlike the main EU co-ordination rules, the protocol does not extend to Iceland, Liechtenstein, Norway and Switzerland. At the time of writing, the UK government was seeking to put in place similar provisions on a reciprocal basis with the EEA states and Switzerland, and had done so on an interim basis with Norway and Switzerland.[29]

When the old co-ordination rules apply

If you are covered by the Withdrawal Agreement protections, in the vast majority of situations the main co-ordination rules[30] will be the rules most likely to apply to you. However, the old co-ordination rules[31] (see p353) can apply if the following applies to you.

- You are receiving a benefit because you claimed it before the main rules came into force.[32] That depends on your nationality (see the relevant dates below). However, if you claimed your benefit before the main rules came into force but did not need to rely on co-ordination rules until after that date (eg, when moving between states), the main rules apply.[33] If the old rules apply to you, they continue to do so during a transitional period of up to 10 years, provided your 'relevant situation remains unchanged'.[34] This question is decided by the state administering your benefit claim, with reference to its national social security legislation.[35] What amounts to a change in your 'relevant situation' that brings you under the main co-ordination rules depends on your circumstances. In one case, a change was making a 'renewal' claim for disability living allowance (DLA) after the relevant date (see below);[36] in another case, a change was moving to another EEA country after the relevant date.[37] However, in one case, the Upper Tribunal held that the old rules continued to apply because the claimant started employment in another EEA country *before* the relevant date and so moving there *after* the relevant date was not a relevant change.[38] The transitional period is intended to protect anyone who might otherwise lose benefit under the main rules. However, you can ask to be transferred and considered under the main rules if that would be better for you. If so, the main rules take effect from the start of the following month.[39] **Note:** it is possible that the old co-ordination rules applied to you and then, subsequently, the main rules applied, so a decision maker or First-tier Tribunal may need to consider both.[40]

- You are a non-EEA (and non-British) national (other than a refugee or member of the family of an EEA or British citizen who is covered by the main rules) who is legally resident in an EEA country or the UK.[41]
- You must have been employed or self-employed and subject to the legislation of an EEA state or the UK because you have paid (or should have paid) national insurance (NI) contributions, or a student and subject to the legislation of the UK or an EEA state. You continue to be covered by the old co-ordination rules if the UK is one of the states where you have legally resided. That is because the UK obtained an opt-out, allowing it not to extend the main rules to nationals of non-EEA states.[42]

Relevant dates

The main co-ordination rules apply to nationals (and members of their family) of:[43]

– the EU member states (and refugees and stateless people) from 1 May 2010;

– Switzerland from 1 April 2012;

– Iceland, Liechtenstein and Norway from 1 June 2012.

As very few claims are now determined under the old current co-ordination rules, this *Handbook* does not cover these. For further information on the old co-ordination rules, see the 2012/13 edition of CPAG's *Welfare Benefits and Tax Credits Handbook.*

Common terms

'Subject to the legislation'

The requirement that you (or the person whose family you are a member of) have been 'subject to a legislation of' one of the states to which the relevant co-ordination rules applies is essential to being covered by those rules. The meaning of the phrase is broadly the same for each of the co-ordination rules, but may be narrower under the UK–EU Protocol.

'Subject to the legislation of'

You have been **'subject to the legislation of'** a state if you have worked in and paid (or should have paid) the equivalent of NI contributions to that state, or you have paid contributions to that state on interest from assets,[44] or you have received any social security benefit (see p363) or special non-contributory benefit (see p367) from that state. You may also be subject to the legislation if you are potentially eligible for any social security benefit or special non-contributory benefit.

'Legislation' is defined as the legislation of each member state relating to the 'social security branches covered', (or under the convention: the benefits specified), in the relevant set of co-ordination rules.[45]

The benefits referred to in this definition include UK benefits that are intended to assist you in the event of one of the risks covered by the co-ordination rules (see p363).[46] Under the main co-ordination rules and the UK–Ireland Convention, examples include attendance allowance (AA), DLA, personal independence payment (PIP), carer's allowance (CA), child benefit and child tax credit.

None of these depend on your being an employee or self-employed at any time. Potentially, therefore, even if you have never worked, including in some circumstances if you are a child, you can be covered by these co-ordination rules. DWP guidance confirms that the personal scope of the main co-ordination rules includes non-economically active people.[47]

Member of the family

A member of the family of someone covered by the each of the co-ordination rules can also rely on, and be affected by, the rules that cover that person (which can vary depending on which rules they are covered by and the type of benefit claimed).[48]

'Member of the family' is defined in broadly the same way in each of the co-ordination rules (see below). However, note that this definition is different to the definition of a 'family member' within free movement residence rights law (see p218). Note, also, the definition can be affected by national social security legislation so can vary among member states.

Note: as economically inactive people, including in some circumstances children, are covered under the main co-ordination rules and the UK–Ireland Convention, and possibly the UK–EU Protocol, you may be covered directly and may not need to rely on being a member of someone else's family. If you are both a member of the family of a person covered by the rules and also covered by the rules yourself, you can usually rely on either coverage. **Note:** the consequences of being a member of someone's family are not always favourable – eg, if it changes which state is competent to pay your benefit (see p369).

Member of the family

You are a '**member of the family**' of a person covered by the co-ordination rules if you are:[49]

- defined or recognised as a member of the family, or designated as a member of the household, by the legislation under which benefits are provided; *or*

- if the legislation under which benefits are provided does not make a distinction between the members of the family and other people to whom it applies, the covered person's spouse or child who is either under the age of majority (18 in England, Wales and Northern Ireland; 16 in Scotland) or older but dependent on the person covered

If, under the legislation in either bullet point above, you are only considered to be a member of the family or member of the household if you are living in the same household as the person, this condition is considered to be satisfied if you are mainly dependent on her/him.

The 'legislation under which benefits are provided' in the above definition covers the legislation providing for the particular benefit you are claiming. Although it may be arguable that a broader category of social security legislation should apply, that has not been accepted to date.

Upper Tribunal decisions

In a case concerning child benefit, the Upper Tribunal found that the relevant legislation was the child benefit legislation and held that the claimant's niece and nephew living in a different EU state did not count as members of the claimant's family.[50] Although this case concerned the old co-ordination rules, it was cited in support of a more recent child benefit decision in which the Upper Tribunal held that the claimant's stepson, for whom it was accepted the claimant was responsible, was not a member of the claimant's family under the main co-ordination rules because the stepson was not the claimant's biological child.[51]

In a case concerning DLA for a child, the Upper Tribunal found that the relevant legislation was the DLA legislation and therefore held that the claimant's sister did not count as a member of his family. However, that did not affect his entitlement because he was covered by the main co-ordination rules himself.[52]

In a case concerning CA, the Upper Tribunal found that the relevant legislation was the CA legislation and since that does not define any particular people as members of the family or household, the claimant's spouse was held to be a member of the family, despite being separated and living in another EEA state.[53]

Note: if you are claiming 'sickness benefits' (eg, AA, CA, DLA care component and PIP daily living component), in limited circumstances a slightly different definition of member of the family member can be relevant under the main co-ordination rules, and rules can apply to determine whether your rights as a member of the family, or any independent rights you have, take priority (see p374).

3. Which benefits are covered

The benefits to which the co-ordination rules apply are referred to as being within the **'material scope'** of the rules.

Each of the rules refer to categories of benefits designed to cover certain 'risks', such as 'old age' or 'maternity'. The UK–Ireland Convention lists the benefits of each state considered to assist with each risk.[54] Under the main co-ordination rules and the UK–European Union (EU) Protocol, most benefits are not specified in the legislation, but member states are required to list the benefits considered to assist with each risk, and those are published by the EU.[55] However, the categorisation of a benefit can be challenged, because ultimately categorisation depends on the benefit's characteristics rather than on how an individual state lists the benefit.

Benefits are also divided into the following types, depending on the conditions of eligibility:

- social security benefits (see below);
- (except under the UK–Ireland Convention) special non-contributory benefits (see p367);
- social and medical assistance (social assistance under the UK–Ireland Convention) (see p368).

Those benefits categorised as social security benefits have the most rights. Special non-contributory benefits provide fewer rights under the main co-ordination rules and are not covered under the UK–EU Protocol. Social and medical assistance is not covered by the co-ordination rules, and the UK–Ireland Convention only covers social assistance in relation to recovery of overpayments.

Social security benefits

Social security benefits are categorised according to the risk against which they are designed to provide financial protection.[56]

The main co-ordination rules and the UK–EU Protocol do not list the benefits that assist with each risk within the legislation, but the UK–Ireland Convention does.[57]

The table below lists the benefits that are accepted as categorised for each risk under the main co-ordination rules (with disputes noted), and the benefits listed in the UK–Ireland Convention. Under the UK–EU Protocol, benefit categorisation should follow that of the main co-ordination rules, unless the protocol specifically provides otherwise. The UK–EU Protocol is the only set of rules that lists benefits that are *not* covered.

The UK–EU Protocol does not apply to:[58]

- family benefits;

- long-term care benefits. These are listed as attendance allowance (AA), disability living allowance (DLA) care component, personal independence payment (PIP) daily living component, carer's allowance (CA), carer's allowance supplement and young carer grant;[59]
- winter fuel or cold weather payments;
- special non-contributory benefits (see p367);
- social and medical assistance (see p368).

Risk	*UK benefits listed under main co-ordination rules*	*UK benefit listed under UK–Ireland Convention*
Sickness	AA DLA care component PIP daily living component CA Carer's allowance supplement (Scotland) Young carer grant (Scotland) Child disability payment (Scotland) care component Statutory sick pay Contributory employment and support allowance (ESA) in the assessment phase (but see below)	Contributory ESA in the assessment phase
Long-term care benefits	Treated as sickness benefits[60]	AA DLA care component PIP daily living component) CA (and see below)
Maternity and paternity	Maternity allowance (MA) Statutory maternity, adoption, paternity and shared parental pay (but see below)	MA

Invalidity	AA, DLA care and mobility components and CA if you were in receipt of benefit before 1 June 1992. If you claimed after this date, see the note below. Long-term incapacity benefit Severe disablement allowance Contributory ESA after the assessment phase Arguably, contributory ESA during the assessment phase (see below)	Contributory ESA after the assessment phase
Old age	State pension Category A, B and D retirement pensions Additional pension Graduated retirement benefit Winter fuel payments Increments – eg, to pensions Increases of retirement pension for an adult Age addition in pensions	State retirement pension
Pre-retirement	None	None
Survivors	Bereavement benefits	Widowed mother's allowance Widow's pension Widowed parent's allowance
Death grants	Bereavement support payment (lump-sum payment)	Bereavement support payment

Accidents at work and occupational diseases	Industrial injuries disablement benefit Constant attendance allowance Exceptionally severe disablement allowance Reduced earnings allowance Retirement allowance	Industrial injuries benefits
Unemployment	Contribution-based jobseeker's allowance (JSA)	Contribution-based JSA
Family benefits (see p386)	Child benefit Guardian's allowance Child tax credit (CTC) Increases in other benefits for an adult or a child Scottish child payment	Child benefit Guardian's allowance CTC

Note:

- If you have a long-term or permanent disability, it is arguable that contributory ESA during the assessment phase, as well as after, should be regarded as an invalidity benefit.[61] Under the main co-ordination rules and the UK–Ireland Convention, in most cases, whether it is classed as an invalidity benefit or a sickness benefit makes no difference to whether you can 'export' contributory ESA. However, under the UK–EU Protocol you cannot export invalidity benefits (see p385).
- The DWP has considered statutory maternity, adoption, paternity and shared parental pay to be pay rather than social security or special non-contributory benefits.[62] However, it is strongly arguable that these benefits should be classed as maternity and paternity benefits or family benefits (see also p340).[63]
- The Department for Work and Pensions (DWP) considers universal credit (UC) to be neither a social security nor a special non-contributory benefit and so the co-ordination rules do not apply to UC.[64] It is arguable that UC should be listed as a social security benefit – eg, the child elements are arguably a family benefit. Get specialist advice if you want to make this argument. Note UC is listed as 'social assistance' in the UK–Ireland Convention (see p368).

Disability and carer's benefits

Under the **main co-ordination rules**, AA, DLA care component, PIP daily living component and CA are categorised as sickness benefits. However, these benefits have been categorised as assisting with different risks at different times. Under the old co-ordination rules and then the main co-ordination rules, these benefits were categorised as invalidity benefits until 1 June 1992. They were then categorised as special non-contributory benefits until that was held to be wrong and they were then re-categorised as sickness benefits.[65] The Court of Justice of the European Union has reconfirmed that DLA care component should be categorised as a sickness, not an invalidity, benefit.[66] For the relevance of the changing categorisations on whether you can be paid one of these benefits in an European Economic Area state, see p330.

The mobility component of DLA continues to be listed as a special non-contributory benefit and that has been held to be lawful.[67] The mobility component of PIP is accepted as a special non-contributory benefit (see below), and it is expected that the mobility component of child disability payment will be as well.

Young carer's grant and carer's allowance supplement have been classified as 'cash sickness benefits' by the EU Administrative Commission and that has been accepted by the Scottish government.[68]

The **UK–Ireland Convention** categorises AA, DLA care component, PIP daily living component and CA as long-term care benefits, but then treats them in broadly the same way as sickness benefits are treated under the main co-ordination rules.[69] Although the young carer grant and carer's allowance supplement are not listed under the convention, the regulations enable you to make a new claim for either payment while resident in Ireland in certain circumstances if you are covered by the convention (see p285).[70]

The **UK–EU Protocol** categorises AA, DLA care component, PIP daily living component, CA, carer's allowance supplement and young carer's grant as long-term care benefits, and the mobility components of DLA and PIP as special non-contributory benefits, and lists both categories as ones to which the protocol does not apply.[71]

Special non-contributory benefits

The **main EU co-ordination rules** and the **UK–EU Protocol** define 'special non-contributory benefits' as:[72]

- intended to provide supplementary or ancillary cover against the risks on p363 and guarantee a minimum subsistence income, or provide specific protection for disabled people closely linked to a person's social environment in the state concerned; *and*
- funded solely from general taxation and do not depend on having made contributions as a condition of entitlement; *and*
- listed as such by each state in an annex to main legislation. The UK benefits listed are below.

In the main EU co-ordination rules, the UK government has only listed pension credit (PC), income-based JSA, income-related ESA and the mobility component of DLA as special non-contributory benefits.[73] However, the UK government has applied for the mobility component of PIP to be listed and that has been agreed by the Administrative Commission for the co-ordination of social security systems, but the listing of PIP has been delayed. Consequently, and since it satisfies all the other conditions, the Upper Tribunal recently held that the mobility component of PIP is a special non-contributory benefit.[74] In any case, the DWP has been treating the mobility component of PIP as such.[75] The UK–EU Protocol lists the mobility component of PIP as a special non-contributory benefit. It is expected that the mobility component of child disability payment (due to be introduced in Scotland in 2021) will also be treated as a special non-contributory benefit. Income-related ESA replaced income support (IS) in the list from 28 June 2012.

Special non-contributory benefits under main co-ordination rules	*Special non-contributory benefits under UK–EU Protocol*
Income-related ESA	Income-based JSA
Income-based JSA	PC
PC	DLA mobility component
DLA mobility component	PIP mobility component
PIP mobility component	Best Start grants
	Best Start foods payment
	Funeral support payment

The **main co-ordination rules** state that special non-contributory benefits can only be paid in the state in which you are 'resident'[76] (see p371 for details of when you count as resident). However, although you cannot 'export' special non-contributory benefits, all the other co-ordination principles apply.[77]

In contrast, under the **UK–EU Protocol**, *none* of the principles apply because the protocol lists special non-contributory benefits as benefits to which the protocol does not apply.[78]

The **UK–Ireland Convention** does not refer to special non-contributory benefits at all, but defines the three means-tested benefits as 'social assistance' (see below), and does not refer to the others at all.

Social and medical assistance

Under the **main co-ordination rules** and the **UK-EU Protocol**, benefits which are neither 'social security' nor 'special non-contributory' benefits are considered to be social assistance and are excluded from the co-ordination rules.[79]

The UK does not specify which benefits it considers to be social assistance under either legislation but has made it clear that the UK does not consider UC to be either a social security or a special non-contributory benefit.[80]

It has also been decided that housing benefit[81] and working tax credit[82] are not social security or special non-contributory benefits. It is likely that the UK government might argue that IS is now also outside the scope of the EU co-ordination rules, since the removal of IS from the list of special non-contributory benefits on 28 June 2012.

Under the **UK–Ireland Convention**, 'social assistance' is defined in relation to UK benefits as UC, PC, IS, income-related ESA and income-based JSA.[83] The only provisions made by the convention for 'social assistance' relate to the recovery of overpayments. If you, or members of your family, have received social assistance in the UK while you were entitled to that assistance under Irish legislation, the convention provides for the UK to request that the Irish benefit authorities recover this 'overpayment' from ongoing payments of the Irish benefit and then forward that to the UK (and vice versa).[84]

4. Principles of co-ordination

The co-ordination rules set out several general principles (see p353). These principles are often the starting point in deciding how the co-ordination rules affect your entitlement.[85] However, there are exceptions to these principles for specific categories of benefits and, in some cases, there are more detailed provisions on how the principles should apply in certain circumstances. The following information provides an overview of the principles, because it is beyond the scope of this *Handbook* to cover all the exceptions and additional provisions in detail. You should, therefore, get specialist advice about the way in which the co-ordination rules apply to your particular circumstances.

The single competent state

In general, under each of the co-ordination rules you can only claim a particular category of benefit from one member state and are only liable to pay national insurance (NI) contributions (or their equivalent) to one state at any one time. That is expressed as the general principle that you can only be subject to the legislation of a single member state.[86] **Note:** the UK–Ireland Convention refers to the 'parties' of the UK and Ireland rather than 'states', and 'competent party' rather than 'competent state' but the same principle applies.

The competent state and competent institution

The **'competent state'** is the state responsible for paying your benefit and to which you must pay NI contributions. It is the state in which the 'competent institution' is situated.[87] The **'competent institution'** is broadly the institution responsible for paying your benefit and to which you are liable to pay NI contributions.[88] In the UK, the competent institutions are the Department for Work and Pensions (DWP) and HM Revenue and Customs.

The general rule is that the **competent state** is the one in which you are:[89]

- employed or self-employed (see the note below);
- a civil servant;
- (other than for the UK–European Union (EU) Protocol) resident while receiving an unemployment benefit under specific provisions;[90] *or*
- (other than for the UK–EU Protocol) a conscripted member of the armed forces or someone doing compulsory civilian service.

If none of the above bullet points apply, the competent state is the state in which you are 'resident' (see below for how this is determined). However, sometimes other co-ordination rules may mean that a different state is deemed competent (see p374).[91] In particular, there are exceptions for 'sickness benefits' if you (or the member of your family who brings you within the co-ordination rules) receive a pension from a state other than the one in which you reside (see p375). There are also exceptions for family benefits if you receive a pension (see p387).

Note:

- For your competent state to be determined on the basis of your employment or self-employment, your earnings do not need to exceed the threshold at which you are liable to pay NI contributions.[92]
- You are treated as still employed or self-employed if, as a result of that activity, you are receiving cash benefits (other than for the risks of old age, occupational diseases and accidents at work or, except under the UK–Ireland Convention, invalidity, sickness or being a survivor).[93]
- If you work simultaneously in the UK and one or more European Economic Area (EEA) states, you are subject to the legislation of the state of residence if you pursue a substantial part (generally, at least 25 per cent) of your activities there.[94]
- If your employer's business is normally in one state but you are sent to another to work and it is anticipated that the posting will last for no more than 24 months, you remain subject to the legislation of the first state. Similarly, if you are self-employed in one state and go to another state to pursue a similar activity as a self-employed person, you remain subject to the legislation of the first state, provided the anticipated duration of your activity in the other state is not more than 24 months.[95] Under the UK–EU Protocol you are referred to as a 'detached worker' and, at the time of writing, all the EU states had just 'opted in' to follow these rules in relation to the UK.[96]
- If you have moved to another EEA state, you may continue to be subject to the legislation of the state where you previously lived and were self-employed if you continue to be self-employed in that previous state.[97]
- If you make a claim, declaration or appeal to the institution in a state that takes the view it is not your competent state, your claim must be forwarded to the relevant institution of the state the institution considers is competent without delay. Your claim, declaration or appeal is treated as if it had been submitted to

the competent state on the date it was originally submitted.[98] For further information, including if there is a dispute between states over which is your competent state, see p372.

How residence is determined

'Residence' is defined in each of the co-ordination rules as 'the place where a person habitually resides'.[99]

Under the **UK–Ireland Convention**, this term is interpreted in accordance with the legislation of the state in which you reside.[100]

Under the **main co-ordination rules** and the **UK–EU Protocol**, the following factors should be considered when determining where you habitually reside. Although this list of factors is in a rule that explains what should be done if there is a difference of views between two states or institutions about where you are resident, it should also be used if there is no such dispute. Firstly, it should be established by common agreement where your centre of interests lies. This is based on an overall assessment of the relevant facts, including:[101]

- the duration and continuity of presence in the state(s) concerned;
- your personal situation, including:
  - the nature and specific characteristics of any activity pursued, in particular the place where such activity is habitually pursued, the stability of the activity, and the duration of any work contract;
  - your family status and family ties;
  - any unpaid activity, such as voluntary work;
  - if you are a student, the source of your income;
  - your housing situation, in particular how permanent it is;
  - the member state in which you are deemed to reside for tax purposes.

If there is still a dispute about your place of residence, your intentions should be considered, especially the reasons why you moved. That is decisive in establishing your actual place of residence.[102]

If there is a dispute between states over which is your competent state, see p372.

When the competent state changes

If you are subject to the legislation of a member state, it continues to be your competent state until a change means that another member state becomes competent.[103]

The main factors that change the competent state are if:

- you start to work in another member state;[104] *or*
- (for 'sickness' or 'family' benefits) you start to receive a 'pension' from another member state (unless you are already receiving a 'pension' in the state you are resident in);

- in some circumstances, a member of your family starts working in, or receiving a pension from, another member state;
- in some circumstances, you move to an EEA state and become resident there.

When the competent state changes can be affected by which co-ordination rules you are covered by and the category of benefit being paid. For example, if you are covered by the main co-ordination rules and are receiving a 'sickness benefit' (see below) from the UK because the UK is the competent state on the basis of your residence in the UK, and you then begin receiving a 'pension' from an EEA state (see p375), this generally means that your competent state ceases to be the UK and becomes the state that pays the pension.[105] On the other hand, if you are covered by the main co-ordination rules and are receiving a 'sickness benefit' from the UK and also a 'pension' from the UK and then you move to an EEA country, the UK remains your competent state. That was confirmed by the Upper Tribunal, which held that a woman continued to be entitled to the care component of disability living allowance (DLA) when she moved from the UK to Finland because she was receiving contributory employment and support allowance (ESA). **Note:** the same decision also held that when her entitlement to contributory ESA expired after a year, she continued to be entitled to DLA care component while living in Finland.[106]

The point at which the UK stops being responsible for paying your benefit if you move to another state is not always clear and much of the caselaw has considered the old co-ordination rules, which differ in significant respects from the main co-ordination rules (see p353).[107] Also, there is no caselaw yet on the new UK–Ireland Convention or the UK–EU Protocol. However, in general, under each of the co-ordination rules, if you continue to be entitled to a UK benefit when you move to an EEA state, the UK remains the competent state for paying that benefit until either you become employed/self-employed in the other state or, in certain circumstances, you start to receive a benefit from that state.[108] If you were self-employed in the UK and move to live in an EEA state, you may, depending on your circumstances, continue to be self-employed in the UK, in which case the UK remains your competent state.[109]

If the decision maker decides the UK is not the competent state

If, when you claim a UK benefit, the decision maker decides the UK is not the competent state to pay that benefit, s/he must, under the main co-ordination rules, forward the claim to the relevant institution in the state that is considered competent without delay, unless there is evidence that state takes a different view (see below). The date you submitted your claim (or appeal) to a state that is not competent is treated as your date of claim (or appeal) by the state that is competent.[110]

If there is a 'difference of views' between the institutions of two (or more) states on which is the competent state for paying a cash benefit or meeting the cost of a benefit in kind, while the issue is being resolved you can, if you meet the other rules of entitlement, get provisional payments from, and under the legislation of, the state in which you are resident (or, for family benefits under the UK–Ireland Convention, the child resides[111]), or (other than under the UK–Ireland Convention) the state where you first applied if you are not resident in any of the states concerned.[112]

If no agreement is reached between the states after one month, the matter can be referred to the EU Administrative Commission (under the main co-ordination rules) or the UK–EU Specialised Committee on Citizen's Rights (under the protocol) for the co-ordination of social security systems, which aims to reconcile disputes within six months.[113] The process is slightly different under the UK–Ireland Convention: an arbitration tribunal gets appointed to resolve the dispute.

If it is established that the state that made provisional payments is not the competent state, it can be reimbursed by the state that is competent (but see below).[114]

Caselaw decided under the main co-ordination rules has established the following points about provisional payments. The rules on provisional payments apply if forwarding your claim triggers a different view and also if there is evidence of a different view when the claim is received, in which case it should not be forwarded.[115] The legislation only requires there to be a 'difference of views'; legislation says nothing about the form in which the view must be expressed, nor the evidence required to prove the difference. If you have written confirmation that the institution of another state takes a different view of which state is competent, provide that to the decision maker (or tribunal).[116] However, the Court of Appeal has held that oral evidence can be accepted if it is sufficient to satisfy the decision maker (or tribunal) that two states hold different views on the issue of competence. The Court of Appeal has also confirmed that the requirement to make provisional payments is unaffected by whether a comparable benefit is paid in the other state or whether the payments would be recouped.[117]

Note: DWP guidance, which states that provisional payments need not be made if the other state does not have a similar benefit, has not been updated since the Court of Appeal decision and should not be followed.

Even if there is clear evidence of a 'difference of views', the benefit authorities do not always comply with their duty to make provisional payments, so you may need to request these in writing, and refer to the relevant legislation and caselaw.

In most cases, the issue is which state is competent to make the payment, but if there is a difference of views between states on which legislation applies, you are provisionally subject to the legislation of one state in the following order of priority:[118]

- if you only work in one state, the state where you work;
- if you either work in two or more states and live in one of them, or do not work, the state where you reside;

- (except under the UK–Ireland Protocol) in all other cases, of the states in which you work, the state to which you first applied.

Sickness benefits

Under the **main co-ordination rules**, attendance allowance (AA), DLA care component, the daily living component of personal independence payment (PIP), carer's allowance (CA), carer's allowance supplement, and the young carer grant and, it is expected, the care component of disabled child payment, are all classed as 'sickness benefits' (see p366). You are only entitled to them if the UK is the competent state for paying 'cash sickness benefits' (for the young carer grant and carer's allowance supplement, that is only a requirement if you are claiming while resident in an EEA state).[119] The UK must be the competent state to pay *your* sickness benefits. So, for example, for you to receive CA, the UK must be the competent state to pay you CA, even if there is a different competent state for paying a sickness benefit to the person for whom you care.[120]

In most cases, the competent state is determined under the general rule explained on p369.

However, if the only basis for the UK being the competent state to pay your sickness benefits is that you are resident in the UK, 'other provisions' of the co-ordination rules may mean that another state is deemed competent.[121] The 'other provisions' that arise most often are if you are claiming a 'sickness benefit' and receive a 'pension' from an EEA state other than the one where you reside (see below).

A different provision, which may change which state is competent is Article 21 of the main co-ordination rules, which provides that an insured person and members of her/his family residing or staying in a state other than the competent state shall be entitled to cash benefits provided by the competent state.[122] The Upper Tribunal held that this provision meant that the UK was not the competent state to pay CA to a woman resident in the UK because her husband (from whom she was separated but not divorced) was working and, therefore, 'insured' in the Netherlands. Since the Netherlands was his competent state, and she was a member of his family residing in another state, the Netherlands was held to be the competent state for her 'sickness' benefit.[123] Similarly, the UK was held not to be the competent state to pay the care component of DLA to a child resident in the UK with her mother who was not working, because her father was self-employed, and therefore 'insured', in Belgium. Consequently, Belgium was held to be the competent state for the child's 'sickness' benefit. The claimant's appeal to the Court of Appeal is due to be heard in April 2021.[124]

An arguably different approach to Article 21 was adopted by the Upper Tribunal, which held that this provision only applies *after* the competent state has been identified and only if that state is not the state of residence. The only circumstance in which it was suggested this could apply is if you are resident in one state and receive a pension from another – ie, if you are covered by the first exception referred to above.[125] In the further appeal from one of these cases, the Court of Appeal also took the view that Article 21 could not apply to the appellant who had claimed CA while resident in Cyprus at a time when he did not work or receive any benefits. That was because his competent state was Cyprus, as his state of residence, and furthermore he was not 'insured' (a finding not altered by his having paid sufficient NI contributions to be entitled, in future, to a UK retirement pension).[126]

Note: two linked cases on whether the claimants' competent state is affected by a member of their family being employed in another state have been due to be heard by the Upper Tribunal for a few years and it is understood they will still be heard.[127] See AskCPAG .org,uk and the *Welfare Rights Bulletin* for updates, and get specialist advice if you think this could affect your entitlement.

The **UK–Ireland Convention** categorises AA, DLA care component, PIP daily living component and CA as long-term care benefits, but then treats them in broadly the same way as sickness benefits are treated under the main co-ordination rules.[128] Although not listed under the convention, the regulations for the young carer grant and carer's allowance supplement require the UK to be the competent state if you are resident in Ireland when you make a new claim for either payment while covered by the convention (see p285).[129]

The **UK–EU Protocol** categorises AA, DLA care component, PIP daily living component, CA, carer's allowance supplement and young carer's grant as long-term care benefits, and the mobility components of DLA and PIP as special non-contributory benefits, and lists both categories as ones to which the protocol does not apply.[130]

If you or a member of your family receive a pension from a European Economic Area state

If you, or the member of your family who brings you within the **main co-ordination rules**, receive a 'pension' (see below) from an EEA (or UK) state other than the one in which you reside, the competent state for paying your cash sickness benefits is the one responsible for meeting the cost of your sickness benefits in kind – eg, in the UK, NHS treatment.[131] **Note:** although you receive sickness benefits in kind in the state where you are resident, the *cost* of these treatments can be borne by another state. This means that to work out which state is competent for paying a cash sickness benefit, you must establish which state must bear the cost of sickness benefits in kind. Various scenarios are set out on p377. It may also be helpful to refer decision makers to the main DWP guidance, *Deciding the Competent State to Pay Cash Sickness Benefits,* and the more recent guidance memos that summarise recent caselaw.[132] The guidance contains the following 'simple hierarchy' to determine which member state is the competent state:[133]

1. The state in which you are working;
2. The state from which you are receiving a pension;

3. The state in which a member of your family is working;
4. The state from which a member of your family is receiving a pension;
5. The state in which you are residing.

Note: while you should refer to this guidance if it is helpful, like all guidance it is not binding. If legislation or caselaw provides that your competent state does not follow this 'simple hierarchy', the law, rather than the guidance, must be followed.

If you are covered by the **UK–Ireland Convention** and you, or a member of your family, receives a pension, the competent state is the state:[134]

- in which you, or the member of your family who receives the pension, is employed or self-employed;
- that pays the pension if there is only one pension in payment;
- the state in which you were subject to the legislation for longest if both the UK and Ireland are paying a pension, or, if the relevant periods are the same, the state to whose legislation you (or the member of your family who receives the pension) were subject most recently.

Pension and pensioner

'Pension', for the purpose of the **main co-ordination rules**, includes more than old age pensions. It includes lump-sum benefits that can be substituted for pensions and reimbursement of contributions, and can include revaluation increases and supplementary allowances.[135] It refers to state payments made under the legislation of an EEA state and does not include private or occupational pensions. Under the old co-ordination rules, it was accepted that a pension can include incapacity benefit (IB), ESA, DLA and severe disablement allowance (SDA).[136] However, a more recent case has held that the care component of DLA is not a pension under the current co-ordination rules. It also held that the term 'pension' must have the same meaning throughout the EU regulations and that a Dutch survivor's benefit is a pension.[137] A further case confirmed that the mobility component of DLA is also not a pension.[138] It may be arguable that the term 'pension' includes pension credit (PC) since this is a supplementary allowance.[139] Although the Upper Tribunal recently commented that PC is not a 'pension', as it is a special non-contributory benefit (see p367),[140] the argument was not considered in depth, and the Court of Justice of the European Union (CJEU) has held that a benefit can be both a special non-contributory benefit and a supplementary allowance.[141] However, the most recent Upper Tribunal decisions have focused on the need for a benefit to be contributory for it to be considered a pension[142] (although contributory ESA awarded on conversion from incapacity benefit in youth was still accepted as a pension, despite the claimant's not having paid contributions).[143] Recent DWP guidance confirms that receipt of contributory ESA, IB, SDA, retirement pension (other than category D), industrial injuries disablement benefit and bereavement benefit (other than a bereavement payment) are all considered UK 'pensions'.[144]

Under the **UK–Ireland Convention,** 'pension' is defined as an old age, invalidity benefit or a survivor's benefit.[145]

'Pensioner' is not defined under the main co-ordination rules, but refers to someone receiving a 'pension'.[146]

Under the UK–Ireland Convention, 'pensioner' is defined as a person receiving a pension.[147]

Who is a member of the family for sickness benefits in kind

Under the main EU co-ordination rules, the definition of 'member of the family' for sickness benefits in kind is slightly different to the general definition (see p361). The difference is highlighted below in *italics*.

You are a member of the family of a person covered by the main co-ordination rules for the purpose of sickness benefits in kind, if:[148]

- you are a person defined or recognised as a member of the family, or designated as a member of the household, by the legislation *of the member state in which you reside; or*
- the legislation under which benefits are provided does not make a distinction between the members of the family and other people to whom it applies, and you are the covered person's spouse or child who is either under the age of majority (18 years old in England, Wales and Northern Ireland; 16 years old in Scotland) or older but dependent on the person covered.

If, under the legislation in either bullet point above, you are only considered to be a member of the family or member of the household if you are living in the same household as the person, this condition is considered to be satisfied if you are mainly dependent on her/him.

If you have a right to benefits in kind as a member of the family, as well as an independent right to benefits in kind, your independent right takes priority unless this is only based on residence.[149] Examples are given below.

Scenarios if a pension is paid by an European Economic Area state

If you are covered by the main co-ordination rules and you, or the member of your family (see p361) who brings you within those rules, receive a 'pension' (see p375) from an EEA state other than the one you are living in, check the possible scenarios, and exceptions, to determine which state is competent for paying your cash sickness benefits (AA, DLA care component, PIP daily living component, CA, carer's allowance supplement, young carer grant and, it is expected, the care component of disabled child payment).

If you reside in the UK (or another state in which entitlement to sickness benefits in kind is on the basis of residence, rather than insurance or employment) and you (or the member of your family who brings you within the co-ordination rules) receive a 'pension' from another state, *but not* from the UK (or the other state of residence), the cost of sickness benefits in kind received in the UK (or other state) is borne by the state that pays the pension, to the extent that you would be entitled to receive sickness benefits in kind from that state if you lived there. Therefore, the state that pays your pension, rather than the state in which you reside, is responsible for paying your cash sickness benefit.[150] If you are already receiving a UK cash sickness benefit and then start receiving a pension from another state, your entitlement to the UK sickness benefit ends.[151] Similarly, if you are living in an EEA state, receiving its cash sickness benefit and start to receive retirement pension from the UK, the UK would become the competent state.[152]

Example

Emil is a Swedish national and receives a small Swedish old age state pension. Emil moves to the UK and claims AA. As he receives a pension from another state (Sweden), that state is responsible to the UK for reimbursing the cost of any NHS treatment he has. Consequently, provided Emil would be entitled to sickness benefits in kind (eg, healthcare) if he were resident in Sweden, he is not entitled to AA (but may be able to claim a Swedish cash sickness benefit).

If you receive a pension from two or more states and one of them is the state in which you reside, that state is responsible for the cost of your sickness benefits in kind (and is therefore the competent state for paying cash sickness benefits).[153]

Example

Emil becomes eligible for and claims a category D retirement pension. He now receives a pension from two or more states, including the one in which he resides (the UK). That state (the UK) is responsible for the cost of his NHS treatment, and is therefore the competent state to pay his cash sickness benefit, so Emil can now be entitled to AA.

If you reside in the UK (or another state in which entitlement to sickness benefits in kind is on the basis of residence) and you receive a pension from two or more states other than the UK (or other state of residence), the cost of your healthcare in kind is met by the state in which you were subject to pensions legislation for the longest period (or if that is more than one state, the state in which you were last subject to its pensions legislation).[154] That state is therefore the competent state for paying your cash sickness benefits.

Example

Jonas worked 10 years in Germany and 18 years in France and now resides in the UK. He receives pensions from both Germany and France. France is the state responsible for the cost of any NHS treatment he has while he lives in the UK and so France is the competent state for paying cash sickness benefits.

If you are the member of the family of a person receiving a pension and reside in a different state to her/him, whichever state must meet the cost of the sickness benefits in kind for her/him must also meet the cost of sickness benefits in kind for you (and is therefore the competent state for paying cash sickness benefits).[155]

However, check whether you also have an independent right to benefits in kind and, if so, whether these take priority. See the second bullet point below.

Example

Reka is a Hungarian national living in the UK. Her husband Roland is a Dutch national. He lives in Ireland and his only income is his Dutch pension. The Netherlands is the state that must meet the cost of the sickness benefits in kind for Roland and, therefore, is also the state that must meet these costs for Reka.

The above rules do not apply in the following cases.

- You (or the member of your family who is a pensioner) are entitled to benefits under the legislation of a state because that state is the competent one on the basis of an activity as an employed or self-employed person.[156] **Note:** the DWP accepts that undertaking activity as an employed or self-employed person in the UK is sufficient to mean that the UK is the competent state for paying cash sickness benefits.[157]

Example

Sophia is Portuguese and lives in the UK. She receives a small pension from Portugal. Sophia works part time as a self-employed cleaner and claims child benefit and child tax credit (CTC) for her disabled granddaughter who lives with her and receives DLA middle rate care component. Sophia can claim CA, as the UK is the competent state for paying benefits to her on the basis of her self-employment here.

- You are the family member of a pensioner, but you have an independent right to benefits in kind, either under the legislation of a state or under the co-ordination rules. Your independent right takes priority, unless it exists solely because of your residence in that state.[158]

Examples

Krista is Latvian and resides in the UK with her Latvian husband Andris. Andris receives a pension from Latvia and Krista receives contributory ESA from the UK. Krista wants to claim the daily living component of PIP. She can do this as her contributory ESA is classed as a 'pension' (see p375),[159] and therefore her independent rights take priority over the rights she has as the member of her husband's family. The UK is the state responsible for the cost of her sickness benefits in kind, and is therefore the competent state for paying cash sickness benefits.

Ryan is a 13-year-old Irish national living in the UK with his Irish mother Megan who receives an invalidity pension from Ireland. Ryan wants to claim the care component of DLA. However, because his independent rights are only based on his residence in the UK, the rights he has as the member of his mother's family take priority. Therefore, Ireland is the state responsible for the cost of his sickness benefits in kind, and is therefore the competent state for paying cash sickness benefits.

To check the sickness benefits payable by EEA states, see 'Your rights country by country' at ec.europa.eu/social.

If the rules exclude you

If you are residing in the UK and you receive a decision that the rules determining the competent state for sickness benefits exclude you from entitlement to AA, DLA care component, the daily living component of PIP, CA, carer's allowance supplement or young carer grant, or you think these rules might exclude you, check the following.

Are you excluded from 'sickness benefits'?

1. If it is suggested that you (or the member of your family who brings you within the co-ordination rules) are receiving a pension from another state, check whether it is a state payment classed as a 'pension'. Private and occupational pensions should not bring you within the above rules. See p375 for the meaning of 'pension'.

2. Do, or could, you (or your family member who brings you within the co-ordination rules) receive a pension from the UK as well as from another state? If so, the UK is responsible for the cost of your NHS treatment and so is the competent state for paying sickness benefits (see the example of Emil above and note that pension can include contributory benefits including contributory ESA).

3. Do, or could, you (or your family member who brings you within the co-ordination rules) work in the UK. The DWP accepts that undertaking activity as an employed or self-employed person in the UK is sufficient to mean that the UK is the competent state for paying cash sickness benefits (see the example of Sophia above and the text above it). **Note**: your earnings do not need to exceed the threshold at which you are liable to pay NI contributions.[160]

4. Do not withdraw your (or the member of your family's) claim for a pension from the other state without getting specialist advice, because that could leave you worse off. Firstly, it could affect your (or her/his) future pension entitlement or you may lose the option to reclaim. Secondly, recent caselaw suggests the DWP may continue to treat the state that paid your pension as the competent state to pay your cash sickness benefit (see p371).[161]

5. If the DWP has decided that the UK is not the competent state, see p372.

6. It may be possible to argue that your particular circumstances mean that the exclusion from AA, DLA care component or the daily living component of PIP on the basis that the UK is not your competent state does not apply.
- If you are the dependent family member of an EEA worker, the exclusion is prohibited by the principle of equal treatment (see below) if the refusal of a disability benefit reduces or impedes her/his ability to work or disadvantages her/him in relation to a British worker.[162] The Upper Tribunal rejected an argument that refusal of AA was disproportionate and discriminatory, but arguably did not fully consider this discrimination argument.[163] However, the argument was considered in a subsequent case when it was put in broad terms.[164] Although the judge dismissed the argument as presented, he left open the possibility that the principle of equal treatment could prohibit excluding a worker's family member from sickness benefits in particular circumstances. Such an argument may be accepted if there is no equivalent sickness benefit payable by the competent state and exclusion would result in your being deprived of any entitlement at all.[165] **Note:** this argument was recently rejected in relation to a child refused DLA, because the competent state was held to be Belgium where her father was self-employed, and not the UK where she lived with her mother, but the appeal from this case is due to be heard in the Court of Appeal in April 2021.[166]
- If you have previously worked and paid taxes in the UK, the co-ordination rules should not deprive you of entitlement to a benefit paid for by taxation. If this would be the result of the co-ordination rules, a state is not prevented from awarding the benefit, even when it is not the competent state for paying it.[167] The Upper Tribunal has considered this line of argument, developed through recent EU caselaw, but decided it did not apply in that particular case as the person had not contributed through general taxation.[168] In the circumstances of this case, it held that the UK was not prevented from excluding the claimant from entitlement to AA if the UK was not the competent state to pay cash sickness benefits.[169]

Equal treatment of people

If you are covered by any of the co-ordination rules, you are entitled to the same benefits under the legislation of the 'competent state' (see p369) as a national of that state.[170] Equal treatment is one of the fundamental rights of EU law,[171] and the principle of non-discrimination prohibits discrimination based on your nationality. Both direct discrimination and, if it cannot be justified as proportionate and in pursuit of a legitimate aim, indirect discrimination are prohibited.

Direct discrimination arises when one person is treated less favourably than another in the same situation. Indirect discrimination arises when rules which, although apparently neutral and non-discriminatory, have, in practice, a greater adverse impact on some people than others – eg, non-nationals of the competent state over nationals of the competent state. For example, the right to reside test in UK law appeared, when the UK was a member of the EU, to apply equally to all

EEA nationals. However, British and Irish citizens always have a right to reside in the common travel area and therefore satisfy the test for means-tested benefits, whereas other EEA nationals only satisfy it in certain circumstances. Therefore, the test is indirectly discriminatory. However, the Supreme Court decided in a case concerning PC that this discrimination is justified and, therefore, legal.[172] Similarly, the CJEU has held that the right to reside test for child benefit and CTC was not directly discriminatory and, although indirectly discriminatory, this was justified.[173] Although a different view was taken by the Northern Ireland Chief Commissioner, who found that the right to reside test for child benefit was directly and indirectly discriminatory, this decision was overturned by the Court of Appeal in Northern Ireland.[174]

Most recently, the exclusion from means-tested benefits of EU nationals who have been granted limited leave under the EU Settlement Scheme (also known as 'pre-settled status'), and who have no other right to reside, was held by a majority in the Court of Appeal to be direct discrimination on nationality grounds and therefore unlawful.[175] This overturned the decision of the High Court that this exclusion was only indirect discrimination and was lawful as it was justified.[176] **Note:** at the time of writing, the DWP was seeking permission to appeal to the Supreme Court (see p153).

Equal treatment of facts and events

Each of the co-ordination rules provide for the 'equal treatment of benefits, income, facts or events'.[177] This provision is sometimes referred to as the 'principle of the assimilation of facts'. This principle is designed to ensure that if the competent state regards the receipt of a particular benefit or income, or the occurrence of certain facts or events, as producing certain legal effects, it should regard the receipt of an equivalent benefit or income from another member state, or the occurrence of particular facts or events in another member state, as producing the same effect. For example, if one state has determined that a person has had an industrial accident, that fact must be accepted, for the purpose of awarding benefit, in another member state.

A benefit paid by a member state is 'equivalent' to a benefit paid by another member state if they are comparable, taking account of the aim of each benefit and the legislation under which they are established. Receipt of a Polish benefit paid on the basis that the claimant was incapable of independent living was accepted in one Upper Tribunal case as equivalent to the middle or higher rate of DLA care component and therefore entitled the claimant's carer to carer's allowance, and in a separate case as equivalent to attendance allowance and therefore entitled the claimant to a severe disability addition within her pension credit.[178]

The Upper Tribunal has held that this principle does not apply to the effects on working tax credit (WTC) because WTC is not a benefit covered by the co-ordination rules (see p363). However, because *other* EU regulations require workers from other EEA states to have the same 'social advantages' as national workers,[179] the regulations on entitlement to the childcare element must be interpreted so as to accept a Dutch invalidity benefit as evidence of a claimant's incapacity.[180] Following this judgment, the WTC regulations were amended to include any benefit paid by an EEA state which is substantially similar to any of the UK benefits listed as evidence of incapacity.[181]

There are exceptions to the general principle of the assimilation of facts, some of which are set out in the co-ordination rules, and others arise as a result of a conflict between this principle and other principles of the co-ordination rules. For example, the assimilation of facts cannot render another member state competent.[182] The competent state should first be determined (see p369) and then that state should assimilate the facts for the purposes of its own legislation.

The assimilation principle should also not interfere with the principle of aggregation (see below).[183] So, the competent state should count periods of insurance in another EEA state (under the aggregation principle) without needing to address the question of whether they count as periods of insurance for the assimilation principle to apply. If it counts as a period of insurance under the legislation of the state in which it took place, that period can be aggregated.

Aggregation

The principle of aggregation for the purpose of acquiring and calculating entitlement to benefits is a key co-ordinating principle in each of the co-ordination rules.[184] To ensure and promote freedom of movement, the aim of this principle is to remove disadvantages that arise when claiming benefit after moving from one member state to another.

'**Aggregation**' means adding together periods of insurance (eg, periods in which you have paid NI contributions in the UK), residence or employment/self-employment completed under the legislation of one or more member states to satisfy the conditions of entitlement for a benefit. For example, if you want to claim a UK contribution-based benefit such as contributory ESA, but you have not paid sufficient NI contributions in the UK, you can rely on contributions you have paid in one or more other member states to satisfy the UK contribution rules.

The competent institution must contact the competent institutions in the other relevant states to determine the periods completed under their legislation.[185]

What constitutes a period of residence, employment or insurance is determined by the legislation of the state in which it took place.[186]

Example

Sancha is a Portuguese national who has worked for many years in Portugal. She leaves her job in Portugal and moves to the UK. She works for three weeks before being made redundant. Sancha is expecting a baby in two months' time and claims maternity allowance (MA). She can be entitled to MA because she can add her periods of employment in Portugal to her period of employment in the UK to satisfy the employment condition of having worked for 26 out of the last 66 weeks.

Note:
if Sancha moved to, and began working in, the UK before 31 December 2020, she would be covered by the main co-ordination rules; if she moved after 31 December 2020, she would be covered by the UK–EU Protocol, but the aggregation principle would apply in either case.

Disability and carer's benefits

The **main co-ordination rules** provide for 'residence' in a member state to be aggregated with presence in Great Britain to satisfy the 'past presence' test for AA, DLA, PIP and CA (see p280).[187] However, the Upper Tribunal has held that 'mere residence' in an EEA state does not count for this purpose, and although in these cases it was not necessary to decide what qualities the residence must have in order to count, it was suggested that insurance-based or contribution-based residence would count.[188] The appeal against this part of the judgment was dropped when the appeal was heard by the Court of Appeal.[189]

The **UK–Ireland Convention** states that, if the UK is your competent state for these benefits, you can be entitled to AA, DLA care component, PIP daily living component and CA while resident in Ireland. However, when determining this entitlement, only periods of residence in Ireland during which you were insured may count towards the past presence requirment.[190]

The **UK–EU Protocol** does not cover these disability and carer's benefits (see p363).

Unemployment benefits

When determining entitlement to unemployment benefits, your periods of insurance (if entitlement depends on insurance) or employment/self-employment (if entitlement depends on employment/self-employment) completed in all member states are only aggregated if you were last insured or you last worked (whichever is required) under the legislation of the state from which you are claiming benefit.[191]

Example
Tomasz is Polish and after working and being insured in Poland for four years became unemployed, and so moved to the UK to look for work. If he claims contribution-based jobseeker's allowance (JSA), he cannot use his periods of insurance from Poland to satisfy the NI contribution conditions. However, if he takes two weeks' full-time temporary work in the UK and then claims contribution-based JSA, he can then aggregate his periods of insurance in Poland and the NI contributions paid in the UK to be able to qualify for contribution-based JSA.

However, this additional condition does not apply if, during your last period of employment or self-employment, you resided in a state other than your competent state. In this case, if you claim an unemployment benefit in the state in which you continue to reside (or have returned to), you *can* aggregate periods of insurance or employment or self-employment in order to be entitled to that benefit.[192]

Example

Monique was employed and insured in Belgium where she resided for a year. She then got a job in France for 18 months. As this involved mainly working from home, she did this work while residing in the UK with her boyfriend. She has been made redundant and wants to claim contribution-based JSA. She can aggregate the contributions paid in both Belgium and France to qualify for contribution-based JSA.

Exporting benefits

Each of the co-ordination rules allows you to 'export' certain social security benefits from one member state to another if you cease to be resident in the state in which your entitlement arose.

This means that certain benefits may not be reduced, modified, suspended, withdrawn or confiscated just because you go to live in a different member state.[193] The rules for exporting vary according to the benefit concerned: some are fully exportable, some may be exportable on a temporary basis, and some are not exportable at all.

Check the individual benefit rules in Chapter 15 to see whether that benefit can be exported. If it can, you should contact the office that pays your benefit well in advance so that arrangements can be made to pay you in the state you are going to. The rules covering periodic reassessments still apply – so, for example, if you export contributory ESA, the DWP continues to assess your limited capability for work and your limited capability for work-related activity. However, any checks and medicals take place in the state in which you are living, with reports then sent to the DWP.[194]

Under the **main co-ordination rules**, and the **UK–Ireland Convention**, all benefits categorised as social security benefits are exportable. However, the **UK–EU Protocol** excludes invalidity and unemployment benefits from export provisions and does not cover family or long-term care benefits at all.[195] See p363 for a list of the UK benefits covered.

The following benefits can be exported indefinitely:

- old age benefits;
- survivor's benefits;
- pensions for accidents at work or occupational diseases;
- (not under the UK–EU Protocol) invalidity benefits;

- (not under the UK–EU Protocol) family benefits (see below);
- death grants.

The following benefits can be exported for a limited period or subject to certain restrictions:
- (not under the UK–EU Protocol) unemployment benefits;
- sickness, maternity and paternity benefits. However, in most cases, these benefits are exportable in a similar way to the fully exportable benefits.

Special non-contributory benefits (see p367) cannot be exported. Under the main co-ordination rules they are paid only in the state in which you are 'resident'.[196] See p371 for details of when you count as resident.

Overlapping benefit rules

A general principle of each of the co-ordination rules is that you should not use one period of compulsory insurance to obtain more than one benefit derived from that period of insurance.[197] In general, you are only insured in one member state for any one period, so you cannot use insurance from that one period to obtain entitlement to benefits of the same kind from more than one state. Usually, benefits are adjusted to ensure that either only one state (the 'competent state' – see p369) pays the benefit, taking into account periods of insurance in other member states, or the benefit is paid pro rata according to the lengths of the periods of insurance in different states.[198]

In certain cases, however, you may be paid both the full level of a UK benefit and a proportion of a benefit from another state, accrued as a result of having paid NI contributions there. Member states are not allowed to prevent their own benefits overlapping with those of other states if this would reduce what you would have received under national law from your periods of contributions in the first state alone.[199]

There are particular overlapping rules on specific categories of benefits – eg, old age and survivor's benefits,[200] and, under the main co-ordination rules and the UK–Ireland Convention, family benefits (see p388).[201]

5. Family benefits

Under the **main co-ordination rules**, family benefits in the UK include child benefit, child tax credit (CTC), guardian's allowance and child dependants' additions in other benefits. Scottish child payment should also be accepted as a family benefit and the rules below should, therefore, also apply to that payment.

If you are covered by the main co-ordination rules, you can export family benefits without any time limit provided the competent state to pay your family benefits has not changed.[202] If you export family benefits, they are uprated in the normal way.

If you are covered by the main co-ordination rules, you may also be entitled to benefits paid in respect of your family living in another European Economic Area (EEA) state (see below).[203] For the definition of 'member of the family', see p361.

If you are entitled to family benefits from more than one EEA state in respect of the same person and for the same period, there are rules that determine which state has priority if your entitlements overlap (see p388).

Note:

- Working tax credit (WTC) has been held not to be a social security benefit or a special non-contributory benefit under the co-ordination rules and, therefore, these rules do not apply to WTC (see p363).[204] However, other provisions of European Union (EU) law can assist you in being paid the childcare element of WTC (see p297 and p382).[205]
- The Department for Work and Pensions (DWP) does not accept that universal credit (UC) is a family benefit and takes the view that the co-ordination rules do not apply to UC. It is arguable that the child elements of UC are a family benefit. Get specialist advice if you want to make this argument.
- Under the **UK–Ireland Convention**, family benefits are listed as child benefit, CTC and guardian's allowance.[206] It contains similar provisions as the main co-ordination rules, but only in relation to the UK and Ireland.[207]
- The **UK–EU Protocol** does not apply to family benefits.[208]

Members of your family resident in another state

If you are covered by the main co-ordination rules or, for situations involving only the UK and Ireland, if you are covered by the UK–Ireland Convention, you are entitled to receive family benefits from your competent state, even when the member of your family for whom you are claiming is resident in another state because s/he is treated as if s/he were resident in the competent state.[209] (You must satisfy the other conditions for that benefit – see the note below). In general, unless you are receiving a pension (see below), your competent state is determined in the usual way (see p369).[210]

It is not necessary for you to be employed or self-employed in the competent state for you to be entitled to the family benefits paid by that state.[211] HM Revenue and Customs (HMRC) have often incorrectly stated, in decisions and appeal submissions, that you need to be working and paying national insurance in the UK to be covered by the current co-ordination rules and that has been confirmed to be wrong by the Upper Tribunal.[212] For details on who is covered by the co-ordination rules, see p355.

Example

Carla is Italian. She works in the UK and sends money to her two children who live in Italy with their grandmother. Carla is entitled to child benefit for her children. She is then made redundant and claims UC. She is awarded UC (on the basis that she has retained her worker status and so satisfies the right to reside requirement), but she is not paid elements for her children as they do not normally live with her. She continues to be entitled to child benefit.

However, if you are receiving a 'pension', the state that is competent for paying this is the one from which you claim family benefits.[213] See p375 for the definition of 'pension'.[214]

Example

Julien is a French national living in the UK, and receiving a state pension from France. Julien's 15-year-old twin daughters live with their uncle (Julien's brother) in Germany, but Julien supports his daughters financially. Julien is not entitled to child benefit for his daughters because he receives a pension from France, and so he is only entitled to claim French family benefits.

Note: although your child is treated as resident in the competent state, you still have to satisfy all the other conditions for that benefit, including, for CTC, that the child is 'normally living with' you, and for child benefit, if the child is not living with you, that you are contributing to the costs of that child an amount at least equal to the amount of child benefit payable for her/him.[215]

Priority when family benefits overlap

There may be entitlement to family benefits under the legislation of more than one EEA state (or under the UK–Ireland Convention, the legislation of both the UK and Ireland) in respect of the same family member and for the same period. This can arise when two people are entitled to benefit for the same child (eg, if a mother resides in one state and the father in another and both can claim family benefits for their child), or if you have an entitlement from more than one state – eg, if you live in one state with your children, but work in another.

To ensure that equivalent family benefits are not paid by more than one state in respect of the same family member for the same period, the main co-ordination rules and the UK–Ireland Convention set out which state has 'priority' – ie, must pay the family benefits.

Note: these priority rules *only* need to be considered if there is an actual overlap of entitlement because a claim has been made for a family benefit in another state (unless entitlement does not require a claim to have been made) – see note below.

The way the priority rules work depends on the basis on which each family benefit is paid and, in some cases, the state in which the child lives.[216]

Different states have different criteria for entitlement. In some, you must reside in that state (family benefits payable on the basis of 'residence'); in others, you must work in that state (family benefits payable on the basis of 'employment or self-employment'); and some states require you to receive a pension (family benefits payable on the basis of 'receipt of a pension'). It can be difficult to work out the basis on which a family benefit is paid, but the European Commission has online information on the conditions for each state.[217] In the majority of states, including the UK, family benefits are mostly payable on the basis of residence – eg, there are no employment conditions or a requirement to receive a pension in order to obtain child benefit or CTC.

If the family benefits from each state are payable on a *different* basis, the state which has priority (ie, must pay) is the one whose family benefits are payable on the first of the following bases:[218]

- activity as an employed or self-employed person. This can include temporary periods not working for reasons such as sickness, maternity or unemployment, provided you receive either wages or benefits other than a 'pension' (see p375);[219]
- receipt of a pension (see p375);
- residence.

If the family benefits from each state are payable on the *same* basis, the state which has priority (ie, must pay) is as follows.[220]

- If family benefits are based on employment/self-employment in both states, the state with priority is the one where the child resides, if you (or if there is another potential claimant, s/he) work there; otherwise, it is the state that pays the highest amount.[221]
- If family benefits are based on receipt of a pension in both states, the state with priority is the one where the child resides if that state also pays the pension; otherwise, it is the state where you (or the other potential claimant) have been insured or resided for the longest period.
- If family benefits are based on residence, the state with priority is the one where the child resides.

If there is an entitlement to family benefits from the state that has priority, the entitlement to family benefits from the other state(s) with lower priority is suspended up to the amount provided under the legislation of the priority state. If this suspension does not wipe out all your entitlement, a supplement is paid to 'top up' the family benefits paid by the priority state.[222] However, this top-up need not be paid for children residing in another state when entitlement to family benefits in both states is based on residence only.[223]

Examples

Marie and her two children moved to the UK from Belgium four months ago when she separated from their father, Arnaud. Marie is looking for work, but has not found a job yet. She claims child benefit. However, Arnaud, who is working in Belgium, is still receiving the Belgian family benefit and sending this money to Marie for the children. The Belgian family benefit is payable on the basis of employment and, therefore, has priority over the UK family benefits, since the latter are based on residence. If the UK family benefits are more than the Belgian family benefits, Marie should be paid the difference to top up the Belgian family benefits.

Alicia moved to the UK from Slovakia to take up a job, but was made redundant after four months. Her husband and their two children stayed in Slovakia. Alicia's husband receives Slovakian family benefits, which are payable on the basis of residence. Alicia claims child benefit. Since this is also payable on the basis of residence, Slovakia has priority since the children live there. The UK does not need to pay a top-up if its family benefits are more generous than the Slovakian ones.

Note: if entitlement to a family benefit in one state depends on a claim having been made and no claim has been made, entitlement to the family benefit that has been claimed in another state cannot be suspended.[224] It is therefore not necessary to consider whether family benefits in another state have priority or are payable at a higher rate if a claim is required for entitlement but no claim has been made.[225]

If family benefits are paid to someone who is not using them to maintain the member(s) of her/his family, the EEA state paying the benefit can make payments to the person who is, in fact, maintaining the member(s) of the family. This is done at the request of, and through, the relevant institution in the state where the person who is maintaining the family member lives.[226]

Administration of family benefits

There are rules that cover the administration of claims for family benefits where more than one state could potentially be involved.[227]

If a claim is submitted to the relevant institution in a state whose legislation is applicable but which does not have priority under the rules above, that institution should make a provisional decision on the priority rules and then forward the claim to the relevant institution in the state with priority without delay. The date of claim is the date it was made to the first state. The relevant institution in the other state should then make a decision within two months. If it fails to do so, benefit should be awarded on the basis of the provisional decision, including any 'top-up' from the state where the benefit was claimed.[228] However, if there is a difference of view between the states about which has priority, provisional payments must be made by the state in which the child resides (or where the benefit was first claimed if the child does not reside in any of the relevant states). If agreement is not reached between the states within a month, the matter may be referred to the EU Administrative Commission for the coordination of social security systems to resolve within six months.[229]

If you are claiming in the UK and HMRC advises you that another state has priority, you may need to remind HMRC of its duty to forward the claim to the relevant institution in the other state. If this has been done and there is evidence of a difference of view between HMRC and the relevant institution in the other state, remind HMRC of its duty to make provisional payments. Although the Upper Tribunal caselaw on provisional payments under the EU co-ordination rules has concerned sickness benefits, it can still be helpful to refer to because it sets out how the rules on provisional payments work (see p372).[230]

It can also be useful to check, and refer to when helpful, HMRC guidance for decision makers, which covers the priority rules, when family benefits can be 'topped up', administrative procedures and provisional payments.[231]

The **UK–Ireland Convention** contains similar rules on the administration of claims for family benefits, including making provisional payments if there is a delay in deciding, or dispute over, whether the UK or Ireland has priority.[232]

Notes

1. **Introduction**

1 Arts 2(e), 126 and 127 WA 2019; ss1A, 1B, 8A and Sch 2 Part 1A EU(W) Act 2018
2 ss1A and 1B EU(W) A 2018
3 s1B(3)(d) and (e) EU(W) A 2018
4 s6 ISSCA 2020; regs 3-4 The Social Security Co-ordination (Revocation of Retained Direct EU Legislation and Related Amendments) (EU Exit) Regulations 2020, No.1508; regs 7-8 The Social Security Co-ordination (EU Exit) (Scotland) (Amendments etc.) Regulations 2020, No.399
5 EU Reg 883/04
6 EU Reg 1408/71
7 Art 65 UK-IC; notification was sent from Ireland on 22 December 2020 and from the UK on 31 December 2020; Explanatory Memo to UK-IC
8 s3 EU(W)A 2018
9 s6 ISSCA 2020; regs 3-4 The Social Security Co-ordination (Revocation of Retained Direct EU Legislation and Related Amendments) (EU Exit) Regulations 2020, No.1508
10 Title III WA 2019; Title III UK-EFTA Agreement; Part 3 UK-Swiss Agreement; ss 7A and 7B EU(W)A 2018
11 Reg 9 The Social Security Co-ordination (Revocation of Retained Direct EU Legislation and Related Amendments) (EU Exit) Regs 2020, No.1508
12 *Bogatu v Minister for Social Protection*, C-322/17 [2019], paras 26-27
13 Art 65 UK-IC; notification was sent from Ireland on 22 December 2020 and from the UK on 31 December 2020; Explanatory Memo to UK-IC

14 s26 European Union (Future Relationship) Act 2020; reg 2 European Union (Future Relationship) Act 2020 (Commencement No1) Regulations 2020, No.1662

2. **Who is covered**

15 Art 3(2)-(4) UK-IC; Ch 1 para 5 DWPWAG
16 Title III WA 2019; Title III UK-EFTA Agreement; Part 3 UK-Swiss Agreement; ss7A and 7B EU(W)A 2018
17 Arts 10, 13, 24, 25 and 30(3)-(5) WA 2019; Arts 9, 12, 23, 24, 19(3)-(5) UK-EFTA Agreement; Arts 10, 12, 19, 20 and 25(3)-(5) UK-Swiss Agreement
18 Art 30(2) WA 2019; Art 29(2) UK-EFTA Agreement; Art 25(2) UK-Swiss Agreement
19 DWPWAG
20 *Petit v Office National de Pensions*, C-153/91 [1992]
21 Art 2 EU Reg 883/04
22 Art 1(g) EU Reg 1408/71
23 Art 2 UK-IC
24 Art 1 UK-IC
25 Art 3(2) UK-IC; Ch 1 para 5 DWPWAG
26 Art SSC2 UK-EUP
27 *Petit v Office National de Pensions*, C-153/91 [1992]
28 Art SSC2 UK-EUP
29 Home Office Policy Paper: Updated impact assessment for EU social security co-ordination (updated 2 March 2021)
30 EU Reg 883/04
31 EU Reg 1408/71
32 Art 87(8) EU Reg 883/04;*Recital (2), Decision H1 of 12 June 2009* of the *Administrative Commission for the Coordination of Social Security Systems* [2010] OJ C-106/13; *SSWP v PW (CA)* [2013] UKUT 296 (AAC)
33 *KG v SSWP (DLA)* [2015] UKUT 146 (AAC)
34 Art 87(8) EU Reg 883/04
35 *Jeltes, Peeters andArnold v Raad van bestuur van het Uitvoeringsinstituut werknemersverzekeringen,* C-443/11, para 59
36 *SSWP v SO*[2019] UKUT 55 (AAC)
37 *KR v SSWP (DLA)* [2019] UKUT 85 (AAC), paras 10-12
38 *SSWP v MC (DLA)* [2019] UKUT 84 (AAC), paras 6 and 21
39 Art 87(8) EU Reg 883/04
40 For example, *SL v SSWP (DLA)* [2014] UKUT 108 (AAC)
41 Art 1 EU Reg 859/2003
42 Recital 18 EU Reg 1231/2010; Ch 3 para 4 and glossary DWPWAG
43 The UK's attempt to challenge this extension of the co-ordination rules failed in relation to:
Switzerland: *UK v Council of the European Union*, C-656/11 [2014]
Iceland, Liechtenstein and Norway: *UK v Council of the European Union*, C-431/11 [2013]
44 *Ministre de l'Économie et des Finances v Ruyter*, C-623/13 [2015]
45 Art 1(l) EU Reg 883/04; Art 1 UK-IC; Art SSC1(q) UK-EUP
46 Art 3 EU Reg 883/04; Art 3 UK-IC; Art SSC3 UK-EUP
47 Vol 2 Ch 7, Part 1 Appendix, para 5 DMG
48 Art 2 EU Reg 883/04; Art 2 UK-IC; Art SSC2 UK-EUP
49 Arts 1(i) and 2 EU Reg 883/04; Art 1(1) UK-IC; Art SSC1(s) UK-EUP
50 *KT v HMRC (CB)* [2013] UKUT 151 (AAC)
51 *HMRC v MB* [2018] UKUT 162 (AAC), reported as [2018] AACR 32
52 *PB v SSWP (DLA)* [2016] UKUT 280 (AAC), paras 8-10
53 *AM v SSWP* [2017] UKUT 26 (AAC), para 15

3. **Which benefits are covered**

54 Art 3 UK-IC
55 Arts 1(l), 3 and 9 EU Reg 883/04; Arts SSC1(q) and SSC3 UK-EUP
56 Art 3 EU Reg 883/04; Art 3 UK-IC; Art SSC3 UK-EUP
57 Art 3 UK-IC
58 Art SSC3(4) UK-EUP
59 Annex SSC-1 Part 2(i) UK-EUP
60 Confirmed in Art 34 EU Reg 883/04
61 *Stewart v SSWP*, C-503/09 [2011]
62 para 070153 DMG
63 *Caisse nationale des prestations familiales v Hiddal and Bernard*, C-216/12 and C-217/12 held that a parental leave allowance was a family benefit under EU Reg 1408/71.
64 SSAC, *Universal Credit and Related Regulations Report and Government Response*, December 2012
65 *Commission of the European Communities v European Parliament and Council of the EU*, C-299/05 [2007]

66 *SSWP v Tolley*, C-430/15 [2017]. This case relates to the old co-ordination rules, but on this point has been held to also apply to the current co-ordination rules in: *LD v SSWP* [2017] UKUT 65 (AAC); *JM v SSWP (CA)* [2018] UKUT 329 (AAC), para 8; *KR v SSWP (DLA)* [2019] UKUT 85 (AAC), para 2; *SSWP v TG (DLA)* [2019] UKUT 86 (AAC), para 3; and *GK v SSWP (CA)* [2019] UKUT 87 (AAC), para 3.
67 *Bartlett and Others v SSWP*, C-537/09 [2011]
68 p2 Policy Note to CASYCG(R)(S) Regs
69 Arts 3, 16, 19 and 20 UK-IC
70 **CAS** s81(2A) and (13) SS(S)A
YCG reg 8(3) and (6) CA(YCG)(S) Regs
71 Arts SSC1(r) and (bb), SSC3(4)(a) and (d), Part 1(i)(c) and (d), and Part 2(i) Annex SSC-1 UK-EUP
72 Art 70(1) and (2) and Annex X EU Reg 883/04; Art SSC1(bb) and Annex SSC-1 Part 1 UK-EUP
73 Annex X EU Reg 883/04
74 *SSWP v DS* [2019] UKUT 238 (AAC)
75 para C2097 and Appendix 1 para 4 ADM
76 Art 70 EU Reg 883/04
77 Art 3(3) EU Reg 883/04; *Dano v Jobcenter Leipzig*, C-333/13 [2014], paras 46-55
78 Art SSC3(4)(a) and Annex SSC-1 Part 1 UK-EUP
79 Art 3(5)(a) EU Reg 883/04; Art SSC3(4)(b) UK-EUP
80 SSAC, *Universal Credit and Related Regulations Report and Government Response*, December 2012
81 CH/1400/2006, paras 37-40
82 *MR v HMRC (TC)* [2011] UKUT 40 (AAC), para 17
83 Art1(1) UK-IC
84 Art 47 UK-IC

4. **Principles of co-ordination**
85 For a recent example, see *J McG v (1) SSWP, (2) HMRC* [2018] UKUT 2 (AAC), paras 19-24
86 Art 11 EU Reg 883/04; Art 9 UK-IC; Art SSC10 UK-EUP
87 Art 1(s) EU Reg 883/04; Art SSC1(i) UK-EUP
88 Art 1(q) EU Reg 883/04; Art SSC1(h) UK-EUP
89 Art 11 EU Reg 883/04; Art 9 UK-IC; Art SSC10 UK-EUP
90 Art 65 EU Reg 883/04; Art 22 UK-IC
91 Art 11(3)(e) EU Reg 883/04; Art 9(4)(e) UK-IC; Art SSC10(3)(c) UK-EUP
92 *JS v SSWP* [2019] UKUT 239 (AAC); Memo ADM 1/20 and DMG 3/20
93 Art 11(2) EU Reg 883/04; Art 9(2) and(3) UK-IC; Art SSC10(2) UK-EUP
94 Art 13 EU Reg 883/04; Art SSC12 and Annex SSC-7, Art SSCI.13(1)-(4) UK-EUP
95 Art 12 EU Reg 883/04; Art 10 UK-IC
96 Art SSC 11 and Annex SSC7, Art SSCI.13(1)-(4) UK-EUP
97 *AR v HMRC (CHB)* [2014] UKUT 553 (AAC); *HB v HMRC (CHB)* [2014] UKUT 554 (AAC), paras 37-39
98 **Main co-ordination rules:** Arts 67, 68 and 81 EU Reg 883/04; Arts 2, 45 and 60 EU Reg 987/2009; *SSWP v AK (AA)* [2015] UKUT 110 (AAC), reported as [2015] AACR 27; *MGL v SSWP (ESA)* [2018] UKUT 352 (AAC)
UK-IC: Art 60
UK-EUP: Art SSC62
99 Art 1(j) EU Reg 883/04; Art 1(1) UK-IC; Art SSC1(aa) UK-EUP
100 Art 1(1) UK-IC
101 Art 11 EU Reg 987/2009; Annex SSC-7, Art SSCI.10 UK-EUP
102 Art 11(2) EU Reg 987/09; Annex SSC-7, Art SSCI.10(3) UK-EUP
103 Arts 11-16 EU Reg 883/04; Arts 9-13 UK-IC ; Arts SSC10-13 UK-EUP
104 See, for example, *SSWP v MC (DLA)* [2019] UKUT 84 (AAC)
105 *LD v SSWP* [2017] UKUT 65 (AAC) – PTA to CA refused; *KS v SSWP* [2018] UKUT 121 (AAC)
106 *KR v SSWP (DLA)* [2019] UKUT 85 (AAC), reported as [2019] AACR 22, paras 18-24
107 See, for example, *Kuusijärvi v Riksförsäkringsverket*, C-275/96 [1998]; *AR v HMRC (CHB)* [2014] UKUT 553 (AAC); *HB v HMRC (CHB)* [2014] UKUT 554 (AAC)
108 See, for example, *Kuusijärvi v Riksförsäkringsverket*, C-275/96 [1998]; *AR v HMRC (CHB)* [2014] UKUT 553 (AAC); *HB v HMRC (CHB)* [2014] UKUT 554 (AAC); *SSWP v Tolley*, C-430/15 [2017]; *SSWP v MC (DLA)* [2019] UKUT 84 (AAC); *KR v SSWP (DLA)* [2019] UKUT 85 (AAC), reported as [2019] AACR 22
109 *AR v HMRC(CHB)* [2014] UKUT 553 (AAC); *HB v HMRC (CHB)* [2014] UKUT 554 (AAC), paras 37-39

110 **Main rules:** Art 81 EU Reg 883/2004; Art 2 EU Reg 987/2009; *SSWP v AK (AA)* [2015] UKUT 110 (AAC), reported as [2015] AACR 27; see also *MGL v SSWP (ESA)* [2018] UKUT 352 (AAC); Vol 2, Ch 7, Part 2 Appendix 4 DMG; Ch C2, Appendix 2 ADM
UK-IC: Art 60
UK-EUP: Art SSC62
111 Art 40(2) UK-IC
112 Art 6(2) EU Reg 987/2009; Art 63(2) UK-IC; Annex SSC-7, Art SSCI.6; *SSWP v HR (AA)* [2014] UKUT 571 (AAC), reported as [2015] AACR 26; *SSWP v SO* [2019] UKUT 55 (AAC)
113 Art 6(3) EU Reg 987/2009; Annex SSC-7, Art SSCI.6(3) UK-EUP
114 Arts 6(4)-(5) and 73 EU Reg 987/2009; Art 63(5) UK-IC; Annex SSC7, Arts SSCI.6(5) and SSCI 57 and Title IV UK-EUP
115 *SSWP v AK (AA)* [2015] UKUT 110 (AAC), reported as [2015] AACR 27, paras 29-30
116 *SSWP v Fileccia* [2017] EWCA Civ 1907, para 46; see also *SSWP v HR (AA)* [2014] UKUT 571 (AAC), reported as [2015] AACR 26, paras 16-19, and *AH v SSWP* [2020] UKUT 53 (AAC), paras 7-19
117 *SSWP v Fileccia* [2017] EWCA Civ 1907, para 45; see also *SSWP v HR (AA)* [2014] UKUT 571 (AAC), reported as [2015] AACR 26, para 18; see also *AH v SSWP* [2020] UKUT 53 (AAC), paras 7-19 – being appealed to CA due to be heard April 2021.
118 Art 6(1) EU Reg 987/2009; Art 63 UK-IC; Annex SSC-7, Art SSCI.6 UK-EUP
119 **AA** s65(7) SSCBA 1992
DLA s72(7B) SSCBA 1992
PIP s84 WRA 2012
CA s70(4A) SSCBA 1992
CASs81(2A) and (9)-(15) SS(S)A 2018
YCGreg 8(3)-(10) CA(YCG)(S) Regs
CDP reg 3(8) DACYP(S) Regs (draft)
120 *SSWP v AH* [2016] UKUT 148 (AAC); linked cases: *JGv SSWP* [2019] UKUT 83 (AAC), paras 41-43; *Konevodv SSWP* [2020] EWCA Civ 809, paras 52-54
121 Art 11(3)(e) EU Reg 883/04
122 Art 21(1) EU Reg 883/04
123 *AM v SSWP* [2017] UKUT 26 (AAC)
124 *AH v SSWP* [2020] UKUT 53 (AAC) – case ref: C3/2020/1399 *Harrington v SSWP* listed for hearing 28-29 April 2021; ADM Memo 17/20 paras 6, 34-36; DMG Memo 16/20 paras 6, 33-35
125 Linked cases: *SSWP v TG (DLA)* [2019] UKUT 86 (AAC), paras 7-8 and 13-18; *GK v SSWP (CA)* [2019] UKUT 87 (AAC), paras 6-7 and 12-17 (appealed to CA – see next footnote)
126 *Konevod v SSWP* [2020] EWCA Civ 809, paras 39-43; ADM Memo 17/20; DMG Memo 16/20
127 File refs: CSDLA/136/2017 and CSG/95/2017
128 Arts 3, 16, 19 and 20 UK-IC
129 **CAS** s81(2A) and (13) SS(S)A 2018 eg 8(3) and (6) CA(YCG)(S) Regs
130 Arts SSC1(r) and (bb), SSC3(4)(a) and (d), Part 1(i)(c) and (d), and Part 2(i) Annex SSC-1 UK-EUP
131 Art 29 EU Reg 883/04
132 Vol 4 Ch 7, part 2 Appendix 3 DMG, note to para 22; Ch C2, Appendix 1 ADM, note to para 22; DMG Memo 16/20; ADM Memo 17/20
133 DMG Memo 16/20, para 37; ADM Memo 17/20, para 38
134 Art 20 UK-IC
135 Art 1(w) EU Reg 883/04
136 *JS v SSWP (DLA)* [2012] AACR 7, para 14; *KS v SSWP (DLA)* [2014] UKUT 19 (AAC), para 81; both in relation to EU Reg 1408/71
137 *LD v SSWP* [2017] UKUT 65 (AAC) – PTA to CA refused
138 *SSWP v SO* [2019] UKUT 55 (AAC), paras 11-12
139 *Perry v Chief Adjudication Officer* [1998]; *EC v SSWP (SPC)* [2010] UKUT 95 (AAC), para 40
140 *IG v SSWP* [2016] UKUT 176 (AAC), reported as [2016] AACR 41, para 25; see also *KS v SSWP* [2018] UKUT 121 (AAC), para 6
141 *Skalka v Sozialversicherungsanstalt der Gewerblichen Wirtschaft,* C-160/02 [2004]; *Naranjo v CRAM Nord-Picardie,* C-265/05 [2007]
142 *SSWP v SO* [2019] UKUT 55 (AAC); *SSWP v TG (DLA)* [2019] UKUT 86 (AAC), para 17; *GK v SSWP (CA)* [2019] UKUT 87 (AAC), para 16
143 *KR v SSWP (DLA)* [2019] UKUT 85 (AAC), reported as [2019] AACR 22, paras 6 and 13-17
144 para C2124 ADM, Vol 2 Ch 7, Part 2 para 071771 DMG; ADM Memo 17/20, para 13 and para 20 examples 1 and 2; DMG Memo 16/20, para 13
145 Art 1(1) UK-IC
146 *SSWP v SO* [2019] UKUT 55 (AAC), para 10

147 Art 1(1) UK-IC
148 Art 1(i)(1) and (ii), (2) and (3) EU Reg 883/04
149 Art 32(1) EU Reg 883/04
150 Art 25 EU Reg 883/04; *SSWP v AK (AA)* [2015] UKUT 110 (AAC), reported as [2015] AACR 27; *KR v SSWP (DLA)* [2019] UKUT 85 (AAC), reported as [2019] AACR 22, paras 13-17; ADM Memo 20/19; DMG Memo 16/19
151 *LD v SSWP* [2017] UKUT 65 (AAC) – PTA to CA refused; *KS v SSWP* [2018] UKUT 121 (AAC)
152 ADM Memo 17/20, para 13; DMG 16/20, para 13
153 Art 23 EU Reg 883/04; *SSWP v HR (AA)* [2013] UKUT 66 (AAC); *SL v SSWP (DLA)* [2014] UKUT 108 (AAC)
154 Arts 24(2)(b) and 25 EU Reg 883/04; *Helder and Farrington v College voor Zorgverzekeringen*, C-321/12 [2013]
155 Art 26 EU Reg 883/04
156 Art 31 EU Reg 883/04
157 Art 11(3)(a) EU Reg 883/04; *JS v SSWP* [2019] UKUT 239 (AAC); Vol 2 Ch 7, Part 2 Appendix 3 DMG, note to para 22; Ch 2 Appendix 1 ADM, note to para 22; ADM Memo 1/20; DMG Memo 3/20
158 Art 32(1) EU Reg 883/04
159 ADM Memo 17/20 para 13 and para 24 examples 1 and 2; DMG Memo 16/20 para 13 and para 24 examples 1 and 2
160 *JS v SSWP* [2019] UKUT 239 (AAC); Memo ADM 1/20 and DMG 3/20
161 *KR v SSWP (DLA)* [2019] UKUT 85 (AAC), reported as [2019] AACR 22, paras 18-24
162 *INASTI v Hervein and Others*, C-393/99 and C-394/99 [2002], para 51; *Leyman v INAMI*, C-3/08 [2009], para 45
163 *SSWP v AK (AA)* [2015] UKUT 110 (AAC), paras 11-12
164 *IG v SSWP* [2016] UKUT 176 (AAC), reported as [2016] AACR 41, paras 11-12
165 *IG v SSWP* [2016] UKUT 176 (AAC), reported as [2016] AACR 41, paras 32 and 40-42 and caselaw cited
166 *AH v SSWP* [2020] UKUT 53 (AAC) – case ref: C3/2020/1399 *Harrington v SSWP* listed for hearing 28-29 April 2021
167 *Hudzinski and Wawrzyniak v Agentur für Arbeit Wesel – Familienkasse*, joined cases C-611/10 and C-612/10 [2012]
168 *IG v SSWP* [2016] UKUT 176 (AAC), reported as [2016] AACR 41, para 32 and caselaw cited
169 *IG v SSWP* [2016] UKUT 176 (AAC), reported as [2016] AACR 41, para 42; see also *JMcG v (1) SSWP, (2) HMRC* [2018] UKUT 2 (AAC) and *KS v SSWP* [2018] UKUT 121 (AAC), paras 14-16
170 Art 4 EU Reg 883/04; Art 4 UK-IC; Art SSC5 UK-EUP
171 Art 18 TFEU; Art 24 EU Dir 2004/38; Art 7 EU Reg 492/2011
172 *Patmalniece v SSWP* [2011] UKSC 11
173 *European Commission v UK*, C-308/14 [2016]
174 *Commissioners for HMRC v Aiga Spiridonova*, 13/115948
175 *Fratila and Tanase v SSWP* [2020] EWCA Civ 1741
176 *Fratila and Tanase v SSWP* [2020] EWHC 998 (Admin)
177 Art 5 EU Reg 883/04; Art 5 UK-IC; Art SSC6 UK-EUP
178 *Knauer v Landeshauptmann von Vorarlberg* C-453/14 [2016]; CG/1346/2018; *HT v SSWP* [2020] UKUT 57 (AAC); DMG Memo 2/20
179 Art 7(1) and (2) EU Reg 492/11
180 *AS v HMRC* [2017] UKUT 361 (AAC), reported as [2018] AACR 14
181 Reg 13(6)(K) WTC(EMR) Regs
182 Recital 11 EU Reg 883/04
183 Recital 10 EU Reg 883/04
184 Art 6 EU Reg 883/04; see also Annex XI UK entry, para 2, and Art 48 TFEU; Art 6 UK-IC; Art SSC7 UK-EUP
185 Art 12 EU Reg 987/09; see *PB v SSWP (DLA)* [2016] UKUT 280 (AAC), para 10, second ground of appeal
186 Arts 1(t)(u) and (v) and 6 EU Reg 883/04; *Decision H6 of 16 December 2010 of the Administrative Commission for the Coordination of Social Security Systems* [2011] OJ C-45/04; Art 6(2) UK-IC; Art SSC7 UK-EUP
187 Art 6 and Annex XI UK entry para 2 EU Reg 883/04; *SSWP v MM and BK v SSWP* [2016] UKUT 547 (AAC), para 25
188 *SSWP v MM and BK v SSWP* [2016] UKUT 547 (AAC), paras 18-27 and 35.
189 *Kavanagh and Another v SSWP* [2019] EWCA Civ 272
190 Art 19 UK-IC
191 Art 61 EU Reg 883/04; see, for example, *ONEM v M and M v ONEM*, C-284/15 [2015]; Art 21(1) and (2) UK-IC; Art SSC56 UK-EUP

192 Arts 61(2) and 65(2) and (5)(a) EU Reg 883/04; Art 21(1) and (2) UK-IC; Art SSC 56(2) UK-EUP; see also *Decision U2 of 12 June 2009 of the Administrative Commission for the Coordination of Social Security Systems* [2012] OJ C-106/12
193 Art 7 EU Reg 883/04; Art 7 UK-IC; Art SSC8 UK-EUP
194 Arts 5, 46 and 82 EU Reg 883/04; Arts 27, 46, 49 and 87 EU Reg 987/2009; Art 59(7) UK-IC; Art SSC63 UK-EUP
195 Arts SSC3(1) and (4) and 8 UK-EUP
196 Art 70 EU Reg 883/04
197 Art 10 EU Reg 883/04; Arts 8 and 31-33 UK-IC; Arts SSC9 and SSC48-50 UK-EUP
198 See, for example, *JMcG v (1) SSWP, (2) HMRC* [2018] UKUT 2 (AAC), paras 15 and 26-31
199 *Teresa and Silvana Petroni v Office National des Pensions Pour Travailleurs Salariés (ONPTS), Bruxelles* 24-75 [1975] ECR I-01149
200 Arts 53-55 EU Reg 883/04; Art 31 UK-IC; Art SSC48(3) UK-EUP
201 Art 68 EU Reg 883/04; Art 39 UK-IC

5. **Family benefits**
202 Arts 7 and 67 EU Reg 883/04; *HB v HMRC (CHB)* [2014] UKUT 554 (AAC); *WC v HMRC* [2019] UKUT 289 (AAC)
203 Art 67 EU Reg 883/04; *HMRC v Ruas* [2010] EWCA Civ 291
204 *MR v HMRC (TC)* [2011] UKUT 40 (AAC), para 17
205 *NB v HMRC (TC)* [2016] NICom 47; Art 56 TFEU
206 Art 3(x) UK-IC
207 Arts 38-42 UK-IC
208 Arts SSC1(k) and SSC3(4)(g) UK-EUP
209 Art 67 EU Reg 883/04; *HMRC v Ruas* [2010] EWCA Civ 291; Art 38 UK-IC
210 *Bogatu v Minister for Social Protection*, C-322/17 [2019]
211 *Bogatu v Minister for Social Protection*, C-322/17 [2019]
212 *BM v HMRC* [2015] UKUT 526 (AAC)
213 Art 67 EU Reg 883/04, second sentence; *Würker v Familienkasse Nurnberg*, C-32/13 [2014]; Art 38(2) UK-IC
214 Art 1(w) EU Reg 883/04; Art 1(1) UK-IC
215 s143(1)(b) SSCBA 1992; s8 TCA; reg 3(1) CTC Regs; *RK v HMRC (CHB)* [2015] UKUT 357 (AAC), reported as [2016] AACR 4; *JL v HMRC (CHB)* [2017] UKUT 193 (AAC); *RI v HMRC (TC)* [2019] UKUT 306 (AAC); *MZ v HMRC* [2020] UKUT 65 (AAC)
216 Art 68 EU Reg 883/04; Art 60 EU Reg 987/09; Art 39 UK-IC
217 'Your rights country by country' at http://ec.europa.eu/social
218 Art 68(1)(a) EU Reg 883/04; Art 60 EU Reg 987/09; Art 39(2) UK-IC
219 *Decision F1 of 12 June 2009 of the Administrative Commission for the Coordination of Social Security Systems* [2010] OJ C-106/04
220 Art 68(1)(b) EU Reg 883/04; Art 60 EU Reg 987/09; Art 39(3) UK-IC
221 See also Art 58 EU Reg 987/2009
222 Art 68(2) EU Reg 883/04; see for example, *Slanina v Unabhängiger Finanzsenat, Außenstelle Wien*, C-363/08 [2009], distinguished in *MZ v HMRC* [2020] UKUT 65 (AAC); Art 39(4) UK-IC
223 Art 68(2) EU Reg 883/04; Art 60 EU Reg 987/09; Art 39(4)(b) UK-IC
224 *Gudrun Schwemmer v Agentur für Arbeit Villingen-Schwenningen – Familienkasse*, C-16/09 [2010]; *Bundesagentur für Arbeit – Familienkasse Sachsen v Trapkowski*, C-378/14 [2015]
225 *JL v HMRC (CHB)* [2017] UKUT 193 (AAC); *WC v HMRC* [2019] UKUT 289 (AAC)
226 Art 68a EU Reg 883/04
227 Art 68(3) EU Reg 883/04; Arts 6 and 58-61 EU Reg 987/2009; see also *MZ v HMRC* [2020] UKUT 65 (AAC) para 12
228 Art 68(3) EU Reg 883/04; Art 60(2) and (3) EU Reg 987/2009
229 Arts 6(2)-(3) and 60(4) EU Reg 987/2009
230 Art 6(2) EU Reg 987/09
231 TCTM 2815-75; paras 10204-13 CBTM
232 Arts 39-42 UK-IC

Chapter 17

International agreements

This chapter covers:

The rules in this chapter may help you to obtain benefits in the UK, or to get your benefit paid in another country. However, if you are moving to or from or within the European Economic Area (EEA), one or more of the sets of European Union (EU) co-ordination rules may apply to you instead. These co-ordination rules are covered in Chapter 16 and are cross-referred to in this chapter where relevant.

In this *Handbook* all references to the EEA are to be read as including Switzerland. The EEA states are listed on p47.

1. Reciprocal agreements

A reciprocal agreement is a two-way agreement made between the UK and another country. Reciprocal agreements are part of UK law and their purpose is to protect your entitlement to benefits if you move from one country that is a party to an agreement to the other.[1] A reciprocal agreement can help you qualify for certain benefits by allowing periods of residence and contributions paid in each country to be added together (this is similar to the 'aggregation principle' in the European Union (EU) co-ordination rules – see p383). It can also mean that you are paid more generously when you go abroad than you would be under the UK rules. In addition, they often specify that you must receive equal treatment with nationals of the country to which you have moved.

In general, a reciprocal agreement only applies if the EU co-ordination rules do not assist you (see p401). Therefore, if you are moving to or from a European Economic Area (EEA) country, you should first check whether you are covered by any of the EU co-ordination rules, whether they apply to the country you are going to or from, and whether they assist with the benefit you are claiming – for the steps to follow, see p352.

You do not need to first check the EU co-ordination rules if you are moving to or from a non-EEA country, Northern Ireland, the Channel Islands or the Isle of Man.

Reciprocal agreements differ in terms of the benefits and people covered and the provisions made. It is therefore crucial to check the individual agreement. You can find the agreements at legislation.gov.uk – search under the relevant country. However, most of the agreements on the website have not been fully updated, so also check for any amendments.

See Appendix 5 for a list of all the countries and the benefits covered.

The following benefits are not covered by any reciprocal agreement:

- housing benefit;
- income support;
- income-based jobseeker's allowance (JSA) (except by the agreement with Northern Ireland – see p399);
- employment and support allowance (ESA) (but see below);
- pension credit;
- personal independence payment (PIP) (but see below);
- social fund payments;
- universal credit;
- child tax credit;
- working tax credit.

Note: although amendments have been made enabling reciprocal agreements to be extended to include ESA and PIP,[2] in general, the necessary amendments to the individual agreements have not been made. However, the agreements with Northern Ireland cover both ESA and PIP (see p399). Most agreements cover your award of contributory ESA if it was converted from incapacity benefit (see p404). It may be arguable that the agreement with the countries of former Yugoslavia (see below) does not need to be amended to cover ESA and PIP because it contains a provision for cover to be extended to 'amendments, supplements and consolidations of listed legislation', provided the parties agree.[3]

The reciprocal agreement between the UK and the former Yugoslavia is a single agreement, but is treated as separate agreements with Bosnia-Herzegovina, Croatia, Kosovo, North Macedonia, Montenegro, Serbia and Slovenia. **Note:** Croatia and Slovenia are members of the EU and therefore EU co-ordination rules may apply.

Agreements with non-European Economic Area countries

The UK has reciprocal agreements with some countries outside the EEA.

Each reciprocal agreement is different in terms of who is covered, which benefits are included and what arrangements are provided.

For a full list of the countries and the benefits covered, see Appendix 5.

Agreements with Ireland, Northern Ireland, the Channel Islands, the Isle of Man and Gibraltar

The rules on most social security benefits only apply in Great Britain – ie, England, Wales and Scotland. This does not include Northern Ireland, the Channel Islands, the Isle of Man or Gibraltar, which have their own social security legislation. There are reciprocal agreements between all of these to ensure you do not lose out if you move between them.

If your situation involves **the UK and Ireland** (eg, you are moving between the two, or you live in one and work in the other), check whether you are covered by the main EU co-ordination rules, the new UK–Ireland Convention on Social Security, or the new UK–EU Protocol on Social Security (see p355), and, if so, whether the benefit you want to claim is covered (see p363).

There is also an agreement with Ireland that applies across the **'common travel area'** (Ireland, the UK, the Channel Islands and the Isle of Man).[4] This agreement only applies if none of the EU co-ordination rules apply to you or to your situation – eg, if you have been working in the Channel Islands or Isle of Man, or moving between either and Ireland.[5]

The Memorandum of Understanding on the Common Travel Area confirms the right of British citizens in Ireland, and Irish citizens in the UK, to the same social security rights as citizens of that state.[6]

Not all benefits and circumstances are covered by any specific agreement, so always check the provisions of the relevant agreement.

Note: although the reciprocal agreement between the UK and the Channel Islands does not cover Sark, there are regulations to ensure you are not disadvantaged by being there.[7]

See p405 for information on retirement pensions and bereavement support payment and Sark and the Isle of Man.

Agreements with Northern Ireland

Reciprocal arrangements between Northern Ireland and Great Britain aim to co-ordinate the social security systems, creating a coherent system of social security throughout the UK.[8] The purpose of the arrangements is to ensure that when you move between the two, you are entitled to the same rights and benefits paid at the same rates, you do not need to make a new claim for the same benefit, and you do not need to return to the previous territory if you appeal a decision made there.[9] The Upper Tribunal considered the operation of the reciprocal agreements in the case of a woman who had moved to Great Britain and was appealing a decision made in Northern Ireland. The judge confirmed her appeal must be heard by the First-tier Tribunal in Great Britain, but that the relevant legislation was that of Northern Ireland.[10]

The reciprocal arrangements between Northern Ireland and Great Britain were replaced on 6 April 2016.[11] The replacement arrangements updated and extended the previous ones.

Although some benefits (many means-tested benefits, tax credits and all statutory payments) are still not covered, the new arrangements now include, from 6 April 2016, ESA (both contributory and income-related), PIP (in addition to attendance allowance, disability living allowance and carer's allowance that continue to be covered), state pension from 27 November 2016, income-based JSA (contribution-based JSA was already covered) from 6 April 2017, bereavement support payment,[12] and from 27 July 2020, universal credit.[13]

There is also guidance aimed at ensuring smooth and efficient co-opertation between the Department for Work and Pensions (DWP), in Great Britain, and the Department for Communities, in Northern Ireland.[14]

Note: before the agreements were extended to ESA, the DWP policy on ESA was to make extra-statutory payments to make up any loss of ESA that resulted from having to make a new claim when moving from Northern Ireland to Great Britain or vice versa.[15] These extra-statutory payments continued after 6 April 2017. If you do not satisfy the contribution conditions for contributory ESA but you have been receiving extra-statutory payments, you are treated as satisfying these conditions and as having made a claim for ESA from 27 November 2016, and your period of limited capability for work is treated as continuous.[16]

Agreements with Gibraltar

Gibraltar is a British overseas territory and the only one which is part of the EU. As the UK is responsible for Gibraltar's external relations, EU law treats Gibraltar as part of the UK for the purposes of the EU social security co-ordination.[17] However, Gibraltar and Great Britain have separate social security systems. The reciprocal agreement between Gibraltar and Great Britain provides for you to be treated as having the same rights and liabilities under the main EU co-ordination rules (except for family benefits) as you would have if the UK and Gibraltar were separate EEA states.[18] Saving regulations ensure that social security co-ordination with Gibraltar continues on the same basis as before the end of the transition period (see p350) until any new agreement is negotiated between the UK and Gibraltar.[19]

If you are covered by this reciprocal agreement and resident in Gibraltar, you can make a new claim for the young carer grant, carer's allowance supplement, and, it is expected, child disability payment, if you can demonstrate a 'genuine and sufficient link' to Scotland and the UK is your competent state (see p285 and p330).

Agreements with European Economic Area states

The UK has reciprocal agreements with most of the EEA member states. For a list of the states with which the UK has social security agreements and the benefits covered by each, see Appendix 5.

In general, until the end of the transition period (see p350), reciprocal agreements could be relied on by EEA nationals if the main (or old) EU co-ordination rules did not apply.[20] This means that, in most cases, you could not qualify for benefits using a reciprocal agreement if you were covered by the main (or old) co-ordination rules (see p355) *and* acquired your right to benefit on, or after, the date those EU co-ordination rules applied.[21] However, it is less clear if you can rely on reciprocal agreements between EEA states if you are not covered by the main (or old) EU co-ordiation rules, but you are covered by the new UK–EU Protocol. Get specialist advice if this could affect you.

Changes due to the UK leaving the European Union

The UK left the EU on 31 January 2020, but the main EU co-ordination rules continued to apply until the end of the transition period at 11pm on 31 December 2020.

From the end of the transition period:

- you can only be covered by the main EU co-ordination rules if you are covered by the Withdrawal Agreement protections (see p356);
- if your situation involves only the UK and Ireland, you may be covered by the new UK–Ireland Convention, which is in force from 1 January 2021 (see p358). This convention broadly reproduces the principles and effects of the main co-ordination rules, but is limited to the UK and Ireland and to specified benefits of each country;
- if your situation only involves the UK and Norway, you may be covered by the new UK–Norway Convention, which is in force from 1 January 2021. This convention amends, updates and replaces an earlier UK–Norway convention and covers Norway, the UK, the Isle of Man and Jersey;[22]
- if you are not covered by the Withdrawal Agreement protections and the main EU co-ordination rules, you may be covered by the UK–EU Protocol, which covers the UK and all the EU member states, but not Iceland, Liechtenstein, Norway and Switzerland (see p359).

If you are not covered by any of the above bullet points, you should check whether a reciprocal agreement covers you and the benefit you are claiming.

For more details on the operation of the EU co-ordination rules after the transition period, and how to check whether they apply, see p350.

People covered by the agreements

Some of the reciprocal agreements cover nationals of the contracting countries, while others apply to 'people going from one member state to another'. This may be particularly significant if you are a non-EEA national who has worked in two or more EEA states but you cannot benefit under the co-ordination rules (see p355). The agreements with Belgium, Denmark, France, Italy and Luxembourg only cover nationals.[23] The convention with the Netherlands covers people who have been subject to the legislation of one or both member states and their family members and survivors.[24]

The reciprocal agreements define who is counted as a national for the purpose of the agreement, where nationality is an issue. In all of these, a UK national is defined as a 'citizen of the United Kingdom and Colonies'.[25]

This category of people disappeared on 1 January 1983 when the British Nationality Act 1981 came into force. On this date, if you previously had citizenship of the UK and Colonies, you might have become:

- a British citizen;
- a British overseas territories citizen (subsequently renamed British dependent territories citizen); *or*
- a British overseas citizen.

You might also have become one of the above after 1 January 1983, including if you were born after this date. The rules on this are beyond the scope of this *Handbook*.

For the purpose of the conventions with Belgium, Denmark, France, Italy and Luxembourg, a UK national now includes anyone in one of the above categories.

The definition of nationality in the agreements with Denmark, Italy and Luxembourg is simply that of a 'Danish' or 'Italian' or 'Luxemburger' national.[26] You have no rights under these agreements if you are not a national of one of these states. The agreement with Belgium, however, covers a 'person having Belgian nationality or a native of the Belgian Congo or Ruanda-Urundi'. The agreement with France refers to 'a person having French nationality' and 'any French-protected person belonging to French Togoland or the French Cameroons'.

When these agreements came into force in 1958, the Belgian Congo and Ruanda-Urundi and French Togoland and the French Cameroons were Belgian and French territories. Which Belgian and French nationals are covered by the agreements is a matter for the Belgian and French authorities. If you come from one of these countries (present-day Democratic Republic of Congo, Rwanda, Burundi, Togolese Republic and the Republic of Cameroon), check with the Belgian or French authorities whether you are covered by these agreements.

The agreements give equal treatment to nationals of the contracting countries, stating that a 'national of one contracting party shall be entitled to receive the benefits of the legislation of the other contracting party under the same conditions as if he were a national of the latter contracting party'.[27]

The reciprocal agreements with Finland, Iceland, Ireland, Portugal, Spain and Sweden are not confined to nationals but give rights to:

- in relation to the Ireland and the UK, persons not covered by the EU co-ordination rules, and in relation to Ireland and Jersey, Guernsey and the Isle of Man, people who have been subject to their legislation (and family members and survivors);[28]
- 'a person subject to the legislation of one contracting party who becomes resident in the territory of the other party' (Portugal);
- 'a national of one contracting party, or a person subject to the legislation of that party, who becomes resident in the territory of the other contracting party' (Spain);
- 'a national of the state and person deriving their rights from such nationals and other people who are, or have been, covered by the legislation of either of the states and people deriving their rights from such a person' (Sweden).

The agreements with Austria and Norway have nationality restrictions that apply to benefits in kind (eg, medical treatment), but not to social security contributions and benefits. A national of the UK is defined as anyone who is recognised by the UK government as a UK national, provided s/he is 'ordinarily resident' in the UK.

The agreement with Germany is not restricted to nationals of either contracting country insofar as social security benefits are concerned. However, a nationality provision applies to contribution liability.

Benefits covered by the agreements

The following benefits are covered by some of the reciprocal agreements. See Appendix 5 for a full list of which benefits apply to which countries.

Unemployment benefits

The relevant benefit in the UK is contribution-based JSA and, for the agreements between Great Britain and Northern Ireland only, also income-based JSA (see p399).

The agreements between Great Britain and Northern Ireland, and between the UK and the Isle of Man, allow you to continue to be paid JSA while absent in the other territory.[29] However, none of the other agreements allow you to receive unemployment benefits outside the country in which you have paid your national insurance (NI) contributions.[30]

Some of the agreements allow NI paid in one country to count towards satisfying the conditions of entitlement in another. This is the case with the UK agreements with Austria, Canada, Cyprus, Finland, Iceland, the Isle of Man, Jersey, Guernsey, Malta, New Zealand, Norway and the agreement with the states of former Yugoslavia (see p397), as well as the agreements between Great Britain and Northern Ireland.

Sickness and invalidity benefits

In the UK, the relevant sickness benefit was short-term incapacity benefit (IB) and the relevant invalidity benefit was long-term IB. In 2008, IB was abolished for new claims and replaced by ESA. There are now very few remaining claimants of long-term IB, but if you still receive this the agreements continue to apply.

Although reciprocal agreements can be amended to apply to ESA,[31] in general, the necessary amendments to the individual agreements have not been made.[32] There are two exceptions. The reciprocal agreements cover:

- contributory ESA if your award was converted from IB. Your ESA is covered by each of the agreements (except the Isle of Man, Israel and Switzerland) that cover invalidity benefits (see Appendix 5);[33]
- both contributory and income-related ESA under the agreement between Great Britain and Northern Ireland (see p399).

It may be arguable that the agreement with the states of former Yugoslavia (see p397) does not need to be amended in order to cover ESA. This is because it allows for the agreement to be extended to 'amendments, supplements and consolidations of listed legislation', provided the contracting parties agree.[34]

The agreements on sickness and invalidity benefits vary. For example, some enable you to be paid in another country, and some enable contributions paid under one country's scheme to be taken into account to help you satisfy the conditions of entitlement in another. The agreements with Austria, Cyprus, Iceland, Norway and Sweden allow you to continue to receive your IB in these countries, subject to medical checks being undertaken in the agreement country. Similarly, you can receive the other country's invalidity benefits in the UK. The agreement with Barbados allows a certificate of permanent incapacity to be issued, permitting you to receive your invalidity benefit without medical checks.

Maternity benefits

In the UK, the relevant maternity benefit is maternity allowance (MA).

If you are entitled to maternity benefits, some of the agreements allow you to receive your benefit in another country. You may be entitled to MA, or continue to be paid MA, when absent from the UK, under the reciprocal agreements with Barbados, Cyprus, Ireland, the Isle of Man, Jersey and Guernsey, Switzerland, Turkey and the countries of the former Republic of Yugoslavia (see p397), and when you have moved from Great Britain to Northern Ireland or vice versa. The circumstances under which you may be able to claim or retain MA differ from agreement to agreement.

Benefits for industrial injuries

The relevant benefits in the UK are industrial injuries disablement benefit (including constant attendance allowance or exceptionally severe disablement allowance), reduced earnings allowance and retirement allowance.

Most of the agreements include industrial injuries benefits. The arrangements determine which country's legislation applies to new accidents or diseases, depending on where you are insured at the time. Many of the agreements allow you to combine industrial injuries incurred in each country when assessing the degree of your latest injury. Also, if you work in one country and remain insured under the other country's scheme and you have an industrial injury, you can be treated as though the injury arose in the country in which you are insured. Most agreements include arrangements to allow you to receive all three UK benefits for industrial injuries indefinitely in the other country.

Retirement pensions and bereavement benefits

All the agreements include retirement pensions and bereavement benefits. In the UK, the relevant benefits are retirement pensions, bereavement support payment and widowed parent's allowance. All the agreements have been amended to include the new state pension from 6 April 2016[35] and bereavement support payment from 6 April 2017.[36]

There is a reciprocal agreement between the Isle of Man and the UK covering arrangements for all retirement pensions.[37] The new UK state pension does not apply in the Isle of Man, so if you reach retirement age on or after 6 April 2016 and have paid contributions in both the UK and the Isle of Man, you must make two claims under the two different systems. If you receive a UK pension while resident in the Isle of Man, or an Isle of Man pension while resident in the UK, it is uprated as if you were resident in the territory that pays the pension.[38] The reciprocal agreement has been amended to take account of the new Manx state pension payable if you reach retirement age on or after 6 April 2019.[39] See gov.im for more details of the Isle of Man and Manx pensions and if you are resident in the Isle of Man.

Note: although the reciprocal agreement between the UK and the Channel Islands does not cover Sark, you are entitled to state pension and bereavement support payment if you are ordinarily resident on Sark.[40]

The provisions of the reciprocal agreements vary. In most cases, the agreements can enable you to receive a retirement pension or bereavement benefit in the agreement country at the same rate as you would be paid in the country where you are insured. However, the agreements with Canada, New Zealand and (for those still covered by the agreement revoked on 1 March 2001, subject to limited savings provisions[41]) Australia do not permit these benefits to be uprated. If you go to live in one of these countries, your retirement pension (and any other long-term benefit) is 'frozen' at the rate payable either when you left the UK or when you became entitled to your pension abroad.

The agreements with Canada, New Zealand and (for those still covered by the agreement revoked on 1 March 2001, subject to limited savings provisions[42]) Australia, allow you to be treated as having paid NI contributions in the UK during periods when you were resident in that country.[43] From 1 April 2015,

periods of habitual residence in an EEA member state or Switzerland count as periods of residence in the UK, for the purpose of these calculations, if you:[44]
- are an EEA national (see p47);
- are covered by the main EU co-ordination rules (see p355); *and*
- have a 'genuine and sufficient link' to the UK (see p283).

The agreement with Chile is limited and relates to the continuing liability to pay NI contributions to your home country if you go to work in the other country for a period of up to five years.[45]

If you do not qualify for a retirement pension or bereavement benefit from either the UK or the other country, or you qualify for a pension or bereavement benefit from one country but not the other, the agreements with the following countries allow you to be paid basic old age and bereavement benefits on a pro rata basis, with your insurance under both schemes taken into account: Austria, Barbados, Bermuda, Cyprus, Finland, Iceland, Israel, Jamaica, Malta, Mauritius, Norway, the Philippines, Sweden, Switzerland, Turkey, the USA and the countries of the former Yugoslavia (see p397).[46]

Family benefits

In the UK, the relevant family benefits are child benefit and guardian's allowance. The provisions concerning these two benefits enable periods of residence and/or presence in the other country to be treated as residence and/or presence in Great Britain. Arguably, these provisions could enable you to to use periods of residence in the other country to satisfy the requirement for child benefit to have been living in the UK for the past three months (see p127). The extent to which reciprocity exists varies, however, according to the particular agreement. For example, residence or contributions paid in Cyprus, Jamaica, Jersey/Guernsey, the Isle of Man, Israel, Mauritius and Turkey count towards your satisfying UK residence conditions for guardian's allowance.

If you are a 'person subject to immigration control' (see p81) and you are covered by a reciprocal agreement for child benefit, your immigration status does not exclude you from entitlement to child benefit (see p100). In practice, this is most helpful if you are covered by the agreement with the former Yugoslavia (a single agreement, which is treated as separate agreements with Bosnia-Herzegovina, Croatia, Kosovo, North Macedonia, Montenegro, Serbia and Slovenia).[47] You must still meet the other conditions of entitlement, including the residence and presence requirements (see p277).

Dependants' benefits

In the UK, a dependant's benefit is an increase to the benefit covered by the agreement. Dependants' increases can be paid if the dependant is in either country to the agreement.

2. Council of Europe conventions and agreements

There are a number of European conventions and agreements, prepared and negotiated within the Council of Europe – eg, the European Convention on Human Rights. The purpose of these conventions is to address issues of common concern in economic, social, cultural, scientific, legal and administrative matters and in human rights. The agreements and conventions are not legally binding in the UK unless they are incorporated into UK law, or legislation is enacted to give specific effect to the treaty obligations in question – eg, the Human Rights Act incorporates the rights set out in the European Convention on Human Rights into UK law. They are statements of intent of the individual countries that are signatories. The UK is a signatory to a number of these agreements, including two that are significant for social security.

The **European Convention on Social and Medical Assistance** has been in force since 1954. It requires ratifying states to provide social assistance in cash and in kind to nationals of other ratifying states who are lawfully present in their territories and who are without sufficient resources on the same conditions as their own nationals. It also prevents ratifying states from repatriating a lawfully present national of other ratifying states simply because s/he is in need of assistance.

The **1961 European Social Charter** is a similar agreement, giving similar access to UK social security benefits to nationals of ratifying states who are lawfully present. It is only the 1961 Charter that has the effect below. If you are a national of a country that has signed a later charter only, that will not assist you.

The countries that have ratified one or both of these agreements are all the EEA countries (*except* Bulgaria, Liechtenstein, Lithuania, Romania and Slovenia), as well as the non-EEA countries of Turkey and North Macedonia. For a list of the EEA countries, see p47.

Effect on benefit entitlements

The main effect of the above agreements is if you are defined as a 'person subject to immigration control' (see p81). If you are a national of one of the countries that has ratified either of the above agreements, and you are lawfully present, you are exempt from being excluded from working tax credit (see p102) or any of the means-tested benefits *other than*, for claims made on or after 1 January 2021, universal credit (UC) (see p97). **Note:** it may be arguable that excluding UC claimants from this exemption is unlawful on the basis that UC should, like the other means-tested benefits, be defined as 'social assistance' under these agreements.[48]

You can only benefit from the above agreements if you are **'lawfully present'** in the UK. In practice, this means you must be within a period in which you have leave to enter or remain in the UK.

Note: if your leave is subject to a 'no recourse to public funds' condition, claiming benefit as a result of being covered by this exemption is not regarded by the Home Office as having recourse to public funds and so does not breach that condition (see p87).[49]

You still must satisfy the other conditions of entitlement, including, for means-tested benefits, having a right to reside (see p151).[50] If you are within a period of leave, you are both lawfully present and have a right to reside (see p166). However, although the House of Lords held that an asylum seeker with temporary admission is 'lawfully present' and so potentially able to benefit from this exemption,[51] temporary admission does not give you a right to reside.[52] (Temporary admission was replaced by immigration bail from 15 January 2018, but the same arguments are likely to apply.)

3. European Union co-operation and association agreements

The Treaty on the Functioning of the European Union provides for agreements to be made with countries outside the European Union (EU).[53] The EU has a number of co-operation and association agreements which can be divided into those that include a rule on equal treatment and have quite a wide scope (see below), and those that do not include an equal treatment rule and whose scope is much narrower (see p410).

These co-operation and association agreements were directly applicable in UK law until the end of the transition period (31 December 2020). Since then most of these have been replaced by new Trade and Continuity Agreements, which are intended to replicate the effects of the previous agreements with bilateral agreements with the UK that reproduce similar provisions in relation to social security rights.

Agreements with equal treatment provisions

The EU agreements that most directly affected benefit entitlement in the UK are those with Algeria,[54] Morocco,[55] San Marino, Tunisia and Turkey.[56]

All these agreements specified that there must be equal treatment for those covered by the agreement in matters of 'social security'. They also contain provisions for aggregating, for the purposes of entitlement to certain social security benefits, periods of insurance or employment completed in one or more EU countries when someone covered by the agreement moves between EU states.

The Court of Justice of the European Union (CJEU) found, in one case, the Turkish agreement and, in another, the Algerian agreement, to be inspired by the old EU co-ordination rules and that these rules should be looked to for guidance in interpreting the agreements. The CJEU held that the benefits covered by these agreements were those classed as 'social security benefits' under the co-ordination rules.[57] See p363 for a full list of these benefits.

UK regulations specified that if you are defined as a 'person subject to immigration control' (see p81) but you are covered by one of these agreements (see below), you are exempt from the exclusion from certain non-contributory benefits (see p98) and tax credits (see p102) that would otherwise apply. If your claim began before 1 January 2021, these rules continue to apply.

If your claim began on or after 1 January 2021, you are a national of Morocco, San Marino, Tunisia or Turkey and you are lawfully working in the UK, you are covered by equivalent rules that mean you are not excluded from the specified benefits despite being defined as a 'person subject to immigration control'. At the time of writing, the UK was seeking an agreement with Algeria, which was expected to have a similar effect. Check whether such an agreement has been reached if that could affect you.

The Upper Tribunal held that the equal treatment provisions in relation to family benefits meant that a Moroccan national who was lawfully working in the UK, and therefore covered by the agreement, could not be excluded from child benefit and child tax credit on the basis that her only right to reside in the UK was as the primary carer of a British citizen (see p157).[58] As a result of this decision, the child benefit and child tax credit regulations were amended, and have been subsequently amended to take account of the changing agreements.[59]

Note: at the time of writing, the UK had signed, but not implemented, a partnership, trade and co-operation agreement with **Albania**, which was understood to include social security provisions.[60] It was understood these included provisions on family benefits that could enable you to be entitled to child benefit despite being defined as a a 'person subject to immigration control' (see p99). Get up-to-date advice if that could affect you.

Who is covered

To benefit from the previous or current agreements, you must, at the relevant time, be within their 'personal scope' – ie, you must be a national of Morocco, Tunisia, San Marino or Turkey (or for claims made before 1 January 2021, Algeria) and you must be lawfully working in the UK.

Lawfully working

'Lawfully working' in the previous agreements was equated with being an 'insured person' under the EU co-ordination rules. In broad terms, this means that you must have been insured by paying, or being credited with, national insurance (NI) contributions.[61] However, this interpretation does not necessarily apply to the new agreements. It is likely that you will only be accepted as 'lawfully working' if your work does not breach any work restrictions attached to your leave or, if you are an asylum seeker, you have permission to work from the Home Office.

Other agreements: Israel

The EU also has various agreements with other countries. In general, these do not contain any provisions on the co-ordination of social security schemes, except for the agreement with Israel.[62]

The agreement with Israel covers nationals of the European Economic Area (EEA) and Israel who are legally working in the EEA (for Israelis) or Israel (for EEA nationals) and members of their family who are legally resident.

It covers benefits designed to protect against the risks of old age, invalidity and accidents at work, benefits for survivors and family benefits. The interpretation of these categories is similar to the EU co-ordination rules (see p363).

This agreement would have ceased to apply at the end of the transition period. However, its effects are reproduced in a new Trade and Partnership Agreement which incorporates the previous agreement, subject to some modifications.[63]

If you are covered by the agreement:[64]

- for Israelis, all your periods of residence, insurance and employment in the UK and EEA states are totalled for the purpose of working out your entitlement to the benefits covered;
- the benefits covered (except non-contributory benefits) can be exported to (for Israelis) Israel or (for UK and EEA nationals) from Israel to the UK or EEA.

Israel also has a reciprocal agreement with the UK.[65] See Appendix 5 for the benefits covered.

Notes

1. **Reciprocal agreements**
   1 s179 SSAA 1992
   2 s179(3), (4) and (5) SSAA 1992
   3 Art 2 FANIII(Y)O
   4 The Social Security (Ireland) Order 2007, No.2122
   5 Art 2 The Social Security (Ireland) Order 2007, No.2122; paras 4-6 Ch 1 DWPWAG; Explanatory Memo to UK-IC
   6 *Memorandum of Understanding between Ireland and the UK concerning the Common Travel Area and associated reciprocal rights and privileges*, May 2019, para 10
   7 In particular, reg 12, SS(PA) Regs
   8 s87 Northern Ireland Act 1998; SS(NIRA) Regs; SS(GBRA)(NI) Regs

9 Sch para 2 SS(NIRA) Regs; Explanatory memorandum to SS(NIRA) Regs, para 4.2; see also *AG v The Department for Communities (DLA)* [2017] UKUT 442 (AAC), paras 15-24
10 *AG v The Department for Communities (DLA)* [2017] UKUT 442 (AAC), paras 15-24
11 SS(NIRA) Regs; SS(GBRA)(NI) Regs
12 SS(NIRA)(A) Regs; SS(GBRA)(A)NI Regs; see also DMG Memo 1/17
13 **UC** (GBRA) Regs; UC(NIRA) Regs; see also ADM Memo 18/20
14 *Concordat between the Department for Work and Pensions and the Department for Communities*, 4 June 2018
15 DWP guidance, *Extra-statutory Payments for Claimants Moving from Northern Ireland to Great Britain*, available at cpag.org.uk/welfare-rights/resources/article/dwp-guidance-relating-extra-statutory-payments-esa-claimants-who
16 Sch Arts 2A-2B SS(NIRA) Regs; Sch Arts 2A-2B SS(GBRA)(NI) Regs; see also DMG Memo 1/17, paras 4-7
17 Art 355(3) TFEU; Vol 2 Ch 7, para 070040 DMG; para C1005 ADM;
18 Sch para 2 The Family Allowances, National Insurance and Industrial Injuries (Gibraltar) Order 1974, No.555; see also Vol 2 Ch 7, paras 070044 and 070331 DMG; para C1005 ADM; *SSWP v Garland* [2014] EWCA Civ 1550, para 33
19 reg 8 Social Security Co-ordination (Revocation of Retained Direct EU Legislation and Related Amendments) (EU Exit) Regs 2020, 1508
20 See, for example, Art 8 EU Reg 883/04, Art 2 The Social Security (Ireland) Order 2007, No.2122 and the Explanatory Memo to the UK-IC
21 *Walder v Bestuur der Sociale Verzekeringsbank*, C-82/72 [1973]; *Galinsky v Insurance Officer*, C-99/80 [1981]; R(P) 1/81; *Jean-Louis Thévenon and Stadt Speyer-Sozialamt v Landesversicherungsanstalt Rheinland-Pfalz*, C-475/93 [1995]; *Balazs v Casa Judeteana de Pensii Cluj*, C-401/13 [2015]
22 The Social Security (Norway) Order 2020, No.1597 (revokes the Social Security (Norway) Order 1992, No.3212)
23 Art 3 to each of the relevant reciprocal agreements
24 Art 2 The Social Security (Netherlands) Order 2007, No.631
25 Art 1 to each of the relevant reciprocal agreements
26 Art 1 to each of the relevant reciprocal agreements
27 Art 1 to each of the relevant reciprocal agreements
28 Art 2 The Social Security (Ireland) Order 2007, No.2122
29 Sch para 2 SS(NIRA) Regs; Sch para 2 SS(GBRA)(NI) Regs; Sch 1 para 2(1) The Social Security (Isle of Man) Order 1977, No.2150
30 Confirmed in Vol 2 Ch 7, para 070338 DMG
31 s179(3), (4) and (5) SSAA 1992
32 para 070312 DMG
33 SS(RA)O
34 Art 2 FANIII(Y)O
35 SS(NIRA) Regs
36 The Social Security (Reciprocal Agreements) Order 2017, No.159
37 The Social Security (Reciprocal Agreement) (Isle of Man) Order 2016, No.157
38 Art 10, The Social Security (Reciprocal Agreement) (Isle of Man) Order 2016, No.157
39 The Social Security (Reciprocal Agreement) (Isle of Man) (Amendment) Order 2018, No.1359
40 Reg 8 The Bereavement Support Payment Regulations 2017, No.410
41 s299 Pensions Act 2004
42 s299 Pensions Act 2004
43 For the relevance of this for periods of residence in Australia before 1 March 2001, see *FE v SSWP (RP)* [2019] UKUT 61 (AAC).
44 The Social Security (Application of Reciprocal Agreements with Australia, Canada and New Zealand) (EEA States and Switzerland) Regulations 2015, No.349
45 Convention on Social Security Between the Government of the United Kingdom of Great Britain and Northern Ireland and the Government of the Republic of Chile, reproduced as Schedule to The Social Security (Contributions) (Republic of Chile) Order 2015, No.828
46 FANYIII(Y)O; *AP v SSWP(RP)* [2011] UKUT 64 (AAC)
47 FANIII(Y)O

2. **Council of Europe conventions and agreements**

48 See justification for exclusion in Explanatory Memo to SSCBCTC(A) Regs, para 7.8
49 para 6.2, notes under 'public funds' definition, IR
50 *Yesiloz v London Borough of Camden and DWP* [2009] EWCA Civ 415
51 *Szoma v SSWP* [2005] UKHL 64; [2006] 1 All ER 1, reported as R(IS) 2/06; *Yesiloz v London Borough of Camden* [2009] EWCA Civ 415
52 R(IS) 3/08

3. **European Union co-operation and association agreements**

53 Art 217 TFEU
54 Euro-Mediterranean Agreement establishing an Association between the European Community and its Member States, of the one part, and the People's Democratic Republic of Algeria, of the other part, 2005/690/EC, 18 July 2005
55 Euro-Mediterranean Agreement between the European Communities and the Kingdom of Morocco, 26 February 1996
56 Decision No.3/80 of the Council of Association, set up under the EEC-Turkey Association Agreement (sometimes referred to as the 'Ankara Agreement')
57 *Sema Sürül v Bundesanstalt für Arbeit*, C-262/96 [1999] ECR I-02685; *Babahenini v Belgian State*, C-113/97 [1998] ECR I-00183; see also CFC/2613/1997
58 *HMRC v HEH and SSWP (TC and CHB)* [2018] UKUT 237 (AAC)
59 **CB** Reg 1(3), 23(4)(b) and (4A) CB Regs
CTC Reg 3(5)(b)(ii), (5A) and (12) TC(R) Regs
60 Partnership, Trade and Cooperation Agreement between UK and Albania – signed 5 February 2021
61 *Sema Sürül v Bundesanstalt für Arbeit*, C-262/96 [1999], in particular paras 85-86 and 93
62 Euro-Mediterranean Agreement establishing an Association between the European Communities and their Member States, of the one part, and the State of Israel, of the other part, 2000/384/EC, 20 November 1995. In force on 1 June 2000; The European Communities (Definition of Treaties) (Euro-Mediterranean Agreement establishing an Association between the European Communities and their Member States and the State of Israel) Order 1997, No.863
63 The Trade and Partnership Agreement between the UK and Israel (18 February 2019)
64 Title VIII Euro-Mediterranean Agreement.
65 The National Insurance and Industrial Injuries (Israel) Order 1957, No.1879

Part 7

Benefit claims and getting paid

Chapter 18

Delays

This chapter covers:

Coronavirus

During the coronavirus pandemic, there has been an increase in new benefit claims and changes in the ways that claims, assessments and challenges are handled. You should not experience any delays in how the your claim or award is handled because the government has increased capacity and made better use of data sharing within and among government departments. The DWP has said that it will exercise greater 'trust' when seeking evidence and information related to a claim or award of benefits, but the DWP might review awards made on this basis at a later date. If you do experience delays, the information in this chapter is still relevant, and the pandemic should not in itself be used as an excuse for any delays you experience.

1. Dealing with delays

All the benefit authorities should act promptly to process your claim, to process any challenge you make to a decision and to issue payments due to you.

Although all benefit claimants can experience delays in the administration of their benefits and tax credits, you are more likely to experience delays if you are a migrant or if someone included in your claim is a migrant.

If you experience a delay, to resolve the matter it can be helpful if you:

- can establish the reasons for the delay (see below);
- are clear at which stage the delay has occurred (see p416).

The reasons for the delay

There can be many reasons for delays in benefit and tax credit administration. These are broadly due to the need for decision makers to have sufficient information, which can take time to collect, and the volume of work that decision makers have.

If you or your family member have moved to or from the UK or are not British, a delay in the administration of your benefit or tax credit could be because of the following.

- The complexity of the rules on immigration status, residence and presence, and the effect of the European Union (EU) co-ordination rules. This complexity means that decisions may be made by specialist decision makers, who often have a backlog.
- The initial benefit or tax credit claim form may not ask for all the information that the decision maker needs in relation to the effect of the rules on immigration status, residence, presence and EU co-ordination. S/he must therefore write to you or to other agencies requesting further information, and this takes extra time.
- You may have difficulties providing evidence that the decision maker has requested – eg, about your immigration status or residence rights. See Chapter 20 for more details on this and what you can do in this situation.
- If you are covered by the EU co-ordination rules, information may need to be obtained from benefit authorities in European Economic Area (EEA) countries, and that can take a long time.
- There may be a query about whether you need or have, or have applied for, a national insurance (NI) number. See Chapter 19 for more information on NI numbers.

When the delay occurs

What you can do to resolve a delay depends on the benefit you have claimed and also the stage at which the delay occurs. Delays can occur when :

- you have made a claim for benefit and are waiting for a decision on it (see below);
- you have challenged a decision on your entitlement (see p429);
- you are awaiting payment (see p434).

Note: although the information in this chapter focuses on delays in decisions on claims, challenges to refusals of claims and payments, similar issues arise if there is a delay in superseding a decision on your claim – eg, to award you increased benefit after you have reported your partner or child moving into your household. For information about supersessions, including the date they take effect, see CPAG's *Welfare Benefits and Tax Credits Handbook*.

2. Waiting for a decision on a claim

If you have been waiting for a decision on your claim, what you can do depends on which benefit or tax credit you have claimed.

Are you waiting for a decision on your claim?

1. Check that your claim has been received. If it has not, if possible provide the benefit authority with a copy of the claim and/or any evidence you previously submitted. If the benefit authority says that it has not received your claim and you have no copy, submit a new claim and ask for it to be backdated. See CPAG's *Welfare Benefits and Tax Credits Handbook* for details on the backdating rules for the different benefits and tax credits.
2. If your claim has been received, but not dealt with, ask why.
3. If the decision maker is not making a decision on your claim because there is a test case pending, see p428.
4. It is helpful to show the history of your previous contact when trying to resolve delays, so keep a copy of any letters sent or received and screenshots of any communication online with the benefit authorities. Take the name and job title of anyone you speak to on the phone and note the date and time.
5. In all communication, give your national insurance (NI) number (if you have one).

Note: administrative policy guidance is sometimes issued to decision makers on the processes to be followed when determining claims from particular groups of migrants – eg, to fast track certain claims or accept certain standard pieces of evidence. It can be helpful to refer to this guidance to ensure that it is properly applied. For an example of such a policy on the habitual residence test, see p140. Although this guidance is often internal, organisations that work with particular groups (such as recently arrived refugees) may be able to give you details of current decision-making policies and practices.

Benefits administered by the DWP and HM Revenue and Customs

The rules about making decisions on claims for benefits and tax credits administered by the DWP or HM Revenue and Customs (HMRC) – ie, all benefits except housing benefit (HB; see p424) and those devolved to the Scottish government (see p425) – do not state how long it should take to determine a claim and issue a decision. However, the decision maker must decide claims for benefit within 'a reasonable time'.[1]

Whether or not the decision maker has taken longer than 'a reasonable time' to make a decision on your claim depends on:

- the volume of claims waiting to be decided and number of available decision makers;[2]

- the facts of your case, including how long you have waited for a decision and the effect of that wait. For example, if you have no income while you wait, this delay is more serious than if the benefit would top up an existing income. Similarly, it may be relevant if you or a family member have a health condition that is exacerbated by the lack of income.

If there are specific reasons why the delay is making things particularly difficult for you or your family, tell the decision maker and suggest that it is not appropriate for your claim to be dealt with as part of a normal queuing system (whereby claims are determined in the order they are received).

If a delay continues, you could:

- request a universal credit (UC) advance or other short-term advance (certain benefits only) (see p419);
- request an interim payment of child benefit and guardian's allowance (see p424);
- apply for help from your local welfare assistance scheme (see p579);
- make a complaint in writing, follow the complaints procedure and consider requesting help from your MP (see p425);
- obtain legal advice about possible judicial review (see p428);
- check whether you can get provisional payments if the delay is due to a dispute about which is the competent state to pay your benefit or tax credit under the European Union (EU) co-ordination rules (see p372).

You can pursue more than one of these options – eg, you can make a complaint and if that does not resolve the delay, obtain legal advice about judicial review.

Is the delay due to the DWP determining whether you have a right to reside for universal credit?

If you are making a new claim for UC and have been receiving one of the benefits that UC replaces, your right to reside will have already been accepted by a decision maker, unless you have been receiving only working tax credit (WTC) or you have been in receipt of benefit continuously since April 2004 and had transitional protection. Therefore, unless there has been a change of circumstances that caused you to lose this right to reside (and provided it is not one that is excluded for UC), the fact that you have already been accepted as having a right to reside should be taken into account by the decision maker when deciding whether you have a right to reside for your UC claim. If you are applying for a UC advance, it must *appear* to the decision maker that you are entitled to UC, so your previous right to reside is relevant.

Note: if you have been receiving income support (IS), HB, child tax credit (CTC) or WTC and the DWP has not yet decided whether you have a right to reside for your UC claim or it refuses your UC claim on the basis that you do not have a right to reside, this decision does not end your award of IS, HB, CTC or WTC (see p272).

Official targets

If there are published targets for the time in which a claim should be processed, it can be helpful to refer to these. They should be taken into account when determining whether or not your claim has been dealt with as soon as is reasonably practicable.

HMRC publications state that its target for processing new child benefit and tax credit claims and changes of circumstances for UK claimants is within an average of 22 days, and for international claimants within an average of 92 days.[3] The DWP states that its claim processing time is five days for IS and 10 days for jobseeker's allowance (JSA) and employment and support allowance. For UC, the target is to make a full first payment on time after the first monthly assessment period.[4]

You may be able to argue (in a judicial review) that policy stating that it will take substantially longer to deal with non-UK national claims is unlawful if you are either covered by the EU co-ordination rules (see p355) or you are a European Economic Area (EEA) national exercising your rights as a 'worker' (see p189). The argument is that you should receive equal treatment and/or should not be deterred from exercising your right of free movement between EEA states as a worker.[5] For more information on equal treatment, see p381.

Advance payments

If you are waiting for a decision on your claim, or you are waiting to be paid (either your first or increased payments) and you are in 'financial need' (see below for what this means), you may be able to get an advance payment of your future benefit award. For UC, this is called a 'universal credit advance' and, for other benefits, a 'short-term advance'.

Advance payments are discretionary – ie, the decision maker does not have to give you an advance but must take all the circumstances of your case into account when making her/his decision – therefore, it is helpful to refer to DWP's guidance.[6]

Note: the decision maker should always determine your benefit claim and pay any benefit due, if possible, before considering an advance.[7] Consequently, requesting an advance can be a way of getting your claim processed and benefit paid.

The decision maker can only make an advance payment if:[8]

- you have made a claim for a benefit for which you can be paid an advance (see below). The only exception to this requirement is if you are not required to make a claim for benefit to be entitled, which only applies in limited circumstances; *and*
- you are in 'financial need' (see below). **Note:** if you are moving to UC from one of the benefits it replaces, you do not need to show you are in financial need to get an advance; *and*[9]

- either:
  - your claim has not been determined, but it appears likely to the decision maker that you are entitled to the benefit; *or*
  - your claim has been determined and you have been awarded benefit but:
    - you are waiting for your first payment; *or*
    - you have received your first payment, but it was for a shorter period than subsequent payments will be paid for and you are waiting for your next payment; *or*
    - you have had a change of circumstances that increases your entitlement, but your benefit has not yet been increased and paid to you; *or*
    - you are entitled to a payment, but it is impracticable to pay some or all of it on the date on which it is due.

You cannot get an advance payment if there is an appeal pending on the benefit in respect of which the advance would otherwise be paid.[10]

You can get an advance payment of any benefit *except*: [11]

- HB, although if your HB is delayed and you are a private or housing association tenant, you might be able to get a 'payment on account' (see p425);
- attendance allowance;
- disability living allowance;
- personal independence payment;
- child benefit or guardian's allowance, although you might be able to get an interim payment (see p424);
- statutory sick pay, statutory maternity pay, statutory adoption pay, statutory paternity pay or statutory shared parental pay;
- tax credits.

Financial need

'Financial need' means that there is a serious risk of damage to your health or safety or a member of your family's health or safety.[12] Guidance notes that situations that are considered 'serious risk' are not easily defined, but that examples include fleeing domestic violence and being without money for food or for gas/electricity meters.[13] The examples given in the information on UC advances on the gov.uk website are if you cannot afford to pay your rent or buy food.[14]

'Family' means your partner and any child in your household for whom you or your partner are responsible.[15]

Applications and decisions

Provided you have verified your identity, you can apply for a UC advance at your initial interview, at a subsequent meeting with your work coach, by phoning the UC helpline on 0800 328 5644 (textphone 0800 328 1344) or via your online account. You can only apply online if you are in your first assessment period.[16]

You can request a short-term advance of other benefits in person at, or by writing (by post, fax or email) to, your local job centre, or by telephoning the number for the specific benefit (see gov.uk/short-term-benefit-advance).

Explain in your application how you meet the criteria. You should give the relevant history of your benefit claim and explain how you satisfy all the conditions of entitlement, including the immigration status, residence and presence requirements. Provide evidence for any areas in which there may be a doubt – eg, the basis of your right to reside (see Chapter 12 and also p422) or the reason why you are not a 'person subject to immigration control' (see Chapter 7). You must also explain why you are in financial need (see above).

Before considering your application, DWP guidance confirms that the decision maker should always check whether s/he can simply determine your claim and issue you a payment. If so, the DWP should phone you to let you know.[17] If your benefit cannot be paid, s/he should determine your application for an advance and tell you the decision, usually on the same day or by 10am the next day.[18] This decision is notified to you on your online UC journal, or the DWP contacts you by phone (or text) for other benefits to either give you the decision or request more information.[19] If you do not have a phone, provide the DWP with the number of a friend or relative. If you cannot, the DWP will tell you to ring the benefit enquiry line after a certain period of time for an update on your request.[20]

If you are offered an advance, you are asked to accept the amount and the repayment terms. You should explain any problems with these. If you do not accept the offer, you are not given the advance.

There are no rules on how much an advance payment should be. However, the DWP considers how much you have asked for, how much you can afford to repay within the time period (see below) and what your benefit entitlement will be. Usually you can get a UC advance of up to 100 per cent of your estimated award (or estimated increase in your award due a change of circumstances).[21] The potential maximum short-term advance of other benefits is usually based on 60 per cent of your daily personal allowance multiplied by the number of days until your benefit is due to be paid.[22]

Repayments

Advance payments are recovered either in one lump-sum deduction from your next benefit payment or by smaller deductions from your regular benefit payments. You (and your partner if it is an advance of UC) must be notified of your liability to repay the advance.[23]

A UC advance is usually recovered within 24 months.[24] From April 2021, DWP policy is to recover at up to 25 per cent of your monthly UC standard allowance. However, the regulations only provide for recovery at a rate of 15 per cent of your UC standard monthly allowance, or 25 per cent if you have earned income (unless it is a 'benefit transfer' advance paid because you have recently moved from one of the benefits that UC replaces).[25] In 'exceptional circumstances', after you have been awarded the advance, you can request that recovery be deferred for up to three months.[26] 'Exceptional circumstances' are not defined, so you should contact the UC helpline and explain how a three-month deferment would help.

A short-term advance of other benefits is usually recovered within 12 weeks at no more than 25 per cent of your benefit.[27] Recovery can be deferred by up to 12 weeks if you are fleeing domestic violence.[28] In exceptional circumstances, you can request that recovery be rescheduled, over a maximum of 24 weeks. The DWP guidance gives a list of examples, including if your benefit has been reduced as a result of a sanction or separation from a partner, and an unforseen and unavoidable event.[29]

There is no right of appeal against a decision on the rate of repayments of advances (unless it is a UC benefit transfer advance).[30] You can ask for the rate of recovery to be reconsidered but if refused, your only legal remedy is judicial review (see p428). If your advance is recovered as a lump sum from arrears of benefit, you can appeal against this decision.[31]

If you are refused an advance payment

You cannot appeal against a refusal to award you an advance payment, unless it is a 'benefit transfer' advance when you move to UC from one of the benefits it replaces.[32] The only legal remedy is judicial review (see p428). However, you can ask for the decision to be reconsidered. If you are notified of the decision by phone, ask for it to be reconsidered during that phone call; if you wait until later, you could be asked to make a new application.[33] If possible, provide any additional information to support your application, and if you are aware that the decision was based on incorrect information, correct that during the call. The decision maker should then reconsider your application based on the revised information.

You can also make a complaint to the DWP (see p426), including if you were prevented from requesting an advance, and that can be effective in either obtaining an advance or in getting your claim processed.

You can contact your MP to see whether s/he can help with either a complaint or to get the decision reconsidered.

Note: you may be able to get help from your local welfare assistance scheme (see p579) as well as, or instead of, an advance. However, you should not be prevented from requesting an advance just because local welfare assistance is available.

Are you having problems getting an advance payment?

1. Be aware of the DWP's guidance on advance payments and refer to it when helpful.
2. There is no minimum period of time you must wait before applying.
3. You may be told to seek help from your local welfare assistance scheme (see p579) or you may be referred to a food bank (see p592) instead. If you consider that you meet the criteria for an advance payment, insist on your application being passed to a decision maker. Decisions on advances must be made by a decision maker, not frontline staff.

4. The decision maker who considers your application may not be an expert on the benefit rules for migrants. This lack of expertise can be a problem because a decision maker can only make an advance payment if it appears you are likely to be entitled to the benefit. It may therefore assist your application if you set out clearly how you satisfy the relevant immigration status, residence and presence conditions.

5. If you are told you cannot receive an advance because the habitual residence test has not yet been applied to you, explain how you satisfy (or are exempt from) this and ask the decision maker to reconsider her/his decision. Although DWP guidance includes an outstanding habitual residence test as an example of when it is likely someone would not be entitled to benefit and therefore when an advance should be refused,[34] decision makers should not refuse your request without considering all your circumstances. Taking such a 'blanket' approach is contrary to earlier paragraphs in the guidance and is arguably unlawful.[35] If you are making a new claim for UC and have been receiving one of the means-tested benefits that UC replaces, your habitual residence (including your right to reside) will have previously been accepted by a decision maker. That is relevant to your application for a UC advance since it must *appear* to the decision maker that you are entitled to UC (see p418 for more information).

6. If the reason your claim cannot be processed is because you are waiting to obtain evidence showing that you satisfy all the conditions of entitlement, it may help to explain the cause of the delay, summarise any other evidence that you have already submitted and explain how it is consistent with the evidence for which you are waiting. For more information on the evidence required for the immigration status and residence tests, see Chapter 20.

7. The decision maker may suggest that you are not entitled to an advance because you do not have an NI number. If that happens, point out that the DWP guidance states that a short-term advance should still be considered, provided you can prove your identity and are complying with other requests for evidence.[36] The guidance also states that the DWP must ensure that all necessary action to allocate an NI number is taken promptly to ensure the claim can be finalised and paid.[37] See Chapter 19 for further information on the NI requirement.

8. If you are, or think you might be, refused an advance on the grounds that you cannot repay it within the usual timescale, note the following.

- The regulations do not require you to be able repay the advance within any particular period.
- DWP guidance covers circumstances in which the standard repayment rates can be varied. For example, you can agree to maker higher repayments to pay back the advance over a shorter period and, in exceptional circumstances, recovery can be rescheduled over a longer period or deferred (see p421).[38]
- Make sure the decision maker is aware if your circumstances are likely to change in the future and improve your ability to repay the advance.

Interim payments of child benefit and guardian's allowance

An interim payment of child benefit or guardian's allowance can be made if it appears to HMRC that you may be entitled to benefit and:[39]

- you have not claimed correctly and it is impracticable for such a claim to be made immediately; *or*
- you have claimed correctly and all the conditions of entitlement are satisfied *except* the NI number requirement (see p442) and it is impracticable for that to be satisfied immediately; *or*
- you have claimed correctly, but it is impracticable for the claim to be dealt with immediately; *or*
- you have been awarded benefit, but it is impracticable to pay you immediately, other than by an interim payment.

Note:

- You cannot appeal against a refusal to award you an interim payment. The only legal remedy is judicial review (see p428). You can ask HMRC to reconsider its refusal and you can complain. You can also contact your MP to see whether s/he can help to get the decision reconsidered.
- An interim payment can be deducted from any later payment of the benefit and, if it is more than your actual entitlement, the overpayment can be recovered. You should be notified of this in advance.[40]
- An interim payment cannot be paid if you have an appeal pending.[41]

Housing benefit

Your HB claim must be determined within 14 days (or as soon as reasonably practicable after that) of your submitting a valid claim and providing all the information and evidence requested and reasonably required by the local authority.[42]

What counts as 'as soon as reasonably practicable' is the same as for benefits administered by the DWP and HMRC (see p417). In addition, the fact that your home may be at risk of repossession if the rent is not paid can often be a relevant factor in determining how long it should take to make a decision.

If you experience a delay in the local authority deciding your claim for HB, you can:

- request a 'payment on account' if you are a private or housing association tenant (see below);
- make a written complaint (see p427);
- obtain legal advice about a judicial review (see p428).

You can pursue more than one of these options – eg, you can complain and if that does not resolve the delay, get legal advice about seeking a judicial review.

Note: HB guidance advising local authorities to refer claimants from the 'Windrush generation' (see p70) who are unable to provide evidence of their immigration status to the Home Office taskforce and then 'wait at least two weeks' before processing their claims is unlawful.[43] CPAG had been advised that the DWP was reviewing its procedures and taking legal advice on this point.[44] If you are a Commonwealth citizen and do not have documents showing your right to remain in the UK, get specialist immigration advice *before* contacting the Home Office as the rules are complex (see p70).

Payments on account

The local authority must make an interim payment (a 'payment on account') if:[45]

- you have claimed HB as a private or housing association tenant; *and*
- it is impracticable for it to make a decision on your claim within 14 days of its being made; *and*
- you have provided any information and evidence requested, or there is a good cause for your failure to do so.

A payment on account is not discretionary. The local authority *must* pay the amount it considers reasonable based on the information it has about your circumstances. If your actual entitlement is less, the local authority recovers the overpayment, or pays arrears if your entitlement is greater.[46] The local authority must notify you of the amount of a payment on account and that it can recover any overpayment resulting from your actual HB entitlement being lower.[47]

You do not need to ask the local authority to make a payment on account or make a separate claim.[48] However, in practice, it is often necessary to write and request a payment on account, and/or make a complaint (see below), and/or write to the solicitor for the local authority and threaten judicial review (see p428) in order to get a payment.

Scottish benefits

The rules for making decisions about benefits devolved to the Scottish government and administered by Social Security Scotland (SSS) do not state how long it should take to determine a claim and issue a decision. However, SSS aims to make decisions on Best Start grants and Best Start foods applications in 21 days, funeral support payments in 10 days (or request further information) and young carer grants in 14 days (or request further information).[49] There are no rules that allow advance or interim payments if SSS takes longer to make a decision on your application, but you can make a complaint.

Making a complaint

Making a complaint when there is an ongoing problem (such as a claim that has not been decided) is different from making a complaint about a situation that you think should not have happened but which is no longer producing a problem – eg, if your claim has been decided, but you are unhappy it took so long. The information in this section is aimed at enabling you to use the complaints process to get the situation resolved (ie, to get a decision on your claim), rather than at seeking compensation or highlighting to the decision maker the hardship it has caused after a delay has been resolved.

When you make a complaint to try to resolve an ongoing delay, it is important to highlight that the problem persists, that this is therefore an urgent matter and be clear what you want to be done about it – eg, ask for your claim to be determined within X number of days. If the complaint is about your UC housing costs or HB claim, include any relevant details of steps your landlord is taking to obtain possession of the property as a consequence of the rent arrears arising from the delay.

The DWP, HMRC and SSS have different procedures for complaining. Local authorities should have their own complaints procedures. These procedures are outlined briefly below, but see CPAG's *Welfare Benefits and Tax Credits Handbook* for more detailed information about making a complaint.

Sometimes your local MP or councillor can help when there are problems with your claim or if you are getting no response to a complaint. If you want to complain about the DWP or HMRC to the Ombudsman, you must first ask your MP for help. If you do not know who your local MP is or how to contact her/him you can call 0800 112 4272 or 020 7219 4272 or see members.parliament.uk. If your complaint is about SSS, your MSP may be able to help (see parliament.scot/msps.aspx). You should be able find out who your local councillors are and how to contact them by contacting your local authority.

Complaints about the DWP

If you want to complain about how the DWP has dealt with your case, first contact the office that is dealing with your claim. If you are unsure which office is dealing with your claim, contact numbers and information about the complaints procedure are provided on the DWP website.[50] You can also make a complaint about UC or JSA online at makeacomplaint.dwp.gov.uk.

If you are still unhappy after you get the initial response to your complaint, you can ask that your complaint be passed to the DWP Complaints Team. A dedicated complaints handler may contact you to discuss your complaint, which should normally be dealt with within 15 working days.

If you are still not satisifed, see CPAG's *Welfare Benefits and Tax Credits Handbook* for information about escalating your complaint to the Independent Case Examiner or the Parliamentary and Health Service Ombudsman.

Complaints about HM Revenue and Customs

You can complain about how HMRC has dealt with your claim for tax credits, child benefit or guardian's allowance online, by phone or in writing. See gov.uk/complain-about-hmrc.

If you are not happy with the initial response, ask HMRC to review your complaint.

If you are not happy with HMRC's reply, you can ask the Adjudicator's Office to investigate.

If you are still unhappy, you can ask your MP to consider referring your concerns to the Parliamentary and Health Service Ombudsman.

For further details on complaints see CPAG's *Welfare Benefits and Tax Credits Handbook*. If your complaint is about tax credits, also see CPAG's *Tax Credits and Complaints* factsheet.[51]

Complaints about Social Security Scotland

You can complain about how SSS has dealt with your application for a Scottish benefit or if you feel a SSS policy affects you unfairly or received poor advice from SSS. Complaints can be made by phone or in writing. Complaints must normally be made within six months. See mygov.scot/complain-social-security-scotland.

If you have had your final response from SSS but remain unsatisfied, you can take your complaint to the Scottish Public Services Ombudsman.

If SSS refuses to accept a benefit application because SSS decides you did not claim or ask for a redetermination in the right way, or you did not provide the required evidence, or did not have a good reason for missing the time limit to request a redetermination, you can appeal instead. These are called 'process decision' appeals.[52] You do not need to ask for a redetermination first but otherwise the rules are mostly the same as for appeals against Scottish benefit entitlement decisions, except that you have no right to appeal to the Upper Tribunal if the First-tier Tribunal does not uphold your appeal. Your only option if it does not is to seek judical review (see p428).

Complaints about housing benefit

Local authorities make HB decisions. They must have an effective complaints procedure, which should be made available to the public. If you are unhappy about the actions of your local authority and wish to make a complaint, ask for a copy of its complaints policy. If you are unable to get the policy or there is no formal complaints procedure, write to the supervisor of the person dealing with your claim, making it clear why you are dissatisfied. If you do not receive a satisfactory reply, take up the matter with someone more senior in the department and, ultimately, the principal officer. Send a copy of any letters to your ward councillors and to the councillor who chairs the relevant committee responsible for HB. If this does not produce results, or if the delay is causing you severe hardship, consider a complaint to the Local Government and Social Care Ombudsman in England or the Public Services Ombudsman in Scotland and Wales, or obtain legal advice about a judicial review (see p428). Government departments also monitor local authorities, so you could contact your MP (see p426) or write to the relevant minister.

Judicial review

Judicial review is a process by which you can ask a court to look at an action (or, in the case of delay, inaction) of any public authority that affects you, on the grounds that such (in)action is unlawful. If the High Court (Court of Session in Scotland) accepts that the (in)action is unlawful, it can order the decision maker to determine your benefit claim or otherwise resolve the issue.

Get legal advice as soon as possible if you are considering a judicial review. The time limit in England and Wales is 'promptly and in any event within three months after the grounds to make the claim first arose'.[53] The time limit in Scotland is also within three months, although there is limited discretion for the court to extend this limit.[54] It is strongly advisable that you only take judicial review proceedings with legal help. The process is complex and you risk having to pay the legal costs of the benefits authority (which could be thousands of pounds) if your challenge is unsuccessful.

However, in cases of benefit delay, often a 'pre-action letter', in which your adviser states that judicial review action will start unless your claim is determined by a certain date, can lead to your claim being decided promptly. The letter should be sent to the solicitor for the DWP, HMRC, SSS or local authority, together with a copy to the manager of the section responsible for dealing with your claim. Although a pre-action letter is currently only a requirement in England and Wales, it can also be used in Scotland to help resolve delays.

A template for a pre-action letter (for use in England and Wales) is available online.[55] See also CPAG's Judicial Review Project (cpag.org.uk/welfare-rights/judicial-review) for more information and advice about judical review and a series of template pre-action letters for use in England and Wales (with notes about how to adapt them for use in Scotland) and how to use them effectively.

Pending test cases

The general rules on deciding your claim do not apply if there is an appeal pending against a decision of the Upper Tribunal or a court in a 'test case' that deals with issues relevant to your claim. If this applies, the decision maker must consider whether it is possible that the outcome of the test case would mean you would have no entitlement. If so, the decision maker can postpone ('stay', or 'sist' in Scotland) making a decision on your claim (or revision or supersession request) until the test case is decided.[56] This prevents you appealing until a decision is made in the test case. Once a decision is made in the test case, the decision maker then makes a decision on your claim (or revision or supersession).[57]

If you would be entitled to benefit even if the test case were decided against you, the decision maker can make a decision.[58] This is done on the assumption that the test case has been decided in the way that is most unfavourable to you. However, this does mean that you are at least paid something while you wait for the result of the test case. Then, if the decision in the test case is in your favour, the decision maker revises her/his decision.

If you already have a decision in your favour, the decision maker can suspend payment of your benefit (see p437).

If you have already appealed to the First-tier Tribunal, see p430.

3. Delays when challenging a decision

If you have challenged a decision on your entitlement to a benefit or tax credit, there can be a delay while the:

- decision maker considers whether or not to revise (or review or redetermine) the decision (see below);
- decision maker prepares the appeal to send to the First-tier Tribunal (see p430); *or*
- appeal is with the First-tier Tribunal waiting for a hearing date.

For benefits other than housing benefit (HB), if you want to appeal to the First-tier Tribunal, you usually have to first apply for a revision (or, for tax credits, a review, or for Scottish benefits, a redetermination) of the decision.[59] The DWP and HM Revenue and Customs (HMRC) call this a 'mandatory reconsideration'.

The DWP or HMRC gives or sends you a 'mandatory reconsideration notice', telling you the result of your application for a revision or review. The notice is proof that it has accepted and considered your application. You usually must send a copy of this to the tribunal when you appeal. If the DWP or HMRC only provides a mandatory reconsideration notice after a long delay, that may put you at a disadvantage – eg, if the delay makes it difficult to obtain evidence to support your appeal. The tribunal should take that into account if you subsequently appeal, so you should explain how you think the delay has affected your chances of winning your appeal.[60] For Scottish benefits, you can appeal if Social Security Scotland (SSS) has failed to make a redetermination within 16 working days. For further information on challenging decisions, see CPAG's *Welfare Benefits and Tax Credits Handbook*.

Delay in carrying out a revision

When you submit your request for a revision to the DWP, make it clear that you are asking for a revision, including the fact that this is also referred to as a 'mandatory reconsideration'. The Dispute Resolution Team should then decide whether or not the decision will be revised and will send you the mandatory reconsideration notice. If the DWP responds to your revision request with a letter telling you that the decision has been looked at again, but not changed, and either inviting you to request a mandatory reconsideration or informing you that your request is being forwarded to a Dispute Resolution Team, you should argue that you can now appeal. However, to safeguard your appeal rights, you should also continue with the mandatory reconsideration process and resubmit a further revision request, explaining what has happened and clearly asking that it be sent immediately to a Dispute Resolution Team. You should also submit a complaint, because you should not need to request a mandatory reconsideration twice.

There are no specified legal time limits for how long a decision maker should take to carry out a revision (or, for tax credits, a review). However, revision requests should be dealt with within a reasonable time. Tax credit reviews should be carried out as soon as is 'reasonably practicable', and HMRC's stated target is 42 days.[61] See p417 for the factors that are relevant when determining what is reasonable. You should ensure that you highlight any specific circumstances of your case that mean it is urgent for you, and therefore not appropriate for your request to be dealt with in the order in which it was received.

If a delay in carrying out a revision or review continues, the options for resolving it are the same as those for resolving a delay in determining a claim (see p417 for benefits administered by the DWP or HMRC and p424 for HB).

You can also try to make an appeal application, but normally you need a mandatory reconsideration notice before you can that. However, if you have done everything correctly and your case is urgent and either there is an unreasonable delay in carrying out the revision (or review) or sending you the mandatory reconsideration notice, the tribunal can waive the normal rules, if it would be in the interest of justice to do so.[62] It might also use its powers to issue a direction requiring the DWP to provide a mandatory reconsideration notice.[63] Make sure that your application clearly states that it is being made without an accompanying mandatory reconsideration notice, that you want the tribunal to use its power to either waive that requirement or to issue a direction requiring the DWP or HMRC to provide one, and that you want this request to be considered by a tribunal judge rather than the clerk.

For Best Start grants, young carer grants and funeral support payments, there is a time limit of 16 working days in which SSS should make its redetermination.[64]

Note:

- The decision maker can postpone making a decision on your request for a revision if there is a 'test case' pending (see p428).
- The DWP publishes quarterly statistics online that show average clearance times for work capability assessment mandatory reconsiderations.[65]
- HMRC has a target of processing 80 per cent of all post within 15 days and 95 per cent of all online forms within seven days.[66]

Delay while an appeal is prepared

The rules on the time in which the decision maker must send her/his response to the First-tier Tribunal and the possible solutions if there are delays depend on whether or not you were required to request a mandatory reconsideration or redetermination before appealing.

If your appeal concerns your rights under European Union (EU) law (eg, your right to reside under EU law or the effect of the EU co-ordination rules), see also p437 for a possible argument that some payments should be paid to you while you wait for your appeal to be heard.

Delay following a mandatory reconsideration or redetermination

Once you have sent your appeal to HM Courts and Tribunals Service (HMCTS), you may experience a delay in its being progressed.

You should first establish what stage the appeal has reached. If your appeal is about universal credit (UC), employment and support allowance (ESA), personal independence payment (PIP) and you have requested an oral hearing, you can register for an email and text notification service called 'Track Your Appeal' by calling 0300 123 1142. For all other appeals (or if the stage of your appeal is not clear from the notifications), contact HMCTS and check whether:

- your appeal has been received. You may wish to obtain proof of receipt – eg, by sending the appeal by a postal service that requires a signature or using the Royal Mail tracking service. Once your appeal has been received by the tribunal, it is responsible for ensuring that the case is dealt with 'fairly and justly', which includes 'avoiding delay so far as compatible with proper consideration of the issues';[67]
- your appeal has been sent on to the DWP, HMRC or SSS and, if so, on what date;
- the DWP/HMRC/SSS has responded (see below). A copy of this response should be sent to you and/or your representative;
- you have been sent an enquiry form or, if you have returned this, whether it has been received; *and*
- if you have requested an oral hearing, your appeal is ready to be listed for a hearing date.

The decision maker must send her/his response to your appeal to the First-tier Tribunal within 28 days (31 days if SSS) of having received the appeal.[68] If the DWP/HMRC/SSS has not responded to your appeal, you can ask the tribunal to make a direction that the DWP/HMRC/SSS does so within a further short period, after which time the appeal is listed and the DWP/HMRC/SSS is barred from taking any further part in proceedings.[69]

If your situation is particularly urgent, you can ask the tribunal to 'expedite' matters by shortening the 28-day (or 31-day) time limit.[70]

If the DWP/HMRC/SSS applies for a direction to extend the time limit, you should be notified of this in writing and you can then apply for a direction setting this direction aside.[71]

If you apply for a direction, explain the consequences for you of a continuing delay and why it would be fair and just to determine the case more quickly than would otherwise happen.

If you request that your appeal be dealt with quickly in this way, you must also be as flexible as possible in preparing your case quickly and making yourself, and any representative, available for hearings at short notice.

If the tribunal refuses to expedite your appeal, and it is arguable that this means your case is not being dealt with fairly and justly, get advice on whether there are grounds for a judicial review (see p428).

If your appeal is delayed because of a pending 'test case', see p433.

Delay without a mandatory reconsideration

You do not need to request a revision of an HB decision before appealing. Instead, you send your appeal to the decision maker in the local authority. It is a good idea to keep a copy of your application and any documents accompanying it. If there is a delay in your appeal being processed, first establish what stage the appeal has reached. Contact the local authority and check whether:

- your appeal has been received;
- the decision maker has written her/his response and sent it to HMCTS. A copy should also be sent to you and/or your representative;
- you have been sent an enquiry form or, if you have returned this, whether it has been received; *and*
- your appeal is ready to be listed for a hearing date.

The decision maker must send her/his response to your appeal to HMCTS as soon as reasonably practicable. You are entitled to have your appeal heard within a reasonable period of time, so the decision maker should prepare the response and send it to the First-tier Tribunal without delay.[72] Following a complaint about an HB appeal, the Ombudsman said that the local authority should forward an appeal within 28 days.[73]

If your appeal has been received but has not been sent to HMCTS, request that this be done. You can complain about the delay (see p425).

If a DWP decision does not say you have to ask for a revision or mandatory reconsideration first before having a right to appeal, you can apply for permission to appeal directly to HMCTS.[74] If you then experience delays with how HMCTS handles your appeal, see above.

If there are special reasons why your appeal should be dealt with urgently or there has already been significant delay, write to the First-tier Tribunal asking it to direct the decision maker to produce the response and/or list the appeal for a hearing.[75] Set out the history of the appeal, what you have done to try to get the matter resolved and the effect of the delay on you and your family as clearly as possible and include all documents that you have about the decision. Bear in mind that the tribunal expects normal procedures to be followed in the vast majority of cases, but, if necessary, can deal with your appeal differently. This includes admitting the appeal directly if it has not yet been received from the decision maker or prioritising the hearing date, so it is not listed in the order in which the appeal was received.

How should you ask the tribunal to deal with your appeal if it has not been sent by the decision maker?

If you write to the First-tier Tribunal, there is a risk of a misunderstanding. The tribunal clerk may be confused if s/he receives documents concerning an appeal that the decision maker has not told the tribunal about. To minimise the chances of confusion, do the following.

1. Clearly head your letter 'Application for a Direction under Rule 6 of the Tribunal Procedure Rules' and mark it 'urgent'.
2. Explain at the start of the letter that the papers have not been sent by the decision maker and you would like the case to be referred to a tribunal judge to give a direction to resolve this problem.
3. Set out the history of when your appeal was submitted and the contact you have had with the benefit authority since then. If possible, enclose a copy of your appeal request and any accompanying documents.
4. Refer to the caselaw that confirms that HMCTS has the power to issue directions in relation to an unnotified appeal.[76]
5. Clearly explain the consequences for you of a continuing delay and why it would be fair and just to determine the case more quickly than would otherwise happen.
6. Follow up your letter with a phone call to the tribunal to establish that it has been received and passed to a judge.
7. See CPAG's website for a sample letter, which you may want to adapt.[77] This does not specify timescales, because what is reasonable depends on the facts of your case and the consequences of the continued delay. For example, if you are at imminent risk of losing your home as a consequence of HB or UC housing costs not being awarded, the timescale should reflect that.

If you request that your appeal be dealt with quickly in this way, you must then be as flexible as possible in preparing your case quickly and making yourself, and any representative, available for hearings at short notice.

If a tribunal judge refuses to direct the decision maker to submit her/his response to the tribunal and to expedite the appeal, you should consider whether there are grounds for a judicial review against this refusal (see p428). Depending on the particular facts, it may be arguable that a failure to give such directions has resulted in procedural impropriety because the tribunal has failed to deal with your case fairly and justly as required.[78]

Appeal delayed because of a pending test case

If you have appealed to the First-tier or Upper Tribunal and there is a 'test case' pending against a decision of the Upper Tribunal or a court that deals with issues raised in your case, the decision maker can serve a notice requiring the tribunal in your appeal:[79]

- not to make a decision and to refer your case back to her/him; *or*
- to deal with your appeal by either:
  - postponing making a decision (known as 'stay' or, in Scotland, 'sist') until the test case is decided; *or*
  - deciding your appeal as if the test case had been decided in the way most unfavourable to you, but only if this is in your interests – eg, you will get some benefit paid as opposed to none. If that happens and the test case is eventually decided in your favour, the decision maker must make a new decision superseding the decision of the tribunal in the light of the decision in the test case.

If the decision on your appeal has been postponed, once a decision has been made in the test case, the decision is made on your appeal.

If your appeal concerns European law, see p437.

4. **Delays getting paid**

Once you have a positive decision stating that you are entitled to benefit, there may be delays in the benefit authority implementing it and making any payments due.

It is important to check first that a decision has been made to award you a specified amount of benefit (see below). If so, unless payments can be suspended (see p435), payment should be made to you as soon as reasonably practicable.[80]

For DWP-administered benefits, if you do not have a bank account, you should be paid through the payment exception service, which enables you to collect your payment from a PayPoint outlet.[81]

If benefit is not paid promptly, you can start action in the county court (England and Wales) or sheriff court (Scotland) for payment of the money owed.[82] However, it is extremely rare that this action is required to obtain benefit that has been awarded but not paid.

The decision awarding you benefit

In most cases, it is clear that there has been a decision awarding you a specified amount of benefit. However, in some cases, you may get a decision that does not award benefit but only decides one or more conditions of entitlement. For example, if you appeal against the DWP's decision that it cannot pay you universal credit (UC) because you do not have a right to reside, although the tribunal can decide that you do have a right to reside (and so you win your appeal), that is not a decision awarding you benefit, because it only relates to one condition of entitlement. The tribunal's decision is sent to the DWP and the decision maker must then decide whether you meet all the other conditions of entitlement to UC and whether to award you a specified amount of benefit. 'Process decision' appeals against Scottish benefits decisions are not about entitlement so if your appeal is upheld, the decision is sent to Social Security Scotland (SSS) to decide your entitlement.

If your appeal about one condition of your entitlement is allowed and there is then a delay in a decision being made to award you benefit, do the following.

- Check whether the decision maker has received notification of the tribunal's decision.
- If the decision maker has received notification, establish the cause of the delay. A long time may have elapsed since your initial claim was made, and so to ensure that you have met the other conditions of entitlement since your date of claim, the decision maker may write asking you to confirm this, often by completing a claim or review form. Any further delays can be reduced if you provide the information or complete and return any forms as soon as you can.
- If you are advised that the decision maker has all the information s/he requires, but there is still a delay in deciding your claim, your options are the same as for someone who experiences a delay in getting a decision on an initial claim (see p417). You should include in any correspondence the fact that you have already had a significant wait while your appeal was determined.

Suspension of benefit

In certain circumstances, a decision maker can suspend payment of part, or all, of your benefit or tax credits. In this case, you have no right to the payment (and so cannot appeal). See CPAG's *Welfare Benefits and Tax Credits Handbook* for all the circumstances in which benefit can be suspended. Note that there are currently no rules that allow payments of Scottish benefits to be suspended.

The situations when payment of benefit or tax credits can be suspended that are most relevant for migrants are:

- because the decision maker wants more information to decide whether you continue to be entitled to benefit (see below); *and*
- while an appeal against a positive decision is pending (see p437).

Has your benefit been suspended?

1. You cannot appeal to the First-tier Tribunal against the decision to suspend your benefit. The only way to change the decision is to negotiate to get your benefit reinstated or to challenge the decision by a judicial review (see p428).
2. If you receive a letter telling you that your benefit has been suspended, write explaining how the suspension affects you and ask for the suspension decision to be reconsidered. There may be other arguments why your benefit should not be suspended, based on the information below.

3. The decision maker may be willing to continue to pay your benefit, or at least some of it, if you can show that you will experience hardship otherwise. Guidance to decision makers is clear that, in almost all decisions to suspend benefit, consideration must be given to whether hardship would result and whether that would make the suspension unacceptable. In addition, the decision to suspend your benefit can be reconsidered if the decision maker receives additional information.[83]

The decision maker requires further information

You can be required to supply information or evidence if the decision maker needs this to determine whether your award of benefit should be revised or superseded.[84]

If you do not provide the information and evidence, payment of all or part of your benefit can be suspended if:[85]

- a question has arisen about your entitlement or whether a decision should be revised or superseded;[86] *or*
- you apply for a revision or supersession; *or*
- you do not provide certificates, documents, evidence or other information about the facts of your case as required.[87]

If the decision maker wants you to provide information or evidence, s/he must notify you in writing. Within 14 days (or one month for child benefit, guardian's allowance and housing benefit (HB), seven days for contribution-based jobseeker's allowance if you come under the UC system, or by the date specified, which must not be less than 30 days after the date of the notice, for tax credits) of being sent the request, you must:

- supply the information or evidence.[88] You can be given more time if the decision maker is satisfied that this is necessary; *or*
- satisfy the decision maker that the information does not exist or you cannot obtain it.[89]

If the decision maker has not already done so, your benefit can be suspended if you do not provide the information or evidence within the relevant time limit.[90] Similarly, your tax credits can be suspended if you do not provide information or evidence by the date requested.[91]

The complexity of the immigration status, residence, presence and European Union (EU) co-ordination rules, together with the additional information and evidence requirements these rules generate, means that the likelihood of your benefit being suspended on the above grounds is increased. For information on some of the practical issues involved in satisfying the information and evidence requirements, see Chapter 20.

If an appeal is pending

Your benefit or tax credit can be suspended if the DWP, HMRC or local authority is appealing (or considering an appeal) against:[92]

- a decision of the First-tier Tribunal, Upper Tribunal or court to award you benefit (or to reinstate benefit); *or*
- a decision of the Upper Tribunal or court about someone else's appeal if the issue could affect your claim – ie, a 'test case'. For HB only, the other case must also be about an HB issue.

The DWP, HMRC or local authority must (although for tax credits this is only guidance[93]) give you written notice as soon as reasonably practicable if it intends to:[94]

- request the statement of reasons for the First-tier Tribunal's decision; *or*
- apply for leave to appeal; *or*
- appeal.

The decision maker must then take that action within the usual time limits for doing so (generally within one month in each case). If s/he does not, the suspended benefit must be paid to you.[95] The suspended benefit must also be paid to you if the decision maker withdraws an application for leave to appeal, withdraws the appeal or is refused leave to appeal and it is not possible for her/him to renew the application.

The decision maker still has discretion not to suspend your benefit or tax credits if s/he considers it would result in hardship, and s/he should keep her/his decision under review so that the suspension can be lifted if your circumstances, including the level of hardship experienced, change.[96] You should therefore write to the relevant benefit authority if the suspension will cause, or is causing, you hardship.

Suspension on this ground is particularly common following appeals about the right to reside requirement. This is due to decision makers appealing to the Upper Tribunal against a First-tier Tribunal's decision, and the large number of ongoing cases about right to reside that are in the higher courts.

If your appeal concerns your rights under EU law (eg, your right to reside or the effect of the EU co-ordination rules), see below.

If your appeal concerns European law

If the issue in your appeal concerns EU law, and the rights you are exercising are still covered by EU law (see Chapters 12 and 16 for when EU law may still apply to you), you may be able to argue that your benefit or tax credit should not be suspended, or that you should receive some form of interim payment. European caselaw has established that national governments cannot automatically refuse requests for interim relief to people seeking to exercise their rights under European law, and that national courts must be able to grant interim relief to ensure EU rights are respected.[97]

This argument could be used, for example, if the issue in your appeal is whether you have a right to reside in EU law (see Chapter 12) or whether you are entitled to benefit because of the EU co-ordination rules (see Chapter 16).

It may be possible to make this argument in the following circumstances.

- If you are waiting for your appeal to be heard by the First-tier Tribunal, you may be able to argue that you should be paid an advance payment or that you should receive some form of interim payment while waiting. You must request a payment outside the benefit rules from the benefit authority, because its decision is that you are not entitled under the rules.
- If action on your appeal has been deferred (known as your appeal having been 'stayed', or, in Scotland, 'sisted') because there is a test case pending (see p433), you may be able to argue either that these rules deferring action should not be applied or that you should receive some form of interim payment until your appeal can be determined.
- If you have won your First-tier Tribunal appeal and the decision maker suspends payment of your benefit or tax credit because s/he has appealed, or intends to appeal, to the Upper Tribunal, you may be able to argue that your benefit should not be suspended, or that you should receive some form of interim payment pending the further appeal.

If there is a difference of views over which state is the competent state under the EU co-ordination rules for paying your benefit or tax credit, you may be entitled to receive provisional payments (see p372).

Note: the benefit authorities can still lift the suspension of your benefit on grounds of hardship (see p437).

Notes

2. **Waiting for a decision on a claim**

1 *SSHD v R (S)* [2007] EWCA Civ 546, para 51

2 *R v Secretary of State for Social Services and Chief Adjudication Officer ex parte Child Poverty Action Group* [1990] 2 QB 540

3 See for example, *HMRC Single Departmental Plan,* available at gov.uk.

4 DWP, *Single Departmental Plan: 2018 to 2022 headline indicators technical detail,* updated 17 February 2020

5 Art SSC.5 PSSC;Art 4 EU Reg 883/04; Arts 18 and 45 TFEU; Art 24 EU Dir 2004/38; Art 7 EU Reg 492/2011

6 DWP guidance for UC advances can be found at rightsnet.org.uk/universal-credit-guidance and summarised at gov.uk/guidance/universal-credit-advances, but these do not include policy changes announced in the March 2020 Budget to extend the standard repayment period to 24, rather than 12, months from October 2021.

7 DWP guidance, *Short Term Benefit Advances: benefit centres*, paras 3, 5, 55 and 80, available at whatdotheyknow.com/request/operational_guidance_for_benefit
8 Regs 5 and 6 SS(PAB) Regs
9 Reg 17 UC(TP) Regs
10 Reg 4(2) SS(PAB) Regs
11 Reg 3 SS(PAB) Regs
12 Reg 7 SS(PAB) Regs
13 DWP guidance, *Short Term Benefit Advances: benefit centres,* paras 22-23, available at whatdotheyknow.com. Search for 'benefit advances operational guidance'.
14 gov.uk/guidance/universal-credit-advances
15 Reg 7 SS(PAB) Regs; s137 SSCBA 1992
16 gov.uk/guidance/universal-credit-advances
17 DWP guidance, *Short Term Benefit Advances: benefit centres*, paras 3, 5, 55, 80 and 90, available at whatdotheyknow.com/request/operational_guidance_for_benefit
18 gov.uk/guidance/universal-credit-advances; DWP guidance, *Short Term Benefit Advances: benefit centres*, para 116, available at whatdotheyknow.com/request/operational_guidance_for_benefit
19 DWP guidance, *Short Term Benefit Advances: benefit centres*, paras 89-94, whatdotheyknow.com/request/operational_guidance_for_benefit
20 DWP guidance, *Short Term Benefit Advances: benefit centres*, para 93, available at whatdotheyknow.com/request/operational_guidance_for_benefit
21 gov.uk/guidance/universal-credit-advances
22 DWP guidance, *Short Term Benefit Advances: benefit centres*, para 35, available at whatdotheyknow.com/request/operational_guidance_for_benefit
23 Reg 8 SS(PAB) Regs
24 As announced in the March 2021 budget, the 24-month period applies from April 2021. Prior to this budget, the period was 12 months.
25 Reg 11 The Social Security (Overpayments and Recovery) Regulations 2013, No.384. This does not apply to UC 'benefit transfer' advance payments made under reg 17 UC(TP) Regs.
26 gov.uk/guidance/universal-credit-advances
27 DWP guidance, *Short Term Benefit Advances: benefit centres,* para 29, available at whatdotheyknow.com/request/operational_guidance_for_benefit.
28 DWP guidance, *Short Term Benefit Advances: benefit centres,* paras 16 and 29-32, available at whatdotheyknow.com/request/operational_guidance_for_benefit
29 DWP guidance, *Short Term Benefit Advances: benefit centres*, paras 175-81, available at whatdotheyknow.com/request/operational_guidance_for_benefit
30 Sch 3 para 15 UC,PIP,JSA&ESA(DA) Regs; Sch 2 para 20 SS&CS(DA) Regs. This does not apply to UC 'benefit transfer' advance payments made under reg 17 UC(TP) Regs.
31 Sch 3 para 14 UC,PIP,JSA&ESA(DA) Regs and Sch 2 para 20A SS&CS(DA) Regs allow a right of appeal against decisions on deductions under reg 10 SS(PAB) Regs.
32 Sch 3 para 14 UC,PIP,JSA&ESA(DA) Regs; Sch 2 para 20A SS&CS(DA) Regs; UC advances when transferring are made under reg 17 UC(TP) Regs and not the SS(PAB) Regs.
33 gov.uk/short-term-benefit-advance; DWP guidance, *Short Term Benefit Advances: benefit centres*, paras 193-95, available at whatdotheyknow.com/request/operational_guidance_for_benefit.
34 DWP guidance, *Short Term Benefit Advances: benefit centres*, paras 17 and 72, available at whatdotheyknow.com/request/operational_guidance_for_benefit.
35 DWP guidance, *Short Term Benefit Advances: benefit centres,* paras 7-11, available at whatdotheyknow.com/request/operational_guidance_for_benefit.
36 For UC advances, see DWP, *September 2019: Touchbase edition 137*
37 DWP guidance, *Short Term Benefit Advances: benefit centres,* paras 66-67, available at whatdotheyknow.com. Search for 'benefit advances operational guidance'.

38 gov.uk/guidance/universal-credit-advances and *Short Term Benefit Advances: benefit centres*, paras 16, 29-32 and 175-181, available at whatdotheyknow.com/request/operational_guidance_for_benefit
39 Reg 22 CB&GA(Admin) Regs
40 Regs 22(3), 41 and 42 CB&GA(Admin) Regs
41 Reg 22(2) CB&GA(Admin) Regs
42 Reg 89 HB Regs; reg 70 HB(SPC) Regs
43 Urgent Bulletin U1/2018, p2
44 Email to CPAG, 8 May 2018
45 Reg 93(1) HB Regs; reg 74(1) HB(SPC) Regs
46 Reg 93(2) and (3) HB Regs; reg 74(2) and (3) HB(SPC) Regs
47 Reg 93(2) HB Regs; reg 74(2) HB(SPC) Regs
48 *R v Haringey London Borough Council ex parte Azad Ayub* [1992] 25 HLR 566 (QBD)
49 See mygov.scot/benefits
50 gov.uk/government/organisations/department-for-work-pensions/about/complaints-procedure
51 cpag.org.uk/welfare-rights/resources/factsheet/tax-credits-and-complaints
52 s61 SS(S)A 2018
53 Civil Procedure Rules, part 54.5
54 s27A Court of Session Act 1988
55 justice.gov.uk/courts/procedure-rules/civil/protocol/prot_jrv
56 **HB** Sch 7 para 16 CSPSSA 2000
Other benefits s25 SSA 1998
57 **HB** Sch 7 para 18(2) CSPSSA 2000
Other benefits s27(2) SSA 1998
58 **HB** Sch 7 para 16(3) and (4) CSPSSA 2000; reg 15 HB&CTB(DA) Regs
CB/GA s25(3) and (4) SSA 1998; reg 22 CB&GA(DA) Regs
UC/PIP/JSA&ESAunder UC s25(3) and (4) SSA 1998; reg 53 UC,PIP,JSA&ESA(DA) Regs
Other benefits s25(3) and (4) SSA 1998; reg 21 SS&CS(DA) Regs

3. **Delays when challenging a decision**
59 For benefits administered by the DWP, you only have to ask for a revision before appealing if the decision you want to appeal says so. The Upper Tribunal recently confirmed this in relation to a claim for UC which the DWP 'closed'. See *PP v SSWP (UC)* [2020] UKUT 109 (AAC).
60 *MM v SSWP (PIP)* [2016] UKUT 36 (AAC)
61 s21A(2) TCA 2002; David Gauke MP, Exchequer Secretary to the Treasury, Eighth Delegated Legislation Committee, 26 March 2014, confirmed in HMRC Consultation Group quarterly update email, 14 February 2018.
62 r7(2)(a) TP(FT) Rules
63 r6 TP(FT) Rules
64 s43 SS(S)A 2018; para 2 Sch 1 EYA(BSG)(S) Regs; reg 9(2) CA(YCG)(S) Regs; reg 6(2) FEA(S) Regs
65 DWP, *Employment and Support Allowance: outcomes of work capability assessments*, available at gov.uk
66 HMRC, *Single Departmental Plan*, available at gov.uk
67 r2(2)(e) TP(FT) Rules; r2(2)(e) FFT(S) Rules
68 r24(1)(c) TP(FT) Rules; r21(7) FFT(S) Rules
69 rr2, 5, 6, 7 and 8 TP(FT) Rules; rr2, 4-7 FFT(S) Rules
70 rr5(3)(a) and 6 TP(FT) Rules; rr4(3)(a) and 5 FFT(S) Rules
71 r6(5) TP(FT) Rules; r5(5) FFT(S) Rules
72 Art 6 European Convention on Human Rights; s6 HRA 1998; CH/3497/2005; *MB v Wychavon DC* [2013] UKUT 67 (AAC)
73 Complaint 01/C/13400 against Scarborough Borough Council
74 See *PP v SSWP (UC)* [2020] UKUT 109 (AAC)
75 R(H) 1/07; *FH v Manchester City Council(HB)* [2010] UKUT 43 (AAC)
76 R(H) 1/07; *FH v Manchester City Council (HB)* [2010] UKUT 43 (AAC)
77 cpag.org.uk/sites/default/files/CPAG-How-to-expedite-social-security-appeal-Aug-13.pdf
78 r2(3)(a) TP(FT) Rules
79 **HB** Sch 7 para 17 CSPSSA 2000
Other benefits s26 SSA 1998
Scottish benefits r4(3)(j) FFT(S) Regs.

4. **Delays getting paid**
80 **UC/PIP/ESA&JSA under UC** Reg 45 UC,PIP,JSA&ESA(C&P) Regs
HB Reg 91 HB Regs; reg 72 HB(SPC) Regs
WTC/CTC Regs 8 and 9 TC(PC) Regs
Other benefits Reg 20 SS(C&P) Regs
Scottish benefits s24 SS(S)A 2018
81 gov.uk/payment-exception-service
82 *Murdoch v DWP* [2010] EWHC 1988 (QB), paras 75-79; for HB, see *Jones v Waveney DC* [1999] 33 HLR 3

83 DWP, *Suspension and Termination Guide,* paras 1350, 2050-52 and 2301-02, available at gov.uk
84 **UC/PIP/JSA&ESA under UC** Reg 38(2) UC,PIP,JSA&ESA(C&P) Regs; reg 45 UC,PIP,JSA&ESA(DA) Regs
HB Reg 86(1) HB Regs; reg 67(1) HB(SPC) Regs
CB/GA Reg 23 CB&GA(Admin) Regs
WTC/CTC s16(3) TCA 2002
Other benefits Reg 32(1) SS(C&P) Regs; reg 17 SS&CS(DA) Regs
85 **UC/PIP/JSA&ESA under UC** Reg 45(6) UC,PIP,JSA&ESA(DA) Regs
HB Reg 13 HB&CTB(DA) Regs
CB/GA Reg 19 CB&GA(DA) Regs
WTC/CTC Reg 11 TC(PC) Regs (the word 'postponement' is used, rather than 'suspension')
Other benefits Reg 17(2) SS&CS(DA) Regs
86 **UC/PIP/JSA&ESA under UC** Reg 44(2)(a)(i) UC,PIP,JSA&ESA(DA) Regs
HB Reg 11(2)(a)(i) HB&CTB(DA) Regs
CB/GA Reg 18(2)(a) CB&GA(DA) Regs
WTC/CTC Reg 11(3A) TC(PC) Regs
Other benefits Reg 16(3)(a) SS&CS(DA) Regs
87 **UC/PIP/JSA&ESA under UC** Reg 38(2) UC,PIP,JSA&ESA(C&P) Regs
HB Reg 86(1) HB Regs; reg 67(1) HB(SPC) Regs
CB/GA Reg 23 CB&GA(Admin) Regs
WTC/CTC Reg 11(3A) TC(PC) Regs
Other benefits Reg 32(1) SS(C&P) Regs
88 **UC/PIP/JSA&ESA under UC** Reg 45(4)(a) UC,PIP,JSA&ESA(DA) Regs
HB Reg 13(4)(a) HB&CTB(DA) Regs
CB/GA Reg 19(2) CB&GA(DA) Regs
WTC/CTC Reg 32 TC(CN) Regs
Other benefits Reg 17(4)(a) SS&CS(DA) Regs
89 **UC/PIP/JSA&ESA under UC** Reg 45(4)(b) UC,PIP,JSA&ESA(DA) Regs
HB Reg 13(4)(b) HB&CTB(DA) Regs
CB/GA Reg 19(2)(b) CB&GA(DA) Regs
WTC/CTC HMRC leaflet WTC/FS9, *Tax Credits: suspension of payments*, March 2019
Other benefits Reg 17(4)(b) SS&CS(DA) Regs
90 **UC/PIP/JSA&ESA under UC** Reg 45(6) UC,PIP,JSA&ESA(DA) Regs
HB Reg 13(4) HB&CTB(DA) Regs
CB/GA Reg 19(5) CB&GA(DA) Regs
Other benefits Reg 17(5) SS&CS(DA) Regs
91 Reg 11 TC(PC) Regs
92 **UC/PIP/JSA&ESA under UC** Reg 44(2)(b) and (c) UC,PIP,JSA&ESA(DA) Regs
HB Sch 7 para 13(2) CSPSSA 2000; reg 11(2)(b) HB&CTB(DA) Regs
CB/GA Reg 18(3) CB&GA(DA) Regs
WTC/CTC Reg 11 TC(PC) Regs
Other benefits s21(2)(c) and (d) SSA 1998; reg 16(3)(b) SS&CS(DA) Regs
93 TCM 0014360 Step 1
94 **UC/PIP/JSA&ESA under UC** Reg 44(5) UC,PIP,JSA&ESA(DA) Regs
HB Reg 11(3) HB&CTB(DA) Regs
CB/GA Reg 18(4) and (5) CB&GA(DA) Regs
Other benefits Reg 16(4) SS&CS(DA) Regs
95 **UC/PIP/JSA&ESA under UC** Reg 46(b) and (c) UC,PIP,JSA&ESA(DA) Regs
HB Reg 12(1)(b) HB&CTB(DA) Regs
CB/GA Reg 21 CB&GA(DA) Regs
Other benefits Reg 20(2) and (3) SS&CS(DA) Regs
96 DWP, *Suspension and Termination Guide,* paras 2050-52 and 2354
97 *The Queen v Secretary of State for Transport ex parte Factortame and Others,* C-213/89 [1990] ECR I-02433, para 23; *Unibet (London) Ltd and Unibet (International) Ltd v Justitiekanslern,* C-432/05 [2007] ECR I-02271, especially para 77; see also *obiter* (not binding) comments in *R (Sanneh) v SSWP and HMRC* [2013] EWHC 793 (Admin), paras 104-14

Chapter 19

National insurance numbers

This chapter covers:

1. The national insurance number requirement (below)
2. Obtaining a national insurance number (p445)
3. Common problems (p448)

This chapter covers the rules on the national insurance number requirement for benefits and tax credits and the issues that arise in satisfying them, particularly if you or a member of your family are not British.

1. The national insurance number requirement

In general, to be entitled to any social security benefit or tax credit (or, in England and Wales, council tax reduction – see p575), you must satisfy the national insurance (NI) number requirement.[1] You and any partner included in your claim must:

- provide an NI number, together with evidence to show that it is the one allocated to you; *or*
- provide evidence or information to enable your NI number to be traced; *or*
- make an application for an NI number, accompanied by sufficient information or evidence for one to be allocated. **Note:** there is no requirement for an NI number to have been allocated to you (see p448).

Certain groups of people are exempt from the requirement (see p443).

There are no specific NI number requirements when claiming any Scottish benefits.

Note: in addition to satisfying the NI number requirement, in most cases you must also make a valid claim and prove your identity. For general information on these requirements, see p454. For detailed information on the requirements for each benefit and tax credit, see CPAG's *Welfare Benefits and Tax Credits Handbook*.

When the requirement applies

The NI requirement applies when you make a claim for benefit. It also applies when someone who will be included in your *existing* award of benefit joins your family – eg, if your partner joins you from abroad. Your benefit award must be 'superseded' and, if your partner does not satisfy the NI requirement, it ceases.[2]

The requirement applies to you, and also to your partner if you are claiming means-tested benefits or tax credits as a couple.[3] That is the case even if, for income support (IS), income-based jobseeker's allowance (JSA) or income-related employment and support allowance (ESA), you are not going to receive any extra benefit for her/him because s/he is a 'person subject to immigration control' for benefit purposes.[4]

However, if you are claiming universal credit (UC) and your partner either is defined as a person subject to immigration control (and not in an exempt group) or fails the habitual residence test (see p139), you are awarded UC as a single person and, consequently, your partner does not need to satisfy the NI requirement.[5] (**Note:** your partner's presence may still affect your UC entitlement.)

If you are claiming pension credit (PC) and your partner is a person subject to immigration control, s/he is treated as not being part of your household and so does not need to satisfy the NI requirement. If your partner fails the habitual residence test, s/he is still included in your claim, you are paid PC as a couple and s/he must satisfy the NI requirement.

For the definition of 'person subject to immigration control', see p81, and for more information about your entitlement if your partner is a person subject to immigration control, see p104 for means-tested benefits and p107 for tax credits.

See below for when your partner does not have to satisfy the NI number requirement.

Who is exempt

You do not need to satisfy the NI number requirement:

- if you are under 16 and you are claiming disability living allowance;[6]
- for statutory sick pay, statutory maternity pay, statutory paternity pay, statutory shared parental pay, statutory adoption pay or a social fund payment;[7]
- for housing benefit (HB) if you live in a hostel;[8]
- for tax credits if you have a 'reasonable excuse' for failing to satisfy the requirement (see below).[9]

If a child or qualifying young person is included in your claim for benefit, s/he does not need to satisfy the NI number requirement.[10]

If you are the benefit claimant and your partner is included in your claim, your partner does not have to satisfy the NI number requirement if:[11]

- s/he is a 'person subject to immigration control' because s/he requires leave to enter or remain in the UK, but does not have that leave (see p85); *and*
- s/he has not previously been given an NI number; *and*
- you are claiming IS, income-based JSA, income-related ESA or PC and your partner is not entitled to that benefit her/himself, or you are claiming HB and your partner fails the habitual residence test (see p139). In practice, that will always be satisfied if your partner satisfies the first bullet point since s/he does not have a right to reside.

You may still be asked for information about an NI number application for your partner, even though s/he is exempt. An NI number will be refused, but that does not prevent you from being entitled to benefits or tax credits or council tax reduction.[12]

Note:

- The above exemption for partners does not apply to UC. If your partner is defined as a 'person subject to immigration control' (and is not exempt), you are awarded UC as a single person and therefore your partner is not required to have an NI number.[13]
- The above exemptions for partners and for a child or qualifying young person included in your claim also apply to your application for council tax reduction in England or Wales (see p578).[14]
- The above exemptions for children, qualifying young people and partners do not apply to the claimant. For example, if you are a child claiming HB, you are not exempt from the NI number requirement, even though a child included in the claim is exempt.[15]
- There is no specific NI number requirement when claiming Scottish benefits.

Tax credits

The NI number requirement for tax credits is as described above, including the exemption for partners who require but do not have leave to enter or remain in the UK. If you live with your partner, you must make a joint claim for tax credits and both of you must satisfy the NI number requirement unless one of you is exempt because you require but do not have leave. **Note:** in nearly all circumstances, you cannot make a new claim for tax credits (including if you have to make a new claim because your partner either joins or leaves you), but must claim either UC or PC instead. See CPAG's *Welfare Benefits and Tax Credits Handbook* for more information.

The NI number requirement does not apply if the Tax Credit Office is satisfied that you (and/or your partner if it is a joint claim) have a 'reasonable excuse' for not complying with that requirement.[16] A 'reasonable excuse' is not defined: whether or not the Tax Credit Office is satisfied that you have one is a matter of discretion. Guidance to decision makers stresses that their discretionary decision must be reasonable, which includes being fair and taking all relevant considerations, including available evidence, into account.[17] A 'reasonable excuse' could include if you are unable to prove your identity because the Home Office has all your documents and you can show this – eg, with a letter from your solicitor.

If the decision maker decides that you have not made a valid claim because you have not satisfied the NI number requirement and you believe you had a reasonable excuse for not doing so, you can appeal against that decision.[18] You must request a mandatory reconsideration of the decision first (see p450).

2. Obtaining a national insurance number

The DWP allocates national insurance (NI) numbers.

NI numbers are allocated automatically to children shortly before their 16th birthday, provided child benefit is being claimed for them. If you are under 20, you were in the UK when you turned 16 and you did not receive an NI number, you can phone HM Revenue and Customs (HMRC) (tel: 0300 200 3500).

If you have been allocated an NI number but do not know it or if you want written confirmation of your NI number, contact HMRC (see gov.uk/lost-national-insurance-number). If you attend your Jobcentre Plus office with evidence of your identity, a member of staff may be able to tell you your NI number.

If you do not have an NI number, see below.

DWP guidance on tracing or allocating an NI number is available online. As the procedures are often misunderstood and/or not followed, it can be helpful to refer to this. The guidance is split into documents covering specific groups or circumstances, and stages of the procedures. All these are available at gov.uk/government/publications/national-insurance-number-allocations-staff-guide.

NI number applications may be completed as part of the process of applying for immigration leave and/or a biometric immigration document. **Note:** guidance for immigration officers covering the procedures for completing an NI number application during an asylum interview, forwarding the application to the DWP if leave is granted, and notifying you of the NI number if one is allocated was withdrawn on 10 August 2018.[19] Replacement guidance is expected. DWP guidance covers the procedures for tracing or allocating an NI number at the request of the Home Office to enable it to be included in the biometric immigration document.[20] These procedures are not always followed and do not always result in an NI number being allocated.

If an NI number has been allocated before a biometric immigration document is issued, the NI number may be included on this document.[21] If you have not been allocated an NI number as part of the process of your immigration application, you should apply in the usual way (see below).

Guidance to claimants who have been granted leave following an asylum application confirms that if an NI number has been allocated to you, written notification should have been sent to you. It also confirms that if you do not have an NI number, you should not delay making your benefit claim as you do not need an NI number to *claim* benefits, and an NI number application will be made as part of your claim for benefits.[22]

Applying for a national insurance number

You do not need to have obtained an NI number before you make your benefit or tax credit claim. If you have not yet been allocated an NI number, you can apply for one by telephoning the NI number application line on 0800 141 2075 or by contacting your local Jobcentre Plus office. At the time of writing, a new online NI number application system, 'Apply for a NINo', is being tested and may be rolled out at the end of March 2021.

Coronavirus

During the coronavirus pandemic, the DWP is not offering appointments at Jobcentre Plus offices and so you need to call the NI number application line to apply. CPAG has heard from a number of advisers about problems claimants are having getting through to the NI number application line. If you are affected by these problems, especially if it means that you cannot be paid your benefit, get advice and also see CPAG's Judicial Review Project webpages (cpag.org.uk/welfare-rights/judicial-review) for template letters and guidance about getting paid your benefit while waiting for a NI number to be allocated.

There are a number of other reasons why you may need an NI number, including for employment purposes, for a student loan and to open an Individual Savings Account (ISA).[23]

If you claim a benefit or tax credit, or you apply for a supersession of an award of benefit (eg, to include your partner) and you (or s/he) do not have an NI number, the benefit authority should complete Form DCI1 and send it to the NI number centre.[24] This counts as your having made an application for an NI number. It is advisable to state clearly on the form or letter that you do not have an NI number and you wish to apply for one.

Note: if your partner is a 'person subject to immigration control' because s/he has leave which is subject to a 'no recourse to public funds' condition and s/he is included in your claim, s/he can be allocated an NI number even if you do not receive an increased amount of benefit for her/him.[25]

When the NI number centre receives Form DCI1, it carries out a number of checks to ensure that you do not already have an NI number. It should then contact you to arrange an interview at your local DWP office if this is required (usually the case for European Economic Area (EEA) nationals). Otherwise, the application can be processed without the need for an interview (often the case for non-EEA nationals who have leave to enter or remain in the UK, or if you or your partner included in your claim are living outside the UK). DWP guidance states that whether or not you have a right to work in the UK is 'not a consideration' when this interview is carried out for the purpose of claiming benefit.[26]

The interview is sometimes referred to as an 'evidence of identity interview' and you should be told which documents to take with you. It is important to take as many as possible that establish your identity.

The section on gov.uk on applying for an NI number lists the following examples of documents that prove your identity, often referred to as 'primary evidence documents':[27]

- passport;
- identity card;
- residence permit;
- birth or adoption certificate;
- marriage or civil partnership certificate;
- driving licence.

If you have any of the above, take them to your interview. If not, take any documents you have that could help prove your identity (often referred to as 'secondary evidence documents'). These could include:[28]

- an immigration status or biometric immigration document;
- Home Office 'cessation letter' confirming the end of your asylum support;
- a current travel document issued by any national government, including the UK;
- a residence document issued to EEA nationals (see p465);
- a certificate of registration or naturalisation as a British citizen;
- a standard acknowledgement letter issued by the Home Office;
- an application registration card issued by the Home Office to an asylum seeker;
- an expired passport, travel document or EEA identity card;
- a local authority rent book or card, or a tenancy agreement;
- council tax documents;
- life assurance/insurance policies;
- mortgage repayment documents;
- recent fuel or phone bills in your name;
- NHS medical card;
- divorce or annulment papers;
- a wage slip from a recent employer;
- a trade union membership card;
- a travel pass with a photograph;
- vehicle registration or insurance documents;
- a work permit.

If you have other documents that are not in the above list, these may also help. Photocopies of documents can be relied on to establish your identity, but you should take the originals if you have them. If not, explain why you do not have them. For example, if some of your documents are with the Home Office, explain and, if possible, provide proof in the form of a solicitor's letter or some other evidence. The DWP should not ask you to provide documents which you obviously do not have.[29]

If you are unable to provide any documentary evidence of your identity (eg, because you are homeless or fleeing domestic violence), a decision should be made on the information that you are able to provide.

At the interview, you are asked to complete Form CA5400. The DWP may also ask you to complete a form allowing it to contact third parties to establish your identity.

An NI number might be refused for various reasons – eg, if you:

- have been unable to prove your identity or the documents you provided are not considered genuine;
- have failed to provide sufficient information; *or*
- failed to attend an evidence of identity interview (you should be given two opportunities to attend[30]) or respond to correspondence.

If your application for an NI number is refused, the reason should be recorded and notified to you.

You cannot appeal directly against a decision not to allocate you an NI number.[31] However, you can appeal against a decision to refuse you benefit because the NI number requirement is not met (see p450).

3. Common problems

Migrants often have problems with the national insurance (NI) number requirement because, unlike most British citizens, they are not issued with an NI number when they turn 16. The three most common problems are:

- being told you cannot apply for benefit unless you have an NI number (see below);
- delays in benefit payment because of the NI number requirement (see p449);
- being refused benefit on the grounds that the NI number requirement is not met (see p450).

Making a claim

If you (or your partner if s/he is included in your claim) do not have an NI number, you may be told by Jobcentre Plus, HM Revenue and Customs or the local authority that you cannot claim a benefit or tax credit. Similarly, except for universal credit (UC), you may find it impossible to claim online if you cannot provide an NI number.

You do not need to have an NI number in order to claim a benefit or tax credit. You should not be prevented from making a claim and your claim should be treated as the first stage in your NI number application (see p442).[32]

You are not required to provide an NI number as part of your online claim for UC. On receiving your claim, the DWP usually tells you to make an appointment at your local job centre to provide proof of your identity and other information to support your claim.

For all other benefits, if you are unable to make your claim online because you do not have an NI number, you should be able to claim by telephone or on a paper claim form.

Have you been told you cannot apply for benefit because you do not have a national insurance number?

If you have lost benefit entitlement because you were prevented from making a claim because you did not have an NI number, you may be able to get a new claim backdated. If the rules for the benefit or tax credit you are claiming do not allow backdating at all, or for the full period, or if the arrears do not cover the full amount lost, consider requesting compensation. For the rules on backdating and further information on obtaining compensation, see CPAG's *Welfare Benefits and Tax Credits Handbook*.

Delays

Payment of benefit or tax credits can often be delayed because you (or your partner) need to satisfy the NI number requirement or you are waiting for an NI number to be allocated. You can satisfy the NI number requirement by applying for an NI number and providing sufficient information or evidence for one to be allocated (see p442).[33]

Is your benefit delayed?

1. Check whether you or your partner are exempt from the requirement to have an NI number (see p443).
2. If you or your partner have applied for an NI number, but there is a delay in one being allocated, ask that your claim be determined, as there is no requirement for a number to be allocated (see p442). It is likely that your claim will have to be processed clerically before the NI number has been allocated, but that should not prevent payment.
3. If it is a new claim for benefit, or you are adding a partner to your claim that will result in your award increasing, you may be able to obtain an advance payment (see p419). That can be paid if you do not have an NI number, provided you meet the usual conditions, including that the decision maker considers it likely you will be entitled to the benefit.[34] The guidance on short-term advances states they should be considered if you do not have

an NI number, provided you can prove your identity and are complying with other requests for evidence. This guidance also states that the DWP should ensure that all action needed to allocate an NI number is taken promptly.[35] While this guidance only applies to the benefits that UC is replacing, the same principles should apply to UC advances, so applying for an advance payment may be a way of getting your NI number allocated more quickly.

4. If you have made a new claim for child benefit and/or guardian's allowance, you may be able to obtain an interim payment (see p424).
5. If you have made a new claim for housing benefit (HB), you may be able to obtain a 'payment on account' (see p425).
6. If you are adding your partner to your existing claim and s/he does not have an NI number, your benefit may be suspended (see p435). You may be able to argue that payment should not be suspended if it is clear that the NI number requirement is likely to be met and the only factor is a question of time.

For further information on your options if your benefit or tax credit payments are delayed, see Chapter 18.

Benefit is refused

You cannot appeal against a decision not to allocate you an NI number.[36] However, if you are refused benefit or tax credits (or are refused an increase when your partner joins your household) because you (or s/he) do not satisfy the NI number requirement, you can ask for a mandatory reconsideration of the decision and then appeal if the decision is not changed. For HB, you can appeal directly or ask for a revision and then appeal if the decision is not changed. In your mandatory reconsideration, revision or appeal, you can argue that the NI number requirement was met.[37] DWP guidance confirms that if an NI number is provided after a decision to disallow your benefit, a reconsideration may be appropriate.[38]

Usually, if benefit is refused because the benefit authority says the NI number requirement is not met, the issue in dispute is whether your application was accompanied by sufficient information or evidence to enable a number to be allocated, even if the benefit authority has not identified the issue as such.[39]

Even if you have been refused an NI number, it is possible to argue successfully that you still satisfy the NI number requirement if your application was accompanied by sufficient information or evidence to enable a number to be allocated.

The decision maker should accept that you satisfy the NI number requirement for your benefit claim if you applied for an NI number because you are employed or self-employed in Great Britain and you provided:[40]

- a birth or adoption certificate issued in the common travel area (UK, Ireland, Channel Islands and Isle of Man); *or*
- an immigration status document or letter issued by the Home Office indicating that you are allowed to be in the UK without a time limit, or that you are allowed to do that employment or self-employment.

Note: it is only a requirement to provide one of these documents if you apply for an NI number because you are employed or self-employed (or you wish to pay class 3 contributions). If you are applying for an NI number to claim benefits, you can provide other documents that prove your identity and you do not need to show you have the right to work (see p446).

If you have been refused an NI number after failing to attend an interview, the reasons why you failed to attend are relevant, so refer to them in any challenge if you are refused benefit as a result.[41]

Have you been refused tax credits?

If the decision maker decides you have not made a valid claim for tax credits because you or your partner do not satisfy the NI number requirement, you can challenge this decision. The Upper Tribunal has held that you have a right of appeal if the basis of your appeal is that your partner is exempt from the NI number requirement because s/he requires but does not have leave to enter or remain in the UK (see p443).[42] In a subsequent case, the Upper Tribunal went further and held that there is also a right of appeal if you or your partner had a reasonable excuse for not satisfying the NI number requirement (see p444).[43] You must request a mandatory reconsideration before you can appeal.

Other remedies

If you are refused an NI number, you can write to your MP and ask her/him to help. Your MP can also complain to the Parliamentary and Health Service Ombudsman on your behalf. See CPAG's *Welfare Benefits and Tax Credits Handbook* for more information.

Problems with NI numbers also raise issues about race discrimination since, in practice, the NI number requirement often prejudices black and minority ethnic communities. You may therefore want to refer to the DWP's Equality and Diversity statement when you contact it.[44] The Equality Advisory and Support Service may be able to advise or, in certain cases, take up the issue (see Appendix 2).

Notes

1. The national insurance number requirement

1 **TC** Reg 5(4) TC(CN) Regs
CB/GA s13(1A) and (1B) SSAA 1992
Other benefits s1(1A) and (1B) SSAA 1992
2 s1(1A) and (1B) SSAA 1992; reg 5(4) TC(CN) Regs; *Leicester City Council v OA* [2009] UKUT 74 (AAC), paras 27 and 28; Vol 1 Ch 2, para 02182 DMG; Ch A2, para A2151 ADM
3 s1(1A) SSAA 1992; reg 5(4) TC(CN) Regs
4 *SSWP v Wilson* [2006] EWCA Civ 882, reported as R(H) 7/06
5 Confirmed in Ch A2, para A2154 ADM
6 Reg 1A SS(DLA) Regs
7 s1(4) SSAA 1992 and s122 SSCBA 1992
8 Reg 4(a) HB Regs; reg 4(a) HB(SPC) Regs
9 Reg 5(6) TC(CN) Regs
10 **UC** Reg 5 UC,PIP,JSA&ESA(C&P) Regs
IS Reg 2A(a) IS Regs continues to apply in these cases due to the transitional protection in reg 1(3) SS(WTCCTC)(CA) Regs.
JSA Reg 2A(a) JSA Regs continues to apply in these cases due to the transitional protection in reg 1(7) SS(WTCCTC)(CA) Regs.
HB Reg 4(b) HB Regs; reg 4(b) HB(SPC) Regs
11 **IS** Reg 2A IS Regs
JSA Reg 2A JSA Regs
ESA Reg 2A ESA Regs
PC Reg 1A SPC Regs
HB Reg 4(c) HB Regs; reg 4(c) HB(SPC) Regs
TC Reg 5(8) TC(CN) Regs
Bereavement benefits and retirement pensions Reg 1A(c) SS(WB&RP) Regs
12 Vol 1, paras 02184-86 DMG; Ch A2, para A2153 ADM; TCTM 06110
13 Confirmed in Ch A2, paras A2153-4 ADM
14 **E** Sch 8 para 7(3) CTRS(PR)E Regs
W Sch para 111(3) CTRS(DS)W Regs; Sch 13 para 5(3) CTRSPR(W) Regs
15 *Westminster City Council v AT & SSWP (HB)* [2013] UKUT 321 (AAC)
16 Reg 5(6) TC(CN) Regs
17 TCTM 06110
18 *CI v HMRC(TC)* [2014] UKUT 158 (AAC)

2. Obtaining a national insurance number

19 Home Office guidance, *Procedures for Issuing a NINO to Asylum Claimants Granted Leave to Enter or Remain in the UK*, available at gov.uk
20 gov.uk/government/publications/national-insurance-number-allocations-staff-guide
21 Reg 15 The Immigration (Biometric Registration) Regulations 2008, No.3048, as amended by reg 13 The Immigration (Biometric Registration) (Amendment) Regulations 2015, No.433
22 gov.uk/government/publications/refugees-guidance-about-benefits-and-pensions/help-available-from-the-department-for-work-and-pensions-for-people-who-have-been-granted-leave-to-remain-in-the-uk and DWP, *LA Welfare Direct 3/2020* available at gov.uk
23 gov.uk/national-insurance/your-national-insurance-number; DWP guidance, *National Insurance Number Instructions for Staff: introduction to national insurance number allocation*, para 13
24 CH/4085/2007; HB/CTB Circular A13/2010, paras 14 and 15; TCM 0066140 and 0316020; DWP guidance, *National Insurance Number Instructions for Staff: benefit inspired evidence of identity (DCI1 Process)*, *National Insurance Number Instructions for Staff: contact centre appointment booking process*, para 92, and *National Insurance Number Instructions for Staff: completing the eDCI1 form*, all available at gov.uk
25 DWP guidance, *National Insurance Number Instructions for Staff: completing the eDCI1 form*, para 43, scenario 1
26 DWP guidance, *National Insurance Number Instructions for Staff: benefit inspired evidence of identity (DCI1 process)*, para 23

27 gov.uk/apply-national-insurance-number
28 DWP guidance, *National Insurance Number Instructions for Staff:documentary evidence and checks*, para 12
29 DWP guidance, *National Insurance Number Instructions for Staff: documentary evidence and checks*, paras 101 and 102
30 DWP guidance, *National Insurance Number Instructions for Staff:benefit inspired evidence of identity (DCI1 Process)*, para 19
31 CH/4085/2007, paras 19-22; *Leicester City Council v OA* [2009] UKUT 74 (AAC), para 33; *OM v HMRC* [2018] UKUT 50 (AAC), para 35; reg 9 and Sch 1 The Social Security (Crediting and Treatment of Contributions, and National Insurance Numbers) Regulations 2001, No.769

3. **Common problems**
32 CH/4085/2007; TCM 0066140 and 0316020; DWP guidance, *National Insurance Number Instructions for Staff: benefit inspired evidence of identity (DCI1 process),National Insurance Number Instructions for Staff: contact centre appointment booking process*, para 92, and *National Insurance Number Instructions for Staff: completing the eDCI1 form*; gov.uk/government/publications/refugees-guidance-about-benefits-and-pensions/help-available-from-the-department-for-work-and-pensions-for-people-who-have-been-granted-leave-to-remain-in-the-uk, para 8; DWP, LA Welfare Direct 3/2020 available at gov.uk
33 See for example, *OM v HMRC* [2018] UKUT 50 (AAC)
34 Reg 5 SS(PAB) Regs
35 DWP guidance, *Short Term Benefit Advances: benefit centres*, paras 66-67, available at whatdotheyknow.com/request/operational_guidance_for_benefit. Note this guidance does not apply to UC advances.

36 CH/4085/2007, paras 19-22; *Leicester City Council v OA* [2009] UKUT 74 (AAC), para 33; *OM v HMRC* [2018] UKUT 50 (AAC), para 35
37 CH/1231/2004; CH/4085/2007; Leicester City Council v OA [2009] UKUT 74 (AAC)
38 Ch A2, para A2150 ADM
39 CH/1231/2004
40 *OM v HMRC* [2018] UKUT 50 (AAC); reg 9 and Sch 1 The Social Security (Crediting and Treatment of Contributions, and National Insurance Numbers) Regulations 2001, No.769
41 CH/4085/2007, in particular paras 30-36; but see also *Leicester CC v OA* [2009] UKUT 74 (AAC), para 35, which held that you must have attended the interview, and *OM v HMRC* [2018] UKUT 50 (AAC), paras 36-38 on changes in the regulations that mean the position is different if you required an NI number to work.
42 *ZM and AB v HMRC(TC)* [2013] UKUT 547 (AAC)
43 *CI v HMRC(TC)* [2014] UKUT 158 (AAC)
44 gov.uk/government/organisations/department-for-work-pensions/about/equality-and-diversity

Chapter 20

Providing evidence

This chapter covers:

This chapter covers some of the issues that arise when you are required to provide evidence to show that you satisfy the immigration conditions (see Part 3), the residence conditions (see Part 4) or that you are covered by the European Union co-ordination rules (see Chapter 16).

1. General points about evidence

Evidence required when you make your claim

When you claim a benefit or tax credit, you must normally:
- satisfy the national insurance (NI) number requirement (see Chapter 19); *and*
- provide proof of your identity, if required (see below); *and*
- ensure your claim is valid (see p455).

To determine your claim, the decision maker needs evidence that you satisfy all the conditions of entitlement (see p456) and that you are not covered by any of the exceptions that mean you are not entitled (see p457). You are usually asked for evidence to show that you satisfy all the conditions of entitlement, including the immigration, residence or presence conditions, or that the European Union (EU) co-ordination rules apply to you.

Coronavirus

During the coronavirus pandemic, the DWP is not usually asking claimants to attend interviews at job centres but gathering information and evidence by telephone instead. This may make it difficult for you to provide evidence and documents needed by a decision maker in connection with you meeting immigration, residence or presence conditions. The DWP has said that during this period it will use information and evidence it already holds from any previous claims you have made and also attempt to obtain information and evidence from other sources such as the Home Office to confirm you meet any relevant conditions. Failing that, the DWP has said it may use a policy of 'trust' in relation to evidence but will later review any decisions based on such a policy. You should provide the DWP with as much and as accurate information as you can by telephone or online, and tell the DWP if information or evidence is not available to you but may be held by a government department.

Proving your identity

You may be asked to produce documents, or other evidence, that prove your identity. If your partner is included in your claim, even if you do not receive an amount for her/him (eg, because s/he is a 'person subject to immigration control' – see p104), you may also be asked to prove her/his identity. In addition, if your claim includes an amount for your child, you may be asked to prove her/his identity.

There are various documents that you can provide to the benefit authorities as proof of your identity. You should not be asked to supply any document that is unreasonable for you to have or obtain, and you should not be refused a benefit or tax credit simply because you can not provide a particular document. Be prepared to ask for an explanation of what is required and why, and challenge any unreasonable requests as well as a decision refusing your benefit.

The gov.uk website on applying for an NI number has a list of examples of documents that prove your identity, and you should provide one or more of these if possible (see p446). It can be helpful to provide details of anyone who can confirm what you have stated – eg, your solicitor or other legal representative or official organisation.

Note: if you are claiming universal credit (UC), you may be required to prove your identity online using the Verify system. This uses various private companies to check your identity. If you cannot prove your identity online, you must do so at the job centre. If possible, take one of the 'primary evidence documents' and two of the 'secondary evidence documents' on p446 with you. If you do not have sufficient documentary evidence, you are asked a series of security questions. If you fail to answer the security questions correctly, the DWP can approach a third party, with your consent, to validate your identity.[1]

Making a valid claim

To be entitled to a benefit or tax credit, you must make a valid claim. You must claim in the correct way and your claim must not be 'defective'. The relevant benefit authority should inform you if your claim is defective and must give you the opportunity to correct the defect.

What counts as a valid claim varies between the individual benefits and tax credits. What you are required to do to make your claim in the correct way is also affected by the method by which you can make your claim – ie, in writing, only on a certain form, online and/or by telephone. You may also have to attend an interview to complete your claim, or be sent a written statement to sign and return. The rules for each benefit and tax credit are covered in CPAG's *Welfare Benefits and Tax Credits Handbook*.

If your claim is refused because it is not valid, you can challenge that decision.

Note: your right to challenge a decision that your claim for tax credits is not valid is based on caselaw, rather than legislation.[2]

In all cases, if you challenge a decision that your claim is not valid, you should also make a fresh claim.

If your claim is accepted as valid, the decision maker must make a decision on your entitlement and you may still be required to provide additional documentation and evidence. If you fail to do so within the time allowed (this can be extended if it is reasonable), the decision maker may conclude that you are not entitled (but see below).

Evidence that you are entitled

When you claim a benefit or tax credit, you must generally show, on the balance of probabilities, that you meet the conditions of entitlement.[3] That is confirmed in DWP guidance as a general principle[4] and also in specific cases. For example, guidance (now withdrawn) on means-tested benefits for Commonwealth citizens who are long- term residents of the UK (sometimes referred to as the 'Windrush generation' – see p70), but who do not have documentary evidence of their immigration status, confirms that their entitlement can be accepted if the evidence indicates on the balance of probabilities that they are likely to have legal and habitual residence.

If you do not meet the conditions of entitlement under the UK rules but you do under the EU co-ordination rules, you must provide evidence of this.

The inquisitorial nature of benefit adjudication means that decision makers, who know what information and evidence is needed to decide whether you satisfy the conditions of entitlement, must ask you for that information. If you have been asked for information or evidence that, to the best of your abilities, you fail to provide, the decision maker can assume that you do not meet that particular condition of entitlement. However, s/he cannot do that if s/he fails to ask the relevant questions and does not give you a reasonable opportunity to provide the necessary information and evidence.[5] The decision maker should also take into account alternative likely explanations for why you have not provided the information or evidence before concluding that you are not entitled.[6]

You should always submit any documentary evidence you have showing that you meet the entitlement conditions. However, if you cannot do so, your own verbal or written evidence, given in the process of making your claim or subsequently, can be accepted without being corroborated.

Corroborative evidence is not necessary unless there are reasons to doubt your evidence – eg, if it is self-contradictory or inherently improbable.[7]

If you are asked for a particular document that you do not have, ask why it is needed so that you have the opportunity to provide alternatives. If you cannot provide any documentary proof of a particular fact, explain why not (eg, because all your documents are with the Home Office) and, if possible, provide proof of this – eg, a letter from your legal representative. If you consider any requests for information are unreasonable, you can complain. Get advice if you think you have experienced discrimination – eg, from the Equality Advisory and Support Service (see Appendix 2).

Evidence that you are not excluded

If there is an exception to entitlement that excludes you from a benefit or a tax credit to which you would otherwise be entitled (eg, because you are not habitually resident or because you are defined as a 'person subject to immigration control'), the burden of proving that this applies to you lies with the relevant benefit authority.[8]

You should always submit any evidence you have that an exception does not apply to your situation.

If you do not provide evidence that you are not excluded from entitlement when you make your claim, the decision maker must ask you for the information and evidence required for her/him to make a decision. Because the process of benefit adjudication is inquisitorial, the decision maker knows what information is required to determine whether you are entitled to benefit or whether you are excluded from entitlement, and s/he must therefore ask for that information.[9]

If some relevant facts are still unknown after all the enquiries have been made, the question of whether an exception applies that excludes you from entitlement should be decided in your favour.[10]

If the decision maker failed to ask all the relevant questions and you appeal, the First-tier Tribunal must ask you those questions.[11] If you have evidence that an exception does not apply to you, submit this in advance of the hearing if possible.

If you cannot provide the evidence required to determine whether or not you are excluded, but that evidence is available to the benefit authorities, see p460.

Decisions to end your entitlement

If you are receiving benefits or tax credits and your award is terminated on the basis that you no longer satisfy the immigration, residence or presence rules, the burden of proof is on the benefit authority to show the evidence on which this decision is based. If the decision maker has not shown this evidence and based her/his decision on the fact that you failed to provide evidence that nothing has changed, you should challenge the decision, pointing out that the burden of proof lies with the benefit authority. Set out clearly the reasons why you continue not to be excluded from entitlement.

The same burden of proof applies to the First-tier Tribunal.

There are a number of Upper Tribunal decisions concerning tax credits that confirm that the burden of proof is on HM Revenue and Customs (HMRC) to establish that there are grounds for revising a decision that you are entitled to tax credits, and that the same burden of proof applies to the First-tier Tribunal. That applies if HMRC wants to revise an entitlement decision for the current year[12] or previous year for which the award has already been finalised.[13] However, if HMRC decides that you have ceased to be entitled during the tax credit renewal period, the onus of proof is on you to show your continued entitlement.[14]

Example

Nardos is an Eritrean national with discretionary leave to remain in the UK, with no restriction on receiving public funds, for two and a half years. She claimed child tax credit (CTC), provided proof of her leave and was awarded CTC. Her leave was due to expire two months ago, but before it did Nardos applied for a further period of discretionary leave. She received an acknowledgement letter from the Home Office and forwarded a copy of this to the Tax Credit Office, but has not yet had a decision from the Home Office. Her discretionary leave to remain is extended while she waits for the Home Office to decide her application for further leave (see p463).

The Tax Credit Office wrote to Nardos asking her to provide evidence that she was entitled to receive public funds – both now and since the start of her claim. Nardos did not know how she could show this and so did not reply. She then received a decision letter, informing her that, as she has not shown she can receive public funds, HMRC has decided she is a 'person subject to immigration control' (see p81) and not entitled to CTC. Her award was terminated and HMRC decided to recover the overpaid CTC since the start of her claim.

Nardos can challenge this decision, by requesting a mandatory reconsideration. HMRC has not provided any evidence to show that her entitlement has ended, nor that the original decision awarding her CTC was incorrect. The evidence that Nardos had already given HMRC shows that she has leave to remain in the UK with no restriction on receiving public funds. She does not need to provide any further evidence that she is not excluded by her immigration status because it has not changed. She should explain this in her mandatory reconsideration request and remind HMRC that the Upper Tribunal has confirmed that the onus of proof is on the HMRC to show the evidence relied on in its decision that she is not entitled to CTC and has not been since the start of her claim.

For information on when a decision to award you benefits or tax credits can be revised or superseded, see CPAG's *Welfare Benefits and Tax Credits Handbook*.

If you make another benefit claim

If you make another benefit claim, either for a different benefit or for the same benefit at a later date, a previous decision about whether you satisfied the immigration status, residence or presence requirements, or whether the EU co-ordination rules applied to you, is not conclusive.[15] However, it is a factor that should be taken into account.

There are limited exceptions to this, including if you claim housing benefit (HB) and the DWP has made a decision to award you income support (IS), income-related employment and support allowance or pension credit. In this case, you are exempt from the habitual residence test for the purpose of HB (see p142).

In practice, if you have had a successful previous benefit claim, mandatory reconsideration or appeal, it is helpful to tell that to the benefit authority or First-tier Tribunal. If you have a written decision, provide a copy to support your case, even if you think the decision maker already has access to this. If some time has passed since the earlier decision, explain why it is still relevant to your current situation.

Example

Carmen is a Spanish national and in 2016 she claimed IS. Her claim was initially refused on the grounds that she did not satisfy the habitual residence test as she had no right to reside, but Carmen was subsequently awarded IS after she requested a mandatory reconsideration. The decision maker decided that Carmen had a right to reside because she had acquired a permanent right to reside as a result of having worker status in the UK from 2010 to 2016. When her daughter turns five, Carmen is no longer entitled to IS and so she makes a new claim for UC. She submits a copy of the IS mandatory reconsideration decision to the UC decision maker, together with evidence that she has not been out of the UK for a continuous period of two years to show that she has not lost her right of permanent residence (see p142).

If a decision on a previous claim was not favourable to you and you make a separate claim, or challenge a refusal of a separate claim, it may be helpful to remind the decision maker (or tribunal) that the earlier decision does not prevent her/him from making a different decision. Explain why the earlier decision was wrong or incomplete, note any challenge that you have submitted or intend to submit, and be clear whether the previous circumstances still apply and whether there have been any relevant changes.

If you are a European Economic Area (EEA) national and you claim HB and have been awarded income-based jobseeker's allowance (JSA), the DWP may have only recorded that you have a right to reside as an EEA jobseeker. Although the local authority can take the DWP's findings into account, they are not conclusive and it must make its own decision on whether you have another right to reside (as the right to reside as a jobseeker is an excluded residence right for HB – see p152), including, for example, whether you have retained worker status.[16]

Note: if the DWP has supplied information, including evidence, which was used in connection with a DWP benefit claim to a local authority, it should be accepted without its accuracy being verified for the purpose of the HB claim. This does not apply if the information was supplied more than 12 months after being used or if there are reasonable grounds for believing it has changed. This also applies in reverse – ie, if the local authority supplied information to the DWP.[17] However, this does not prevent the decision maker from requesting additional information – eg, if the information supplied is insufficient to determine your entitlement.

If evidence is not available to you

If your potential exclusion from benefit entitlement depends on evidence that is not available to you, but which is available to the benefit authority, the benefit authority must take the necessary steps to obtain it. If it fails to do so and so it is not known whether or not you are excluded from benefit, the matter must be decided in your favour – ie, that you are not excluded.[18]

This principle was established by the House of Lords in the case of *Kerr*[19] and is significant for migrants. For example, if the decision maker needs evidence of your immigration status which the Home Office has but you do not, s/he must use her/his channels of communication with the Home Office to obtain it.[20]

The principle is also significant if your entitlement depends on someone else's circumstances and the relevant information about these is not available to you, but it could be available to the benefit authority if the decision maker made enquiries or checked records. For example, the decision maker may need evidence of your right to reside which depends on the current or past economic activity of a family member (see p220), but you cannot contact her/him or s/he will not provide you with the information you need.

If this applies to you, you should provide as much information as possible to the benefit authority to enable it to trace the evidence you cannot provide, but which could be available to the decision maker if s/he made enquiries or checked records.

Example

Kristina is a 19-year-old Slovakian national who came to the UK in October 2020 and has been granted pre-settled status. She is due to give birth next week and wants the support of her father, Pavol, who has been in the UK for two years. However, Pavol disapproves of Kristina's pregnancy and has said that he never wants to hear from her again. Kristina is sleeping on a friend's sofa and has claimed UC. If Pavol has 'worker' status, Kristina, as his family member, is exempt from the habitual residence test for UC.

Kristina has her own birth certificate, which names Pavol as her father and confirms his nationality. However, she cannot get evidence of Pavol's worker status from him. Kristina has heard that Pavol was made redundant two months ago and is now claiming JSA. Therefore, if she can provide sufficient information to the DWP for it to be able to trace Pavol's JSA claim, the DWP will be able to obtain details of his previous work from the claim and assess whether that work gave him worker status and whether he has retained that status while claiming JSA. The DWP holds this information and therefore must take the necessary steps to enable it to be traced. If the DWP does not do so, Kristina can argue that she cannot be excluded from UC on the basis of not being habitually resident, as that has not been proven by the DWP.

How do you get the benefit authority to check someone's residence rights?

If your right to reside depends on someone else's residence rights, but you cannot obtain proof of these, ask the benefit authority to carry out the necessary investigations.

1. Although there is a duty on the benefit authority to take the necessary steps to trace information that is available to the authority and not you, it is unlikely to do so unless you clearly ask it to. Explain why you are unable to obtain the necessary information and remind the benefit authority of its duty to trace the information, citing the principles established in the *Kerr* case.[21]

2. Explain your right to reside, how this results from your relationship with the other person (eg, as her/his family member or primary carer of her/his child) and what information needs to be obtained – eg, evidence of current or past employment.

3. Provide as much information as possible on the relevant person's:
- name;
- date of birth;
- NI number;
- last known address;
- last known place of work;
- nationality;
- previous benefit claims.

4. The benefit authority must then take the necessary steps to trace the information, by checking records of any benefit claims or NI contributions. **Note:** guidance confirms that decision makers should use additional records available to them (eg, NI contribution records) to confirm whether a claimant has permanent residence.[22]

5. If the benefit authority fails to make the necessary investigations, you cannot be excluded from benefit on the basis of not having a right to reside, as the burden of proof is on the benefit authority to show that you do not have a right to reside (see p457).

6. If the benefit authority tells you it is prohibited from carrying out the investigations under data protection legislation, it may be arguable that this is incorrect as there are exemptions in the Data Protection Act.[23] However, in any event, you should appeal if the benefit authority refuses to carry out the investigations and ask the First-tier Tribunal for a direction requiring the decision maker to carry out the necessary investigations. It can

make such a direction once you have appealed.[24] The Data Protection Act permits disclosure of personal data if it is required by an order of a court or tribunal.[25]
Asking for a direction before your appeal hearing avoids the need for the hearing to be adjourned. It can also mean that, once the necessary information has been traced, the decision refusing your claim is revised, you are awarded benefit and your appeal lapses.

2. **Evidence of immigration status**

If you are claiming any of the benefits or tax credits listed on p95, the decision maker needs evidence of your immigration status to determine whether you are a 'person subject to immigration control' (see p81). If you are an EEA national, you may need to provide evidence that you have 'pre-settled' or 'settled' status under UK immigration law (see p49) rather than rights under European Union law to claim benefits or tax credits.

If you are claiming means-tested benefits or tax credits and your partner lives with you, the decision maker also needs evidence of her/his immigration status to determine whether s/he is a 'person subject to immigration control' (see p104).

It is rare for a decision maker to need evidence of your child's immigration status, as this does not affect whether or not you can be paid for her/him. However, if your child is the claimant (eg, for disability living allowance), evidence of her/his immigration status is required to determine whether s/he is a 'person subject to immigration control'.

Note: if your partner or child has leave which is subject to a 'no recourse to public funds' condition, this may be breached if s/he is included in your (or someone else's) claim and could jeopardise her/his immigration status (see p87).

Further information on checking your immigration status is in Chapter 6. If you are unclear about the status of anyone who may be included in your benefits or tax credits claim, get immigration advice (see Appendix 2) before claiming.

Problems with evidence

Problems can arise if you do not have documentary evidence or if the documents you have are unclear. The general points about evidence all apply (see p454). You should not be refused benefit because you cannot provide a particular document, and you should ask why a document is being requested so you can provide the evidence in a different way. If you cannot provide a document (eg, because it is with the Home Office), it can help if you provide a letter confirming this from your legal representative. S/he may also be able to confirm your current immigration status and the significance of any applications you have pending.

If evidence of immigration status is not available to you, but is available to the decision maker (eg, by emailing the Home Office), s/he must take the necessary steps to obtain this (see p460).

DWP guidance (now withdrawn) on means-tested benefits for Commonwealth citizens who are long-term residents of the UK (sometimes referred to as the 'Windrush generation' – see p70) but who lack documentary evidence of their immigration status refers the decision maker to the Home Office 'task force'. However, the guidance to housing benefit decision makers suggests that claimants be referred to the task force and that decision makers should only contact the Home Office directly if a claimant is experiencing unacceptable delays in resolving her/his status. The guidance for other means-tested benefits confirms that your entitlement should be assessed if the evidence held by the DWP and Home Office indicates, on the balance of probabilities, that you have legal and habitual residence.[26]

Note: if you are unsure of or you do not have documents to prove your immigration status, get independent immigration advice (see Appendix 2) before either contacting the Home Office or making a claim for benefits.

Changes in immigration status

If you have time-limited leave to enter or remain, you can apply to extend your leave or apply for further leave to remain on a different basis. Provided you apply before your existing leave expires, this leave is extended until your application is decided by the Home Office.[27] If your original leave was not subject to a no recourse to public funds condition, you were not a 'person subject to immigration control' and were therefore entitled to all benefits and tax credits, subject to the usual rules of entitlement. When your leave is extended, you continue not to be a person subject to immigration control and your benefit entitlement remains the same. It is important to notify the benefit authorities, as otherwise they may assume your leave has expired and that you are no longer entitled to benefit (because you are now a person subject to immigration control on the basis of being someone who requires but does not have leave – see p81).

The benefit authorities need evidence that you applied to vary your leave before your existing leave ended. If possible, you should submit documents showing when your leave was due to expire, which the benefit authorities may already have on your file, together with confirmation of the date when your application to vary that leave was submitted – eg, a letter from a legal representative who helped you with the application, proof of date of posting and any letter confirming the date your application was received. Although it should not be necessary, in practice it also helps if you submit a covering letter. In this, explain that your previous leave is extended because you applied to vary your leave before your previous leave expired, you therefore continue not to be a person subject to immigration control, and so your benefit or tax credit entitlement also continues. Include the relevant legal references in your letter.

Note: if your application to vary your leave is refused and your leave is extended while your appeal against that refusal is pending, you *may* count as a person subject to immigration control (see p92).

3. Evidence of residence rights

In many circumstances, providing evidence of your residence rights will require you to provide evidence of your nationality and, if you are not a British or Irish citizen, evidence of your immigration status.

However, if you are a European Economic Area (EEA) national resident in the UK before 1 January 2021, or a family member of such an EEA national, or you had a derivative right to reside before that date, and you do not have indefinite leave granted under the European Union (EU) Settlement Scheme (also known as settled status), you may need to provide evidence of your European free movement residence rights, and also evidence that you are in one of the protected groups that can have such rights. This can be complex and can involve several steps, each requiring certain conditions to be met. It is advisable to set out to the decision maker the basis on which you are in a protected group, and the basis of your free movement residence right, as clearly as you can and, wherever possible, provide evidence of every requirement. If you do not have documentary evidence of one requirement but you have provided evidence of others, it is more likely that the decision maker will accept your uncorroborated evidence on the remaining one (see p456).

If you have limited leave granted under the EU Settlement Scheme (also known as pre-settled status), you are in a protected group that can have a free movement right to reside. **Note:** the Court of Appeal recently held that pre-settled status is itself a qualifying right to reside for EU citizens claiming means-tested benefits. However, due to delays in this decision being implemented and the Department for Work and Pensions seeking to challenge it further, you should always provide evidence of a free movement right to reside if possible. For details of the steps to follow if you have pre-settled status, and other exemptions, see p152 for means-tested benefits and p157 for child benefit and child tax credit.

For information on how to prove your EU Settlement Scheme settled or pre-settled status to the benefit authorities, see p165.

If you do not have pre-setted status, whether you are in a protected group that can have free movement residence rights will depend on you (or the person that you are a 'relevant family member' of) having had a free movement right to reside on 31 December 2020. You should provide evidence of that if you can, but if you cannot, you should ask the benefit authority to make its own investigations – eg, by checking HM Revenue and Customs records for evidence of work), and provide sufficient information to enable it to do so (see p460).[28]

For details of the protected groups, including their duration, see p168.

See p171 for a summary of European free movement rights.

Residence documents

The only circumstance when you need a residence document in order to have a European free movement right to reside is if you are an 'extended family member' (see p223). In this case, you must have a family permit, registration certificate or residence card, which remains in force, in order to be *treated as* a 'family member' of someone who can confer a right of residence on you (see p223).

For any other right to reside, you do not need a residence document because your right to reside depends on the facts of your situation. Documentation only confirms your residence rights; it cannot give you a right to reside if, for instance, it was issued in error or if it correctly confirmed your right to reside when it was issued, but your circumstances have now changed so that you no longer have a right to reside.[29]

You can be issued with the following residence documents if you applied before the end of the transition period (11pm on 31 December 2020) (or if the exception for a family permit applies to you).

- **A registration certificate** if you are an EEA national with a right of residence under the EEA Regulations.[30]
- **A residence card** if you are a non-EEA national and you have a right to reside as the family member of an EEA 'qualified person' (see p172) or an EEA national with a permanent right of residence.[31]
- **A derivative residence card** if you have a derivative right to reside (see p233).[32]
- **A document certifying a permanent right of residence** if you are an EEA national with a permanent right of residence, or a **permanent residence card** if you are a non-EEA national with permanent residency.[33]
- **A residence document,** issued, or treated as issued, under previous EEA Regulations. These are treated as issued under the current EEA Regulations.[34]
- **A family permit** issued for entry to the UK if you are a family member of an EEA national with a free movement right of residence in the UK and either:[35]
  - you applied before the end of the transition period; *or*
  - you are in a protected group that can continue to have a free movement right to reside until at least 30 June 2021 (for details of these protections, including their duration, see p168). If you are an 'extended family member', a family permit may only be granted on this basis if you are the EEA national's partner in a durable relationship.

4. Other types of evidence

Certain types of evidence are of particular significance for migrants and are discussed below. Depending on your circumstances and the benefit or tax credit being claimed, this evidence may be required by all claimants to satisfy the entitlement conditions, or because it affects the amount to which you are entitled. You should not be required to submit more evidence because you are a migrant than would be required of a British person in the same circumstances. If you are asked for more evidence because you are not British, you may want to get advice from the Equality Advisory and Support Service (see Appendix 2).

It can be helpful to check the guidance issued to decision makers on acceptable evidence and refer to this when it supports your situation. Check the guidance on evidence in general,[36] on specific types of evidence (eg, of age, marriage and death[37]), and the guidance specific to migrants,[38] including on the right to reside and habitual residence tests.[39]

Evidence from other countries

If your documentary evidence is from another country and is not in English, it can be helpful to submit an authorised translation. If obtaining a translation will cause any delay, you should make sure you do not miss any deadlines for submitting evidence. For example, you could take the original document to a local benefit office to take an authorised copy and accompany this with a letter explaining that you are obtaining a translation.

The authenticity of a document issued outside the UK should not automatically be questioned. Decision makers are reminded in their guidance that certificates of birth, marriage, civil partnerships and deaths issued abroad can all be accepted as evidence of that event, unless there is a reason to doubt their authenticity.[40]

Even if a document is from a country in which it is relatively easy to obtain fraudulent documents, a decision maker (or First-tier Tribunal) cannot presume your document is not genuine. While the decision maker (or tribunal) may conclude on the balance of probabilities that a document is not genuine, s/he still needs to decide the 'weight' given to that document by considering any evidence of the accuracy of record keeping by the issuing body, whether other evidence corroborates the document and your overall credibility.[41]

Evidence of nationality

The most common acceptable evidence of your nationality is a current passport, a current European Economic Area (EEA) identity card or, if you are a non-EEA national, a current travel document or biometric residence permit. However, if you cannot provide one of these, other official documents should be accepted (see p446). As with all evidence requirements, it helps if you can provide more than one form of evidence of your nationality.

If you are relying on someone else's nationality for your own rights (eg, to argue you have a right to reside as the family member of an EEA worker), you must provide evidence of her/his nationality – eg, to show s/he is an EEA national.

Evidence of a relationship

If your rights are based on being someone's family member or primary carer, you must provide evidence of this relationship. You must also provide evidence of the other factors that are relevant. For example, if you need to show you are the family member of an EEA worker, in addition to evidence that you are her/his family member, you must also provide evidence of her/his EEA nationality and her/his employment.

Non-European Economic Area nationals

If you entered the UK as the family member of an EEA national who is in the UK exercising her/his treaty rights (eg, as a worker), you usually have an entry clearance document that states this. You should provide this document to the benefit authority, as it is the most significant documentary evidence required. However, depending on your circumstances, the benefit authority may also want evidence that you are still her/his family member, or that you come within limited circumstances that enable you to retain residence rights as a former family member (see p228).

If you are a non-EEA national and are the primary carer of someone who confers a derivative right to reside on you (see p233), the benefit authorities require evidence of each requirement that must be satisfied for you to have this right to reside. For example, if you are asserting that you are the primary carer of a worker's child in education, you must show:

- you are the primary carer of the child (see p239);
- s/he is currently in education (see p237);
- one of her/his parents (or step-parents) is an EEA national (see p466);
- that parent (or step-parent) had worker status in the UK (see p237) while the child was in the UK.

Note: if you are a non-EEA national and are the family member of an EEA national who confers residence rights on you, you may not be a 'person subject to immigration control' (see p81).

Evidence of marriage or civil partnership

If you have been given leave to enter or remain on the basis of being a spouse or civil partner of someone, evidence of that leave is generally accepted as sufficient evidence of your relationship for the purposes of proving your entitlement to a benefit or tax credit.

Spouses and civil partners have far greater rights under European Union (EU) law than partners who are not married or who are not civil partners. Consequently, it can be important to show that someone is your spouse or civil partner – eg, when s/he can confer residence rights on you. If you need to prove that you are someone's spouse or civil partner, you must show that you are still married or in a civil partnership. If you have separated and are no longer living together or in a relationship, you are still her/his spouse or civil partner until you are finally divorced or the civil partnership is finally dissolved.[42]

A marriage or civil partnership certificate is the best evidence. If the certificate was issued outside the UK by the appropriate registration authority, it should be accepted as valid evidence (see p466).[43]

If you do not have a marriage or civil partnership certificate, other evidence confirming your marriage or civil partnership can be accepted. Official documents that refer to your marriage or civil partnership, as well as official correspondence confirming you live together, can be be taken into account.

There is extensive guidance for decision makers on evidence of marriage and civil partnerships, including religious and national variations.[44]

If you are refused benefits or tax credits because your marriage or civil partnership is not recognised or is deemed to have been a marriage or civil partnership 'of convenience', get specialist immigration advice.

Evidence of parentage

If you have been given leave to enter or remain on the basis of being a parent or child of someone, evidence of that leave is generally accepted as sufficient evidence of your relationship for the purposes of proving your entitlement to benefits and tax credits.

If you are the child of someone who can confer residence rights on you under EU law, you must show that s/he is your parent and either you are aged under 21 or you are dependent on her/him. If you are the parent of someone who can confer residence rights on you, you must show that you are her/his parent and you are dependent on her/him.

A birth certificate, or official DNA test results, that name both child and parent should be sufficient evidence. If the document is from outside the UK, see p466.

If you do not have a birth certificate or official DNA test results, other documents can also be accepted. If you do not have anything decisive, submit the evidence you have to back up your own written or verbal evidence and ask for the decision maker to decide on the balance of probabilities (see p456).

Example

Nadifa is 18 and a Dutch national. She has health problems and wants to claim universal credit (UC). She came to the UK four years ago with her mother, who is also a Dutch national, having acquired Dutch citizenship after fleeing to the Netherlands as a refugee 15 years ago. Nadifa's mother is a self-employed translator and has extensive evidence of this. However, Nadifa does not have any evidence that she is her mother's daughter. Her mother fled to the Netherlands without any documents. Nadifa therefore submits evidence of her mother's Dutch nationality and self-employment, together with a letter setting out the relevant details of her life history and documents showing that she was given leave to remain in the Netherlands as a dependant on her mother's asylum claim, evidence that she travelled with her mother to the UK four years ago and letters from her GP and dermatologist discussing Nadifa's eczema and the likelihood of its being linked to her mother's eczema.

Note: if you are trying to show that you are someone's father or that someone is your father, until officially declared otherwise, a man is deemed to be a child's father if he was married to the child's mother at the time of the child's birth or his name was registered on the birth certificate.[45]

Evidence of age

Your age (or someone else's age) can affect whether or not you meet the basic conditions of entitlement to a benefit, and the amount to which you are entitled. Your age (or someone else's age) can also affect your residence rights, whether your immigration status excludes you from benefits and tax credits and/or whether you are covered by the EU co-ordination rules. In addition, age can affect whether you (or someone else) are defined as a 'family member' or as 'dependent'.

A birth certificate, passport or identity card is usually accepted as proof of your date of birth. Other evidence that can show your date of birth includes school, medical or army records. Guidance to decision makers states that the 'primary' or best evidence of age is a certified copy of an entry which must be made in a register by law, such as a birth certificate or adoption certificate.[46] If you were born abroad and have a certificate issued by the appropriate registration authority, that should be accepted unless there is reason to doubt its validity (see p466).[47] See also the other evidence that can be accepted as proof of your identity on p446, and guidance to decision makers on 'secondary' evidence of age.[48]

You may be able to show your date of birth by referring to the accepted birth dates of other relatives, such as siblings.[49] For example, if you are recorded as the eldest child and your sister has been accepted as born in 1995, you must have been born before then.

If you have no record of your date of birth, or there is conflicting evidence, it is possible for an age assessment to be carried out. However, there is no accurate scientific test that can establish a person's age, and such an assessment can be disputed. See p513 for age assessments for unaccompanied asylum-seeking children. Guidance to decision makers covers the possibility of arranging a physical examination of an adult, but notes that this is generally only reliable five years either way.[50] However, getting your GP to state her/his opinion of your age, together with her/his reasons, can be helpful supporting evidence, particularly if it is clear that the GP has known you for some time and is familiar with your medical conditions.[51]

A common problem is conflicting evidence due to past errors. Your date of birth may have been wrongly recorded in your passport when it was issued – eg, because you gave the wrong date or because of an administrative error. The date in the passport may then have been used in many other official documents and it may be difficult to persuade the benefit authorities that all these dates are wrong. You should explain that all these dates come from one document and give a detailed account about how the wrong date came to be recorded. This explanation counts as evidence, but you should submit any other evidence you have (or can obtain) showing that date is not correct.[52]

While each piece of evidence must be considered, the oldest documents may be more reliable, since they were made nearer to the time of the events to which they refer.

Passports and other immigration documents are commonly recorded as '1 January' when your exact date of birth is unclear. However, if you obtain evidence of your exact date of birth later, this can be accepted.

The decision maker (or First-tier Tribunal) should weigh up all the available evidence and determine your age on the balance of probabilities.[53]

If there is no documentary evidence, the benefit authorities should accept your own statements, unless they are contradictory or improbable (see p456).

Evidence of work

Evidence of your (or someone else's) current or past employment or self-employment can be required to prove that you satisfy, or are exempt from, immigration or residence conditions, or that you are covered by the EU co-ordination rules. The exact evidence required depends on what you need to prove, so it is essential that you check the rules for the specific condition you need to satisfy or be exempt from.

Examples

Hassan is a Turkish national and is in the UK to study. He has a student visa, which gives him leave to be in the UK for the next two years, subject to the condition that he does not have recourse to public funds. Hassan is therefore a 'person subject to immigration control' (see p81). He works 15 hours a week, which is permitted under his student visa. Hassan wants to claim child benefit and UC because his girlfriend's 14-year-old French son has come to live with him while she goes to Canada for a year. Hassan can claim both child benefit and UC if he can show that he is 'lawfully working' and 'lawfully present', because this means he is exempt from the exclusion that would otherwise apply to him as a 'person subject to immigration control' (see p99 for child benefit and p97 for UC). Hassan must provide HM Revenue and Customs (HMRC) with evidence of his employment (eg, a payslip or letter from his employer), together with confirmation that his work is allowed under the conditions of his immigration leave, and both HMRC and DWP with proof of his Turkish nationality and his student visa.

Dimitra is a Greek national who wants to claim UC as she is due to have a baby in three weeks. She came to the UK six years ago and got a job after being here a month. She worked in this job until three months ago, when she stopped work to care for her four-year-old son. If Dimitra can show that she had a right to reside as a 'worker' for a continuous period of five years, she will have a permanent right to reside (see p245), which satisfies the right to reside requirement for UC. Dimitra must provide evidence that she was in an employment relationship (see p192) doing 'genuine and effective' work (see p194) for a continuous period of five years. Dimitra should also apply for 'settled' status (see p49), which would satisfy the right to reside requirement for UC (see p152).

There is no definitive list of what counts as acceptable evidence. The evidence of work is considered stronger if it has several ways of showing it relates to you – eg, if it shows your full name, your date of birth, your address and your national insurance (NI) number, rather than just one or two of these.

Evidence of employment includes:

- a contract of employment;
- payslips;
- correspondence from your employer to you – eg, offering you the job or confirming a change in hours;
- a letter from an employer confirming your employment;
- documents relating to your total pay and tax over a period, such as P60 and P45 forms;
- bank statements showing wages being paid in from the employer or, if you are paid 'cash in hand', showing you have deposited your wages on a regular basis.

If you are not actually working (eg, because you are on sick leave or maternity leave), you may not have ceased to have a right to reside as a 'worker' (see p195). You need to provide evidence that you are still under a contract of employment, such as a letter from your employer stating this. Alternatively, if you have ceased to be a worker, you may be able to retain your worker status and must provide evidence of the basis of this (see p201) in addition to the evidence of the worker status you had.

Evidence of self-employment includes:

- documents from HMRC confirming your registration as self-employed;
- evidence of paying class 2 NI contributions;
- bank statements showing payments from your customers;
- business accounts;
- samples of marketing;
- documents showing you have bought the required equipment needed.

If you want to demonstrate that you have a right to reside as a self-employed person, it should be enough to show that you have established yourself to undertake activity as a self-employed person (see p198). The Upper Tribunal has considered how self-employment should be evaluated for the purpose of working tax credit entitlement and, although this context differs from the context of having a right to reside as a self-employed person, these decisions give useful guidance.[54]

If you are not actually working, you may not have ceased to have a right to reside as a self-employed person. You must provide evidence of all the factors that are relevant in your circumstances (see p199).

You may be able to retain your self-employed status (see p201) and need to provide evidence of this in addition to the evidence of your self-employment.

If you need evidence of your past employment or self-employment, you can submit a 'subject access' request to HMRC, asking for a summary of your employment history for a specified period.[55]

If your right to reside depends on someone else being, or having been, a worker or self-employed, all the above points apply to evidence of their work. If you do not have any documentary evidence of this because you cannot contact the person or s/he will not provide you with the evidence, you may be able to argue that the benefit authorities should obtain this evidence (see p460).

Croatian, A2 and A8 nationals

Restrictions, which could affect your residence rights based on employment, previously applied to Croatian, A2 nationals and A8 nationals (see p176). If these applied to you, you must supply additional evidence. If you need to show that you had a right to reside as a 'worker', or that you had retained 'worker' status, you must show that, at the time of working, you:

- were exempt from restrictions (see p178 for Croatian and A2 nationals, and p179 for A8 nationals); *or*
- (for Croatian and A2 nationals) worked in accordance with a valid authorisation document (see p177); *or*
- (for A8 nationals) worked for an 'authorised employer' (see p180). **Note:** a registration certificate that was applied for after the first month of work is not retrospective, and so is only evidence that you were working for an authorised employer from the date it was issued.[56] Also, because you were classed as working for an authorised employer for the first month of any employment, you do not need to provide a registration certificate for this first month.

If you are unable to provide your authorisation document or registration certificate because it has been lost or stolen, you should provide the benefit authority with as much information as you can about your employment and when it was authorised or registered, and ask the decision maker to confirm this through her/his contacts with the Home Office. You can also submit a 'subject access' request to the Home Office, asking for the details of your authorisation or registration(s). For details of how to do this, see gov.uk/government/publications/requests-for-personal-data-uk-visas-and-immigration.

Your employer at the relevant time may also be able to assist you with evidence confirming your authorisation or registration.

Do not delay making your claim while you gather evidence of your worker authorisation or registration(s).

Note: there were no additional restrictions, and therefore no additional evidence requirements, if you (or the person whose right to reside you are relying on) was self-employed.

Evidence of jobseeking

To retain your worker status while involuntarily unemployed (see p202),[57] you must provide evidence that you are seeking employment, but under the EEA Regulations, to have a right to reside as a jobseeker (see p182), you must also have a 'genuine chance of being engaged'.

These requirements are similar to the requirements to be 'actively seeking' and 'available for' work for jobseeker's allowance (JSA) or NI credits, and to the work search and work availability requirements under the UC system. In most cases, if the decision maker accepts that you have provided evidence that satisfies these work-related requirements, this evidence should also be accepted as satisfying the requirements for you to have a right to reside as a jobseeker. For the circumstances when this might not apply and for more information on the type of work you must be seeking, see p187.

Note: you do not need to receive, or claim, benefit to have a right to reside as a jobseeker, as long as you provide evidence that you are seeking employment and have a 'genuine chance of being engaged' (see p187).[58]

Under EU law, there is no time limit on how long you can have a right to reside as a jobseeker – it continues for as long as you provide evidence that you are looking for work and have a genuine chance of being engaged.[59] There is also no time limit on how long you can retain your worker or self-employed status while involuntarily unemployed, provided you were employed for at least a year (see p204).[60]

However, under the EEA Regulations, in order to continue to have a right to reside as a jobseeker for longer than 91 days, the evidence that you are seeking employment and have a genuine chance of being engaged must be 'compelling'.[61] This requirement is referred to as the 'genuine prospects of work test'.

Examples of evidence

Evidence that you are seeking employment could include details of all your:

- work search activities;
- enquiries made to potential employers;

- applications for employment, together with responses;
- requests to attend interviews, together with responses.

Evidence that you have a genuine chance of being engaged could include evidence of:
- your work history in the UK and elsewhere;
- your qualifications and other training undertaken;
- voluntary work (in the UK and abroad);
- your language skills;
- security checks you have satisfied;
- your proximity to potential employers;
- completion of a course on obtaining work as part of an employability programme;
- the broad range of types of work you are looking for and/or the hours of work you are able to do;
- your arrangements for adequate childcare to enable you to attend interviews and take up employment.

Whether you have a genuine chance of being engaged also depends on future events,[62] so you should provide evidence of any qualifications you hope to obtain and experience you will gain in the near future. If you have appealed against a decision that you are not entitled to benefit because you did not show that you had a genuine chance of being engaged, and by the date your appeal is heard you have obtained employment, the tribunal can take this into account as evidence of your *chance* of being engaged on the date of the decision.[63]

Although it is arguable that you should not be required to change the quality of your evidence after a particular length of time, in practice, the longer you have been a jobseeker without obtaining work, the more likely it is that the decision maker will argue that this shows you do not have a genuine chance of getting work. The Upper Tribunal has held that if you have been seeking employment without success for at least six months, this is relevant, but is only one factor that must be considered and can be outweighed by others.[64] You should therefore provide as much evidence as possible to demonstrate that, on the balance of probabilities, you have a genuine chance of being engaged, despite the long period of unemployment.

Notes

1. **General points about evidence**
1 DWP, *Identity Verification*, version 10, available at rightsnet.org.uk/universal-credit-guidance
2 *CI v HMRC (TC)* [2014] UKUT 158 (AAC)
3 *LS v SSWP(SPC)* [2014] UKUT 249 (AAC); see also *KS v SSWP* [2016] UKUT 269 (AAC), paras 10-14 and *DH v SSWP* [2018] UKUT 185 (AAC), para 6
4 Vol 1 Ch 1, paras 01343-5 DMG; Ch A1, paras A1340-2 ADM
5 *Kerr v Department for Social Development (Northern Ireland)* [2004] UKHL 23, paras 15-17 and 61-63; *SS v HMRC(TC)* [2014] UKUT 383 (AAC), paras 28-30; *DD v HMRC and SSWP (CB)* [2020] UKUT 66 (AAC), para 28
6 *SSWP v HS (JSA)* [2016] UKUT 272 (AAC), reported as [2017] AACR 29
7 R(I) 2/51, paras 6 and 7; R(SB) 33/85, para 14; *EP v SSWP (JSA)* [2016] UKUT 445 (AAC), para 21
8 R(IS) 6/96, para 15; see also *Kerr v Department for Social Development (Northern Ireland)* [2004] UKHL 23, paras 16-17 and 61-69; CIS/1697/2004, paras 18-20; R(PC) 1/09, paras 16-18
9 *R v Medical Appeal Tribunal (North Midland Region) ex parte Hubble* [1958] 2 QB 228; *Kerr v Department for Social Development (Northern Ireland)* [2004] UKHL 23, paras 15-17 and 61-63; R(PC) 1/09, paras 16-20; *DD v HMRC and SSWP (CB)* [2020] UKUT 66 (AAC), para 28
10 *Kerr v Department for Social Development (Northern Ireland)* [2004] UKHL 23, paras 61-69; R(PC) 1/09, para 19
11 R(IS) 11/99; *AS v SSWP (UC)* [2018] UKUT 260 (AAC)
12 s16(1) TCA 2002; *NI v HMRC (TC)* [2015] UKUT 490 (AAC) – see also caselaw listed in para 4; *JR v HMRC (TC)* [2015] UKUT 192 (AAC)
13 s19 TCA 2002; *CS v HMRC (TC)* [2015] UKUT 407 (AAC), para 23; *TS v HMRC (TC)* [2015] UKUT 507 (AAC); *VO v HMRC (TC)* [2017] UKUT 343 (AAC), para 41
14 s14 TCA 2002; *SB v HMRC (TC)* [2014] UKUT 543 (AAC), para 12
15 See for example, s17 SSA 1998; Sch 7 para 11 CSPSSA 2000
16 *EP v SSWP (JSA)* [2016] UKUT 445 (AAC), paras 24-27
17 The Social Security (Claims and Information) Regulations 2007, No.2911
18 *Kerr v Department for Social Development(Northern Ireland)* [2004] UKHL 23, paras 61-69; R(PC) 1/09, paras 16-19
19 ADM Memo 30/20, para 42
20 R(PC) 1/09, paras 16-19
21 *Kerr v Department for Social Development (Northern Ireland)* [2004] UKHL 23, paras 61-69; ADM Memo 30/20 para 42
22 Vol 2, para 073431 DMG; Ch C1, para C1810 ADM
23 Sch 2 para 5(3)(c) Data Protection Act 2018 (and s94(6) may also be relevant)
24 rr5, 6 and 15 TP(FT) Rules; *PM v SSWP (IS)* [2014] UKUT 474 (AAC)
25 s35 Data Protection Act 1998 until 24 May 2018; Sch 2 para 5(2) Data Protection Act 2018 from 25 May 2018; *TM v HMRC (TC)* [2013] UKUT 444 (AAC), para 6

2. **Evidence of immigration status**
26 **HB** U1/2018, paras 6-10
27 s3C(2)(a) IA 1971

3. **Evidence of residence rights**
28 Reg 13 CR(ADTP) Regs; *Kerr v DSDNI* [2004] UKHL 23, paras 62-69; ADM Memo 30/20, para 42; DMG Memo 26/20, para 42
29 *SSWP v Dias*, C-325/09 [2011] ECR I-06387; *EM and KN v SSWP* [2009] UKUT 44 (AAC); *MD v SSWP (SPC)* [2016] UKUT 319 (AAC); regs 17(8), 18(7), 19(4) and 20(5) I(EEA) Regs
30 Reg 17 I(EEA) Regs; Sch 3 para 3(3) ISSC Regs
31 Reg 18 I(EEA) Regs; Sch 3 para 3(4) ISSC Regs
32 Reg 20 I(EEA) Regs; Sch 3 para 3(6) ISSC Regs

33 Reg 19 I(EEA) Regs; Sch 3 para 3(5) ISSC Regs
34 Reg 45 and Sch 6 para 2 I(EEA) Regs; Reg 10 CR(ADTP) Regs
35 Reg 12 I(EEA) Regs; regs 3(4)-(6), 4(2) and (5)-(8) and 6(b) CR(ADTP) Regs; sch 3 para 3(1) and (2) ISSC Regs

4. **Other types of evidence**
36 For example, Vol 1 Ch 1 DMG or Ch A1 ADM
37 For example, Vol 3 Ch 10 DMG or Ch B3 ADM
38 For example, Vol 2 DMG or Ch 20 CCM
39 For example, Vol 2 Ch 7 DMG
40 See, for example, Vol 3 Ch 10 DMG
41 *SW v SSWP (SPC)* [2016] UKUT 163 (AAC), in particular paras 28 and 41
42 *Diatta v Land Berlin,* C-267/83 [1985] ECR I-00567
43 Vol 3 Ch 10, para 10155 DMG
44 For example, Vol 3 Ch 10, paras 10120-43 DMG
45 **EW** ss2 and 4 CA 1989
S s3 C(S)A 1995
46 Vol 3 Ch 10, paras 10030 and 10064-65 DMG; para B3016 ADM
47 Vol 3 Ch 10, para 10035 DMG; para B3021 ADM; *SW v SSWP (SPC)* [2016] UKUT 163 (AAC), in particular paras 28 and 41
48 Vol 3 Ch 10, paras 10036 and 10070-73 DMG; paras B3022 and B3051-58 ADM
49 Vol 3 Ch 10, para 10071 example 10 DMG; para B3051 example ADM
50 Vol 3 Ch 10, paras 10098-102 DMG; paras B3073-74 and B3086-89 ADM
51 For example, *SW v SSWP (SPC)* [2016] UKUT 163 (AAC)
52 For example, *SW v SSWP (SPC)* [2016] UKUT 163 (AAC)
53 *LS v SSWP(SPC)* [2014] UKUT 249 (AAC), para 5
54 *JF v HMRC (TC)* [2017] UKUT 334 (AAC), paras 30-31; *VO v HMRC (TC)* [2017] UKUT 343 (AAC)
55 For guidance on how HMRC records of national insurance records and contributions should be interpreted, see *SSWP v LM (ESA)* [2017] UKUT 485 (AAC), para 2 and Appendix 1.
56 *SSWP v ZA* [2009] UKUT 294 (AAC); *Szpak v SSWP* [2013] EWCA Civ 46
57 Reg 6(1), (2), (5) and (6) I(EEA) Regs; art 7(3) EU Dir 2004/38; KH v Bury MBC and SSWO (HB) [2020] UKUT 50 (AAC); ADM Memo 31/20
58 *The Queen v Immigration Appeal Tribunal, ex parte Antonissen,* C-292/89 [1991] ECR I-00745, para 21; R(IS) 8/08, para 5; *GE v SSWP (ESA)* [2017] UKUT 145 (AAC), para 46
59 *The Queen v Immigration Appeal Tribunal, ex parte Antonissen,* C-292/89 [1991] ECR I-00745, para 21
60 Art 7(3)(b) EU Dir 2004/38; ADM Memo 31/20 para 14
61 Reg 6(1), (5), (6) and (7) I(EEA) Regs. Previously, DWP applied these requirements to those retaining worker and self-employed status while involuntarily unemployed, but see *KH v Bury MBC and SSWP (HB)* [2020] UKUT 50 (AAC); ADM Memo 31/20'
62 *SSWP v MB (JSA) (and linked cases)* [2016] UKUT 372 (AAC), reported as [2017] AACR 6, para 47
63 *OS v SSWP (JSA)* [2017] UKUT 107 (AAC), paras 5-7 and caselaw cited; see also *AMS v SSWP (PC) (final decision)* [2017] UKUT 381 (AAC), para 26
64 *SSWP v MB (JSA) (and linked cases)* [2016] UKUT 372 (AAC), reported as [2017] AACR 6, paras 49-60; *KH v Bury MBC and SSWP (HB)* [2020] UKUT 50 (AAC)

Part 8

Support for asylum seekers

Chapter 21

Asylum support overview

This chapter covers:

1. Introduction

Types of support for asylum seekers

Asylum seekers are excluded from claiming social security benefits on the basis of being 'persons subject to immigration control' (see p81).[1] Instead, there are three main types of government support for people who have applied for asylum in the UK.

- Support for an asylum seeker and her/his dependants for a period until a final decision on an asylum application is made. This is known as **section 95 support.** It consists of accommodation and cash or the option of cash only (see p481).[2]
- **Temporary support** (often called 'section 98', 'initial accommodation' or 'emergency support'), which is available to asylum seekers and their dependants waiting for a decision on their application for section 95 support. This support **comprises full-board accommodation** (see p492).[3]
- **Section 4 support** is for people whose asylum application has been rejected. It consists of accommodation and a payment card, known as an ASPEN card (see p493).[4]

In certain limited circumstances, people who have applied for asylum are eligible for:

- local authority support for people who have claimed asylum (see p509); *and*
- discretionary support for people on immigration bail (see p507).

The section on local authority support includes support that has exceptionally been made available to homeless asylum seekers by local authorities in response to the coronavirus pandemic (see p513).

Home Office agencies

Since the Immigration and Asylum Act 1999 came into force, the responsibility for providing accommodation and support to asylum seekers has passed between several different Home Office agencies. Until April 2006, the support scheme for asylum seekers and refused asylum seekers was administered by the National Asylum Support Service (NASS). In April 2006, NASS ceased to exist and its role was taken over by the Border and Immigration Agency (BIA). On 7 April 2008, the UK Border Agency (UKBA) was formed, taking over the support role of the BIA, as well as the immigration and asylum functions of the Immigration and Nationality Directorate. The UKBA was abolished on 26 March 2013 and all its functions were returned to the Home Office. Asylum support applications are now dealt with by the UK Visas and Immigration (UKVI) department in the Home Office. For simplicity, we refer to the 'Home Office' in this *Handbook*.

You may find that some advisers and even officials still refer to asylum support as 'NASS' or 'UKBA' support, even though these agencies no longer exist.

Home Office guidance

The Home Office publishes internal guidance for its decision makers on deciding and processing applications for asylum support at gov.uk/government/collections/asylum-support-asylum-instructions. It is important to be familiar with the guidance in addition to the law. The guidance is regularly amended, so always check the website for the latest versions. The guidance published online by the Home Office at the time of writing included the following documents:

- *Allocation of Accommodation Policy;*
- *Applications for Additional Support;*
- *Assessing Destitution;*
- *Asylum Seekers with Care Needs;*
- *Asylum Support Applications: EU nationals or people with refugee status abroad;*
- *Asylum Support Instructions: policy bulletins;*
- *Asylum Support: section 4(1) handling transitional cases;*
- *Asylum Support, Section 4(2): policy and process;*
- *Breach of Conditions Instruction;*
- *Ceasing Asylum Support Instruction;*
- *Change of Address;*
- *Children Turning 18 Years Old;*
- *Dependants on an Asylum Support Application;*
- *Discontinuing Asylum Support after Failure to Report with an ARC.*

- *Domestic Abuse: responding to reports of domestic abuse from asylum seekers;*
- *Healthcare Needs and Pregnancy Dispersal Policy; and*
- *Section 55 Guidance.*

In addition, simpler practical guides for asylum seekers are published by the Home Office, including:

- *Asylum Support: rights and expectations in the UK; and*
- *Living in Asylum Accommodation.*

Two of the above documents give an overview of the main types of asylum support, and are a useful starting point: one dealing with section 95 support (*Asylum Support Instructions: policy bulletins*) and the other with section 4 support (*Asylum Support: section 4(2) policy*). The guidance is not law but gives a strong indication of how applications are likely to be processed by the Home Office. The law requires the Home Office to follow its own written policies unless there is good reason to depart from them. If in any particular case, however, there is a conflict between the law and Home Office guidance, you can argue that the law must prevail.

Asylum Help

Asylum Help UK is a national confidential and impartial advice service for asylum seekers, funded by the Home Office and provided by the charity Migrant Help. The Asylum Help service can help you apply for support and give general advice about the asylum process and associated matters such as housing problems, dealing with agencies such as social services, finding English language classes, questions about asylum support, getting legal representation, finding schools and returning home. The level of advice provided is generally low. For contact details and a list of other organisations that provide advice services to asylum seekers, see Appendix 2.

2. Support for asylum seekers

You are entitled to asylum support under section 95 of the Immigration and Asylum Act 1999 (known as **section 95 support**) if:[5]

- you are an asylum seeker or a dependant of an asylum seeker; *and*
- you are destitute or likely to become destitute.

Note: while the Home Office considers your application for section 95 support, you may be able to get temporary support (see p492).

Who is excluded from support

The following people are excluded from section 95 support:[6]

- people with refugee status granted by a European Economic Area (EEA) state and their dependants;[7]
- EEA nationals and their dependants.[8]

Note: a child cannot be excluded from support, nor can someone if the provision of support is necessary to avoid a breach of human rights.[9]

You can also be excluded from getting support if:[10]

- you are not excluded from getting social security benefits because of your immigration status (see p96);[11]
- you are not being treated as an asylum seeker or the dependant of an asylum seeker for immigration purposes;[12]
- you apply for support as part of a group and every person is excluded under either of the above.[13]

If you do not have dependent children and you apply for cash-only support and not accommodation (see p538), you can also be excluded if you did not claim asylum 'as soon as reasonably practicable' on entering the UK.[14] However, support should not be withheld if to do so would breach a person's human rights.[15]

There is no statutory definition of the term 'as soon as reasonably practicable'. When the rule was first introduced in 2003, it led to substantial numbers of in-country asylum seekers (ie, people who did not claim asylum at the port of entry but only after they had entered UK) being refused support, and subsequent judicial review cases in the High Court. The Home Office has since issued a policy stating that any claim made within three days of arrival is treated as having been made 'as soon as reasonably practicable'.[16]

Before support can be withheld on this basis, the Home Office should invite you to what is known as 'a section 55 interview', at which you will be asked about the timing of your asylum claim, and (if the Home Office concludes that you did not claim asylum as soon as reasonably practicable) whether you can access food and other basic living essentials from specific persons you may be living with or from charities. This information is relevant to whether withholding support would be a breach of your human rights. The Supreme Court has held that leaving destitute asylum seekers who have no right to work or claim benefits without food and shelter would be a breach of their human rights.[17]

Who is an asylum seeker for support purposes

For the purposes of asylum support, you are an asylum seeker if:[18]

- you are over 18 years of age; *and*
- you have made an application for asylum; *and*
- your application has been recorded by the Secretary of State (see below); *and*
- the application has not yet been determined (see below).

For asylum support purposes, an 'asylum application' is an application made either under the 1951 Refugee Convention (see p12) or under Article 3 of the European Convention on Human Rights. If you have made a different type of application, such as under Article 8 of the European Convention on Human Rights or an application for indefinite leave to remain on non-asylum grounds (see p29), and you have not also made an asylum or Article 3 application, you cannot claim section 95 support. You may be eligible for support from your local authority (see p507). For further details on asylum applications, see p39.

Throughout this part of the book, references to an 'asylum claim' should be understood to include either a claim that your return to your country of origin would be in breach of the Refugee Convention or that it would be in breach of Article 3 of the European Convention on Human Rights.

When an asylum application is recorded

Asylum applications made 'at port' (ie, on entry to the UK) are recorded immediately. If you are already in the UK and making an 'in-country' asylum application for the first time, it is processed at the Home Office's Asylum Intake Unit (AIU) in Croydon. You must make an appointment to attend the AIU by telephone in advance, unless you have nowhere to live, in which case you can turn up at the AIU and apply on the same day. Your application is normally 'recorded' at your screening interview on the same day.

If your asylum application has been refused and your appeal rights are exhausted, you may be able to apply to make a fresh asylum application. Such an application is not recorded as a fresh asylum claim (which confers eligibility for section 95 support) until the Home Office accepts that it meets the relevant test – ie, it is 'significantly different' to the material considered but rejected in your first asylum application. It will be significantly different' if the new material taken together with the previously considered material creates a realistic prospect of success.[19] Applications for a fresh asylum claim had to be made in person by appointment at the Home Office's Further Submissions Unit in Liverpool, until 18 March 2020. On that date in-person appointments ceased to be offered because of the coronavirus pandemic. At the time of writing, applications for a fresh asylum claim can only be submitted by email or post. While you are waiting for your further representations to be considered, you may be eligible for section 4 support (see p493).

When an asylum application is determined

For support purposes, until your asylum claim is determined, you remain an asylum seeker and eligible for section 95 support from the time your asylum claim is recorded (see above); or any further representations are accepted by the Home Office as constituting a 'fresh asylum claim' (see p498).

Your asylum claim remains undetermined:

- until you leave the UK (if you leave before it is allowed); *or*

- until you withdraw your claim in writing; *or*
- until the Home Office treats your claim as having been impliedly withdrawn; *or*
- if your asylum claim is refused during the time allowed for any appeal to be brought, and during any appeal brought within that time to the First-tier Tribunal, or a further appeal to the Upper Tribunal or Court of Appeal.

If your asylum claim is refused and you bring any subsequent appeal after the time for appealing has expired, you will cease to be an asylum seeker for asylum support purposes until the appeal is accepted by the relevant tribunal or court – ie until permission to extend time for bringing the appeal is granted. Once permission to extend time for appealing has been granted, you will be treated as an asylum seeker again, as above.

If your immigration application is successful, you will continue to be treated as an asylum seeker for 28 days after:[20]

- your application for asylum is granted; *or*
- your application for asylum is refused but you are granted limited leave to enter or remain; *or*
- your asylum appeal is allowed.

If your immigration application is unsuccessful, you will continue to be treated as an asylum seeker for asylum support purposes for 21 days after your asylum claim has been refused by the Home Office, or, if there is an appeal, for 21 days after the appeal is finally dismissed.

Section 95 for families with children

If you have a dependent child when your application for asylum is determined, you continue to be treated as an asylum seeker for support purposes until her/his 18th birthday, provided s/he remains in the UK.[21] Therefore, families with children aged under 18 continue to receive section 95 support, even after their asylum application has been refused. To remain eligible for section 95 support until your youngest child reaches 18, it does not matter whether you are receiving asylum support at the time your asylum application is determined but you must have a dependent child on this date.

This provision does not apply if your children were born after your asylum application was refused and you had exhausted all your rights of appeal. In this case, you cease to be an asylum seeker for support purposes and are no longer eligible for section 95 support. However, you and your children may be eligible for section 4 support as a refused asylum seeker (see p493) or for support under the Children Act 1989 (see p509).

It is open to the Home Office to withdraw section 95 support from failed asylum-seeker families who, in its opinion, have not taken steps to leave the UK voluntarily.[22] In such a case, you would be expected to demonstrate that you are taking steps to arrange your departure from the UK to return home. However, although this power was piloted across the UK in 2005, it has not been adopted as general practice. If the Home Office decides to withdraw your support because it says that you are not taking steps to leave the UK with your family, you can appeal against this decision to the Asylum Support Tribunal. For more information, see Chapter 24.

Who is a dependant for support purposes

Support is provided to asylum seekers and their dependants, provided they are destitute. You are a 'dependant' of an asylum seeker if you are:[23]

- her/his spouse or civil partner; *or*
- a child aged under 18 years of the asylum seeker or of her/his spouse/civil partner, and you are dependent on the asylum seeker; *or*
- a child aged under 18 years of the close family of the asylum seeker/spouse/ civil partner (you do not have to be dependent on the asylum seeker); *or*
- a child aged under 18 years and you have lived in the asylum seeker's household for six out of the last 12 months, or since birth; *or*
- now over 18 years old, but you were under 18 and came within one of the above categories when the asylum support application was made or when you entered the UK; *or*
- a close family member, or someone who has lived with the asylum seeker for six out of the last 12 months (or since birth), and you are disabled and in need of care and attention from a member of the household (regardless of your age); *or*
- the asylum seeker's partner and you were living with her/him as an unmarried (mixed or same-sex) couple for at least two of the three years before the application for support or before entering the UK.[24] If you are in an unmarried couple and want to be included as a dependant in your partner's existing asylum support, it can be difficult to comply with this condition. You may be caught in a 'catch-22' situation – eg, your relationship may have started at a time when either you or your partner were already on asylum support and you will not have been allowed to join her/his household. Therefore, you will have never been able to build up two years of having lived together before the application for support; *or*
- someone who has applied to the Home Office to remain in the UK as a dependant on another person's asylum claim.

Note: being a dependant for support purposes is not always the same as being a dependant on another person's asylum application. Whether the Home Office allows you to be a dependant on someone else's asylum application (and whether this would be in your interests) and, therefore, whether you can be a dependant on her/his asylum support application, is not always simple. You should obtain specialist advice if that affects you. See the official guidance for who is considered a dependant for asylum purposes[25] and for asylum support purposes.[26] Further information is in the Asylum Support Appeals Project Factsheet 11, *Asylum Support for Dependants*.[27]

The definition of destitute (section 95)

You are considered destitute if:[28]

- you do not have adequate accommodation or any means of obtaining it (whether or not you can meet your other essential living needs); *or*
- you have adequate accommodation or the means of obtaining it but cannot meet your other essential living needs.

When you make an application for support, you are regarded as destitute if you appear to the Home Office to be destitute now or if there is a likelihood of destitution within 14 days.[29] If you already receive support, you continue to be regarded as destitute if there is a likelihood of destitution within 56 days.[30]

See p520 for what income and assets are taken into account when deciding whether or not you are destitute.

Conditions on which section 95 and section 98 support is granted

Section 95 support is granted on certain conditions – eg, that you live at the address the Home Office has provided, and that you behave in accordance with the rules applying in your particular accommodation.[31] These conditions must be set out in writing[32] and given to the person who is being supported.[33]

Even if you have only applied for financial support and not accommodation (eg, because a friend has offered to let you stay with her/him), you must inform the Home Office of your address for support purposes, and that becomes your authorised address. You must tell the Home Office if you need to leave this address, and you are not allowed to leave the address for more than 14 days.

The Home Office may take into account any previous breach of conditions when deciding whether or not to provide you with support, whether to continue to provide support, and in deciding the level or kind of support to be provided.[34]

Note: the above provisions also apply to section 98 support (see p492).

Change of circumstances in relation to section 95 support

If you are provided with section 95 support, in addition to complying with the conditions on which support was granted (see above), you must notify the Home Office of certain relevant changes in your circumstances.[35] These are if you (or any of your dependants):[36]

- are joined in the UK by a dependant;

- receive or obtain access to any money or savings, investments, land, cars or other vehicles, or goods for the purposes of trade or other business, which you have not previously declared;
- become employed or unemployed;
- change your name;
- get married or divorced;
- begin living with another person as if you were married to her/him, or if you separate from a spouse or from a person with whom you have been living as if you were married;
- become pregnant or have a child;
- leave school;
- begin to share your accommodation with another person;
- move to a different address or otherwise leave your accommodation;
- go into hospital;
- go into to prison or some other form of custody;
- leave the UK; *and/or*
- die.

If there is a relevant change of circumstances, a decision may be made to change the nature or level of the existing support, to withdraw support or to provide support to different individual/s.

Note: it may be a criminal offence not to notify the Home Office of a change in circumstances (see p492).[37]

Termination of section 95 support

Section 95 support is terminated if:

- the Home Office decides that you cease to be entitled – ie, that you cease to be destitute and/or cease to be an asylum seeker; *or*
- your section 95 support is suspended or discontinued because the Home Office believes you have broken the rules.

The usual law on security of tenure does not apply to Home Office accommodation.[38]

Tenancies or licences created when Home Office support is provided can come to an end when asylum support is terminated – ie if:[39]

- you are no longer destitute; *or*
- your application for asylum has been determined; *or*
- you have moved to
- be supported in other accommodation; *or*
- your support has been suspended or discontinued (see below).

In any of the above circumstances, any tenancy or licence is terminated at the end of the period (minimum of seven days) specified in a 'notice to quit' given to you.[40]

When section 95 or section 98 support can be suspended or discontinued

If you have been granted section 95 support, the Home Office may discontinue or suspend it in certain circumstances. Support can be suspended or discontinued if:[41]

- the Home Office has reason to believe that you are accommodated in 'collective accommodation' (eg, a hostel or shared house) and you or your dependant have committed a serious breach of the accommodation's rules.[42] Each accommodation provider is likely to have a set of 'house rules', which everyone must follow – eg, to be respectful of other residents and not to make any noise late at night; *or*
- the Home Office has reason to believe that you or your dependant have committed an act of seriously violent behaviour;[43] *or*
- you or your dependant have committed a criminal offence under Part VI of the Immigration and Asylum Act 1999.[44] That includes making a false claim to get support and failing to report a change of circumstances to the Home Office – eg, a change in your financial resources; *or*
- you fail within a reasonable period (being no less than five working days) to provide the Home Office with information about an application for, or receipt of, support in response to a request by the Home Office;[45] *or*
- you fail to attend an interview relating to your or your dependant's support and do not have a reasonable excuse;[46] *or*
- you fail within a reasonable period (being no less than 10 working days) to provide information about your dependant's asylum application in response to a request by the Home Office;[47] *or*
- the Home Office has reason to believe that you or your dependant have concealed financial resources and unduly benefited from asylum support;[48] *or*
- you or your dependant fail to comply with reporting requirements;[49] *or*
- the Home Office has reason to believe that you or your dependant have made, or you attempted to make, a second application for asylum before the first application is determined;[50] *or*
- there are 'reasonable grounds' to suspect that you have abandoned your 'authorised address' (see p543) without first informing the Home Office or without its permission;[51] *or*
- your support is provided on condition that you reside at a specific place, and you or your dependant have failed without reasonable excuse to comply with that condition.[52]

Your support may be suspended (for a period up to 30 days)[53] if the Home Office requires time or more information to decide whether to discontinue (ie, terminate) your support. If the Home Office is satisfied that there has been a breach of conditions, the Home Office must take into account the extent of the breach when deciding whether or not to continue to provide support. In making this assessment, the Asylum Support Tribunal usually[54] applies the reasoning of the Court of Appeal in relation to the approach local authorities should take towards asylum seekers who breach the conditions of the support they receive from the local authority, namely that support should not be terminated unless the asylum seeker's breaches of conditions are 'persistent and unequivocal' and a warning letter has been sent.[55]

Note: even if the grounds to suspend or discontinue your support are established, you can still retain your entitlement to support if you can show that you are destitute and require support to avoid a breach of your human rights. However, if you are a refused asylum seeker in receipt of section 95 support because you have a dependent child younger than 18 (see p486), you will be in a vulnerable position. The Home Office may argue that there is nothing preventing you from avoiding a breach of your human rights by making a voluntary return to your country.

If you apply for support again after it has been discontinued, unless there are exceptional circumstances, the Home Office may refuse to consider your application if there has been no 'material change in circumstances' since the original decision to suspend or discontinue the support.[56] A 'material change' is any change in any of the circumstances that you need to notify the Home Office about if you were receiving section 95 support (see p517).[57] If the Home Office decides to consider your application for support in these circumstances, you may still be refused support.[58] **Note:** the above provisions also apply to section 98 support (see p493).

A decision to refuse or discontinue support can be appealed to the Asylum Support Tribunal (see Chapter 24). It is not possible to appeal either:

- a decision to suspend s95 support; *or*
- a decision to refuse, suspend or discontinue s98 support (see p493).

Such decisions can only be challenged by judicial review.

A decision to suspend support cannot be appealed and can only be challenged by judicial review. **Note**: contrary to the position with section 4 appeals,[59] there is nothing to prevent you from being evicted from your accommodation, despite having lodged an appeal against a refusal or discontinuation of section 95 support. However, in practice most appellants are allowed to remain in initial accommodation until their appeal is heard, particularly if dependent minors are being accommodated.

Discontinutation of support to families with children

When considering whether to discontinue section 95 support for families with children younger than 18, the Home Office must discharge its duty under section 55 of the Borders, Citizenship and Immigration Act 2009 to ensure that the decision has regard to the need to safeguard and promote the welfare of children who are in the UK. Any decision to discontinue support must be proportionate. Accordingly, support should not be discontinued if a breach of conditions is minor – eg, a failure to report. If a breach of conditions is serious (eg, extreme violence or vandalism) and a decision to discontinue support is taken, the Home Office must nevertheless discharge its duty to safeguard and promote the welfare of the children. The Home Office guidance states:[60]

> Before any action is taken to begin the process to discontinue support, the case worker should liaise with the local authority, notifying them that the Home Office plans to discontinue support from the family, and request that the local authority provides alternative support. If the local authority makes an offer of support, the provision of support under Section 95 should be discontinued as soon as the family transfers in to local authority care.[61]

Recovery of section 95 or section 98 support

There are four circumstances in which you may be required to repay your asylum support. **Note:** all apply to section 95 support and some apply to section 98 as well (see below). None apply to section 4 support, so there is no power for the Home Office to force you to repay any section 4 support you have received. The Home Office may require you to repay your section 95 or 98 support if:

- you had assets at the time of your application for support that you can now convert into money (see below); *or*
- you have been overpaid support as a result of an error (see p491); *or*
- you have misrepresented or failed to disclose a 'material fact' (see p491); *or*
- it transpires that you were not destitute.

In addition, the Home Office may try to recover any support provided to you from a person who has sponsored your stay in the UK (see p33). The Home Office can recover the support through deductions from your existing asylum support or through the civil courts.

You have convertible assets

The Home Office can[62] require you to repay the value of asylum support you have received if, at the time of your application for support, you had assets (eg, savings, investments, property or shares) either in the UK or abroad that you could not then convert into money but which you can convert to money now (even if you have not done so).

The Home Office cannot require you to repay more than either:

- the total monetary value of all the support provided to you up to the date that it asks you to make a repayment; *or*
- if it is a lesser amount, the total monetary value of the assets that you had at the time of the application for support and that you have since been able to convert into money.

You were overpaid section 95 and / or 98 support

The Home Office may[63] require you to repay any section 95 and/or section 98 support that has been provided to you as a result of an 'error' by the Home Office. Unlike recovery of overpayments of most social security benefits, you do not need to have been responsible for the overpayment.

The Home Office may recover the support from you by deductions from support if you are still being supported[64] or as a debt, if you are no longer being supported.[65] The Home Office cannot recover more than the total monetary value of the support provided to you as a result of its mistake.

You have mispresented or failed to disclose

If the Home Office believes that you have received section 95 and/or section 98 support as a result of misrepresenting or failing disclose a material fact, the Home Office may apply to a county court (or, in Scotland, the sheriff) for an order requiring you (or the person who made the misrepresentation, or who was responsible for the failure to disclose) to repay the support.[66] Recovery is possible from people other than yourself and your dependants. The total amount that the court can order to be repaid is the monetary value of the support paid as a result of the misrepresentation or failure to disclose, which would not have been provided had there not been that misrepresentation or failure to disclose.

Recovery of section 95 support from sponsor

Section 95 support may be recovered from a sponsor of someone who receives the support.[67] A 'sponsor' is a person who has given a written undertaking under the Immigration Rules to be responsible for the maintenance and accommodation of someone seeking to enter or remain in the UK (see p33). This form of recovery is intended to deal with the situation in which someone obtains admission to the UK under a sponsorship agreement in a non-asylum capacity and then applies for asylum and becomes entitled to asylum support during the application process. The sponsor is only liable to repay payments for the period during which the undertaking was in effect. S/he should not, therefore, be liable for payments for any period of leave given subsequent to the original leave for which the undertaking was given, unless a further undertaking was also given. The sponsor is not liable for payments during any period of residence without leave.

To recover asylum support, the Home Office must apply for an order at a magistrates' court (in Scotland, the sheriff court). The court may order the sponsor to make weekly payments to the Home Office of an amount the court thinks is appropriate, taking into account all the circumstances of the case and, in particular, the sponsor's own income. The weekly sum must not be more than the weekly value of the support being provided to the asylum seeker. The court can order that payments be made to cover any period before the time the Home Office applied to the court. In such cases, the Home Office must take into account the sponsor's income during the period concerned, rather than her/his current income. The order can be enforced in the same way as a maintenance order.

Offences relating to sections 95 and section 98

It is a criminal offence[68] if, with a view to obtaining support under section 95 or section 98:

- you make a statement or representation (knowingly or otherwise) that is false; *or*
- you produce or cause to be produced any document or information that is false in a material particular; *or*
- you fail to notify the Home Office of a change in circumstances when required to do so (see p486); *or*
- you cause another person to fail to notify a change in circumstances that the other person was required to notify the Home Office about.

Note: these offences do not apply to similar acts and omissions with a view to obtaining section 4 support. To the best of the author's knowledge, prosecutions for these offences have been rare.

3. Temporary support

While considering your application for section 95 support, the Home Office can provide a temporary form of support to you or your dependant(s) under section 98 of the Immigration and Asylum Act 1999. This is known as **section 98 support** and is also commonly called 'emergency support' or 'initial accommodation'.

Temporary asylum support can be provided if it appears that you *may* be destitute at the time of the application – ie, even if there is some uncertainty.[69] The definition of 'destitution' is the same as for section 95 support (see p520),[70] except that temporary support can only be provided on the basis that you may be destitute now and not on the basis that you are likely to become destitute within 14 days.[71] Temporary support can be provided at short notice. It can be authorised outside of office hours if you are considered to be particularly vulnerable – eg, you are a visibly pregnant woman or are able to prove you are pregnant, or you are part of a family with a dependent child younger than 18 or you are disabled.[72]

Temporary support may be provided subject to conditions, which must be given in writing. It can only be provided until the Home Office makes a decision on whether or not to give you section 95 support. If the Home Office refuses section 95 support, temporary support ends at the same time.

There is no right of appeal to the First-tier Tribunal (see p553) against a refusal or withdrawal of temporary support.[73] The only method of challenging such a decision is by judicial review proceedings.

Who is excluded from temporary support

You are excluded from temporary support if:[74]

- you are not excluded from getting social security benefits because of your immigration status (see p96); *or*
- you apply for asylum support as a dependant, but you are not being treated as a dependant of an asylum seeker for immigration purposes; *or*
- you apply as part of a group and every person in the group is excluded under either of the above bullet points.

Termination of section 98 support

Your section 98 support will be terminated:

- after the Home Office takes a decision on your application for section 95 support. If your section 95 application is refused, you will have a right of appeal against that decision (see p552), and support might continue pending the appeal (especially if you have dependent children). If your section 95 application is granted, your section 98 support will end once you are dispersed to your section 95 accommodation (see p543). If you are granted asylum while in receipt of section 98 support, you will be given 28 days' notice to quit the initial accommodation; *or*
- if the Home Office suspends or discontinues your section 98 support for breach of conditions (see p486) or for another reason specified in the regulations[75] (see p487).

Recovery of section 98 support and offences

See p490.

4. Support for refused asylum seekers

If your asylum application has been unsuccessful and you have exhausted all your appeal rights (in these circumstances, referred to as a 'refused asylum seeker' in this *Handbook*), the general rule is that you are expected to return to your country of origin and are not entitled to support from the Home Office. However, if there is some bar to you leaving, you may be able to claim support under section 4(2) of the Immigration and Asylum Act 1999. That is known as **section 4 support**.

To get section 4 support you must:

- be a person who was but is no longer an asylum seeker and whose claim for asylum was rejected;[76] *or*
- be destitute (see below);[77] *and*
- meet one of the five criteria for support (see p495).[78]

Who is excluded from support

Certain people are excluded from section 4 support. They are the same people who are excluded from section 95 support (see p482). The following other classes of people are also excluded from section 4 support:

- refused asylum seekers who have not complied with removal directions and their dependants;[79] *and*
- refused asylum seekers with children who the Secretary of State says have failed, without reasonable excuse, to take reasonable steps to leave, or place themselves in a position to leave, the UK (although this exclusion is rarely used).[80]

However, people in these categories should not be excluded if section 4 support is necessary to avoid a breach of their human rights.[81]

The definition of destitute

The definition of 'destitute' is the same as for section 95 support (see p486).[82] In deciding whether you are destitute, the Home Office considers the time that has elapsed since you were in receipt of section 95 support and, if you have had any access to accommodation or financial support since then, evidence about whether that support is still available. If there has been no gap in your asylum support, the Home Office is likely, in practice, to accept that you remain destitute.[83] However, if you have not recently had support, the Home Office expects you to prove that you are now destitute, and requires detailed information on how you have survived and how your situation has now changed to leave you destitute. In these circumstances, the Home Office asks you to provide evidence, such as letters from friends, family and charities, explaining what support they have given you in the past and why that cannot continue. You may have survived from working (legally or illegally) in the past and so may need to explain this to the Home Office, so that it can fully understand your new situation. If this evidence cannot be obtained, tell the Home Office (and the Asylum Support Tribunal in any appeal) why this is the case – eg, the friendship may have now deteriorated because you have overstayed your welcome.

Note: the test of destitution is set out in regulations (see p486).[84] If you have relied on friends and relatives, you may still have been destitute within the meaning of these regulations, even while receiving that help – eg, you may have spent nights sleeping on various friends' floors without a key to gain access, and walking the streets during the day, or have had no money and/or little food. In this situation, you have been destitute under the regulations throughout this period, as you have not had adequate accommodation and/or have been unable to meet your essential living needs. When applying for section 4 support in these circumstances, it is important to give full details about what support has been made available in the past. A 'self-statement' that fully explains your circumstances is recommended, with as much supporting evidence as possible (the Home Office frequently disbelieves uncorroborated statements by applicants).

Criteria for support

As well as being destitute, to qualify for section 4 support, you must also prove (see p531) that you are in one of the following situations.

- You are taking all reasonable steps to leave the UK (see below).
- You are unable to leave the UK because a medical condition prevents you from travelling (see p496).
- You are unable to leave the UK because there is no viable route of return (see p496).
- You have applied for judicial review of a decision in relation to your asylum claim (see p497).
- Section 4 support is necessary to avoid a breach of human rights (see p497).

You are taking all reasonable steps to leave the UK

To qualify for section 4 support, you must be taking all reasonable steps to leave the UK or place yourself in a position in which you are able to leave the UK, including, if relevant, applying for a travel document.[85]

The Home Office runs a 'voluntary returns service', through which refused asylum seekers and others without leave to remain in the UK can receive assistance and, in some cases, cash, to return home. If you apply to the Home Office for assisted or voluntary return, that alone may not be sufficient to satisfy the requirement for section 4 support.

The Home Office will expect you to be proactive in arranging your return, for example, from keeping appointments with your embassy to attempting to get a travel document.

After granting support, the Home Office expects you to be able to leave the UK within three months.[86] Therefore, if it is going to take you longer than that to leave, you should provide the Home Office with an explanation supported by evidence for the delay, otherwise your support will be discontinued. It is advisable to keep a diary of the steps you take. It is also important to keep copies of all letters and emails, and notes of telephone calls, emails and visits to, for example, the voluntary returns service and your embassy.

If you are refused support on this basis, or your support is discontinued, you should appeal to the Asylum Support Tribunal. See Chapter 24 for details.

Support is often withdrawn on the grounds that someone has not taken *all* reasonable steps. It could be argued that the Home Office's view on this is often unrealistic, bearing in mind that applicants are destitute, desperate and may speak little English. However, on appeal, the Asylum Support Tribunal may take the view that if any reasonable step can be identified that you have not taken, even if you did not previously think of taking that step, you have not satisfied the requirement and should be refused support. Each case should be considered on its own merits.

Note: evidence required to prove you have taken all reasonable steps to leave the UK is explained on p531.

You are unable to leave the UK because a medical condition prevents you from travelling

To get section 4 support, you must be unable to travel (ie, to make a single journey from the UK to your country of origin) because of 'a physical impediment' or other medical reason.[87] 'Unable' has been interpreted to mean more than 'unreasonable' or 'undesirable' but not 'impossible'.[88]

If you apply for support on this ground, you must submit a completed medical declaration ('Section 4(2) medical declaration'), available on gov.uk. If you cannot find the declaration form on this website and the Home Office does not send one to you, a copy can be obtained from local support agencies or the Asylum Support Appeals Project. Arguably, a letter containing the same information on headed paper should be sufficient, but it is highly likely that the Home office will insist on a completed medical declaration form (see p531).

Note: evidence required to prove that you are unable to leave the UK due to a medical condition is explained on p531.

You are unable to leave the UK because there is no viable route of return

To qualify for section 4 support under this ground, the Secretary of State must have made a declaration that, in her/his opinion, there is no viable route to a particular country.[89]

At the time of writing, there is no country to which that applies. Irrespective of your personal circumstances, therefore, you will not succeed in claiming support under this criterion unless, by the time of your application, the Secretary of State has made a declaration that there is no safe route. The only time the Secretary of State has made such a declaration was in 2005 for a six-month period with regard to Iraq. If the Secretary of State refuses to make a declaration where there is evidence that there is no viable route of return to a country (eg, because there are no flights to that country from the UK), then it may be possible to challenge the Secretary of State's refusal by way of judicial review (see p569).

You have applied for a judicial review of a decision relating to your asylum claim

To get section 4 support under this ground, you must have lodged an application for judicial review to challenge a decision relating to your application for asylum and, in England and Wales, you must have been granted permission to proceed (or leave to proceed in Northern Ireland).[90] Simply lodging a judicial review application at court in Scotland is sufficient.

Note: If you have lodged an application and are waiting for the court to consider whether to grant permission, you are likely to be able to receive support to avoid a breach of your human rights (see p500).

Note: evidence required to prove that you have applied for judicial review is explained on p532.

Section 4 support is necessary to avoid a breach of human rights

You qualify for section 4 support if you can show that the provision of accommodation is necessary to avoid a breach of human rights.[91] The courts have said that denying support to asylum seekers whose claims are outstanding, in the context in which they are not allowed to work or claim benefits, constitutes 'inhuman and degrading treatment'.[92] That is prohibited under Article 3 of the European Convention on Human Rights. If you are freely able to return to your home country to avoid destitution, however, your human rights are not breached if support is withheld. If you have an outstanding asylum claim, the Home Office will accept that you are cannot be expected to return to your country voluntarily to avoid destitution, since your fear of ill treatment may be well founded as far as the Home Office is concerned. However, the possibility of a voluntary return is always a central issue whenever an application for section 4 support is made by a refused asylum seeker (since the Home Office will proceed on the basis that a refused asylum seeker can return to their country of origin without problem). The law has developed some principles for deciding when a person whose asylum claim has been rejected should be granted support rather than asked to make a voluntary departure from the UK.

This category of cases covers a wide range of scenarios. The Home Office's current policy[93] provides for section 4 support to be granted in cases which there are 'legal or practical obstacles' to a voluntary return. The policy is unclear about constitutes a practical obstacle. The policy states that whether there is a 'legal obstacle' should be considered on a case-by-case basis but accepts that two scenarios will usually meet the test:

- you have submitted further representations against the refusal of your asylum claim, which remain outstanding; *and*
- you have appealed out of time against the refusal of your asylum claim and the First-tier Tribunal is considering whether to allow the appeal to proceed out of time.

However, the law also recognises additional scenarios that are not referred to in the Home Office's policy, and which are considered below.

Note: some judges of the Asylum Support Tribunal continue to apply the test in the previous Home Office policy of whether it is reasonable to expect you to make a voluntary departure.[94] Sometimes, this test may be easier to apply to the facts of your case than the restrictive and arguably harder to apply test of whether there are legal or practical obstacles to a voluntary return.

Section 4 support is most likely granted to cases in which:

- you have made fresh representations to the Home Office in support of your asylum or human rights claim, and the representations are not hopeless or abusive (see below); *or*
- you have made an application for leave under Article 8 of the European Convention on Human Rights (see p43); *or*
- you have made an 'out-of-time' appeal against the refusal of your asylum claim to the First-tier Tribunal (Immigration and Asylum Chamber) (see p500); *or*
- you have issued or threatened judicial review proceedings in relation to your asylum claim (generally to challenge a refusal to treat your fresh representations as a fresh asylum claim (see p500); *or*
- you have applied for leave to enter or remain as a stateless person (see p501); *or*
- you have an outstanding application to the European Court of Human Rights (see p501).

Each of these scenarios is considered below.

Note: for each of the scenarios considered below, the evidence you should provide in support of your application is explained on p530.

You have made fresh representations to the Home Office

This is the most usual situation in which a refused asylum seeker is given support to avoid a breach of her/his human rights. You must show that:

- you have made a further application to the Home Office to remain in the UK in support of your asylum claim, or in support of your claim that your removal from the UK would breach Article 3 of the European Convention on Human Rights (see p46). That is usually in the form of further representations and evidence that you want the Home Office to accept as a fresh asylum claim, or a fresh claim made under Article 3 of the European Convention on Human Rights; *and*
- this application is still outstanding – eg, the Home Office has not yet decided whether it amounts to a fresh asylum application;[95] *and*
- it would not be reasonable for you to leave the UK at this stage, and to be left destitute while you remain would be a breach of your human rights (under Article 3).

The High Court has stated that section 4 support should be provided in the above circumstances,[96] provided the further representations are not clearly hopeless and abusive (see below).

If you want to make further representations, you must address them to the Further Submissions Unit (FSU) of the Home Office in Liverpool. Up until 18 March 2020, such applications could only be made in person by appointment except if there were exceptional reasons why you could not travel to Liverpool, such as illness, disability or childcare difficulties. However, since 18 March 2020, the FSU has been closed to attendees because of the coronavirus pandemic, and all further representations have had to be submitted by email or post.

The First-tier Tribunal has granted support on human rights grounds if someone has prepared fresh representations and has an appointment to attend the FSU and submit them on a future date and, in exceptional cases, if further submissions are still being prepared.[97] That is because the applicant has done all that s/he reasonably can to submit the fresh representations. However, the approaches of the Asylum Support Tribunal judges vary, and some may refuse support unless the representations have already been submitted. If you are applying for section 4 support but still have not submitted your further representations, it is important, if possible, to put evidence before the Home Office and the Asylum Support Tribunal to demonstrate that any delay in submitting your further representations is not your fault, and that the fresh claim, when finalised, is not hopeless or abusive. To do that, it might be necessary to produce a draft version of the further representations from your immigration solicitor, or a note setting out their intent, and why the further representations contain new material and have a realistic prospect of success.

Even if the representations have been submitted, the Home Office can refuse support if the fresh claim is considered to be hopeless or abusive – eg:

- the fresh claim or representations contain no detail whatsoever – eg, if you are still fearful of returning to your country of origin but do not give any further information or simply state that you will send new information later; *or*
- the evidence or arguments that you have submitted as part of your fresh claim have already been seen and rejected by the Home Office, or rejected on appeal, and do not rely on any change in the law or the factual circumstances of your claim since the previous refusal.

Once the Home Office has looked at any fresh representations, you are informed in writing whether they have been accepted as a new asylum application. If they are accepted, a fresh asylum application is recorded. At this point, you become an asylum seeker again and should reapply for section 95 support (see p481). If your representations are not accepted as a fresh asylum application, your section 4 support is discontinued unless you can prove that you meet one of the other criteria for support.

Note: the evidence you should consider providing to prove you have made fresh representations to the Home Office is considered on p533.

You have made an 'out-of-time' appeal to the First-tier Tribunal

If you want to appeal against the refusal of your asylum application but the time for appealing has expired, you must ask the First-tier Tribunal (Immigration and Asylum Chamber) for permission for an 'out-of-time' appeal to proceed. If you have made such an application, the Home Office and the First-tier Tribunal (Asylum Support) usually grant section 4 support on the basis that it would be unreasonable to expect you to leave the UK in the meantime.

If the First-tier Tribunal (Immigration and Asylum Chamber) gives you permission to appeal out of time, you become an asylum seeker again and are eligible for section 95 support (and, at that stage, no longer eligible for section 4 support).

If you appeal within the prescribed time limits, you are still considered to be an asylum seeker and so you will still be eligible for section 95 support (see p481).

Note: the evidence you should provide to prove you have made an out-of-time appeal is given on p534.

You have issued or threatened judicial review proceedings

If your further representations are not treated as a fresh asylum claim by the Home Office, you can challenge the Home Office's decision by judicial review. While you are preparing to bring a claim for judicial review, you may be eligible for support to avoid a breach of your human rights.

A judicial review in the High Court on this issue in 2009 held that it would be a breach of human rights to withhold section 4 support in a variety of factual circumstances even if (in England, Wales and Northern Ireland) permission to apply for judicial review has not yet been granted. The judge did not define these circumstances, but the judgment implies that they include when your solicitor has sent the required 'pre-action' letter to the Home Office threatening judicial review proceedings or when you have already issued proceedings and are waiting for a decision on whether you can proceed.[98] You must show that your case is not 'entirely without merit'. If you have been granted legal aid to pursue your judicial review, that can be used as a persuasive, if not conclusive, argument of your case having some merit.

Note: the evidence you can provide to prove that you have issued or threatened judicial review proceedings is considered on p532.

You have made an application for leave under Article 8 of the European Convention on Human Rights

You may qualify for section 4 support if you have an outstanding application for leave under Article 8 of the European Convention on Human Rights (see p43), provided your application has some merit and is not obviously hopeless or abusive.[99]

You have applied for leave to remain as a stateless person

Refused asylum seekers who later apply to the Home Office for leave to remain because they are stateless are eligible for section 4 support on the basis that they have an outstanding application and it is not reasonable to leave until it has been decided. There is a prescribed form on which to apply for leave to remain as a stateless person. If your application is refused, there is no right of appeal, so the only remedy is judicial review. If you apply for a judicial review of the refusal of your statelessness application, you can continue to receive section 4 support.

You have applied to the European Court of Human Rights

Refused asylum seekers who have exhausted their appeal rights in the UK but who claim that their removal would lead to a breach of their human rights can apply to the European Court of Human Rights in Strasbourg for an order preventing their imminent removal (called a Rule 39 order).

If that applies to you and you are waiting for a decision from the European Court and you are destitute, you may be eligible for section 4 support. In a decision in 2011, a judge in the Asylum Support Tribunal gave criteria for deciding when support should be granted.[100] You must show that:

- your application to the European Court 'has some merit'. This includes showing that it contains details and these are specific to your case. The level of detail required depends on the case; *and*
- you exhausted all remedies in the UK before applying to the European Court, including making a fresh application for asylum and challenging any refusal by judicial review. However, there is no need to have applied for a remedy if it was 'bound to fail'. So, for example, if you have been refused legal aid for a judicial review because of existing UK caselaw, you may still satisfy this ground. Alternatively, you should have evidence (eg, from your immigration solicitor) that any unexhausted domestic remedies were bound to fail and, therefore, were pointless to initiate before you applied to the European Court of Human Rights.

Other scenarios in which withholding section 4 may breach human rights

Depending on the facts of your case and the available evidence, you may be able to argue that because of your personal circumstances (potentially including your medical condition, practical barriers to travel and legal commitments in the UK), it is unreasonable to expect you to return home voluntarily, so withholding support would breach your human rights. However, such arguments do not routinely succeed. In the lack of powerful supporting evidence, the tribunal is liable to conclude that, even though you may be reluctant to leave the UK, there is no legal or practical obstacle to you doing so.

However, each case is considered on its own facts. By way of example, the Asylum Support Tribunal has granted section 4 support on human rights grounds when a medical condition makes travel risky or harmful but does not make someone 'unable to travel', including to a mentally ill person on the basis that he should remain on support while still in the UK, pending forced removal.[101] In another case, the tribunal decided that a refused asylum seeker could not be expected to leave the UK while on probation and subjected to reporting requirements and medical tests because of drug offences. Leaving the UK would have meant that he could not comply with the probation order made by the court, and section 4 support was therefore required to prevent his destitution. Similarly, a grant of bail requiring a section 4 applicant to attend a criminal trial in the magistrates court on a date to be fixed was held by the Asylum Support Tribunal to be a legal obstacle to a voluntary return, confering eligibility for section 4 support.[102]

COVID-19-related grounds for support under regulation 3(2)(e)

On 27 March 2020, the government confirmed that due to the coronavirus pandemic, those asylum seekers whose support would ordinarily have been stopped because their asylum claims had been finally determined and refused would not be evicted from their asylum support accommodation. After this announcement:

- Asylum seekers who had been supported under section 95 but whose eligibility under section 95 had ended because their asylum claims had been finally determined and refused, were automatically transferred on to section 4 support without needing to make an application or vacate their accommodation.
- Refused asylum seekers who applied for section 4 support were generally granted that support provided they could prove they were destitute and without having to demonstrate that they met one of the criteria for support (see p495).

Refused asylum seekers who had been granted section 4 support did not have their section 4 support discontinued. Those asylum seekers who had been supported under section 95 and whose asylum claims succeeded (and who were therefore recognised as refugees) were not required to leave their section 95 accommodation in light of the difficulty they would have in accessing mainstream benefits and alternative accommodation during lockdown.

After the end of the initial lockdown, discontinuations of support for those accepted by the Home Office as destitute commenced:

- in August 2020, for those recognised as refugees; *and*
- in October 2020, for those on section 95 support whose appeals were finally determined and refused; *and*

- in October 2020, the Home Office ceased to accept that withholding support would be a breach of human rights due to the effect of COVID-19 alone. Accordingly, the Home Office required new applicants for section 4 support to show that they qualified for section 4 for another reason, and refused the applications of applicants that the Home Office considered had failed to do so. Similarly, if existing recipients of section 4 support could not show eligibility for a non-COVID-related reason, the Home Office discontinued their support.

On 16 October 2020, the principal judge of the Asylum Support Tribunal determined two linked appeals in which the only issue was whether it would be a breach of human rights for support to be withheld because of the effect of the COVID-19 pandemic. At that time, England had been divided into three tiers, each of which had different restrictions on freedoms, such as freedom of movement and assembly, reflecting the differing rates of COVID-19 infection and the consequential strains on public health (from Tier 1: medium risk to Tier 3: very high risk). The principal judge held that in Tier 1 and Tier 2 areas, it would not be a breach of human rights for section 4 support to be withheld, because in those areas, applicants could be expected to make a voluntary return to their countries. In Tier 3 areas, however, the judge held that section 4 support should not be discontinued, since the high risk of COVID-19 infection and transmission meant that to withhold support would be a breach of both the appellants' human rights and the human rights of the wider community.[103]

On 2 November 2020, in related judicial review litigation,[104] the Administrative Court ordered that the Home Office cease discontinuations of section 4 support, pending disposal of the judicial review proceedings.

At the time of writing (January 2020), the judicial review proceedings remain pending, the Administrative Court's order of 2 November 2020 remains in place, and the Asylum Support Tribunal judges have applied the principal judge's decision to appeals against refusals of applications for section 4 support as well as appeals against discontinuations.

Termination of section 4 support

Your section 4 support may be terminated in one of two ways, namely:

- you have breached the conditions on which section 4 support was granted; *or*
- your entitlement to section 4 has been reviewed, and a decision taken that you are no longer entitled.

Conditions of section 4 support

Section 4 support is granted subject to conditions. The conditions must be given to you in writing and must involve:[105]

- specified standards of behaviour; *or*
- a reporting requirement; *or*

- a requirement:
  - to reside at an authorised address; *or*
  - if absent from an authorised address without the Home Office's permission, to ensure that the absence is for no more than seven consecutive days and nights or for no more than a total of 14 days and nights in any six-month period; *or*
- specified steps to facilitate your departure from the UK.

The Home Office usually writes to you about an alleged breach of conditions before terminating your support.

When support can be suspended or discontinued

In contrast to section 95 support, the Home Office has no power to suspend section 4 support. The Home Office can only review your entitlement and discontinue your support if it considers you are no longer entitled.

The Home Office may decide you are no longer destitute or no longer eligible – eg, because you are not taking all reasonable steps to leave the UK, your further representations for asylum have been refused or your application for judicial review has failed.

The Home Office's policy is to review section 4 support:[106]

- three months after it is granted on the basis that you are taking all reasonable steps to leave the UK; *or*
- six weeks after the birth of a baby if you have received support on the basis of late pregnancy or birth of a baby (the Home Office accepts that a woman cannot travel six weeks before or six weeks after giving birth); *or*
- at the end of the period estimated by the Home Office medical adviser or your doctor as the period within which you should recover sufficiently from an illness or disability that has prevented you from travelling earlier.

You can appeal against the decision to discontinue your support. See Chapter 24.

The best interests of children

The Home Office has a duty to ensure that all its decisions take into account the need to safeguard and promote the welfare of children.[107] In practice, it tends not to discontinue section 4 support for families who would otherwise be destitute. However, the wording in the policy guidance does not make this practice clear.[108]

If the breach of conditions is a minor one, it may not be appropriate to discontinue support. If the Home Office does decide to terminate your support, it should liaise with the local authority so that social services can carry out a child in need assessment, with a view to taking over the support. However, Home Office policy states that it is not necessary to liaise with the local authority if support has been discontinued because the Home Office believes you are no longer destitute.

Recovery of section 4 support and offences

In contrast to the position with section 95 and section 98 support (see p492), there are no specific offences in the Immigration and Asylum Act 1999 relating to obtaining section 4 support. The Home Office does not have any powers to recover the costs of section 4 support that has already been paid.

5. Support for those whose asylum claims have been withdrawn

Sometimes people claim asylum but then expressly or impliedly withdraw their claim. Typically, they may claim asylum on or soon after arrival in the UK but cease contact with the Home Office before their asylum claim is determined. They may re-establish contact with the Home Office years later in circumstances in which they need support. This section addresses the circumstances in which asylum support may be available to them.

Your asylum claim will be treated as withdrawn if:

- you have expressly withdrawn your application (in writing on a prescribed form); *or*
- the Home Office decides that you have impliedly withdrawn your application:
  - - by leaving the UK; *or*
  - - by failing to complete an asylum questionnaire when requested to; *or*
  - - by failing to attend your asylum interview, unless you can show that was due to circumstances beyond your control.

If you fall into any of these categories, then depending on your circumstances, it may not be possible for you to claim either section 95 or section 4 support because:

- your asylum claim is treated as no longer existing and so is not now recorded, which is a pre-condition for entitlement to section 95 support (see p482); *and*
- the Home Office and some judges of the Asylum Support Tribunal (different judges have taken different positions on this point) are liable to decide that your asylum claim was never rejected, which is a pre-condition for section 4 support (see p494).

Therefore, the general rule is that if your asylum claim has been withdrawn, then you:

- are not eligible for section 95 or section 4 support (although see below for exceptions); *and*
- you may be eligible for what is known as 'Schedule 10' support if you have been granted bail (see p507).

Exceptions to this general rule inlclude the following.

- You succeed in reopening your asylum claim. The rules require you to do that by lodging further representations with the Home Office's Further Submissions Unit. The Home Office then makes a decision on whether your asylum claim has been reopened. If the Home Office decides to reopen your case, you will be eligible for section 95 support if you are destitute.
- You have a child in your household younger than 18 *and* you were in receipt of section 95 support before your asylum claim was treated as withdrawn. You should remain entitled to section 95 support if you are destitute until the child reaches 18. If you were not on section 95 support when your asylum claim was withdrawn, the position is more complicated, and you should seek expert advice.
- You applied for asylum before 7 April 2008, or between 7 April 2008 and 27 February 2015. The rules changed on those dates. If you applied for asylum before 7 April 2008, your claim is likely to have been refused rather than treated as withdrawn, so you may be entitled to section 4 support provided all other conditions of eligibility are met. If you applied for asylum between 7 April 2008 and 27 February 2015, your claim will only have been treated as impliedly withdrawn if you failed to attend your asylum interview.
- Some judges of the Asylum Support Tribunal have held that a decision by the Home Office to treat an asylum claim as withdrawn means that the claim has been rejected. That means that you may be entitled to section 4 support if you appeal, depending on which judge hears your appeal.[109] However, that is not the view of the Home Office and probably not the majority view of the Asylum Support Judiciary.[110]

There are other potential arguments in third-country cases in which the Home Office refers the asylum claim to another state for the claim to be considered there instead of in the UK, pursuant to the Dublin III regulations. In such cases, the Home Office is required to certify the asylum claim once the third country has accepted the referral. It is arguable that the Home Office certification should be treated as a rejection of the asylum claim, even if the asylum seeker subsequently absconded, making it possible to potentially claim section 4 support. There are also arguments about entitlement to section 95 being retained if the Home Office has failed to follow the correct procedures for treating the claim as withdrawn.

Overall, this is a complicated area, and expert advice should be sought.

If your claim has been treated as withdrawn and none of the above exceptions to the general rule apply (and if you appeal to the Asylum Support Tribunal but do not get one of the minority of judges who is willing to treat a decision by the Home Office to treat your asylum claim as withdrawn as a 'rejection' of the claim), you will not be entitled to either section 95 or section 4 support. However, if you have been granted bail, you may still be able to apply for what is known as 'Schedule 10' support. That is addressed below.

6. Discretionary support for people on immigration bail

This section applies to anyone who has been granted immigration bail, not solely people who have claimed asylum. It may be relevant to people who have claimed asylum who are not eligible for either section 95 or section 4 support – eg, people (a) who claimed asylum but whose asylum claims have been treated as withdrawn, or (b) who claimed asylum as children, became appeal-rights exhausted before reaching 18 years old, and who are seeking to pursue their asylum claims as adults.

Before 15 January 2018, a number of different categories of people could apply for accommodation and support from the Home Office under section 4(1) of the Immigration and Asylum Act 1999.

Entitlement to support under section 4(1) did not depend on being an asylum seeker or refused asylum seeker. The people who could apply included:

- people who had been granted forms of release from real or potential immigration detention known as 'temporary admission', or 'temporary release'; *and*
- people released from immigration detention on bail; *and*
- people in immigration detention intending to seek bail.

However, on 15 January 2018, section 4(1) was repealed by the Immigration Act 2016. The same act also abolished temporary admission and release. The power for the Home Office to grant support under section 4(1) was replaced by a new power to provide support for people who have been granted immigration bail in Schedule 10 to the Immigration Act 2016.[111] This new form of support is called 'Schedule 10 support'.

Who is entitled to Schedule 10 support

You will be entitled to Schedule 10 support if:

- you have been granted immigration bail; *and*
- you are required by your bail condition to live at a certain address (whether or not that address has yet been specified, bail can be granted in principle on condition that the applicant provides an acceptable address);[112] *and*
- you would not be able to support yourself at the address unless Schedule 10 support is granted;[113] *and*
- the Secretary of State accepts there are exceptional circumstances that justify the provision of support.

The Home Office's policy on granting support under Schedule 10 is contained in its policy on immigration bail.[114] Three types of cases are accepted as being generally exceptional, and therefore to be potentially appropriate for Schedule 10 support:[115]

- Special Immigration Appeals Commission cases, which involve national security; *or*
- harm cases, involving:
  - people, including foreign National offenders (FNOs), who are granted bail and who are assessed as being at a high or very high risk of causing serious harm to the public;*or*
  - FNOs at high risk of harmful reoffending against an individual (eg, offences of domestic burglary, robbery, sexual assaults and violence) who are assessed using the Offender Group Reconviction Scale (OGRS) with a minimum score of 70 per cent; if that person has nowhere suitable to live in accordance with her/his probation licence and/or multi-agency public protection arrangements (for a limited period, or otherwise at the discretion of the Home Office in the interest of public protection); *or*
- cases in which failure to provide support will be a breach of human rights.

Exceptional circumstances

For the circumstances in which a denial of support would lead to a breach of human rights, see p497. That section concerns the circumstances in which section 4 support is necessary to avoid a breach of human rights. Similar general considerations apply in Schedule 10 cases except that, unlike with section 4, the class of applicants for Schedule 10 support is not limited to refused asylum seekers. Nonetheless, the Home Office's policy[116] requires applicants for Schedule 10 support to also show that there is some legal or practical obstacle to returning to their home country. In the absence of such an obstacle, the Home Office is likely to conclude that it will not be a breach of your human rights to withhold support, because you could avoid that prospect by voluntarily returning to your country of origin.

Procedure for applying

If you are applying for Schedule 10 support under the human rights criteria, you should use form BAIL409, unless you are an FNO being considered for deportation, in which case there is no published application process and you must contact your Criminal Casework Directorate case owner. Note that an application for Schedule 10 support should be made in liaison with your immigration solicitor.

Award

If support is granted, it is likely to be the same as section 4 support – ie, cash will not be provided, but instead the weekly allowance (£36.93 at the time of writing) will be put on an 'ASPEN' card to be used in designated shops.

Exclusions from Schedule 10 support

You will not be entitled to Schedule 10 support if you are eligible for another type of support. Asylum seekers and refused asylum seekers should in general apply for section 95 or section 4 support (unless their claims have been treated as withdrawn – see p505), and those with children or care needs should seek support from the local authority (see below). There is no provision for dependants to be supported under Schedule 10. Partners and other dependants need to apply for support in their own right (if necessary, to the local authority – see p502).

7. Support from your local authority

If you are an asylum seeker or refused asylum seeker, and you have care needs, or have a child or children, are a child, you may be entitled to support from your local authority.

Note: this is a complex area of law and detailed consideration is beyond the scope of this *Handbook*. What follows is an overview of the general forms of local authority support, followed by a summary of the ways in which asylum seekers and refused asylum seekers can access them.

If you believe that you may be entitled to support from your local authority, get expert advice from a children's law or community care adviser.

If you are an asylum seeker or a refused asylum seeker, the local authority may be under a duty to provide accommodation and financial support you if:
- you have accommodation-related care needs; *or*
- you have a child that the local authority has assessed as being a 'child in need' for the purposes of the Children Act 1989; *or*
- you are an unaccompanied asylum-seeking child.

Asylum seekers with accommodation-related care needs

The legislation governing support for people with care needs changed in 2015, although it is generally considered that many of the previously established legal principles continue to apply. Different laws apply in the different regions of the United Kingdom.
- In England, local authorities' duties to assess any person who appears to need care and support, and provide appropriate care in accordance with their assessment, are set out in the Care Act 2014.
- In Wales, the equivalent legislation is the Social Services and Well-being (Wales) Act 2014.
- In Scotland, it is the Social Work (Scotland) Act 1968.
- In Northern Ireland, it is Article 15 of the Health and Personal Social Services Order 1972.

All the legislation follows the same broad principle by which local authorities assess and then meet the needs of those in their area who appear to be in need of care and support. There is provision for urgent assessment when a person presents with apparently urgent needs.

Who is excluded from support

Local authorities are prevented by statute[117] from meeting the needs for care and support of an asylum seeker:

> whose needs for care and support have arisen solely because (a) the adult is destitute or (b) of the physical effects, or anticipated physical effects, of being destitute.

The meaning of the statutory language arose in a series of cases in the early 2000s between the Home Office and local authorities to determine responsibility for funding the accommodation of asylum seekers with care needs. As Lord Justice Simon Brown famously observed in one of those cases:[118]

> The word "solely" is a strong one and its purpose there seems to be evident. Assistance under the Act ... is, it hardly need be emphasised, the last resort for the destitute. If there are to be immigrant beggars on our streets, then let them at least not be old, ill or disabled.

In practice, therefore, the courts have held that there is a distinction between:

- asylum seekers who require care and attention solely because of the effects of destitution (and for no other reason); *and*
- asylum seekers whose need for care and attention arises independently of whether or not they may be destitute – eg, because of some disability.

The law prevents a local authority from supporting people in the first group but requires local authorities to meet the assessed needs of those in the second. The meaning of 'care and attention' (the previous statutory duty referred to 'care and attention' rather than 'care and support') was considered by the House of Lords in a subsequent case. Lady Hale held that:[119]

> ...the natural and ordinary meaning of the words 'care and attention' in this context is 'looking after'. Looking after means doing something for the person being cared for which he cannot or should not be expected to do for himself: it might be household tasks which an old person can no longer perform or can only perform with great difficulty; it might be protection from risks which a mentally disabled person cannot perceive; it might be personal care, such as feeding, washing or toileting. This is not an exhaustive list. The provision of medical care is expressly excluded.

In practice, this judgment has meant that to receive support from the local authority, an asylum seeker's need for care and support must be accommodation related.

Refused asylum seekers with accommodation-related care needs

The duties owed by local authorities to refused asylum seekers with accommodation-related care needs are generally the same as are owed to asylum seekers (see above), with one further restriction. Schedule 3 to the Nationality, Immigration and Asylum Act 2002 prevents local authorities providing care and support to refused asylum seekers except in relation to children, or if support is necessary to prevent a breach of human rights.[120]

If you are a refused asylum seeker who has accommodation-related care needs, and you seek care and support from the local authority, the local authority may decline to help if you are able to make a voluntary return to your country. The local authority may argue that if you decide to remain and thereby face destitution, your destitution will be caused by your choice not to return to your country not by its decision to withhold support. The court has ruled this approach to be generally lawful.[121] However, if you are a refused asylum seeker with accommodation-related needs for care and support, it may be a breach of your human rights to require you have leave the UK if you have a pending immigration application that:

- can only be pursued from within the UK; *and*
- is not hopeless.[122]

The considerations that apply in these cases are similar to those considered in relation to section 4 (see p497). If you need care and support from the local authority, and (1) you have an outstanding application for leave to enter or remain (2) that cannot be pursued from outside the UK, you will need to satisfy the local authority of (1) and (2) and, in addition, that there is some merit in the outstanding application. To do that, you will likely need a letter from your immigration solicitor to support your request to the local authority.

Asylum-seeking families with a child in need

Local authorities have a duty to safeguard and promote the welfare of children who are 'in need'. If you are destitute and have children, you may therefore be eligible for accommodation or support from your local authority under the Children Act 1989 (in Scotland, the Children (Scotland) Act 1995). A child who is destitute is generally considered to be 'in need', but a child can also be in need if s/he is disabled or if s/he is unlikely to achieve or maintain a reasonable standard of health or development without the provision of services by a local authority. The duty to support the child extends to supporting parents or other family members if that is in the child's best interests.

However, asylum seekers are eligible for support under section 95. This eligibility takes precedence over support under the Children Act: if a local authority has reasonable grounds for believing that a family is eligible for, and would be granted, section 95 support if applied for, the local authority is prevented[123] from providing welfare to a child of the family. If an asylum seeker with a child younger than 18 receives a negative asylum decision (whether on first application or appeal) the asylum seeker is treated as though the asylum claim was not determined, and remains on section 95 support while the child is younger than 18 and the family remains in the UK.[124]

The majority of asylum seekers with children remain on section 95 support for some time after making a claim if their claims are unsuccessfully finally determined. However, if a child is born to an asylum seeker after the asylum claim has been finally determined, the family is not entitled to section 95 support. In those circumstances, the asylum seeker may be able to apply for section 4 support if destitute and eligible under regulation 3(2)(a)-(e) of the Immigration and Asylum (Provision of Accommodation to Failed Asylum-Seekers) Regulations 2005 (see p502). Once section 4 support is granted to a destitute family with children, the Home Office's unpublished policy[125] appears to be that it will not be discontinued unless the asylum seeker is no longer destitute or has breached other conditions of her/his support package.

Note: before any decision can be taken to remove section 4 support from a family with a child, the Home Office should demonstrate, under section 55 of the Borders, Citizenship and Immigration Act 2009, how it has discharged its duties in relation to the safety and welfare of the child. The fact that you may be eligible for section 4 support (see p495) does not exclude you from claiming Children Act support if your child has particular welfare needs that would not otherwise be met. Unlike section 95 support – eligibility for which prevents local authorities from providing Children Act support (see) – section 4 is a 'residual power' and any duty to provide support under the Children Act should take priority. Despite that, some local authorities might still refuse support on the basis that you should apply for section 4 support before approaching the local authority. If that happens, you should get expert advice, because it may be possible to challenge the local authority's refusal by judicial review.[126]

If you are a refused asylum seeker with a child in need supported by the local authority, the local authority may attempt to discharge its duty to the child by offering to fund the your and your child's journey to your home country. An attempt to terminate Children Act support for that reason has been held to be unlawful if the mother of a child in need had an outstanding immigration application that was not hopeless and that would have been treated as withdrawn if the family had left the UK.[127]

Unaccompanied asylum-seeking children

Local authorities are responsible for supporting children younger than 18 who arrive in the UK alone and claim asylum (who are often referred to as 'unaccompanied minors'). Unaccompanied asylum-seeker children are dispersed around the country. The local authority in the new area should then make arrangements for suitable accommodation, which can include foster care.

If you have already been supported by a local authority as an unaccompanied minor, the authority may continue to have a duty to provide you with support when you reach 18 under the Children (Leaving Care) Act 2000. That allows for a needs assessment and potential support up to the age of 21, or 24 if you continue in education.

There may be a dispute about your age. If you claim asylum as an unaccompanied minor, the Home Office should refer you to social services for support unless it strongly believes that you are older than 18. If the social services department (in Scotland, social work department) has any doubt about your age, it can carry out an age assessment. See p469 for more information on proving your age. You should seek specialist advice if your age has been disputed; refugee organisations, such as the Refugee Council, may be able to assist you (see Appendix 2).

Local authority support during the coronavirus pandemic

In March 2020, as part of its response to the coronavirus pandemic, the UK government made funding available to local authorities and devolved governments to accommodate all rough sleepers: 'to protect their health and stop wider transmission'.[128] Those so accommodated included asylum seekers and failed asylum seekers who might, if destitute, have been eligible for asylum support. The precise support arrangements made by local authorities in response to this government initiative varied by local authority and by region (as housing is a devolved issue). Despite making funding available, the government did not legislate to give local authorities new powers to achieve this aim. In relation to homeless people with no recourse to public funds, Luke Hall (then Minister for Local Government and Homelessness) stated on 22 April 2020:

> ...funding has been provided to help local authorities to reduce risks to public health and to support individuals on the basis of need. The legal position on those with no recourse to public funds has not been amended. The government recognises that these are unprecedented times, and expects local authorities to support people who are sleeping rough.

At the time of writing, the legal basis on which homeless asylum seekers and refused asylum seekers were accommodated by local authorities has not been clarified. Asylum seekers and refused asylum seekers are in general excluded from housing assistance by local authorities. In England, it has been suggested that local authorities retained a power under section 1 of the Localism Act 2011 to accommodate such people to prevent a breach of their human rights. Those asylum seekers and refused asylum seekers accommodated by local authorities had no access to mainstream benefits, and faced a number of practical problems, including:

- people needing to self-isolate with no access to facilities that were not shared;
- inadequate or no provision made for subsistence; *and*
- requiring accommodated persons to collect subsistence payments in person but not paying their travel expenses.

These problems led to applications for asylum support being made to the Home Office by people in local authority accommodation. Although government policy is to move those people who were so entitled out of local authority accommodation into asylum support, some applications for asylum support were refused by the Home Office on the basis that the applicants were in local authority accommodation and therefore not destitute. On appeal, different judges of the Asylum Support Tribunal have decided this point in conflicting ways. If you were homeless and received local authority support during the pandemic but you wish to apply for asylum support under section 95 or section 4, you should therefore seek expert advice.

Notes

1. **Introduction**

1 ss115(1) and (3) IAA 1999 bar persons subject to immigration control from specified benefits. There are exceptions set out in regulations made under s115(4) but none of them apply to asylum seekers.
2 s95 IAA 1999
3 s98 IAA 1999
4 s4 IAA 1999

2. **Support for asylum seekers**

5 s95(1) IAA 1999
6 Sch 3 NIAA 2002
7 Sch 3 para 4 NIAA 2002
8 Sch 3 para 5 NIAA 2002
9 Sch 3 paras 2 and 3 NIAA 2002
10 s95(2) IAA 1999; reg 4 AS Regs
11 Reg 4(4)(b) AS Regs
12 Reg 4(4)(c) AS Regs
13 Reg 4(3) AS Regs
14 s55(1) NIAA 2002
15 s55(5)(a) NIAA 2002.
16 Home Office guidance, 'Asylum Support (Asylum Instructions)', *Asylum Support: policy bulletins – instructions*, Ch 5
17 R *v SSHD ex p Limbuela and others* [2005] UKHL 66
18 ss94(1) and 95(1) IAA 1999
19 para 353 IR
20 s94(3) IAA 1999; regs 2 and 2A AS Regs
21 s94(5) IAA 1999
22 Sch 3 para 7A NIAA 2002
23 s94(1) IAA 1999; reg 2 (4) AS Regs; Home Office guidance, 'Asylum Support (Asylum Instructions)', *Dependants on an Asylum Support Application*
24 Reg 2(4)(f) and (6)(a) and (b) AS Regs

25 Home Office, *Asylum Policy Instruction: dependants and former dependants*, May 2014
26 Home Office guidance, 'Asylum Support (Asylum Instructions)', Dependants on an Asylum Support Application, available at gov.uk/government/collections/asylum-support-asylum-instructions
27 Available at asaproject.org/uploads/Factsheet_11-_Asylum_support_for_dependants.pdf
28 s95(3) IAA 1999
29 Reg 7(a) AS Regs
30 Reg 7(b) AS Regs
31 s95(9) IAA 1999; regs 19 and 20 AS Regs
32 s95(10) IAA 1999
33 s95(11) IAA 1999
34 Reg 19 AS Regs
35 Reg 15(1) AS Regs
36 Reg 15(2) AS Regs
37 ss105(1)(c) and 106(1)(c) IAA 1999
38 They are 'excluded tenancies' under s3A (7A) Protection from Eviction Act 1977.
39 Reg 22(2) AS Regs
40 Reg 22(3) AS Regs
41 Reg 20(1) AS Regs
42 Reg 20(1)(a) AS Regs
43 Reg 20(1)(b) AS Regs
44 Reg 20(1)(c) AS Regs
45 Reg 20(1)(e) AS Regs
46 Reg 20(1)(f) AS Regs
47 Reg 20(1)(g) AS Regs
48 Reg 20(1)(h) AS Regs
49 Reg 20(1)(i) AS Regs
50 Reg 20(1)(j) AS Regs
51 Reg 20(1)(d) AS Regs
52 Reg 20(1)(k) AS Regs
53 Home Office guidance, 'Asylum Support (Asylum Instructions)', *Ceasing Asylum Support Instruction*, para 2.7
54 For example, *JKV v SSHD*, AS/12/03/28234
55 *R v Kensington and Chelsea RLBA ex p Kujtim* [1999] All ER 161, para 35
56 Reg 21(1) AS Regs
57 Reg 21(1)(c) and (2) AS Regs, with reference to reg 15 AS Regs
58 Reg 21(3) AS Regs
59 Home Office guidance, 'Asylum Support (Asylum Instructions)', *policy bulletins instruction*, para 6.6
60 Home Office guidance, 'Asylum Support (Asylum Instructions)', *policy bulletins instruction*, para 25.2.1
61 *ZN v SSHD*, AS/17/09/37288
62 Reg 17 AS Regs
63 s114 IAA 1999
64 Reg 18 AS Regs
65 s114(3) IAA 1999
66 s112 IAA 1999
67 s113 IAA 1999
68 ss105-106

3. **Temporary support**
69 s98(1) IAA 1999
70 s98(3) IAA 1999, applying s95(3)
71 See s98(3), which provides that the 'likely to become destitute' provision in s95(1) does not apply for the purposes of s98.
72 Home Office guidance, *Asylum Support (Asylum Instructions), policy bulletins instruction*, para 1.1, available at gov.uk/government/collections/asylum-support-asylum-instructions
73 That is because s103 IAA 1999, which deals with appeals, does not refer to s98 support.
74 Reg 4(8)(9) AS Regs
75 Reg 20A AS Regs

4. **Support for refused asylum seekers**
76 s4(2) IAA 1999
77 Reg 3(1)(a) IA(PAFAS) Regs
78 Reg 3(1)(b) and (2) IA(PAFAS) Regs
79 **NI** AA, Sch 3, para 6
80 **NI** AA, Sch 3, para 7A
81 **NI** AA, Sch 3, para 3
82 Reg 2 IA(PAFAS) Regs
83 Home Office guidance, 'Asylum Support (Asylum Instructions)', Asylum Support, Section 4(2): policy and process, p9, available at gov.uk/government/collections/asylum-support-asylum-instructions
84 Regs 6-9 AS Regs
85 Reg 3(2)(a) IA(PAFAS) Regs
86 Home Office guidance, 'Asylum Support (Asylum Instructions)', *Asylum Support, Section 4(2): policy and process*, p10, available at gov.uk/government/collections/asylum-support-asylum-instructions
87 Reg 3(2)(b) IA(PAFAS) Regs
88 *R (SSHD) v ASA and Osman, Yillah, Ahmad and Musemwa (interested parties)* [2006] EWHC 1248
89 Reg 3(2)(c) IA(PAFAS) Regs
90 Reg 3(2)(d) IA PAFAS) Regs
91 Reg 3(2)(e) IA(PAFAS) Regs
92 *R (Limbuela and Others (Shelter intervener)) v SSHD* [2005] UKHL 66

93 Home Office guidance, 'Asylum Support (Asylum Instructions)', *Asylum Support, Section 4(2): policy and process*, p13, available at gov.uk/government/collections/asylum-support-asylum-instructions
94 For example. a decision of the principal judge dated 23 October 2020, AS/20/09/42386 and 42397, at para 47
95 The significance of whether the Home Office accept that your representations amount to a 'fresh' claim, is that if the representations are refused but the Home Office accept them as constituting a fresh claim, you will be granted a fresh right of appeal.
96 *R (MK and another) v SSHD* [2012] EWHC 1896 (Admin), paras 166-169 and *R (Nigatu) v SSHD* [2004] EWHC 1806 (Admin), para 20
97 See AS/14/11/32141 at para 31, but also AS/19/07/40099 at paras 19-20
98 *R (NS) v First-tier Tribunal* [2009] EWHC 3819 (Admin)
99 *R (Mulumba) v First-tier Tribunal (Asylum Support)*, unreported. The Home Office conceded in the 2015 judicial review that 'provision of s4 may in any particular case be necessary to avoid a breach of a person's Article 8 rights'. See also AS/14/11/32141. The basis of that decision was that if the applicant was required to leave the UK, the Article 8 claim would be treated by the Home Office as withdrawn (see *Birmingham City Council v Clue* [2010] EWCA Civ 460, para 65).
100 AS/11/06/26857, 18 August 2011
101 AS/15/09/34157, 8 October 2015
102 AS/20/11/42538 at para 25
103 AS/20/09/42386 and 4239 at paras 47-49
104 R(QBB) v SSHD (CO/3986/2020)
105 Reg 6 IA(PAFAS) Regs
106 Home Office guidance, 'Asylum Support (Asylum Instructions)', *Asylum Support, Section 4(2): policy and process*, p15
107 s55 Borders, Citizenship and Immigration Act 2009
108 Home Office guidance, 'Asylum Support (Asylum Instructions)', *Asylum Support, Section 4(2): policy and process*, p16

5. **Support for those whose asylum claims have been withdrawn**

109 AS/19/11/40826 at para 26, and AS/19/11/40868 at para 21
110 eg AS/13/07/30183'

6. **Discretionary support for people on immigration bail**

111 Sch 10 para 9 IA 2016,
112 Sch 10 para 9(1)(a) IA 2016
113 Sch 10 para 9(1)(b) IA 2016
114 Home Office, *Immigration Bail*, p53, available at assets.publishing.service.gov.uk/government/uploads/system/uploads/attachment_data/file/919793/Immigration-bail-v5.0ext.pdf
115 Sch 10 para 9(3) IA 2016
116 Home Office, *Immigration Bail*, p56, available at assets.publishing.service.gov.uk/government/uploads/system/uploads/attachment_data/file/919793/Immigration-bail-v5.0ext.pdf

7. **Support from your local authority**

117 s21 Care Act 2014 (for England). Analogous provisions for Wales and Scotland are: Social Services and Well-being (Wales) Act 2014 and s13A Social Work (Scotland) Act 1968.
118 *R v Wandsworth London Borough Council, Ex parte O, R v Leicester City Council, Ex parte Bhikha* [2000] 1 WLR 2539
119 *R (On the Application of M) (Fc) v Slough Borough Council* [2008] UKHL 52
120 Sch 3 NIAA 2002, paras 1, 3 and 6
121 *Kimani v Lambeth Borough Council* [2004] 1 WLR 272
122 *Birmingham City Council v Clue* [2010] EWCA Civ 460
123 s122(5) IAA 1999
124 s94(5) IAA 1999
125 Disclosed following a High Court case (*MK and AH v SSHD* [2012] EWHC 1896 (Admin))
126 See *R (VC and others) v Newcastle City Council and SSHD* [2011] EWHC 2673 (Admin), paras 91-92
127 *Birmingham City Council v Clue* [2010] EWCA Civ 460
128 Letter dated 26 March 2020 from Luke Hall MP, Minister for Local Government and Homelessness, to local authorities, available at assets.publishing.service.gov.uk/government/uploads/system/uploads/attachment_data/file/928780/Letter_from_Minister_Hall_to_Local_Authorities.pdf

Chapter 22

Applying for asylum support

This chapter covers:

1. Section 95 support

If you are either an asylum seeker or a dependant of an asylum seeker for support purposes, you can apply for section 95 support from the Home Office.[1] The application can be for you alone, or for yourself and your dependants.[2] **Note:** the procedure for applying is essentially the same if you are a refused asylum seeker who is applying for section 4 support (see p529).

Under section 95, you can apply for accommodation and cash support or, if you have somewhere to live and can prove this to the Home Office, just for the cash support to meet your 'essential needs' (known as **'subsistence-only support'**). In rare circumstances, you may wish to apply for accommodation only.[3] Most people apply for both.

You must apply for support on Form ASF1, available from the Asylum Help service at Migrant Help (see p481) and from gov.uk/asylum-support/how-to-claim.[4] Even if the application is for both yourself and your dependants, you only need to complete one form. If you wish to apply for support as a dependant of a person who is already being supported by the Home Office, it is not technically necessary for you to complete the application form again – the Home Office considers providing additional support for you if notified of your existence in writing.[5] However, in this situation, it is advisable for you to complete a separate application form, because that should ensure that any subsequent refusal is issued in writing, thereby giving you a right of appeal. An asylum seeker is under a duty to notify the Home Office if s/he has been joined by a dependant – but without a formal application, the mere act of notifying the Home Office may be insufficient to generate a written decision on a dependant's claim.

Migrant Help can help you complete Form ASF1 and submit it to the Home Office. **Note:** in recent years the Home Office has shown as increased readiness to refuse applications for section 95 support on the basis that applicants have undisclosed resources or access to undisclosed resources, and so are 'not destitute'. You are, therefore, strongly advised to obtain specialist help with completing Form ASF1 from a local advice agency or, failing that, Migrant Help. If you fail to provide all the necessary documents with your initial application, it is likely to be refused. If that happens, you may need to appeal against the Home Office's decision (see Chapter 24).

You must complete the application form in full and in English.[6] There are detailed notes accompanying the form that give further information about the application procedure and guidance on how to complete the form.[7] The form asks for details of the stage your asylum application has reached, the kind of support you need, your current accommodation, any other kind of support you receive (including support from friends or relatives, details of cash, savings, investments or other property you own in the UK and abroad, any employment you have and state benefits you receive, both for yourself and your dependants), and details of any disabilities or special needs you have.

If you can, you must send documentary evidence to corroborate the information you give. **Note**: a false statement to obtain asylum support is a criminal offence (although, to the author's knowledge, prosecutions brought by the Home Office are rare).[8]

Form ASF1 can be downloaded, printed and filled in by hand, or completed and saved to a computer. Whatever format is used, the completed form must be emailed, faxed or posted to the Home Office. At the time of writing, all applications, whether by email, fax or post, must be sent via Migrant Help. The address for this purpose is Asylum Support Casework Team, PO Box 471, Dover CT16 9FN or ascorrespondence@migranthelpuk.org. The methods of, and addresses for, communicating with the Home Office frequently change, and if it is unclear from the website how to submit the form, contact a specialist agency for advice.

The Home Office may ask you for further information on any of the details contained in the application form.[9] It is important that you respond to any such questions because the Home Office has the power not to consider your application if the Home Office thinks that you have not completed the form properly or accurately, or if you have not co-operated with enquiries.[10] Such a refusal to consider an application is known as a 'section 57 decision'. There is no right of appeal against a section 57 decision, so it is therefore important to answer all further questions from the Home Office (known as 'further information requests') as best you can and within the time limit given to you.

If you have done your best but have been unable to provide all the information requested by the Home Office, and you have explained why you cannot provide the missing information, but the Home Office has nevertheless refused to entertain your application, you should seek urgent expert advice on whether to file a notice of appeal against the Home Office's decision. In some cases, the Asylum Support Tribunal has treated what the Home Office describes in correspondence as a 's57 decision' (ie, a refusal to entertain an application) as a substantive refusal, with the result that there is a right of appeal after all, which the tribunal can proceed to determine in an appellant's favour.[11]

Alternatively, you may be able to bring a claim for judicial review. This is a potentially lengthy and uncertain procedure of last resort, which will require you in due course to answer the Home Office's query anyway.

Proving you are entitled to section 95 support

To be entitled to section 95 support, you must prove:

- you are an asylum seeker (see below); *and*
- you are destitute.

Together, these provide entitlement (see p520).

Proving you are an asylum seeker

If you have applied for asylum and are awaiting a decision, the Home Office will be able to determine that you are an asylum seeker from your Port and Home Office reference numbers, which you must include with your application for asylum support. It is straightforward for the Home Office to determine your status as an asylum seeker, if:

- your asylum claim has been refused; *and*
- you have appealed; *and*
- you have lodged your appeal within the time permitted.

In both these scenarios, there should be no need to provide additional evidence to prove that you are an asylum seeker. However, you may need additional evidence to prove that you are an asylum seeker for asylum support purposes (see p483) if you are claiming asylum support after:

- having appealed to a tribunal or court out of time against a negative decision on your asylum claim; *or*
- having made further representations to the Home Office, which you have asked the Home Office to treat as a fresh claim for asylum; *or*
- having absconded, which means the Home Office may have treated your claim as impliedly withdrawn; *or*
- having left the UK before a decision was taken on your asylum claim, and then returned; *or*
- if you appealed against a negative asylum decision out of time: evidence that time for bringing an appeal against the refusal of your asylum claim has been extended; *or*

- if you submitted further representations to the Home Office: evidence that the Home Office has agreed to treat further representations you have submitted as a fresh asylum claim.

The evidence you require may need to be obtained from your immigration solicitor. You should seek expert advice on your asylum support application if necessary.

Proving you are destitute

If you apply for section 95 support for yourself, you must prove to the Home Office that you are 'destitute'. If you apply for support for yourself and your dependants, you must prove that the group as a whole is destitute.[12] The same applies to applications for section 4 support (p529).

Being 'destitute' means either that you are destitute now or that you are 'likely to become destitute within (for new applicants) 14 days'.[13] You are destitute if either:[14]

- you do not have 'adequate accommodation' (see p525), or any means of getting adequate accommodation; *or*
- you cannot meet your essential living needs (see p538), even if you have adequate accommodation.

It is an either/or test, so you are 'destitute' and therefore eligible for both accommodation and cash support, if you are without adequate accommodation *or* without the means to feed yourself.

The Home Office must follow regulations that set out what is and what is not relevant in deciding these questions. These apply from the time you make an application for support up until the Home Office decision (or the tribunal decision, if there is an appeal), and at any time thereafter if there is a question of whether support should continue. It is important to be aware of Home Office policy in addition to the regulations.[15]

When considering whether you are destitute, the Home Office must take into account those resources (known as 'assets') that are available to you, or likely to be available to you over the next 14 days (for a new application). The **only** resources that the law permits the Home Office to take into account are:[16]

- cash;
- savings;
- investments;
- land;
- vehicles;
- goods for trade or business.

Any of the above assets held by a dependant on your asylum support claim must also be declared and will be taken into account. Your dependants include any children under the age of 18, any adult children who are disabled and in need of care or attention, your spouse/civil partner or your unmarried partner, provided you have been living together for at least two of the three preceding years.[17]

This 'other support' might include support from friends and relatives in the UK (or abroad, depending on the facts) or from voluntary sector organisations. Land may include property, such as a house and other outbuildings. Investments include business investments, income bonds, life assurance policies, pension schemes, stocks and shares, and unit trusts. Your land, assets and investments could be in the UK or abroad and must all be disclosed on Form ASF1.

When deciding whether you are destitute, the Home Office must ignore any:

- assets you or your dependants have that are not listed above;[18] *and*
- Home Office support that you are receiving.[19]

Note: there is nothing in the regulations that require you to sell your personal possessions such as your jewellery.[20] However if you choose to sell them when you are receiving section 95 support, you must declare the proceeds of the sale to the Home Office, who will review your eligibility for asylum support if it considers that you may no longer be destitute.[21]

Providing evidence of your resources

You should not assume that the Home Office will accept any information you include in your application form as credible without supporting evidence. As a general rule, the Home Office is likely to treat any significant gaps in your supporting evidence (particularly if the gaps are unexplained) and/or any inconsistencies in the evidence you do submit as providing grounds for doubting the credibility of your claim to be destitute. That said, the amount and quality of evidence you are able to include with your asylum support application to show that you are destitute will depend on your circumstances. If you are destitute and your application is urgent, then you may be able to provide further evidence later in the process in response to Home Office requests for further information or (if your application is refused) while you are preparing your appeal.

Bank and credit card accounts

You must disclose all bank and credit card accounts in the UK and abroad. **Note**: the Home Office regularly conducts Experian credit checks on applicants, which reveal all bank and credit card accounts held in the UK. If you do not disclose a bank account that is subsequently revealed through a Home Office Experian check, the Home Office is likely to conclude that you have concealed your resources and may be disinclined to believe that you are destitute.

Bank and credit card statements

The Home Office will want to see evidence of your income and savings, both in the UK and in your home country, to exclude the possibility that you have built up and retained savings from which you can now support yourself. You should, therefore, provide the Home Office with bank and credit card statements for the previous six months. You may want to include a summary explanation of all debits and credits of £50 or more. Evidence of bank accounts and savings abroad may be required to show that you do not have resources at home that could be used to fund your support in the UK. If you are unable to obtain statements in relation to accounts held abroad, you should explain why – eg, by providing evidence of unsuccessful attempts to obtain bank statements, such as email correspondence with the bank. The Home Office will expect you to use online banking facilities if they are available.

Earlier visa applications

Note: if you claim asylum after entering the UK on a visa, the Home Office examines the information contained in your visa application and compares it with the information on Form ASF1. For example, you may have come to the UK on a student or visitor's visa and then claimed asylum. That process can lead to problems if you entered the UK on an illegally procured visa, which may typically have been granted on the basis of manufactured evidence that your resources in your home country were greater that they were in reality. In most cases the Home Office will rely on the resources disclosed on your visa application, and dispute the credibility of your asylum-support application if you disclose lesser resources in Form ASF1. This is a complicated issue that usually arises on appeal, and you should seek expert advice if this situation applies to you.

Evidence of employment

Evidence of any income you received in your home country from employment (or otherwise) may be required to show that that income stream is no longer available to you or would be insufficient to support you in the UK. If you have been working in the UK, you should explain how much you have earned and provide evidence of your income, such as a P60 or a wage slip. Working in the UK without permission to work is a criminal offence, and disclosing such work could expose you to criminal prosecution. That said, as far as the author is aware, criminal prosecutions of asylum support applicants who have revealed details of illegal working in their applications are rare. This is a sensitive issue and must be carefully presented, and if you have supported yourself by working illegally in the UK, you should seek expert advice.

Support from friends, family and charitable bodies

If you receive support from friends, family or charitable bodies, you should provide evidence (eg, a letter) from anyone supporting you, specifying what sort of support they provide and how much. If you are living with, or are partially supported by close family members, you should consider providing evidence of their savings, income and outgoings to demonstrate why it is not reasonable for them to meet all your accommodation costs and/or essential living needs.

If your partner receives benefits

If your partner receives universal credit or another social security benefit, you must disclose his/her income in your application. The Home Office will refer to your household as a 'mixed household', and will apply its policy[22] on mixed households to determine the proportion of your partner's benefit that will be treated as reasonably available to you. These calculations can be complicated and are beyond the scope of this *Handbook*. Expert advice should be sought.

If you are a lone parent

If you are a lone parent, the Home Office may ask you for evidence that you have taken steps to seek maintenance from the other parent.

Support may be granted on condition you take steps to dispose of relevant assets

Even if you have declared relevant assets (eg, savings, investments, land, vehicles, goods for trade or business – see p520) to a substantial value, you may still qualify as destitute if you can show that you cannot realise the value of those assets within the relevant period (14 days for new applications). Proving that can be a contentious issue if you have property abroad that could be sold to pay for your support in the UK. The Home Office may provide you with support on a limited basis to allow you time to sell items of property – eg, six months to sell a house abroad. The Home Office would then treat the money received from the sale as cash or savings and would take it into account when deciding whether or not to continue to provide support. If you do not consider it reasonable that you should have to sell your property (eg, there are family members still living in the property who would be homeless if they had to leave), you should give your reasons and any supporting evidence when you send in your application form.

Evidence of essential living needs

Home Office policy lists those expenses that the Home Office generally considers make up an individual's essential living needs. The policy states:[23]

> The cash allowance [which is paid to asylum support claimants and is intended to cover essential living needs] should generally be sufficient to cover the following needs: food, clothing, toiletries, non-prescription medication, household cleaning items, communications, travel, and the ability to access social, cultural and religious life, which is covered by the funding provision for communications and travel. The level of the cash allowance takes into consideration that other essential living needs (eg, warmth, cooking, lighting) are covered by the provision of accommodation that is free of both rent and utility bills (fuel and water) and is also fully furnished and equipped with both

household goods (eg, kitchenware, access to laundry services) and linens (eg, towels and sheets).

If you have adequate accommodation but claim that you are destitute because you cannot meet your essential living needs, it will therefore be relevant if you have to contribute to rent and utility bills, the cost of essential household goods and access to laundry services. You should provide evidence of the amount you are required to contribute to each such expense.

When the Home Office decides whether you can meet your essential living needs, the regulations state that certain items are treated as not essential[24] – eg, it is not relevant whether or not you can pay for the following items:

- the cost of sending or receiving faxes, photocopying or buying or using computer facilities; *or*
- travelling expenses; *or*
- toys and other recreational items; *or*
- entertainment expenses.

When deciding whether you can meet your essential living needs in terms of clothing, the Home Office cannot take into account your personal preferences.[25] However, the Home Office can take into account your individual circumstances when deciding whether you can meet your clothing requirements. The level of support necessary to meet the essential living need for clothing was considered by the High Court in a case brought by Refugee Action.[26] The court held that essential living needs include the 'provision of suitable clothing to avoid any danger of illness'. Health-related clothing issues might include:

- whether you can afford to provide clothes for yourself that are suitable for the different weather conditions in the UK; *and*
- whether you have sufficient changes of clothes required for cleanliness and personal hygiene; *and*
- whether you have clothes that are suitable for any particular health needs that you have.

In relation to school uniforms, the court held that[27] 'School uniform grants are often provided by local authorities but all other clothing for asylum seekers and their dependent children has to be paid for out of the s.96(1)(b) cash support. To the extent that school uniform is not provided in a particular case, this would fall for consideration as an exceptional case.'

If you are granted support, the cost of travelling to your new accommodation is paid for by the Home Office.

If, because of your specific circumstances, you have another need that is not referred to in the regulations, the Home Office must decide whether the need is essential,[28] taking into account your individual circumstances. Once you are in receipt of support, it is possible to apply for additional support if your needs are 'exceptional'.[29] Any such claim should be supported by evidence.

Evidence of not having adequate accommodation

If you are applying for support but you have some form of accommodation, the Home Office must decide whether or not this is 'adequate'. The Home Office must take into account whether:[30]

- it is 'reasonable' for you to continue to occupy the accommodation (see below); *and*
- you can afford to pay for the accommodation (see below); *and*
- you can gain entry to the accommodation (see below); *and*
- if the accommodation is a houseboat, a caravan or some other moveable structure that can be lived in, there is somewhere you can locate, and have permission to live in, the accommodation; *and*
- you can live in the accommodation with your dependants; *and*
- you or your dependants are likely to experience harassment, threats or violence if you continue to live in the accommodation (see below).

Note: even if the accommodation is adequate, you are still destitute if you cannot meet your essential living needs. If you have told the Home Office that you want to stay in your current accommodation and only want financial assistance, the factors listed above are not taken into account when deciding whether you are destitute, except for the question of whether you can afford the accommodation.[31]

Note: in England, if you have sufficient savings to be able to rent accommodation for yourself, you must first obtain permission from the Home Office for the 'right to rent'.[32] Landlords can only legally grant tenancies or rent rooms to those with a right to rent. At the request of the landlord, the Home Office checks that you are still a current asylum seeker and may grant permission for you to rent a property. If you have been unable to rent a property because landlords will not apply for the right to rent on your behalf, you will need to provide evidence that you have been unable to obtain permission to rent. The Home Office policy states that 'permission to rent is normally granted to asylum seekers if their asylum claim, or appeal against refusal of the claim, is still outstanding'.[33]

Is it reasonable for you to continue to occupy the accommodation

The Home Office must consider whether it is 'reasonable' for you to continue to occupy the accommodation.[34] You will need to provide evidence of your personal circumstances, such as letters, medical reports and photos. For example, it may not be reasonable for you to continue to occupy accommodation if you are staying with a friend and sleeping on her/his floor, or if you cannot gain entry during the day, or if it is unsuitable for you because of your health needs or a physical disability.

The Home Office may also take into account the general housing circumstances in the district of the local government housing authority in which the accommodation is situated.[35] To prove that it is not reasonable for you to continue to live there, you may have to provide evidence that your accommodation is worse or more overcrowded than other accommodation generally is within the area in which you live.

Can you afford to pay for the accommodation

The Home Office must consider whether you can afford to pay for your existing accommodation.[36] It must take into account:[37]

- any income or assets (other than from Home Office support or temporary support – see p520) available to you or any of your dependants or which might be expected to be available; *and*
- the costs of living in the accommodation; *and*
- your other reasonable living expenses.

All your living expenses in relation to the accommodation (eg, your rent and any utility or other bills) should be evidenced (see p523).

Do you have access to the accommodation

You can be considered not to have access to your accommodation if you do not have access during the day. For example, a friend may allow you to sleep in her/his home but require you to leave during the day, or you may be staying in a hostel where occupants cannot remain during the day.

Are you likely to experience harassment, threats or violence

The Home Office must consider whether it is 'probable' that your continued occupation of the accommodation will lead to domestic abuse against you or any of your dependants.[38] The domestic abuse must be:

- from a person who is, or who has been, a 'close family member'; *and*
- in the form of either actual violence or threats of violence that are likely to be carried out.

There is no definition of 'close family member'. Depending on the circumstances, it may cover a married or unmarried partner and ex-partner, those to whom you have a blood relationship, in-laws, relatives of your partner and others who live (or have lived) in your household. **Note:** the family member does not have to live with you.[39] You may fear that because your address is known to her/him, your continued occupation of that accommodation is likely to lead to domestic violence.

Although the asylum support rules only specifically refer to *domestic* violence, it is arguable that other forms of violence or threats you have received from anyone not normally associated with you are also relevant when deciding whether your current accommodation is adequate. This abuse may be in the form of racial harassment or attacks,[40] sexual abuse or harassment, and harassment because of your religion or for other reasons.

If you are affected by domestic abuse or violence, contact Migrant Help or your accommodation provider. Alternatively, you can contact a Home Office safeguarding team directly.[41] If there is time and it is safe to do so, you should seek an expert adviser who has the relevant contact details and may be able to advocate on your behalf.[42]

How the Home Office determines your section 95 application

To determine whether you are entitled to section 95 support, the Home Office uses the information and evidence contained in your completed Form ASF1 and supporting documents to decide whether:

- you are an asylum seeker; *and*
- you are able to:[43]
  - meet your essential living needs (if you have adequate accommodation and are only seeking financial support); *or*
  - secure adequate accommodation and also be able to meet your essential living needs (if you are seeking accommodation *and* financial support).

To determine whether you are an asylum seeker, the Home Office will generally just check its records. In some cases, that may be complicated (eg, if you made an out of time appeal or absconded before a decision was taken on your claim – see p535), and you may need to provide the Home Office with additional evidence. To determine whether you are destitute, the steps the Home Office takes depend on the facts of your case and what you are applying for. If you have existing accommodation that you claim is not adequate, the Home Office considers the information and evidence in your application to determine whether the accommodation is adequate (see p525). If you do not have adequate accommodation, the Home Office determines whether you have the means to pay for your own accommodation.

To do that, the Home Office's policy states:

> 'As a general rule, the cost of obtaining adequate accommodation, which will vary by region, should be established by obtaining an average price for bed and breakfast in the local area. Bed and breakfast establishments offer simple and easily accessible accommodation and are relatively affordable compared to hotels. The majority of bed-and-breakfast establishments will have their own websites, containing price lists for varying types of room to suit singles, couples or families.'[44]

From websites such as booking.com, it is relatively simple for the Home Office to determine the cost of a room for you and any dependants, for your asylum support claim, in a bed and breakfast near where you are currently staying for the next 14 days. Such research will give the Home Office a figure for the likely cost of your accommodation.

To calculate the cost of meeting your essential living needs, the Home Office calculates the amount of cash that you and any dependants would each receive in respect of essential living needs if your application for section 95 support was successful. This amount is set out in regulations as a weekly cash sum that the Home Office has calculated should meet essential living needs for a week.[45] The Home Office then multiplies the weekly amount by the number of people needing support (you and any dependants) to give the total weekly cost of meeting the essential living needs for your household. That figure is then multiplied by two to give the total cost over the next 14 days. If you are applying for accommodation and subsistence, the Home Office will add together (a) the likely cost of bed and breakfast accommodation in your local area, and (b) the cost of meeting your essential living needs for you and any dependants over the next 14 days. That gives a figure that the Home Office refers to as the 'destitution threshold'. If you are applying for subsistence only, (a) is ignored. To determine whether you are to be treated as destitute, the Home Office will simply compare your available resources over 14 days with the destitution threshold. If your available resources are less in value than the destitution threshold, you will be treated as destitute, and will be entitled to section 95 support while your asylum application is determined.

2. **Section 98 support**

While you are waiting for a decision on your application for section 95 support, you should be provided with temporary support under section 98 of the Immigration and Asylum Act 1999 (see p492) if it appears to the Home Office that 'you may be destitute'.[46] The accommodation that is provided as part of temporary support is often called 'initial accommodation'. It is temporary full board or self-catering accommodation intended for short-term use.

There is no application form for temporary support but there is an initial accommodation referral form that Migrant Help will complete on your behalf, if that charity is helping you.

Temporary support can be offered quickly, including out of normal office hours if you are particularly vulnerable. The Home Office will treat you as particularly vulnerable if you are:

- part of a family with a dependent child or children younger than 18 years old; *or*
- a visibly pregnant woman, or a woman able to prove that she is pregnant; *or*
- an asylum seeker who is disabled but is not considered to have clear and urgent care needs; *or*
- an asylum seeker whose individual needs appear to require special consideration.[47]

If you apply for asylum on arrival or shortly afterwards at the Asylum Screening Unit in Croydon and are street homeless, you should be given initial accommodation (usually, a full-board hostel). If you need to apply for support at a later stage and also need to apply for temporary support, you can apply via Migrant Help, although it is also possible to apply via other voluntary sector organisations.

Concerns have been expressed that the Home Office sometimes adopts an overly restrictive test of whether it appears that applicants 'may' be destitute.[48] If the Home Office refuses you temporary support, it will email its reasons to Migrant Help, which will communicate them to you. There is no right of appeal: the only method of challenging a decision to refuse temporary support is by judicial review. If temporary support is granted, initial accommodation will continue until, either:

- (if your application for section 95 support is granted) the day on which you travel to your dispersal accommodation; *or*
- shortly (sometimes the next working day) after your application for section 95 is refused (although, in practice, many appellants are permitted to remain in initial accommodation until after their appeal, particularly if they have minor children dependants); *or*
- 28 days after your asylum claim is granted by the Home Office or on appeal; *or*
- 21 days after your application for asylum claim has been refused by the Home Office or on appeal.

3. Section 4 support

The procedure for applying for section 4 support is very similar to applying for section 95 support (see p517). You use the same Form ASF1, which can be obtained from Migrant Help or online from gov.uk/asylum-support/how-to-claim. There are additional sections at the end of Form ASF1 that you should complete to show the grounds on which you are eligible for section 4 support.

Most section 4 applications are dealt with by a centralised team in Leeds. As with section 95 applications, communication with the Home Office is via Migrant Help (see p481). If and when the Home Office decides that you should receive support and has made the necessary arrangements with an accommodation provider, you will be notified of the travel arrangements to the dispersal area (see p548). There is no interim or emergency support available. It is, therefore, crucial to submit all the necessary information and documentation with your application form, since if you supply insufficient or ambiguous information, your application will be rejected or the Home Office will write to you requesting more information, which will delay any support that may be provided.

Significant administrative delays are an unfortunate feature of section 4 decision making. Although the Home Office should provide support as soon as your eligibility is established, there are routine delays. Home Office policy has been to give accommodation providers up to 14 days in which to provide accommodation once entitlement has been established, but that often takes longer.

There are also specific timescales for making decisions on applications for section 4 support based on further submissions (see p499). Home Office policy is to make such decisions within five working days and, for priority applicants, within two working days. Priority applicants include people who are street homeless, families with minors, disabled people, elderly people, pregnant women, persons who have been subjected to torture, rape or other serious forms of psychological, physical or sexual violence, and potential victims of trafficking.[49]

Proving you are entitled to section 4 support

To be entitled to section 4 support, you must prove:

- you are destitute (see p520); *and*
- you are eligible – ie:
  - (a) you have made a claim for asylum that was rejected; *and*
  - (b) you fall into one of the categories set out in regulations 3(2)(a)–(e) of the Immigration and Asylum (Provision of Accommodation to Failed Asylum-Seekers) Regulations 2005 (see p495).

Proving you are destitute for section 4 support

The evidence you need to submit to prove that you are destitute is the same as for a section 95 application (see p520).

Proving you are eligible for section 4 support

You need to show that:

- you are a person who has made an asylum claim that has been rejected (see below); *and*
- you meet one of the section 4 criteria for support (see p531).

Proving your asylum claim has been rejected

This is generally straightforward because in the vast majority of cases, Home Office records show that your asylum claim was refused, and any appeal against the refusal has been dismissed. In general, therefore, no specific evidence of this fact is required in addition to your completed Form ASF1.

Occasionally, cases arise in which there is some uncertainty about whether an asylum claim has been 'rejected'.

- If you lodged an appeal against a negative asylum decision out of time, your asylum claim is treated as having been determined (see p483). That is, unless and until permission is granted to extend time for appealing, following which you will be treated as an asylum seeker again, and eligible for section 95 support.
- If you claimed asylum and then absconded, your claim may subsequently have been treated by the Home Office as impliedly withdrawn. If you later claim

asylum support (possibly years later), your eligibility for section 4 support depends on whether your impliedly withdrawn asylum claim was 'rejected',[50] and that might not be clear from the papers in your possession.

In a minority of such cases, it is complicated to prove that you are a rejected asylum seeker, and you should seek expert advice.

Proving you meet one of section 4 criteria for support

The section 4 criteria for support are set out in regulation 3(2)(a)–(e) of the Immigration and Asylum (Provision of Accommodation to Failed Asylum-Seekers) Regulations 2005 (see p495). The onus is on you to show that you meet the criteria, and a substantial amount of work may be necessary to do so. **Note:** for each of the scenarios considered at p497, the evidence you should consider providing in support of your application is considered below.

Proving you are taking all reasonable steps to leave the UK

You must show you are taking all reasonable steps to leave the UK or place yourself in a position in which you are able to leave the UK. This involves providing evidence that your approach has been proactive. If the Home Office can show that there is just one reasonable step that you could have taken but didn't, your claim is liable to be refused.

Reasonable steps might include:

- applying to the Home Office for voluntary departure;
- complying with the Home Office's re-documentation process – eg providing bio-data or attending an interview;
- asking the Home Office for assistance in obtaining a travel document;
- contacting and/or attending your embassy to request a travel document;
- completing an application for a travel document; *and*
- contacting the authorities or family members in your home country for help in obtaining identity documents so that a travel document can be issued to you.

It is important to carefully itemise the steps you have taken and to provide supporting evidence if possible, such as copies of any letters or emails you have sent, and documents you have signed in connection with a voluntary return, or an application for an identity or travel document. You should also keep a written record of all your dealings by telephone and in person with Home Office or Immigration Service officials, and officials in your home country in the UK and abroad.

Proving that you are unable to leave UK for medical reasons

If you apply for support on this ground, you must submit a completed medical declaration ('section 4(2) medical declaration'), available on gov.uk. The medical declaration must be completed by your GP or a specialist medical practitioner. The declaration must state that you are unable to leave the UK because of your medical condition. The Home Office pays a fee to doctors for completing this form.[51]

When asking the medical professional to complete the declaration, point out the method of travel (eg, by plane) and how many hours it will take to travel to and wait at the UK international airport as well as the number of hours to travel by air to your country of origin and home area. When deciding whether to grant support, the Home Office does not consider your doctor's opinion that you should be allowed to stay in the UK on compassionate grounds or to finish a course of treatment or to get medical treatment that may be unavailable in your own country. If your doctor says that, the Home Office might discount the report, believing that your doctor has applied the wrong test.

The Home Office accepts that a woman cannot travel during the period of 'around' six weeks before the expected date of giving birth and six weeks after the birth.[52] You must provide medical documentation (usually Form MAT B1 issued by your GP or midwife) to confirm the pregnancy and expected date of birth or the birth certificate with your application form. The Home Office recognises that a woman may be unable to travel for a longer period if there are particular medical problems with the pregnancy, so you may be eligible for section 4 support earlier in your pregnancy. You can also argue that, according to the NHS, 'the length of a normal pregnancy varies between about 37 and 42 weeks', although the expected delivery date is 'calculated at 40 weeks from the first day of your last period'.[53] However, only 5 per cent of babies are born on their due date; a substantial number of babies are born up to three weeks before their expected due date. The Asylum Support Tribunal has accepted this argument, in combination with evidence of complications in pregnancy, as evidence of the need to provide support earlier than six weeks before the expected date of delivery.

You should also consider providing evidence of how your social circumstances are affecting your pregnancy. So, for example, if you are experiencing any form of abuse or if you are unable to sleep and eat properly, include this information on the application form.

Proving that there is no viable route of return

At the time of writing, there is no country to which this provision applies (see p496).

Proving that you have applied for a judicial review

Although this is a free-standing ground in regulation 3(2)(d), in practice it is almost always simpler to rely on judicial review proceedings under regulation 3(2)(e) (see below). Unlike under reg 3(2)(d), under reg 3(2)(e), provided that a pre-action protocol letter has been sent and you are awaiting a reply, there is no express requirement that permission to apply for judicial review has been granted or even that proceedings have been issued. That applies in England, Wales and Northern Ireland; there is no such express requirement in Scotland. See p534.

Proving that section 4 support is necessary to prevent breach of human rights

This category of cases covers a wide range of scenarios. In each case, the law recognises that it would be unreasonable to expect you to make a voluntary return (and, by so doing, avoid destitution). **Note:** the Asylum Support Tribunal continues on occasion to apply the test of whether it is reasonable to expect you to make a voluntary departure.[54] For section 4 applicants, this test is likely to be easier to apply to the facts of your case than the test in the current policy[55] of 'legal or practical obstacles' to returning home (although the meaning is essentially the same and both tests are still used).

Precisely what evidence you need depends on the facts of your case, but as a general rule, some objective evidence, including evidence from your medical practitioner and/or from your immigration solicitor, to support your claim will be necessary.

Proving a fresh claim for asylum

If you have made or intend to make fresh representations to the Home Office with a request that they be considered as a fresh claim for asylum, the Home Office (or, if your application is refused and you appeal, the Asylum Support Tribunal) considers whether:

- you have already made further representations; *and*
- whether those further representations, when considered with the material you previously submitted in support of your asylum claim, are hopeless – ie, bound to fail.

Although the Asylum Support Tribunal has indicated that it will not generally allow appeals on the basis of a mere intention to submit further representations (ie, they have not yet been submitted to the Home Office), there are frequent exceptions to this rule. If you are applying for section 4 support but still have not submitted your further representations, it is crucial, if possible, to put evidence before the Home Office and the Asylum Support Tribunal to demonstrate that any delay in submitting your further representations is not your fault. For example, delays that might justify a departure from the general rule that further representations need already to have been submitted before you can rely on their existence to claim section 4 support might include:

- there was a delay in obtaining an appointment from the Home Office's Further Submissions Unit, particularly if the delay was lengthy and the further representations were ready and clearly had merit; at the time of writing, due to the COVID-19 pandemic, this argument is not possible because further representations are no longer submitted at a face-to-face appointment; *or*

- a medical report could not be completed because the medical expert cancelled an appointment (through no fault of yours); *or*
- there was a delay due to your immigration solicitor's error (particularly if a date for submission of the fresh claim has been fixed and is imminent).

To demonstrate that your further representations are not hopeless, it is important to obtain a letter from your immigration solicitor:

- enclosing a copy of the further representations (in draft if not yet submitted), or at least the gist of the proposed representations if they have not yet been drafted;
- enclosing a copy of the determination of the First-tier Tribunal (Immigration and Asylum Chamber) dismissing your appeal against the refusal of your asylum claim. That is necessary because the immigration judge's findings are the starting point in determining the merit of your further representations, so both the Home Office and the Asylum Support Tribunal consider the immigration judge's findings to determine whether your further representations are hopeless;
- identifying the fresh evidence or development you rely on, explaining, in as much detail as possible what is new, and why, despite the immigration judge's findings, the new material means that your asylum claim has a realistic prospect of success; *and*
- (if the further representations have not yet been finalised or submitted), estimating when those things will be done.

Proving an out of time appeal

Obtain a letter from your immigration solicitor explaining that an appeal was made out of time, and remains under consideration by the tribunal or court to which you are seeking to appeal. You should also enclose documentary evidence that your out of time application was received by the tribunal or court concerned.

Proving judicial review

If you have issued or threatened judicial review proceedings, you should obtain a letter from your judicial review solicitor, enclosing a copy of your judicial review claim form. If the claim has not yet been issued, a copy of the solicitor's judicial review pre-action protocol letter and any response received. You must show that you are progressing a claim if one has not yet been issued (eg, by showing that your solicitors have applied for legal aid and are awaiting a decision), and that your judicial review claim has some merit. A letter addressing these issues from your immigration solicitor is likely to be helpful.

Proving you have applied for leave to enter or remain under Article 8 of the European Convention on Human Rights

You should obtain a letter from your immigration solicitor, as above, enclosing a copy of the application and explaining why it is not hopeless.

Proving you have applied for leave as a stateless person

You should obtain a letter from your immigration solicitor enclosing a copy of your statelessness application, and confirming the stage it has reached. If the application has been refused and you have challenged the refusal by way of judicial review, you should provide evidence of the judicial review claim, as above.

Proving you have applied to the European Court of Human Rights

You should obtain a letter from your immigration solicitor enclosing a copy of your application to the European Court of Human Rights (ECtHR), explaining the stage at which your application has reached, its merits, and confirming that you exhausted all remedies in the UK before applying to the ECtHR.

---

4. Decisions on applications

If your application is granted

If the Home Office decides to provide you with support, it informs you in writing that your application has been accepted and about the package of support you will receive. Unless you applied for subsistence-only section 95 support (see p517), your package of support will consist of accommodation that is:

- generally provided outside London and the southeast of England (see p543);
- subject to conditions, breach of which can in some cases lead to you being prosecuted (see p492) and/or evicted (see p488);
- subject to termination in certain specified circumstances (see p487 and p503).

See Chapter 23 for what support you will get.

If your application is refused

If your application is refused, you will receive a letter explaining why, and informing you of your right of appeal, together with an appeal form. See Chapter 24 for information about bringing an appeal (p553) and about further applications for support (p570).

Notes

1. Section 95 support

1 Reg 3(1) AS Regs
2 Reg 3(2) AS Regs
3 See *MYA v SSHD* AS/19/02/39259, 5 March 2019, for an example of the Asylum Support Tribunal awarding accommodation only.
4 Reg 3(3) AS Regs
5 Reg 3(6) AS Regs
6 Reg 3(3) AS Regs
7 Form ASF1 and the accompanying guidance are available at: gov.uk/government/publications/application-for-asylum-support-form-asf1
8 ss105-07 IAA 1999
9 Reg 3(5) AS Regs
10 s57 NIAA 2002; reg 3(5A)-(5B) AS Regs; see also Home Office guidance, 'Asylum Support (Asylum Instructions)', *Asylum Support: policy bulletins – instructions,* Ch 10, available at: gov.uk/government/collections/asylum-support-asylum-instructions
11 For example, see Asylum Support Tribunal appeal ref: AS/17/03/36540. The wording of the Home Office s57 letter usually plays a crucial role in this type of appeal. Further information is available in Asylum Support Appeals Project, *Briefing Note on When It Is Possible To Appeal a Decision under Section 75 of the Nationality and Immigration Act 2002*, September 2016, available at asaproject.org/resources/briefing-notes.
12 s95(4) IAA 1999; reg 5(1) AS Regs
13 Reg 7(a) AS Regs. Note that if you are required to prove that you are destitute at a time when you already being supported (eg, if the Home Office considers discontinuing your support), the time in which you have to prove that you are likely to become destitute is 56, not 14, days (Reg 7(b) AS Regs).
14 s95(3) IAA 1999
15 Home Office guidance, *Assessing Destitution*, available at gov.uk/government/publications/assessing-destitution-instruction
16 s95 (7) IAA 1999 and reg 6(4)-(5) AS Regs
17 Reg 2(4) and 6(4) AS Regs
18 Reg 6(6) AS Regs
19 Reg 6(3) AS Regs
20 However, the Asylum Support Tribunal has held in one case that: 'As a general rule, however, if an item of personal possession can be easily converted into cash (and vice versa) e.g. gold jewellery, or stocks and shares, it may be reasonable to treat such possessions as cash, savings or investments because they are easily converted into cash' (*ZN v SSHD* AS/17/09/37288 at para 24). Since all possessions can be easily sold, this general proposition would drive a coach and horses through regulation 6 of the Asylum Support Regulations 2000, and, in the author's view, must be wrong. Chapter 20 of the Home Office guidance 'Asylum Support (Asylum Instructions)', *Asylum Support: policy bulletins – instructions,* is devoted to asylum seekers' 'possessions', and is inconsistent with the general principle that such possessions need to be sold to fund asylum support.
21 While the duty to report a change of circumstances and the criminal consequences of failing to do so are clear if you are receiving s95 support, the extent of any such duty is not so clear if you are receiving s4 support. That said, obtaining s4 support to which you are not entitled (eg, if you cease to be destitute) may well be a criminal offence, although this specific issue is beyond the scope of this book.
22 'Asylum Support (Asylum Instructions)', *Asylum Support: policy bulletins*, Ch 7.2
23 Home Office guidance, 'Asylum Support (Asylum Instructions)', *Applications for Additional Support*, p4
24 s95(7)(b) IAA 1999 and Reg 9 AS Regs
25 s95(7)(b) IAA 1999; reg 9(1) and (2) AS Regs
26 *R (Refugee Action) v SSHD* [2014] EWHC 1033, para 96

27 *R (Refugee Action) v SSHD* [2014] EWHC 1033, para 95
28 Reg 9(6) AS Regs
29 Home Office policy, *Applications for additional support*
30 s95(5)(a) IAA 1999; reg 8(1)(a)-(b) and (3) AS Regs
31 Reg 8(2) AS Regs
32 IA 2014
33 Home Office guidance, 'Asylum Support (Asylum Instructions)', *Assessing Destitution (v8)*, p15. In relation to eligibility for s4 support, the guidance states: 'Failed asylum seekers who can satisfy one of the conditions set out in the regulation 3(2) of the Immigration and Asylum (Provision of Accommodation to Failed Asylum-Seekers) Regulations 2005 will also normally be granted permission to rent.'
34 Reg 8(3)(a) AS Regs
35 Reg 8(4) AS Regs. 'District', for these purposes, has the same meaning as in s217(3) Housing Act 1996 (Reg 8(6)(b) AS Regs)
36 Reg 8(3)(b) AS Regs
37 Reg 8(5)(a)-(c) AS Regs
38 Reg 8(3)(g) and (6)(a) AS Regs; Home Office guidance, 'Asylum Support (Asylum Instructions)', *Domestic Abuse: responding to reports of domestic abuse from asylum seekers*
39 Although Form ASF1 guidance notes ask for information if you are in fear of 'a person who normally stays with you as a member of your family'.
40 See Home Office guidance, 'Asylum Support (Asylum Instructions)', *Asylum Support: policy bulletins – instructions,* Ch 17
41 Their contact details can be found in the Home Office guidance, 'Asylum Support (Asylum Instructions)', *Domestic Abuse: responding to reports of domestic abuse from asylum seekers*, July 2019.
42 See Asylum Support Appeals Project Factsheet 18: *Asylum Support for Survivors of Domestic Abuse*, available at: asaproject.org/resources
43 Over the next 14 days (on a new application for support), or over the next 56 days (if the Home Office is minded to discontinue your existing support).
44 Home Office guidance, 'Asylum Support (Asylum Instructions)', *Assessing Destitution*, p14
45 At the time of writing, the weekly amount per person is £39.63 (also at the time of writing,the government has confirmed that reg 10(2) AS Regs will shortly be amended to reflect this figure). Additional sums may be claimed in certain circumstances (see Home Office guidance, 'Asylum Support (Asylum Instructions)', *Applications for Additional Support*).

2. **Section 98 support**

46 You can also apply for temporary support before you have submitted an application for section 95 support in completed Form ASF1. If you apply for temporary support before you submit Form ASF1, the Home Office may grant support on condition that a completed Form ASF1 is submitted to the Home Office within two working days.
47 'Asylum Support (Asylum Instructions)', *Asylum Support: policy bulletin – instructions*, para 1.1.1
48 For example, see Refugee Action's July 2017 report, *Slipping through the cracks*, available at: refugee-action.org.uk/resource/asylum-support-delays-report

3. **Section 4 support**

49 'Asylum Support (Asylum Instructions)', *Asylum Support, Section 4(2): policy and process*, p14
50 See *HMA v SSHD*: AS/20/08/42323, available at gov.uk/asylum-support-tribunal-decisions, for an analysis of the legal position by the Asylum Support Tribunal.
51 Home Office guidance, 'Asylum Support (Asylum Instructions)', *Asylum Support, Section 4(2): policy and process*, p11, available at gov.uk/government/collections/asylum-support-asylum-instructions
52 Home Office guidance, 'Asylum Support (Asylum Instructions)', *Asylum Support, Section 4(2): policy and process*, p11, available at gov.uk/government/collections/asylum-support-asylum-instructions
53 See 'Your pregnancy and baby guide' at nhs.uk
54 For example, a decision of the Principal Judge dated 23 October 2020, AS/20/09/42386 and 42397, at para 47
55 Home Office guidance, 'Asylum Support (Asylum Instructions)', Asylum Support, Section 4(2): policy and process, p13

Chapter 23

Asylum support: payment and accommodation

This chapter covers:

1. Section 95 support

Section 95 asylum support is provided in one of the following ways:[1]

- accommodation and 'subsistence' (cash, via an ASPEN card; see p539) to cover your and your dependants' essential living needs; *or*
- subsistence-only support for your essential living needs if you already have accommodation; *or*
- expenses (other than legal expenses) in connection with your asylum application; *or*
- if your circumstances are exceptional, any other form of support that the Home Office thinks is necessary.[2]

Note: the Home Office does not have to take into account any preference you or your dependants have as to how the support is provided or arranged.[3]

When deciding what support to give you, the Home Office must take into account any income, support or assets (see p520) that you or your dependants have, or which might reasonably be available to you.[4]

Support to meet your essential living needs

If the Home Office decides you need support for your essential living needs, the general rule is that you are provided with cash on an ASPEN card (see below) on a weekly basis.[5]

Amount of support

The Home Office reviews the amount of support annually. Since 10 August 2015, there has been a flat rate per person, regardless of age. The current rate is £39.63. This figure was set out in a letter dated 27 October 2020 from Home Office minister Chris Philp MP and was broken down in an annex to the minister's letter:

Categories of 'need'	ONS Expenditure data from 2018/19 (adjusted for single person) / 2020 market research	After Home Office adjustment and inflation
Food and non-alcoholic drinks	£25.23	£26.49
Adjusted for inflation since the data was collected – CPI as at March 2020 (1.5%)	2020 market research	£26.89
Toiletries	2020 market research	£0.69
Non-prescription medicines	2020 market research	£0.35
Laundry/toilet paper	2020 market research	£0.43
Clothing and footwear	2020 market research	£3.01
Travel	2020 market research	£4.70
Communications	2020 market research	£3.56
Subtotal		£12.74
Total		£39.63

Home Office guidance states that this:

> should generally be sufficient to cover the following needs: food, clothing, toiletries, non-prescription medication, household cleaning items, communications, travel, and the ability to access social, cultural and religious life (covered by the funding provision for communications and travel).

Furthermore: "the level of the cash allowance takes into consideration that other essential living needs (for example, warmth, cooking, lighting) are covered by the provision of accommodation that is free of both rent and utility bills (fuel and water) and is also fully furnished and equipped with both household goods (for example kitchenware, access to laundry services) and linens (towels and sheets, for example).'[6]

There are additional payments of:[7]

- £3 a week for pregnant women; *and*
- £5 a week for babies under one; *and*
- £3 a week for children between the ages of one and three.

In 2017, the Home Office introduced a new method of issuing financial support called an 'ASPEN' card. This replaced cash payments received by asylum seekers on a weekly basis from a designated post office. The ASPEN card is a pre-paid visa chip and pin and can be used in the same way as a debit card to pay for items in shops or to withdraw cash from most ATMs. The support is uploaded onto the card weekly. There is no limit on the amount that can be carried over from one week to the next, but the Home Office monitors spending. It can also monitor the location of where the ASPEN card has been used and is therefore alerted if you have spent time away from the place where you have been provided with accommodation.

Legal challenges to the rates of asylum support

Before August 2015, the rates of asylum support were based on the equivalent of 70 per cent of the applicable amount of income support (IS), without any premiums, to which an adult would otherwise be entitled if s/he qualified for IS and had no other income (see CPAG'S *Welfare Benefits and Tax Credits Handbook* for more details). Initially, the rates were increased in April every year, but from April 2011 the rates were frozen, meaning a cut in real terms over several years.

In 2013, the charity Refugee Action brought a judicial review challenge against the Home Secretary's decision to freeze the rate of asylum support. This was upheld by the High Court in April 2014,[8] which ruled that the Home Secretary had acted irrationally and failed to take all relevant factors into account, in accordance with her duties under the European Union Reception Directive and the Immigration and Asylum Act 1999 to provide for asylum seekers' essential living needs. Following the judgment, the Home Secretary reconsidered the level of support, but decided it should remain unchanged. In April 2015, the rate for single asylum seekers over 18 was increased by by 33 pence and then, from August 2015, the rates were cut to £36.95, representing a significant reduction in the rate previously paid for children in families (which had previously been £52.96 per week). In 2016, there was a further challenge to the level of support, but the Home Office's methodology for setting the rates was found to be lawful.[9]

Exceptional payments

The Home Office can provide additional support if the normal rate of support is not enough to meet your essential living needs and you can show that your particular circumstances are 'exceptional'.[10] The Home Office's ability to provide exceptional payments was a key part of its case in the Refugee Action judicial review (see above), and so you should not hesitate to apply for exceptional payments if you need any. For example, the High Court found that it was unreasonable to refuse a separated father help with the travel costs he incurred in visiting his young child because the Home Office was unable to provide him with accommodation closer than 130 miles away.[11] The court suggested that reasonable travel costs should enable him to visit his son at least fortnightly.

The Home Office has an application form (Form ASF2)[12] and guidance that allows asylum seekers to apply for exceptional payments for any 'exceptional needs'. You must give details on the form of your needs and circumstances, the support required and its likely duration, together with documentary evidence to support your application.

If your application is refused, the Home Office should provide the reasons in writing. However, if an application is refused, the only remedy is judicial review.

Health benefits

As part of your section 95 support package, the Home Office should issue you with a certificate (HC2), enabling you to get free NHS prescriptions, dental treatment, sight tests and wigs together with vouchers towards the cost of glasses and contact lenses. The HC2 certificate itself tells you how to use it and what you can use it for. If you have already paid for any of the above items or for travel to and from hospital for NHS treatment, you may be able to claim the money back.

Maternity payments

You may be eligible for a one-off maternity payment of £300.[13] You must apply in writing between eight weeks before the expected birth and six weeks after, enclosing evidence – eg, a birth certificate, Form MAT B1 from your GP or some other original formal evidence. A payment can also be made if you are a supported parent or a parent applying for support and you have a child under three months old who was born outside the UK. It is important to make this application in time. If it is made late, your application is likely to be refused. The Home Office policy bulletin that allows maternity payments does not say whether or not it is possible to make a late claim, but there is scope for payment in exceptional circumstances, so it may be worth applying if you can give good reasons for the delay.[14]

Expenses in connection with your asylum application

The Home Office may meet some of the expenses connected to your asylum application.[15] These do not include 'legal' expenses – eg, the costs of paying your lawyer to prepare your case and represent you.

Eligible expenses include the cost of preparing and copying documents and travelling to Home Office interviews,[16] and may include the cost of:

- sending letters and faxes to obtain further evidence; *and*
- your travel expenses (or those of your witnesses) to attend your appeal; *and*
- medical or other examinations in connection with your application.

Note: you may also be able to apply for exceptional payments (see p540).

Although not paid as asylum support, the cost of your fares incurred in travelling to comply with any immigration reporting requirements can be reclaimed from the Home Office if you live more than three miles from the reporting centre.[17] You must claim these at the reporting centre. It is only possible to claim the travel costs for attending your next reporting date (ie, in advance), not costs already incurred. Some reporting centres are very strict in applying the wording of the guidance. This says that the test is a three-mile 'radius', interpreted as the straight-line distance between the reporting centre and your accommodation, not whether the distance that you must travel is more than three miles. If necessary, you should argue that the guidance should be interpreted more sensibly.

Education and sports facilities

If you are receiving asylum support, the Home Office has the power to provide funding for the following services:[18]

- adult education, including English language lessons; *and*
- sporting or other developmental activities.

The Home Office is not under a duty to fund these services, which vary in each dispersal region.

Your children must attend school if they are aged five to 17. All state schools are free of charge and your children may be able to get free school meals and a clothing grant. You should check with your local authority.

Backdating support

There is often a delay between applying for support and getting paid. This delay can be serious if you are without support in the meantime. Unlike social security benefits, there are no rules in the legislation identifying the date from when support must be provided.

It is arguable that support should be payable from the date the Home Office receives a full and valid claim – ie, an application that shows that you are destitute and eligible for support. That should be the case no matter what delays are caused by the Home Office or the appeal procedure.

However, in practice, the Home Office does not backdate support to the date of the application. Support may sometimes be backdated to the date of the decision if there was then a further delay before payment started. If you have applied for subsistence-only support, you may be able to argue that a back payment should be made to your ASPEN card to the date your support should have started. If you have applied for accommodation and subsistence, you may, in any event, be in a full-board hostel until the date you are moved to your dispersal accommodation and your subsistence payments start. If you are not in full-board accommodation, the Home Office pays you a daily subsistence through your accommodation provider until you are dispersed.

Once you are getting support, the Home Office recognises in its policy guidance[19] that awards of asylum support can be backdated if payments have been missed through no fault of the applicant. The guidance gives examples of what the Home Office accepts are legitimate reasons why an applicant may not have collected her/his support that include, but are not limited to, the following:

- reporting event/asylum interview; *and*
- illness; *and*
- hospitalisation; *and*
- travel difficulties; *and*
- difficulties with your application registration card.

Note: this policy relates to missed payments of support *after* a favourable decision on eligibility has already been made, not to Home Office delays in processing an initial application for support *before* a favourable decision has been made.

Contributions to support

When deciding what level of support to give you as a destitute asylum seeker, the Home Office must take into account any income, support and assets that are available (or might reasonably be expected to be available) to you or any dependant (see p485).[20] If you have income and/or assets, it can decide that you should make a contribution to the cost of your support rather than reducing the level of support provided.[21] If that is the case, you are notified of the amount and you must make payments directly to the Home Office. If you are required to make a contribution, the Home Office may also make it a condition of your support that you pay your contributions promptly.[22] In practice, the Home Office tends to delay the start of the financial support or deduct the relevant amount from the initial support payment.

Note: If you have, in the past, litigated against the Home Office about something other than a protection claim or a nationality dispute, and have been ordered to pay the Home Office's costs, you may be required to contribute towards your litigation debt from your asylum support. See Home Office guidance, *Suitability: unpaid litigation costs*.

Section 95 accommodation and dispersal

The Home Office does not own and provide accommodation but makes arrangements with private contractors that provide the accommodation throughout the UK.[23]

When deciding the location and nature of the accom~odation you are given, the Home Office must consider:[24]

- you are only being provided with accommodation on a temporary basis until your application for asylum has been dealt with (including any period during which you are appealing); *and*
- it is desirable to provide accommodation for asylum seekers in areas where there is a good supply of accommodation – eg, outside London, given that there is an acute shortage of affordable accommodation in the London area.

The Home Office does not take into account your preferences on:

- the area in which you would like the accommodation to be located;[25] *or*
- the nature of the accommodation to be provided;[26] *or*
- the nature and standard of the fixtures and fittings in the accommodation.[27]

However, the Home Office may still take into account your individual circumstances if they relate to your accommodation needs.[28]

The majority of applications for asylum and asylum support are made in the southeast of England. The Home Office has a strict policy of 'dispersal', which makes it difficult to succeed in arguing against being moved away from London and the South East or against being moved away from the area in which you already live (see p543).

However, there are exceptions to the general rule, which are considered by reference to the Home Office's policy on dispersal.[29] Potentially relevant factors include:[30]

- disruption to existing medical treatment or disability assistance; *or*
- disruption to a child's final school or college year, leading up to GCSE, Scottish Highers, AS or A-level exams (or their equivalents), provided the child has been enrolled at that school for a significant part of the previous school year.'

The above list is not exhaustive, so the Home Office may consider delaying dispersal in other circumstances. If you need to be accommodated in a particular location, you should carefully consider the Home Office's allocation of accommodation and healthcare needs and pregnancy dispersal policies, and seek specialist advice before submitting a location request to the Home Office.

Helen Bamber Foundation and Freedom from Torture

If you are awaiting assessment from Helen Bamber Foundation or Freedom from Torture (both of which have London offices), the Home Office may delay dispersal pending a decision by those organisations about whether to offer you treatment. If you are receiving treatment from either organisation, the Home Office may provide you with accommodation in London travel zones 1–6 or within a one-hour travelling distance from one of Freedom from Torture's regional offices in Birmingham, Manchester, Newcastle or Glasgow.[31]

Healthcare needs and pregnancy

The Home Office may delay dispersal on medical grounds, if you can provide evidence either that the medical treatment you are receiving is not available elsewhere or that transferring your care to a dispersal area would be unreasonably disruptive.

Note: as a general rule, some disruption to your healthcare may be insufficient, to delay dispersal because the guidance states: 'the degree of disruption [should be balanced] against the overriding principle of allocating accommodation on a "no choice basis" and outside London and the South East'.[32] However there is detailed guidance about specific health scenarios that should be carefully considered (see below).

The following are some of the circumstances in which the Home Office may delay dispersal:

- HIV;[33] *or*
- active TB;[34] *or*
- severe mental health problems;[35] *or*
- pregnancy;[36] *or*
- if treatment is ongoing and available only in the area where the applicant is living;[37] *or*
- if replication of treatment is difficult to implement, particularly in cases where the treatment is broad in its nature – eg, in cases which an applicant has more than one ailment that requires more than one specialist to provide treatment, and the individual has an active support network in that area;[38] *or*
- if the applicant is in receipt of specialist treatment that may be hard to replicate at advanced stages of treatment, especially if invasive surgery or intensive treatment is required;[39] *or*
- if invasive surgery has been booked to take place within a month or a person is recovering from an operation. If the applicant is recovering from an operation, dispersal that requires long-distance travel should not take place until the individual has been medically assessed as fit to undertake the journey;[40] *or*
- if invasive surgery has been booked to take place in excess of a month's time but evidence has been supplied that there will be a delay in rebooking the surgery at an alternative hospital, and the delay would have an adverse impact on the health of the applicant, and travel from out of area dispersal accommodation to the treating hospital is not appropriate;[41] *or*
- if it is necessary to arrange continuity of care – eg, a person is undergoing kidney dialysis;[42] *or*
- if there is a presence, or suspicion, of infectious and notifiable diseases – see patient.info/doctor/notifiable-diseases;[43] *or*
- if referral or admission to secondary care services is necessary due to acute need.[44]

The above list is not exhaustive.

Family ties

It is possible to request that accommodation be provided near to family if dispersal away from the area would disrupt family relationships. The Home Office must have regard to the right to respect for family life protected by Article 8 of the European Convention on Human Rights. The right to respect family for life is a qualified right, which needs to be balanced against the public interest and does not prevail if the state's countervailing action (eg, to disperse you away from your family members) is necessary and proportionate in the public interest. The guidance observes that disruption to relationships with friends and family does not usually outweigh public interest in dispersal out of London and south-east England. If dispersal would interfere with the rights of a parent and a child to maintain regular contact, that may be taken into account in dispersal decisions, including in some cases by the payment of travel expenses to enable regular visits to be made.[45]

Children's education

Requests for accommodation in a particular area to maintain continuity in a child's education are not usually successful but may be considered favourably if:[46]

- the child has started her/his final school or college year leading up to her/his GCSE, Scottish Highers, AS or A-level exams (or their equivalents), provided s/he has been enrolled at that school for a significant part of the previous school year;
- a child with special educational needs has gained entry to an appropriate school, unless it is clear that accommodation can be arranged near to another location where there is an appropriate school to which the child can be transferred.

Other factors

The guidance lists other factors that might be the subject of a request to be accommodated in a particular area, including the wish to remain close to other members of your ethnic group, your place of worship or your current solicitors. It will be difficult to succeed with a request for accommodation in a particular area based on these factors alone because you are likely to be able to access members of your community, a suitable place of worship and new solicitors in most dispersal areas.

2. Section 98 support

Section 98, or 'temporary' support (see p492), is intended for asylum seekers who appear to the Home Office to be destitute and require short-term accommodation while a section 95 application is being processed. It is generally provided in a full-board Home Office hostel. However, in some locations, the accommodation is self-catering and cash is provided to buy food (see p528).

3. Section 4 support

Section 4 support is provided as a package of accommodation and financial support. There is no subsistence-only support. The Home Office issues section 4 support recipients with ASPEN cards (see p539). These can be used to make payments in participating shops. Unlike section 95 support, section 4 recipients cannot use their ASPEN card to withdraw cash from ATMs.

Unlike section 95 support, there are no specific provisions to reduce the value of any support provided under section 4, to require you to make contributions, or to recover the value of support if it has been provided to someone who is not entitled to support.

Financial element of section 4 support

The amount of the financial element of section 4 support is not fixed in the legislation but is decided by the Secretary of State for the Home Department. When the regulations were made in 2005, the value of the vouchers was set at £35 per individual – ie, for each adult and child. The amount is now the same as the section 95 allowance (£39.63 at the time of writing). See p539 for more information about how that figure is broken down.

It is possible to carry your balance over from one week to the next – eg, to save for more expensive items. However, if too much balance is accrued, the Home Office may query whether you are destitute.

Applying for additional section 4 support

There has been criticism of the low level of financial support provided under section 4 and, to comply with a European Directive, the government introduced additional section 4 support in 2007.[47] This additional support can be claimed by refused asylum seekers (and/or their dependants) in certain prescribed circumstances.[48] **Note**: this additional support is not provided automatically. You must make an application to the Home Office, using the form *Application for Provision of Services or Facilities for Section 4 Service Users*. Guidance on what can be claimed and what evidence is required is contained in the guidance notes accompanying the application form[49] and in the Home Office's separate policy document on section 4.[50]

You can claim additional support:[51]

- for the costs of travel to receive healthcare treatment if a 'qualifying journey' is necessary. A **'qualifying journey'** is a single journey of at least three miles, or of any distance if:
  - you or your child are unable, or virtually unable, to walk up to three miles because of a physical impediment or for some other reason; *or*
  - you have at least one dependant aged under five years;
- for the costs of travel to register a birth;
- to obtain a child's full birth certificate;
- for telephone calls and letters (ie, stationery and postage) about medical treatment or care and to communicate with:
  - the Home Office;

  - a 'qualified person' – ie, a solicitor, barrister or authorised immigration adviser;
  - a court or tribunal;
  - a voluntary sector partner;
  - a Citizens Advice office;
  - a local authority;
  - an immigration officer;
  - the Secretary of State;
- if you are pregnant (up to £3 a week);
- if you have a child under one year (up to £5 a week);
- if you have a child between one and five years (up to £3 a week);
- for clothing for a child under 16 years old (up to £5 a week);
- for exceptional specific needs. The Home Office must be satisfied that there is an exceptional need (which may not be met by the above) for travel, telephone calls, stationery and postage, or essential living needs. These specific needs could include travel to your embassy.

There is also a one-off additional payment for pregnant women and new mothers similar to the maternity payment that can be made with section 95 support (see p541). The amount is £250 (£500 for twins) provided as a credit on your payment card. You should apply on the application form, with a MAT B1 certificate or birth certificate. You must apply between eight weeks before the expected due date and six weeks after the birth.

Many refused asylum seekers and others in receipt of section 4 support are required to sign in at an immigration reporting centre at regular intervals and may be able to reclaim their travel costs (see p14).

Section 4 accommodation and dispersal

Section 4 accommodation is in general provided on a no-choice basis. However, Home Office policy on section 4 states that:[52]

> The caseworker may exceptionally consider providing accommodation in a particular location if there are particular reasons to do so, for example medical reasons. The Asylum Support Medical Adviser is able to provide advice on: the general availability of medical treatment in a particular region of the UK that the person may need to access; the person's fitness to travel to the region; any specific type of accommodation the person may need to be provided with because of a medical reason.

The guidance proceeds to state that: 'Further information may be found in the Healthcare needs and pregnancy dispersal guidance', which is stated to apply to section 95 only. The policy determining the scope for requests for a departure from the general rule requiring dispersal is therefore the same as for section 95 (see p543).

No subsistence-only support

Subsistence-only support is not available under section 4. If you have friends or family who can provide you with accommodation but who cannot support you, the Home Office cannot provide you with the financial element of section 4 support unless you occupy Home Office accommodation.[53] You must therefore take up the offer of Home Office accommodation to receive payment card credits.

This situation can cause severe hardship and can seem absurd. You may have friends who can provide you with accommodation, companionship and social, psychological and moral support that may be crucial to you, and, it would be substantially less expensive for the government simply to provide you with the payment card without accommodation. You may, therefore, have to choose between living with your friends but remaining destitute (with the risk that your friends may then refuse to accommodate you), or possibly being relocated far from your friends to a place where you know no one and, if you are a single person, where you may have to share a room with strangers.

The Home Office has split adults (ie, older than 18 years) from their families in this way when they have had separate asylum applications. It is, therefore, important that you obtain advice from your immigration lawyer on whether to include a family member in your asylum claim as a dependant.

In one case, the High Court found that a refusal to provide support to a refused asylum seeker in a way that allowed him to continue to live with his British partner and child did not breach their right to family life under Article 8 of the European Convention on Human Rights, but the Home Office stated that it would make 'every effort' to house the applicant within a 'reasonable walking distance' of close family members.[54] If you are dispersed to accommodation that is a long distance from your family, you may still be able to claim travel expenses to visit close family members (see p547). If the familial relationship is strong and your dispersal very disruptive, you can challenge the dispersal by judicial review.

Notes

1. Section 95 support

1 s96(1) IAA 1999
2 s96(2) IAA 1999
3 s97(7) IAA 1999
4 Reg 12(3) AS Regs
5 Reg 10(1)(2) AS Regs
6 Home Office guidance, 'Asylum Support (Asylum Instructions)', *Applications for Additional Support*, p4
7 Reg 10A AS Regs, introduced by The Asylum Support (Amendment) Regulations 2003, No.241; see also Home Office guidance, 'Asylum Support (Asylum Instructions)', *Asylum Support: policy bulletins – instructions*, para 25.5, available at gov.uk/government/collections/asylum-support-asylum-instructions
8 *R (Refugee Action) v SSHD* [2014] EWHC 1033 (Admin)
9 *R (Ghulam, K, YT and RG) v SSHD* [2016] EWHC 2639 (Admin)
10 s96(2) IAA 1999
11 *R (MG) v SSHD* [2015] EWHC 3142 (Admin)
12 Available at gov.uk/government/publications/application-for-additional-asylum-support-form-asf2
13 Home Office guidance, 'Asylum Support (Asylum Instructions)', *Asylum Support: policy bulletins – instructions*, para 24.2, available at gov.uk/government/collections/asylum-support-asylum-instructions
14 Home Office guidance, 'Asylum Support (Asylum Instructions)', *Asylum Support: policy bulletins – instructions*, para 24.3, available at gov.uk/government/collections/asylum-support-asylum-instructions
15 s96(1)(c) IAA 1999
16 Expressly included in IAA 1999, Explanatory Notes, para 300 available at legislation.gov.uk/ukpga/1999/33/notes/division/5/14/1
17 Home Office, *Enforcement Instructions and Guidance*, Ch 22, para 22a.3.3, available at gov.uk/government/collections/enforcement-instructions-and-guidance
18 Sch 8 para 4 IAA 1999; reg 14 AS Regs
19 Home Office guidance, 'Asylum Support (Asylum Instructions)', *Asylum Support: policy bulletins – instructions*, Ch 15, available at gov.uk/government/collections/asylum-support-asylum-instructions
20 Reg 12(3) AS Regs
21 Reg 16(2) AS Regs
22 Reg 16(4) AS Regs. Conditions may generally be imposed under s95(9)-(12) IAA 1999.
23 ss99-100 IAA 1999
24 s97(1) IAA 1999
25 s97(2)(a) IAA 1999
26 Reg 13(2)(a) AS Regs
27 Reg 13(2)(b) AS Regs
28 Reg 13(2) AS Regs
29 Home Office guidance, 'Asylum Support (Asylum Instructions)', *Allocation of Accommodation Policy*
30 Home Office guidance, 'Asylum Support (Asylum Instructions)', *Allocation of Accommodation Policy*, available at gov.uk/government/collections/asylum-support-asylum-instructions
31 Home Office guidance, 'Asylum Support (Asylum Instructions)', *Allocation of Accommodation Policy*, pp11-13
32 Home Office guidance, 'Asylum Support (Asylum Instructions)', *Allocation of Accommodation Policy*, p8 available at gov.uk/government/collections/asylum-support-asylum-instructions
33 Home Office guidance, 'Asylum Support (Asylum Instructions)', *Healthcare Needs and Pregnancy Dispersal Policy*, pp19 and 31
34 Home Office guidance, 'Asylum Support (Asylum Instructions)', *Healthcare Needs and Pregnancy Dispersal Policy*, pp19 and 34
35 Home Office guidance, 'Asylum Support (Asylum Instructions)', *Healthcare Needs and Pregnancy Dispersal Policy*, pp19 and 35
36 Home Office guidance, 'Asylum Support (Asylum Instructions)', *Healthcare Needs and Pregnancy Dispersal Policy*, pp19 and 37

37 Home Office guidance, 'Asylum Support (Asylum Instructions)', *Healthcare Needs and Pregnancy Dispersal Policy*, p19
38 Home Office guidance, 'Asylum Support (Asylum Instructions)', *Healthcare Needs and Pregnancy Dispersal Policy*, p19
39 Home Office guidance, 'Asylum Support (Asylum Instructions)', *Healthcare Needs and Pregnancy Dispersal Policy*, p19
40 Home Office guidance, 'Asylum Support (Asylum Instructions)', *Healthcare Needs and Pregnancy Dispersal Policy*, p19
41 Home Office guidance, 'Asylum Support (Asylum Instructions)', *Healthcare Needs and Pregnancy Dispersal Policy*, p19
42 Home Office guidance, 'Asylum Support (Asylum Instructions)', *Healthcare Needs and Pregnancy Dispersal Policy*, p20
43 Home Office guidance, 'Asylum Support (Asylum Instructions)', *Healthcare Needs and Pregnancy Dispersal Policy*, p20
44 Home Office guidance, 'Asylum Support (Asylum Instructions)', *Healthcare Needs and Pregnancy Dispersal Policy*, p20
45 Home Office guidance, 'Asylum Support (Asylum Instructions)', *Allocation of Accommodation Policy*, p9
46 Home Office guidance, 'Asylum Support (Asylum Instructions)', *Allocation of Accommodation Policy*, p9

3. **Section 4 support**

47 The Immigration and Asylum (Provision of Services or Facilities) Regulations 2007, No.3627; Home Office guidance, 'Asylum Support (Asylum Instructions)', *Asylum Support, Section 4(2): policy and process*, p18, available at gov.uk/government/collections/asylum-support-asylum-instructions
48 Prescribed by the Immigration and Asylum (Provision of Services or Facilities) Regulations 2007, No.3627
49 gov.uk/government/application-for-section-4-extra-services-or-facilities
50 Home Office guidance, 'Asylum Support (Asylum Instructions)', *Asylum Support, Section 4(2): policy and process*, pp18-22
51 Home Office guidance, 'Asylum Support (Asylum Instructions)', *Asylum Support,Section 4(2): policy and process*, p18, available at gov.uk/government/collections/asylum-support-asylum-instructions
52 Home Office guidance, 'Asylum Support (Asylum Instructions)', *Asylum Support, Section 4(2): policy and process*, p6
53 *R (Kiana and Musgrove) v SSHD* [2010] EWHC 1002 (Admin); *MK v SSHD* [2011] EWCA Civ 671; s4(2), (10) and (11)
54 *R (Kiana and Musgrove) v SSHD* [2010] EWHC 1002 (Admin), para 45

24

Chapter 24

Asylum support – appeals

This chapter covers:

1. Introduction

If your application for either section 95 support or section 4 support is refused by the Home Office or, in some circumstances, if your support is discontinued, you can appeal to the independent First-tier Tribunal (Asylum Support), which is based in east London.

A decision of the Asylum Support Tribunal cannot be appealed to the Upper Tribunal and can only be legally challenged by judicial review, except in limited circumstances in which the Asylum Support Tribunal can 'set aside' its own decisions (see p568).

The Tribunal Procedure (First-tier Tribunal) (Social Entitlement Chamber) Rules 2008 (referred to as the 'tribunal rules' in this chapter) contain the rules for appeals in the Social Entitlement Chamber.[1] Most of these are common to all tribunals in the Social Entitlement Chamber but a few[2] refer solely to the Asylum Support Tribunal.

In all asylum support appeals, a single judge considers the appeal and makes the decisions. Tribunal judges have no power to make an order relating to the parties' costs, so even if you lose your appeal, you cannot be ordered to pay any legal costs to the Home Office or to the tribunal.

2. The right to appeal

The circumstances in which you have the right to appeal to the Asylum Support Tribunal are limited. You can only appeal if you have been refused support by the Home Office or your support has been stopped – ie:[3]

- you have applied for section 95 or section 4 support and it has been refused; *or*
- your asylum support has been discontinued – ie, your section 95 support has been stopped prematurely while you are still an asylum seeker,[4] or your section 4 support has been stopped for any reason.

Further information is in Asylum Support Appeals Project Factsheet 3, *Appealing to the Asylum Support Tribunal*.[5]

There is no right of appeal against any other Home Office decision about your support (such as the level of support or the place of dispersal) or *any* decision about temporary support. In addition, it is not possible to appeal a decision to refuse your application for support (or to refuse to consider it) if the reason for the refusal is that:

- you failed to provide complete or accurate information in connection with your application;[6] *or*
- you failed to co-operate with enquiries made in respect of the support application;[7] *or*
- you did not make your application for asylum as soon as reasonably possible.[8]

These decisions can only be challenged by judicial review, although the Home Office may be willing to reconsider an application if missing information is later provided.

Note: if you are appealing a discontinuation of your section 4 support and you appeal within the time limits (or a late appeal is accepted) while you are still living in the section 4 accommodation, your support should continue until the day of the appeal.[9] Although there is no equivalent written policy in respect of section 95, in practice many section 95 appellants remain on support until their appeal is heard, particularly if there are dependent minor children.

3. Bringing an appeal

If the Home Office refuses your application for support or terminates your support, it gives you a written decision with its reasons. It also informs you in the decision letter whether you have a right of appeal and, if so, provides an appeal form. You can also get an appeal form (Form EO9) from the tribunal website at gov.uk/government/publications/form-t200-notice-of-appeal-form-eo9. The Home Office does not always get this process right. If your application for support is unsuccessful or your support has been discontinued and you want to appeal, but the Home Office says you do not have the right to appeal, get legal advice immediately.

The appeal timetable

The tribunal rules set out a timetable for appeals to the Asylum Support Tribunal, a summary of which is set out below.[10]

Day	*Event*
Day one	Notice of decision is received by you.
Day four (latest)	Notice of appeal must be received by the tribunal. Delivery of a notice of appeal at any time up to midnight on the relevant day is sufficient. If not lodged in time, you must apply for an extension of time (see p558).
Day four or day five	Tribunal sends notice of appeal to the Home Office.
Day seven (latest)	You and the tribunal receive the Home Office's response to the notice of appeal, contained in a bundle of relevant documents, often called 'the Home Office bundle'.
Day seven or thereafter 'with the minimum of delay'	Tribunal judge decides whether to hold an oral hearing or to direct a paper determination instead, and fixes the hearing date for the oral hearing or paper determination, giving both parties one to five days' notice. It is likely that, at the same time, directions are given (see p560). If the judge believes the appeal should be 'struck out' (eg, if the tribunal does not have jurisdiction – see p566), s/he must give you an opportunity to make representations.
Day nine or thereafter 'with the minimum of delay'	Oral hearing held. The tribunal judge notifies the decision to you and the Home Office at the end of the hearing or, if not present, sends a decision notice. If the appeal is determined on the papers, the decision made and a statement of reasons are sent.
Within three days after an oral hearing	Tribunal judge sends a statement of reasons for the decision to you and the Home Office.

As part of its overriding duty to deal with cases fairly and justly, the tribunal must process appeals to avoid delay so far as compatible with proper consideration of the issues.[11] In practice,the tribunal usually holds an oral hearing within approximately two weeks of receiving your notice of appeal, depending on the volume of cases at any particular time.

Notices or documents can be sent to the tribunal by post, fax or email or given by hand.[12]

If a time limit expires on a non-working day (Saturday, Sunday and bank holidays), it is treated as expiring on the next working day.[13]

Note: the above timetable has been affected by new procedures implemented on the suspension of face-to-face hearings due to the coronavirus pandemic (see p509). At the time of writing, the appeal procedure is under review by the tribunal and is subject to change, depending partly on coronavirus-related factors.

Notice of appeal

You must use the prescribed form if you want to appeal.[14] It must be completed in English (or in Welsh).[15] This is known as the **'notice of appeal'**. See Asylum Support Appeals Project (ASAP) Factsheet 4, *Filling in the Notice of Appeal during the Covid-19 Period*,[16] for more information.

You must state the grounds for your appeal on the form (ie, why you disagree with the Home Office's decision) and attach a copy of the decision you are appealing against. If your notice of appeal does not include all the necessary information and/or is not accompanied by the written Home Office decision, the tribunal will write to you or your representative requesting that you complete the information or provide the relevant documents.[17]

If you have any further information or evidence relating to your application for support or your appeal, you should (if possible) send copies of the relevant documents to the tribunal with the notice of appeal. However, do not delay submitting your appeal to obtain any further evidence, which can be sent to the tribunal later. It is very important that you provide the tribunal with any evidence that proves you are entitled to support. For example, if the Home Office does not accept that you are destitute, you may want to provide letters from one or more people who have been providing you with support but who cannot continue to do so, or a letter from a volluntary agency or from anyone else who has direct knowledge of your circumstances and is willing to give evidence in support of your appeal. Any supporting letters or statements should:

- contain a means of identifying the writer – eg, name, address, telephone number, passport number; *and*
- be signed (unless sent by email); *and*
- be in English if possible.

If it is not possible for supporting evidence to be produced in English, you should submit the evidence if relevant. You should explain what the document is, why it is relevant to your appeal, and why it has not been possible for you to obtain a translation. The Home Office generally refuses to take any document not submitted in English into account. However, if you cannot pay for the document to be professionally translated, the tribunal may find a way of taking it into account, including by asking the court interpreter to provide a translation during the hearing.

You should be aware that any supporting evidence you submit is scrutinised carefully by the Home Office and the tribunal. If any aspect of the evidence is inconsistent with your claimed circumstances, the inconsistency is liable to be taken as a sign that you and/or your witness are not telling the truth. This can be a particular problem if the witness is not a native English speaker, because inconsistencies due to language difficulties are not necessarily accepted by the Home Office or the tribunal.

There is a database of the most significant Asylum Support Tribunal decisions at gov.uk/asylum-support-tribunal-decisions, which you may want to use to see how the tribunal has dealt with similar issues in the past. Although past tribunal decisions are not legally binding on the judge who decides your appeal, the decisions may be persuasive and help support your appeal.

Once you have completed the appeal form, you[18] (or your representative – see p559[19]) must sign the form. You can send it to the tribunal by email, fax or post.[20]

Deciding whether to request an oral hearing

The notice of appeal form asks whether you want to attend, or be represented at, an oral hearing or whether you are content for the appeal to be decided on the papers submitted to the tribunal. You must also state whether you will need an interpreter at the hearing and, if so, in what language and dialect. If you have any difficulties with the English language, you should ask for an interpreter. If required, an interpreter is paid for and supplied by HM Courts and Tribunals Service. Although it always depends on the particular circumstances of your case, it is usually advisable to request an oral hearing because the tribunal judge is better able to understand your case if you explain your situation in person. That is especially true if what you have claimed in your application has been disbelieved by the Home Office. Success rates are generally higher following an oral hearing than a paper determination.

Since March 2020, face-to-face hearings have been suspended due to the coronaviurus pandemic. At the time of writing, it is not known when they will be resumed. Face-to-face hearings have been replaced by telephone hearings, and there have been procedural changes that affect the circumstances in which an oral (telephone) hearing is granted. In this section, the old procedure is first described followed by the new procedure, which has temporarily replaced the former process.

Pre-COVID-19-pandemic hearings

Under the old procedure, if you asked for an oral hearing in the notice of appeal, the tribunal would grant your request and you would receive notice of a hearing date in due course. An appeal could still be decided on the papers without a hearing if both sides agreed and the tribunal believed it could make a decision that way.[21] Even if you asked for your appeal to be determined without an oral hearing, the tribunal could still hold an oral hearing if there were issues to be explored that were raised but not explained in the papers (see p563). If you chose to have an oral hearing, the Home Office would send you tickets to travel to London for the hearing (see p564). If it was difficult to travel to the hearing (eg, because of medical problems, pregnancy or lack of childcare), you could request on the notice of appeal for the appeal to be heard by video link. If the tribunal approved, you would be invited to attend a court in your local area, with a video line linking you to the tribunal in London, where the interpreter, Home Office representative and judge would attend.

COVID-19 pandemic hearings

Following the outbreak of the pandemic, the tribunal procedure rules were changed to remove the right to an oral hearing in certain cases. The tribunal issued guidance in October 2020:[22]

> The tribunal will . . . proceed on the basis that an appellant who seeks an oral hearing of their appeal will be offered an oral hearing, unless a duty judge provisionally decides that:
> (i) the appeal can be decided in the appellant's favour without the need for an oral hearing; *or*
> (ii) oral evidence would add nothing to the appellant's case; *or*
> (iii) the tribunal lacks jurisdiction; *or*
> (iv) there is no reasonable prospect of the appellant's case succeeding.

This means that, even if you ask for an oral hearing in your notice of appeal, your appeal could be listed for determination on the papers. That can be difficult for those who do not read or write in English, or who do not have the facilities to prepare detailed written evidence – eg, appellants who are homeless.

A provisional decision to decide your appeal on the papers will be made by a judge when directions are given. It is, therefore, important that you read the directions notice carefully to understand what the judge has decided. There are three procedural rules (1–3 below) that the tribunal can use to dispense with an oral hearing.

1) Under rule 5A,[23] an oral hearing can be dispensed with if three conditions are satisfied:

- the matter is urgent; *and*
- it is not reasonably practicable for there to be a hearing, including a hearing by videolink or telephone; *and*
- it is in the interests of justice to dispense with an oral hearing.

2) Under rule 8(3),[24] the appellant's case can be struck out if:

- the appellant has failed to comply with a direction or otherwise failed to cooperate with the tribunal to such an extent that the tribunal cannot deal with the appeal fairly and justly; *or*

- the tribunal considers there is no reasonable prospect of the appellant's case succeeding.

3) Under rule 27(1),[25] the tribunal does not need to hold a hearing if:
- each party has consented to, or has not objected to, the matter being decided without a hearing; *and*
- the tribunal considers that it is able to decide the matter without a hearing.

When you receive the directions notice, you may find that your appeal will be decided on the papers without a hearing following one of the above three rules. If that happens, and you want an oral hearing, you should seek urgent advice if possible. In any event, you should consider urgently writing to the tribunal to object to your appeal being determined on the papers.

Depending on which one of the above three rules the judge has relied on to dispense with a hearing, your letter should address the relevant matters set out in the rule, as well as the reasons given by the judge for deciding that the appeal could be fairly decided without a hearing.

If you are not represented, cannot write in English, and/or have no access to word-processing facilities to prepare documents to send to the tribunal, these might be obvious reasons why it would not be fair to decide your appeal without an oral hearing in which you can make your case orally with the services of an interpreter provided by the tribunal.

Representation, including preparing submissions requesting an oral hearing may be available from ASAP. However, ASAP's capacity to assist appellants is limited, so if you require representation before the tribunal (including if your appeal has been listed for paper determination but you would like an oral hearing), you should contact ASAP as soon as possible after you lodge your notice of appeal.[26]

Once granted, an oral hearing (whether face-to-face or a telephone hearing), you should ensure that your witnesses are aware of the hearing date and that they attend. Your witnesses may be able to give direct evidence about how you have been supported or about any aspect of your case that the Home Office disputes in the letter refusing your support claim.

Applications for an extension of time for appealing

Your notice of appeal must be received by the Asylum Support Tribunal within three working days of the day on which you received the notice of the decision on your asylum support application.[27] If you receive the Home Office's decision letter more than two days after the date it was written, it is advisable to state in your notice of appeal the date on which you received the letter to show that you are not (or not fully) responsible for any delay. You can submit the notice of appeal to the tribunal by email, fax or post – the details are on the appeal form.

If you do not appeal in time, you can ask the tribunal in the notice of appeal to extend the time limit for appealing.[28] You should explain why you could not appeal earlier – eg, if you were ill and incapable of dealing with your affairs at the time you received the notice, if you needed advice, or if there was a delay before you received the Home Office refusal letter. The tribunal usually treats applications for an extension of time favourably, provided sufficient explanation is given for the delay. Judges recognise that the time limit to appeal is very short, and an extension of a two or three days (or longer) is often granted, especially for destitute people who may not speak English and may be relying for advice on an advice agency that is only open during certain hours. The judge must consider your application fairly and justly,[29] and must take into account why you (or your representative) could not comply with the time limit.

If the tribunal refuses to extend the time limit, your only alternative is to seek judicial review of the decision on your asylum application and/or of the decision of the Asylum Support Tribunal to refuse to give you more time (see p569). Alternatively, you may be able to reapply for support (see p570).

Confirming whether you have a representative

You may be represented throughout the appeal procedure by a representative of your choice. S/he does not have to be legally qualified.[30] If you are represented, the name and address of your representative must be given in writing to the First-tier Tribunal.[31] This can be done by including the details in the notice of appeal. If your representative is unable to attend the hearing with you, you should tick 'no' when asked this question on the notice of appeal.

It is generally understood that 'representation' implies an ongoing responsibility for the prompt conduct of all stages of the appeal, including:

- securing and preparing all available relevant evidence and submitting it to the tribunal; *and*
- dealing with all correspondence with the tribunal and the Home Office; *and*
- responding in writing to the directions given by the tribunal; *and*
- advising you on each of these steps and at every stage; *and*
- representing you or arranging for a legal adviser to represent you at the tribunal; *and*
- advising you on the outcome of the appeal and on any steps to be taken – eg, to secure support if the appeal has been successful or any further challenge (eg, by judicial review) if the appeal was unsuccessful.

An adviser should therefore *not* state that s/he is your representative if s/he is simply helping you to complete and submit the notice of appeal, and perhaps acting as a mailbox for you. In those circumstances, s/he should make it clear on the notice of appeal that this is the limit of her/his involvement.

If you state that you have a representative, the tribunal must give her/his details to the Home Office. Any documents that the Home Office is required to serve must be served on the representative (and need not be served on you).[32] Anyone else who accompanies you to the appeal hearing cannot assist in presenting your case without the tribunal's approval.[33]

Legal aid may be available in asylum support cases if you are at risk of homelessness, but only for advice to prepare your case **not** to represent you at a hearing.[34]

ASAP provides free representation and advice before the Asylum Support Tribunal for as many people as possible (see Appendix 2). This service is provided by ASAP staff and volunteer solicitors and barristers. You can ask ASAP to represent you at any time before your hearing (although the later you refer your case, the less likely it is that ASAP will have capacity to represent you). Alternatively, and preferably, you can ask your representative (if you have one) to refer your case to ASAP in advance. If you do not have a representative, you can make the referral yourself. If your named representative on the notice of appeal is a firm of solicitors (and not an advice agency), the tribunal may not allow ASAP to represent you, unless you or your solicitor refer the case to ASAP in advance of the hearing.

The Home Office bundle

On the same day as the tribunal receives your notice of appeal or, if this is not reasonably practicable, as soon as possible on the next day, the tribunal must send a copy to the Home Office, together with any supporting documents that you sent with the appeal.[35]

By the third day after your notice of appeal is received by the tribunal, the Home Office must send to the tribunal:[36]

- a statement saying whether or not it opposes the appeal; *and*
- a copy of the decision letter refusing or withdrawing support; *and*
- any other evidence that it took into account when refusing you support; *and*
- any other grounds and reasons for the decision that have not been included in the decision letter; *and*
- copies of all documents it has that are relevant to the case.

At the same time, the Home Office must provide you (or your representative) with a copy of all the above information and documents.[37]

This material is commonly referred to as the 'Home Office bundle'. It is important that you receive a copy of the bundle before the hearing so that you are aware of all the evidence in the appeal. If you or your representative have not received the bundle on time, you should alert the tribunal and/or contact the Home Office.

Tribunal directions and notification of the hearing date

If an oral hearing is listed, the tribunal must promptly inform the parties of the time and date. It is likely that the hearing will take place within two weeks or so of the tribunal's receiving your notice of appeal.

When sending out the notice of a hearing date, the tribunal also sends a 'directions notice' to both you and the Home Office usually requiring you (and sometimes the Home Office) to produce further evidence that the judge giving directions considers will help resolve issues in dispute in the appeal.[38] The evidence you are required to produce is evidence that a judge who has had a preliminary look at the papers (not necessarily the same judge who will hear your appeal) considers will be useful for a fair decision to be made when the appeal is finally determined. You may be asked to produce evidence relating to your destitution (eg, bank statements), medical evidence or copies of any missing documents that the tribunal considers may be relevant.

If an agency or solicitor has helped you to complete the appeal form, the directions notice may be sent to her/him, so it is important to keep in regular contact to check that they have been received and whether your adviser/solicitor can help you respond.

Responding to directions and submitting further evidence

The directions notice is an important document as it indicates how the tribunal is thinking about your appeal and what it considers to be the crucial issues. If possible, you should send any documents that the tribunal has requested to the tribunal and to the Home Office before the hearing. The directions notice tells you to send the information by midday on the day before the hearing.[39] Even if you cannot meet this deadline, you should still send the information and the documents whenever you can, and (if face-to face hearings are resumed) take the papers to the appeal hearing. It is important to comply with any directions, because if you do not, the tribunal may not have all the evidence it considers necessary to make a decision on your appeal, and the judge may hold the lack of evidence against your case. However, if you cannot answer all the questions or provide all the evidence that has been requested, you should provide what information and evidence you can and provide an explanation for what is missing.

You should also note what further information the Home Office has been directed to provide and make sure you see the Home Office's response. Be aware that the Home Office does not always respond in time to the directions notice, and may only produce the information that the tribunal has requested at the hearing, if at all.

If you want to submit more evidence in support of your appeal that you did not send with your notice of appeal, you may still send it to the tribunal to be considered. In particular, you may wish to rely on evidence that shows a change in your circumstances after the date of the Home Office decision or which has only now come into your possession, or evidence that rebuts a new point that the Home Office has raised against you in the letter refusing your support, or in its response to directions. You should send this evidence to the tribunal judge before the date of the hearing, or the date on which you have been notified that s/he will proceed to determine the appeal. You should do this immediately and by fax or email if possible, especially if no oral hearing is to be held, because the tribunal may determine the appeal very quickly after the date specified in the directions notice.

You should also send a copy of any further evidence to the Home Office. Although the tribunal rules no longer require you to do so, the tribunal judge will want to ensure that the Home Office has seen any further evidence, and there is a (very small) risk that the judge will refuse to allow evidence that is provided late and which has not been seen by the Home Office.[40]

During the appeal hearing, you should make sure that you have copies with you of all the appeal papers, including your evidence and the Home Office's documents and any new evidence, because you may need to refer to them. At the start of the hearing, you should also ensure that none of the papers have gone astray and that the judge has all your evidence.

The Home Office can also send further evidence to the tribunal before the appeal is determined. It is likely that the Home Office and/or the tribunal will send copies to you (or your representative) or, if there is not sufficient time, provide you with copies at the hearing. In any event, you must be provided with copies of any documents on which the Home Office intends to rely at the hearing and you must have time to consider them.

Withdrawing an appeal

If, at any stage before the hearing, you decide you do not wish to carry on with your appeal, you can give written notice of withdrawal.[41] If you give notice of the withdrawal orally 'at the hearing', the judge's consent is required.[42] The tribunal rules state that if either party withdraws from the case in writing before the hearing, the consent of a judge is not required and therefore no reasons need be given. However, if you give written notice of withdrawal on the day of the hearing, some judges may want you to attend the hearing to explain why you want to withdraw (although the lawful basis to require you to attend the hearing if you have given notice of withdrawal in writing beforehand is not clear).

If the Home Office withdraws, that can be unfair on you because, unless the Home Office immediately substitutes its negative decision with a positive one awarding you support, you still need your appeal to go ahead to get support.

If the Home Office withdraws from an appeal when you are not yet receiving support, you should refer it to its policy on withdrawals.[43] Under this policy, if the Home Office serves a notice of withdrawal before 12 noon on the day before the hearing, the Home Office should immediately make a fresh decision, which must be posted or faxed to you or your representative. If this decision is again negative (but for a different reason than the first), you need to appeal immediately again. This process will have caused a delay in your getting support (assuming you win your eventual appeal). You should make sure that you compare the two decisions and if there is no substantial difference, draw that to the tribunal's attention when you appeal.

Under the withdrawal policy, if the Home Office withdraws after 12 noon on the day before the hearing, it must apply to do so at the hearing itself. The judge only consents to the withdrawal if:

- the Home Office confirms in writing that the decision under appeal is being withdrawn and you are to be granted support immediately; *or*
- the Home Office serves you with a copy of a fresh refusal or discontinuation decision letter, and you or your representative agree that the hearing can proceed on the basis of this new decision; *or*
- you agree with the Home Office to adjourn the proceedings (for no longer than 14 days) and the Home Office confirms in writing that you will be provided with support in the meantime.

In practice, the tribunal allows the Home Office to withdraw from appeals at any time before the day of the hearing (as opposed to only up to midday) without providing reasons and it is difficult to prevent this. If you are not immediately provided with a new decision letter, whether positive or negative, refer the Home Office to its policy and consider bringing a claim for judicial review (see p569) if there continues to be a significant delay.

Paper determinations

After it receives the Home Office's response, the tribunal judge must consider all the documents and decide whether it is necessary to hold an oral hearing, or whether the appeal can be determined simply by considering the papers. At the time of writing, this decision remains affected by the March 2020 suspension of face-to-face hearings due to the coronavirus pandemic, as a result of which it is now possible that your appeal will be listed for paper determination even if you requested an oral hearing in the notice of appeal (see below).

If your case is listed for a paper determination, you can write to the tribunal to object to your appeal being decided on the papers and to request an oral hearing. See p561 for the issues you should address in your submissions to the tribunal.

You may have stated on the notice of appeal form that you did not want an oral hearing, but you may not have been aware of all of the information or evidence relied on by the Home Office until afterwards – eg, new papers might subsequently be disclosed to you by the Home Office or the tribunal. If, having seen any new material, you change your mind and decide that you want an oral hearing at which to make direct representations to the tribunal, you should notify the tribunal as soon as possible by fax, email or telephone. The judge must then take this into account when deciding whether to grant an oral hearing. If you want to make written representations to the tribunal about this further evidence, you should do so as soon as possible.

Oral hearings

Travel to the hearing

Face-to-face hearings were suspended by the tribunal in March 2020 due to the coronavirus pandemic and were replaced by telephone hearings. Hearings by video link were also suspended due to appellants' difficulty in accessing video-link facilities on account of coronavirus-related travel restrictions. At the time of writing, the tribunal has indicated that it is considering a resumption of video-link and face-to-face hearings when circumstances permit.

Prior to the suspension of face-to-face hearings, the procedure was as follows. You were sent tickets for your travel to and from the hearing. If you lived too far away from East London, where the Asylum Support Tribunal is situated, to travel on the day and arrive on time for your hearing, overnight accommodation was arranged and paid for by the Home Office. Unless you specifically requested help with travel for a witness and the tribunal directed the Home Office to comply with your request, you were only sent travel tickets for yourself. (That would have affected you if, for example, you had a British national partner with leave to remain who was in receipt of social security benefits and it was important for her/him to attend the appeal to be able to give full details with documentary evidence of her/his benefits and to explain why s/he cannot support you.)

The hearing

Prior to the suspension of face-to-face hearings, oral hearings before the Asylum Support Tribunal took place, in principle, in public, although it was extremely rare for members of the public to attend.[44] The tribunal judge could decide that a hearing, or part of it, should be in private and could exclude anyone who was likely to cause a disruption or defeat the purpose of the hearing. In practice, judges checked who was present in the hearing room to ensure that there was no one present who might intimidate the appellant or otherwise hinder a fair hearing. If, for any reason, an appellant thought that someone should be excluded, it was open to her/him to tell the tribunal either before or at the start of the hearing. The position at the time of writing is that oral hearings are conducted by telephone due to COVID-19. Before the start of the hearing, you or your representative, if you have one, must inform the tribunal of your telephone number as well as the telephone number of your representative, anyone who you wish to give evidence in support of your appeal, and anyone who wishes to observe the proceedings. A court interpreter will also attend by telephone.

The procedure that must be adopted at the oral hearing is decided by the tribunal judge. S/he should explain the procedure to you at the outset. There are no strict rules on evidence, and so hearsay and letters from third parties can be considered. You can provide oral evidence and call any witnesses to give oral evidence in support of your case. The Home Office is usually represented by a 'presenting officer', who sets out its case and asks you questions. Sometimes the

Home Office is unrepresented at the hearing. You or your representative must also have the opportunity of directly addressing the tribunal about the decision it should make and commenting on all of the evidence, documentary or oral. If witnesses are called, they may be required to give their evidence under oath or affirmation.[45]

If either you or the Home Office attend the hearing with further evidence that has not previously been provided, the other party must be given the opportunity to look at and comment on this evidence before the hearing proceeds, although that can be difficult in practice if the hearing is a telephone hearing and you are unrepresented and do not have access to email facilities. The judge often checks at the beginning of the hearing whether any further documents need to be made available to the parties.

If possible, take notes of what is said at the hearing. It is usual for the judge to make her/his own written record. If you later want to challenge the decision by judicial review, you can request a copy of this record.

If you are not present at the time of the hearing, it may go ahead without you (or in the absence of a Home Office representative) if the judge:[46]

- is satisfied that you/the Home Office have been notified of the hearing or that reasonable steps have been taken to notify you/the Home Office of the hearing; *and*
- considers that it is in the interests of justice to proceed.

The judge usually waits 30 minutes from the listed start time before starting the appeal without you.

Burden and standard of proof

The tribunal judges decide issues of fact on the balance of probabilities. This simply means deciding which facts in your case are more likely than not to be true. In appeals against a *refusal* of an application for support, it is up to you to prove, on the balance of probabilities, that you are entitled to support and meet the relevant criteria. If you are appealing a decision to *withdraw* support, it is up to the Home Office to establish, on the balance of probabilities, that your support should be terminated.

The tribunal can take into account any change of circumstances that took place between the date on which the decision of the Home Office was made and the date of the appeal.

The tribunal sometimes hears cases in which people are not sure of their immigration status, which may have changed since their appeal was lodged. If is is apparent at the hearing that you have applied for the wrong form of support (eg, the you are eligible for section 95 support as an asylum seeker, but you applied for section 4 support as a refused asylum seeker or vice versa), most judges are willing to grant section 95 support if eligibility is established, even if you applied for the wrong type of support.[47]

Giving the decision

In all cases, the tribunal will reach a decision with the minimum of delay.

If there is an oral hearing, the judge may retire for a period to consider the decision. However, s/he must tell you and the Home Office representative the decision that has been reached at the end of the hearing, and (unless the judge decides to adjourn the appeal or reserve her/his decision until another day), must provide notice of the decision the same day.[48] The notice does not give any reasons for the decision, but simply states whether the appeal has been allowed, dismissed or remitted (see below). This notice is an important document if you win, because it is evidence of the outcome of your appeal that will be accepted by the Home Office and accommodation providers. The notice is also sent on the same day to any party (ie, you or the Home Office) who was not present at the hearing. Unless the appeal has been adjourned or a decision reserved by the judge to another day, the judge announces a final decision at the hearing, and then prepares written reasons, which the judge must send to the parties within three days after the hearing.

If there is no oral hearing, the appeal is determined on the papers on or after the date notified in the directions notice (see p560), which will be a date following the time limit for complying with the directions. Unless the appeal has been adjourned, the tribunal must send a copy of the decision notice together with the judge's written statement of reasons for the decision to both parties on the same day as the appeal is decided.[49]

4. Decisions the Asylum Support Tribunal can make

When deciding an appeal, an Asylum Support Tribunal judge can:[50]

- substitute her/his own decision for the decision made by the Home Office and thus allow the appeal, so you are entitled to support; *or*
- dismiss your appeal, so that the decision of the Home Office stands; *or*
- require the Home Office to reconsider the matter. The Asylum Support Tribunal calls this 'remitting' the appeal (see below).

If your appeal is allowed

If your appeal is successful, the Home Office must provide support on that day. However, if you attend your appeal hearing,[51] you may be left with a difficult choice. In practice, the Home Office is likely to offer 'emergency' accommodation situated in a hostel in south-east London while you wait to be allocated 'dispersal' accommodation elsewhere in the UK.[52] This emergency accommodation can be requested from the Home Office representative at the hearing or, if the Home

Office did not attend your hearing, you can ask the tribunal clerk to put you in contact with the representative on duty that day. The accommodation is offered on condition that you stay there on the night of your appeal. If you are then allocated accommodation in a different part of the UK to where you were previously living, the Home Office does not provide travel costs to allow you to return to collect any belongings.

Alternatively, after the hearing, you can return to the town in which you were living, using the return ticket provided by the Home Office. The Home Office should then contact you directly, or through your advice agency, to arrange your accommodation. This usually takes two to three days to arrange, in some cases even longer, during which time you may be left homeless. You are given travel tickets to get to your new accommodation. This option is therefore more appropriate if you need to collect belongings and you have somewhere to stay and the ability to feed yourself in the short term.

This arrangement is particularly unsatisfactory if you are street homeless but have left belongings (eg, medication) in the town where you were sleeping. Further information is in Asylum Support Appeals Project Factsheet 16, *Acommodation After a Successful Section 4 Appeal*.[53]

If there is any delay by the Home Office in providing support immediately after a successful appeal, the Home Office may be acting unlawfully, and you may be able to challenge the delay by bringing a claim for judicial review (see p569).

If your appeal was heard by video link, the Home Office can provide emergency accommodation at your nearest initial accommodation centre. You should request this at the end of the hearing.

If your appeal is dismissed

If your appeal is dismissed and if you are currently receiving asylum support, your support will be terminated soon; if you are not receiving asylum support, you will remain without support.

If your appeal is remitted

The effect of remitting a decision is to set aside the decision of the Home Office. This requires the Home Office to reconsider and come to a new decision on whether you should be provided with support. This puts you back into the position you were in before the decision was made. If you had been receiving support and the Home Office's decision to withdraw your support is remitted by the tribunal, the Home Office must immediately reinstate the support until it comes to a new decision. If you were previously without support and are appealing the Home Office's decision to refuse your application, a tribunal decision to remit that refusal decision leaves you in your previous position of being without support, at least until the Home Office comes to a new decision.[54]

Other types of tribunal decisions

The tribunal can make other types of decision.

- Adjourning the appeal, often at the same time giving directions for the future conduct of the case. Adjournments are relatively rare as tribunal judges tend to treat asylum support cases as urgent.
- Striking out an appeal, thereby determining in favour of the Home Office. A tribunal 'strikes out' your appeal by taking a decision that your appeal cannot continue to a final hearing, either following a hearing about whether or not to strike your appeal out or even before a hearing has taken place. The tribunal must strike out your appeal if it does not have jurisdiction to decide the matter – eg, the tribunal cannot consider an appeal about how much asylum support the Home Office should pay you each week. The tribunal may also strike out your appeal without a hearing if it considers your case has no reasonable prospect of success. Before striking out your appeal, the tribunal must give you the opportunity to make representations. It may direct you to make these in writing by a certain deadline, following which a decision is made by the judge 'on the papers'. Alternatively, the tribunal may fix a date for you and the Home Office to attend to make any representations about whether the appeal should be struck out. If, following such a hearing, and, if the appeal is not struck out, the appeal then proceeds to a full hearing, usually on the same day.

5. After the decision

There is no right of appeal against the Asylum Support Tribunal's decision. If you are dissatisfied with the decision, in limited circumstances you can ask the tribunal to set it aside (see below). Otherwise, the only way of challenging the decision is by judicial review (see p569).

Setting aside a decision

The Asylum Support Tribunal can only set aside its own decision and make a new decision (or set aside and remake part of a decision) if:[55]

- it was a decision 'disposing of the proceedings' – ie, a final decision or a decision to strike out the appeal, and:
  - a document relating to the proceedings was not sent or was not received at an appropriate time by either party or her/his representative; *or*
  - a document relating to the proceedings was not sent to the tribunal at an appropriate time; *or*
  - a party or representative was not present at a hearing; *or*
  - there has been some other procedural irregularity in the proceedings; *and*
- the tribunal considers that it is in the interests of justice to do so.

You cannot, therefore, ask the Asylum Support Tribunal to set aside a decision because you do not agree with the decision. Bear in mind that, even if one of these conditions does apply, the tribunal may still decide that it is not in the interests of justice to set aside the decision. For example, even if you did not receive a relevant document at the appropriate time, the tribunal may still consider that this did not make any difference to the decision that was eventually made, and so it is not in the interests of justice to set the decision aside.

If you wish to apply to set aside a decision, your application must be in writing and received by the Asylum Support Tribunal no later than one month after the date on which it sent the decision to you.[56]

Challenging the tribunal's decision by judicial review

Judicial review is a type of procedure by which a High Court or Upper Tribunal judge considers the lawfulness of a decision of a public body, including a decision of the Asylum Support Tribunal. There must be an error in law for an application for judicial review to succeed – it is not enough that you do not agree with the decision the judge made. Whether there is an error of law in the judge's decision is a complicated matter beyond the scope of this book. To be successful in judicial review proceedings, you will need help from a public law solicitor.

An application for judicial review must be made promptly and, in any event, within three months of the decision you want to be reviewed. The application must be in writing, laying out the facts and legal arguments, and be accompanied by copies of all relevant documents.

Judicial review is a two-stage procedure. You must first get the permission of a High Court judge to proceed with the claim. At this stage, a judge gives preliminary consideration to the case to establish whether there is an arguable error of law. If the judge concludes the decision maker made an arguable error of law, s/he grants permission for the judicial review proceedings to proceed to a full hearing.

If the judge is not persuaded that there is an arguable error of law, s/he will refuse you permission to proceed. In any event, a judge has a discretion to refuse you permission (or to reject your case at the full hearing) if s/he does not think an order should be made. Judicial review proceedings are relatively expensive, and although the court can intervene quickly in an emergency, the proceedings can take months or even years to be determined. Unless legal aid is granted, an unsuccessful judicial review applicant is liable to pay the Home Office's legal costs if the judicial review claim is refused. In many cases, a further application for asylum support may be a more practical remedy than judicial review and legal aid is available. If you think judicial review might be appropriate in your case, you should immediately get legal advice from a solicitor specialising in judicial review. If your case is strong, legal aid should be available to pay the solicitor's fees.

Making a new application for support

Following an unsuccessful appeal, the Home Office cannot consider any further application for support from you, unless the Home Office is satisfied that there has been a 'material change in the circumstances' between the time of the appeal and the new application.[57] If you are destitute, you should not just submit an identical application to that which was dismissed on appeal. However, you should reapply if you have new evidence of destitution that could be a material change of circumstances – eg, street homelessness following your appeal. The Home Office and tribunal will want to see evidence that your situation has changed since the last decision. If you decide to reapply for support after a dismissed appeal, make sure your application deals with the points raised in the 'statement of reasons', including by providing information or evidence that the previous judge considered was missing, or otherwise found to be unsatisfactory, and by addressing the reasons why the previous judge dismissed your appeal.

Responding to a fresh Home Office decision following a tribunal decision to remit

If the Asylum Support Tribunal decides to remit the matter (see p566) and the Home Office then makes a new decision refusing you support, you may appeal again against the new decision.

Notes

1. **Introduction**
 1 TP(FT) Rules
 2 For example, rr29(2)(a) and 33(3) TP(FT) Rules

2. **The right to appeal**
 3 s103(1)-(3) IAA 1999
 4 s103(2) IAA 1999. The legislation provides a right of appeal if a decision is made to stop providing support 'before that support would otherwise have come to an end'. The intention is to allow a right of appeal in any case where support is terminated before the asylum seeker has ceased to be an asylum seeker for support purposes. See IAA 1999, Explanatory Notes, para 317.
 5 Available at asaproject.org/resources
 6 s57 NIAA 2002
 7 s57 NIAA 2002
 8 s55 NIAA 2002
 9 Home Office guidance, 'Asylum Support (Asylum Instructions)', *Asylum Support: policy bulletins – instructions*, para 6.6, p26, available at gov.uk/government/collections/asylum-support-asylum-instructions

3. **Bringing an appeal**
 10 rr22(2)(a) and (7)(a), 24(1)(a), 29, 33 and 34 TP(FT) Rules
 11 r2(2)(e) TP(FT) Rules
 12 r13(1) TP(FT) Rules
 13 r12(2) and (3) TP(FT) Rules
 14 Tribunals Judiciary, Practice Direction, 'First-tier Tribunal Social Entitlement Chamber, Asylum Support Cases', 30 October 2008
 15 r22(3) TP(FT) Rules
 16 Available at asaproject.org/resources

17 The Asylum Support Tribunal has agreed to list appeals in which appellants only have an eviction notice but no Home Office decision letter.
18 r22(3) TP(FT) Rules
19 r11(5) TP(FT) Rules
20 r13(1) TP(FT) Rules
21 r27(1) TP(FT) Rules
22 judiciary.uk/wp-content/uploads/2020/10/Asylum-Support-Guidance-Note.02October2020.FINAL_.pdf
23 r5A TP(FT) Rules
24 r8(3) TP(FT) Rules
25 r27(1) TP(FT) Rules
26 See ASAP's Factsheet 4A, *How to Request an Oral Hearing*
27 rr12 and 22(2)(a) TP(FT) Rules
28 rr5(3)(a) and 22(6) TP(FT) Rules
29 r2 TP(FT) Rules
30 r11(1) TP(FT) Rules. Note also that asylum support law is not immigration law, and so an adviser does not have to be registered with the Office of the Immigration Services Commissioner.
31 r11(2) TP(FT) Rules
32 r11(6a) TP(FT) Rules
33 r11(7) TP(FT) Rules
34 Sch 1 Part 1, para 31 Legal Aid, Sentencing and Punishment of Offenders Act 2012
35 r22(7)(a) TP(FT) Rules
36 r24(1)(a), (2) and (4) TP(FT) Rules
37 r24(5) TP(FT) Rules
38 r15 TP(FT) Rules
39 At the time of writing, this deadline had been brought forward due to COVID-related changes to the tribunal's procedure.
40 r15(2)(b) TP(FT) Rules
41 r17(1) TP(FT) Rules
42 r17(2) and (3)(c) TP(FT) Rules
43 Home Office guidance, 'Asylum Support (Asylum Instructions)', *Asylum Support: policy bulletins – instructions*, para 6.5, available at gov.uk/government/collections/asylum-support-asylum-instructions
44 r30(1) TP(FT) Rules
45 r15(3) TP(FT) Rules
46 r31 TP(FT) Rules
47 See *Razai & Ors* [2010] EWHC 3151 (Admin), para 29
48 rr33(3) and 34(1)(a) TP(FT) Rules
49 rr33(3) and 34(1)(b) TP(FT) Rules

4. **Decisions the Asylum Support Tribunal can make**

50 s103(3) IAA 1999
51 At the time of writing, face-to-face hearings had been suspended due to the coronavirus pandemic.
52 Home Office guidance, 'Asylum Support (Asylum Instructions)', *Asylum Support, Section 4(2): policy and process*, p6, available at: gov.uk/government/collections/asylum-support-asylum-instructions
53 Available at asaproject.org/resources
54 On an application for section 95 support you could, in theory, receive temporary support under s98 IAA 1999 until a new decision is made.

5. **After the decision**

55 r37(1) TP(FT) Rules
56 r37(3) TP(FT) Rules
57 s103(6) IAA 1999

Part 9

Other sources of help

Chapter 25

Other sources of help

This chapter covers:

1. Council tax reduction

If you need help to pay your council tax, you may be able to get help under your local authority's council tax reduction scheme. **Note:** council tax reduction is not a social security benefit or a tax credit, and how the scheme operates depends on where you live.[1]

- In England and Wales, local authorities can devise their own local schemes, which must meet minimum requirements. In Wales, if a local authority does not set up its own scheme, a default scheme applies. Check with your local authority whether it has its own local scheme or whether the default scheme applies.
- In Scotland, there is a national scheme, administered by local authorities.

The regulations for all the schemes are in CPAG's *Housing Benefit and Council Tax Reduction Legislation* and see CPAG's *Council Tax Handbook* for more information.

All the schemes have immigration and residence rules. To be entitled to council tax reduction, you must:

- not be defined as a 'person subject to immigration control' (see below); *and*
- be habitually resident in, including having a right to reside in, the common travel area (see p577), unless you are exempt.

You are not entitled to council tax reduction if you are absent from the property, although certain temporary absences are disregarded. These rules can be affected by whether your absence is in, or outside, Great Britain (see p578).

To be entitled to council tax reduction in England and Wales you, and anyone included in your application, must satisfy the national insurance (NI) number requirement (see p578).

People subject to immigration control

You are usually not entitled to council tax reduction if you are defined as a 'person subject to immigration control' (see p81).[2]

However, you are not excluded from council tax reduction on the basis of being a person subject to immigration control if you are:[3]

- a national of a country that has ratified either the European Convention on Social and Medical Assistance or the European Social Charter (1961). The only non-European Economic Area (EEA) countries to which this applies are Turkey and North Macedonia; *and*
- lawfully present in the UK. You satisfy this if you currently have leave to enter or remain in the UK. However, see below if your leave is subject to a condition that you do not have recourse to public funds.

Note: you must satisfy all the other conditions of entitlement for council tax reduction, including the requirement to have a right to reside (see below). **Note:** the courts have held that although asylum seekers with temporary admission are 'lawfully present' in the UK, they do not have a right to reside. Temporary admission was replaced by immigration bail on 15 January 2018, but the same arguments are likely to apply.[4]

Public funds

Council tax reduction is defined as a public fund in the Immigration Rules.[5]

If your leave to enter or remain in the UK is subject to a condition that you do not have recourse to public funds, you are defined as a 'person subject to immigration control' (see p87) and (unless you are covered by the above exception) you are not entitled to council tax reduction.

If you are exempt, and are therefore entitled to council tax reduction, this may still be regarded as having recourse to public funds. Receiving council tax reduction breaches this condition of your leave and could affect your right to remain in the UK (see p87).[6]

If your leave is subject to a no recourse to public funds condition, you should also avoid being included in someone else's claim because if s/he receives a larger council tax reduction because of your presence (eg, if s/he loses the single person discount and becomes liable for 100 per cent of the council tax), this may breach your no recourse to public funds condition and could affect your right to remain in the UK (see p28).[7]

Note: although council tax reduction is defined as a public fund, a discount in your council tax liability is not. If you get a discount (eg, a single person discount because you live alone), this does not breach any condition not to have recourse to public funds.

Asylum support

In Wales and Scotland only, asylum support counts as income for council tax reduction purposes, unless you are defined as a 'pensioner'.[8] In England, some local authorities also treat asylum support as income, so you should check your local scheme. If you are included in someone else's council tax reduction claim, your asylum support may be taken into account when calculating her/his entitlement.

Residence requirements

To be entitled to council tax reduction, you must satisfy both parts of the habitual residence test: you must be 'habitually resident in fact' (see p146), and have a non-excluded right to reside (see below), in the 'common travel area' (ie, the UK, Ireland, Channel Islands and the Isle of Man), unless you are exempt from the habitual residence test.[9]

The same exemptions from the habitual residence test for housing benefit (see p142) apply to council tax reduction, except if you:[10]

- in England and Wales only, are the 'extended family member' (see p223) of an EEA 'worker' (see p189) or 'self-employed person' (see p196), including someone who retains either status (see p201), you are not exempt; *or*
- in England and Wales only, are a Crown servant or member of HM forces posted overseas and immediately before your posting you were habitually resident in the UK, you are also exempt; *or*
- in Scotland only, receive income-based jobseeker's allowance (JSA), you are exempt.

Note: receipt of pension credit (PC) does not exempt you from the habitual residence test for council tax reduction.

If you are not exempt from, or do not satisfy, the habitual residence test, you are treated as not being in Great Britain and so are not entitled to council tax reduction.

Note: a local authority cannot require you to have resided in that local authority area for a set period of time before you can be entitled to council tax reduction.[11]

Right to reside

To satisfy the right to reside requirement for council tax reduction, you must have a right to reside in the common travel area, other than as:[12]

- an EEA national with an initial right of residence during your first three months in the UK (see p181); *or*
- a family member of the above; *or*
- (except Scotland) an EEA jobseeker (see p182); *or*
- (except Scotland) a family member of an EEA jobseeker; *or*
- (except Scotland) a person granted 'pre-settled status' (see p49); *or*
- (except Scotland) the primary carer of a British citizen who is dependent on you and would have to leave the European Union (EU) if you were required to leave (see p240).

For information on who has a right to reside, see Chapter 12.

National insurance number requirement

If you apply for council tax reduction in England and Wales, you and anyone included in your application must satisfy an NI number requirement that is similar to that for benefits (see p442).[13] However, that does not apply to a child or young person, or if:[14]

- you are defined as a 'person subject to immigration control' because you require leave but do not have it (see p85); *and*
- you have not previously had an NI number; *and*
- you do not satisfy the habitual residence test. **Note:** this is always likely to apply if you satisfy the first point, as you do not have a right to reside (see p577).

Absences abroad

Although you must be living in your property to qualify for council tax reduction, certain temporary absences are allowed. An overview of the rules is provided below, but you should also check the details of your local or national scheme.

In England if you are a 'pensioner' (ie, you have reached pension age and you are not receiving universal credit, income support, income-related employment and support allowance or income-based JSA), you continue to receive council tax reduction during an absence for up to:[15]

- **four weeks** if you are absent from Great Britain, provided the absence is unlikely to exceed four weeks. This can be extended by up to four weeks if the absence is in connection with the death of your partner, a child for whom you (or your partner) are responsible, or a close relative of you or your partner or child, and it is unreasonable for you to return within the first four weeks;
- **13 weeks** if you are absent in Great Britain and the absence is not intended to be longer or is due to your being in residential accommodation;
- **26 weeks** if you are absent from Great Britain and you are a member of HM forces posted overseas, a mariner or a continental shelf worker, and the absence is unlikely to exceed 26 weeks;

- **52 weeks** in limited circumstances. Those include if you, your partner or dependent child are a hospital inpatient, you are undergoing or recovering from medical treatment, or you are absent from home because of domestic violence.

If you are not a 'pensioner', there are no prescribed rules on absences, so check the details of your local scheme.

In Wales, you can continue to receive council tax reduction during an absence for up to:[16]

- **13 weeks** if your absence is not intended to be longer or is due to your being in residential accommodation;
- **52 weeks** in limited circumstances. Those include if you, your partner or dependent child are a hospital inpatient, you are undergoing or recovering from medical treatment, or you are absent from home because of domestic violence.

In Scotland, you can continue to receive council tax reduction during an absence for up to:[17]

- **one month** if you are absent from Great Britain, provided you have not been absent on more than two occasions in the previous 52 weeks. This may be extended by a further month if the absence abroad is in connection with the death of your partner or a child for whom you (or your partner) are responsible;
- **13 weeks** if you are absent in Great Britain, provided your absence is not intended to be longer or is due to your being in residential accommodation;
- **six months** if the absence is abroad solely in connection with your treatment, or recovery from treatment, for an illness or disability, or you are accompanying someone else for such treatment;
- **52 weeks** in limited circumstances. Those include if you, your partner or dependent child are a hospital inpatient, you are undergoing or recovering from medical treatment, or you are absent from home because of domestic violence;
- **indefinitely** if you are abroad in your capacity as (or accompanying your partner in her/his capacity as) an aircraft worker, mariner, continental shelf worker, Crown servant or member of HM forces and you satisfy, or are exempt from, the habitual residence test (see p577).

2. **Local welfare assistance schemes**

Help may be available under local welfare assistance schemes set up by your local authority (in England) or by the Scottish and Welsh governments. The Department for Work and Pensions may refer to this as 'local welfare provision'.

Depending on your circumstances and where you live, you may qualify if you need help, for example:

- with immediate short-term needs in a crisis – eg, if you do not have sufficient resources, or you need help with expenses in an emergency or as a result of a disaster, such as a fire or flood in your home;
- to establish yourself in the community following a stay in institutional or residential accommodation, or to help you remain in the community;
- to set up a home in the community as part of a planned resettlement programme;
- to ease exceptional pressure on your family;
- to enable you to care for a prisoner or young offender on temporary release;
- with certain travel expenses – eg, to visit someone in hospital, to attend a funeral, to ease a domestic crisis, to visit a child living with her/his other parent or to move to suitable accommodation.

In **Wales**, the Discretionary Assistance Fund for Wales offers non-repayable emergency assistance payments and individual assistance payments.

In **Scotland**, the Scottish Welfare Fund is a national scheme administered in accordance with the Scottish government's national guidance, but local authorities have some discretion. You can apply to your local authority for community care grants and crisis grants, and can be entitled if you are (or are about to be) resident in the local authority's area, homeless or stranded in the area, or if there are other exceptional circumstances.[18] The guidance excludes you from the scheme if you are an asylum seeker, despite there being no such exclusion in legislation.[19] You can claim a family reunion crisis grant if you have been granted refugee leave or humanitarian protection and your family members have been granted permission to join you under the family reunion provisions (see p114). You can apply before they arrive for assistance with living costs and essential items to help your family settle into the community.[20]

In **England**, the local scheme is entirely at your local authority's discretion. Check with your local authority to find out what help is available, whether you qualify and how to apply. It is arguable that a local authority cannot require you to have resided in that local authority area for a set period of time before you can be entitled to assistance under the local scheme. This argument is based on a High Court case in which it was held to be unlawful for a local authority to require you to have resided in its area for a set period of time before you can be entitled to council tax reduction (see p577).

Public funds

Local welfare assistance scheme payments, other than from the Discretionary Assistance Fund in Wales, have been defined as 'public funds' under the Immigration Rules since 6 April 2016.[21] If you have leave to enter or remain in the

UK which is subject to a condition that you do not have recourse to public funds (see p31), you will breach this condition if you receive a payment from one of these schemes on or after this date. Get immigration advice before you make a claim. The guidance on the Scottish Welfare Fund specifically excludes 'expenses to meet the needs of people who have no recourse to public funds'.[22]

3. Early years food and vitamins

If you are pregnant or have a young child, in England and Wales you can qualify for Healthy Start food and vitamins. In Scotland, you can qualify for Best Start foods and can also register with your midwife while pregnant to receive a free 'baby box' of essential items.

Healthy Start and Best Start food

If you qualify for Healthy Start food (see below):[23]

- you get weekly vouchers (currently worth £3.10) that can be exchanged for 'Healthy Start food' at registered shops; *or*
- you are paid an amount equal to the value of the vouchers if there is no registered shop within a reasonable distance of your home.

If you qualify for Best Start foods (see below), you are issued with a payment card credited with £4.25 (£8.50 while a child is younger than one year old or within a year of the child's expected date of birth, whichever is later) every week to be spent on 'Best Start foods'.[24]

Healthy Start and Best Start food[25]

'Healthy Start food' and **'Best Start foods'** are liquid cow's milk and cow's (or goat's in Scotland) milk-based infant formula, fresh or frozen (or canned in Scotland) fruit and vegetables including loose, pre-packed, whole, sliced, chopped or mixed fruit or vegetables (but not fruit or vegetables to which fat, salt, sugar, flavouring or any other ingredients have been added). In Scotland, Best Start foods also includes fresh, dried or canned pulses (but not those to which fat, salt, sugar or flavouring or other ingredients has been added) and fresh eggs.

Who can qualify

You qualify for a Healthy Start voucher or Best Start foods credit in *each* of the following situations that apply to you.[26]

- You are more than 10 weeks pregnant, or in Scotland as soon as you are pregnant provided you are 'ordinarily resident' (see p131), and you are:

  - aged 18 or over and are entitled to (or you are a member of the family, or in Scotland the partner or dependant, of someone who is entitled to) a 'qualifying benefit' (see below); *or*
  - in England and Wales, younger than 18, unless you are defined as a 'person subject to immigration control' (see p81); *or*
  - in Scotland, younger than 18 (including if you turn 18 while still pregnant) and you are habitually resident (see p139). However, if you are, or your partner or someone you are the dependant of, is entitled to a 'qualifying benefit' (see below), the habitual residence requirement does not apply.
- In England and Wales, you are a mother who has 'parental responsibility' (see below) for a child and:
  - you are aged 16 or older and entitled to (or you are a member of the family of someone who is entitled to) a qualifying benefit other than income-related employment and support allowance (ESA). If you are entitled to universal credit (UC), your child must be younger than one year old. For other qualifying benefits, your child must be younger than one or there must be less than a year since her/his expected date of birth. Therefore, you can continue to qualify for vouchers for a period after your child is one – ie, if s/he was born prematurely; *or*
  - it is less than four months since your baby's expected date of birth and you have not yet notified Healthy Start that s/he was born. You must have been getting a qualifying benefit before your baby was born. That allows your entitlement to vouchers to continue until you notify Healthy Start of the birth. Once you do, you can then qualify under the rule above (if you are 16 or older). **Note:** as long as you provided the notification within the four-month period, you can also get extra vouchers for your child from her/his date of birth.
- If you qualify for vouchers for more than one child under this rule (eg, you have twins), you get a voucher for each. If you do not have parental responsibility but would otherwise qualify for vouchers, your child qualifies instead of you.
- In England and Wales, you get a voucher for a child younger than four years old who is a member of your family (see below), and if you or a member of your family are entitled to a 'qualifying benefit' (see below) other than income-related ESA.
- In Scotland, you are ordinarily resident in Scotland (see p131) and 'responsible' (see below) for a child who is:
  - younger than three years old and you are (or you are the partner or dependant of someone who is) entitled to a 'qualifying benefit' (see below); *or*
  - younger than the age of one or has not yet reached the first anniversary of her/his expected date of birth – eg, if born prematurely. You must also be

younger than 18 or have turned 18 before the child's first birthday and be 'habitually resident' (see p139).

In practical terms, each week you could get one voucher or credit for each of your children aged between one and four (three in Scotland), two vouchers (or the higher credit in Scotland) for each child younger than one (or within one year of her/his expected date of birth), plus one voucher or credit if you are pregnant.

Definitions

The following are **'qualifying benefits'**:[27]

- UC if, during the last complete assessment period (or the one before), you (and your partner if you have a joint claim) had earned income of £408 (£610 in Scotland) or less. If your earned income subsequently increases to more than £408/£610, you continue to qualify for a further eight weeks after the last complete assessment period;
- income support, income-based jobseeker's allowance and (in some cases) income-related ESA. In Scotland, also housing benefit, provided your income is not more than £311 a week, and pension credit (PC);
- child tax credit (CTC), provided your gross income for CTC purposes is not more than £16,190. In England and Wales, you must not be entitled to working tax credit (WTC) as well, other than during the four-week WTC 'run-on' period. In Scotland, you can be entitled to both CTC and WTC provided your income for tax credit purposes is less than £7,320.

'Parental responsibility' is as defined in section 3(1) of the Children Act 1989 (in England or Wales).[28]

Being **'responsible'** for a child means:[29]

- s/he is 'dependent' (see below) on you; *or*
- you are the child's parent, the child normally lives with you, and you are younger than 20 and are the 'dependant' (see below) of another person; *or*
- you are legally recognised as the child's adoptive parent or the child has been placed with you by an adoption agency; *or*
- you are the child's legal guardian; *or*
- you are the child's kinship carer.

'Family' means a person and her/his partner and any child or qualifying young person who is a member of her/his household and for whom s/he or her/his partner counts as responsible.[30] So, for example, if you are not entitled to a qualifying benefit, but are included in your parent's claim for one of these, you can qualify for Healthy Start food vouchers.

Being the **'dependant'** of someone means s/he is:[31]

- your kinship carer; *or*
- awarded child benefit, CTC or PC for that week, or UC for the assessment period including that week or for the previous assessment period, and you are treated as a child or qualifying young person for that benefit, even if no benefit is actually paid for you.

Claims

You must make an initial claim for Healthy Start food vouchers in writing, and must provide specified information and evidence.[32] You can:

- complete the form in the Healthy Start leaflet (HS01), available from midwives, health visitors, maternity clinics and some doctors' surgeries or from 0345 607 6823; *or*
- download, complete and print out a form online or email yourself a form from healthystart.nhs.uk/healthy-start-vouchers/how-to-apply. From 6 April 2020, the form no longer needs to be countersigned by a health professional. If you are younger than 16, your claim must also be signed by your parent or carer. Send the completed form to: Healthy Start Issuing Unit, Freepost RRTR-SYAE-JKCR, PO Box 1067, Warrington WA55 1EG.

You must apply for Best Start foods credits in the same way that you apply for a Best Start grant (see mygov.scot/best-start-grant-best-start-foods). You do not need to make a separate application; one application is used to work out your entitlement to both. Remember to apply when you are first pregnant as you can qualify for Best Start foods immediately, even if you do not qualify for a Best Start grant until later.

If you are getting Healthy Start food vouchers or Best Start foods credits while you are pregnant and then inform Healthy Start or Social Security Scotland of your baby's birth while s/he is younger than four months old, you can get additional vouchers for her/him from her/his date of birth.[33] You may need to make a claim for UC, PC, CTC or child benefit for her/him (or add her/him to your existing CTC, UC or PC claim) to ensure that you continue to get the vouchers or credits.

If you do not get vouchers or credits to which you think you are entitled, or have any other problems with these, contact the Healthy Start helpline on 0345 607 6823 or Social Security Scotland on 0800 182 2222.

Vitamins

If you qualify for Healthy Start food vouchers, you also qualify for Healthy Start vitamins.[34]

In Scotland, with the introduction of Best Start foods, all pregnant women should still be entitled to free vitamins (see mygov.scot/free-vitamins-pregnant).

Mothers and pregnant women are entitled to 56 vitamin tablets, and children younger than four to 10 millilitres of vitamin drops, every eight weeks.

You do not have to make a separate claim for Healthy Start vitamins; you are sent Healthy Start vitamin coupons with your Healthy Start food vouchers. However, you must show evidence to the vitamin supplier that you are entitled (ie, the letter to which your most recent Healthy Start vouchers were attached) and, if requested, proof of your child's age.[35]

The ways that vitamins are made available vary through out the UK. For details see healthystart.nhs.uk. Ask your health professional what the local arrangements are for getting your free vitamins.

4. **Free milk for children**

Children younger than five are entitled to 189–200 millilitres of free milk on each day they are looked after for two hours or more:[36]

- by a registered childminder or daycare provider; *or*
- in a school, playcentre or workplace nursery which is exempt from registration; *or*
- in local authority daycare.

Children younger than one are allowed fresh or dried milk.

In Wales, children in key stage one are entitled to free milk if the school has chosen to participate in the scheme.

In Scotland, free milk may be provided to school-age children by the local authority (see mygov.scot/school-meals).

5. **Education benefits**

Financial help is available from your local authority if you are in school or are a student, or if you have a child in school or college.

Free school lunches

School children are entitled to free school lunches if their families receive:[37]

- universal credit (UC). In Scotland, a parent on UC (whether single or in a couple) must not be earning more than £610 a month. In England and Wales, your earnings (and those of your partner if you make a joint claim) must not exceed:
  - £616.67 in the UC assessment period immediately before the date you claim free school lunches; *or*
  - £1,233.34 in the two UC assessment periods immediately before the date you claim free school lunches; *or*
  - £1,850 in the three UC assessment periods immediately before the date you claim free school lunches; *or*
- income support (IS), income-based jobseeker's allowance or income-related employment and support allowance (ESA);
- child tax credit (CTC) and have annual taxable income of £16,190 in England and Wales, £16,105 in Scotland, or less. That does not apply if the family is entitled to working tax credit (WTC) unless:

- this is during the four-week 'WTC run-on' period. See CPAG's *Welfare Benefits and Tax Credits Handbook* for when this applies; *or*
- in Scotland only, the WTC award is based on annual taxable income of £7,330 or less;
- in England and Wales, the guarantee credit of pension credit (PC). In Scotland, entitlement has not yet been extended to families who get PC including a child addition but local authorities have the discretion to provide free school lunches in these circumstances.[38]

Also entitled are:
- 16–18 year olds receiving the above benefits or tax credits in their own right;[39]
- asylum seekers in receipt of asylum support (see p481);[40]
- in Scotland, a child attending early learning and childcare who is entitled under any of the bullet points above or, at the local authority's discretion, if her/his family receives PC, incapacity benefit or severe disablement allowance, or if since the age of two s/he has been looked after by a local authority or is the subject of a kinship care or guardianship order.[41] Free meals are also provided to all children who are in 'funded early learning and childcare' settings in Scotland (see mygov.scot/school-meals).

Note:
- In England and Scotland, free school lunches are provided to all children during the first three years of primary school. By August 2022, free school lunches will be provided to all primary school children in Scotland.
- In Wales, free school breakfasts are provided to all children in primary schools maintained by the local authority.[42]
- In England, pupils eligible for free school lunches on or after 31 March 2018 remain entitled until 31 March 2022, and in Wales, pupils eligible on or after 31 March 2019 remain entitled until 31 December 2023, whether or not they (or their parents) continue to be entitled to a qualifying benefit. Those entitled to free school lunches on 31 March 2022 in England, or 31 December 2023 in Wales, continue to be entitled until they finish their current stage of education – eg, primary or secondary school.[43]

School transport and school clothes

Local authorities must provide **free transport to school** for pupils aged five to 16 if it is considered necessary to enable that pupil to get to the 'nearest suitable school'. This applies if s/he lives more than a set distance from that school. However, if there is no safe walking route, a pupil must be given free transport irrespective of how far away s/he lives from the nearest suitable school. Free school transport must also be be provided to pupils with special educational needs and to those whose parents are on a low income – ie, if they receive a benefit that would qualify them for free school lunches or the maximum rate of WTC.

Local authorities can give **grants for school uniforms and other school clothes.** Each authority determines its own eligibility rules. In Scotland, the minimum school clothing grant for 2020/21 is £100.

Some school governing bodies or parents' associations also provide help with school clothing.

Education maintenance allowance and 16 to 19 bursaries

Education maintenance allowance is a means-tested payment for young people who are aged 16 to 19, are resident in Wales or Scotland, and who stay on in further education. Payments are made directly to the young person and are conditional on regular course attendance. The young person receives a weekly allowance during term time. The amount depends on the household income. Entitlement depends on your being 'ordinarily resident' in Wales or Scotland. That is not solely determined by where you live but can also be affected by your nationality and immigration status. For further details of each scheme, see studentfinancewales.co.uk/fe/ema or mygov.scot/ema.

16 to 19 bursaries are payments for young people aged 16 to 19 who stay on in further education or training in England, available through the school, college or training provider. Certain vulnerable young people (eg, young people in care, care leavers, young people who get UC or IS, or who get ESA and either disability living allowance or personal independence payment) can get the maximum bursary. Discretionary bursaries are available to those in financial difficulty. You should apply as close to the start of the academic year as possible, or as soon as you become in financial need if this is later. See gov.uk/1619-bursary-fund for further information.

Neither payment counts as income for any benefits or tax credits the parent may be getting. They are also not affected by any income the young person has from part-time work.

Note: if you are a student, to find out what help is available to finance your studies, contact your local authority or college or university, or see gov.uk/student-finance. Also see AskCPAG.org.uk and CPAG's *Student Support and Benefits Handbook* and *Benefits for Students in Scotland Handbook*.

6. Community care support from the local authority

If you have care needs, you may be able to get support, including accommodation, from your local authority or NHS primary care trust under community care legislation.

This is a complex area of law and beyond the scope of this *Handbook*, but see p509 for a brief description of the support available for asylum seekers and refused asylum seekers under the Care Act 2014.

There are restrictions and exclusions that affect all groups of migrants, but there are also exceptions to these rules that mean you may still be able to get support.

Note: community care support is not listed as a 'public fund' in the Immigration Rules. Therefore, if you have leave to enter or remain in the UK that is subject to a 'no recourse to public funds' condition, receiving community care support does not breach this condition. For more information on public funds, see p31.

Community care support is often misunderstood and poorly administered by local authorities and other providers. Get specialist advice before applying to your local authority for support or if you have been refused support.

Adults with care and support needs

Local authorities can provide support, including accommodation, to adults who have a need for care and support. However, if you are defined as a 'person subject to immigration control' (see p81), you are excluded if your need for care and support is solely as a result of being destitute or the physical effects, or anticipated physical effects, of being destitute.[44] Even if you are destitute, there must be another reason for your needing the care and support – eg, because of your age, disability, or physical or mental health problem. This test has become known as the 'destitution plus' test.

There are other exclusions that may also mean you cannot access support. For a summary of the exclusions that affect migrants, see p510.

For a summary of local authority support available to adults, see p509.

Other types of support

There are a number of other types of community care support that may be available from local authority social services departments or from NHS primary care trusts. The type of support available depends on your individual circumstances. The support may be services but could include accommodation – eg, if you have been detained, admitted or transferred to hospital under various sections of the Mental Health Act 1983, you are now no longer detained and you leave hospital, the clinical commissioning group, primary care trust or local health board and the local social services department have joint duties to provide you with aftercare services, which can include accommodation. A summary of the different community care provisions is in the *Disability Rights Handbook*, published annually by Disability Rights UK. The legislation under which these types of support can be provided is complex and frequently misunderstood. Get expert advice from a specialist community care adviser.

7. Support under the Children Act 1989

Local authorities have a duty to safeguard and promote the welfare of children who are 'in need' in their area.[45] If you are destitute and have children, you may be eligible for accommodation or support from your local authority under the Children Act 1989 (in Scotland, the Children (Scotland) Act 1995). A child who is destitute is generally considered to be 'in need', but a child can also be in need if s/he is disabled, or if s/he is unlikely to achieve or maintain a reasonable standard of health or development without the provision of services by a local authority.[46] Although the duty is to support the child, it extends to supporting parents or other family members if that is in the child's best interests.[47]

Some people are excluded from Children Act support, including some groups of adult migrants, but there are also exceptions. Children are always eligible for support under the Children Act regardless of immigration status.[48]

The provision of support can be complex, and is often misunderstood and poorly administered by local authorities. Get specialist advice before applying to your local authority for support, if you have been refused support or if the local authority tells you it can only accommodate your child but not you as well.

This *Handbook* does not cover support available under the Children Act. However, for limited further information about the rules affecting this support for asylum seekers and refused asylum seekers, see p511. For specialist advice on support available for destitute migrant families in England and Wales, contact Project 17 (see Appendix 2).

8. NHS healthcare

The UK's NHS is a residence-based healthcare system. However, not all healthcare is provided free of charge to everyone, and the charges can be considerable. Since 23 October 2017, providers of chargeable NHS services must charge patients who are chargeable, *in advance* of providing the service, unless doing so would prevent or delay services that are urgent or immediately necessary. All maternity care is classed as immediately necessary. If the service is chargeable but cannot be charged in advance, an invoice is issued after the care has been provided.

The legislation setting out the rules for NHS charges is different in England, Wales and Scotland. The legislation and guidance on how it should be implemented is not always applied correctly by the relevant NHS bodies. Get advice if you have been told that you will be charged, if you want to challenge charges or you have been refused treatment due to charges. The following information gives a broad overview.

There is a charge for hospital healthcare service, unless:

- the specific service is exempt (see below); *or*
- you are not chargeable (see p591).

NHS services are not listed in the definition of 'public funds' in the Immigration Rules (see p31). If you have leave to enter or remain in the UK on condition that you do not have recourse to public funds, you have not breached this condition if you receive NHS services. However, if the Home Office is notified that you have one or more NHS charges amounting to at least £500, this can be a reason for it to refuse an application for most types of immigration leave.[49] The NHS has a duty to notify the Home Office about debts of more than £500 that have been outstanding for more than two months. However, it should only notify the Home Office about the debt if certain criteria are met, including that there is no genuine outstanding challenge to the debt and no meaningful repayment plan is being adhered to .[50] If all the criteria cease to be met, the NHS should update the Home Office immediately.

Services exempt from charges

Health services that are currently exempt from charges, regardless of immigration or residence status, are broadly:[51]

- accident and emergency services, but not any provided after you have been admitted as an inpatient or at a follow-up outpatient appointment;
- services not provided in a hospital and not provided by staff employed to work in, or under the direction of, a hospital;
- services for diagnosing and treating specified conditions, including food poisoning, HIV, measles, malaria, tuberculosis, viral hepatitis, whooping cough and coronavirus;[52]
- services for diagnosing and treating sexually transmitted infections;
- services for treating conditions caused by torture, female genital mutilation, domestic violence or sexual violence, provided you have not travelled to the UK for the purpose of seeking that treatment;
- in England only, family planning services (this does not include maternity services or services providing terminations of pregnancies).

Note: there are no residence-related charges for primary healthcare, including services delivered through GP practices, NHS walk-in centres, dentists, pharmacists and optometrists. However, some of these services have other charges (eg, for dental care or prescriptions), and these have different exemption criteria. For details of who is exempt from these charges, see CPAG's *Welfare Benefits and Tax Credits Handbook.*

Who is not chargeable

You are charged for NHS hospital services unless, at the time you receive the NHS care, you are 'ordinarily resident' in the UK or you are exempt from charges. The exempt groups and the interpretation of 'ordinarily resident' vary between England, Wales and Scotland. The rules are complex and can be affected by many factors, including your nationality.

Who can be ordinarily resident in the UK

If you are 'ordinarily resident' in the UK you are entitled to free NHS care.[53]

Whether you 'ordinarily resident' in the UK for the purposes of NHS charging, depends on your nationality and the quality of your residence. You must be voluntarily and lawfully resident in the UK and be properly settled in the UK for the time being.

You can be ordinarily resident if you are a British citizen or have indefinite leave to enter or remain in the UK.

Until the end of the transition period (11pm on 31 December 2020 – see p164), you could also be ordinarily resident if you are a European Economic Area (EEA) national living in the UK in a settled way. However, since that date the rules for EEA nationals, and non-EEA family members of EEA nationals, have become more complex. Check whether you are covered by one of the groups exempt from NHS charges below and otherwise get advice on your individual circumstances.

Which groups are exempt from NHS charges

The groups that are exempt from NHS charges are numerous and the rules vary between England, Scotland and Wales, but the groups include those listed below. You will be exempt from NHS charges if at the time you receive your NHS care you:[54]

- have been granted leave under the European Union Settlement Scheme (see p49);
- are covered by a reciprocal healthcare agreement;
- (except, in England, for assisted conception services) are within a period of leave to enter or remain in the UK, in respect of which you have paid the 'immigration health surcharge' (or it was waived) (see p20);
- are an asylum seeker;
- have been granted refugee leave or humanitarian protection;
- are a refused asylum seeker – in England only you must also be in receipt of section 4 asylum support (see p493) or Care Act support (see p588);
- are receiving local authority support as a looked after child;
- are in immigration detention.

Further information

JCWI (Joint Council for the Welfare of Immigrants) has produced a short guide on NHS charging and also a detailed toolkit for advisers.[55]

Maternity Action has produced factsheets on the NHS charging rules and provide an email and telephone advice service on NHS maternity care and charging.[56]

Useful information on accessing healthcare in the UK, including if you are having difficulties in registering with a GP, is available online from Doctors of the World.[57]

9. Other financial help

Other financial help is available, especially if you are on a low income, have children, are an older person, or have an illness, disability or other special needs.

See the *Disability Rights Handbook*, published by Disability Rights UK, for other help if you have needs resulting from disability, health problems or caring responsibilities.

Food banks

If you are experiencing severe financial hardship (eg, caused by debt, or by having your benefits delayed or refused), you may be able to get vouchers for food that can be redeemed at a food bank. Vouchers are available from frontline care professionals, such as doctors, health visitors, social workers and advice workers. Jobcentre Plus staff may also provide vouchers. Further information and contact details for many food banks can be found at trusselltrust.org or by contacting your local authority.

You may be able to get help with food or meals through local community groups that are part of the FareShare network. Further information is available at fareshare.org.uk.

Repairs, home improvements and energy efficiency

Your local authority may be able to provide you with a grant to help with the cost of improving your home. The main types of grant available are:

- home improvement grants; *and*
- disabled facilities grants.

You may also be able to get:

- assistance from a home improvement agency (a local not-for-profit organisation) to repair, improve, maintain or adapt your home – sometimes called 'care and repair' or 'staying put' schemes – or with small repairs, safety checks and odd jobs from a handyperson service. For information see, in England, foundations.uk.com, in Wales, careandrepair.org.uk and in Scotland, careandrepairscotland.co.uk;

- a grant for help with insulation and other energy efficiency measures in your home. Help with fuel bills may also be available. Different schemes operate in England, Wales and Scotland. For further information, contact in England, Simple Energy Advice on 0800 444 202 (simpleenergyadvice.org.uk), in Wales, Nest on 0808 808 2244, (nest.gov.wales) in Scotland, Home Energy Scotland on 0808 808 2282 (homeenergyscotland.org) or visit energysavingtrust.org.uk. For more details, see CPAG's *Fuel Rights Handbook*.

Special funds for sick or disabled people

A range of help is available for people with an illness or disability to assist with things like paying for care services in their own home, equipment, holidays, furniture and transport needs, and for people with haemophilia or HIV contracted via haemophilia treatment. Grants are also available for practical support to help people do their jobs – eg, to pay for specialist equipment and travel. For more information, see the *Disability Rights Handbook*, published by Disability Rights UK.

Payments for former members of the armed forces

If you are a former member of the UK armed forces, or your spouse or civil partner died while in service, you may be able to claim under the one of the various schemes administered by the Ministry of Defence. The benefits and lump-sum payments include pensions, disablement benefits and compensation payments. Your entitlement depends on your circumstances, including the dates of service and, if relevant, the degree and effect of any disablement or ill health and the final salary. Further details are available from Veterans UK (gov.uk/government/organisations/veterans-uk).

Charities

There are many charities that provide various types of help to people in need. Your local authority social services department or local advice centre may know of appropriate charities that could assist you, or in your local library you can consult publications, such as *The Guide to Grants for Individuals in Need* and *Charitiy Choice* (see charitychoice.co.uk/bookstore). The organisation Turn2us has a website (turn2us.org.uk) with an A–Z of charities that can provide financial help. In many cases, applications for support can be made directly from the website. Information on grants available for individuals can also be found at fundsonline.org.uk.

Notes

1. Council tax reduction

1 **E** CTRS(PR)E Regs
W CTRS(DS)W Regs; CTRSPR(W) Regs
S CTR(S) Regs; CTR(SPC)S Regs
2 **E** Reg 13 CTRS(PR)E Regs
W Reg 29 CTRSPR(W) Regs; Sch para 20 CTRS(DS)W Regs
S Reg 19 CTR(SPC)S Regs; reg 19 CTR(S) Regs
3 **E** Reg 13(1A) CTRS(PR)E Regs
W Reg 29(2) CTRSPR(W) Regs; Sch para 20(2) CTRS(DS)W Regs
S Reg 19(2) CTR(SPC)S Regs; reg 19(2) CTR(S) Regs
4 *Szoma v SSWP* [2005] UKHL 64, reported as R(IS) 2/06; *Yesiloz v London Borough of Camden* [2009] EWCA Civ 415
5 para 6.2(b) IR
6 para 6.2(b) notes under 'public funds' definition, IR. Council tax reduction is not included in the regulations that are referred to in the notes that disregard claims made as a result of exemptions.
7 para 6.2(b) IR
8 **S** Reg 39(11) CTR(S) Regs
W Sch 6 para 17(10) CTRSPR(W) Regs; Sch para 51(10) CTRS(DS)W Regs
9 **E** Reg 12 CTRS(PR)E Regs
W Reg 28 CTRSPR(W) Regs; Sch para 19 CTRS(DS)W Regs
S Reg 16 CTR(SPC)S Regs; reg 16 CTR(S) Regs
10 **E** Reg 12 CTRS(PR)E Regs; reg 3 The Council Tax Reduction Schemes (Prescribed Requirements) (England) (Amendment) (No.2) Regulations 2014, No.3312
W Reg 28 CTRSPR(W) Regs; Sch para 19 CTRS(DS)W Regs; reg 31 The Council Tax Reduction Schemes (Prescribed Requirements and Default Scheme) (Wales) (Amendment) Regulations 2015, No.44
S Reg 16 CTR(SPC)S Regs; reg 16 CTR(S) Regs
11 *R (Winder and Others) v Sandwell MBC* [2014] EWHC 2617 (Admin)
12 **E** Reg 12 CTRS(PR)E Regs
W Reg 28 CTRSPR(W) Regs; Sch para 19 CTRS(DS)W Regs
S Reg 16 CTR(SPC)S Regs; reg 16 CTR(S) Regs
13 **E** Sch 8 para 7 CTRS(PR)E Regs
W Sch 13 para 5 CTRSPR(W) Regs; Sch para 111 CTRS(DS)W Regs
14 **E** Sch 8 para 7(3) CTRS(PR)E Regs
W Sch 13 para 5(3) CTRSPR(W) Regs; Sch para 111(3) CTRS(DS)W Regs
15 Sch 1 para 5 CTRS(PR)E Regs
16 Reg 26 CTRSPR(W) Regs; Sch para 17 CTRS(DS)W Regs
17 Regs 15, 17 and 18 CTR(SPC)S Regs; regs 15, 17 and 18 CTR(S) Regs

2. Local welfare assistance schemes

18 Welfare Funds (Scotland) Act 2015; reg 4 The Welfare Funds (Scotland) Regulations 2016, No.107; Scottish government, *Scottish Welfare Fund: statutory guidance*, May 2019, paras 4.3-4.10
19 Scottish government, *Scottish Welfare Fund: statutory guidance*, May 2019, para 6.8
20 Scottish government, *Scottish Welfare Fund; statutory guidance*, May 2019, section 10
21 para 6.2(b) IR
22 Scottish government, *Scottish Welfare Fund: statutory guidance*, May 2019, Annex A para 19; see also para 6.7

3. Early years food and vitamins

23 Regs 5(2) and 8 HSS&WF(A) Regs
24 Regs 13 and 14 WF(BSF) Regs
25 Regs 2(1) and 5(1) and Sch 3 HSS&WF(A) Regs; HSS(DHSF)(W) Regs; reg 2 and Sch 1 WF(BSF) Regs
26 **EW** Reg 3 HSS&WF(A) Regs
S Regs 7 and 8 WF(BSF) Regs
27 **EW** Reg 3 HSS&WF(A) Regs
S Regs 6(3) and 10 WF(BSF) Regs
28 Reg 2(1) HSSWF(A) Regs
29 Reg 4 WF(BSF) Regs
30 Reg 2(1) HSS&WF(A) Regs
31 Reg 5 WF(BSF) Regs
32 Reg 4 and Sch 2 HSS&WF(A) Regs

33 **EW** Reg 4(2) and (3A) HSS&WF(A) Regs
S Reg 11(2) WF(BSF) Regs
34 Reg 3 HSS&WF(A) Regs
35 Reg 8A HSS&WF(A) Regs

4. **Free milk for children**
36 Reg 18 WF Regs

5. **Education benefits**
37 **E** s512ZB Education Act 1996; The Education (Free School Lunches) (Prescribed Tax Credits) (England) Order 2003, No.383; The Free School Lunches and Milk (Universal Credit) (England) Order 2013, No.650
W s512ZB Education Act 1996; The Education (Free School Lunches) (Prescribed Tax Credits) (Wales) Order 2003, No.879 (W.110); The Free School Lunches and Milk (Universal Credit) (Wales) Order 2019, No.187 (W.47)
S s53(3) Education (Scotland) Act 1980; The Education (School Lunches) (Scotland) Regulations 2009, No.178
38 s53(3)-(5) Education (Scotland) Act 1980
39 For CTC, the legislation only provides for this in Scotland.
40 Provided under Part VI of IAA 1999
41 The Education (School Lunches) (Scotland) Regulations 2015, No.269
42 s88 School Standards and Organisation (Wales) Act 2013
43 The Welfare Reform Act 2012 (Commencement No.30 and Transitory Provisions) Order 2018, No.145; Art 3 The Free School Lunches and Milk (Universal Credit) (Wales) Order 2019, No.187 (W.47)

6. **Community care support from the local authority**
44 **E** s21 CA 2014
W s46 Social Services and Well-being (Wales) Act 2014
S s12(2A) Social Work (Scotland) Act 1968

7. **Support under the Children Act 1989**
45 s17 CA 1989; s22 C(S)A 1995
46 s17(10) CA 1989
47 s17(3) CA 1989; s22(3) C(S)A 1995
48 Sch 3 para 2(1)(b) NIAA 2002

8. **NHS healthcare**
49 See, for example, paras S-EC.3.2, S-LTR.4.5, S-ILR.4.5 Appendix FM IR
50 Department of Health and Social Care, *Overseas Chargeable Patients, NHS Debt and Immigration Rules: guidance on administration and data sharing*, 26 March 2019, s4
51 **E** Regs 8 and 9 NHS(COV) Regs 2015
W Reg 3 NHS(COV) Regs 1989
S Reg 3 NHS(COV)(S) Regs
52 **E** Sch 1 NHS(COV) Regs 2015
W Sch 1 NHS(COV) Regs 1989
S Sch 1 NHS(COV)(S) Regs 1989
53 s39 IA 2014
E Regs 2 and 7 NHS(COV) Regs 2015
W Regs 1 and 2 NHS(COV) Regs 1989
S Regs 1 and 2 NHS(COV)(S) Regs 1989
54 s.39 IA 2014
E NHS(COV) Regs 2015
W NHS(COV) Regs 1989
S NHS(COV)(S) Regs 1989
55 jcwi.org.uk/nhs-charging-toolkits
56 maternityaction.org.uk
57 doctorsoftheworld.org.uk/useful-resources

Appendices

Appendix 1

Glossary of terms

A2 national. A national of the European Union member states Romania and Bulgaria.

A8 national. A national of the European Union member states Czech Republic, Estonia, Hungary, Latvia, Lithuania, Poland, Slovakia and Slovenia.

Absent. Not physically in an area such as Great Britain; the alternative to present.

Accession states. The newer members of the European Union: Croatia, the A2 states and the A8 states.

Administrative removal. A legal mechanism used to remove foreign nationals who have entered the UK illegally, including by deception, or to remove those who have breached the conditions of their leave, including overstaying.

Applicable amount. The maximum amount of benefit set by the government, taking account of certain factors such as age and whether someone is single or part of a couple.

Application registration card. The form of identification for those who have claimed asylum.

ASPEN card. A pre-paid visa chip and pin card, given to asylum seekers in receipt of asylum support. It is credited by the Home Office and can be used in a similar way to a debit card to pay for items in shops or (for those getting section 95 support) to withdraw cash from most ATMs.

Association agreement. A treaty signed between the European Union and a country outside the European Union, giving reciprocal rights and obligations.

Asylum. Leave to enter or remain in the UK as a refugee, given under the Refugee Convention or Article 3 of the European Convention on Human Rights (including protection under the Refugee Qualification Directive).

Asylum seeker. A person who has applied for asylum and whose application has yet to be decided, or whose appeal against a refusal of an asylum application remains outstanding.

Asylum support. Support provided by the Home Office to various categories of asylum seekers and failed asylum seekers. In the past, this was provided by a section of the Home Office called the National Asylum Support Service (NASS). This was abolished in 2007, but the term 'NASS support' continues to be used.

Certificate of entitlement. A certificate of entitlement to the right of abode demonstrates that a person has the right of abode – ie, the right to travel freely to and from the UK. British citizens have the right of abode and can demonstrate this by producing their passports. A few Commonwealth nationals also have the right of abode and can obtain a certificate of entitlement, endorsed in their own national passport, to demonstrate this.

Common travel area. The UK, Ireland, Isle of Man and the Channel Islands.

Commonwealth countries. Antigua and Barbuda, Australia, Bahamas, Bangladesh, Barbados, Belize, Botswana, Brunei Darussalam, Cameroon, Canada, Cyprus, Dominica, Fiji Islands, Gambia, Ghana, Grenada, Guyana, India, Jamaica, Kenya, Kiribati, Lesotho, Malawi, Malaysia, Maldives, Malta, Mauritius, Mozambique, Namibia, Nauru, New Zealand, Nigeria, Pakistan, Papua New Guinea, Rwanda, Saint Lucia, Samoa, Seychelles, Sierra Leone, Singapore, Solomon Islands, South Africa, Sri Lanka, St Kitts and Nevis, St Vincent and the Grenadines, Swaziland, Tanzania, Tonga, Trinidad and Tobago, Tuvalu, Uganda, United Kingdom, Vanuatu and Zambia.

Competent state. The European Economic Area country responsible under the European Union co-ordination rules for paying your benefit and to which you are liable to pay national insurance contributions.

Court of Justice of the European Union. The European Union institution that ensures that European Union law is observed by member states. It sits in Luxembourg. Previously known as the **European Court of Justice**.

Deportation. A legal mechanism used to remove a foreign national on the recommendation of a criminal court following her/his conviction for a criminal offence, or if the Home Secretary has decided that a person's presence in the UK is 'not conducive to the public good'. If an order has been signed to deport a foreign national, s/he may not return unless and until the order has been revoked.

Derivative right to reside. The term given to certain residence rights that are derived from someone else in specific ways.

Destitute. For asylum support purposes, someone who does not have access to adequate accommodation or who cannot meet her/his essential living needs.

Destitution domestic violence concession. A provision under which people who have immigration leave on the basis of a relationship, but which has broken down as a result of domestic violence, can be granted three months' leave in which to apply for indefinite leave to remain.

Digital- only status. A digital/electronic record of immigration status and conditions that can be viewed by inputting data into a Home Office website.

Discretionary leave. Permission to enter or remain in the UK given to a person outside the Immigration Rules or to someone who is refused asylum but who cannot be removed under another Article of the European Convention on Human Rights or for other humanitarian reasons.

eGate. An electronic immigration barrier at a UK port. See also 'passport eGate'.

Enforcement. A term used to refer to any of the different ways in which a person can be forced to leave the UK for immigration reasons – ie, having been refused entry at a port, having been declared an illegal entrant, or having been notified that s/he is someone who is liable for administrative removal, or who is being deported.

Entry clearance officer. An official at a British post overseas who deals with immigration applications made to that post.

European Community. The European Union was previously known as the European Community and, before that, the European Economic Community. In this *Handbook*, the legislation of all three is referred to as European Union law.

European Convention on Human Rights. An international instrument agreed by the Council of Europe. The rights guaranteed by it have now largely been incorporated into UK law by the Human Rights Act 1998.

European Convention on Social and Medical Assistance. An agreement signed by all the European Economic Area states, plus Turkey, requiring the ratifying states to provide assistance in cash and kind to nationals of other ratifying states who are lawfully present in their territory and who are without sufficient resources on the same conditions as their own nationals.

European Economic Area. Covers all European Union states plus Iceland, Liechtenstein and Norway. European Economic Area nationals have free movement within these and all European Union member states. From 1 June 2002, the right to free movement also applies to Switzerland.

European Union Settlement Scheme. The scheme administered by the Home Office under which European Economic Area nationals and their family members can apply for leave, enabling them to remain lawfully in the UK following the UK's departure from the European Union.

European Social Charter. The 1961 Council of Europe Social Charter, signed by all the European Economic Area countries, plus Macedonia and Turkey.

European Union. Austria, Belgium, Bulgaria, Croatia, Cyprus, Czechia, Denmark, Estonia, Finland, France, Germany, Greece, Hungary, Ireland, Italy, Latvia, Lithuania, Luxembourg, Malta, Netherlands, Poland, Portugal, Romania, Slovakia, Slovenia, Spain and Sweden .

European Union/European Economic Area national. The term used in this *Handbook* to describe citizens of European Union member states/European Economic Area countries.

eVisa. A printed electronic visa.

Exceptional leave. A form of leave to remain granted outside the Immigration Rules that has now been replaced with humanitarian protection and discretionary leave for those seeking asylum.

First-tier Tribunal (Asylum Support). The tribunal that decides appeals against the refusal or termination of asylum support. It sits in east London, but hears appeals nationwide (by video link if necessary).

First-tier Tribunal (Immigration and Asylum Chamber). The tribunal that hears and determines appeals against decisions made by the Secretary of State for the Home Department about asylum, immigration and nationality.

First-tier Tribunal (Social Entitlement Chamber). The tribunal that hears and determines appeals against decisions made by the Department for Work and Pensions and local authorities about benefit entitlement.

Great Britain. Comprises England, Wales and Scotland.

Habitual residence. The type of residence someone must usually have to get income support, income-based jobseeker's allowance, income-related employment and support allowance, housing benefit, pension credit, universal credit, attendance allowance, disability living allowance, carer's allowance and personal independence payment. The term 'habitually resident' is not defined in the benefit regulations and is determined by looking at all the person's circumstances.

Home Office. The government department responsible for asylum, immigration and nationality issues.

Humanitarian protection. Permission to enter or remain in the UK given to a person who needs to be protected from harm, but whose case does not fit the criteria for refugee status.

Illegal entrant. A person who immigration officials decide has entered the UK in breach of the immigration laws. This could be by deception or clandestinely.

Immigration bail. A form of lawful immigration status given as an alternative to detention and with certain restrictions on the person's liberty to work and sometimes requiring her/him to live at a known address and/or report to an immigration enforcement office at specified times. Commonly given to people who have been refused asylum.

Immigration judge. A person who determines appeals in the First-tier Tribunal (Immigration and Asylum Chamber) or Upper Tribunal (Immigration and Asylum Chamber).

Immigration officer. An official, usually stationed at a British port of entry, who decides whether to grant or refuse leave to enter. Immigration officers also have responsibility for enforcing immigration control.

Immigration Rules. Rules made by the Home Secretary, setting out the requirements for granting or refusing entry clearance, leave to enter and leave to remain to people applying in the different categories.

Indefinite leave. Permission to enter or remain that has no time limit.

Integration loan. An interest-free loan made to assist people who have recently been given refugee status or humanitarian protection to integrate into UK society.

Lawfully working. Depending on the context, either working with the permission of the Home Office or, for accession state nationals, working in accordance with any employment restrictions that apply.

Limited leave. Permission to enter or remain that is given for a certain period of time only. Also referred to as 'time-limited leave'.

Maintenance undertaking. A written undertaking given by someone under the Immigration Rules to be responsible for the maintenance and accommodation of another person who is applying to come to or stay in the UK.

Ordinarily resident. A residence requirement for several benefits and tax credits. A person is ordinarily resident where s/he has her/his home that s/he has adopted for a settled purpose and where s/he lives for the time being.

Passport eGate (also **ePassport gate**). Automated self-service barriers, operated by the Home Office, using facial recognition technology to verify a traveller's identity against the data stored in the chip in her/his biometric passport.

Past presence test. A requirement for some benefits to have been present in Great Britain for a period of time before the date of claim.

Person from abroad. A social security definition that refers to a person who has failed the habitual residence test for the purposes of income support, income-based jobseeker's allowance, income-related employment and support allowance or housing benefit.

Person subject to immigration control. A person in one of four specific groups of non-European Economic Area nationals who are excluded from entitlement to most social security benefits and whose entitlement to support under the Care Act 2014 is restricted.

Points-based system. The system of controlling migration to the UK from outside the European Union for economic purposes or studies.

Present. Physically in an area such as Great Britain; the alternative to absent.

Pre-settled status. Limited leave to remain granted under the EU Settlement Scheme to European Economic Area nationals, their family members and those with derivative residence rights who have lived in the UK for less than five years.

Public funds. These are defined in the Immigration Rules as: housing provided by local authorities, either for homeless people or allocated from the local authority's housing register; attendance allowance; carer's allowance; child benefit; child tax credit; council tax benefit; council tax reduction; disability living allowance; income-related employment and support allowance; housing benefit; income support; income-based jobseeker's allowance; local welfare assistance (except the Discretionary Assistance Fund for Wales); pension credit; personal independence payment; severe disablement allowance; social fund payments; working tax credit; and universal credit.

Reciprocal agreement. A bilateral agreement made between the UK and another country, with the purpose of protecting benefit entitlement for people moving between the two.

Refugee. A person who satisfies the definition of someone who needs international protection under Article 1A(2) of the 1951 Convention Relating to the Status of Refugees.

Refugee Convention. The 1951 United Nations Convention Relating to the Status of Refugees, a multilateral treaty defining who is a refugee and setting out the rights of people who are granted asylum.

Removal. The final procedure for sending a person refused entry, or who is being treated as an illegal entrant, or who is subject to the administrative removal or deportation process, away from the UK.

Resident. A requirement of a category D retirement pension and a necessary part of ordinary residence and habitual residence. Residence is more than presence and is usually where you have your home for the time being.

Restricted leave. Leave to remain given outside the Immigration Rules to someone who is excluded from refugee or humanitarian protection leave but who cannot be removed from the UK for human rights reasons. Replaced discretionary leave.

Right of abode. The right to enter, remain, leave and return freely to the UK without needing to obtain leave from the immigration authorities. All British citizens, and some Commonwealth nationals, have the right of abode.

Right to reside. A residence requirement for entitlement to some benefits and tax credits. For child benefit and child tax credit, a person must have a right to reside in the UK, and, to satisfy the habitual residence test for means-tested benefits, s/he must have a right to reside in the common travel area. The right to reside depends on someone's nationality, immigration status and whether s/he has rights under European Union law.

Secretary of State for the Home Department (the Home Secretary). The government minister with primary responsibility for decisions made by the Home Office on immigration, asylum and nationality.

Section 4 support. A form of asylum support for destitute asylum seekers whose asylum application has been refused and who fit certain eligibility criteria.

Section 95 support. A form of support for people who have made an application for asylum in the UK.

Settlement/settled status. Defined in immigration law as being ordinarily resident in the UK without any restrictions on the time the person is able to remain here.

Generally used to refer to those with indefinite leave, including when granted under the EU Settlement Scheme.

Sponsor. The person (usually a relative) with whom someone is applying to join, or remain with, in the UK, and/or a person who is to be responsible for the applicant's maintenance and accommodation in the UK.

Stateless person. Someone who is not considered a national by any country.

Subject to immigration control. Often used to refer to those who need leave to enter or remain in the UK – and this is the definition given in the Asylum and Immigration Act 1996. However, the Immigration and Asylum Act 1999 gives a different, narrower, definition, which is used to exclude people from most benefits and tax credits and certain services provided by local authorities' social services departments. This *Handbook* uses the term as it is defined in the 1999 Act.

Temporary admission. A temporary licence given to people before 15 January 2018 to be in the UK while they are waiting for a decision to be made on their immigration status or while they are waiting to be removed from the UK. The alternative to temporary admission is detention.

Third country. Usually used to refer to a country to which the Home Office wishes to send an asylum seeker for her/his application for asylum to be considered, other than the country of which s/he is a national, rather than in the UK.

The United Kingdom. Comprises England, Wales, Scotland and Northern Ireland. The Channel Islands of Jersey and Guernsey, and the Isle of Man, are Crown dependencies and not part of the UK.

UK Visas and Immigration. The Home Office department that deals with immigration control.

Unmarried partners. A term used in the Immigration Rules to refer to couples (heterosexual or same-sex) who have been together for two or more years, who are in a relationship 'akin to marriage' and who cannot marry according to the law – eg, because they are of the same sex or one of them is already married. The

Immigration Rules give unmarried partners some rights to enter and remain in the UK if one partner is settled in the UK or has limited leave to enter or remain here.

Upper Tribunal (Immigration and Asylum Chamber). The tribunal that hears and determines appeals against determinations made by the First-tier Tribunal (Immigration and Asylum Chamber) and most immigration-related applications for judicial review.

Upper Tribunal (Social Entitlement Chamber). The tribunal that hears and determines appeals against decisions made by the First-tier Tribunal (Social Entitlement Chamber) about benefit entitlement.

Visa national. A person who must obtain entry clearance before travelling to the UK for most purposes, unless s/he is a person with indefinite leave returning within two years or returning within a period of earlier leave granted for more than six months. For a list of countries covered, see Appendix 1 to the Immigration Rules.

Work permit. A document issued by UK Visas and Immigration to employers, allowing them to employ a named individual in a particular job.

Appendix 2

Information and advice

Immigration and asylum

If you need help with an immigration problem, you can obtain advice from your local law centre, a solicitor specialising in immigration work or one of the agencies listed below.

Note: anyone who gives immigration advice must be professionally regulated. For further details, see p7.

AIRE Centre (Advice on Individual Rights in Europe)

Room 505
Charles Clore House
17 Russell Square
London WC1B 5DR
Tel: 020 7831 4276
info@airecentre.org
airecentre.org

Promotes awareness of European legal rights and assists people to assert these.

Asylum Support Appeals Project (ASAP)

Studio 11/12
Container City Building
48 Trinity Buoy Wharf
London E14 0FN
Tel: 07903 630 392
Advice line (advisers only): 020 3716 0283 (Mon, Wed and Fri 2pm–4pm)
asaproject.org

Offers free legal representation and advice to asylum seekers on appeal at Asylum Support Tribunal, and provides advice to frontline organisations and advisers.

British Red Cross

44 Moorfields
London EC2Y 9AL
Tel: 0344 871 1111
For help during the coronavirus pandemic: 0808 196 3651
contactus@redcross.org.uk
redcross.org.uk

Provides urgent support for refugees and vulnerable migrants in specific areas across the UK.

Civil Legal Advice

Tel: 0345 345 4345
Minicom: 0345 609 6677
(Mon–Fri 9am–8pm; Sat 9am–12.30pm)
gov.uk/civil-legal-advice
gov.uk/check-legal-aid

A legal aid eligibility checker: find-legal-advice.justice.gov.uk

A directory of legal aid suppliers in England and Wales.

Consonant (formerly Asylum Aid and Migrants Resource Centre)

Berol House
25 Ashley Road
London N17 9LJ
Tel: 020 7354 9631
legal@consonant.org.uk
legal.consonant.org.uk

Specialists in immigration law offering advice.

Doctors of the World

29th Floor
One Canada Square
London E14 5AA
Tel: 020 7167 5789
Advice line for the public: 0808 164 7686 (Mon–Fri 10am–12pm)
Advice line for organisations: 020 7078 9629
clinic@doctorsoftheworld.org.uk
doctorsoftheworld.org.uk

Runs clinics and advocacy programmes in London to groups such as destitute migrants.

Greater Manchester Immigration Aid Unit

1 Delaunays Road
Crumpsall Green
Manchester M8 4QS
Tel: 0161 740 7722
info@gmiau.org
gmiau.org

Provides free, confidential immigration and asylum legal advice and representation to people in the local community.

Immigration Law Practitioners' Association

Lindsey House
40–42 Charterhouse Street
London EC1M 6JN
Tel: 020 7251 8383
info@ilpa.org.uk
ilpa.org.uk

A professional association aiming to promote and improve advice and representation in immigration, nationality and asylum law.

Joint Council for the Welfare of Immigrants

115 Old Street
London EC1V 9RT
Tel: 020 7251 8708
Irregular migrants helpline: 020 7553 7470 (Monday, Tuesday and Thursday 10am–1pm)
info@jcwi.org.uk

jcwi.org.uk

Supports individuals and families with legal advice and challenges unjust laws and practices.

Law Centres Network

Floor 1, Tavis House
1–6 Tavistock Square
London WC1H 9NA
Tel: 020 3637 1330
lawcentres.org.uk

Does not give advice but can provide details of your nearest law centre.

Maternity Action

Migrant Women's Rights Service
Second floor
3–4 Wells Terrace
London N4 3JU
020 7251 6189 (Monday and Thursday 2–4pm)
migrantwomensrights@maternityaction.org.uk
maternityaction.org.uk/migrant-womens-rights-service

Advises supporters of migrant women who are pregnant or new mothers.

Migrant Help

Charlton House
Dour Street
Dover CT16 1AT
Tel: 01304 203 977
Free asylum helpline: 0808 801 0 503
info@migranthelpuk.org

migranthelpuk.org

Delivers support and advice services to migrants in the UK.

Migrant Legal Action

53 Addington Square
London SE5 7LB
Tel: 020 7701 0141
Advice line: 020 3150 1470 (Mon–Fri 2–4pm)
info@migrantlegalaction.org.uk
southwarkadvice.org.uk

Provides a specialist legal service, free of charge.

Project 17

St Joseph's Hospice
Mare St
London E8 4SA
Tel: 07963 509 044
Advice line (advisers only): 07701 330 016
info@project17.org.uk
project17.org.uk

Works to end destitution among migrant children. Helps families experiencing exceptional poverty to improve their access to local authority support.

Refugee Action

Victoria Charity Centre
11 Belgrave Road
London SW1V 1RB
Tel: 020 7952 1511
info@refugee-action.org.uk
refugee-action.org.uk/our-services/help-and-advice

Refugee Action has projects in London, Birmingham, Coventry, Stoke-on-Trent, Manchester and Merseyside.

Refugee Council

PO Box 68614
London E15 1NS
Tel: 020 7346 6700
Infoline (for help finding support during the COVID-19 pandemic): 0808 196 7272
info@refugeecouncil.org.uk
refugeecouncil.org.uk

Provides asylum seekers and refugees with crisis advice and practical support.

Rights of Women

52–54 Featherstone Street
London EC1Y 8RT
Tel: 020 7251 6575
info@row.org.uk
Advice line for women: 020 7490 7689 (Mon and Thur 10am–1pm and 2pm–5pm)
Professionals advice line: 020 8138 8028 (fortnightly on Friday 10am–12pm)
rightsofwomen.org.uk/get-advice/immigration-and-asylum-law

Advises on immigration and asylum law, with a focus on supporting survivors of domestic abuse.

Scottish Refugee Council

6th Floor, Portland House
17 Renfield Street
Glasgow G2 5AH
Tel: 0141 248 9799
Advice line: 0808 196 7274 (Mondays, Tuesdays, Thursdays and Fridays 10am–1pm and 2–4pm; Wednesdays 2–4pm)
info@scottishrefugeecouncil.org.uk
scottishrefugeecouncil.org.uk

Welsh Refugee Council

120–122 Broadway
Cardiff CF24 1NJ
Tel: 0808 196 7273
info@wrc.wales
wrc.wales

Social security

Independent advice and representation

It is often difficult for unsupported individuals to get a positive response from the Department for Work and Pensions, local authority or HM Revenue and Customs (HMRC). It can help if you obtain advice about your entitlement and how you can demonstrate this. If you can get good-quality assistance from an adviser who will take on your case, this is even more helpful, particularly if you need to challenge a decision. The following may be able to assist.

- Advicelocal (advicelocal.uk) has details of advice organisations in your area.
- Citizens Advice. You can find out where your local office is from the Citizens Advice website at citizensadvice.org.uk (England and Wales) or cas.org.uk (Scotland).
- Law centres. You can find your nearest law centre at lawcentres.org.uk.
- LawWorks (lawworks.org.uk) has details of local legal advice centres that give free advice.
- Housing association welfare rights services for tenants.
- Local authority welfare rights services.
- Local and national organisations for particular groups of claimants may offer help. For instance, there are unemployed centres, pensioners' groups and organisations for people with disabilities.

Advice from CPAG

Unfortunately, CPAG is unable to deal with enquiries directly from members of the public, but if you are an adviser you can phone or email for help with advising your client.

Advisers in England, Wales and Northern Ireland can call from 10am to 12pm and from 2pm to 4pm (Monday to Friday) on 020 7812 5231. Email advice is now limited to enquiries that are specifically about universal credit, child benefit and tax credits. Our email address is advice@cpag.org.uk. For more information, see cpag.org.uk/welfare-rights.

Advisers in Scotland can call us from 10am to 4pm (Monday to Thursday) and from 10am to 12pm (Friday) on 0141 552 0552, or email advice@cpagscotland.org.uk.

CPAG's Upper Tribunal assistance project can provide help to advisers helping claimants challenge tribunal decisions. See cpag.org.uk/welfare-rights/upper-tribunal-assistance-project. We also provide training and advice to support advisers to pursue judicial review remedies. See cpag.org.uk/welfare-rights/judicial-review.

AskCPAG is a new information and solutions platform for advisers, including a digital version of the *Welfare Benefits and Tax CreditsHandbook*, fully searchable and updated throughout the year. See AskCPAG.org.uk.

CPAG takes on a small number of test cases each year. We focus on cases that have the potential to improve the lives of families with children in poverty. If you are an adviser and would like to refer a test case to us, see cpag.org.uk/welfare-rights/legal-test-cases.

Human rights

Equality Advisory and Support Service

FREEPOST EASS HELPLINE FPN6521
Tel: 0808 800 0082
Textphone: 0808 800 0084
equalityadvisoryservice.com

Information, advice and support on discrimination and human rights issues, and the relevant law.

Appendix 3

Useful addresses

Immigration and asylum

UK Visas and Immigration

Lunar House
40 Wellesley Road
Croydon CR9 2BY
gov.uk/government/organisations/uk-visas-and-immigration

UK Visas and Immigration Contact Centre

Tel: 0300 790 6268

Asylum support

Tel: 0808 801 0503

Voluntary returns service

Tel: 0300 004 0202
gov.uk/return-home-voluntarily

Note: contacting the Home Office directly to discuss your assisted voluntary return may have an impact on any outstanding protection or human rights-based claim that you have made. You may therefore wish to obtain independent advice before doing so.

Enquiries from European citizens

Tel: 0300 790 6268

EU Settlement Scheme

Tel: 0300 123 7379 (Mon–Fri 8am–8pm, Sat–Sun 9.30am–4.30pm)
Advisers tel: 0300 790 0566 (Mon–Fri 8am–8pm, Sat–Sun 9.30am–4.30pm)
Online applications: gov.uk/settled-status-eu-citizens-families

Employer and educational institution helpline

Tel: 0300 123 4699
businesshelpdesk@homeoffice.gov.uk
educatorshelpdesk@homeoffice.gov.uk

Citizenship and nationality

Tel: 0300 790 6268
nationalityenquiries@homeoffice.gov.uk

Passport Office

PO Box 767
Southport
PR8 9PW
Tel: 0300 222 0000
gov.uk/government/organisations/hm-passport-office

Independent Chief Inspector of Borders and Immigration

5th Floor
Globe House
89 Eccleston Square
London SW1V 1PN
chiefinspector@icibi.gov.uk
gov.uk/government/organisations/independent-chief-inspector-of-borders-and-immigration

First-tier Tribunal (Immigration and Asylum Chamber)

PO Box 6987
Leceister LE1 6ZX
Tel: 0300 123 1711
customer.service@justice.gov.uk
gov.uk/immigration-asylum-tribunal

Note: urgent appeals must be addressed to:
Expedite Requests for The First-tier Tribunal
Office of the Duty Judge
Expedited Appeal Hearing Requests
First-tier Tribunal (Immigration and Asylum Chamber)
PO Box 6987
Leicester LE1 6ZX
Fax: 0870 739 5895
customer.service@justice.gov.uk

Upper Tribunal (Immigration and Asylum Chamber)

1A Field House
15–25 Breams Buildings
London EC4A 1DZ
Tel: 0300 123 1711
Fax: 0870 324 0095
fieldhousecorrespondence@justice.gov.uk
gov.uk/upper-tribunal-immigration-asylum

First-tier Tribunal (Asylum Support)

2nd Floor
Import Building
2 Clove Crescent
London E14 2BE
Freephone: 0800 681 6509
asylumsupporttribunals@justice.gov.uk
gov.uk/appeal-first-tier-asylum-support-tribunal
gov.uk/courts-tribunals/first-tier-tribunal-asylum-support

Office of the Immigration Services Commissioner

5th Floor
21 Bloomsbury Street
London WC1B 3HF
Tel: 0345 000 0046
info@oisc.gov.uk
gov.uk/government/organisations/office-of-the-immigration-services-commissioner

Solicitors Regulation Authority

The Cube
199 Wharfside Street
Birmingham B1 1RN
Tel: 0370 606 2555
sra.org.uk

Legal Ombudsman

PO Box 6806
Wolverhampton WV1 9WJ
Tel: 0300 555 0333
enquiries@legalombudsman.org.uk
legalombudsman.org.uk

For complaints about lawyers.

European Delegation to the UK

Europe House
32 Smith Square
London SW1P 3EU
Tel: 020 7973 1992
Freephone: 00 800 67891011
Fax: 020 7973 1900
delegation-united-kingdom@eeas.europa.eu
eeas.europa.eu/delegations/united-kingdom_en

Social security

HM Courts and Tribunals Service

Tribunal areas

Birmingham
Administrative Support Centre
PO Box 14620
Birmingham B16 6FR
Tel: 0300 123 1142
ascbirmingham@justice.gov.uk

Bradford
Phoenix House
Rushden Avenue
Thornbury
Bradford BD3 7BH
Tel: 0300 123 1142
sscs_Bradford@justice.gov.uk

Cardiff
Eastgate House
35–43 Newport Road
Cardiff CF24 0ABYP
Tel: 0300 123 1142
sscsa-cardiff@justice.gov.uk

Glasgow
Glasgow Tribunals Centre
20 York Street
Glasgow G2 2GT
Tel: 0300 790 6234
sscsa-glasgow@justice.gov.uk

Leeds
York House
31 York Place
Leeds LS1 2ED
Tel: 0300 123 1142
sscsa-leeds@justice.gov.uk

Liverpool
36 Dale Street
Liverpool L2 5UZ
Tel: 0300 123 1142
sscsa-liverpool@justice.gov.uk

Newcastle
Newcastle Civil and Family Courts and Tribunals Centre
Barras Bridge
Newcastle upon Tyne
NE1 8QF
Tel: 0300 123 1142
sscsa-newcastle@justice.gov.uk

Sutton
Copthall House
9 The Pavement
Grove Road
Sutton SM1 1DA
Tel: 0300 123 1142
sscsa-sutton@justice.gov.uk

Direct lodgement of appeals

England and Wales

HMCTS SSCS Appeals Centre
PO Box 1203
Bradford BD1 9WP

Scotland

HMCTS SSCS Appeals Centre
PO Box 27080
Glasgow G2 9HQ

First-tier Tribunal (Tax Chamber)

PO Box 16972
Birmingham B16 6TZ
Tel: 0300 123 1024
taxappeals@justice.gov.uk
gov.uk/tax-tribunal

The Upper Tribunal (Administrative Appeals Chamber)

England and Wales

5th Floor
7 Rolls Buildings
Fetter Lane
London EC4A 1NL
Tel: 020 7071 5662
adminappeals@justice.gov.uk
gov.uk/administrative-appeals-tribunal

Scotland

George House
126 George Street
Edinburgh EH2 4HH
Tel: 0131 271 4310
utaacmailbox@gov.scot
gov.uk/administrative-appeals-tribunal

Northern Ireland

Tribunal Hearing Centre
2nd Floor
Royal Courts of Justice
Chichester Street
Belfast BT1 3JF
Tel: 028 9072 4848
gov.uk/administrative-appeals-tribunal

The Upper Tribunal (Tax and Chancery Chamber)

England and Wales

5th Floor
7 Rolls Buildings
Fetter Lane
London EC4A 1NL
Tel: 020 7612 9730
uttc@justice.gov.uk
gov.uk/tax-upper-tribunal

Scotland

Upper Tribunal for Scotland
The Glasgow Tribunals Centre
20 York Street
Glasgow G2 8GT
Tel: 0141 302 5880
uppertribunalforscotland@scotcourtstribunals.gov.uk
scotcourts.gov.uk/the-courts/court-locations/the-upper-tribunal-for-scotland

Department for Work and Pensions

Caxton House
Tothill Street
London SW1H 9NA
gov.uk/government/organisations/department-for-work-pensions

Government Legal Department

102 Petty France
London SW1H 9GL
Tel: 020 7210 3000
Litigation enquiries: 020 7210 8500
thetreasurysolicitor@governmentlegal.gov.uk
gov.uk/government/organisations/government-legal-department

Department of Health and Social Care (Overseas Healthcare)

Overseas Healthcare Services
NHS Business Services Authority
Bridge House
152 Pilgrim Street
Newcastle upon Tyne NE1 6SN
Tel: 0191 218 1999
nhsbsa.ohsregistrations@nhs.net

NHS healthcare information for visitors and residents from EEA and Switzerland and for UK citizens living in the EU, EEA and Switzerland.

Disability and Carers Service

Attendance Allowance Service Centre

Freepost DWP Attendance Allowance
Tel: 0800 731 0122
Textphone: 0800 731 0317
gov.uk/attendance-allowance

Disability Living Allowance Unit

Claimants born on or before 8 April 1948:
Freepost Disability Living Allowance 65
Tel: 0800 731 0122
Textphone: 0800 731 0317
gov.uk/dla-disability-living-allowance-benefit

Claimants born after 8 April 1948 who are over 16 years old:
Disability Living Allowance
Warbreck House
Warbreck Hill Road
Blackpool FY2 0YE
Tel: 0800 121 4600
Textphone: 0800 121 4523
gov.uk/dla-disability-living-allowance-benefit

Claimants aged under 16 years:
Disability Benefit Centre 4
Post Handling Site B
Wolverhampton WV99 1BY
Tel: 0800 121 4600
Textphone: 0800 121 4523
gov.uk/disability-living-allowance-children

Personal Independence Payment Unit

Personal Independence Payment New Claims
Post Handling Site B
Wolverhampton WV99 1AH
Claims: 0800 917 2222; textphone 0800 917 7777
Helpline: 0800 121 4433; textphone 0800 121 4493
gov.uk/pip

Carer's Allowance Unit

Mail Handling Site A
Wolverhampton
WV98 2AB
Tel: 0800 731 0297
Textphone: 0800 731 0317
gov.uk/carers-allowance

Exporting benefits overseas

Exportability Co-ordinator
Room B215
Pension, Disability and Carers Service
Warbreck House
Warbreck Hill Road
Blackpool FY2 0YE
gov.uk/claim-benefits-abroad/disability-benefits

Jobcentre Plus

New benefit claims

Tel: 0800 055 6688
Welsh language: 0800 012 1888
Textphone: 0800 023 4888
gov.uk/contact-jobcentre-plus/new-benefit-claims

Enquiries about ongoing claims

Tel: 0800 169 0310
Welsh language: 0800 328 1744
Textphone: 0800 169 0314
gov.uk/contact-jobcentre-plus/existing-benefit-claims

Universal credit

Tel: 0800 328 5644
Textphone: 0800 328 1344
Welsh language: 0800 328 1744
gov.uk/universal-credit

Social fund

Tel: 0800 169 0140
Textphone: 0800 169 0286
Welsh language: 0800 169 0240

Maternity allowance

Tel: 0800 169 0283
Textphone: 0800 169 0286
Welsh language: 0800 169 0296
gov.uk/maternity-allowance

Bereavement benefits

Tel: 0800 731 0139
Textphone: 0800 169 0314
Welsh language: 0800 731 0453

The Pension Service

New claims tel: 0800 731 7898
Textphone: 0800 731 7339
Welsh language new claims: 0800 731 7936
Welsh language textphone: 0800 731 7013
Change of circumstances tel: 0800 731 0469
Textphone: 0800 731 0464
Welsh language change of circumstances: 0800 731 0453
Welsh language textphone: 0800 731 0456
gov.uk/contact-pension-service

Winter fuel payments

Winter Fuel Payment Centre
Mail Handling Site A
Wolverhampton WV98 1LR
Tel: 0800 731 0160
Textphone: 0800 731 0176
gov.uk/winter-fuel-payment

International Pension Centre

The Pension Service 11
Mail Handling Site A
Wolverhampton WV98 1LW
Tel: 0191 218 7777
Textphone: 0191 218 7280
gov.uk/international-pension-centre

HM Revenue and Customs (tax credits)

Tax Credit Office

HM Revenue and Customs
Tax Credit Office
BX9 1ER
gov.uk/child-tax-credit
gov.uk/working-tax-credit

Tax credit helpline

Tel: 0345 300 3900
Textphone: 0345 300 3909
Intermediaries advice line for voluntary and charitable organisations: 0345 300 3943

HM Revenue and Customs (child benefit and guardian's allowance)

Child benefit

Child Benefit Office
PO Box 1
Newcastle upon Tyne NE88 1AA
Tel: 0300 200 3100
Textphone: 0300 200 3103
Welsh language: 0300 200 3103
gov.uk/child-benefit

Guardian's allowance

Guardian's Allowance Unit
PO Box 1
Newcastle upon Tyne NE88 1AA
Tel: 0300 322 9080
Textphone: 0300 200 3103
gov.uk/guardians-allowance

HM Revenue and Customs (national insurance)

PT Operations North East England
HM Revenue and Customs
BX9 1AN
Tel: 0300 200 3500
Textphone: 0300 200 3519
gov.uk/topic/personal-tax/national-insurance

HM Revenue and Customs (Statutory Payment Dispute Team)

PT Operations North East England
HM Revenue and Customs
BX9 1AN
Tel: 0300 322 9422
Textphone: 0300 200 3212
gov.uk/guidance/statutory-pay-entitlement-how-to-deal-with-disagreements

NHS Business Services Authority (Help with NHS Costs)

NHS Help with Health Costs
Bridge House
152 Pilgrim Street
Newcastle upon Tyne NE1 6SN
Low income scheme: 0300 330 1343
Medical and maternity exemption certificates: 0300 330 1341
NHS tax credit exemption certificates: 0300 330 1347
nhsbsa.nhs.uk/nhs-help-health-costs

Local Government and Social Care Ombudsman

England

Tel: 0300 061 0614
lgo.org.uk

Scottish Public Services Ombudsman

Bridgeside House
99 McDonald Road
Edinburgh EH7 4NS
Postal address: Freepost SPSO
Tel: 0800 377 7330 / 0131 225 5300
Fax: 0800 377 7331
spso.org.uk

Public Services Ombudsman for Wales

1 Ffordd yr Hen Gae
Pencoed CF35 5LJ
Tel: 0300 790 0203
ask@ombudsman.wales
ombudsman.wales

Parliamentary and Health Service Ombudsman

Millbank Tower
30 Millbank
London SW1P 4QP
Tel: 0345 015 4033
ombudsman.org.uk

The Adjudicator

The Adjudicator's Office
PO Box 10280
Nottingham NG2 9PF
Tel: 0300 057 1111
gov.uk/government/organisations/the-adjudicator-s-office

Independent Case Examiner

The Independent Case Examiner
PO Box 209
Bootle L20 7WA
Tel: 0800 414 8529
Fax: 0151 221 6601
ice@dwp.gov.uk
gov.uk/government/organisations/independent-case-examiner

Judicial Conduct Investigations Office

81–82 Queens Building
Royal Courts of Justice
Strand
London WC2A 2LL
Tel: 020 7073 4719
general.enquiries@judicialconduct.gov.uk (no longer accepting complaints by email)
complaints.judicialconduct.gov.uk

Standards Commission for Scotland

Room T2.21
Scottish Parliament
Edinburgh EH99 1SP
Tel: 0131 348 6666
enquiries@standardscommission.org.uk
standardscommissionscotland.org.uk

Commissioner for Ethical Standards in Public Life in Scotland

Thistle House
91 Haymarket Terrace
Edinburgh EH12 5HE
Tel: 0300 011 0550
info@ethicalstandards.org.uk
ethicalstandards.org.uk

Appendix 4

Useful publications

Many of the books listed here will be in your local public library. You can find Stationery Office books at Stationery Office bookshops or order them by telephone, email or online (tel: 0333 202 5070; email: customer.services@tso.co.uk; web: tsoshop.co.uk). To pay by cheque, select the 'Pay by post' option from the TSO Shop online checkout section, then print your order form and post it to TSO Customer Services, 18 Central Avenue, St Andrews Business Park, Norwich NR7 0HR. Many publications listed in this appendix are available from CPAG; see below for order details, or order from cpag.org.uk/shop.

Immigration, nationality and asylum

Immigration Law Handbook (10th edition), M Phelan and J Gillespie, Oxford University Press, 2018

Best Practice Guide to Asylum and Human Rights Appeals, M Henderson, R Moffatt and A Pickup, Immigration Law Practitioners' Association and the Electronic Immigration Network, 2020 (available only from ein.org.uk) Children

Children in Need: local authority support for children and families (2nd edition), I Wise QC and others, Legal Action Group, 2013

Caselaw and legislation

The Law Relating to Social Security

All the legislation but without any commentary. Known as the 'Blue Book'. Available at lawvolumes.dwp.gov.uk and updated up until October 2015. Check also legislation.gov.uk.

Social Security Legislation, Volume I: Non-Means-Tested Benefits and Employment and Support Allowance

D Bonner, I Hooker and R White (Sweet & Maxwell)

Legislation with commentary. 2021/22 edition (September 2021).

Social Security Legislation, Volume II: Income Support, Jobseeker's Allowance, State Pension Credit and the Social Fund

J Mesher, P Wood, R Poynter, N Wikeley and D Bonner (Sweet & Maxwell)

Legislation with commentary. 2021/22 edition (September 2021).

Social Security Legislation, Volume III: Administration, Adjudication and the European Dimension
M Rowland and R White (Sweet & Maxwell)
Legislation with commentary. 2021/22 edition (September 2021).

Social Security Legislation, Volume IV: Tax Credits and HMRC-administered Social Security Benefits
N Wikeley and D Williams (Sweet & Maxwell)
Legislation with commentary. 2021/22 edition (September 2021).

Social Security Legislation, Volume V: Universal Credit
P Wood, R Poynter and N Wikeley (Sweet & Maxwell)
Legislation with commentary. 2021/22 edition (September 2021).

Social Security Legislation – updating supplement
(Sweet & Maxwell)
The spring 2020 update to the 2020/21 main volumes.

Housing Benefit and Council Tax Reduction Legislation
L Findlay, R Poynter, S Wright, C George, M Williams, S Mitchell and M Brough (CPAG)
Legislation with detailed commentary. 2021/22, 34th edition (winter 2021): £140 including Supplement (£119.00 members). The 33rd edition (2020/21) is still available, £128 per set (£108.80 members).

Official guidance

Decision Makers' Guide: staff guide
Available at gov.uk/government/collections/decision-makers-guide-staff-guide.

Advice for Decision Making: staff guide
Available at gov.uk/government/publications/advice-for-decision-making-staff-guide.

Housing Benefit Guidance Manual
Available at gov.uk/government/collections/housing-benefit-claims-processing-and-good-practice-for-local-authority-staff.

Discretionary Housing Payments Guidance Manual
Available at gov.uk/government/publications/discretionary-housing-payments-guidance-manual.

Healthcare professionals: information from DWP
Available at gov.uk/government/collections/healthcare-practitioners-guidance-and-information-from-dwp.

Work Capability Assessment (WCA) Handbook: for healthcare professionals
Available at gov.uk/government/publications/work-capability-assessment-handbook-for-healthcare-professionals.

Tax Credits Technical Manual
Available at hmrc.gov.uk/manuals/tctmanual.

Budgeting Loan Guide
Available at gov.uk/government/publications/budgeting-loan-guide-for-decision-makers-reviewing-officers-and-further-reviewing-officers.

Personal Independence Payment (PIP) Assessment Guide for Assessment Providers
Available at gov.uk/government/publications/personal-independence-payment-assessment-guide-for-assessment-providers.

Leaflets

The DWP publishes many leaflets, available free from your local DWP or Jobcentre Plus office. To order DWP leaflets, or receive information about new leaflets, contact APS, Unit C, Orion Business Park, Bird Hall Lane, Cheadle Heath SK3 0RT, email: DWPCST@theapsgroup.com or complete the order form at gov.uk/government/publications/dwp-leaflets-order-form. Leaflets on housing benefit are available from your local council.

Periodicals

Welfare Rights Bulletin (CPAG, bi-monthly)
Covers developments in social security law, including Upper Tribunal decisions, and updates this *Handbook* between editions. The annual subscription is £49 (£41.65 for members) but it is sent automatically to CPAG members and welfare rights subscribers (more information at cpag.org.uk/membership).

Articles on social security can also be found in *Legal Action* (Legal Action Group), *Adviser* (Citizens Advice) and the *Journal of Social Security Law* (Sweet & Maxwell).

Other publications

AskCPAG
The full text of the *Welfare Benefits and Tax Credits Handbook* online and updated throughout the year. Annual subscription £69 per user (£58.65 members).

AskCPAG+
CPAG's full digital package which includes the full text of the *Welfare Benefits and Tax Credits Handbook* updated throughout the year, the *Welfare Rights Bulletin*, *Poverty* journal and decision-making tools and appeal letter generators. Annual subscription £138 per user (£117.30 members).

Universal Credit: what you need to know (CPAG)
6th edition, September 2020: £15 (£12.75 members)

Financial Help for Families: what you need to know (CPAG)
2nd edition, November 2020: £15 (£12.75 members)

Personal Independence Payment: what you need to know (CPAG)
3rd edition, autumn 2021: £16 (£13.60 members)

Winning Your Benefit Appeal: what you need to know (CPAG)
4th edition, summer 2021: £16 (£13.60 members)

Child Support Handbook (CPAG)
29th edition, summer 2021: £45 (£38.25 members)

Debt Advice Handbook (CPAG)
14th edition, winter 2021: £35 (£29.75 members)
Available free online at AskCPAG.org.uk.

Fuel Rights Handbook (CPAG)
20th edition, winter 2021: £35 (£29.75 members)

Student Support and Benefits Handbook (CPAG)
18th edition, winter 2021: £35 (£29.75 members)
Available free online at AskCPAG.org.uk.

Benefits for Students in Scotland Handbook (CPAG)
19th edition, autumn 2021: £35 (£29.75 members)
Available free online at AskCPAG.org.uk.

Council Tax Handbook (CPAG)
13th edition, March 2021: £31 (£26.35 members)

Benefits for Migrants Handbook (CPAG)
13th edition, December 2021 2021: £45 (£38.25 members)

Children's Handbook Scotland: a benefits guide for children living away from their parents (CPAG)
14th edition, autumn 2021: £35 (£29.75 members)
Available free online at AskCPAG.org.uk

Help with Housing Costs Vol 1: Guide to universal credit and council tax rebates 2021/22 (Shelter)
£43.50 (June 2021)

Help with Housing Costs Vol 2: Guide to housing benefit 2021/22 (Shelter)
£43.50 (June 2021)

Disability Rights Handbook 2021/22 (Disability Rights UK)
£37 (46th edition, May 2021)

Disabled Children: A legal handbook (Legal Action Group)
£50 (3rd edition, December 2019)

For CPAG titles and most other publications contact:

CPAG, 30 Micawber St, London N1 7TB (tel: 020 7837 7979, email: bookorders@cpag.org.uk). Discounts on CPAG publications are available to CPAG members and Citizens Advice. Order forms are available at cpag.org.uk/shop. Postage and packing: free for online subscriptions and orders up to £10 in value; for order value £10.01–£100, add a flat rate charge of £3.99; for order value £100.01–£400, add £7.49; for order value over £400, add £11.49.

Appendix 5

Reciprocal agreements

Reciprocal agreements with European Economic Area states

State	*Retirement pension*	*Bereavement benefits*	*Guardian's allowance*	*'Sickness benefit'*	*Incapacity benefit*	*Contribution-based jobseeker's allowance*	*Maternity allowance*	*Disablement benefit*	*Industrial injuries benefits*	*Child benefit*	*Attendance allowance and disability living allowance*	*Carer's allowance*
Austria	✓	✓	✓	✓	✓	✓	✓	✓	✓	✓	–	–
Belgium	✓	✓	✓	✓	✓	✓	✓	✓	✓	✓	–	–
Croatia	✓	✓	–	✓	✓	✓	✓	✓	✓	✓	–	–
Cyprus	✓	✓	✓	✓	✓	✓	✓	✓	✓	–	–	–
Denmark	–	✓	✓	✓	✓	✓	✓	✓	✓	✓	✓	–
Finland	✓	✓	–	✓	✓	✓	✓	✓	✓	✓	–	–
France	✓	✓	–	✓	✓	✓	✓	✓	✓	✓	–	–
Germany	–	✓	✓	✓	✓	✓	✓	✓	✓	✓	✓	–
Iceland	✓	✓	✓	✓	✓	✓	–	✓	✓	–	–	–
Ireland	✓	✓	✓	✓	✓*	✓	✓	✓	✓	–	–	–
Italy	✓	✓	✓	✓	✓	✓	✓	✓	✓	–	–	–
Luxembourg	✓	✓	✓	✓	✓	–	✓	✓	✓	–	–	–
Malta	✓	✓	✓	✓	✓	✓	–	✓	✓	–	–	–
Netherlands	✓	✓	✓	✓	✓	✓	✓	✓	✓	–	–	–
Norway	✓	✓	✓	✓	✓	✓	✓	✓	✓	✓	✓	–
Portugal	✓	✓	✓	✓	✓	✓	✓	✓	✓	✓	–	–
Slovenia	✓	✓	–	✓	✓	✓	✓	✓	✓	✓	–	–
Spain	✓	✓	✓	✓	✓	✓	✓	✓	✓	✓	–	–
Sweden	✓	✓	✓	✓	✓	✓	✓	✓	✓	✓	–	–
Northern Ireland**	✓	✓	✓	✓	✓	✓	✓	✓	✓	✓	✓	✓

* In addition to the reciprocal agreement between the UK and Ireland, a new Convention on Social Security came into effect on 1 January 2021, which co-ordinates the social security systems between these two countries. For further details, see p399 and Chapter 16.

**Although Northern Ireland is part of the UK, there are reciprocal agreements between Great Britain and Northern Ireland. That is because benefits in Northern Ireland and Great Britain are separate and administered under different social security legislation. For details of these agreements, see p399.

There is an agreement with Gibraltar, which treats the UK and Gibraltar as separate countries (except for child benefit) for the purposes of the European Union co-ordination rules. For further details, see p399.

Reciprocal agreements with non-European Economic Area states

State	*Retirement pension*	*Bereavement benefits*	*Guardian's allowance*	*'Sickness benefit'*	*Incapacity benefit and 'converted' employment and support allowance*	*Contribution-based jobseeker's allowance*	*Maternity allowance*	*Disablement benefit*	*Industrial injuries benefits*	*Child benefit*	*Attendance allowance and disability living allowance*	*Carer's allowance*
Barbados	✓	✓	✓	✓	✓	–	✓	✓	✓	✓	–	–
Bermuda	✓	✓	–	–	–	–	–	✓	✓	–	–	–
Bosnia-Herzegovina	✓	✓	–	✓	✓	✓	✓	✓	✓	✓	–	–
Canada	✓	–	–	–	–	✓	–	–	–	✓	–	–
Chile	✓	✓	–	–	–	–	–	–	–	–	–	–
Israel	✓	✓	✓	✓	✓*	–	✓	✓	✓	✓	–	–
Jamaica	✓	✓	✓	–	✓	–	–	✓	✓	–	–	–
Kosovo	✓	✓	–	✓	✓	✓	✓	✓	✓	✓	–	–
Macedonia	✓	✓	–	✓	✓	✓	✓	✓	✓	✓	–	–
Mauritius	✓	✓	✓	–	–	–	–	✓	✓	✓	–	–
Montenegro	✓	✓	–	✓	✓	✓	✓	✓	✓	✓	–	–
New Zealand	✓	✓	✓	✓	–	✓	–	–	–	✓	–	–
Philippines	✓	✓	–	–	–	–	–	✓	✓	–	–	–
Serbia	✓	✓	–	✓	✓	✓	✓	✓	✓	✓	–	–
Switzerland	✓	✓	✓	✓	✓*	–	✓	✓	✓	✓	–	–
Turkey	✓	✓	✓	✓	✓	–	✓	✓	✓	–	–	–
USA	✓	✓	✓	✓	✓	–	–	–	–	–	–	–
Isle of Man	✓	✓	✓	✓	✓*	✓	✓	✓	✓	✓	✓	✓
Guernsey	✓	✓	✓	✓	✓	✓	✓	✓	✓	✓	✓	–
Jersey	✓	✓	✓	✓	✓	–	✓	✓	✓	✓	✓	–

You can find the agreements at legislation.gov.uk and search for the relevant country.

The UK also has other types of agreements with other countries. For more information on all agreements, see Chapter 17.

The agreement with Chile has only been in force since 1 June 2015.

The agreements with Bosnia-Herzegovina, Croatia, Kosovo, North Macedonia, Montenegro and Serbia are in a single agreement with former Yugolsavia, but are treated as separate agreements.

Until 1 March 2001, there was an agreement with Australia. This was then revoked, subject to limited savings provisions in relation to retirement pensions and bereavement benefits.

There is an agreement with Japan, but it only covers liability for contributions.

Appendix 6

Passport stamps and other endorsements

Figure 1: UK passport

Note: from March 2020, blue UK passports were issued. See the Home Office's video at youtu.be/M5GWYaUQEDI.

Figure 2: Certificates certifying naturalisation and registration as a British citizen

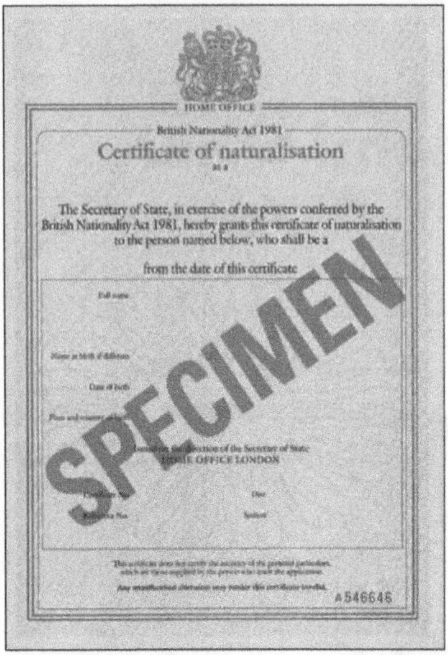
HOME OFFICE

British Nationality Act 1981

Certificate of naturalisation

as a

The Secretary of State, in exercise of the powers conferred by the British Nationality Act 1981, hereby grants this certificate of naturalisation to the person named below, who shall be a

from the date of this certificate

HOME OFFICE LONDON

SPECIMEN

A 546646

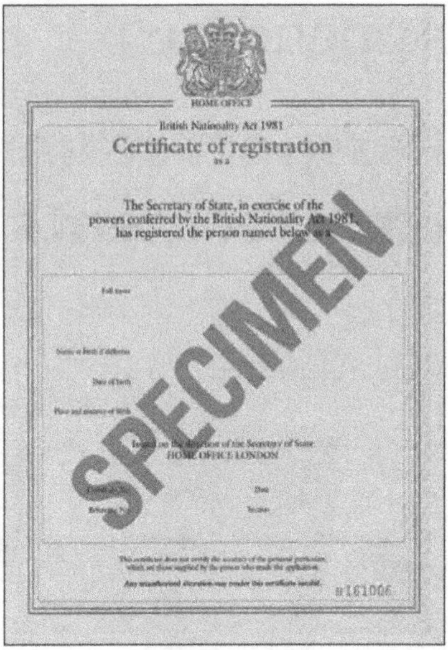
HOME OFFICE

British Nationality Act 1981

Certificate of registration

as a

The Secretary of State, in exercise of the powers conferred by the British Nationality Act 1981, has registered the person named below as a

Issued on the direction of the Secretary of State
HOME OFFICE LONDON

SPECIMEN

B 161006

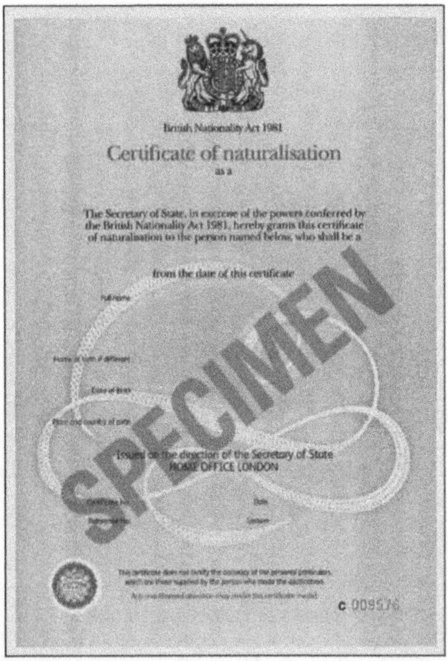
British Nationality Act 1981

Certificate of naturalisation

as a

The Secretary of State, in exercise of the powers conferred by the British Nationality Act 1981, hereby grants this certificate of naturalisation to the person named below, who shall be a

from the date of this certificate

Issued on the direction of the Secretary of State
HOME OFFICE LONDON

SPECIMEN

C 009576

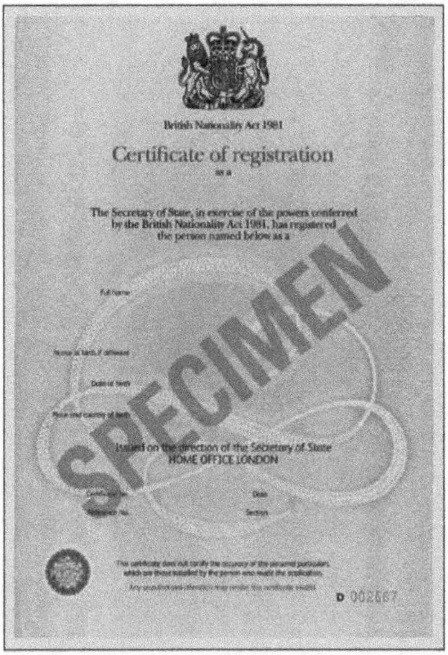
British Nationality Act 1981

Certificate of registration

as a

The Secretary of State, in exercise of the powers conferred by the British Nationality Act 1981, has registered the person named below as a

Issued on the direction of the Secretary of State
HOME OFFICE LONDON

SPECIMEN

D 002667

Figure 3: Certificate of entitlement to the right of abode

Figure 4: Immigration status document

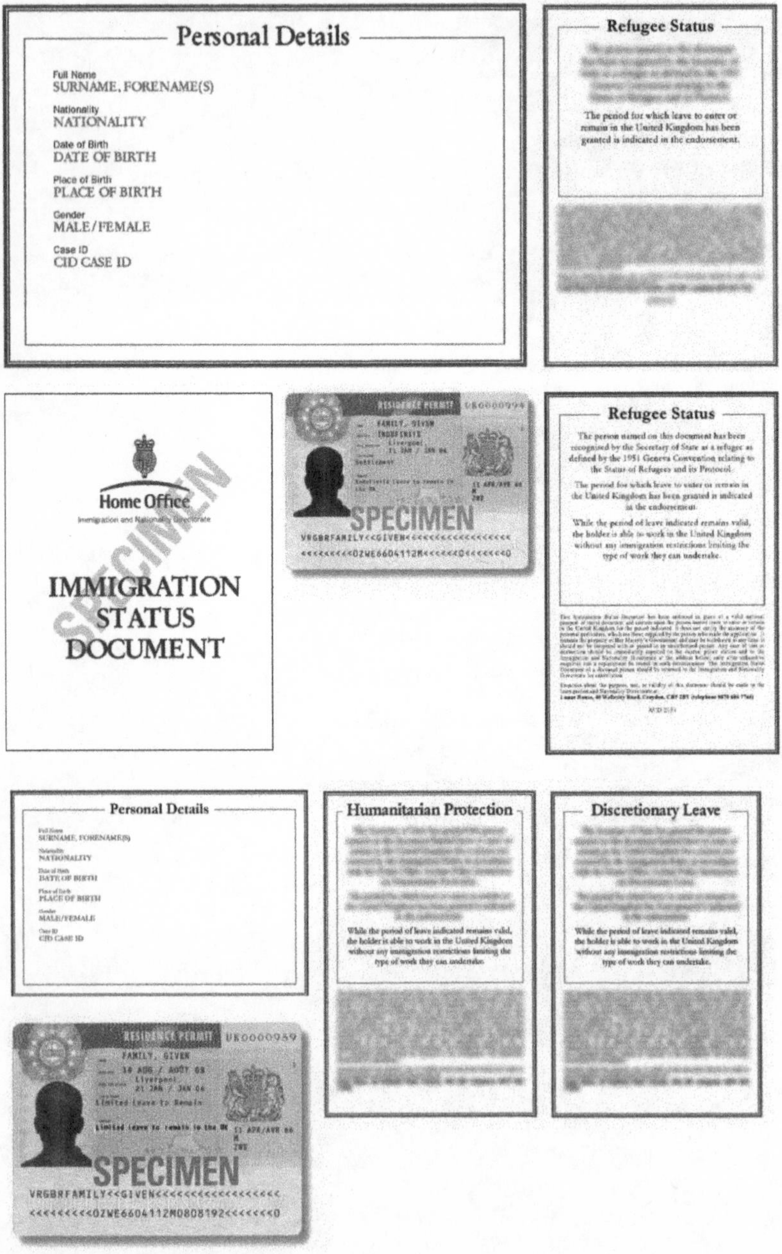

Figure 5: Biometric residence permit

The card's design is set by European Union (EU) regulation. It is a standard credit card size (86mm x 54mm) and will look similar to identity cards issued by other EU countries. The card is made from polycarbonate plastic and contains a chip to make it more secure against forgery and abuse.

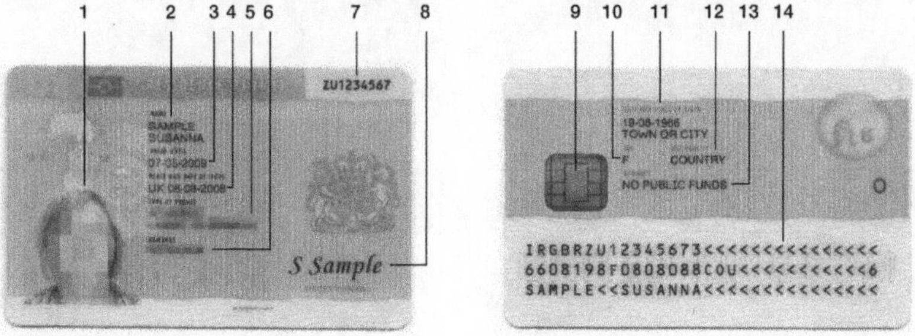

1. Holder's digital image
2. Holder's name
3. Valid until – the date the card expires. This date is at the end of the time the holder is allowed to stay; or five or 10 years if the holder has been given permission to settle in the United Kingdom (known as indefinite leave to remain)
4. Place and date of issue – this is the UK followed by the date the card was issued
5. Type of permit – this is the immigration category the holder is in (for example, STUDENT)
6. Remarks – these are the immigration entitlements for the length of the holder's stay, and may continue on the back of the card
7. ZU1234567 – unique card number
8. Holder's signature
9. Biometric chip
10. Holder's gender
11. Holder's date and place of birth
12. Holder's nationality
13. Remarks – this is a continuation of immigration entitlements for the length of time of the holder's stay (see 6 above)
14. Machine readable zone (MRZ) – this area allows information printed on the card to be read quickly by machine

Figure 6: Registration certificate or document certifying permanent residence

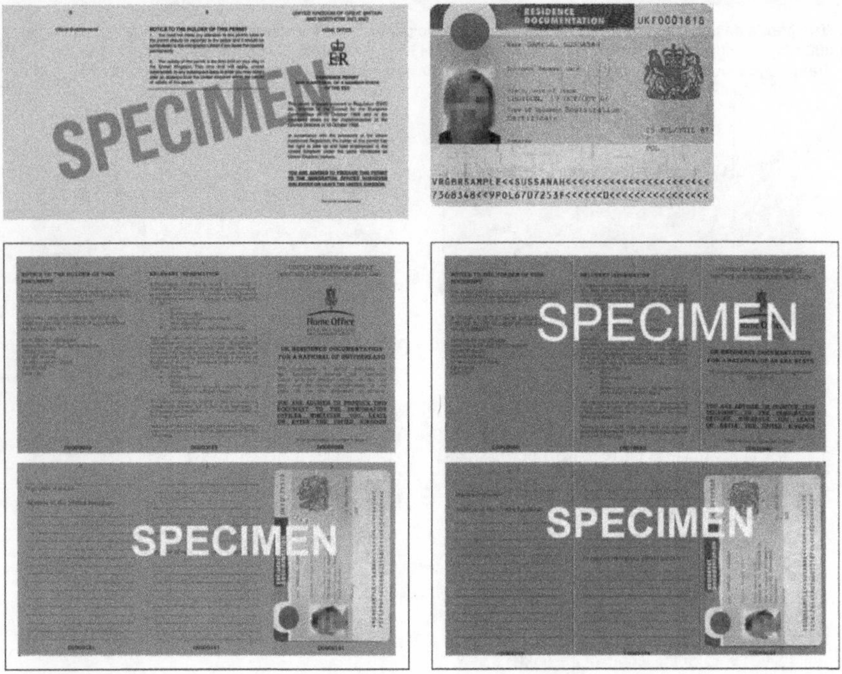

Figure 7: Residence card (including an accession residence card or a derivative residence card) issued by the Home Office to a non-European Economic Area national who is a family member of a national of a European Economic Area country or Switzerland or who has a derivative right of residence

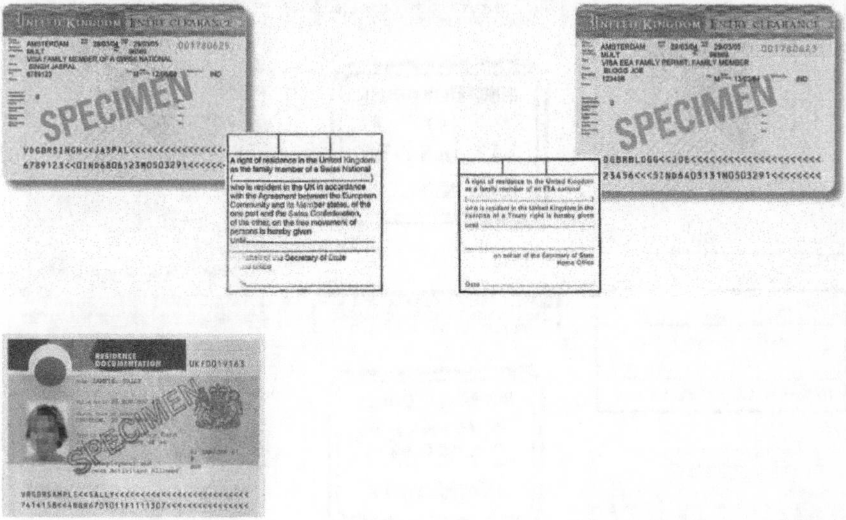

Figure 8: Historic ink stamp endorsements (top left, top middle and bottom left), application registration card (top right and bottom right), visa vignettes (bottom middle and bottom left), and residence permit vignette

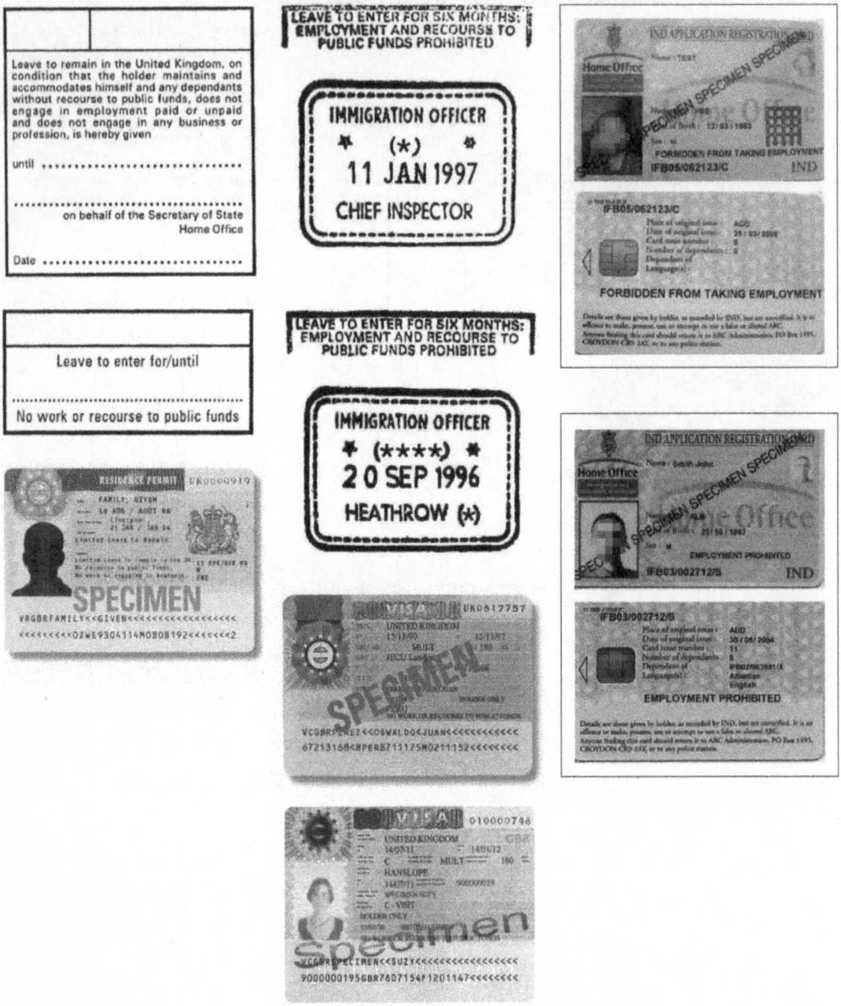

Figure 9: Entry clearance vignette

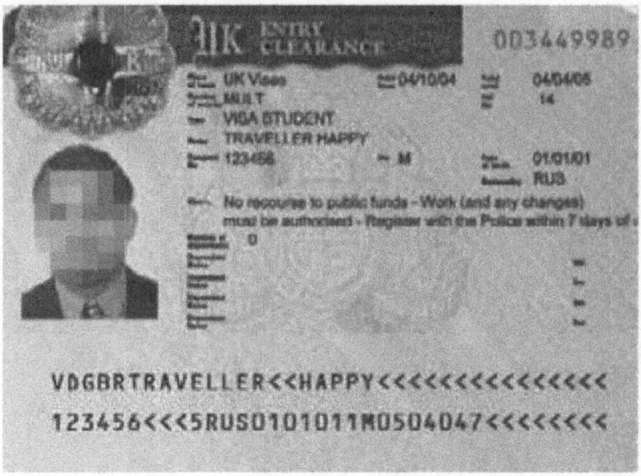

Figure 10: Date stamp on entry clearance vignette

Figure 11: Refugee Convention travel document

Figure 12: Notice of removal

Home Office

Home Office

NOTICE OF IMMIGRATION DECISION

NOTICE OF REMOVAL

Home Office Reference: [redacted]

To: [redacted]

You are a person with no leave to enter or remain in the United Kingdom (UK). You have not given any reasons as to why you should be granted leave to remain or why you should not require leave to remain. Therefore you are liable for removal.

REASONS FOR DECISION

The following reasons are given:

You are specifically considered a person who has been unable to show evidence of lawful entry because you cannot produce the passport on which you claim to have entered the UK.

LIABILITY FOR REMOVAL

Persons who require, but no longer have leave to enter or remain are liable to removal from the United Kingdom under section 10 of the Immigration and Asylum Act 1999 (as amended by the Immigration Act 2014).

If you do not leave the United Kingdom as required you will be liable to enforced removal to Jamaica. We may remove you via a transit point in an EU member state.

You may be detained or placed on reporting conditions.

If you wish to seek legal advice you must do so now.

Tick one box	
☒	You will not be removed for the first seven calendar days after you receive this notice. Following the end of this seven day period, and for up to three months from the date of this notice, you may be removed without further notice.
☐	You will not be removed before **(insert date and time)**. After this time, and for up to three months from the date of this notice, you may be removed without further notice.
☐	You will be given further notice of when you will be removed.

Please Note: Limited information about you such as relevant medical or behavioural issues will be shared with the relevant parties involved in the enforced removal process where necessary to facilitate your safe removal from the UK.

CONSEQUENCES OF ILLEGALLY STAYING IN THE UK

RED.0001 1

Figure 13: Notice of immigration bail

BAIL 201

Home Office

Per ID: [redacted]
Port Ref:
HO Ref: [redacted]

Becket House
60-68 St Thomas Street
London
SE1 3QU
Tel: 0207 238 0084 Fax: 0207 238 1411

NOTIFICATION OF GRANT/VARIATION OF IMMIGRATION BAIL[1] TO A PERSON DETAINED[2] OR LIABLE TO BE DETAINED[3]

To: [redacted]

[redacted]

Date of Birth: [redacted]
Nationality: [redacted]

[redacted]

This notice is given to you because your immigration bail is being varied

The Secretary of State may grant immigration bail to a person who is detained, or who is liable to be detained, for the reasons listed below. The following reason applies to you:

Mark one box		
A	☐	You are liable to be detained pending examination because you are a person required to submit to examination / pending a decision to give, refuse, or cancel leave to enter.
B	☐	You are liable to be detained because you are a person who has been refused leave to enter the United Kingdom.
C	☒	You are liable to be detained because you are a person without leave who has been served with a notice of liability to removal, or are a dependant of such a person.
D	☐	You are liable to be detained because there is reasonable suspicion that you may be liable to removal from the United Kingdom.
E	☐	You are liable to be detained pending a decision to deport you / because a decision has been made to deport you.
F	☐	You are detained pending [a decision to issue directions for] your removal from the United Kingdom.
G	☐	You are the subject of a deportation order and are detained pending your deportation from the United Kingdom.
H	☐	You are detained / liable to be detained for the following reason:

[1] Schedule 10 to the Immigration Act 2016
[2] Paragraph 1 of Schedule 10 to the Immigration Act 2016
[3] Paragraph 2 of Schedule 10 to the Immigration Act 2016

BAIL 201

BAIL 201

☐ You have made a claim for asylum:

A ☐ I hereby grant you immigration bail subject to the following conditions or

B ☒ I hereby vary your conditions of immigration bail as follows

☒ You are not allowed to WORK

CONDITIONS

You will be subject to at least one bail condition. A marked box indicates the bail condition(s) applicable to you.

☒	You **must** REPORT to **an immigration official** at: Becket House 60-68 St Thomas Street London SE1 3QU On [redacted] Between 09:00 and 11:30 Hrs And then fortnightly on Tuesday until further notice

ANY CHANGE OF CONDITION

You must not change your conditions without the agreement of the Secretary of State. If these conditions are to be changed, you will be notified. This notice is correct at time of service and is recorded on Home Office systems.

- Although you may have been granted immigration bail, you remain liable to be detained
- This document must not be accepted by employers as evidence of a right to work or by landlords as evidence of a right to rent (this does not apply to EEA nationals, or the family member of an EEA national, exercising an EU treaty right).
- You have NOT been given leave to enter the United Kingdom within the meaning of the Immigration Act 1971

FAILURE TO COMPLY WITH CONDITIONS

Failure to comply with any of the above conditions may lead to arrest, your conditions being varied, the requirement to pay money under any financial condition, and/or your detention.

Failure to comply with any of the above conditions, without reasonable excuse, is also a criminal offence which may be punished by a fine or a prison sentence[1].

Any unresolved application which you may have made for leave to enter may be refused.

Your details may also be placed on the Police National Computer (PNC).
Should you have difficulty in being able to comply with any of your conditions, you must immediately contact [Becket House] and give your reason.

IMMIGRATION BAIL AUTOMATICALLY ENDS WHEN:

BAIL 201

BAIL 201

- You are no longer liable to be detained and the Secretary of State is not considering whether to make a deportation order against you,
- You are granted leave to enter or remain in the United Kingdom,
- You are detained, or
- You are removed or otherwise leave the United Kingdom.

HELP AND SUPPORT ON RETURNING HOME VOLUNTARILY

The Home Office Voluntary Returns Service can be contacted for help on returning home.

The team can discuss your return, help to obtain your travel document and send it to the port of departure, help with the cost of your tickets, and in some cases provided other financial and practical assistance to use once you have returned to your home country.

Please note that if your documents are held by the Home Office please contact the voluntary returns service before you book your flight if you are paying for your own return, this will help us ensure that your passport is available for your flight.

Contact the voluntary Returns Service

Telephone: 0300 004 0202 (Monday – Friday between 9:00 and 17:30)

Web: https://www.gov.uk/return-home-voluntarily/who-can-get-help

Date [redacted]

[redacted] **On behalf of the Secretary of State**

[1] Section 24(1)(h) Immigration Act 1971

BAIL 201

Figure 14: Embarkation stamp

Appendix 7

Abbreviations used in the notes

AAC	Administrative Appeals Chamber
AACR	Administrative Appeals Chamber Reports
AC	Appeal Cases
Admin	Administrative Court
AG	Advocate General
All ER	All England Law Reports
All ER(D)	All England Law Reports (Digest)
Art(s)	Article(s)
CA	Court of Appeal
Ch	chapter
Civ	Civil Division
CJEU	Court of Justice of the European Union
Crim App R	Criminal Appeal Reports
CSIH	Court of Session, Inner House
CSOH	Court of Session, Outer House
Dir	Directive
EC	European Community
ECJ	European Court of Justice
ECR	European Court Reports
ECHR	European Court of Human Rights
EEA	European Economic Area
EFTACR	European Free Trade Association Court Reports
EU	European Union
EWCA	England and Wales Court of Appeal
EWHC	England and Wales High Court
FLR	Family Law Reports
HLR	Housing Law Reports
IAC	Immigration and Asylum Chamber
Imm AR	Immigration Appeal Reports

IR	Immigration Rules
NICom	Northern Ireland Commissioner
NIQB	Northern Ireland Queen's Bench Division
OJ	Official Journal of the European Union
p(p)	page(s)
para(s)	paragraphs(s)
PTA	Permission to appeal
QB	Queen's Bench Reports
QBD	Queen's Bench Division
r(r)	rule(s)
Reg(s)	regulation(s)
s(s)	section(s)
Sch(s)	Schedule(s)
SLT	Scots Law Times
SSAC	Social Security Advisory Committee
SSC	Social Security Protocol
SSH	Secretary of State for Health
SSHD	Secretary of State for the Home Department
SSWP	Secretary of State for Work and Pensions
TFEU	Treaty on the Functioning of the European Union
UKAIT	United Kingdom Asylum and Immigration Tribunal
UKHL	United Kingdom House of Lords
UKSC	United Kingdom Supreme Court
UKUT	United Kingdom Upper Tribunal
Vol	volume
WLR	Weekly Law Reports

Agreements and conventions

UK-EFTA	Agreement on arrangements between Iceland, the Principality of Liechtenstein, the Kingdom of Norway and the United Kingdom of Great Britain and Northern Ireland following the withdrawal of the United Kingdom from the European Union, the EEA Agreement and other agreements applicable between the United Kingdom and the EEA EFTA States by virtue of the United Kingdom's membership of the European Union
UK-EUP	Trade And Cooperation Agreement between The EU and The European Atomic Energy Community, of the one part, and the UK of the other part: Protocol on Social Security Coordination

UK-IC	Convention on Social Security Between the Government of the United Kingdom of Great Britain and Northern Ireland and the Government of Ireland, 1 February 2019 – reproduced in Sch 1 of The Social Security (Ireland) Order 2019, No.622
UK-Swiss Agreement	Agreement between the United Kingdom Of Great Britain and Northern Ireland and the Swiss Confederation on Citizens' Rights following the Withdrawal of the United Kingdom from the European Union and the Free Movement of Persons Agreement
WA 2019	Agreement on the withdrawal of the United Kingdom of Great Britain and Northern Ireland from the European Union and the European Atomic Energy Community, 19 October 2019

Acts of Parliament

AI(TC)A 2004	Asylum and Immigration (Treatment of Claimants, etc.) Act 2004
BNA 1981	British Nationality Act 1981
CA 1989	Children Act 1989
CA 2014	Care Act 2014
C(S)A 1995	Children (Scotland) Act 1995
CSPSSA 2000	Child Support, Pensions and Social Security Act 2000
EU(W)A 2018	European Union (Withdrawal) Act 2018
EU(W)A 2020	European Union (Withdrawal) Act 2020
HRA 1998	Human Rights Act 1998
IA 1971	Immigration Act 1971
IA 1978	Interpretation Act 1978
IA 1988	Immigration Act 1988
IA 2014	Immigration Act 2014
IA 2016	Immigration Act 2016
IAA 1999	Immigration and Asylum Act 1999
ISSCA 2020	Immigration and Social Security Co-ordination (EU Withdrawal) Act
JSA 1995	Jobseekers Act 1995
NAA 1948	National Assistance Act 1948
NIAA 2002	Nationality, Immigration and Asylum Act 2002
PA 2014	Pensions Act 2014
SPCA 2002	State Pension Credit Act 2002

SSA 1975	Social Security Act 1975
SSA 1998	Social Security Act 1998
SSAA 1992	Social Security Administration Act 1992
SSCBA 1992	Social Security Contributions and Benefits Act 1992
SS(S)A 2018	Social Social Security (Scotland) Act 2018
TCA 2002	Tax Credits Act 2002
TCEA 2007	Tribunals, Courts and Enforcement Act 2007
WRA 2007	Welfare Reform Act 2007
WRA 2012	Welfare Reform Act 2012

Regulations and other statutory instruments

Each set of regulations has a statutory instrument (SI) number and date. You can find all regulations at legislation.gov.uk.

A(IWA) Regs	The Accession (Immigration and Worker Authorisation) Regulations 2006 No.3317
A(IWR) Regs	The Accession (Immigration and Worker Registration) Regulations 2004 No.1219
AC(IWA) Regs	The Accession of Croatia (Immigration and Worker Authorisation) Regulations 2013 No.1460
AS Regs	The Asylum Support Regulations 2000 No.704
ASPP(G) Regs	The Additional Statutory Paternity Pay (General) Regulations 2010 No.1056
CA(YCG)(R)(S) Regs	The Carer's Assistance (Young Carer Grants) (Scotland) Regulations 2019 No.324
CASYCG(R)(S) Regs	The Carer's Allowance Supplement and Young Carer Grants (Residence Requirements and Procedural Provisions) (EU Exit) (Scotland) Regulations 2020 No.475
CB Regs	The Child Benefit (General) Regulations 2006 No.223
CB&GA(Admin) Regs	The Child Benefit and Guardian's Allowance (Administration) Regulations 2003 No.492
CB&GA(DA) Regs	The Child Benefit and Guardian's Allowance (Decisions and Appeals) Regulations 2003 No.916
CR(ADTP) Regs	The Citizens' Rights (Application Deadline and Temporary Protection) (EU Exit) Regulations 2020 No.1209
CR(FW) Regs	The Citizens' Rights (Frontier Workers) (EU Exit) Regulations 2020 No.1213

CTC Regs	The Child Tax Credit Regulations 2002 No.2007
CTR(S) Regs	The Council Tax Reduction (Scotland) Regulations 2012 No.303
CTR(SPC)S Regs	The Council Tax Reduction (State Pension Credit) (Scotland) Regulations 2012 No.319
CTRS(DS)E Regs	The Council Tax Reduction Schemes (Default Scheme) (England) Regulations 2012 No.2886
CTRS(DS)W Regs	The Council Tax Reduction Schemes (Default Scheme) (Wales) Regulations 2013 No.3035 (W.303)
CTRS(PR)E Regs	The Council Tax Reduction Schemes (Prescribed Requirements) (England) Regulations 2012 No.2885
CTRSPR(W) Regs	The Council Tax Reduction Schemes and Prescribed Requirements (Wales) Regulations 2013 No.3029 (W.301)
DACYP(S) Regs	Disability Assistance for Children and Young People (Consequential Amendment and Transitional Provision)(Scotland) Regulations 2021 No.73
EA(BSG)(S) Regs	The Early Years Assistance (Best Start Grants) (Scotland) Regulations 2018 No.370
ESA Regs	The Employment and Support Allowance Regulations 2008 No.794
ESA Regs 2013	The Employment and Support Allowance Regulations 2013 No.379
ESA(TP)(EA) Regs	The Employment and Support Allowance (Transitional Provisions, Housing Benefit and Council Tax Benefit) (Existing Awards) (No.2) Regulations 2010 No.1907
FANIII(Y)O	The Family Allowances, National Insurance and Industrial Injuries (Yugoslavia) Order 1958 No.1263
FEA(S) Regs	The Funeral Expense Assistance (Scotland) Regulations 2019 No.292
FTT(S) Rules	The First-tier Tribunal for Scotland Social Security Chamber (Procedure) Regulations 2018 No.273
GA(Gen) Regs	The Guardian's Allowance (General) Regulations 2003 No.495
HB Regs	The Housing Benefit Regulations 2006 No.213

HB(HR)A Regs	The Housing Benefit (Habitual Residence) Amendment Regulations 2014 No.539
HB(SPC) Regs	The Housing Benefit (Persons who have attained the qualifying age for state pension credit) Regulations 2006 No.214
HB&CTB(DA) Regs	The Housing Benefit and Council Tax Benefit (Decisions and Appeals) Regulations 2001 No.1002
HSS(DHSF)(W) Regs	The Healthy Start Scheme (Description of Healthy Start Food) (Wales) Regulations 2006 No.3108 (W.287)
HSS&WF(A) Regs	The Healthy Start Scheme and Welfare Food (Amendment) Regulations 2005 No.3262
I(EEA) Regs	The Immigration (European Economic Area) Regulations 2016 No.1052
I(EEA) Regs 2006	The Immigration (European Economic Area) Regulations 2006 No.1003
I(EEA)A Regs 2012	The Immigration (European Economic Area) (Amendment) Regulations 2012 No.1547
I(EEA)A Regs 2018	The Immigration (European Economic Area)(Amendment) Regulations 2018 No.801
IA(PAFAS) Regs	The Immigration and Asylum (Provision of Accommodation to Failed Asylum-Seekers) Regulations 2005 No.930
ILRFO Regs	The Integration Loans for Refugees and Others Regulations 2007 No.1598
IS Regs	The Income Support (General) Regulations 1987 No.1967
ISSC Regs	The Immigration and Social Security Co-ordination (EU Withdrawal) Act 2020 (Consequential, Saving, Transitional and Transitory Provisions) (EU Exit) Regulations 2020 No.1309
ISSCA(C) Regs	The Immigration and Social Security Co-ordination (EU Withdrawal) Act 2020 (Commencement) Regulations 2020 No.1279
JSA Regs	The Jobseeker's Allowance Regulations 1996 No.207
JSA Regs 2013	The Jobseeker's Allowance Regulations 2013 No.378
NHS(COV) Regs 1989	The National Health Service (Charges to Overseas Visitors) Regulations 1989 No.306

NHS(COV) Regs 2015	The National Health Service (Charges to Overseas Visitors) Regulations 2015 No.238
NHS(COV)(S) Regs	The National Health Service (Charges to Overseas Visitors) (Scotland) Regulations 1989 No.364
SCP Regs	The Scottish Child Payment Regulations 2020 No.351
SFM&FE Regs	The Social Fund Maternity and Funeral Expenses (General) Regulations 2005 No.3061
SFWFP Regs	The Social Fund Winter Fuel Payment Regulations 2000 No.729
SMP Regs	The Statutory Maternity Pay (General) Regulations 1986 No.1960
SMP(PAM) Regs	The Statutory Maternity Pay (Persons Abroad and Mariners) Regulations 1987 No.418
SPBP(PAM) Regs	The Statutory Parental Bereavement Pay (Persons Abroad and Mariners) Regulations 2020 No.252
SPC Regs	The State Pension Credit Regulations 2002 No.1792
SPPSAP(G) Regs	The Statutory Paternity Pay and Statutory Adoption Pay (General) Regulations 2002 No.2822
SPPSAP(PAM) Regs	The Statutory Paternity Pay and Statutory Adoption Pay (Persons Abroad and Mariners) Regulations 2002 No.2821
SS(AA) Regs	The Social Security (Attendance Allowance) Regulations 1991 No.2740
SS(C&P) Regs	The Social Security (Claims and Payments) Regulations 1987 No.1968
SS(DLA) Regs	The Social Security (Disability Living Allowance) Regulations 1991 No.2890
SS(GBRA)(A)NI Regs	The Social Security (Great Britain Reciprocal Arrangements) (Amendment) Regulations (Northern Ireland) 2016 No.393
SS(GBRA)(NI) Regs	The Social Security (Great Britain Reciprocal Arrangements) Regulations (Northern Ireland) 2016 No.149
SS(HR)A Regs	The Social Security (Habitual Residence) Amendment Regulations 2004 No.1232
SS(IA)CA Regs	The Social Security (Immigration and Asylum) Consequential Amendments Regulations 2000 No.636

SS(IB) Regs	The Social Security (Incapacity Benefit) Regulations 1994 No.2946
SS(IB-ID) Regs	The Social Security (Incapacity Benefit – Increases for Dependants) Regulations 1994 No.2945
SS(ICA) Regs	The Social Security (Invalid Care Allowance) Regulations 1976 No.409
SS(II)(AB) Regs	The Social Security (Industrial Injuries) (Airmen's Benefits) Regulations 1975 No.469
SS(II)(MB) Regs	The Social Security (Industrial Injuries) (Mariners' Benefits) Regulations 1975 No.470
SS(IIPD) Regs	The Social Security (Industrial Injuries) (Prescribed Diseases) Regulations 1985 No.967
SS(NIRA) Regs	The Social Security (Northern Ireland Reciprocal Arrangements) Regulations 2016 No. 287
SS(NIRA)(A) Regs	The Social Security (Northern Ireland Reciprocal Arrangements) (Amendment) Regulations 2016 No.1050
SS(PA) Regs	The Social Security Benefit (Persons Abroad) Regulations 1975 No.563
SS(PA)A Regs	The Social Security (Persons from Abroad) Amendment Regulations 2006 No.1026
SS(PAB) Regs	The Social Security (Payments on Account of Benefit) Regulations 2013 No.383
SS(PFA)MA Regs	The Social Security (Persons From Abroad) Miscellaneous Amendments Regulations 1996 No.30
SS(PIP) Regs	The Social Security (Personal Independence Payment) Regulations 2013 No. 377
SS(RA)O	The Social Security (Reciprocal Agreements) Order 2012 No.360
SS(SDA) Regs	The Social Security (Severe Disablement Allowance) Regulations 1984 No.1303
SS(WB&RP) Regs	The Social Security (Widow's Benefit and Retirement Pensions) Regulations 1979 No.642
SS(WTCCTC)(CA) Regs	The Social Security (Working Tax Credit and Child Tax Credit) (Consequential Amendments) Regulations 2003 No.455
SSB(Dep) Regs	The Social Security Benefit (Dependency) Regulations 1977 No.343
SSB(PA) Regs	The Social Security Benefit (Persons Abroad) Regulations 1975 No.563

SSB(PRT) Regs	The Social Security Benefit (Persons Residing Together) Regulations 1977 No.956
SSCBCTC(A) Regs	The Social Security, Child Benefit and Child Tax Credit (Amendment) (EU Exit) Regulations 2020 No.1505
SS&CS(DA) Regs	The Social Security and Child Support (Decisions and Appeals) Regulations 1999 No.991
SSP Regs	The Statutory Sick Pay (General) Regulations 1982 No.894
SSP(MAPA) Regs	The Statutory Sick Pay (Mariners, Airmen and Persons Abroad) Regulations 1982 No.1349
SSPP(G) Regs	The Statutory Shared Parental Pay (General) Regulations 2014 No.3051
SSPP(PAM) Regs	The Statutory Shared Parental Pay (Persons Abroad and Mariners) Regulations 2014 No.3134
TC(CN) Regs	The Tax Credits (Claims and Notifications) Regulations 2002 No.2014
TC(DCI) Regs	The Tax Credits (Definition and Calculation of Income) Regulations 2002 No.2006
TC(Imm) Regs	The Tax Credits (Immigration) Regulations 2003 No.653
TC(PC) Regs	The Tax Credits (Payments by the Commissioners) Regulations 2002 No. 2173
TC(R) Regs	The Tax Credits (Residence) Regulations 2003 No.654
TP(FT) Rules	The Tribunal Procedure (First-tier Tribunal) (Social Entitlement Chamber) Rules 2008 No.2685
UC Regs	The Universal Credit Regulations 2013 No. 376
UC(GBRA)Regs	The Universal Credit (Great Britain Reciprocal Arrangements) Regulations (Northern Ireland) 2020 No.129
UC(NIRA) Regs	The Universal Credit (Northern Ireland Reciprocal Arrangements) Regulations 2020 No.677
UC(TP) Regs	The Universal Credit (Transitional Provisions) Regulations 2014 No.1230
U-C,PIP,JSA&ESA(C&P) Regs	The Universal Credit, Personal Independence Payment, Jobseeker's Allowance and Employment and Support Allowance (Claims and Payments) Regulations 2013 No.380

UC,PIP,JSA&ESA(DA) Regs	The Universal Credit, Personal Independence Payment, Jobseeker's Allowance and Employment and Support Allowance (Decisions and Appeals) Regulations 2013 No. 381
WRA(No.31)O	The Welfare Reform Act 2012 (Commencement No.31 and Savings and Transitional Provisions and Commencement No.21 and 23 and Transitional and Transitory Provisions (Amendment)) Order 2019 No.37
WRA(No.32)O	The Welfare Reform Act 2012 (Commencement No.32 and Savings and Transitional Provisions) Order 2019 No.167
WF Regs	The Welfare Food Regulations 1996 No.1434
WF(BSF) Regs	Welfare Food (Best Start Foods) (Scotland) Regulations 2019 No.193
WTC(EMR) Regs	The Working Tax Credit (Entitlement and Maximum Rate) Regulations 2002 No. 2005

Other information

ADM	*Advice for Decision Making*
CBTM	*Child Benefit Technical Manual*
CCM	*Claimant Compliance Manual* (HMRC guidance on investigation of tax credit claims)
DMG	*Decision Makers' Guide*
DWPWAG	DWP *Guidance Relating to the UK's Operational Implementation of the Social Security Coordination Provisions of Part 2 of the EU Withdrawal Agreement: citizens' rights* (11 November 2020)
GM	*Housing Benefit/Council Tax Benefit Guidance Manual*
HB	*Housing Benefit Bulletin*
IDI	Immigration Directorate Instructions
IR	Immigration Rules
TCM	*Tax Credits Manual*
TCTM	*Tax Credits Technical Manual*

References like CIS/142/1990 and R(IS) 1/07 are to commissioners' decisions.
References like *TG v SSWP (PC)* [2015] UKUT 50 (AAC) are references to decisions of the Upper Tribunal.
References like ASA/02/02/1877 are references to decisions of the First-tier Tribunal (Asylum Support).

Index

How to use this Index

Entries against the bold headings direct you to the general information on the subject, or where the subject is covered most fully. Sub-entries are listed alphabetically and direct you to specific aspects of the subject. The following abbreviations are used in the index:

AA	Attendance allowance
CA	Carer's allowance
C-ESA	Contributory employment and support allowance
C-JSA	Contribution-based jobseeker's allowance
CTA	Common travel area
CTC	Child tax credit
DLA	Disability living allowance
EC	European Community
EEA	European Economic Area
ESA	Employment and support allowance
EU	European Union
HB	Housing benefit
IB	Incapacity benefit
IS	Income support
I-ESA	Income-related employment and support allowance
I-JSA	Income-based jobseeker's allowance
JSA	Jobseeker's allowance
MA	Maternity allowance
NI	National insurance
PC	Pension credit
PIP	Personal independence payment
SAP	Statutory adoption pay
SMP	Statutory maternity pay
SPP	Statutory paternity pay
SSP	Statutory sick pay
SSPP	Statutory shared parental pay
UC	Universal credit
WTC	Working tax credit